Enterprise Java™
with UML™

Second Edition

C.T. Arrington
Syed Rayhan

WILEY

Wiley Publishing, Inc.

Publisher: Joe Wikert
Editor: Robert Elliott
Assistant Developmental Editor: Adaobi Obi Tulton
Editorial Manager: Kathryn A. Malm
Senior Production Editor: Angela Smith
Text Design & Composition: Wiley Composition Services

This book is printed on acid-free paper. ∞

For general information on our other products and services please contact our Customer Care Department within the United States at (800) 762-2974, outside the United States at (317) 572-3993 or fax (317) 572-4002.

Wiley also publishes its books in a variety of electronic formats. Some content that appears in print may not be available in electronic books.

Library of Congress Cataloging-in-Publication Data: Available from Publisher

ISBN: 0-471-26778-3

Printed in the United States of America

10 9 8 7 6 5 4 3 2 1

Enterprise Java™ with UML™

Second Edition

OMG Press Books in Print

For complete information about current and upcoming titles, go to www.wiley.com/compbooks/omg.

- *Building Business Objects* by Peter Eeles and Oliver Sims, ISBN: 0-471-19176-0.
- *Business Component Factory: A Comprehensive Overview of Component-Based Development for the Enterprise* by Peter Herzum and Oliver Sims, ISBN: 0-471-32760-3.
- *Business Modeling with UML: Business Patterns at Work* by Hans-Erik Eriksson and Magnus Penker, ISBN: 0-471-29551-5.
- *CORBA 3 Fundamentals and Programming, 2nd Edition* by Jon Siegel, ISBN: 0-471-29518-3.
- *CORBA Design Patterns* by Thomas J. Mowbray and Raphael C. Malveau, ISBN: 0-471-15882-8.
- *Enterprise Application Integration with CORBA: Component and Web-Based Solutions* by Ron Zahavi, ISBN: 0-471-32720-4.
- *Enterprise Integration: An Architecture for Enterprise Application and Systems Integration* by Fred A. Cummins, ISBN: 0-471-40010-6.
- *Enterprise Java with UML* by CT Arrington, ISBN: 0-471-38680-4.
- *Enterprise Security with EJB and CORBA* by Bret Hartman, Donald J. Flinn and Konstantin Beznosov, ISBN: 0-471-15076-2.
- *The Essential CORBA: Systems Integration Using Distributed Objects* by Thomas J. Mowbray and Ron Zahavi, ISBN: 0-471-10611-9.
- *Instant CORBA* by Robert Orfali, Dan Harkey and Jeri Edwards, ISBN: 0-471-18333-4.
- *Integrating CORBA and COM Applications* by Michael Rosen and David Curtis, ISBN: 0-471-19827-7.

- *Java Programming with CORBA, Third Edition* by Gerald Brose, Andreas Vogel and Keith Duddy, ISBN: 0-471-24765-0.

- *Mastering XMI: Java Programming with XMI, XML, and UML* by Timothy J. Grose, Gary C. Doney and Stephen A. Brodskey, ISBN: 0-471-38429-1.

- *The Object Technology Casebook: Lessons from Award-Winning Business Applications* by Paul Harmon and William Morrisey, ISBN: 0-471-14717-6.

- *The Object Technology Revolution* by Michael Guttman and Jason Matthews, ISBN: 0-471-60679-0.

- *Programming with Enterprise JavaBeans, JTS and OTS: Building Distributed Transactions with Java and C++* by Andreas Vogel and Madhavan Rangarao, ISBN: 0-471-31972-4.

- *Programming with Java IDL* by Geoffrey Lewis, Steven Barber and Ellen Siegel, ISBN: 0-471-24797-9.

- *Quick CORBA 3* by Jon Siegel, ISBN: 0-471-38935-8.

- *UML Toolkit* by Hans-Erik Eriksson and Magnus Penker, ISBN: 0-471-19161-2.

About the OMG

The Object Management Group (OMG) is an open membership, not-for-profit consortium that produces and maintains computer industry specifications for interoperable applications. To achieve this goal, the OMG specifies open standards for every aspect of distributed computing from analysis and design, through infrastructure, to application objects and components defined on virtually every enterprise middleware platform. OMG's membership roster includes virtually every large company in the computer industry, and hundreds of smaller ones. Most of the companies that shape enterprise and Internet computing today are represented on OMG's Board of Directors.

OMG's flagship specification, and the basis for future OMG specifications, is the multi-platform Model Driven Architecture (MDA). Unifying the modeling and middleware spaces, the MDA supports applications over their entire lifecycle from Analysis and Design, through implementation and deployment, to maintenance and evolution. Based on normative, platform-independent Unified Modeling Language (UML) models, MDA-based applications and standards may be expressed and implemented, equivalently, on multiple middleware platforms; implementation are produced automatically, for the most part, by MDA-enabled tools which also generate cross-platform invocations making for a truly interoperable environment. Because the UML models remain stable as the technological landscape changes around them over time, MDA-based development maximizes software ROI as it integrates applications across the enterprise, and one enterprise with another. Adopted by members as the basis for OMG specifications in September 2001, the MDA is truly a unique advance in distributed computing. To learn more about the MDA, see www.omg.org/mda.

OMG's modeling specifications form the foundation for the MDA. These include the UML, the MetaObject Facility (MOF), XML Metadata Interchange (XMI), and the Common Warehouse Metamodel (CWM). The industry's standard for representation of analysis and design, the UML defines Use Case and Activity diagrams for requirements gathering, Class and Object diagrams for design, Package and Subsystem diagrams for deployment, and six other diagram types. The MOF defines a standard metamodel for applications, allowing UML models to be interchanged among tools and repositories; and XMI standardizes the format for these interchanges. Finally, CWM establishes metamodels in the field of data warehousing, completing OMG's standardization in the modeling space.

The Common Object Request Broker Architecture (CORBA) is OMG's vendor-neutral, system-independent middleware standard. Based on the OMG/ISO Interface Definition language (OMG IDL) and the Internet Inter-ORB Protocol (IIOP), CORBA is a mature technology represented on the market by more than 70 ORBs (Object Request Brokers) plus hundreds of other products. Scalable to Internet and Enterprise levels, CORBA more than meets business computing requirements through its robust services providing directory, distributed event handling, transactionality, fault tolerance, and security. Specialized versions of CORBA form the basis for distributed Realtime computing, and distributed embedded systems.

Building on this foundation, OMG Domain Facilities standardize common objects throughout the supply and service chains in industries such as Telecommunications, Healthcare, Manufacturing, Transportation, Finance/Insurance, Biotechnology, Utilities, Space, and Military and Civil Defense Logistics. OMG members are now extending these Domain Facilities, originally written in OMG IDL and restricted to CORBA, into the MDA by constructing UML models corresponding to their underlying architecture; standard MDA procedures will then produce standards and implementations on such platforms as Web Services, XML/SOAP, Enterprise JavaBeans, and others. OMG's first MDA-based specification, the Gene Expression Facility, was adopted less than six months after the organization embraced the MDA; based on a detailed UML model, this specification is implemented entirely in the popular language XML.

In summary, the OMG provides the computing industry with an open, vendor-neutral, proven process for establishing and promoting standards. OMG makes all of its specifications available without charge from its Web site, www.omg.org. Delegates from the hundreds of OMG member companies convene at week-long meetings held five times each year at varying sites around the world, to advance OMG technologies. The OMG welcomes guests to their meetings; for an invitation, send your email request to info@omg.org or see www.omg.org/news/meetings/tc/guest.htm.

Membership in OMG is open to any company, educational institution, or government agency. For more information on the OMG, contact OMG headquarters by telephone at +1-781-444-0404, by fax at +1-781-444-0320, by email to info@omg.org, or on the Web at www.omg.org.

2003 OMG Press Advisory Board

Contents

Acknowledgments

Many thanks to the fine professionals from John Wiley and Sons: Terri Hudson, Kathryn Malm, Angela Smith, Jeri Freedman, and especially Adaobi Obi Tulton.

Thanks to our friends and coworkers at Capital One, who provided encouragement and careful reviews of the manuscript; Irwan Budianto, Rebecca A. Weingard, and Mel Riffe.

Thanks to Justin Gaspard, who reviewed the new chapters and also dramatically improved the Web site by providing the Ant deployment scripts and porting the sample application to JBoss and Weblogic.

C. T.: Thanks to my parents, for fostering a lifetime obsession with the printed word.

Thanks to Syed for collaborating with me on this project – I enjoyed working with him and the book definitely benefited from his efforts and insights.

I will never be able to sufficiently thank my family for permitting me this most selfish endeavor. That said I had better try . . . How many evenings and weekends did I take away? How many mornings did I wake bleary eyed and grumpy from too little sleep and too little progress? This book truly was an amazing opportunity for the skinny (formerly) kid who read too much, and you two made it possible. Thank you!

Syed: Thanks to my wife for encouraging me to pursue this project and supporting me along the way. Without her constant support and sacrifice, this would not have been successful.

I am grateful to my mother for trading her happiness for her children's. I would not be here without her sacrifice.

Thanks to C. T. and the publisher for giving me the opportunity to experience this wonderful journey of becoming an author.

About the Authors

C.T. Arrington is an architect and development manager with Capital One, where he specializes in architecting *n*-tier systems in Java. He has spent the last 11 years developing software for a wide variety of applications and hopes to continue for another forty! He is also a former Rational Software certified instructor and a Sun certified Java Programmer, Developer, and Architect.

Syed Rayhan is an architect specializing in enterprise applications in Java. He is currently working as a consultant for a Fortune 100 financial company, where he is implementing a J2EE system to support the client's complex mortgage business. He has spent his last 9 years developing enterprise applications mostly for Fortune 500 financial companies. His interests in technology include distributed application architecture, object-oriented (OO) analysis and design, design patterns, and now Web services. His interest in IT management is to study the challenges that the IT managers face regarding build vs. buy, reuse, outsourcing, and the software development process that works in the context of new technologies.

CHAPTER

1

Introduction to Modeling Java with the UML

As Java completes its move from a novelty language to the language of choice for Web-enabled enterprise computing, Java developers are faced with many opportunities as well as many challenges. We must produce systems that scale as the underlying business grows and evolves at Web speed. Our customers' appetite for functionality, scalability, usability, extensibility, and reliability rises each year.

Fortunately, Java provides a lot of support as we struggle to meet these demands. First, and perhaps foremost, Java is a small, tightly written object-oriented (OO) language with excellent support for exception handling and concurrency built in. Of course, this language runs on a platform-independent virtual machine that allows Java systems to run on everything from a PalmPilot to a Web browser to an AS400, with about a dozen operating systems in between. From this solid foundation, Sun built and evolved one of the most impressive class libraries you could ever ask for, including support for internationalization, calendar management, database access, image manipulation, networking, user interfaces, 2-D and 3-D graphics, and more. Finally, Enterprise JavaBeans and Java 2 Enterprise Edition provide specifications for true cross-platform enterprise computing. Many of the problems that have plagued enterprise developers for decades, such as object-to-relational persistence, object caching, data integrity, and resource management, are being addressed with newfound vigor. These specifications, and the application servers that implement them, allow us to leverage a wealth of academic research and practical experience. We are better equipped to develop enterprise systems than ever before.

However, powerful tools do not guarantee success. Before developers can harness the enormous power of enterprise Java technology, they need a clear understanding of the problem and a clear plan for the solution. In order to develop this understanding, they need a way to visualize the system and communicate their decisions and creations to a wide audience. Fortunately, the last few decades have also seen dramatic progress in our ability to understand and model object-oriented systems. The Unified Modeling Language (UML) is an open standard notation that allows developers to build visual representations of software systems. These models enable developers to devise elegant solutions, share ideas, and track decisions throughout the entire development cycle. Also, tools for creating, reverse-engineering, and distributing software models in UML have matured greatly over the past 2 years, to the point where modeling can be a seamless part of a development life cycle.

This book describes software modeling with the UML, and demonstrates how developers can use UML throughout the software development process to create better enterprise Java systems and more livable enterprise Java projects. The remainder of this chapter discusses software modeling in more detail and presents some object-oriented terminology and UML notation as a foundation for the rest of the book.

NOTE **This is a book for Java developers who are interested in modeling software before they build it. It is based on our own practical experience as software developers, both painful and euphoric.**

When you finish this book, you will be able to:

- Communicate an understanding of OO modeling theory and practice to others
- Communicate an understanding of UML notation to others
- Critically review a wide variety of UML software models
- Use UML to create a detailed understanding of the problem from the user's perspective
- Use UML to visualize and document a balanced solution using the full suite of Java technologies
- Use UML to describe other technologies and class libraries

What Is Modeling?

A model is a simplification with a purpose. It uses a precisely defined notation to describe and simplify a complex and interesting structure, phenomenon, or relationship. We create models to avoid drowning in complexity and so that we can understand and control the world around us. Consider a few examples from the real world. Mathematical models of our solar system allow mere mortals to calculate the positions of the planets. Engineers use sophisticated modeling techniques to design everything from aircraft carriers to circuit boards. Meteorologists use mathematical models to predict the weather.

Models of software systems help developers visualize, communicate, and validate a system before significant amounts of money are spent. Software models also help structure and coordinate the efforts of a software development team. The following sections describe some characteristics of models and how they contribute to software development.

Simplification

A model of a system is far less complex, and therefore far more accessible, than the actual code and components that make up the final system. It is much easier for a developer to build, extend, and evaluate a visual model than to work directly in the code. Think of all the decisions that you make while coding. Every time you code, you must decide which parameters to pass, what type of return value to use, where to put certain functionality, and a host of other questions. Once these decisions are made in code, they tend to stay made. With modeling, and especially with a visual modeling tool, these decisions can be made and revised quickly and efficiently. The software model serves the same purpose as an artist's rough sketch. It is a quick and relatively cheap way to get a feel for the actual solution.

The inherent simplicity of models also makes them the perfect mechanism for collaboration and review. It is very difficult to involve more than one other developer during the coding process. Committing to regular code reviews requires a great deal of discipline in the face of ubiquitous schedule pressure. A particular piece of a software model can be reviewed for quality, understandability, and consistency with the rest of the model. Preparation time for reviews of a model is dramatically lower than for a comparable code walkthrough. An experienced developer can assimilate a detailed model of an entire subsystem in a day. Assimilating the actual code for the same subsystem can easily take weeks. This allows more developers to collaborate and review more of the whole model. In general, collaboration and review of software models leads to lower defect rates and fewer difficulties during integration. Also, software models dramatically decrease the time required to assimilate and review code.

Varying Perspectives

A single model of a software system can describe the system from different perspectives. One view might show how major parts of the system interact and cooperate. Another view might zoom in on the details of a particular piece of the system. Yet another view might describe the system from the users' perspective. Having these different views helps developers manage complexity, because high-level views provide context and navigation. Once the developer has found an area of interest, he or she can zoom in and assimilate the details for that area. Newly acquired developers find this especially useful as they learn their way around a system.

We use this technique in the real world. Consider the common street map, which models the streets and buildings of a city. One part of the map might show the major highways and thoroughfares of the entire city, while another part might zoom in on the downtown area to show each street in detail. Both views are correct and valuable, in different ways.

Common Notation

A common notation allows developers to move past arguments over the meaning of a proposed solution and focus on the merits of the solution. Of course, this requires consistent use and understanding of the common notation. Many other disciplines use a common notation to facilitate communication. Experienced musicians do not argue over the meanings of their symbols. They can depend on the notation to provide a precise description of the sounds, which frees them to collaborate to find the right sounds.

A precise software model in a common notation allows developers to combine their efforts and to work in parallel. As long as each contribution fits the model, the parts can be combined into the final system. Modern manufacturing uses this technique to lower costs and decrease production schedules. Based on a vehicle's design, an automotive manufacturer can purchase parts from hundreds of suppliers. As long as each part meets the specifications described in the design model, it will fit nicely into the final product.

UML

The Unified Modeling Language (UML) is a language for specifying, visualizing, constructing, and documenting the artifacts of software systems. UML provides the precise notation that we need when modeling software systems. It is important to note that the UML is not just a way to document existing ideas. The UML helps developers create ideas, as well as communicate them.

The UML was not the first notation for modeling object-oriented software systems. In fact, UML was created to end the confusion between competing notations. Many of the best and brightest academics and practitioners in the field of object-oriented software development joined together in the mid- to late-1990s to create a common notation. It is now the international standard for modeling object-oriented systems.

The UML is an open standard controlled by the Object Management Group (OMG), rather than any one individual or company.

> **NOTE** As you read this book, you may wish to return to this chapter. It describes the basic UML terminology and notation.

The Basics

Before we dive into modeling your system using UML, there are a few object-oriented concepts that you need to understand before you start.

Abstraction

An *abstraction* is a simplification or model of a complex concept, process, or real-world object. As humans, we need abstractions to survive. Abstractions allow us to simplify our understanding of the world so that our understanding is useful without becoming overwhelming. Do you thoroughly understand personal computers, televisions, CD players, or even a simple transistor radio? Can the same person understand these electronic devices and also conquer the mysteries of cellular biology and human physiology? How about the details of any two human endeavors, such as coal mining and professional football?

An abstraction is a simplification or mental model that helps a person understand something at an appropriate level. This implies that different people would build radically different abstractions for the same concept. For example, I see my refrigerator as a big box with a door, some food inside, and a little wheel that lets me set the temperature. A design engineer sees my refrigerator as a complex system with an evaporator fan, an evaporator, a defrost heater, a compressor, and a condenser fan, all working together to move heat from the inside of the equipment to my kitchen. The design engineer needs this rich view of the fridge to design an efficient and effective refrigerator. I, on the other hand, am needlessly burdened by such details. I just want a cold glass of soda.

A good abstraction highlights the relevant characteristics and behavior of something that is too complex to understand in its entirety. The needs and interests of the abstraction's creator determine the level of detail and emphasis of the abstraction.

Abstractions are even more useful when they help us understand how different parts of a larger model interact together. In the object-oriented world, the interacting parts of a model are called *objects*.

Encapsulation

According to my dusty old copy of Webster's, to encapsulate means "to enclose in or as if in a capsule." For object-oriented systems, the specifics of the data and behavioral logic are hidden within each type of object. Think of encapsulation as a counterpoint to abstraction. An abstraction highlights the important aspects of an object, while encapsulation hides the cumbersome internal details of the object. Encapsulation is a very powerful tool in our effort to make reusable, extensible, and comprehensible systems.

First, encapsulating the nasty details inside of a system makes the system easier to understand and to reuse. In many cases, another developer may not care how an object works, as long as it provides the desired functionality. The less he or she needs to know about the object in order to use it, the more likely that developer is to reuse it. In short, encapsulation reduces the burden of adopting a class or class library for use in a system.

Also, encapsulation makes a system more extensible. A well-encapsulated object allows other objects to use it without depending on any internal details. Consequently, new requirements may be met by changing the encapsulated details, without affecting the code that uses the object.

Object

An object is a particular and finite element in a larger model. An object may be very concrete, such as a particular automobile in a car dealer's inventory system. An object may be invisible, such as an individual's bank account in a banking system. An object may have a short life, such as a transaction in a banking system.

It is important to distinguish between the abstraction that similar objects in a system share and the objects themselves. For example, the abstraction comprising cars in a dealer's inventory system certainly includes the make, model, mileage, year, color, purchase price, and condition. The object, which is a particular car in the inventory, might be a light blue 1996 Honda Accord, in good condition, with 54,000 miles on the odometer.

All objects have *state*, which describes their characteristics and current condition. Some characteristics, such as the make and model of the car, never change. Other parts of a car's state, such as mileage, change over time.

Objects also have *behavior*, which defines the actions that other objects may perform on the object. For instance, a bank account may allow a customer object to withdraw money or deposit money. A customer initiates a withdrawal, but the logic for performing the withdrawal lives inside of the account object. Behavior may depend on an object's state. For example, a car with no gas is unlikely to provide desirable behavior.

Moreover, each object in a system must be uniquely identifiable within the system. There must be some characteristic or group of characteristics that sets each object apart. To continue the car example, each car has a unique vehicle identification number.

In the UML, an object is represented as a rectangle with the name underlined, as in Figure 1.1

The work in an object-oriented system is divided up among many objects. Each object is configured for its particular role in the system. Since each object has a fairly narrow set of responsibilities, the objects must cooperate to accomplish larger goals. Consider a customer who wants to transfer money from one account to another at an ATM. This fairly trivial example requires a user interface object, a customer object, a checking account object, and a savings account object. This combination of narrow specialization and cooperation allows the objects to stay simple and easy to understand. A *method* is a service or responsibility that an object exposes to other objects. Thus, one object can call another object's methods. A method is loosely analogous to a function or subroutine in procedural programming, except that the method is called on a specific object that has its own state. This tight integration between data and behavior is one of the key distinguishing features of object-oriented software development.

Class

A class is a group of objects that have something in common. A class captures a particular abstraction and provides a template for object creation. By convention, class names start with an uppercase letter and use mixed case to mark word boundaries. Each object created from the class is identical in the following ways:

- The type of data that the object can hold. For instance, a car class might specify that each car object have string data for the color, make, and model.

- The type and number of objects that the object knows about. A car class might specify that every car object know about one or more previous owners.

- The logic for any behavior that the object provides.

myHondaAccord:

Figure 1.1 A car object.

The actual values for the data are left to the objects. This means that one car may be a blue Honda Accord with one previous owner, while another car might be a green Subaru Outback with two previous owners. Also, since the behavior may be state-dependent, two different objects may respond differently to the same request. However, two objects with identical state must respond identically.

Consider a more detailed and completely silly analogy. Toy soldiers are created by melting either green or brown plastic and injecting the molten plastic into little molds. The shape of the mold determines the height and shape of the toy soldier, as well as its ability to grasp a tiny rifle and carry a radio on its back. The purchaser cannot change the height of the toy or outfit it with a flamethrower. The class—I mean mold—does not support these configurations.

However, there is still work for purchasers of the toy soldier. They may provide or withhold the rifle and radio, and they may organize the toys into squads for deployment against the hated Ken doll. They are configuring the objects—oops, I mean soldiers—and determining the associations between them.

Objects provide the real value in an object-oriented system. They hold the data and perform the work. Classes, like molds, are important for the creation of the objects, though no one ever plays with them.

In the UML, a class is represented as a rectangle with the name in the top compartment, the data in the next compartment, and the behavior in the third compartment. Figure 1.2 shows a UML representation of the ToySoldier class. Notice that, unlike the UML representation of an object, the name is not underlined.

Relationships between Objects

Object-oriented systems are populated by many distinct objects that cooperate to accomplish various tasks. Each object has a narrowly defined set of responsibilities, so they must work together to fulfill their collective goals. In order to cooperate, objects must have relationships that allow them to communicate with one another.

Recall that the state and behavior for an object are determined and constrained by the object's class. The class controls the state that the object possesses, the behavior that it provides, and the other objects that it has relationships with. With this in mind, it is logical to describe the relationships between objects in a class diagram.

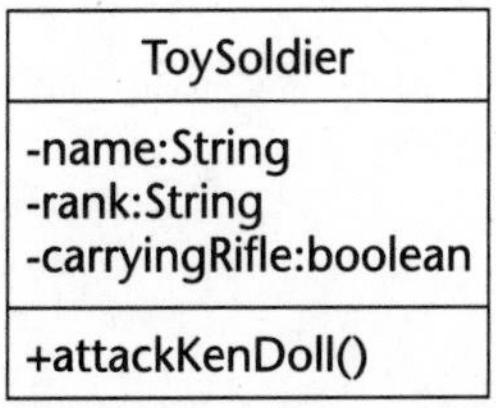

```
+-----------------------------+
|         ToySoldier          |
+-----------------------------+
| -name:String                |
| -rank:String                |
| -carryingRifle:boolean      |
+-----------------------------+
| +attackKenDoll()            |
+-----------------------------+
```

Figure 1.2   The ToySoldier class in the UML.

There are four types of relationships:

- Dependency
- Association
- Aggregation
- Composition

Dependency

Dependency is the weakest relationship between objects. An object depends on an object if it has a short-term relationship with the object. During this short-lived relationship, the dependent object may call methods on the other object to obtain services or configure the object. Real life is full of dependency relationships. We depend on the cashier at the grocery store to sell us food, but we do not have a long-term relationship with that person. In the UML, dependency is represented by a dashed line with an arrow pointing to the depended-upon class.

Dependency relationships in object-oriented systems follow a few common patterns. An object may create an object as part of a method, ask it to perform some function, and then forget about it. An object may create an object as part of a method, configure it, and pass the object to the method caller as a return value. An object may receive an object as a parameter to a method, use it or modify it, then forget about it when the method ends.

Figure 1.3 shows a dependency relationship between the Customer class and the Cashier class. This relationship reads as: "Each Customer object depends on Cashier objects." Changes to the interface of the Cashier class may affect the Customer class.

Association

An association is a long-term relationship between objects. In an association, an object keeps a reference to another object and can call the object's methods, as it needs them. Real life is replete with association relationships. Consider people with their automobiles. As long as they remember where they left their car, the car will let them in and take them to their destination. In the UML, association is represented by a solid line between the two classes.

In some cases an object may instantiate another object and keep a reference to it for future use. An object may also receive an object as a parameter to a configuration method and keep a reference to the object.

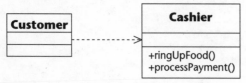

Figure 1.3   Sample dependency relationship.

Figure 1.4 Sample association relationship.

Figure 1.4 shows an association relationship between the Person class and the Car class. The relationship is read as: "Every Person object is associated with an unspecified number of Car objects," and "every Car object is associated with an unspecified number of Person objects." It may help to think of this as a "knows-about-a" relationship, as in "each Person object knows about some Car objects."

Aggregation

An aggregation relationship indicates that an object is part of a greater whole. The contained object may participate in more than one aggregation relationship, and exists independently of the whole. For example, a software developer may be part of two project teams and continues to function even if both teams dissolve. Figure 1.5 shows this aggregation relationship.

In the UML, aggregation is indicated by decorating an association line with a hollow diamond next to the "whole" class. The relationship is read as: "Each ProjectTeam object has some SoftwareDeveloper objects," and "each SoftwareDeveloper object belongs to one or more ProjectTeam objects."

Composition

A composition relationship indicates that an object is owned by a greater whole. The contained object may not participate in more than one composition relationship and cannot exist independently of the whole. The part is created as part of the creation of the whole, and is destroyed when the whole is destroyed. In the UML, composition is indicated by decorating an association with a solid diamond next to the "whole" class.

Consider a small gear deep in the oily bowels of an internal combustion engine. It is inextricably part of the engine. It is not worth the cost of removal when the engine finally expires, and it is not accessible for replacement. Figure 1.6 shows this composition relationship. The relationship is read as: "Each Engine object always contains a SmallGear object," and "Each SmallGear object always belongs to a single Engine object."

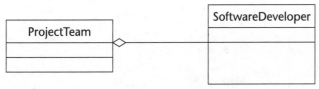

Figure 1.5 Sample aggregation relationship.

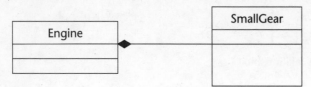

Figure 1.6   Sample composition relationship.

TIP It may be difficult to remember which relationship is aggregation and which is composition. We offer a simple and somewhat silly mnemonic device for aggregation. Aggregation sounds a lot like congregation, as in members of a church. People may exist before joining a church. People may belong to more than one church, or they may change churches. Likewise, people continue to exist after leaving the church or after the church disbands or merges with another church. As for composition, well, it is the other one. Sorry.

Navigability

Relationships between objects are often one-sided. For instance, in any car that I can afford, the Car object controls the Wheel objects, but the Wheel objects are unable to control the Car. Figure 1.7 shows an association relationship between the Car class and the Wheel class. The arrow pointing to the Wheel class indicates that the Car may send messages to the Wheel, but that the Wheel cannot send messages to the Car. This means that a Car object may call the getSpinSpeed method on its Wheel objects and that the Wheel object may return a value from that method; but the Wheel does not have a reference to the Car object, so it cannot call the startEngine method.

According to the UML specification, an association line with no arrows can have one of two meanings. Developers on a project may agree that the absence of arrows means that the association is not navigable. Alternatively, developers on a project may agree that the absence of arrows means that the association is bidirectional.

Since there is no reason to have an association that is not navigable, the first interpretation of an association with no arrows generally means that the navigability has not been determined. In this case, an arrow on each side of the line indicates bidirectional navigability.

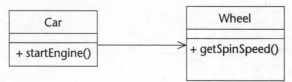

Figure 1.7   Sample association with one-way navigability.

Developers on a project may agree that a line with no arrows represents bidirectional navigability. In this case, the double-arrow notation is never used, and there is no way to indicate an unspecified or not-navigable association.

For this book, we use double arrows to indicate bidirectional navigability. We prefer this option because it allows us to defer consideration of the navigability of an association without confusion.

Multiplicity

One object may have an association with a single object, with a certain number of objects, or with an unlimited number of objects. Figure 1.8 shows several relationships with the multiplicity determined. In the UML, the multiplicity describes the object that it is next to. So, an Engine object may have zero or many SmallGear objects, but each SmallGear object belongs to exactly one Engine object. Each Car object is associated with one or more Person objects, and each Person object may be associated with zero or more Car objects. Also, each Car object has exactly one Engine object, and different Car objects never share an Engine object.

NOTE There is no default multiplicity. The absence of a multiplicity for an association indicates that the multiplicity has not been determined.

Interface

An interface defines a set of related behavior, but does not specify the actual implementation for the behavior. To be more specific, each interface completely specifies the signature of one or more methods, complete with parameters and return type. An interface captures an abstraction, without addressing any implementation details.

A class realizes an interface by implementing each method in the interface. The interface defines a set of behaviors. The class makes it real.

Interfaces provide flexibility when specifying the relationship between objects. Rather than specifying that each instance of a class has a relationship with an instance of a specific class, we can specify that each instance of a class has a relationship with an instance of some class that realizes a particular interface. As we will see throughout this book, creative use of this feature provides an amazing amount of flexibility and extensibility.

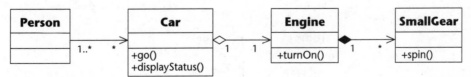

Figure 1.8 Sample associations with multiplicity.

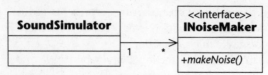

Figure 1.9   Sample interface.

For instance, a game might contain a sound simulator object that is responsible for collecting and playing the sounds that emanate from various objects in a virtual world. Each SoundSimulator object is associated with zero or more objects whose classes realize the INoiseMaker interface. From the SoundSimulator's perspective, the specific type of noisemaker is completely irrelevant. Figure 1.9 shows this relationship.

Polymorphism

Polymorphism, according to our dictionary, means having more than one form. In object-oriented circles, polymorphism refers to multiple implementations of a single abstraction. Abstractions are captured in classes and in interfaces. So, we can get polymorphism by having more than one class inherit from a base class. Each class could simply override the default implementation provided by the base class. We can also get polymorphism by having more than one class realize an interface. Each class must provide an implementation for each method in the interface.

To continue our sound simulator example for polymorphism through interfaces, consider two classes that make noise, Trumpet and Tiger. Both implement the makeNoise method and realize the INoiseMaker interface. Each SoundSimulator object is associated with some objects whose classes realize INoiseMaker. The sound simulator does not need to know the specific class for each object. Instead, the sound simulator just asks the object to make some noise. Figure 1.10 shows the two classes that realize the INoiseMaker interface and the relationship between SoundSimulator and INoiseMaker.

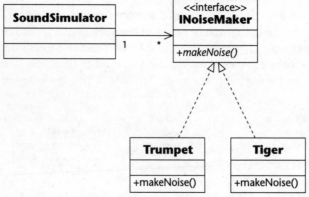

Figure 1.10   Polymorphism through realization.

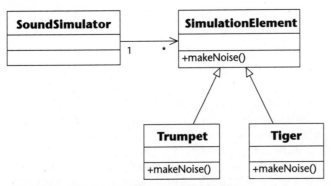

Figure 1.11 Polymorphism through inheritance.

Multiple implementations of an abstraction can also be achieved by having more than one subclass override the default implementation provided by the base class. Figure 1.11 shows an alternate approach in which each SoundSimulator object is associated with some objects that instantiate SimulationElement or a subclass of SimulationElement. As before, the SoundSimulator knows that the object on the other end of the association implements the makeNoise method, but does not know what sound to expect.

Polymorphism has two very significant benefits. First, polymorphism allows unlimited flexibility within a running system. Different implementations of an abstraction can be mixed and matched to achieve very interesting effects. The second benefit is long-term extensibility for the system. As long as the abstraction is unchanged, new implementations can be introduced without affecting the code that depends on an interface. For example, adding a new class that realizes INoiseMaker does not affect the SoundSimulator class in any way.

Modeling Software Systems with the UML

UML enables developers to build a single coherent model that describes a software system from several perspectives. This combination of internal consistency and distinct views means that a variety of participants can use the same model and speak the same language throughout the development process. Granted, some participants will only use part of the model, but they can still follow the overall structure of the model.

The Customer's Perspective

Most customers are relatively disinterested in technology. They are far more interested in the value that the system provides for them, that is, how it increases their productivity and makes their lives easier. Developers should gather requirements from the customer's perspective, considering how the customer will interact with the system to obtain value. This allows the customer to review and validate the requirements from a very natural perspective, his or her own. The customer can also measure development progress from an individual perspective.

UML provides several mechanisms for documenting system requirements from the user's perspective. They are the use case diagram, a text description for each use case, and an activity diagram for each use case.

- A *use case* defines and describes a discrete way in which users get value from the system. A user might perform a series of fairly complex steps to obtain a desirable result, such as withdrawing funds from an ATM or purchasing a book online. Alternatively, a user may simply press a large red button labeled Run Quarterly Sales Report. User effort is not the determining factor. Instead, the independent usefulness of the result is the key. A *use case diagram* models all interactions between the user and a system in a single high-level diagram. This diagram allows customers and developers to capture the intent and scope of the system in a very accessible format. The use cases can then be used to track development progress and to guide development activities.

- The *text description* of each use case describes the use case, including the details of the interactions between the user and the system.

- An *activity diagram* is a visual description of the interactions between the system and the user for a use case.

Together, these diagrams help the customers and developers to fully understand the system problem from the customer's perspective.

The Developer's Perspective

Developers must first understand the problem, then the solution, from their own perspective. Object-oriented systems force developers to describe a system in terms of objects that cooperate to provide functionality to the users, so object-oriented developers focus on the objects that populate the system and the classes that define the objects.

UML provides several mechanisms for documenting a system from the developer's perspective: class diagrams, state chart diagrams, package diagrams, sequence diagrams, and collaboration diagrams.

- A *class diagram* defines and constrains a group of objects in detail. It shows the state, behavior, and relationships with other objects that are mandated for each object that instantiates the class.

- A *state chart diagram* describes the state-dependent behavior for a class. Specifically, it describes how an object responds to different requests depending on the object's internal configuration.

- A *package diagram* describes how different parts of a system depend on one another based on the relationships between objects that reside in different parts of the system.

- A *sequence diagram* shows how objects interact with one another to provide functionality. A sequence diagram clearly indicates the order of the interaction; it is less useful for determining the relationships between objects.

- A *collaboration diagram* also shows how objects interact with one another to provide functionality. Collaboration diagrams provide a counterpoint to sequence diagrams by clearly revealing the relationships between objects. However, they are less useful for determining the sequence of interactions.

Modeling Process

UML is used to gradually evolve the understanding of a system. First, the developers and customers use the UML to understand the problem from the customer's point of view. Next, the developers use UML to understand the problem from their own point of view. This clear understanding of the problem allows the developers to use UML as they invent a solution to the problem. Finally, the UML model is used as a resource by the implementers of the system. The chapters in this book mimic the stages of the modeling process.

Requirements Gathering

When gathering requirements, developers seek to understand the problem from the customer's perspective, without concern for technology or system design. This ensures that the developers are focused on the correct problem. While no system is immune to requirements change or "scope creep," adopting this perspective can prevent misunderstandings and dramatically reduce the severity of requirements changes.

In this process, developers create use case diagrams, text use case descriptions, and activity diagrams. We introduce requirements gathering in Chapter 2, "Gathering Requirements with UML." In Chapter 3, "Gathering Requirements for the Timecard Application," we begin gathering requirements for a sample application.

Analysis

In analysis, developers seek to understand the problem from their own perspective, still without concern for technology. Building on the understanding of the problem created during requirements gathering, they discover the roles and responsibilities that must be filled in the system. This builds a solid foundation for technology selection and design of the system.

In the analysis process, developers create class diagrams, sequence diagrams, and collaboration diagrams. We introduce analysis in Chapter 4, "A Brief Introduction to Object-Oriented Analysis with the UML." In Chapter 5, "Analysis Model for the Timecard Application," we demonstrate analysis in an example.

Technology Selection

During technology selection, developers categorize the system in terms of its technological requirements, then select the most appropriate technologies to fulfill these well-defined needs. This orderly and disciplined approach to selecting technology trades a fairly large upfront effort for decreased risk over the life of the project.

In the technology selection process, developers use all of the existing documents and diagrams. They produce a high-level summary of the technological requirements and a list of appropriate technologies for the system. No additional UML diagrams are produced.

Technology selection is covered in several chapters. In Chapter 6, "Describing the System for Technology Selection," we explain the process for describing the technology needs of a system, and reinforce these ideas by example. In Chapters 7 through 12, we present different technologies and describe their suitability, before selecting appropriate technologies for the example system.

Architecture

In architecture, developers describe the system at a high level, and decompose the system into smaller parts, such as subsystems. Relationships between parts are highlighted, while the details of each part are deferred. Technology selections are clearly shown as part of the architecture. Providing a high-level view of the system and its component parts makes it possible for a large number of participants to evaluate the feasibility of the architecture. Also, during design and implementation, the architecture serves as an invaluable high-level guide to developers as they struggle to understand the system as a whole.

Architecture builds on the cumulative understanding of the system as described in the use case model and in the technology selection. During architecture, developers produce primarily class diagrams and package diagrams.

We cover architecture in a single chapter: Chapter 13, "Software Architecture," explains the process and demonstrates it through the sample system.

Design and Implementation

In design, developers use all of the results from the previous steps as they create an intricate model of the objects that interact to provide the system's functionality. A detailed design provides the last chance to validate the solution before the extremely expensive and labor-intensive implementation process begins. In about a day, a small group of developers who are familiar with UML and with the system can prepare for a thorough design review of a major subsystem. Compare this to the weeks that are required to read and understand the code for a major subsystem. A detailed design can be created, reviewed, and revised in a fraction of the time it takes to write the code.

Once the design is complete, it serves as a valuable foundation for implementation. Developers are free to focus their efforts on the details of the implementation technologies, without constantly worrying whether their efforts will fit within the larger system. As long as they follow the design, or reconcile any changes to the design with other developers, their work will not be wasted.

Design and implementation is invariably an iterative process, as the implementation always evolves from the design, and the design for the next incarnation of the system builds on the current implementation. Fortunately for us, modern UML modeling tools allow us to easily shift our emphasis from design to code and back to design.

We cover design and implementation in the remainder of the book: In Chapter 14, "Introduction to Design," we explain the process; we dedicate Chapter 15, "Design for the TimecardDomain and TimecardWorkflow," Chapter 16, "Design for the TimecardUI Package," and Chapter 17, "Design for the BillingSystemInterface," to designs for different parts of the system.

What's on the Web Site

The book's companion Web site contains all the design documents and the source code for the sample Timecard application that you'll work on throughout the book. You'll also find instructions for installing and running the sample Timecard application with Sun's J2EE reference implementation.

The Next Step

Now that we have established a basic understanding of the terminology and the processes involved, we can start with requirements gathering, which seeks to understand the problem from the customer's perspective.

Gathering Requirements with UML

The first step to designing any enterprise application is to gather requirements for the system. A system's requirements consist of a document (or a collection of documents) that describes the functionality that the system provides. It is an agreement between the end user, the developer, and the system's sponsor as to what the system should and can do.

Requirements gathering is an interactive process whereby business analysts and developers gather system requirements by interacting with end users, domain experts, and other stakeholders. This highly iterative process is a combination of problem discovery and consensus building that lays the foundation for the project's success.

In this chapter, we'll show you how the Unified Modeling Language (UML) can be used in a requirements-gathering process. We'll outline several classic paths that lead to poor requirements, then suggest ways that you can detect and avoid them.

> **NOTE** The UML notation and requirements-gathering techniques introduced here will be used to capture requirements for a sample application in Chapter 3, "Gathering Requirements for the Timecard Application." We will use this sample application throughout the book, so even if you are an expert in requirements gathering, it might be useful to skim this chapter and read Chapter 3.

Are You Ready?

Before you can gather requirements, you need to do two things:

1. Create a clear vision of the system.

2. Determine who has the decision-making authority for the project.

The first step is to create a clear vision for the system. This vision is described in the *vision document,* a text document that presents an extremely high-level explanation of the goals and scope of the system. The vision document can be in any format. In one company, the vision document may be two paragraphs transferred from the napkins that were handy during the dinner when the principals spawned the idea for the company. In another organization, it may be a formal document that presents an exhaustive business case, complete with revenue projections, return-on-investment calculations, and four-color graphs on fancy paper. However it is presented, a success-ful vision document describes the system, its goals, and how the organization benefits from it. The system goals are described at a fairly high level to give the developers and the customers the flexibility to clarify the system vision. The document also highlights any known scope limitations.

The second step is to identify a *sponsor* or *sponsors* for the project. Gathering require-ments without sponsors is painful at best and disastrous at worst, because they are the people who make final decisions regarding budget, features, and schedule. Ideally, the sponsors form a small decisive group that has the authority and vision needed to set-tle disputes and to keep a clear focus for the project. In any system, compromises must be made. For example, some desired functionality might be deferred to a later release to meet the schedule. Different groups of users may have different needs and goals that pull the system in different directions. Without a clear decision-making authority, it is difficult to resolve issues and to keep them resolved. When decisions are made and remade in a frustrating cycle in an attempt to please everyone, developers often end up overcommitting themselves and, subsequently, end up disappointing everyone.

What Are Good Requirements?

Good requirements clearly and unambiguously state what the system does and for whom. They answer questions such as: Who uses the system? What value do users receive from their use of the system? These questions must be answered before con-sidering technology selection, architecture, and design, otherwise, developers will be doomed to solve the wrong problems and be unable to make informed decisions about technology and architecture.

Requirements gathering involves five key steps:

1. Find the people who can help you understand the system.

2. Listen to these stakeholders and understand the system from their perspective.

3. Capture the way customers want to use the system, along with the value provided, in an accessible model.

4. Create a detailed description of the interactions between the system and the customers and between the system and other external systems.

5. Refactor the detailed descriptions to maintain readability and accessibility.

These steps are repeated until a solid consensus on what the system should do is reached. Notice that the goal is a *solid* consensus, not a 100 percent perfect consensus. Gathering requirements, like any creative and collaborative endeavor, never reaches a clear conclusion, because each iteration raises new subtleties and a new layer of details. Requirements must not become an end in themselves. Requirements are useful only as a form of communication and as a consensus-building process; they are not artistic works with intrinsic value. Each additional refinement of the requirements yields less and less value. At some point, the project must move on.

Find the Right People

In order to gather requirements, you must solicit input from people at different levels within the organization or user group. One group may understand the problem domain and strategic goals, but they may not actually use the system. Another group may not see the big picture, but may be intimately familiar with the day-to-day activities. These people are the system's stakeholders, those who have a significant interest in the project's direction and success. Stakeholders include everyone from the end user to the development team to the senior managers who control the budget. It is up to you to establish a reasonable rapport with a wide variety of stakeholders, for they will provide you with the information you'll need to develop the requirements document.

Domain Experts

The domain experts are the strategic thinkers. They understand the organization and the system. They set the goals for the system as well as lend insight to their particular domain. These people are usually easy to identify, as they generally have a high profile and occupy nice offices. They may have advanced degrees, many years of experience in their field, and a senior position, such as CEO, vice president, or senior research fellow. Unfortunately, they also tend to be incredibly busy, talk too fast, and assume that everyone else knows and loves their field. To build the system that they need, you must understand them. To achieve that, you must make sure that they appreciate this simple truth and be confident that you will treat their time with care. Whenever possible, prepare by learning the relevant terminology and concepts inherent to their field before meeting with them, then baseline their expectations by explaining your limited background.

Subsequently, it is a good idea to verify your understanding of the conversations by paraphrasing them back to the source, preferably both verbally and in writing. Persistence and humility are key ingredients to your success.

End Users

Another important source of information is the actual end user. After all, it is the end users who must accept and use the final product. Their importance seems obvious, yet, remarkably, many organizations fail to solicit their input. Therefore, in some cases, you may need to push for access to a representative group of users. Sometimes the reluctance of management to grant access to the end users is evidence of an honest effort to protect the end users' time. In other cases, institutional traditions and rigid hierarchies erect the barrier. A medical doctor, for example, may balk at the idea that a licensed practical nurse may have valuable insights into the actual use of a medical data-tracking system. A manager with 20 years of experience may not realize that it has been 15 years since he or she actually did the work, and that a new hire may have a valuable perspective.

Be firm; excluding the actual users is not a viable option. Remember, developers must understand the day-to-day pragmatics as well as the strategic value of the system.

WARNING Never forget the end user.

Listen to the Stakeholders

Developers need insight and knowledge from the stakeholders. To facilitate this dialogue, you must temporarily suppress your own perspective and inclinations so that you can hear these stakeholders. In most cases, domain experts and end users are not concerned with cool technologies or object-oriented design principles; they want to know how they will benefit from the system. They are not interested in scarce technical resources or the risks of adopting new technology; they need a solid schedule that they can plan around. They are not interested in user interface design techniques; they just want a system that makes them more efficient.

Until you can clearly restate the customer's needs in your own words, do not plan the solution or consider the impact on the schedule. Above all, be positive, and try to think of the system in terms of the value that it provides to people. This is not an intuitive perspective for most developers, ourselves included. Our training and natural inclinations often make the solution more interesting than the problem. Also, there is a natural tendency to consider the impact on our personal and professional lives. We must overcome this mind-set—at least long enough to understand the needs of the people on the other side of the table.

It is important to remember that considering the other stakeholders' perspective does not mean committing to an impossible system or schedule. It means that developers are obligated to completely understand the requests and needs before contemplating feasibility and negotiating the schedule.

TIP Gathering requirements sets the stage for development, and makes—or breaks—every development team's relationship with the customer and domain experts.

Considering the customer's point of view in this initial stage often yields amazing dividends. In addition to high-quality requirements, you can gain the trust and goodwill of the stakeholders. Then, later in the process, stakeholders may consider the developer's perspective when considering requests to defer features or adjust the schedule.

The dialogue between you and the clients should be captured via meeting notes or transcribed recordings. Transcribed recordings are more accurate, but may make many people uncomfortable. In any case, a written dialogue that can be verified and built upon is an essential tool.

Develop Accessible Requirements

Requirements are useful if and only if people use them. If the user finds them turgid and/or incomprehensible, then they cannot tell you if you are specifying the right system. If developers find them obtuse and irrelevant, then the actual system will radically deviate from the requirements. While even the best requirements document is unlikely to find itself on the *New York Times* best-seller list, a requirements document must be readable and accessible to a wide audience. Describing how the system is used at a high level is an important step toward this goal.

TIP Requirements are useful if and only if people use them.

The high-level diagrams within the use case model in UML provide an excellent mechanism for this purpose. *Use case diagrams* show discrete groups of system users as they interact with the system. There are three steps to creating a use case model.

1. Identify the groups of people who will use the system.

2. Determine how these groups of people will get value from the system.

3. Provide a simple and accessible view of the users and their use of the system.

The next sections take a closer look at each of these steps.

Find Actors

The first step to requirements gathering is to identify the distinct groups of people who will use the system. In UML, a distinct group is referred to as an *actor*. Other systems that use the system or are used by the system are also actors. So, an actor is a group of people or a system that is outside of the system and interacts with the system. To qualify as an actor, the group must use the system in a different way.

It is important to note that differences in the real world may not be relevant within the system requirements. For example, managers often are considered a distinct group of people in the real world, whereas in many systems, they are not separate actors because they do not use the system in a manner that is different from the way an employee uses the system. Consider a simple timecard system, in which every employee enters his or her hours. A select few add valid charge codes. It is possible that some employees who add charge codes are managers, but that some are not. So managers, in this case, do not need separate representation. Examples of reasonable actors from various domains will help clarify this distinction. The following groups are separate actors in the given problem domain.

- Bank customers and bank tellers are separate actors because they have very different needs and privileges in a banking system. For instance, customers cannot see other customers' records.

- Traveling salespeople and back-office personnel are separate actors because they have different needs and different access methods for a sales-tracking system.

- Students and the registrar are separate actors because they have very different needs and privileges in a course registration system.

The following groups do not need to be treated as separate actors.

- Republicans and Democrats do not need to be treated as separate actors in a system that gathers votes for an election. Party affiliation might be noted for each voter, but it does not change the way voters use the system.

- Doctors and nurses do not need to be treated as separate actors in a system that records quantitative medical data, such as heart rate, blood pressure, and temperature. Both groups are well qualified to obtain and record the information, and there are no differences in the way that they perform the activities.

- Men and women do not need to be treated as separate actors in most computer games.

Once you have identified the actors, you are ready to move on to the next step.

Find Use Cases

The next step is to identify the ways the actors get value from the system. In the UML, the manner in which the system provides a discrete value to an actor is called a *use case*. A user might perform a series of fairly complex steps to obtain a desirable result, such as withdrawing funds from an ATM or purchasing a book online. Alternatively, a user may simply press a large red button labeled Run Quarterly Sales Report. User effort is not the determining factor. Rather, the independent *usefulness* of the result is the key.'

It is important to keep each use case well focused, with a single, clear purpose. Use cases divide the requirements into sections, so focused use cases make the documents easier to navigate and to understand. Use cases are also used for scheduling and estimation, so tightly focused use cases facilitate accurate estimation and precise tracking. Each use case is also used as a basis for a test case, so well-focused use cases convert nicely to a useful test plan and provide the basis for objective progress tracking. Monolithic use cases mean fewer divisions in the requirements documents and fewer milestones.

If you can answer yes to the following questions, a use case is well focused. Otherwise, the use case may need to be split into several use cases.

- Does the use case provide a single discrete benefit?

- Can you describe that benefit in 20 to 30 words, without adding several occurrences of "and" or "or"?

- Does the actor tend to complete the use case in a single session or sitting?
- Can you imagine the use case as a single test case in a coherent test plan?

Each use case must be significant and provide value in isolation. A use case may depend on other use cases or be part of a larger workflow, but the user must obtain a significant value from the use case alone. Individual steps, such as accepting user input, validating user input, retrieving data from a database, and formatting a result are not good candidates for use cases. They simply do not make sense separately.

If you can answer yes to the following questions, then the use case is probably significant and well isolated. Otherwise, the use case may really be part of some other use case.

- Does the actor either gain significant information or change the system in some measurable way?
- Could an actor perform the use case and then stop using the system for a significant time? This may not be the normal case, but it must be plausible.

Let's take a look at the use cases for a banking system as an example. A banking system with the functions enter amount, select account, withdraw funds, deposit funds, select source account, select destination account, and transfer funds as separate use cases is too granular. The use cases do not make sense in isolation. For example, no user would select an account and then walk away satisfied. Each of these activities is actually part of one or more use cases.

The same system with a single use case—manage money—is too ambiguous. A good use case provides specific value to one or more specific actors. Manage money sounds like a vision for any number of systems, not a particular use case in a banking system.

Instead, a bank system might reasonably have these use cases: deposit funds, withdraw funds, and transfer funds. Each of these use cases provides concrete benefit to the bank customer, because each moves the customer's money around in a useful and distinct way. Each of these use cases makes sense in isolation. For instance, the user might comfortably walk away from the system after depositing money, and return some other day to withdraw funds.

Describe Actors and Use Cases

Once you have identified the actors and use cases for the system, the next step is to indicate which actors depend on which use cases. In the UML, a stick figure represents an actor, and a labeled oval represents a use case. A solid arrow pointing from an actor to a use case indicates that the actor initiates the use case. Figure 2.1 shows that the Customer actor uses the Purchase Book use case.

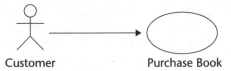

Customer   Purchase Book

Figure 2.1   An example use case diagram.

This type of diagram serves as a very accessible view of the overall use of the system. It allows developers and stakeholders to keep their bearings as they navigate through a large requirements document. It also helps end users to identify areas that affect them, so they can efficiently contribute to those areas. As we will see in the next section, the full requirements document contains a wealth of information for each use case.

Describe Detailed and Complete Requirements

There are two ways to describe the requirements: Use a text document to describe the use case in detail, along with the interactions between the actor and the system for each use case; or describe the requirements using a UML *activity diagram*. The UML activity diagram shows the same interactions as described in the text document, but in a visual form. The two documents have a similar purpose and contain similar information, and reinforce one another quite well. Certainly, different people learn in very different ways, so having a readable text description and a highly precise visual description is an advantage.

Each use case includes three elements:

- Use case description
- One or more flow of events
- Activity diagram

Let's take a look at each of these elements.

Use Case Description

A use case description provides an overview of the use case, and specifies any special features, such as preconditions, postconditions, performance requirements, security requirements, and deployment constraints. Preconditions include any use cases that must be completed before the actor may start the use case. Postconditions include any changes to the system that must be accomplished during the use case. Finally, deployment constraints describe limitations on how the use case is accessed. For instance, the actor may need to interact with the system through a firewall or from a highly portable device. These constraints specify needs while leaving the solution as open as possible.

Flow of Events

A flow of events describes a sequence of interactions that occurs as the actor attempts to complete the use case. A flow of events does not describe different variations; instead, it follows a single path all of the way through the use case. Other paths through the use case are described by other flows of events.

Each interaction in the flow is a text description of the actor's input and the response from the system. Consider the interactions involved in the Withdraw Funds use case from a banking system when the actor does everything right and the system performs as expected.

1. Customer inserts card and enters his or her personal identification number (PIN). The system greets the customer by name, and presents a list of options, consisting of withdraw funds, deposit funds, and transfer funds.

2. User selects withdraw funds. The system presents a list of accounts for the customer to choose from.

3. The customer chooses an account. The system asks the user to enter the amount of money for withdrawal.

4. The customer enters a positive multiple of $20. The system asks the customer if the amount is correct.

5. The customer responds that the amount is correct. The system thanks the user, distributes the money, prints a receipt, and returns the customer's card.

To restate: This first flow of events describes the interactions when everything goes well. Certainly, there are other less favorable possibilities, but it is often best to describe the normal flow before tackling the details of other possible flows, including disaster scenarios. For example, think about what happens when you give driving directions to a new arrival to your town or city. Most people describe the most direct route first, then provide alternative routes on request. This logic holds for use cases. Someone who is new to the system needs to understand the normal flow before he or she considers more complex flows.

There are three types of flows through every use case:

Normal, or baseline flow.   Captures the purpose of the use case by describing the interactions when everything proceeds according to plan. The flow above for the Withdraw Funds use case is an example of a normal flow.

Alternative flows.   Describes variation by the actor. For example, the actor may abort the session or become confused and wander through the system for a while. Or the actor may enter invalid data and be forced to correct it before he or she can continue. One use case may require several alternative flows. Alternative flows for the Withdraw Funds use case include the entry of an invalid PIN and a request to overdraw the account.

Exception flows.   Describes variation by the system. Since systems are generally prized for their consistency, these variations are errors. For example, the system may be prevented from completing its normal response due to network failure, disk errors, or resource limitations. Most use cases have at least a few exception flows.

Activity Diagrams

An activity diagram is a UML diagram that shows all of the flows of events for a use case in one place. To accomplish this, activity diagrams show different activities that the system performs and how different results cause the system to take different paths. Activity diagrams depict a start state, activities that the system performs, decisions that determine which activity is performed next, and one or more end points. Activity diagrams also have notation to describe activities that are performed in parallel.

Figure 2.2 shows the activity diagram for the Withdraw Funds use case. The solid circle represents the start of the use case; the round-cornered rectangles represent activities that the system performs. Each arrow represents a transition from one activity to another. So, the first activity is the system asking the actor to enter his or her PIN, as shown in the Ask for PIN activity. The labeled arrow from the Ask for PIN activity to the Validate PIN activity represents the transition between the two activities that occurs when the actor enters his or her PIN. Since there are two outcomes from the Validate PIN activity, the next transition includes a diamond-shaped decision symbol. Each of the outcomes is labeled with the associated decision criteria. If the PIN is valid, the transition goes to the Present Options activity; otherwise, the transition goes to the Check for Too Many Retries activity. Following the path straight down, the actor selects an account to transition from the Present Accounts activity to the Request Amount activity. From there, the actor enters an amount to cause the transition from the Request Amount activity. This transition contains a decision, with one outcome leading back to the Request Amount activity and the other outcome leading down to the Dispense Money activity.

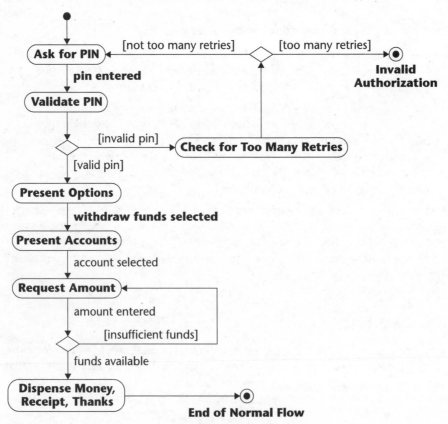

Figure 2.2   Activity diagram for the Withdraw Funds use case.

The straight path from the Ask for PIN activity to the Dispense Money activity is the normal flow. The side paths for invalid logins and for overdrawn accounts are alternative flows. No exception flows are shown.

NOTE An activity diagram is not a flowchart. While they look very similar and share much of the same notation, they have very different purposes. Flowcharts help implementers develop code by precisely describing the control logic for the code. An activity diagram helps stakeholders understand the requirements at a very precise level, and helps developers design the system, by precisely describing how the actor uses the system and how the system responds. Flowcharts describe the solution; activity diagrams describe the problem.

Some project teams limit the creation of activity diagrams to very complex use cases. This is generally not a good idea. If the use case really is simple, developing an activity diagram is straightforward and does not consume much time. Also, creating the activity diagram often unearths interesting issues that might not surface in a text description of the interaction. Finally, creating activity diagrams for the simple use cases also familiarizes developers and stakeholders with the mechanism on easy use cases.

Refactor the Use Case Model

After each use case is fleshed out, the requirements gatherers must revisit and often revise the use case model as a whole. Using the guidelines for isolation and focus, use cases may need to be split up, merged, or clarified. Excessively complex use cases must be identified and fixed.

In some cases, a use case may seem well focused and isolated, but still be too complex. This is often found in use cases that consist of complex workflows. The system may not provide any value unless the entire workflow is completed, yet it may be difficult to comprehend the entire process at once. For example, consider the process of ordering a book online. The use case that provides the value is Purchase Book. That does not, however, specify the steps involved: The customer must find a book, consider any reviews, enter his or her payment information and shipping information, and, finally, purchase the book. No mere mortal could understand the activity diagram for this monolithic use case. Few organizations own a sufficiently large plotter to print it. Writing or even reading this huge flow of events from the beginning to the end would be exhausting. Finding a specific issue in a flow of events would be difficult. Despite the theoretical correctness of the use case, it fails the ultimate test; it is not useful to the stakeholders.

There are several mechanisms that manage this sort of complexity. The first splits up the use case and uses preconditions to describe the workflow. Another mechanism uses the *include* and *extend* relationships as specified by the UML. Also, variability can be expressed by actor and use case generalization. Let's consider these mechanisms as applied to a simple book-ordering example.

Split up the Use Case

First, an unwieldy use case may be deleted and its functionality split into several use cases. These use cases are connected by preconditions and postconditions. Preconditions include any use cases that must be completed before the actor may start the use case. Postconditions include any changes to the system that must be accomplished during the use case. Figure 2.3 shows the Purchase Book use case split into many use cases. Find a Book allows the customer to search for a book by different criteria; it has no preconditions. View Reviews displays the reviews for a selected book; it has successful completion of Find a Book as a precondition. Since each customer must enter payment information at least once and each customer may buy many books, the Enter Payment Information use case is an optional part of the workflow. The same is true of Enter Shipping Information. The Complete Purchase use case has completion of the Enter Payment Information use case and the Enter Shipping Information use case as preconditions. All preconditions for a use case are described in the description of that use case.

This approach has several advantages. First and foremost, it breaks the use case model into manageable pieces. Each new use case has significantly smaller flows of events. The activity diagrams for the use cases no longer require an expensive plotter and a magnifying glass. The overall use case model is far easier to navigate and to understand.

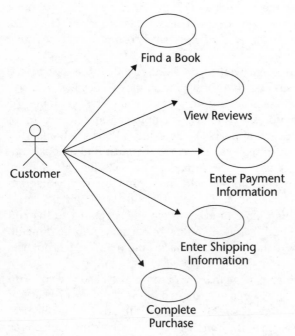

Figure 2.3   Use cases for the Purchase Book workflow.

Unfortunately, some information is hidden in this process. A reviewer must check the preconditions to determine the order and dependencies of the use cases in the workflow. There is no way to determine which use cases are optional and which use cases are essential to the workflow. While the layout of the diagram provides some visual clues, it is not a precise or clear description.

Use of Include and Extend Relationships

The UML provides two powerful and, at times, confusing relationships between use cases. The *extend* relationship allows a use case to be included as an option in another, or base, use case. The other relationship, *include*, allows a use case to always include another base use case.

Include

In an include relationship, the base use case depends on the included use case because it absorbs its behavior. An include relationship is represented by a dashed arrow pointing from the base use case to the included use case. The relationship is stereotyped by enclosing the word "include" within double angle brackets. The flow of events proceeds along in the base use case until the inclusion point is reached. At this point, the flow of events for the included use case is followed until it is completed. After completion of the included use case, the rest of the base flow of events is followed to completion. The inclusion is not optional; when the base use case reaches the inclusion point, the included use case takes over the flow. Also, the included use case may be abstract, such that different forms of the use case can be included without changing the base use case.

Include has two major advantages. First, the base use case is simplified, since the included use case is pulled out. Second, a use case may be included in more than one base use case, so that common flows can be abstracted out. However, in order to qualify, the included use case must fit the definition of a use case. Specifically, it must provide some isolated value to the actor.

Extend

In an extend relationship, the base use case does not include the subordinate use case. Instead, the extension use case depends on the base use case and optionally adds its flow of events to the base use case's flow of events. An extend relationship is represented by a dashed arrow pointing from the extension case to the base use case. The relationship is stereotyped by enclosing the word "extend" within double angle brackets. The base use case defines one or more extension points in its flow of events. Each extension use case specifies the extension point at which it may be inserted, along with the conditions that must hold for the insertion to take place. As the base use case's flow of events progresses to an insertion point, the conditions are checked for the extension use case. If the conditions are met, the extension use case's flow of events is followed to completion. Next, the base use case's flow of events picks up just after the extension point.

In an extend relationship, the dependency is from the extension use case to the base use case, as opposed to an include relationship, in which the dependency is from the base use case to the included use case. Extend use cases are optional, while include use cases must take over the flow if the base use case reaches the inclusion point.

Example

Let's take a look at an example. Figure 2.4 shows the Customer actor initiating the Purchase Book use case. The include relationship between the Purchase Book use case and the Find a Book use case indicates that the flow of events for the Purchase Book use case always includes the flow of the Find a Book use case. Similarly, the include relationship between the Purchase Book use case and the Complete Purchase use case indicates that the flow of events for the Complete Purchase use case is always followed, if the flow of events for the Purchase Book use case reaches the inclusion point.

The extend relationships between the Purchase Book use case and the remaining use cases indicate that they are optional. For instance, the customer may have already entered shipping and payment information and be quite content with it.

There are advantages to using the include and extend relationships. The original use case is simplified because the flows of events in the base use case implement the include or extend use cases. Also, the relationships between the original use case and the subordinate use cases are far more precise and visually apparent than is the case for independent use cases and preconditions.

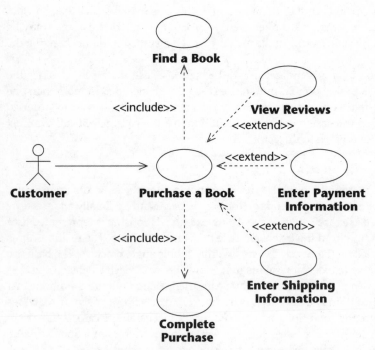

Figure 2.4   Purchase Book use case with include and extend.

However, the precision of include and extend comes with a price. It is not always easy to explain the concepts; and, as noted earlier, a use case must be written for a wide audience. Imagine a requirements review with 30 people in attendance. Now, picture trying to explain the include and extend relationships on the spot. If your use case model benefits from this more advanced notation, then it may be necessary to educate the stakeholders in small groups. Alternatively, it may be possible to show a simplified use case model that omits the inclusion and extension use cases to the wide audience, and reserve the more complex model for carefully targeted groups.

Use Case Generalization

In some situations, a use case may have several distinct paths. For example, there may be two ways in which to find a book. Customers who have a clear idea of their needs can search by title, subject, or even ISBN. Otherwise, customers browse in broad categories, such as mystery novels or home and garden. They may jump from book to book, by following links to similar books.

This combination of searching and browsing in one use case makes the Find a Book use case very difficult to develop and to understand. Fortunately, UML provides a mechanism for exactly this situation. The Find a Book use case is converted into an abstract use case, which means that it defines the value that is obtained by the actor, but does not specify the interactions that are used to reach the goal. Next, multiple concrete use cases are written, with each one specifying a set of interactions that reach the goal defined by the abstract use case. For the Find a Book use case, one concrete use case might be Search for a Book and the other might be Browse for a Book. Figure 2.5 shows the abstract Find a Book use case as a generalization of the two concrete use cases.

Use case generalization can help divide a complex use case into more manageable pieces. In many cases, just the act of creating the activity diagram identifies good candidates for use case generalization. Look for parallel paths that have the same basic purpose.

WARNING Do not implement use case generalization based on use case size and complexity alone.

It is often tempting to split up a use case as the activity diagram and flow of events becomes unwieldy. Discipline and an understanding of the different mechanisms must temper this natural instinct. Arbitrary use of sophisticated mechanisms leads to confusion and eliminates many of the benefits of use cases.

When appropriate, use case generalization makes a use case model more precise without making it much more complex. It is an excellent mechanism when there are high-level alternatives in a use case, but both alternatives serve the same basic purpose.

That said, as with include and extend, use case generalization requires more sophistication from the consumers of the use case model. In my experience, the concept is significantly easier to explain than include and extend. Also, it is very easy to produce a high-level use case model that simply excludes the concrete use cases.

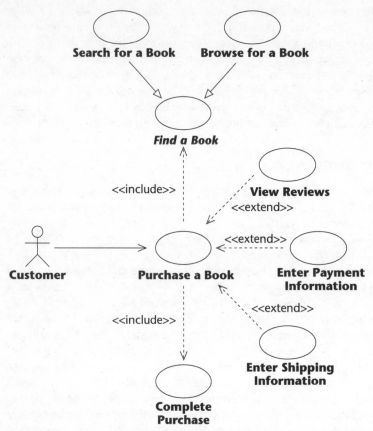

Figure 2.5   The Find a Book use case with use case generalization.

Actor Generalization

In many use case models, one actor is very similar to another actor, yet still has additional obligations or responsibilities. In the UML, an actor is shown as a special type of another actor by drawing a generalization arrow to the more general actor. The generalization relationship is intended to document real-world differences and similarities between user groups. The more specific actor must initiate all of the use cases that the more generic actor initiates; thus the more specific actor is actually a type of the generalized actor.

Consider a simple hiring process, in which managers and employees both participate in the interview and selection processes, but in which only the manager discusses salary and makes the final hiring decision. Both perform the Interview Candidate and Evaluate Candidate use cases, but only the manager performs the Tender Offer and Reject Candidate use cases. Figure 2.6 shows the first two use cases initiated by the Employee actor and the second two use cases initiated by the Manager actor. But note, since the Employee actor is a generalization of the Manager actor, the Manager actor also initiates the Interview Candidate and Evaluate Candidate use cases.

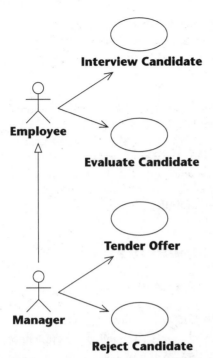

Figure 2.6   Use of actor generalization.

Actor generalization is appropriate only if the actor uses all of the use cases that the generalized actor uses, thus really is a special type of the generalized actor. Consider an example with technical experts and managers. In most companies, there is no generalization relationship between the actors. Not all managers are technical experts and not all technical experts are managers. There is no reason to force this into a generalization relationship. Instead, simply show the actors separately, as in Figure 2.7.

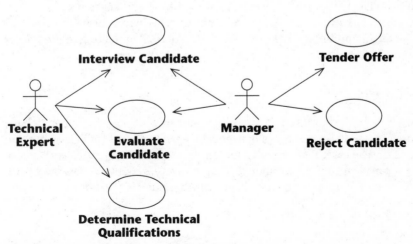

Figure 2.7   Separate actors, no generalization.

WARNING Actor generalization can become needlessly complex. Don't impose a relationship where none exists. Remember, you can always eliminate the actor generalization and simply show the relationships between each actor and use case.

Actor generalization can simplify a use case model, especially if a new version of an actor adds a few use cases while initiating many existing use cases. However, actor generalization does add complexity and demand some incremental sophistication from the consumers of the use case model. If the actors' names are well chosen, and the relationships are not excessively complex, most stakeholders find the underlying idea quite reasonable. After all, the relationships between actors reflect and highlight real-world differences and similarities among user communities.

Guidelines for Gathering Requirements

It is important to keep the requirements at a consistent level of detail and to be thorough. That said, it is also important to make sure that the requirements-gathering process does not become an end unto itself. Striking this balance between too little and too much will result in a solid foundation for the entire development process. The following guidelines give general advice on the requirements-gathering process as a whole.

Focus on the Problem

Remember to concentrate on what the system does, and ignore questions about how it works. For example, it is inappropriate to choose between two competing technologies in a requirements document, but it is necessary to include any known deployment constraints. The customer may require access to certain functionality from a Web browser, which is a requirement and so must be noted for each use case. However, the decision to use Java servlets as opposed to JavaServer Pages (JSP) is inappropriate in a requirements document. Later, when the project focuses on technology selection and architecture, the requirements provide valuable information that shapes these difficult and crucial decisions. Attempting to make the decisions while still gathering requirements leads to hasty decisions that are based on incomplete information.

Don't Give Up

Perseverance is often the hardest part of use case modeling. A large system may have dozens of use cases with several flows of events for each use case. There is an activity diagram for each use case. Be complete, and strive to maintain a consistent level of quality and detail. The collective understanding of every system evolves over time, and requires countless hours of review of the meeting notes and updates to the use case model.

It often helps to develop the requirements in stages. First, develop the high-level use case model, which identifies the actors and use cases. Validating this model with the user builds consensus and clarifies the boundaries of the system. Next, develop descriptions and flows of events for some strategically important use cases. It may be appropriate to review this material with some of the stakeholders as you proceed. Continue this process until you have at least a description and the normal flow for each use case in the model. After validating this model with the stakeholders, identify a few use cases for further exploration and dig in. At this stage, it is appropriate to spend several days on each use case, developing alternate and exception flows of events and consolidating the flows in an activity diagram. After a few use cases have elaborated, it may be necessary to refactor the high-level use case model, using techniques such as the include and extend relationships between use cases or use case generalization. After reviewing this block of work with the stakeholders, you must decide to design and develop the well-defined use cases or elaborate additional use cases.

A commitment to complete requirements does not preclude other concurrent efforts. For instance, once each use case has been described and reviewed, parallel efforts for screen design, technology selection, and architecture may coexist with refinement of the use case model. Obviously, these processes must not start too early; but judicious overlapping of these activities is relatively safe and often provides valuable insight. On the other hand, it is very dangerous to consolidate the various documents or consolidate the efforts. Each effort has separate goals and deserves a separate schedule and separate reviews.

Don't Go Too Far

Authors and speakers, ourselves included, use statistics to frighten developers into gathering comprehensive requirements. Having seen the effects of inadequate requirements, we believe that this tactic is justifiable. Nevertheless, requirements gathering can be overemphasized and drawn out past its usefulness. Remember, requirements are not an end unto themselves. They are a foundation for the rest of the development process. Foundations must be strong and durable; they do not need to be artistic masterpieces.

In some cases the requirements-gathering process drags on and on due to a reluctance to move forward or a desire to achieve perfect requirements. This tendency may be exacerbated by a demanding or indecisive customer or by uncertainty about the next step. Developers are especially vulnerable on their first project with a new methodology or with new technology. We have seen some projects become mired in requirements long after the benefits stopped, because it was easier to continue to impress the stakeholders with another round of requirements than to face an uncertain future. Of course, this never works out well, because the next step must eventually be taken, and time spent endlessly refining requirements cannot be used on prototyping or technology training that might remove some of the uncertainty.

Believe in the Process

Solid requirements are essential to your project's success. Without them, you are doomed to solve the wrong problems, repeat your efforts, and anger your customer. Attempting to save time by neglecting requirements invariably leads to extending the duration of the project and higher costs. As Benjamin Franklin put it, "Haste makes waste." Discovering a missing or misunderstood requirement during system testing is often catastrophic. Fixing an omission or mistake may require weeks or months of development. In the meantime, marketing schedules are destroyed, expensive production hardware sits unused, business opportunities are missed, and credibility is lost forever. In some cases, projects, jobs, even entire companies are lost. At best, developers pour their hearts into a year's effort and produce a system that the customers think they can live with, although they don't really see what that one screen is for and they really wish that it worked differently.

Poor requirements lead to project failure in several ways:

Customer confidence in the development process and the developers erodes with each misunderstanding.   Each failure raises the pressure for the next attempt; hence, communication between developers and stakeholders deteriorates rapidly. Once communication breaks down, the misunderstandings grow, and an adversarial cloud settles over the project. It is very difficult to reverse this trend once it starts.

The software base bloats as it expands to accommodate an ever-changing view of the system.   New requirements and new understandings of existing requirements add layer after layer to the implementation. Continued over months and years, this process can mean a tedious death of a project by a thousand cuts.

Developers' morale collapses as they realize that they are spending more and more time but accomplishing less and less.   Each time a developer spends time solving the wrong problem, his or her faith in the process and hope for success diminishes.

On the other hand, a good use case model is a solid foundation for the rest of the project because:

Developers begin analysis, architecture, and design with confidence.   They know that the requirements will not shift radically beneath their feet, and they have a clear source of information as they proceed. Certainly, they expect to ask questions and refine the requirements as they go, but the core value is complete. This allows them to focus their attention on the solution. Technology selection and architecture decisions are based on complete information. Also, since the overall problem is well understood, developers may comfortably focus on a few use cases at a time.

Project managers treat each use case as a unit of work for scheduling, risk tracking, and estimation.   Developers produce effort estimates and identify risks for each use case in turn. This allows the project manager and the senior technical staff to develop a very sophisticated project plan that identifies and attacks risks early in the project, by targeting particular use cases. For example, one use case may be identified as a high priority due to its complex processing or a challenging user interface. Also, many project teams are new to the solution technologies. Selecting simple use cases for the initial development effort may help alleviate this common and serious risk. It is better to build on success than to overreach and live with failure. So, project managers should leverage the use case model as they estimate and schedule development, manage risks, and grow their team.

Testers treat each use case as a basis for a section in the test plan.   A well-written flow of events form easily evolves into a test case. Remember, the flow of events describes the interactions between the actor and the system. In the test case, the actor's requests and inputs become test directions, and the system's responses become the expected result. Of course, the use case is written without consideration for particular screens or technology, so additional instructions must be added. However, the basic structure and narrative flow often remains unchanged in the evolution from flow of events to test case. This creates an interesting side effect: People with experience developing test plans may be very proficient at reviewing and writing use cases.

Stakeholders track progress objectively; either the latest release supports a use case or it doesn't.   Objective measurement tends to reduce tensions between developers and stakeholders. Having clearly understood bad news is still better than being completely in the dark. Completing three out of the five use cases is a clear, if partial, success. Everyone knows what is complete and what is not complete. Compare this to the equivalent measurement of a milestone being 60 percent complete. Stakeholders tend to feel frustrated and misled, because the system's progress is a mystery to them, and the percent-complete numbers never quite move as expected.

How to Detect Poor Requirements

If gathering requirements is key to project success, then everyone must be doing it. Tragically, this is not the case. Many organizations, both large and small, skim past requirements or develop them so poorly that all benefit is lost. There are several common rationalizations for this negligence:

- Excessive schedule pressure
- No clear vision
- Premature architecture and design

The following sections describe these common paths to poor requirements, including symptoms and remedies.

Path 1: Excessive Schedule Pressure

Excessive schedule pressure is the most common rationale for skipping or skimming through the requirements-gathering process. It is also the worst possible combination: The development team does not know what it is trying to accomplish, but they are working too fast to notice. The pressure to get something, anything, out the door is overwhelming. In the end, very bright people spend nights and weekends paying the price.

There are two distinct variants on this path. In one, management is almost completely uninvolved. Their only concern is the final milestone, so the constant refrain is "When will you be done?" The alternate version is micromanaged pressure. In this version, management obsessively tracks the schedule and misuses schedule-oriented practices, such as commitment-based scheduling and time-boxing.

Symptoms

- Hard deadlines are determined before the objectives are defined.
- Developers make feature decisions as they code.
- Everyone is coding, but there is no coherent or readable requirements document.

Solution

Education, redirection of energy, and verification are the keys to avoiding this path. Managers, developers, and the stakeholders must understand the process and the importance of gathering requirements, and requirements reviews must be used to ensure that requirements are complete before moving forward. If the schedule is truly important, managers and the entire development staff must redirect their energies toward practices that do work.

First, both developers and managers need to understand that trying to save time by skimping on requirements is a dangerous and counterproductive practice. Reinforce the following points:

- Incomplete requirements lead to expensive and time-consuming reworking.
- Work that is invalidated by a new requirement or a new interpretation is completely wasted.
- The longer it takes to catch missing or incorrect requirements, the longer it will take to undo the damage.
- A commitment to gathering solid requirements eliminates reworking, thereby shortening the actual schedule.
- Fostering positive relations with the other stakeholders during requirements gathering sets the stage for win-win compromises on the schedule and features.

Once everyone understands the need for good requirements, they must commit to producing them. Specifically, managers must schedule time for requirements gathering, and ensure that the requirement gatherers have access to the right stakeholders. The requirements gatherers must be thorough and persistent. Requirements must be reviewed for quality and completeness at scheduled intervals. At least some of these reviews must include a wide range of stakeholders. Gathering requirements takes skill and a great deal of persistence. With a little practice and a lot of willpower, every project team can excel at this process.

Path 2: No Clear Vision

In this situation, the development team gathers requirements for a poorly defined system. Without a solid system scope and vision, requirements tend to change and grow at each requirements meeting. If there is no clear system sponsor, requirements change as developers attempt to please various potential sponsors. A lack of vision often leads to requirements artifacts of unusually large size. These intricate creations grow, but rarely improve. I have seen over $1 million (U.S.) spent gathering requirements and prototyping, all without a clear vision of the system. At best, the time is simply wasted. At worst, the final set of requirements actually impedes progress because it is burdened by obsolete or contradictory requirements. Ironically, the requirements-gathering process and the developers often receive the blame.

Symptoms

- Requirements documents are very large and very convoluted.
- Requirements are contradictory.
- Frequent changes are made to requirements.
- Requirements are unstable: They are included, excluded, and reinstated in a bizarre birth, death, and reincarnation cycle.
- Corporate politics are an integral part of requirements meetings.

Solution

Developers can raise awareness of the risks associated with gathering requirements without a clear vision. Unfortunately, the underlying political barriers to commitment may be very real. Perhaps the budget is fragmented among different departments. Perhaps the most likely sponsor swore off commitment to risky software development projects as part of a New Year's resolution.

The first goal is to find or create a sponsor. In some cases, there are stakeholders who face severe consequences if the project does not succeed. These stakeholders may listen to reason and become the sponsor. As always, finding receptive people and educating them about risks and dangers is a delicate task. But the alternative is worse.

If no sponsor can be found, the developers may still be able to bring some order to the chaos. Rather than having one set of requirements that has pieces of each vision, try to maintain a distinct document for each major vision. This may help the stakeholders see the dilemma. At the very least, the developers' lives will improve, because each document stays relatively simple.

Path 3: Premature Architecture and Design

In times of adversity, we revert to what we know and believe. Is it surprising when developers forsake tedious and often contentious requirements meetings in favor of technology selection, design, and code? It is difficult to spend endless hours establishing the details of the system requirements when design and code beckon with the promise of quick progress, objective results, and intellectual stimulation. As a result, requirements documents either atrophy from neglect or evolve to resemble architecture and design documents. Either way, the quick progress is often illusory, because it is progress in a poorly defined direction.

Symptoms

- The requirements-gathering process ends with no closure or consensus.
- Requirements documents contain implementation details.

Solution

There are two solutions to this situation. First, educate and encourage developers to make requirements a priority. Second, make gathering requirements as easy as possible for developers.

Developers must understand the benefits of requirements and the dangers of developing software without them.

Reinforce the following points at every opportunity:

- Incomplete requirements lead to poor technology selection and architecture decisions. The time spent making these decisions and implementing them cannot be recovered.

- Solid requirements make estimating, scheduling, and testing possible. All of these activities help the developer coexist with the other stakeholders, by baselining expectations and providing project visibility.

These messages are especially powerful when combined with commitment-based scheduling. In this scenario, a developer develops requirements for part of a system, then produces an effort estimate based on the requirements. This allows developers to benefit from their own diligence.

In many organizations, gathering requirements is unnecessarily burdensome for developers. For instance, tedious formatting standards can be relaxed or the work may be shifted to other personnel. Dedicated business analysts can interact with the customer and start the process.

The Next Step

This chapter established a number of steps and guidelines for gathering requirements, including gathering raw requirements, creating a high-level view of the requirements, and describing the details of the requirements. Chapter 3 introduces a simple sample application to demonstrate how you can use these techniques.

Gathering Requirements for the Timecard Application

In this chapter, we'll simulate the requirements-gathering process for a simple time-tracking application, using the process introduced in Chapter 2, "Gathering Requirements with UML." We'll use this example throughout this book.

NOTE For the purposes of this book, we had to keep the example simple, so please keep in mind that while this book describes techniques that are appropriate for much larger systems, demonstrating these real-world techniques against a fairly small problem often forced us to overengineer the sample solutions. Another caveat: To keep the example small, the simulated customer is unbelievably compliant and helpful.

In this example, the developer discovers that the primary stakeholder is the operations manager who manages the time-tracking process for the client organization. Next, the developer works with the operations manager and an end user to understand the system, then describes the system in a high-level use case model. Based on feedback from the customer, the developer refines the use case model and increases the level of detail. Finally, the developer refactors the use case model to improve readability and accessibility.

The final product of this chapter is a use case model, complete with a high-level use case diagram for navigation, as well as a detailed description of each use case. Together, these elements combine to form a model that is both accessible and complete. Both factors are critical, as stakeholders review the use case model to validate the proposed system, and the development team treats the use case model as a basis for the entire development process, from effort estimation to design and test.

Listen to the Stakeholders

Remember, a system is defined by the value that it provides to people. So, our goal during this phase is to understand the system from the customer's perspective. This section describes a somewhat idealized dialogue between a developer, the operations manager who is responsible for time tracking, and an employee who uses the system. Their goal is to describe the system's functionality and purpose. Certainly, in the real world, such a meeting would involve 5, 10, or even 20 people, all with different needs and perspectives. It might take many meetings over several weeks to reach the first solid understanding of the system.

TIP Raw requirements are the foundation for the whole development process. There is only one way to get them: Go forth and ask—nicely. Then ask if you got it right.

SAMPLE NOTES FROM INITIAL MEETING

DEVELOPER: Who will use the application?

CUSTOMER: Employees will use it to record their billable and nonbillable hours.

DEVELOPER: From where? Here and home and client sites? Behind firewalls?

CUSTOMER: Here at the office. Sometimes from home. Definitely from client sites that are behind firewalls.

DEVELOPER: Okay, that helps. Well, what does the timecard application look like now?

CUSTOMER: It is an Excel spreadsheet for each half-month. Each employee fills in his or her copy and then emails it to me. It is pretty standard: charge codes down the side and days across the top. The employee is able to comment any entry.

DEVELOPER: Where do the charge numbers come from?

CUSTOMER: A separate spreadsheet has a list of valid charge codes, organized by client and activity.

DEVELOPER: So, each charge code has a name, a client, and a project?

CUSTOMER: Yes, and also a type, like billable or nonbillable.

DEVELOPER: Do you think you would ever need a deeper hierarchy?

CUSTOMER: What?

DEVELOPER: Sorry, right now you have client, project, and activity. Would you ever need subprojects or subactivities?

> **CUSTOMER:** No, I wouldn't think so.
>
> **DEVELOPER:** Who manages charge codes?
>
> **CUSTOMER:** Well, I add them as needed, and individual managers tell their people what to bill to. They never really go away.
>
> **DEVELOPER:** Are there any special cases you can think of? For instance, do employees fill information in ahead of time or anything like that?
>
> **CUSTOMER:** Oh, I see. The employee doesn't. If someone is going to be on vacation for a long time, or in the hospital, I take care of his or her timesheets.
>
> **DEVELOPER:** How will the data be used once it is collected?
>
> **CUSTOMER:** Our new billing system uses the data to bill our customers.
>
> **DEVELOPER:** What criteria does the billing system use when it requests data from the Timecard system?
>
> **CUSTOMER:** It should be able to specify the date range, clients, and employees that are included.
>
> **DEVELOPER:** Okay, we should be able to handle that. I'll see if I can track down the details for that.
>
> **DEVELOPER:** Thank you very much for your time; I think we have something to work with. . . . Can we meet again on Tuesday?
>
> **CUSTOMER:** Sounds good.

In this dialogue, the customer and the developer discovered and refined the customer's needs for the system. Notice that the developer asks a question, listens to the answer, then either summarizes the response or asks a clarifying question. In most cases, the customer does not know exactly what he or she wants, and certainly is not expected to anticipate the level of detail required for software development. So, it is up to the developer or requirements analyst to shape the discussion and ensure that the necessary information is gathered.

Based on this dialogue, the developers can begin creating the actual system requirements documents, starting with a high-level use case diagram.

Build a Use Case Diagram

Building a high-level use case diagram has three steps: Identify the actors, identify the use cases, and finally determine the relationships between the actors and use cases.

Remember from Chapter 2:

- An actor usually represents a group of people who gain value by interacting with the system. An actor may also represent a system that is outside of the system and that gains value or provides value by interacting with the system.

In the UML, actors are shown as stick figures. There is no distinction between human actors and external systems.

■ A use case describes a set of interactions between an actor and the system that provides a discrete benefit or value to the actor. The value must be independently significant, yet well focused. In the UML, a use case is shown as a labeled oval.

■ There are only two reasons for an actor to be associated with a use case. First, all use cases are initiated by at least one actor. In order to initiate a use case, the actor must be associated with it. In the UML, this is shown by a solid arrow from the actor to the use case. Once a use case is initiated, it may send notifications to other actors or request information from other actors. This dependence on the other actor(s) is represented in the UML by a solid arrow drawn from the use case to the actor.

Find the Actors

Actors are discovered by reading the raw requirements notes, culling out participants, and determining the distinct groups of users. This first attempt invariably contains redundant names for the same actor, and may miss some actors entirely.

Find Candidate Actors

From the raw notes, the developer highlights the following dialogue:

DEVELOPER: Who will use the application?

CUSTOMER: **Employees** will use it to record their billable and nonbillable hours.

DEVELOPER: Who manages charge codes?

CUSTOMER: Well, I (**operations manager**) add them as needed, and individual **managers** tell their people what to bill to. They never really go away.

DEVELOPER: How will the data be used once it is collected?

CUSTOMER: Our new **billing system** uses the data to bill our customers.

From these excerpts, it appears that the candidate actors are employee, operations manager, manager, and billing system.

Refine the Actors

Refining the list of actors is an interactive process. In many cases, the customers have a clear view of the roles within their organization. Subsequent meetings will be greatly simplified if developers adopt the users' terminology. Also, developers may need to probe a bit to determine if there are differences in the way that different types of people use the system. Remember, actors are determined by their use of the system, not by differences in job titles or organizational hierarchy.

The first actor seems clear. Employees use the system to record their time. The next, operations manager, seems essential, but the name indicates a single person in the organization. What if that person goes on vacation or needs to delegate his or her responsibilities as the organization grows? A brief flurry of emails with the operations manager determines that the actor's real name is "administrative user," with the understanding that currently only one person is filling this role.

A face-to-face meeting is needed to decide whether managers are separate actors. They certainly have a role in the process, because employees must know which projects they can bill to. However, under the current requirements, the managers do not use the system to enforce these decisions. After some discussion, the customers agree that determining who has permission to bill to a charge code is not a requirement for the system. So, managers are eliminated as an actor.

Finally, the billing system is an external system that interacts with the Timecard system, so it is also an actor.

This leaves the following actors: employee, administrative user, and billing system.

Find the Use Cases

Use cases are found by identifying candidate use cases from the raw notes and asking what additional use cases are needed to support the obvious use cases. Then the guidelines established in Chapter 2 are applied to the candidates. These guidelines lead developers to split, merge, and eliminate use cases until a solid set of use cases is identified.

Find Primary Use Cases

These are the use cases that characterize the system. From the raw notes, the developer highlights the following dialogue:

DEVELOPER: Who will use the application?

CUSTOMER: Employees will use it to **record their billable and nonbillable hours**.

CUSTOMER: It is an Excel spreadsheet for each half-month. Each employee fills in his or her copy and then emails it to me. It is pretty standard: charge codes down the side and days across the top. The employee is able to **comment any entry**.

DEVELOPER: Who manages charge codes?

CUSTOMER: Well, I (operations manager) **add them as needed**, and individual managers tell their people what to bill to. They never really go away.

DEVELOPER: How will the data be used once it is collected?

CUSTOMER: Our new billing system uses the data to **bill our customers**.

DEVELOPER: What criteria does the billing system use when it requests data from the Timecard system?

CUSTOMER: It should be able to specify the date range, clients, and employees that are included.

DEVELOPER: Okay; we should be able to handle that. I'll see if I can track down the details for that.

The first excerpt leads to the Record Time use case. The second leads to the Comment Time Entry use case. The third excerpt leads to the Create Charge Code use case. Finally, the last excerpt leads to the Extract Time Entries use case.

At first glance, Bill Client is an attractive use case. However, it is part of the billing system rather than the Timecard system, so it does not belong in the requirements of our Timecard system.

> **TIP** Use short active phrases when naming a use case. When reading the use case diagram, a reviewer should be able to say the name of the actor followed by the use case and have it sound almost like a sentence. For example, a diagram that shows the Employee actor initiating the Record Time use case reads as *the employee records time*.

Find Supporting Use Cases

Supporting use cases are not mentioned in the dialogue. They are found by asking what the system needs before it can accomplish each use case. Consider the Record Time use case. Before an employee can record his or her hours, the system needs a list of charge codes and a list of employees. The first part, the charge codes, is already provided by the Create Charge Code use case, but the existence of the employee is unexplained. So, a new use case, Create Employee, is needed. The other use cases, Comment Time Entry and Extract Time Entries, are supported by the Record Time use case.

The new list of candidate use cases includes Create Employee, Create Charge Code, Record Time, Comment Time Entry, and Extract Time Entries.

Evaluate Use Cases

Each use case must meet the isolation and focus guidelines described in Chapter 2. To summarize, each use case must be significant, so that it has value in isolation. However, it must also be well focused, so that it does not provide more than one distinct benefit to the actor. Each use case is considered independently before checking the whole use case model for consistency.

The Create Employee use case has a single benefit, as it only allows an administrator to add an employee to the system. So, the Create Employee use case meets our guidelines for focus. It is easy to imagine an administrative user receiving a request from a new hire's manager and adding the new hire to the system as a single task. Also, the system is significantly changed, as it has gained a new end user, so the Create Employee use case meets our guidelines for independent value.

The Create Charge Code use case also has a single benefit, as it only allows the administrative user to add a charge code to the system. It is easy to imagine the administrative user receiving a request from a project manager and adding the new charge code as a single task. Also, the system is significantly changed, as it has gained a new charge code that may be used by the end users. So, the Create Charge Code use case meets our guidelines.

The Record Time use case seems slightly less focused, since it allows an employee to view, update, and add time entries. However, none of these activities seems independently valuable. Record Time has a single distinct value, despite its distinct subactivities. When a use case seems too large, but the subactivities are clearly too small, it is wise to keep the high-level use case. As we will see later in this chapter, there are several techniques that simplify complex use cases without losing their coherence. Certainly the Record Time use case has value in isolation, as it is the motivation for the entire system.

The Comment Time Entry use case certainly meets the guidelines for focus, because it has a very concrete benefit. However, it fails the test for value in isolation. Commenting an entry is part of a larger activity, recording time. So, the Comment Time Entry use case is deleted as a use case and becomes part of the details for the Record Time use case.

The Extract Time Entries use case clearly has a well-defined and valuable purpose, because it allows the billing system to access the Timecard system's data.

This process trims our list of use cases to Create Employee, Create Charge Code, Record Time, and Extract Time Entries.

Determine the Actor-to-Use-Case Relationships

Each actor initiates one or more use cases, and each use case is initiated by one or more actors. Our final step in creating the high-level use case diagram is to describe these relationships for the actors and use cases. A solid arrow from the actor to the use case indicates that the actor initiates the use case.

Consider each actor in turn. Based on the dialogue with the customers, the Employee actor cannot initiate the Create Employee, Create Charge Code, or Extract Time Entries use cases. Certainly, the Employee actor must initiate the Record Time use case on a regular basis.

The Administrative User actor clearly initiates the Create Employee and Create Charge Code use cases. The person who fills the role of the Administrative User actor is almost certainly an employee of the organization and therefore must record his or her time. However, he or she does so in the role of an employee. The only reason a person would need to record time as an Administrative User would be to record another employee's time. Revisiting the meeting notes, it is clear that this is a requirement, as the administrative user records time for sick or vacationing employees.

The Billing System actor initiates the Extract Time Entries use case. It cannot initiate any of the other use cases.

Figure 3.1 shows these relationships; it is the first draft of the high-level use case diagram. At this point, you should confirm the accuracy of the model with the customer. The customer must recognize all of the actors and use cases. At this meeting, your customer should provide a valuable sanity check, and point out any missing features. Remember, a good use case model serves as a friendly and readable entry point into your requirements. Your customer must be able to easily understand it.

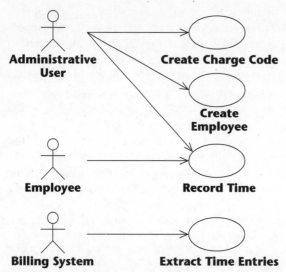

Figure 3.1   High-level use case diagram for the Timecard system.

Describe the Details

A use case diagram provides a high-level view of the entire system, but this is not a sufficient foundation for design. For each use case, you need to determine exactly how the customer uses the system. Again, the emphasis is on the value and the workflow, not on specific solutions.

Guidelines for Describing the Details

Any known deployment constraints are included at this point. For instance, if the end user accesses the system from behind a firewall or from a portable device, you must capture that requirement for any affected use cases. However, technology selection decisions are not included, so it would be inappropriate to propose solutions to the deployment constraints. Another common mistake is to think of a use case in terms of screen design. This is dangerous, because some screens may support many use cases and one use case may use several screens in the final design.

  Developing a flow of events requires a developer or requirements analyst to play the role of the end user and ask a series of questions. How does the flow start? What information does the system demand from the actor? How does the system respond? How does the flow end? The answers are captured in a list of inputs to the system and responses from the system. A flow of events resembles a test plan without any details about the screens or the format of the responses. In some cases, the developer can interact with the end users during this process, understanding their needs for each use case. Otherwise, the developer must develop reasonable flows of events and have the end users validate them.

It is a common belief that you come away with a very clear understanding of the system after the initial meeting with the customer. In fact, often, filling in the details for each use case is a humbling and enlightening experience. As you develop each flow of events and attempt to describe the preconditions and deployment constraints, you will discover relevant questions and open issues. These can be listed as part of the use case documentation and resolved at the first review of the entire use case model.

Each use case should follow a template. Though no two projects follow the same template, it should look something like this:

Name of use case.   A brief active phrase that captures the purpose of the use case.

Description.   A brief paragraph that explains the purpose of the use case, with an emphasis on the value to the actors. If this information cannot be conveyed in a brief paragraph, the use case may not be clearly focused.

Preconditions.   A brief paragraph that lists any use cases that must succeed before the use case is initiated and that describes the dependencies.

Deployment constraints.   A brief paragraph that describes how the system will be used to fulfill the use case. For instance, a particular use case may be initiated by an Employee actor who is behind the firewall that protects the employee's client. Because neglecting this sort of constraint can have serious consequences, the information must be captured as early as possible.

Normal flow of events.   An ordered list of interactions that describes all inputs to the system and responses from the system that make up the normal path through the use case. The normal flow of events captures the intent of the use case by showing the interactions when everything proceeds according to plan. This flow of events is also referred to as the *happy flow*.

Alternate flow of events.   An ordered list of interactions that describes all inputs to the system and responses from the system that make up a single alternate path through the use case. An alternate flow of events captures the system's response to variations by the user, such as entering invalid data or attempting to perform steps in a workflow in an unusual order. This section is repeated for each alternate flow of events.

Exception or error flow of events.   An ordered list of interactions that describes all inputs to the system and responses from the system that make up a single exception path through the use case. An exception flow of events captures the system's response to errors, such as unavailable system or external resources. This section is repeated for each exception flow of events.

Activity diagram.   Shows all of the flows of events for the use case in one diagram. It complements the flows of events and provides a valuable way to measure the complexity of a use case.

Nonfunctional requirements.   A brief paragraph or two that describes any success criteria for the use case that are not easily embedded in the flows of events. For instance, the system might need to provide a response for the use case in less than 3 seconds; or there might be an upper limit of seven mouse clicks to navigate through any flow of events for the use case.

Notes (optional).   A list of resolved issues that don't fit well in any other category. These may include restrictions on the system's functionality.

Open issues (optional).   A list of questions for the stakeholders.

Let's take a look at the use case documentation for our Timecard application.

Sample Use Case Documentation for Create Charge Code

Name of use case.   Create Charge Code

Description.   The Administrative User actor uses the Create Charge Code use case to populate the time-tracking system with charge codes. Once added, a charge code is available to all employees as they enter their hours.

Preconditions.   None

Deployment constraints.   None

Normal flow of events.   Add a charge code to an existing project.

1. The administrative user sees a view of existing charge codes. Charge codes are activities organized by client and project.

2. The administrative user adds a charge code to an existing project. The new charge code appears in the view, and may be used by employees.

Alternate flow of events.   New charge code for a new project for a new client.

1. The administrative user sees a view of existing charge codes. Charge codes are activities organized by client and project.

2. The administrative user adds a client. The new client appears in the view.

3. The administrative user adds a project to the new client. The new project appears in the view.

4. The administrative user adds a charge code to the new project. The new charge code appears in the view and may be used by employees.

Alternate flow of events.   Duplicate charge code.

1. The administrative user sees a view of existing charge codes. Charge codes are activities organized by client and project.

2. The administrative user adds a charge code to an existing project. The charge code already exists for the project.

3. The system informs the administrative user that the charge code already exists. No change to the view.

Exception flow of events.   The system is unable to add the charge code due to a system or communication error.

1. The administrative user sees a view of existing charge codes. Charge codes are activities organized by client and project.

2. The administrative user adds a charge code to an existing project. The system is unable to complete the addition, due to a system or communication error.

3. The system informs the administrative user of the error, complete with available details. The view reverts to the previous state.

4. If possible, an error is added to a log.

Activity diagram.   See Figure 3.2.

Nonfunctional requirements.   None

Open Issues:

- Is there a default set of activities?

- Can an employee bill to a project without specifying the activity?

- Is there information other than the name of the client, project, or activity?

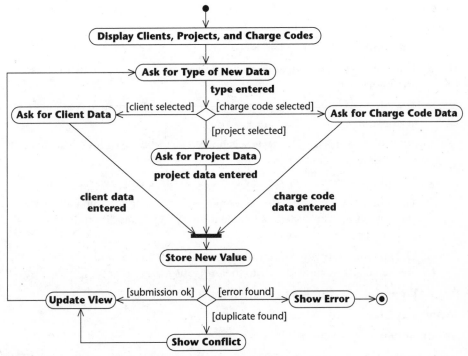

Figure 3.2   Activity diagram for Create Charge Code use case.

Sample Use Case Documentation for Create Employee

Name of use case.   Create Employee

Description.   The Create Employee use case allows the administrative user to add an employee to the time-tracking system. Once employees have been created, they are able to use the system to record their time.

Preconditions.   None

Deployment constraints.   None

Normal flow of events.   The administrative employee adds an employee.

1. The administrator sees a view of all existing employees by name.
2. The administrator adds an employee, with a name, email address, and password.
3. The new employee appears in the view. The employee can record his or her hours.

Alternate flow of events.   Employee exists.

1. The administrative user sees a view of all existing employees by name.
2. The administrative user adds an employee, with a name, email address, and password.
3. The administrative user is notified of the conflict. No change is made to existing data.

Exception flow of events.   The system is unable to add the employee due to a system or communication error.

1. The administrative user sees a view of all existing employees by name.
2. The administrative user adds an employee, with a name, email address, and password. The system is unable to complete the addition due to a system or communication error.
3. The system informs the administrative user of the error and provides available details. The view reverts to the previous state.
4. If possible, an error is added to a log.

Activity diagram.   See Figure 3.3.

Nonfunctional requirements.   None

Open issues:

- Is there information other than the employee's name and password?
- Will the employee need to change his or her password?
- Are employees organized by department or category?

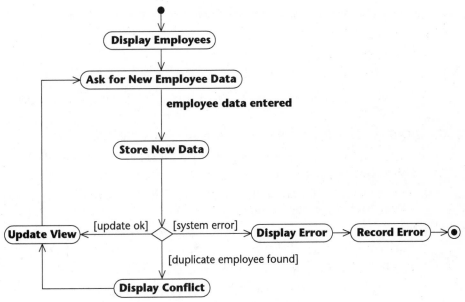

Figure 3.3 Activity diagram for the Create Employee use case.

Sample Use Case Documentation for Record Time

Name of use case. Record Time

Description. The Record Time use case allows employees to track the hours that they work. The Record Time use case allows an administrative user to record hours for any employee.

Preconditions. None

Deployment constraints. The Record Time use case must be accessible from client sites and the employees' homes. In the case of client sites, they will often be behind the client's firewall.

Normal flow of events. An employee records his or her time.

1. The employee sees previously entered data for the current time period.

2. The employee selects a charge number from all available charge numbers, organized by client and project.

3. The employee selects a day from the current time period.

4. The employee enters the hours worked as a positive decimal number.

5. The new hours are added to the view and are seen in any subsequent views.

Alternate flow of events.   An employee updates his or her time.

1. The employee sees previously entered data for the current time period.

2. The employee selects an existing entry.

3. The employee changes the hours worked.

4. The new information is updated in the view and is seen in any subsequent views.

Alternate flow of events.   An administrative user records time for an employee.

1. The administrative user is presented with a list of employees, sorted by name.

2. The administrative user selects an employee and sees previously entered data for the current time period.

3. The administrative user selects a charge number from all available charge numbers, organized by client and project.

4. The administrative user selects a day from the current time period.

5. The administrative user enters the hours worked as a positive decimal number.

6. The new hours are added to the view and are seen in any subsequent views.

Exception flow of events.   The system is unable to add the update to the time-card due to a system or communication error.

1. The employee sees previously entered data for the current time period.

2. The employee selects a charge number from all available charge numbers, organized by client and project.

3. The employee selects a day from the current time period.

4. The employee enters the hours worked as a positive decimal number. The system is unable to complete the addition due to a system or communication error.

5. The system informs the administrative user of the error and provides available details. All additions and edits are undone together. The view reverts to the previous state.

6. If possible, an error is added to a log.

Activity Diagram.   See Figure 3.4.

Nonfunctional requirements.   None

Open issues:

- Can an employee enter hours or edit hours in a previous timecard?

- Can an employee enter hours or edit hours in a future timecard, for example, just before a vacation?

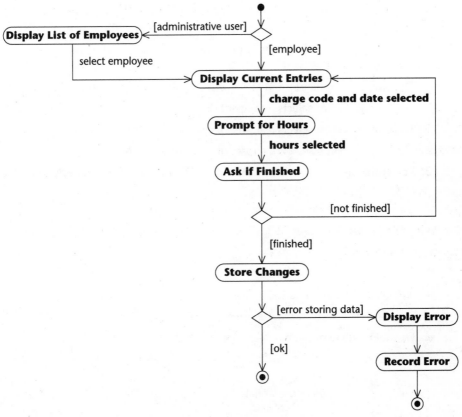

Figure 3.4 Activity diagram for the Record Time use case.

Sample Use Case Documentation for Extract Time Entries

Name of use case.   Extract Time Entries

Description.   The Extract Time Entries use case allows the billing system to retrieve data from the Timecard system.

Preconditions.   None

Deployment constraints.   None

Normal flow of events.   The billing system extracts data from the Timecard system.

1. The billing system authenticates itself to the Timecard system.

2. The billing system selects a range of dates.

3. The billing system selects a subset of clients or all.

4. The billing system selects a subset of employees or all.

5. The data is extracted, formatted, and provided to the billing system.

Exception flow of events.   The system is unable to extract the data due to a system error.

1. The billing system authenticates itself to the Timecard system.

2. The billing system selects a range of dates.

3. The billing system selects a subset of clients or all.

4. The billing system selects a subset of employees or all.

5. The system is unable to extract the data. The billing system is notified of the error.

6. If possible, the error is recorded to a log.

Activity Diagram.   See Figure 3.5.

Nonfunctional requirements.   None

Open issues:

■ Are the data selection criteria sufficient?

■ Are the data selection criteria unnecessarily complex?

■ Do other data extraction formats exist?

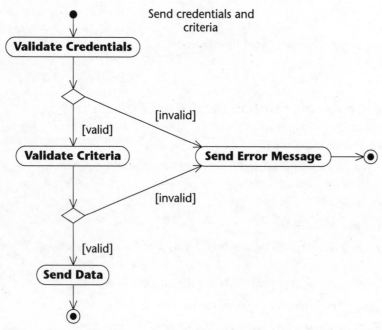

Figure 3.5   Activity diagram for Extract Time Entries use case.

Gathering More Requirements

Creating the detailed flow of events for use cases clarifies your understanding of the problem domain and raises many issues. At some point, you accumulate enough new questions to justify a requirements review meeting with the customer. This meeting has two goals:

- To validate and improve the current use case model, which includes the flow of events

- To resolve most of the outstanding questions and open issues

The key is to understand the system from your customer's perspective. It is important to stay focused on how the system provides value to the customer. But as you describe the system at a lower level of detail, it is easy to start contemplating possible solutions, so it is essential to be disciplined; resist the tendency to start architecture and design at this point. To this end, it is very helpful to avoid user interface design. Discussions concerning the look and feel of the system can easily become discussions of what is and is not possible with particular technologies. Remember, focus on what the customer needs from the system.

This requirements review meeting covers all of the use cases that have been developed. Participants must be prepared to discuss the details of the use cases, including the flows of events, the activity diagram, the deployment constraints, and any open issues. In order to ensure this level of preparedness, the participants must have time to review the documents before the review meeting.

In many cases, the sheer volume of requirements forces the review to be split over several meetings. Marathon meetings, with consecutive 8- to 10-hour days, are impressive sounding, but result in uneven coverage of the requirements. By the end of the second day, the participants are either worn out and apathetic or exhausted and combative. Either way, the time is not well spent. Consider instead meeting every other day or performing smaller more frequent reviews throughout the requirements-gathering process.

As before, the results of the meeting should be captured in written meeting notes, which should be validated by the participants. These notes will form the foundation for the common understanding of the system.

SAMPLE NOTES FROM FOLLOW-UP MEETING

DEVELOPER: Let's start with the Create Charge Code use case. Does the primary flow make sense?

CUSTOMER: Yes. I don't think we would ever need to add a charge code directly to the client. If we do, we can just add a "general" project.

DEVELOPER: Are there other data associated with clients or projects—purchase orders, contact information?

CUSTOMER: Yes, of course, but they are not part of this system.

DEVELOPER: Is there a default set of activities that are common to all projects?

CUSTOMER: No two projects have exactly the same activities, but there are some commonly occurring activities. Could the administrator select some from a list of common activities and type others? That would save a lot of time and avoid people's using alternate spellings or synonyms for the same activity.

DEVELOPER: I'll add that. Can an employee bill to a project without specifying the activity? Or directly to a client?

CUSTOMER: If an employee needs to bill without a project and activity . . . well then we probably have a problem.

DEVELOPER: Are billing rates set for different activities for each client?

CUSTOMER: Billing rates vary by client, project, activity, and employee. But we really don't want that in the Timecard system.

DEVELOPER: Excellent; it helps to know where the system stops. Great. Let's move to the Add Employee use case. What do you think of the main flow?

CUSTOMER: I agree that the employees would be organized by name. There is no need to organize people by department for this application. We haven't thought much about passwords or security. I know I personally hate assigned passwords; people always write them down and post them on their monitors.

DEVELOPER: So, should employees be able to change their passwords? Should they be required to do so on their first login?

CUSTOMER: That would be great. And most of them will be used to that flow from other systems.

DEVELOPER: Okay, I'll add that. Is there other information that we should be tracking—billing rates, contact information?

CUSTOMER: No; we may want to integrate that sort of thing later, but for now we want to keep it very simple.

DEVELOPER: Okay. Is there any other functionality we need here?

CUSTOMER: Well . . . I don't know how hard this would be, but could the system email the new users? Maybe to tell them they can start using the system and to give them their password?

DEVELOPER: We can add that. It's much better to add it to the requirements now.

CUSTOMER: Thanks.

DEVELOPER: Any other issues with this use case?

CUSTOMER: No, I think we have it.

DEVELOPER: Great. Let's move to the Record Time use case. What do you think of the main flow?

CUSTOMER: It makes good sense to me.

DEVELOPER: Can an employee edit previous timecards?

CUSTOMER: That is a tough question. I worry that if we don't let them do it, we will be getting calls from employees saying, "Please, just this one time, I need to add three hours. . . ." And if they don't record them, we can't bill for them. I think that they should be able to look at their previous timecards. They'll need to submit them when they are done.

DEVELOPER: Okay; how about editing future timecards?

CUSTOMER: Yeah, I know that sounds useful, especially for vacations and stuff. On the other hand, we want to avoid prebilling. We definitely should not allow them to fill in next week's timecard. Also, it should not be possible for people to fill in tomorrow's timecard. It may be a pain, but some customers audit our billing practices, and this would really help.

DEVELOPER: Okay, I'll add that. Will a manager or administrator need to add entries for sick or vacationing employees?

CUSTOMER: Oh, I guess so. If the employee is out more than a week, then an administrator needs to fill in the timecard.

DEVELOPER: Can any administrator do any employee's timecard?

CUSTOMER: Sure, let's keep it simple.

DEVELOPER: Any other functionality or issues?

CUSTOMER: No. Interestingly, I thought that was the easy use case, but it brought up a lot of issues.

DEVELOPER: Isn't that just the way? What do you think of the Extract Time Entries use case?

CUSTOMER: I like it. It will make it easy to get information to the billing system. It would be nice if the billing system could request information for a specific project for a specific client.

DEVELOPER: Oh, of course. Any other extraction criteria?

CUSTOMER: No, I can't think of any.

DEVELOPER: Finally, a use case that was as simple as it looked.

CUSTOMER: A nice way to finish out the meeting. Thanks.

DEVELOPER: Thank you. You have really improved my understanding of the system.

In this dialogue, the customers and the developer refined their collective understanding of the system. Specifically, they discovered some missing functionality, excluded other functionality, and validated a significant portion of the use case model. Following the meeting, the use case model must be updated to reflect the new understanding of the system.

Revising the Use Case Model

In many cases, a healthy dialogue with the customer will completely change your understanding of the system. Remember, both you and the customer are discovering and inventing the system as you go. You should notice a shift from discussing basic terms to delving into relatively subtle points. The first meeting and use case model builds a common vocabulary and reaches a consensus on what the system should and should not do. The second meeting uncovers missing pieces and resolves the special cases. This section shows how the use case diagram and the details for each use case are updated from the dialogue.

Revise the Use Case Diagram

Adding new information to the use case diagram follows the same pattern as during its original development. First, mine the dialogue for new actors and new use cases. Then, validate the candidate use cases against the guidelines for narrow focus and independent value. Finally, look for new relationships between actors and use cases.

For this example, the dialogue does not reveal any new actors, so we'll move on to the new use cases.

Find New Use Cases

The following excerpts indicate a need for some new use cases.

CUSTOMER: We haven't thought much about passwords or security. I know I personally hate assigned passwords; people always write them down and post them on their monitors.

DEVELOPER: So, should employees be able to change their passwords? Should they be required to do so on their first login?

CUSTOMER: That would be great. And most of them will be used to that flow from other systems.

The new candidate use cases are Login and Change Password.

Evaluate Candidate Use Cases

Change Password is well focused and certainly has value in isolation, since it protects the employee's privacy and security. So, we add the Change Password use case to the model.

Login is less clear. It is well focused, but it does not provide much value on its own. In general, employees log in as a precursor to performing some more interesting task, such as recording their time. On the other hand, most people describe it as a separate step, as in "I log in, then record my time." Many development teams and UML gurus have spent many hours disputing the status of Login as a use case. That said, no project has ever failed because the wrong choice was made. For now, we'll consider it as a separate use case that is used as part of many more valuable use cases.

Find New Relationships

The following excerpts provide insight into the interactions between the system and the actors.

> CUSTOMER: Well . . . I don't know how hard this would be, but could the **system email the new users**? Maybe to tell them they can start using the system and to give them their password?

> DEVELOPER: We can add that. It's much better to add it to the requirements now.

> CUSTOMER: We haven't thought much about passwords or security. I know I personally hate assigned passwords; people always write them down and post them on their monitors.

> DEVELOPER: So, should employees be able to **change their password**? Should they (the employees) be required to do so on their first login?

> CUSTOMER: That would be great. And most of them will be used to that flow from other systems.

The first excerpt indicates that the Create Employee use case interacts with the Employee actor by sending him or her an email. This is represented in Figure 3.6 by the solid line from the Create Employee use case to the Employee actor. You can verbalize this as, "The Administrative User actor initiates the Create Employee use case. As part of the use case, the system sends information to the Employee actor."

The second excerpt shows that the Employee actor initiates the Change Password use case. Also, the Change Password use case is always included in the Login use case if it is the employee's first login. This is shown by the include relationship (dashed line) from the Login use case to the Change Password use case. Remember, the extend relationship indicates that the subordinate use case is optional. An included use case is always performed if the flow of events reaches the inclusion point.

The second excerpt also reveals that the Employee actor initiates the Login use case. While it is not explicitly stated, it is reasonable to expect administrative users to log in and change their passwords.

At this point, you update the use case diagram to match your new understanding of the system. The updated high-level use case diagram is shown in Figure 3.6.

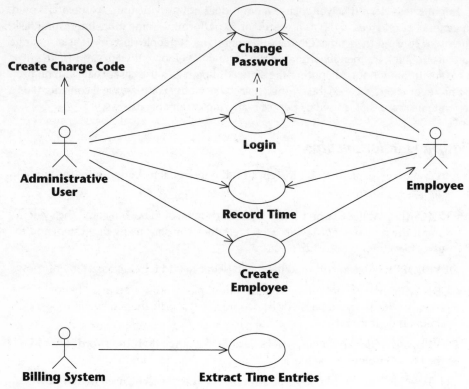

Figure 3.6 Revised use case diagram.

Revising the Use Case Documentation

In many cases, the flow of events for a use case evolves radically from the initial draft. Oddly enough, they never get shorter. Updating a flow of events is a fairly mechanical process of reviewing meeting notes and incorporating the changes. Perseverance is the key. If the list of open issues does not shrink over time, it may be a sign that you lack a clear and stable system vision.

The discussion of the Create Charge Code use case clarified the system's scope. The customer clearly sees the Timecard system as a simple and isolated system. It may seem odd to explicitly exclude functionality in requirements. After all, requirements describe what the system does, right? In my experience, it is well worth the effort to document any known limitations of the system as they are discovered. This simple discipline avoids countless arguments in which the customer contends that certain functionality is clearly within the current schedule, while the developers stare blankly as they consider weekends about to be lost. The flow of events for the Create Charge Code use case limits each client to a name and a list of projects. Each project consists of a name and a charge code. Nothing else is included—no purchase orders, no contact information. This sort of restriction encourages precise thinking by developers and customers. The message should be "speak now or be willing to talk schedule later."

A review of a flow of events may introduce completely new requirements. For example, the Administrative User actor now is able to pick charge codes from a list of previously defined activities. This must be added to the flow of events.

You can see how discussions with the user can lead us to revise existing use cases, add new use cases, place limits on system functionality, and add completely new functionality. In general, this is a positive sign. Hopefully, by this point, everyone's understanding of the system is maturing and converging to a common view. Conversations are increasingly productive, as different parties agree on general principles and common meanings for domain terms. The following samples demonstrate how requirements evolve; they also serve as a foundation for the ongoing sample Timecard application.

Sample Use Case Documentation for Login (New)

Name of use case.   Login

Description.   The Login use case allows employees and the administrative user to access the system.

Preconditions.   None

Deployment constraints.   Employees must be able to log in from any computer, including home, client sites, and on the road. This access may be from behind a client's firewall.

Normal flow of events.   The administrative user or employee's username and password are valid.

1. The administrator or employee supplies a username and password.
2. The user is authenticated as either an administrator or an employee. This is not a choice during the login; it is determined by the username.

Alternate flow of events.   First login.

1. The administrator or employee supplies a username and password.
2. The user is authenticated as either an administrator or an employee. This is not a choice during the login; it is determined by the username.
3. The user is instructed to change his or her password.
4. Include the Change Password use case at this point.

Alternate flow of events.   Invalid authentication information.

1. The administrator or employee supplies a username and password.
2. The user is notified that he or she has entered incorrect login information.
3. The failure is logged by the system.
4. The user is allowed to try again indefinitely.

Activity diagram.   See Figure 3.7.

Nonfunctional requirements.   The user's password must not be passed as plaintext.

Open Issues.   None

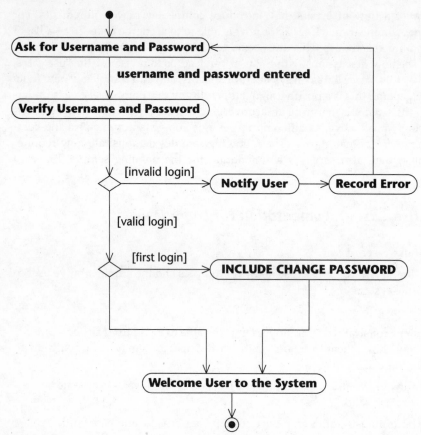

Figure 3.7   Activity diagram for the Login use case.

Sample Use Case Documentation: Change Password (New)

Name of use case.   Change Password

Description.   The Change Password use case allows employees and administrative users to change their password.

Preconditions.   The user must have logged in to the system.

Deployment constraints.   Employees must be able to log in from any computer, including home, client sites, and on the road. This access may be from behind a client's firewall.

Normal flow of events.   An employee changes his or her password.

1. The user enters his or her current password and new password twice.

2. The user is notified that his or her password has been changed.

Alternate flow of events.   Invalid current password.

1. The user enters his or her current password and new password twice.

2. The user is notified that his or her attempt failed.

3. The failure is logged by the system.

4. The user is allowed to try again indefinitely.

Alternate flow of events.   The new passwords do not match.

1. The user enters his or her current password and new password twice.

2. The user is notified that his or her attempt failed.

3. The user is allowed to try again indefinitely.

Exception flow of events.   The system is unable to store the new password due to a system or communication error.

1. The user enters his or her current password and new password twice.

2. The user is notified of the error and provided with any available details.

3. The failure is logged by the system.

Activity diagram.   See Figure 3.8.

Nonfunctional requirements.   The user's password must not be passed as plaintext.

Open Issues.   None

Sample Use Case Documentation for the Create Charge Code Use Case (Revised)

Name of use case.   Create Charge Code

Description.   The Create Charge Code use case allows the administrative user to add a new charge code to the system so that employees can bill to the charge code. Since each charge code is specific to a client and a project, the administrative user may need to add a client or project first.

Preconditions.   The user must be logged in as an administrative user.

Deployment constraints.   None

Normal flow of events.   Add a charge code to an existing project.

1. The administrator sees a view of existing charge codes for a selected project. Charge codes are activities organized by client and project.

2. The administrator selects from a list of common activities or enters a new activity to create a new charge code for the selected project.

3. The new charge code appears in the view and may be used by employees.

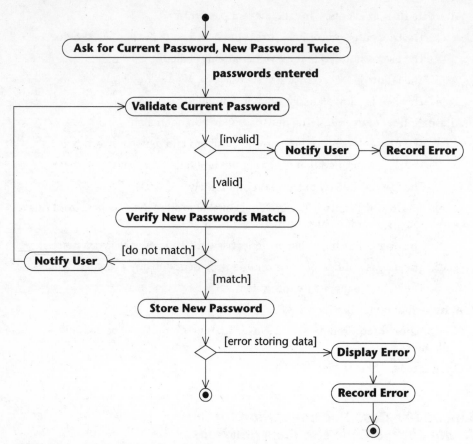

Figure 3.8   Activity diagram for the Change Password use case.

Alternate flow of events.   Administrator adds a new client and project.

1. The administrator sees a view of existing clients.

2. The administrator enters the name of a new client.

3. The administrator selects the new client and enters the name and description for a new project.

4. Employees will not be able to bill to the project until the administrator adds a charge code.

Alternate flow of events.   Duplicate data; input charge code already exists at the specified level.

1. The administrator sees a view of all existing charge codes. Charge codes are activities organized by client and project.

2. The administrator attempts to add a charge code that has the same activity as another charge code for the project. Once the list of common activities that does not include duplicates is created, this will be less likely to happen.

3. The administrator is notified of the conflict. No change is made to the existing data.

Exception flow of events.   The system is unable to store data due to system or communication failure.

1. The administrator sees a view of existing charge codes for a selected project. Charge codes are activities organized by client and project.

2. The administrator selects from a list of common activities or enters a new activity to create a new charge code for the selected project.

3. The system is unable to store the new charge code.

4. The user is notified of the error and provided with any available details.

5. The failure is logged by the system.

Activity diagram.   See Figure 3.9.

Nonfunctional requirements.   None

Notes.   Clients and projects have a name and description. Other information, such as contact information, billing rates, and purchase orders are kept elsewhere.

Open issues.   None

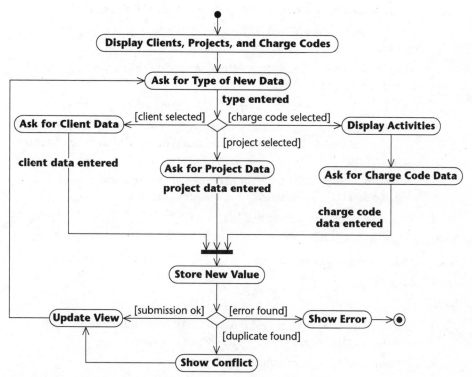

Figure 3.9   Activity diagram for the Create Charge Code use case.

Sample Use Case Documentation for Create Employee (Revised)

Name of use case.   Create Employee

Description.   The Create Employee use case allows the administrative user to add an employee to the system, so that the employee may enter his or her hours into the time-tracking system.

Preconditions.   The user must be logged in as an administrative user.

Deployment constraints.   None

Normal flow of events.   The administrative user adds a new employee.

1. The administrator sees a view of all existing employees by name.

2. The administrator adds an employee, with a name and password.

3. The new employee appears in the view.

4. An email is sent to the employee, instructing him or her to log in and change his or her password.

5. The employee can log in.

Alternate flow of events.   Duplicate data; employee already exists.

1. The administrator sees a view of all existing employees by name.

2. The administrator adds an employee, with a name and password.

3. The administrator is notified of the conflict. No change is made to the existing data.

Exception flow of events.   The system is unable to add the employee due to a system or communication error.

1. The administrative user sees a view of all existing employees by name.

2. The administrative user adds an employee, with a name and a password. The system is unable to complete the addition due to a system or communication error.

3. The system informs the administrative user of the error and provides available details. The view reverts to the previous state.

4. If possible, an error is added to a log.

Activity diagram.   See Figure 3.10.

Nonfunctional requirements.   None

Open issues.   None

Notes:

1. Each employee has a name and password. All other information, such as contact information or billing rates, is kept elsewhere.

2. Employees will not be organized by department.

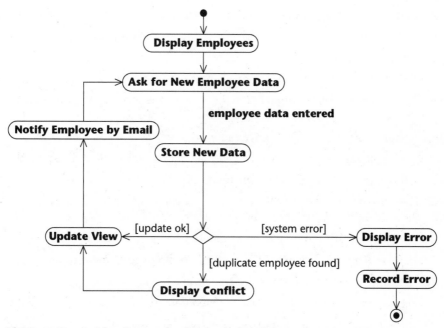

Figure 3.10 Activity diagram for the Create Employee use case.

Sample Use Case Description for Record Time (Revised)

Name of use case. Record Time

Description. The Record Time use case allows any employee to track his or her own hours. Administrative users can record hours for any employee.

Preconditions. The user must be logged in.

Deployment constraints. The Record Time use case must be accessible from client sites and the employees' homes. In the case of client sites, the employee will often be behind the client's firewall.

Normal flow of events. An employee records his or her own time.

1. The employee sees any previously entered data for the current time period.
2. The employee selects a charge number from all available charge numbers, organized by client and project.
3. The employee selects a day from the time period.
4. The employee enters the hours worked as a positive decimal number.
5. The new hours are added to the view and are seen in any subsequent views.

Alternate flow of events.   Employee edits existing data.

1. The employee sees previously entered data for the current time period.

2. The employee selects an existing entry.

3. The employee changes the charge number and/or the hours worked.

4. The new information is updated in the view and is seen in any subsequent views.

Alternate flow of events.   An employee submits a timecard as complete.

1. The employee sees any previously entered data for the current time period.

2. The employee elects to submit the timecard.

3. The employee is asked to confirm his or her choice and is warned that he or she will not be able to edit his or her entries.

4. The timecard is submitted; it is no longer available for editing.

Alternate flow of events.   Administrator edits an employee's timecard.

1. The administrator selects an employee from a list.

2. The administrator sees previously entered data for the current time period.

3. The administrator selects an existing entry.

4. The administrator changes the charge number and/or the hours worked.

5. The update is logged as an unusual activity.

6. The new information is updated in the view and is seen in any subsequent views.

Alternate flow of events.   Administrator submits an employee's timecard as complete.

1. The administrator selects an employee from a list.

2. The administrator sees any previously entered data for the current time period.

3. The administrator elects to submit the timecard.

4. The administrator is asked to confirm his or her choice and is warned that he or she will not be able to edit his or her entries.

5. The submission is logged as an unusual activity

6. The timecard is submitted; it is no longer available for editing.

Activity diagram.   See Figure 3.11.

Nonfunctional requirements.   None

Notes:

1. The employee can only enter data for one timecard at a time. If he or she has not submitted a previous timecard, he or she will not be able to enter hours for the current timecard.

2. Once a timecard has been submitted, it cannot be edited again.

3. Employees cannot enter time for days that have not started.

Open issues.   None

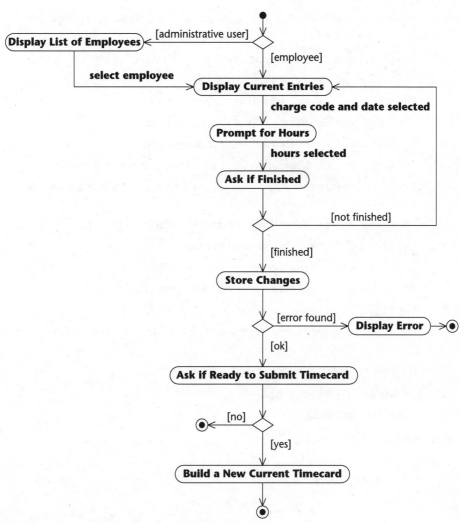

Figure 3.11   Activity diagram for Record Time use case.

Sample Use Case Documentation for Extract Time Entries (Revised)

The only change for this use case is the addition of projects as a selection criteria.

Name of use case.   Extract Time Entries

Description.   The Extract Time Entries use case allows the billing system to retrieve data from the Timecard system.

Preconditions.   The user must be logged in as an administrative user.

Deployment constraints.   None

Normal flow of events.   The billing system extracts data from the Timecard system.

1. The billing system authenticates itself to the Timecard system.
2. The billing system selects a range of dates.
3. The billing system selects a subset of clients or all.
4. The billing system selects a subset of employees or all.
5. The billing system selects a subset of projects or all.
6. The data is extracted, formatted, and provided to the billing system.

Exception flow of events.   The system is unable to extract the data due to a system error.

1. The billing system authenticates itself to the Timecard system.
2. The billing system selects a range of dates.
3. The billing system selects a subset of clients or all.
4. The billing system selects a subset of employees or all.
5. The billing system selects a subset of projects or all.
6. The system is unable to extract the data. The billing system is notified of the error.
7. If possible, the error is recorded to a log.

Activity Diagram.   See Figure 3.12.

Nonfunctional requirements.   None

Open issues.   None

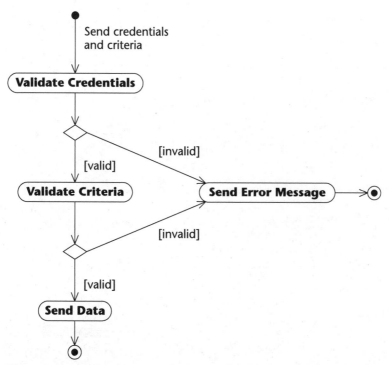

Figure 3.12   Activity diagram for Extract Time Entries use case.

The Next Step

This chapter demonstrated the power of the UML for gathering requirements. A high-level use case diagram makes it fairly easy to understand the system's purpose and its benefit to the people who use it. At a far lower level of detail, the flow of events and activity diagrams for each use case allow developers and stakeholders to reach a consensus on the behavior of the system. The UML provides a precise and expressive notation for building and sharing a collective understanding of the problem that the system must solve.

Now that the problem is well understood from the customer's point of view, the developers can continue development from a solid foundation. There will always be misunderstandings and requirements changes due to new business needs, but the number of surprises can be contained to a reasonably low level. This enables developers to work in a more stable and successful environment. In the next step, analysis, the developers will build an understanding of the problem from a developer's perspective.

A Brief Introduction to Object-Oriented Analysis with the UML

The preceding chapters demonstrated how the UML is used to view a problem from the customer's and end user's perspective. During analysis, though the focus is still on the problem, it is from the developer's perspective. Analysis describes what the system needs to do; it does not determine how it will do it. Thus, the emphasis is still on understanding the problem, rather than on selecting technology to solve the problem. These details are determined later, in the architecture, technology selection, and detailed design steps.

NOTE Our view of object-oriented analysis and design is influenced by the Rational Unified Process, my experiences teaching Rational's object-oriented analysis and design course, and many fine texts by Grady Booch, Martin Fowler, and Peter Coad. Any misinterpretations or oversimplifications are, of course, our own.

Performing analysis for a system is somewhat analogous to staffing a brand-new company. Before collecting resumes and performing interviews, you have to figure out what roles need to be filled. During analysis, you determine the roles and responsibilities of different parts of the system before you evaluate candidate technologies and actually build or purchase the parts.

In this chapter, we will walk through the analysis phase of the project. In Chapter 5, "Analysis Model for the Timecard Application," we'll use the concepts introduced here when we create the analysis model for the Timecard application.

Are You Ready?

Object-oriented analysis is the art and science of finding and documenting the objects that cooperate to meet the system's goal. During analysis, this effort is limited to determining the responsibilities of each object and the interactions among the objects. Analysis is a technology- and implementation-independent description of the objects' roles and interactions, which is then used as a basis for technology selection, architecture, and design.

There are two key steps to prepare to begin analysis. First, you must ensure that the requirements are solidly and consistently defined. Next, if the project is large enough to merit multiple iterations, you must prioritize the use cases based on risk, significance, and the abilities of your project team.

Solid Requirements

To begin analysis, the requirements must be solid, with a high-level use case diagram and documentation for each use case. At a minimum, the documentation for each use case must contain the normal flow of events. Many use cases should be fully specified, with alternate and exception flows of events. However, it is important to recognize that though the requirements are solid, they are not complete.

Working with poorly formed requirements or attempting to achieve perfect requirements ensures failure. Balance is the key. If you discover radically new use cases during analysis, it means that you quit the requirements-gathering phase too soon and that your requirements were not solid. That said, you might find a new use case that supports an existing use case, or realize that an existing use case must be refactored into several use cases. Certainly, you must expect to refine your understanding of each use case during analysis.

Prioritizing Use Cases

Analysis may be performed for all of the use cases at once or for a targeted subset of use cases, as in iterative development. In iterative development, all of the use cases are described during a comprehensive requirements-gathering phase. Next, a set of use cases is identified and a minisystem is developed to meet these requirements. This minisystem is created by performing analysis, architecture, technology selection, design, code, and test for the selected use cases. The process of building the minisystem is an iteration. The entire system is built incrementally, with a new set of use cases added in each iteration.

Prioritizing the use cases makes it possible to attack the most important ones together in the first iteration. Once this first iteration is completed, the remaining use cases are reprioritized, and the process continues. By dividing the use cases in this manner, the overall project risk is minimized, and the project can build a large success from a series of smaller successes, or overcome small failures rather than succumbing to one large failure.

TIP It is always better to plan a series of small successes and accept the occasional minor setback. Planning for one giant success often results in one catastrophic failure.

Risk

Risk provides an important criterion when ordering use cases. It often makes sense to attack risks early in the project. In this approach, a risky use case may cause the first iteration to fail. On the bright side, there is plenty of money left in the budget and plenty of time in the schedule, so you can try other approaches. If the total schedule is going to lengthen, it is better to find out early. Either way, this approach ultimately reduces risk and increases the predictability of the schedule.

There are many types of risk. A use case may push the state of the art for computer science, depend on an intricate set of interactions with the end user, or have very restrictive nonfunctional requirements. Consider a brief example: A credit card company is developing a Web-enabled system that allows customers to check their outstanding balance, view the last month's transactions, pay the current bill, and apply for more credit. Experience and focus groups determine that there is no speed requirement for the first two use cases, View Balance and View Transactions. People are used to waiting several seconds for this sort of information.

In contrast, most people become anxious when money is changing hands. They want the transaction completed and a printable receipt produced. So, the Pay Current Bill use case is risky because it must meet demanding performance requirements. The last use case seems to have a lot of risk, because it requires a computer to apply a complex set of rules to a large amount of data, and produce an important answer. However, this is hardly a new problem in the credit card industry, so in practice there may not be much risk involved.

Significance

Some use cases capture the intent of a system, while other use cases play a supporting role. In many systems, it is important to develop the more significant use cases in the first iteration. The supporting use cases can often be deferred by populating the system with fake data. By developing the more significant use cases first, developers give the other stakeholders a chance to see the system while there is still time and budget to change it.

Team Competency and Team Building

While it is important to pick use cases based on risk and significance, you must not forget the developers. Ignoring team competencies can jeopardize both the project's success and the long-term stability of the development team. Teams in which members are new to one another, new to object-oriented development, and new to some of the candidate technologies must start with a small, simple set of use cases.

What Is Object-Oriented Analysis?

Since objects do the work in an object-oriented system, object-oriented analysis must discover the objects that make up the system, describe their responsibilities, and determine their interactions. Again, this is done without considering the development language or technology that will be used for the objects.

There are two key advantages to deferring technology selection. First, it allows you to solve a simpler and more generic problem. It is easy to become absorbed in the intricacies of a particular technology, and focusing on these details prevents a designer from seeing larger patterns. Also, an implementation-independent analysis model allows for more flexibility as the solution evolves. Strange combinations of technology shortcomings and new requirements can lead to changes in the implementation strategy. An implementation-independent analysis model helps developers to create clear designs and provides insurance against radical changes in the system architecture.

If analysis is not concerned with the specific technologies of the system, then what questions does it answer? Analysis discovers the objects that interact to form the system. When the analysis is completed, you have an understanding of what the objects in the system need to do and, at a logical level, how they will do it. As you discover and evolve this detailed understanding of the system, you invariably notice weak areas in the requirements. It is very common for developers to revisit some use cases with the other stakeholders during analysis.

The Analysis Model

An *analysis model* contains two types of diagrams, which describe the objects and their interactions. These diagrams are organized according to the use case model, with each use case leading to several diagrams.

The first diagram used for analysis is the *class diagram*. This diagram captures each type of object in detail. Remember that the template for creating all objects of a particular type is called a class. So, a class diagram shows the state and describes the behavior that typifies the objects. The second type of diagram is an *interaction diagram*. This diagram describes the interactions between objects. It shows how one object configures another object and how other objects use an object to reach an objective.

These diagrams form two very different views of the objects that make up a system. The first, the class diagram, shows the templates for the objects in great detail. The second diagram, the interaction diagram, shows the object in motion.

Relationship to Use Case Model

Analysis builds on requirements gathering, so the analysis model builds on and is structured by the use case model. Specifically, each use case in an iteration leads to a class diagram that shows all of the different types of objects that participate in the use case. Also, each flow of events for a use case leads to an object interaction diagram that shows how individual objects cooperate to perform the flow of events. Finally, all of the classes from all of the use cases are organized into groups, for consistency.

Considering each use case separately also helps decrease the total effort required for analysis. Obviously, developers must consolidate and refactor their model of the system as additional use cases are considered, which adds to the effort. But the benefits of a divide-and-conquer approach far outweigh the effort spent on refactoring. After all, finding all of the objects for a moderately large system in one pass is impossible for most people. Perhaps there is one genius in a million who, like a chess grand master or brilliant composer, can keep the whole model in his or her head. The rest of us must be content with solving the puzzle a piece at a time.

Steps for Object-Oriented Analysis

Object-oriented analysis can be broken into several discrete steps. For each use case in the current iteration, you need to:

1. Discover candidate objects

2. Describe object interactions

3. Describe the classes

Let's look at each of these steps in more detail.

Discover Candidate Objects

The first step in creating an analysis model is object discovery. In this step, developers find a group of objects that contribute to the solution for a use case. These objects are used as a starting point for the next step, describing behavior.

This section has two parts. The first part enumerates some guidelines for discovering objects. The second part discusses an actual process for discovering objects. Probably, no two developers will perform this creative task in the exact same way; nevertheless, this process can serve as a reasonable starting point for most developers.

In discussing objects, it is difficult to avoid discussing classes. After all, every object is an instance of a particular class. Every class defines a type of object. In the UML, the attributes and behavior common to a group of objects are documented in a class diagram. There is no UML diagram that shows the data and behavior for an individual object. The UML diagrams that show objects are dedicated to showing the interaction and cooperation between objects.

TIP By discovering objects, you are implicitly discovering the classes that the objects instantiate.

Guidelines for Discovering Objects

Before discovering objects, you should have some guidelines for the objects and classes that you will discover. Establishing these guidelines early in the process prevents confusion between developers, and facilitates development of a coherent and consistent analysis model. The following delineations provide some criteria and checkpoints:

- Limit the responsibilities of each analysis class.
- Use clear and consistent names for classes and methods.
- Keep analysis classes simple.

Limit Responsibilities

A good class has a single clear and coherent purpose or responsibility. This makes the class easier to understand, maintain, and extend. Simplicity and clarity of purpose also make it easier for other parts of the system to use the class, which keeps the system lean and elegant. Conversely, allowing large classes with many responsibilities can cripple a project. These classes are difficult to maintain, and over time may grow beyond the comprehension of their creators. This seems to be true for all programming paradigms: If you allow too much functionality to reside in a single function, procedure, subroutine, class, module, or stored procedure, the eventual result is an incomprehensible "hot potato" that is shuffled from developer to developer until everyone retires or leaves the project.

Analysis classes may seem excessively well focused and even contrived. It may seem odd to have a class in analysis with three methods and no data. This discomfort leads many developers to combine analysis classes or to add unrelated responsibilities to an existing analysis class that appears too small. Doing so is dangerous. During detailed design and implementation, a simple analysis class may evolve into a reasonably complicated class or even a group of tightly coupled classes. User interface and system interface classes invariably explode, as their full complexity is understood. In general, creating small well-defined analysis classes is a sound philosophy. To that end, strive to answer yes to the following questions:

1. Does each class have a single clear purpose?
2. Is this purpose clear from a one-paragraph textual description?
3. Does each method fit within the responsibility of its class?

Use Clear and Consistent Names

For a class to be useful to developers, it must be easy to understand from the outside. This means that class names and responsibilities must be clear and unambiguous from the perspective of other developers and, whenever possible, other stakeholders. For instance, a class that describes part of the business problem must make sense to an industry expert. Clear class and method names allow other developers and stakeholders to understand and validate the analysis model. This allows developers and stakeholders to catch mistakes and misunderstandings before they threaten the success of the project.

By definition, an object is an independent system element, with its own data and the capability to provide services as defined by its class. With this in mind, class names should always be nouns that describe the nature or responsibility of the system element. This distinguishes classes and objects from methods. By tradition, class names start with an uppercase letter and use mixed-case letters to highlight word boundaries. Some types of objects are natural nouns. Consider a few examples from different problems, such as Employee, Timecard, LinkedList, BinaryTree, BankAccount, and Mortgage. In other cases, a class name is a noun that originates from a verb. This is often the case when a class is typified by its responsibility for some action. Again, consider a few examples from different problems, such as TaxCalculator, EventListener, PayrollProcessor, and InputValidator. The English language is full of verbs that have mutated into nouns: People who teach are teachers; people who tend gardens are gardeners; people who program computers are programmers; people who instruct are instructors.

Keep It Simple

Don't get too fancy when discovering analysis objects; that is, don't try to determine the relationships between the objects. Don't name roles or create elaborate inheritance hierarchies. Remember, this is your first attempt at a high-level solution. In short, don't spend large amounts of time perfecting the first draft. Discover some objects, review the results, and defer the details until you have found behaviors.

CHECKLIST FOR NAMING OBJECTS

✓ Is the name of each class a noun?

✓ Will the name of each class and method be unambiguous to other developers who are less familiar with the system?

✓ Have you avoided meaningless "filler" names, such as manager, in favor of descriptive names with well-defined meanings?

✓ Is the name of each method a verb or a combination of a verb and a noun?

Process for Discovering Objects

Identifying the objects that make up the system is one of the most difficult parts of analysis. The use case model is large and elaborate, while the *analysis model* is just a blank sheet of paper, waiting to be filled. As with many complex and creative endeavors, the hardest part is getting started. Fortunately, the object-oriented community has identified four commonly occurring types of objects that can be used in almost every analysis model. They are:

- Entity
- Boundary
- Control
- Life cycle

The following sections describe them in detail.

Entity Objects

Entity objects encapsulate the business data and business logic of the system [Jacobson, et al. 1999]. They are generally fairly easy to find, as they are the nouns used to describe significant parts of the problem. There are two ways to find entity objects. One approach is to consider all of the data and behaviors required to solve the problem, then organize the data into related groups. The other approach is to identify the important nouns as entity objects, then determine the data and behavior that each entity object contains. While the latter is closer to object-oriented theory, reality lies somewhere in the middle for most developers. It makes sense to make a list of all data, a list of behaviors, and a list of all the important-sounding nouns, then allocate the data and behaviors to different types of entity objects. During this process, you may find additional entity objects, rename entity objects, or remove entity objects.

For example, let's find the entity objects for our reoccurring example of withdrawing funds from bank accounts, as introduced in Chapter 2, "Gathering Requirements with UML." Working through the normal flow of events and the activity diagram, there are several important-sounding nouns, some data, and some behaviors.

CHECKLIST FOR IDENTIFYING ENTITY OBJECTS

✓ Is the entity object a significant noun in the problem?

✓ Does the entity object contain information that is used to solve the system problem?

✓ Does the entity object contain calculation or validation logic that is used to solve the system problem?

✓ Does the entity object make sense to experts who understand the system's goals?

Nouns (candidate entity objects).   Customer, user, account, money, receipt

Data.   Personal identification number (PIN), customer name, amount for withdrawal

Behaviors.   Validate PIN, withdraw funds, check for sufficient funds, dispense money, print receipt, thank customer

First, we need to clarify the nouns, data, and behaviors that we extracted from the flow of events and the activity diagram. This leads us to perform the following exclusions:

- Customer and user seem interchangeable, so we discard user and keep the more descriptive customer.

- Money seems like part of a more significant entity, not an entity in its own right, so we discard it.

- Receipt does not seem very significant; it seems more oriented toward the interface with the user, so we discard it.

- Dispense money, print receipt, and thank customer all seem to be very specific parts of the interface with the user, not core parts of the terminology of the problem, so we discard them.

After these exclusions, we are left with the following nouns, data, and behaviors:

Nouns (candidate entity objects).   Customer, account

Data.   Personal identification number, customer name, amount for withdrawal

Behaviors.   Validate PIN, withdraw funds, check for sufficient funds

Based on these lists, we can allocate data and behavior to the candidate entity objects, as follows.

- Each customer object knows the name and PIN of the customer that it represents, and can validate the entered PIN.

- Each account object knows how much money is in the account that it represents; it provides withdrawal funds and checks for sufficient funds as services.

- No object seems appropriate to hold the withdrawal amount, so, we introduce a new entity object that represents the transaction.

We have discovered three distinct types of entity objects. Since each type of object is a class in an object-oriented system, we can use the UML notation for classes to capture the work. Figure 4.1 shows all three classes with their data and behaviors. Notice the <<entity>> at the top of each class box.

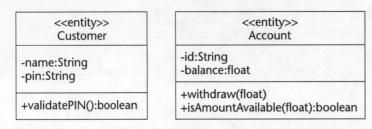

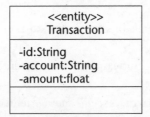

Figure 4.1   Entity classes for banking example.

WARNING In many cases, the industry's terminology may be obscure or even antiquated. You might be tempted to improve the terminology during analysis; you may want to update or generalize a term for the convenience of the developers. Don't. Maintain domain-specific terminology, and educate developers to use it. Changing the terminology makes conversations with the stakeholders difficult, and is generally impolite. After all, a term may have been around for a few hundred years and be part of the culture of the industry.

Boundary Objects

In Chapter 2, the actors in the use case model were defined as those people or systems located outside of the solution system that will interact with the solution system. *Boundary objects* represent how the system will interface with the actors.

Boundary objects are identified by examining the relationships between the actors and the use cases in the use case diagram. As a rule, each actor/use case pair forms a boundary object in the analysis model. There are two types of boundary objects:

User interfaces.   Allow the system to interact with humans

System interfaces.   Allow the system to interact with other systems

For both types, boundary objects have a very narrow focus. User interface objects are responsible only for presenting data to the user and accepting input from the user. System interface objects are responsible for communicating with another system. Business data and business rules belong in entity objects, not in boundary objects [Jacobson, et al. 1999].

CHECKLIST FOR IDENTIFYING BOUNDARY OBJECTS

✓ Does the user interface class describe the information that is displayed and the services that are offered?

✓ Does the user interface analysis class defer all screen design decisions?

✓ Does each system interface class describe the interactions with an external system?

✓ Does the system interface analysis class defer all protocol details?

TIP The analysis model should not contain any user interface design details. However, user interface prototyping may be performed concurrently with analysis, as long as it is treated as a separate effort with a separate deliverable.

Consider the banking example with a Customer actor and two use cases, Withdraw Funds and Transfer Funds. According to the rule of thumb, there is a boundary object for each actor/use case pair, so there are two boundary objects. This leads to two objects: withdrawFundsUI and transferFundsUI. From the normal flow of events and the activity diagram in Chapter 2, we see that the withdrawFundsUI object has the following user interface-related behavior: soliciting a PIN, displaying accounts, allowing the user to select an account, and soliciting the withdrawal amount. As with entity objects, this behavior is captured in a class diagram, since it is available to all instances of the WithdrawFundsUI class. Figure 4.2 shows this behavior in a class diagram. Each method is named from the perspective of the actor or object that uses the object.

TIP Use a consistent naming scheme for user interfaces and external systems. Many projects append the suffix View or UI to the end of the use case name. If more than one actor initiates the use case, the actor's name should be incorporated.

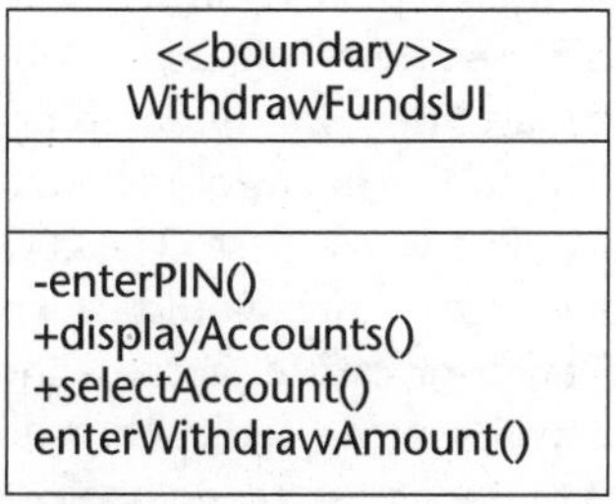

<<boundary>> WithdrawFundsUI
-enterPIN() +displayAccounts() +selectAccount() enterWithdrawAmount()

Figure 4.2 WithdrawFundsUI class.

Boundary objects appear very insubstantial during analysis. They may not have any data and may have easy-sounding responsibilities, such as "display accounts." Resist the urge to discount or ignore boundary objects. In many cases, their functionality is a key criterion during technology selection, and greatly influences the design and architecture of the system. Boundary objects are only "thin" during analysis, because their responsibilities are described at a very high level.

Control Objects

Control objects provide workflow and session services to other objects. The control object bundles the complex series of requests to the entity objects into a common workflow that is easily accessed by the boundary objects. A high-level message from a boundary object to the control object is converted into a series of messages from the control object to the entity objects. This allows the boundary object to concentrate on its responsibilities while the domain object stays simple. As a rule, each use case has one type of control object in the analysis model [Jacobson, et al. 1999].

TIP The easiest way to identify control objects is to consider the system without them.

Entity objects are simple, with a small number of well-focused responsibilities. This means that a boundary object with a complex objective must send a complex series of requests to the simple well-focused entity objects. The trade-off is unpleasant: either to have heavy and less-flexible entity objects or to have complex boundary objects that are tightly coupled with the entity objects. Neither option is acceptable. Entity objects must be simple and flexible, so that they can provide business logic and business data for many use cases. Even well-defined user interface and system interface objects tend to be difficult to extend and to maintain, so adding even more complexity is quite dangerous.

Fortunately, a control object serves as an intermediary between the boundary objects and the entity objects that cooperate in a particular use case. This allows the entity objects to provide a simple set of services, while the boundary objects defer the complexity of interacting with the entity objects to the control object. Several boundary objects may use a single type of control object for a particular use case. For example, a Web interface and a client server interface might share a common type of control object.

Perhaps a real-life example will make this rather abstract idea more concrete. Consider a customer ordering lunch in a sub shop on North Broad Street in Philadelphia, specifically, a nice cheese steak on a freshly baked sub roll with mayo, mushrooms, fried onions, and sweet peppers, but no tomatoes and no lettuce. But we digress. The customer does not shout his or her order to the short-order cook; most shops would frown on such a breach of etiquette. Instead, a designated order taker or cashier accepts the request, queries the customer for additional drink and side preferences, settles the bill, writes down the order on a little piece of paper, and clips it to the greasy range hood.

CHECKLIST FOR IDENTIFYING CONTROL OBJECTS

✓ Does the control object model the application or workflow logic for the use case?

✓ Does the control object delegate the actual business logic to the entity objects?

· This interaction is very simple and convenient for the customers. They do not need to get the cook's attention or direct their efforts in any way. They do not need to separately request fries or the drink from busy employees. Once the order is completed, they wait in quiet anticipation.

The little piece of paper also simplifies the staff's tasks. The fry guy can fill drinks and dish up some fries without worrying about whose order it is. The cook is similarly free to concentrate on the details of sub making: getting the ingredients together and in proper balance, ignoring the customer's preferences, and wrapping the finished product. In the end, the customer gets a delicious cheese steak with mayo, hot peppers, and tomato and lettuce.

So, a simple single point of contact, the order taker, simplifies life for the customer and allows the other employees in the shop to stay focused on their individual tasks. This is exactly the role of a control object. A control object encapsulates the interactions with entity objects so that the boundary object can focus on the actor without making additional demands on the entity objects.

Consider the Withdraw Funds use case. Our simple rule of thumb indicates that there is a single type of control object for each use case. Since the use case describes a simple workflow for withdrawing money, it seems appropriate to introduce a WithdrawFundsWorkflow class, as in Figure 4.3.

The behavior for this type of control object is determined by isolating the behavior that is exposed by the entity objects and used by the boundary objects for the use case. The behavior consists of validating the entered PIN, checking for sufficient funds, and withdrawing funds. Remember, a control object does not actually verify the PIN or withdraw funds. Instead, the control object finds and uses one or more entity objects to process each request.

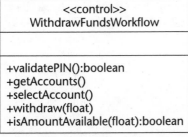

Figure 4.3 The WithdrawFundsWorkflow class.

CHECKLIST FOR IDENTIFYING LIFECYCLE OBJECTS

✓ **Does the lifecycle class locate, create, or destroy entity objects?**

✓ **Is each lifecycle class dedicated to a single type of entity object?**

Object Lifecycle Classes

Object lifecycle classes keep track of entity objects. Object-oriented systems contain hundreds or even thousands of entity objects. These objects must be created, located, and sometimes destroyed. Control or entity objects may need to locate an entity object by different criteria. For example, a WithdrawFundsWorkflow object needs to locate a specific Customer object, given the name or ID of the actual customer. There may be several ways to create an entity object. Since the logic for creating, finding, and destroying a particular type of entity object may be used in many use cases, it is handy to have a single type of lifecycle object for each type of entity object. As the developer considers each use case in turn, the lifecycle class accumulates additional behavior. As a general rule, there is a lifecycle class for each entity class.

NOTE Entity, boundary, and control classes have a long history as analysis classes. Lifecycle classes, at least by this name, lack this pedigree. In fact, as far as we know, we just made up the term. In our experience, almost all designers introduce something similar either late in analysis or very early in design. Most designers use names from the intended implementation technology or from their design experience. Some common examples include *home*, *factory*, and *container*. None of these names seems appropriate for an analysis model, because they all include design assumptions. While in general we frown upon the practice of authors creating their own terms to describe existing ideas, it seems that there is a vacuum to be filled here. So, we refer to such classes as *lifecycle classes.*

For the Withdraw Funds use case, both customer and account objects are located by particular criteria. Figure 4.4 shows that CustomerLocator lifecycle objects can locate Customer objects by ID or name. Similarly, the AccountLocator lifecycle objects can locate accounts for a specified customer.

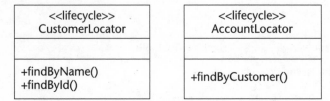

Figure 4.4   The CustomerLocator class.

Describe Behaviors

Once you've identified entity, boundary, and controller classes, the next step is to determine how the associated objects interact, to realize the use cases.

This section has two parts. The first part enumerates some guidelines for describing behaviors. The second part discusses an actual process for describing the interaction between objects. As noted before, probably no two developers will perform this creative task in the exact same way, but this process can serve as a reasonable starting point for most developers.

UML uses two diagrams to describe the interactions between objects: sequence diagrams and collaboration diagrams. *Sequence diagrams* show how objects interact over time. A sequence diagram allows you to track complex message sequences easily, but does not show how objects are connected. *Collaboration diagrams* show connections between objects, but are not very readable for complex sequences.

Objects interact by calling methods in other objects. Objects use this mechanism to send information, request a service, or request information. In object-oriented terminology, these interactions are described as *messages*, which are sent from one object and received by another. While messages are named from the perspective of the calling object, it is important to remember that the implementation is in the receiving object. Think of the receiver as providing some standardized service that can be called by other objects.

> **TIP** To preserve your sanity, we recommend considering use cases one at a time, developing sequence diagrams and a view of participating classes for each use case in turn. As you add more use cases, you inevitably revise your earlier work. For instance, your understanding of the responsibilities of a particular class often changes as you consider its role in various use cases.

Guidelines for Finding Behaviors

There are four rules to follow as you identify the behaviors of objects as they cooperate to fulfill a use case:

- Make sure the messages for each type of object fit together.
- Clearly name each message.
- Completely satisfy the functionality for the use case.
- Keep it simple.

The following subsections explain these guidelines in detail.

Ensure Cohesion between Methods

The methods for a class must form a coherent group, and they must fit the stated responsibilities of the class. For instance, makeToast, makeEggs, and makeJuice are closely related behaviors that combine to fulfill the "make breakfast" responsibility. They make perfect sense as methods in a Cook class. If we add the changeOil method, the methods no longer form a single coherent responsibility.

You will be tempted to add a responsibility to an object that does not fit with the existing responsibilities. The short-term convenience is not worth the long-term confusion.

Use Clear and Unambiguous Method Names

Each method must be named clearly and unambiguously from the perspective of the calling object. A developer who wishes to use your object should not need to read your source code to determine what the methods do. For instance, a class that has getQuantity and getValue as its methods is not likely to earn popularity awards for its developer. You must remember that the audience for your method names includes other current developers, future developers, and *you* after a long vacation.

Most method names can indicate the return type of the method. For instance, getName should return a string that is the name of the object. A method called setHeight is not expected to return anything, and almost certainly accepts a numeric parameter that changes the height of the object.

Completely Satisfy the Use Case

You must ensure that the use case is completely realized by your objects. This requires perseverance and good bookkeeping. Each step in each flow of events, and each activity and condition in the activity diagram for the use case, must be traceable to one or more methods in the objects. Since this is analysis, the method may not be well understood, but it must exist.

Keep It Simple

Don't get too fancy during analysis; that means defer any nonobvious parameters and return types until design. Also, there is no need to determine the source of each object, so don't bother creating elaborate inheritance hierarchies or arguing over the exact relationship between two objects. There is no need to get bogged down in the details when the whole landscape will change and evolve during design. For now, just use classes to hold related behaviors.

A Process for Describing Behaviors

This subsection shows how to find and describe the interactions between objects as they cooperate to fulfill a use case. This process can be separated into three steps:

1. Add the previously identified participating objects to a sequence diagram.
2. Work forward from the actor, finding behaviors as you go.
3. Validate the sequence from the end.

CHECKLIST FOR DESCRIBING BEHAVIORS

✓ Does each method have a clear purpose?

✓ Is each method name a strong combination of a verb and noun?

✓ Have you avoided wishy-washy names?

✓ Are all methods named clearly from the perspective of the calling object?

✓ Will all method names be unambiguous to other developers?

✓ Does the method name indicate what will be returned? For instance, a getDate request might reasonably be expected to return some sort of Date object, while a repaint request would not be expected to return anything.

✓ Are the methods in each class closely related to one another?

✓ Do the methods in each class match the stated responsibility of the class?

✓ Does each class still have a single concrete purpose?

The following subsections build on the Withdraw Funds use case as introduced in Chapter 2, and on the candidate objects found in the *Discover Candidate Objects* section of this chapter.

Add Participating Objects to a Sequence Diagram

Finally, it is time for the players to take the field. First, we add the actor that initiates the use case to the sequence diagram. Next, we add the boundary object, then the control object, then the entity objects. This pattern almost always holds true. Each use case is initiated by an actor, so it makes sense to put the actor on first. Likewise, there is always a single boundary object between the actor and the use case, so it makes sense to show that object next. There is always a single control object that serves as a single point of contact as the boundary object uses the entity objects. Finally, there may be many entity objects, depending on the complexity of the use case. We ignore the lifecycle objects until they are needed.

TIP When arranging the actor and objects for a use case, you can derive the order based on the way objects depend on one another, or you can follow the slightly flawed mnemonic device of "simple as ABCE" for actor, boundary, control, and entity.

Figure 4.5 shows the objects arranged in this simple pattern. Each object may show its name, its type, and its stereotype. The name of an object is the underlined text to the left of the colon. The class that the object instantiates is the underlined text to the right of the colon. The stereotype is at the top of the object box; it is always enclosed inside angle brackets. In many cases, there is no need to name an object. For instance, in this case, there is only one object of type WithdrawFundsUI, so there is no need to name it. But because most customers have a checking and savings account, it may be useful to name the Account object.

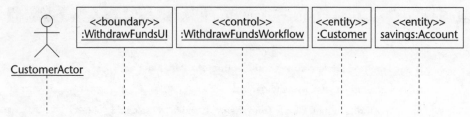

Figure 4.5   Empty sequence diagram for the Withdraw Funds use case.

Work Forward from the Actor

Once the objects are arranged on the sequence diagram, we can show how they interact with one another. Remember, in object-oriented terminology, one object sends a message to another object; the actual method implementation resides inside the receiving object. Each message is named for the method that it calls.

Since the actor always initiates the use case, it must send the first message. A message in UML is depicted as a solid arrow from one object's dashed line to another. The order of messages from top to bottom along the lines indicates the order in which they are sent.

Figure 4.6 shows a first attempt at the sequence diagram for the normal flow of events for the Withdraw Funds use case. The sequence begins when the customer enters his or her PIN. This message is received by a nameless WithdrawFundsUI boundary object that asks a nameless WithdrawFundsWorkflow object to validate the PIN. The WithdrawFundsWorkflow object, like all control objects, does not know how to perform this task directly. Instead, it knows which object to ask. It asks the Customer object that is associated with the user to validate the PIN. The return value of VALID bubbles up to the WithdrawFundsUI object. The return value is explicitly shown because the value affects the sequence.

Next, the WithdrawFundsUI object needs to present a list of accounts to the user. So the WithdrawFundsUI object asks the WithdrawFundsWorkflow object for a list of accounts. The WithdrawFundsWorkflow object asks each account for its name, and returns a list. Notice that the return arrow is not shown for the getName messages, because it is obvious from the method name, and the return result does not affect the flow. The displayAccounts arrow from the WithdrawFundsUI object back to the WithdrawFundsUI object indicates that the object calls a method on itself to display accounts.

Next, the customer selects an account in the WithdrawFundsUI object, which in turn selects an account in the WithdrawFundsWorkflow object. Notice that the WithdrawFundsWorkflow simply absorbs the account selection for future use. Finally, the customer enters an amount, after which the WithdrawFundsUI passes the amount to the WithdrawFundsWorkflow object. The WithdrawFundsWorkflow object asks the savings account if the funds are available, then performs a withdrawal against the savings account.

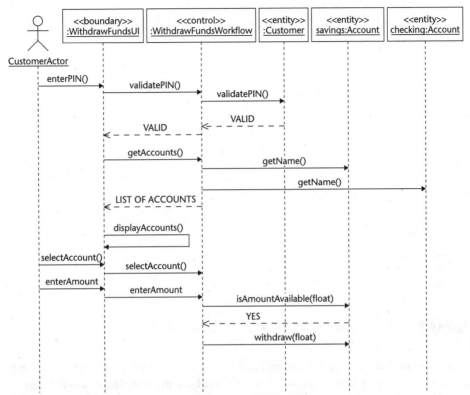

Figure 4.6 Initial sequence diagram for the Withdraw Funds use case.

Validate the Sequence

Finally, when you believe you have discovered the required methods, you must validate the sequence. To do this, work backward from the end of the last sequence, asking whether each object has the information that it needs to provide the desired services.

An account object certainly knows how much money it has, and can remove money from itself, so the last two methods are okay. The beginning of the sequence, where the WithdrawFundsUI object passes the amount along to the WithdrawFundsWorkflow object, seems reasonable—if you assume that the WithdrawFundsUI and the WithdrawFundsWorkflow objects are created as a pair of cooperating objects. The sequence also assumes that the WithdrawFundsWorkflow object remembers the selected account.

The previous sequence, in which the WithdrawFundsUI object passes the account selection to the WithdrawFundsWorkflow object seems similarly reasonable.

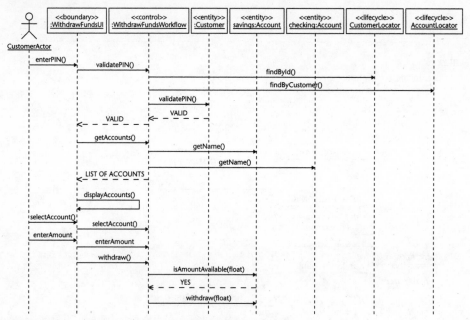

Figure 4.7   Sequence diagram for the Withdraw Funds use case.

Working backward from the display accounts method, it is reasonable to expect each account to know its name. It is not, however, clear how the WithdrawFundsWorkflow object found the savings and checking accounts. There are three alternatives: First, the Customer object can hold a list of its accounts; second, the WithdrawFundsWorkflow object can use a locator object to find the accounts for a given customer; third, you can defer the question until design. As long as you are consistent within your project, any of these approaches is defensible, although I prefer the locator approach, because it provides a convenient list of the ways that each type of object is located.

The first sequence raises a similar question. A Customer object can certainly validate a PIN, but how did the WithdrawFundsWorkflow object find the Customer? Figure 4.7 shows the same sequence diagram with these issues resolved.

Describe the Classes

The previous step used sequence diagrams to describe the interactions between objects for a use case. The interactions between objects require methods in classes and relationships between classes. In UML, this information is captured in a *static class diagram*.

Consider an object that sends a message to another object. In order to send the message, the sender needs a reference to the receiver. This can be a permanent link, where the sender keeps a reference to the receiver; or the sender can create a helper object, send it a few requests, and then lose track of it. Also, the method must exist in the receiving object. Since each class completely determines the data and behavior that its instances have, the method must be defined in the class that was used to instantiate the object.

This section has two parts. The first offers general guidance for describing classes and their relationships. The second part defines and demonstrates a simple process for describing classes based on object interactions.

Guidelines for Describing Classes

There are three rules to follow as you describe the classes that support a use case:

1. Be complete.
2. Keep it simple.
3. Maintain coherent classes.

Be Complete

Each message in a sequence diagram must have a corresponding method in the associated class. Remember, when an object sends a message to another object, it is actually calling a method that is implemented in the receiving object's class. So, every message must match a corresponding method in a class.

In order to send a message, the sending object must have a relationship that is navigable toward the receiving object. The receiving object may reply with a return value without requiring navigability toward the sender.

It is important to establish the direction of relationships between classes. As the system evolves, you need to know how different parts of the system depend on one another.

Keep It Simple

You don't want to miss anything completely, and you do not want to overanalyze the problem during analysis. Remember, analysis provides a useful foundation for design, but the actual diagrams do not need to survive past design. It is simply too difficult to keep the analysis model synchronized as the design and architecture evolves.

However, you should not spend much time seeking out inheritance hierarchies or determining the multiplicity of relationships. Do not spend hours arguing over aggregation or composition for a relationship that may not even exist in the design model.

If information seems obvious, then include it; otherwise, be very conservative as you spend time in analysis. Remember, the purpose of analysis is to discover and allocate responsibilities.

TIP Think of the analysis model as a rough sketch. You must complete it before you start painting with expensive oils on an expensive canvas, but you don't frame the sketch.

Maintain Coherent Classes

Each new flow of events for each use case introduces methods for existing classes. As this effect is multiplied over many flows of events for many use cases, it is difficult to keep the methods in each class consistent. So, after the sequence diagrams are completed and the classes are updated to reflect the behavior discovered through the sequence diagrams, the classes must be reexamined. Some of the methods that accumulated in a class may not fit well together or may vary from the stated responsibility of the class. In this case, the methods must be reallocated, so that each class forms a coherent whole.

Process for Describing Classes

There are three steps in describing classes:

1. Consolidate behaviors from objects to classes.
2. Refactor classes to meet guidelines.
3. Find relationships between classes.

The following subsections explain these steps and demonstrate them against the WithdrawFunds use case.

Consolidate Behaviors

In the WithdrawFunds use case, there is only one sequence diagram, as shown in Figure 4.7. In real systems, there are many sequence diagrams per use case and one class diagram per use case. A class that supports more than one use case will appear in each class diagram.

The implementation for each message is located in the receiving object. Each object's behavior is completely determined by the class it instantiates. So, for each message, we identify the receiving object's class and make sure that the method is in the class. Also, if a class or a method in a class is not used in any sequence diagrams, it should be removed. Figure 4.8 shows the changes to the class diagram. The findByName method in the CustomerLocator class, the isAmountAvailable method in the Withdraw-FundsWorkflow class, and the entire Transaction class have all been removed. Two new methods, enterAmount in the WithdrawFundsWorkflow class and getName in the Account class have been added.

Refactor Classes

You must examine each class to determine if it still has a well-focused responsibility and if the methods are cohesive. WithdrawFundsUI, AccountLocator, and Customer-Locator are all unchanged or reduced, so they pass our criteria.

WithdrawFundsWorkflow gained the enterAmount method and lost isAmount-Available. The responsibility and nature of the WithdrawFundsWorkflow object has not changed. It is still a simple control class that uses entity objects on the Withdraw-FundsUI object's behalf.

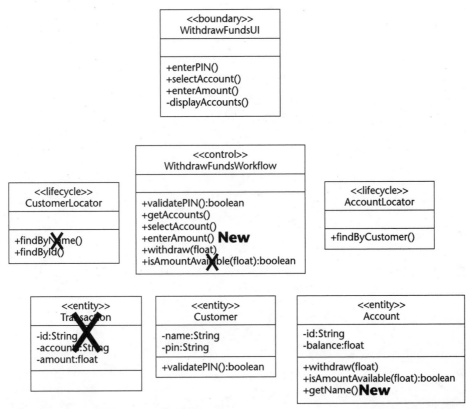

Figure 4.8 Updated class diagram.

Account added the getName method. It seems perfectly reasonable for an account object to know and expose its own name, so Account is still okay.

Find Relationships between Classes

For each message, there is a dependency or association from the class of the sender to the class of the receiver. If the sender remembers the receiver across different messages, it is a form of association. Multiplicity can be used to describe the relationship. An object may share use of an object or may require its undivided attention.

We use the sequence diagram shown in Figure 4.7 to determine interactions between objects. There is a relationship between the WithdrawFundsUI class and the WithdrawFundsWorkflow, because the WithdrawFundsUI object calls the validatePIN, getAccounts, selectAccounts, enterAmount, and withdraw methods on the WithdrawFundsWorkflow object. This relationship is shown in the class diagram in Figure 4.9. Since there are no messages from the WithdrawFundsWorkflow object to the WithdrawFundsUI object, it is a unidirectional relationship. The WithdrawFundsUI object remembers the WithdrawFundsWorkflow object over time, so it does not need to find it each time the actor enters data. It is not clear how the WithdrawFundsUI object gets an initial reference to the WithdrawFundsWorkflow object, but for now, we accept that they are a closely cooperating pair of objects.

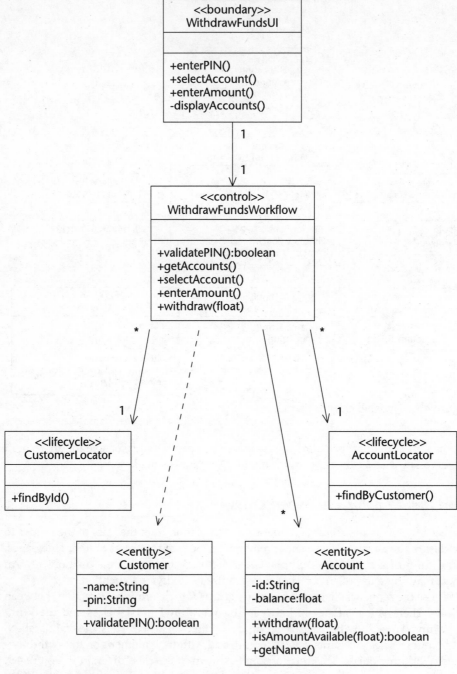

Figure 4.9   Class diagram with relationships.

Notice that the WithdrawFundsWorkflow object remembers information, such as the selected account and the amount to withdraw, for the WithdrawFundsUI. This implies that each WithdrawFundsWorkflow object is dedicated to a single Withdraw-FundsUI. This dedication is captured by the multiplicity number, which is closest to the WithdrawFundsUI class. Reading the relationship from the WithdrawFundsWork-flow to the WithdrawFundsUI results in: "Each WithdrawFundsWorkflow object is known about by exactly one WithdrawFundsUI object." Each WithdrawFundsUI needs to use the same WithdrawFundsWorkflow object every time it receives input from the actor, so it keeps a reference to exactly one WithdrawFundsWorkflow object. This is indicated by the number 1 next to the WithdrawFundsWorkflow class.

There is only one CustomerLocator object that is shared by all WithdrawFunds-Workflow objects. There can, however, be more than one WithdrawFundsWorkflow object at a time, as each actor using the system gets his or her own WithdrawFundsUI object, which in turn gets its own WithdrawFundsWorkflow object. This is indicated by the asterisk (*) next to the WithdrawFundsWorkflow class and the number 1 next to the CustomerLocator class. The same logic determines the relationship between the WithdrawFundsWorkflow class and the AccountLocator class.

Clearly, there is some sort of relationship between the WithdrawFundsWorkflow class and the Customer class, as the WithdrawFundsWorkflow object sends a vali-datePIN method to a Customer object. However, once the validation returns, the With-drawFundsWorkflow object never uses the Customer object again. It is possible in an alternate flow that the WithdrawFundsWorkflow object might remember the Cus-tomer object, perhaps so that it can retry different PINs as the actor enters them. How-ever, we have only one sequence diagram, and it doesn't show any such memory or subsequent use. So, the relationship is a dependency.

There is clearly an association relationship between the WithdrawFundsWorkflow class and the Account class, as the WithdrawFundsWorkflow object locates some Account objects, retrieves their names, then remembers them. Notice that the multi-plicity of the WithdrawFundsWorkflow objects is left unspecified. This process has just raised an interesting question: If a user can log in twice, can there be two Withdraw-FundsUI objects, each with a WithdrawFundsWorkflow object? Each Withdraw-FundsWorkflow object would use the same Account objects. So, if multiple logins are allowed, the multiplicity is *; otherwise, it is 1.

The Next Step

This chapter described and demonstrated techniques for understanding the problem from a developer's perspective. Analysis describes the solution in terms of cooperating objects and the classes that define them. It focuses on the responsibilities and behaviors of these objects, while ignoring the implementation technology.

This provides a solid foundation for subsequent technology selection, architecture, and design efforts. Without analysis, developers are forced to simultaneously under-stand the solution and the problem. This often leads to hasty or flawed decisions.

The next chapter reinforces the techniques and principles covered in this chapter, and continues the sample Timecard system introduced in Chapter 2.

Analysis Model for the Timecard Application

Now, that we've walked through the steps for the analysis phase, let's walk through an example. So far, we've gathered the requirements for our Timecard application. The next step is to analyze the requirements and translate them into a language that the developers can understand. Remember that we're not interested in the specific technologies yet; we're focusing on the model of how the system internals will work.

This chapter expands on the material from Chapter 4, "A Brief Introduction to Object-Oriented Analysis with the UML." It provides a small but fairly representative example of the art and science of object-oriented analysis.

NOTE The example in this chapter is continued throughout the book, so it is recommended that even experienced object-oriented practitioners at least skim the information.

Let's begin by walking through each step, from prioritizing the use cases to discovering candidate objects and interactions to, finally, describing the classes in detail.

Prioritizing the Use Cases

Each use case must be ranked according to its risk, its significance to the user and the architecture, and its suitability given the skills of the team. Once the use cases are ranked in these categories, we must determine which subset of the use cases is most important and makes sense in the first iteration of the system. This process often involves trade-offs and compromises. For example, a use case might be very risky, which would lead us to include it in the first iteration. However, if the team is completely unprepared to succeed with that same use case, then a less risky and more achievable use case must be selected as a compromise.

The Ranking System

To make life easier, risk, significance, and suitability are forced into a simple qualitative ranking system from 1 to 5. The higher the number, the more suitable the use case is for inclusion in the first or next iteration.

In Chapter 3, "Gathering Requirements for the Timecard Application," we identified six use cases for the sample Timecard application. Figure 5.1 shows the high-level use case diagram. We must describe each use case in terms of its risk, significance, and suitability given the current state of the team.

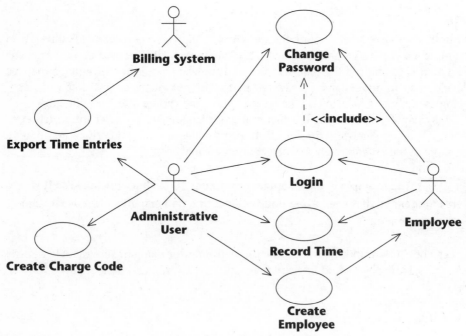

Figure 5.1   High-level use case diagram for the Timecard application.

Risk

When possible, you should attack risky parts of the system early in the development cycle. Then, if the first approach fails, there is still time and opportunity to try alternatives.

Before considering the risks involved with each use case, you must develop a list of risks for the project. The following risks are common to many projects, and so can serve as a starting point as you list the risks for your project.

- Unacceptable system performance
- Unacceptable user interface
- Schedule uncertainty and schedule length
- Inability to adapt to new requirements

After some consideration, we determine that the user interface is fairly straightforward. We also realize that performance may be critical, because the end users are very busy and will not appreciate any delays due to the timecard system. From our experience on previous projects, we know that the stakeholders invariably increase the system's scope over time and that the stakeholders expect the new features to fit seamlessly into the existing system. Therefore, we order the risks as follows, and resolve to consider each use case with respect to the risks.

1. Unacceptable system performance
2. Inability to adapt to new requirements
3. Schedule uncertainty and schedule length
4. Unacceptable user interface

Before we rank each use case according to risk, we need a simple descriptive way of expressing different levels of risk. To that end, we ask developers if they are sure they can solve the problem on their first try, and make them pick from the following to answer:

1. Of course; our project team has solved that problem before.
2. Certainly; our organization has solved that problem before.
3. There are third-party products, training, books, or other technical resources available, but we do not have any in-house experience.
4. Maybe; we have heard of similar problems being solved.
5. I hope so, but we will be breaking new ground.

As we will see in the use case evaluations, this simple risk "spectrum" helps identify high-risk use cases that must be considered for inclusion in the next iteration.

Significance

A use case is significant to the user and to the architecture if it is close to the core vision of the system. A significant use case captures the flavor and intent of a system. Other use cases may be very important, but in a supporting role. For example, the Timecard system cannot function without the Add Employee use case. On the other hand, the Record Time and Extract Time Entries use cases completely capture the intent of the system.

Significance can be measured by asking developers how users would react if the use case were omitted from the iteration or replaced with simulated results. Make them pick from the following to answer this question:

1. They would barely notice, and they could easily use the system without it.
2. They would notice, but with a little imagination, the system would still make perfect sense.
3. Most of the system could exist independently.
4. Some parts of the system could exist independently.
5. The system would be impossible to use without it.

As we will see in the use case evaluations, this simple spectrum helps identify very significant use cases that must be considered for inclusion in the next iteration.

Suitability

A use case is suitable for the current project team if they can start working on it with a minimum of training and a relatively short learning curve. These two criteria are especially important when new technologies, languages, and development techniques are introduced to an organization.

Many organizations adapt to new technologies and techniques by putting their best people on a superhigh-profile project. After all, the hype says that object-oriented development and Java is the wave of the future, so why not invest in a week or two of training for the brightest people in the company and then watch them revolutionize the company under intense schedule pressure? Of course, this is backward thinking, because the company simultaneously alienates their best and brightest, while making them substantially more marketable.

It takes at least six months to become proficient in a completely new way of thinking, and at least two or three months to become truly proficient in a new language and development environment. Development teams need time and practice under relatively low pressure so that they can develop proficiency and confidence in the new techniques.

Since we are picking use cases for the first iteration and have not selected any technologies yet, it may be difficult to determine exactly how much the developers will need to learn. In contrast, in the real world, project teams generally know whether they will be adopting a new technique, such as object-oriented development. Also, they generally know the language or family of languages that will be used. With this in mind, we ask the developers to describe their comfort level with the technology and techniques, and tell them to choose from the following answers:

1. The team definitely needs more seasoning before attempting this use case.

2. The team's capabilities are probably sufficient for this use case, but may improve substantially over the course of a single iteration.

3. The team's capabilities are probably sufficient and are unlikely to improve over the course of a single iteration.

4. There is no need for more seasoning. Either the team is already quite experienced or the use case is sufficiently straightforward.

5. There is no need for more seasoning. The team is experienced and the use case is straightforward. Money in the bank.

As we will see in the use case evaluations, this simple spectrum helps protect the development team by excluding inappropriate use cases from the next iteration.

For our examples, let's assume that we have a reasonably seasoned team. Most of the developers have at least a year of experience with object-oriented development, and almost everyone has at least a year of experience with Java and at least a year of experience developing software that uses relational databases.

Let's walk through each use case and evaluate them according to risk, significance, and suitability. This will tell us which use cases should be included in the first iteration.

Evaluation of the Extract Time Entries Use Case

The Extract Time Entries use case allows the billing system to extract a specified range of time entries from the Timecard system.

Risk

Certainly, there is some performance risk involved, since the system must extract significant blocks of data from a set of data that grows larger with every new employee and with the passage of time. This activity could be performed during off-peak hours.

- This use case must be extensible, because the criteria for extracting timecard entries may evolve and become more sophisticated over time.

- This use case is fairly easy to estimate, since it is simply a matter of finding timecard entries and extracting the data.

Overall, the risk of the use case seems to be quite low. Level 2, "Certainly; our organization has solved that problem before," seems applicable.

Significance

This is a very significant use case. The whole point of a timecard system is to collect and retrieve timecard entries for a variety of purposes. Level 5, "The system would be impossible to use without it," is well justified.

Suitability

This use case is relatively straightforward, and the team is certainly ready. Level 4, "There is no need for more seasoning. Either the team is already quite experienced or the use case is sufficiently straightforward," seems appropriate.

Conclusion

Because of its high significance, this use case is very desirable as part of the first iteration. Including it would build credibility with the customer and provide architecturally significant functionality.

Evaluation of the Create Charge Code Use Case

The Create Charge Code use case allows administrative users to add charge codes for use by the employees as they enter their hours.

Risk

There is virtually no performance risk, since charge codes are added infrequently and contain very small amounts of data.

- The use case seems very well understood, so the extensibility risk is low.
- This use case is fairly easy to estimate, since it is simply a matter of adding data to the system.
- The user interface is very straightforward, so there is no real risk of delivering an overly complex user interface.

Overall, the risk of the use case seems to be quite low. Level 1, "Of course; our project team has solved that problem before," seems applicable.

Significance

While it is certainly very important in the final system, the Create Charge Code use case is more of a support use case. During preliminary iterations, the customer is unlikely to notice the difference between simulated charge codes and charge codes that are entered through the system. Level 1, "They would barely notice, and they could easily use the system without it," describes the likely response.

Suitability

Level 5, "There is no need for more seasoning. The team is experienced and the use case is straightforward. Money in the bank," describes the development team's readiness for this use case.

Conclusion

In the absence of any significant risk or significance, there is no compelling reason to consider this use case for the first iteration.

Evaluation of the Change Password Use Case

The Change Password use case allows any current user to change his or her password.

Risk

There is virtually no performance risk, since passwords are changed infrequently and contain very small amounts of data.

- The use case seems very well understood, so the extensibility risk is low.
- This use case is fairly easy to estimate, since it is simply a matter of changing data in the system.
- The user interface is very straightforward, so there is no real risk of delivering an overly complex user interface.

Overall, the risk of the use case seems to be quite low. Level 1, "Of course; our project team has solved that problem before," seems applicable.

Significance

Like the Create Charge Code use case, the Change Password use case provides supporting functionality. Level 1, "They would barely notice, and they could easily use the system without it," describes the likely response.

Suitability

Level 5, "There is no need for more seasoning. The team is experienced and the use case is straightforward. Money in the bank," describes the development team's readiness for this use case.

Conclusion

The relatively low risk and lack of significance indicates that this use case can be omitted from the first iteration. Certainly, it is important to the project, but it can be deferred without affecting the stakeholders as they evaluate the system or the developers as they design the system.

Evaluation of the Login Use Case

The Login use case allows any current user to validate his or her identity to the system as a prerequisite to performing the other more interesting use cases.

Risk

There is some performance risk, since large numbers of users may log in at the same time. However, logging in is a fairly straightforward process and does not involve a lot of data or calculation. The performance risk is low.

- Login is a very well-understood use case, so there is little extensibility risk.
- Login does not present much schedule risk, since it is very small and well focused.
- There is no risk of an unacceptable user interface.

Level 1, "Of course; our project team has solved that problem before," describes the Login use case perfectly.

Significance

The final system would be completely unacceptable without the Login use case, but the end users could certainly evaluate the system without it. Still, the developers need to make sure that their architecture supports this use case even if it is not included in the first iteration.

Level 2, "They would notice, but with a little imagination, the system would still make perfect sense," seems appropriate.

Suitability

Level 4, "There is no need for more seasoning. Either the team is already quite experienced, or the use case is sufficiently straightforward," seems very appropriate.

Conclusion

With some reservations because of the use case's architectural significance, Login is not essential for the first iteration.

Evaluation of the Record Time Use Case

The Record Time use case allows any user to enter his or her hours for the current time period.

Risk

The performance risk is very significant, because many users will record their time in the last few working hours of each time period. Also, users are rarely willing to accept poor performance while performing "nuisance" tasks. For instance, people may be willing to wait 15 minutes for a funny video clip to download and queue up, but they become aggravated if they have to wait 3 minutes in a grocery store line. Filling in a timecard generally falls into the category of undesirable tasks, so performance problems must be avoided.

- The use case seems very well understood, so the extensibility risk is low.
- Any estimate for this use case will be complicated by the complexity and performance requirements.
- The user interface is fairly complex, with charge code selection, comments for entries, and an editable matrix of time entries.

The Record Time use case is fairly risky, due to the performance requirements and user interface complexity. Level 3, "There are third-party products, training, books, or other technical resources available, but we do not have any in-house experience," is appropriate.

Significance

The Record Time use case is very significant, because it captures the intent of the timecard system. It is difficult to imagine an iteration without this use case. Level 5, "The system would be impossible to use without it," seems completely justified.

Suitability

The same complexity and risk that drives us to include this use case in the first iteration also forces us to carefully evaluate its suitability for the team. Level 2, "The team's capabilities are probably sufficient for this use case, but may improve substantially over the course of a single iteration," seems appropriate.

Conclusion

Clearly, many factors encourage us to include the Record Time use case in the first iteration. However, because of its complexity, we might want to manage the stakeholders' expectations by spreading complete development of the use case over the first two iterations. For example, the first iteration might include the complete user interface but defer performance goals to the next iteration.

Evaluation of the Create Employee Use Case

The Create Employee use case allows an administrative user to add an employee to the system.

Risk

There is virtually no performance risk, since employees are added infrequently, and the process requires very small amounts of data.

- The use case seems very well understood, so the extensibility risk is low.

- This use case is fairly easy to estimate, since it is simply a matter of adding data to the system.

- The user interface is very straightforward, so there is no real risk of delivering an overly complex user interface.

Overall, the risk of the use case seems to be quite low. Level 1, "Of course; our project team has solved that problem before," seems applicable.

Significance

Though very important in the final system, the Create Employee use case is more of a support use case. During preliminary iterations, the customer is unlikely to notice the difference between simulated employees and actual employees entered through the system. Level 1, "They would barely notice, and they could easily use the system without it," describes the likely response.

Suitability

Level 5, "There is no need for more seasoning. The team is experienced and the use case is straightforward. Money in the bank," describes the development team's readiness for this use case.

Conclusion

In the absence of any significant risk or significance, there is no compelling reason to consider this use case for the first iteration.

Select Use Cases for the First Iteration

Given a fairly seasoned development team, we can determine the use cases for the first iteration based on risk and significance. Record Time and Extract Time Entries definitely belong in the first iteration. Create Employee, Create Charge Code, and Change Password should all be deferred. Login could easily be deferred, but we will include it to make the first iteration more realistic.

By putting all of the architecturally significant use cases in a single iteration, we give the stakeholders a clear impression of the system after the first iteration, while the developers can ensure the integration of the solutions to these key use cases.

Now that we have selected the use cases for the first iteration, let's perform the remaining analysis steps for those use cases.

Discover Candidate Objects

In this step, developers find candidate objects that interact to provide the functionality as described in the use cases. Remember, this process is greatly simplified by dividing objects into four categories: entity, boundary, control, and life cycle.

While discovering objects, it is important to limit the responsibilities for each object and to use clear and consistent names for each object and for each method in each object.

Since we are just starting analysis, we will not spend time determining the relationships between objects. These relationships are clarified in the remaining steps of the process. Also, there is no point in specifying the type of every attribute or in creating elaborate inheritance hierarchies. We will keep it simple, and not try to perfect the rough draft.

Discover Entity Objects

For each use case, we search each flow of events to find nouns, data, and behavior. Nouns may become entity objects, the data may become attributes of the objects, and the behavior is allocated to one or more objects. The nouns for each use case are considered separately before considering them together.

Record Time Use Case

Working through the normal flow of events, we highlight the following candidate objects and data:

1. The *employee* sees any *previously entered data* for the current time period.

2. The *employee* selects a *charge number* from all available charge numbers, organized by *client* and *project*.

3. The *employee* selects a day from the *time period*.

4. The *employee* enters the *hours worked* as a positive decimal number.

5. The new *hours* are added to the *view* and are seen in any subsequent views.

The following pieces are highlighted in the first alternate flow of events—employee edits existing data:

1. The *employee* sees *previously entered data* for the current *time period*.

2. The *employee* selects an *existing entry*.

3. The *employee* changes the *charge number* and/or the *hours worked*.

4. The new information is updated in the *view* and is seen in any subsequent views.

The following pieces are highlighted in the next alternate flow of events—employee submits timecard as complete:

1. The employee sees any previously entered data for the current time period.

2. The employee elects to submit the timecard.

3. The employee is asked to confirm his or her choice and is warned that he or she will not be able to edit his or her entries.

4. The timecard is submitted; it is no longer available for editing.

The remaining flows of events do not introduce any new information, so we move on.

Next, we produce a simple alphabetic list of nouns, then judge each one. This process weeds out unneeded and duplicate entity objects. It also identifies nouns that are more appropriate as attributes inside an object as opposed to an independent object.

1. charge code

2. charge number

   Clearly, charge code and charge number are synonyms. Since charge code is more common in the other documentation, we discard charge number and keep charge code as a type of entity object.

3. client

   Client also seems like a reasonable type of entity object.

4. day

   Day does not seem like an independent type of object. Instead, it seems like data within an object.

5. employee

   An employee seems like an independent entity object.

6. existing entry

   An entry in a timecard may be the object that holds the day. We tentatively make this a type of entity object.

7. hours

8. hours worked

   Hours and hours worked are synonyms, but hours worked is far more descriptive, so we discard hours. Hours worked becomes data in the newly discovered entry objects. This convinces us that the entry object is justified.

9. previously entered data

   Previously entered data duplicates entry, so we discard it.

10. project

    Project becomes a type of entity object.

11. timecard

    Timecard becomes a type of entity object.

12. time period

    Time period describes a timecard, so it becomes data inside each timecard object.

13. view

    View objects are boundary objects, so we reject view.

We're done with the Record Time use case. Our entity objects are: charge code, client, employee, existing entry, hours worked, project, and timecard.

Extract Time Entries Use Case

Working through the normal flow of events, we highlight the following candidate objects and data for the Extract Time Entries use case:

1. The *billing system* authenticates itself to the Timecard system.

2. The *billing system* selects a *range of dates*.

3. The *billing system* selects a *subset of clients or all*.

4. The *billing system* selects a *subset of employees or all*.

5. The *billing system* selects a *subset of projects or all*.

6. The data is extracted, formatted, and provided to the *billing system*.

Next, we produce a simple alphabetic list of nouns, then judge each one.

1. billing system

    The billing system is an external actor, and it seems to request data rather than hold data, so it probably does not need representation by an entity object.

2. clients

    Client has already been identified as a type of entity object.

3. data

    This data refers to a group of entries from a group of timecards. Since these are already entity objects, no new objects are needed.

4. employees

    Employee is already a type of entity object.

5. range of dates

    Range of dates sounds like data within another object. We add a new entity object, extract request, even though it did not show up in the flow of events.

So, this use case gives us one new entity object: extract request. Now, let's look at the next use case.

Login Use Case

Working through the normal flow of events, we highlight the following candidate objects and data for the Login use case:

1. The *administrative user* or *employee* supplies a *username* and *password*.

2. The *user* is authenticated as either an *administrative user* or an *employee*. This is not a choice during the login; it is determined by the *username*.

Now, we produce a simple alphabetic list of nouns, then judge each one.

1. administrative user

   Administrative user has already been identified as a type of entity object.

2. employee

   Employee has already been identified as a type of entity object.

3. password

   Password seems more appropriate as data within the employee and administrative user objects.

4. user

   User is just a generic reference to an employee or administrative user.

5. username

   Username seems more appropriate as data within the employee and administrative user objects.

After evaluating this use case, there are no new entity objects to add to our list.

Consolidate the Entity Objects

Our list of entity objects looks like this:

administrative user

charge code

client

employee

existing entry

hours worked

project

timecard

extract request

The only two types of entity objects that seem similar are administrative user and employee. They are both types of users, one with administrative privileges and one without. So, we decide to eliminate both types of objects and add user.

The class diagram in Figure 5.2 shows the different types of the entity objects.

Discover Boundary Objects

Our next step is to identify the boundary objects for our use cases. Remember the rule for boundary objects in analysis: one boundary object per actor/use case pair.

For the Extract Time Entries use case, this leads to a boundary object that serves as an interface between the billing system and the Timecard system.

For the Record Time use case, the rule leads to two boundary objects, one that serves as an interface between the administrative user and the system, and one that serves as an interface between regular employees and the system. This is true despite our earlier decision to merge the administrative user and the employee into a single entity object. Boundary objects are discovered based on the way people or external systems use the system, not on how they are represented inside the system.

For the Login use case, the rule leads to two boundary objects, one that serves as an interface between the administrative user and the system, and one that serves as an interface between employees and the system.

Following a standard naming convention simplifies this process. We use UI as a suffix for any user interface objects and SystemInterface for any system interfaces. If more than one actor initiates the use case, the boundary classes must be named distinctly. Applying these guidelines to the preceding decisions leads to the boundary classes in Figure 5.3.

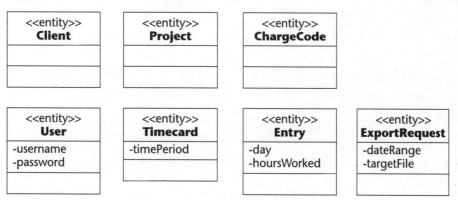

Figure 5.2   Entity classes.

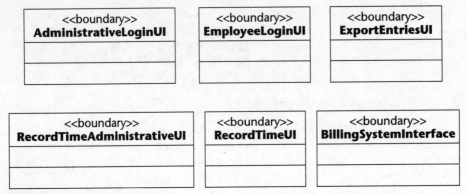

Figure 5.3   Boundary classes.

Discover Control Classes

The rule for control classes in analysis is one type of control object per use case. A control object encapsulates the workflow for the use case. This allows the entity objects to stay well focused, while the control object provides a simple interface to the boundary objects.

When devising a name for a type of control object, remember to keep it simple. It makes sense to pick a reasonable suffix, such as Workflow and stick with it. In many cases, simply adding Workflow to the use case name is sufficient. No points are given for style. Simplicity and consistency are far more important.

- For the Extract Time Entries use case, this leads to a control class called Extract-TimeEntriesWorkflow.

- For the Record Time use case, this leads to a control class called RecordTime-Workflow.

- For the Login use case, this leads to a control class called LoginWorkflow.

Figure 5.4 shows these control classes.

<<control>> **ExportTimeEntriesWorkflow**	<<control>> **RecordTimeWorkflow**	<<control>> **LoginWorkflow**

Figure 5.4   Control classes.

Discover Lifecycle Classes

There is no easy rule for discovering lifecycle classes. A lifecycle object is used to create, locate, and destroy entity objects. In analysis, a lifecycle class allows developers to consolidate the different ways a certain type of entity object is located and created.

In many cases, it makes sense to see how entity objects are used before creating lifecycle classes. Therefore, we will not attempt to discover any lifecycle classes at this point. Instead, we will defer their discovery to the next step, describing object interactions.

Describe Object Interactions

In this step, we use sequence diagrams to model the interaction and cooperation between objects as they fulfill a use case. This requires a sequence diagram for each flow of events and a class diagram for each use case. The class diagram shows all of the classes that define the objects that participate in the sequence diagrams.

During this step, we use the flows of events and the activity diagram for the use case, as well as the entity, boundary, and control classes that we discovered in the previous step.

It is often helpful to discover some behavior for each class before starting the sequence diagrams. These methods often help shape the sequences, and they can always be moved or removed if they do not fit. This is especially true for developers who are migrating to object-oriented development from procedural development. Novice object-oriented developers tend to mutate the objects into verbs and the methods into data, as in a data flow diagram. Finding the objects and some methods in a separate step helps prevent this natural tendency.

WARNING Objects should be nouns, and methods should be verbs. If your sequence diagram has verbs for the objects and nouns for the methods, you are reverting to procedural habits by creating data flow diagrams.

Add Tentative Behavior for Login

Walking through the normal flow in the activity diagram, we see that the system asks for the username and password. Clearly, this must be performed by the LoginUI objects, as they handle all interactions with the external actors. So we add a displayLoginForm method to both user interface classes.

Next, the actor enters values for the username and password. The actor must somehow indicate that he or she is done, so we add a submitNameAndPassword method to the user interface classes.

In the next activity, the system verifies the username and password. Clearly, this business logic does not belong in the boundary objects. We give the responsibility to the LoginWorkflow objects by adding the validateLogin method to the LoginWorkflow class. However, the LoginWorkflow object will not actually know whether a particular name and password pair is valid. Since the user objects already have this information, we make the LoginWorkflow object find the right user and ask him or her to validate the login, so we add a validateLogin method to the User class. For the LoginWorkflow object to find the right user, we need a lifecycle object that searches for users by username, so, we create a UserLocator class with a findByName method.

In the final activity of the normal flow, the system welcomes the user, so we add a displayWelcome method to the user interface classes.

Walking through the activity diagram lets us find behavior and allocate methods to the classes identified earlier. All of these decisions are captured in Figure 5.5. Next, we must use a sequence diagram to visualize and verify this behavior.

Build Sequence Diagrams for Login

Now that we have identified several types of objects, and allocated responsibilities to them, we must show how the objects work together. First, we arrange the initiating actor and the objects on a sequence diagram. Since the actor initiates the sequence, we place the actor in the top left. Since the actor interacts with the system through the boundary object, we place the boundary object to the immediate right of the actor. Since the control object serves as a single point of contact between the boundary object and the entity objects, we place the control object between them.

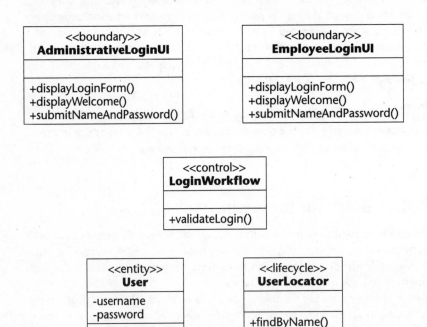

Figure 5.5 Participating classes for Login.

We repeat this process for the normal flow and some of the alternate flows. At some point, the sequence diagrams become repetitive, so we stop making them. Deciding when to stop is a delicate balancing act; including too few sequence diagrams leads to missed behavior, while too many sequence diagrams leads to extra work, as each sequence diagram must be kept up to date and improved throughout the analysis and design process.

Normal Flow for Login

The actor asks the boundary EmployeeLoginUI object to display the login form. The actor then fills in username and password and submits them to the system. The EmployeeLoginUI object asks the control LoginWorkflow object to validate the login workflow. To satisfy this request, the LoginWorkflow object asks the UserLocator object to find the User object that corresponds to the name. Once the LoginWorkflow object gets the right User object, it asks it to validate the password. Once the Login-Workflow object receives a response, it passes it back to the EmployeeLoginUI object. When the EmployeeLoginUI object receives the valid response, it displays a welcome message, and the flow is complete. Figure 5.6 shows this sequence.

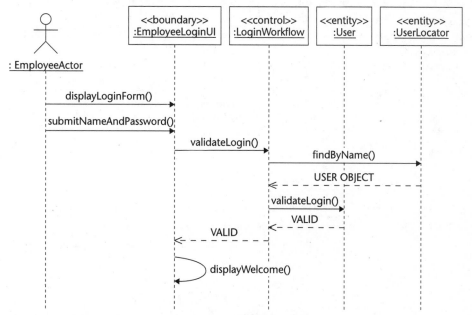

Figure 5.6   Sequence diagram for the normal flow of Login.

Alternate Flow for Invalid Password

This sequence proceeds exactly as in the normal flow, until the User object responds with INVALID to the validateLogin method. This response is propagated up to the EmployeeLoginUI, which must display an invalid password message to the actor. Since there is no method in the EmployeeLoginUI, we add one, displayErrorMessage. Figure 5.7 shows the complete sequence.

Alternate Flow for Unknown User

This sequence proceeds exactly as in the normal flow, until the UserLocator responds with a NULL when asked to locate the user by his or her name. Obviously, the Login-Workflow cannot ask an unknown User object to validate the password, so it returns INVALID to the EmployeeLoginUI object. As in the sequence for the invalid password, the EmployeeLoginUI calls its own displayErrorMessage method. Figure 5.8 shows this sequence.

Validate Sequences for Login

In the previous sequences, we found behavior by following the flow of events forward. Now we must verify the sequences by going backward through each sequence. At each step, we determine whether the object has the information it needs to respond to the request.

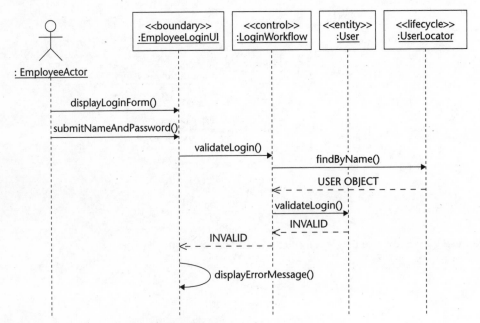

Figure 5.7 Alternate flow for invalid password.

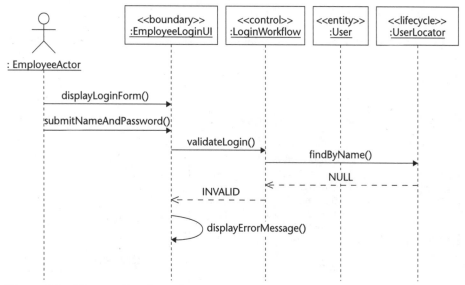

Figure 5.8 Alternate flow for unknown user.

Normal Flow

The last method called is displayWelcome from the EmployeeLoginUI to itself. Certainly, the EmployeeLoginUI can greet the user by his or her username.

The previous method is from the LoginWorkflow object, which asks the User object to validate the login. The LoginWorkflow object knows about the User object because it just asked the UserLocator object to find it. Since each User object has a username and a password, it can easily determine whether the password matches.

The previous method is the LoginWorkflow, which asks the UserLocator to find the User object that corresponds to the username. Though it is not clear how the Login-Workflow object knows the UserLocator object, it is safe to assume that any object can use the dedicated UserLocator object. The details are deferred until design. Certainly, the UserLocator object must be able to locate any User object; that is its job.

The previous method is the EmployeeLoginUI object, which asks the LoginWorkflow object to validate the login. Though it is unclear how the EmployeeLoginUI object knows about the LoginWorkflow object, it is reasonable to assume that these two objects are a cooperating pair, and that either the EmployeeLoginUI created the LoginWorkflow or they were both created by the same application-level object. Again, this detail is deferred until design. While the LoginWorkflow cannot perform this task on its own, it knows where to go for this information. This is the nature of control objects.

Certainly, the EmployeeLoginUI object knows how to display the login form and accept user input. It is unclear how the actor and EmployeeLoginUI are hooked together. This depends on the implementation strategy, and may be profitably deferred until design.

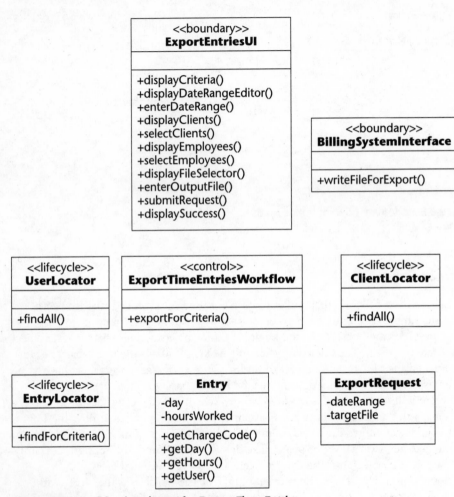

Figure 5.9 Participating classes for Extract Time Entries.

Sequence Diagrams and Class Diagrams for the Remaining Use Cases

The sequence diagrams and class diagrams for the Extract Time Entries and Record Time use cases are shown in Figures 5.9 through 5.13 with little explanation. These diagrams complete the analysis model that is used as a basis for the remainder of the book, but they do not introduce any new techniques or issues.

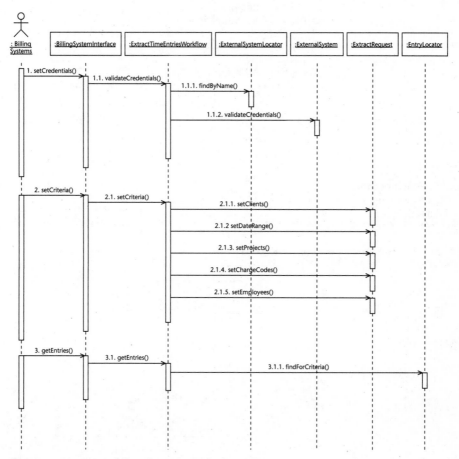

Figure 5.10   Normal flow for Extract Time Entries.

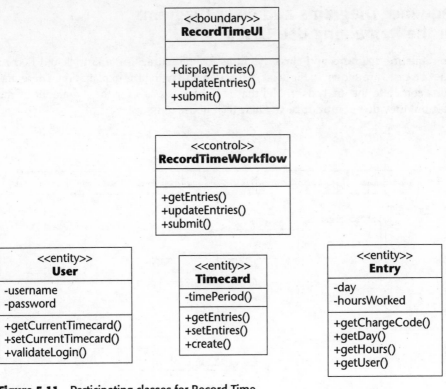

Figure 5.11   Participating classes for Record Time.

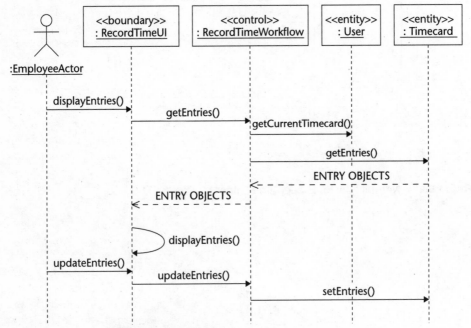

Figure 5.12   Normal flow for Record Time.

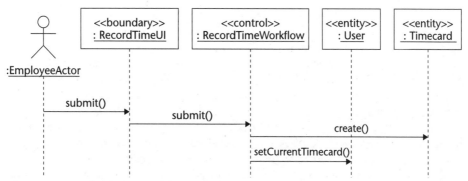

Figure 5.13 Submit timecard flow for Record Time.

Describe Classes

In this step, we determine the relationships between classes that are required to support the interaction between objects in the flow of events. This is accomplished by creating a class diagram for each use case. This means that several sequence diagrams contribute to each class diagram.

Remember, each time an object calls a method in another object, there is a relationship between the objects. This relationship is captured in the class diagram. In analysis, we want to fully specify the relationships between entity classes while loosely specifying the relationships between boundary and control classes and between control and entity classes. Of course, we should determine that a relationship exists and determine its direction. However, any decisions as to multiplicity or type of association are pure speculation. Different technologies and different techniques lead to different patterns of association.

Determining the need for a relationship is simple bookkeeping. Every message from one object to another requires a relationship from the sending object's class to the receiving object's class. Determining the type of the relationship is a bit more complex. It is a dependency if the sending object creates the receiving object, uses it, then loses it, or if the sending object receives the receiving object as a method parameter, uses it, and fails to keep it. During analysis, this may be difficult to determine, since there are no method parameters. Fortunately, these decisions are not important during analysis.

Find Relationships for Login

We find relationships by working forward in the sequence diagram for the normal flow of the Login use case. The EmployeeLoginUI object calls the validateLogin method in the LoginWorkflow object. This implies a relationship from the EmployeeLoginUI class to the LoginWorkflow class. There is also a relationship from the LoginWorkflow class to the User class and the UserLocator class. The return values do not indicate relationships, since an object does not need a reference to provide a response.

Now that we have determined the direction of the relationship, we will consider the type of each relationship. At first, it seems as if there is no reason for the Employee-LoginUI object to keep a reference to the LoginWorkflow object. However, a quick glance at the activity diagram for the Login use case shows that the EmployeeLoginUI object allows the user to reenter his or her username and password. It makes sense for the EmployeeLoginUI object to keep a reference to the LoginWorkflow object, so the relationship is an association.

The relationship between the LoginWorkflow object and the UserLocator object follows the same logic. The LoginWorkflow object should keep a reference in case it needs it for subsequent login attempts, so the relationship is an association.

The LoginWorkflow object does not need to keep a reference to the User object, because the LoginWorkflow object looks up the User object each time, so the relationship is a dependency.

Figure 5.14 shows these relationships.

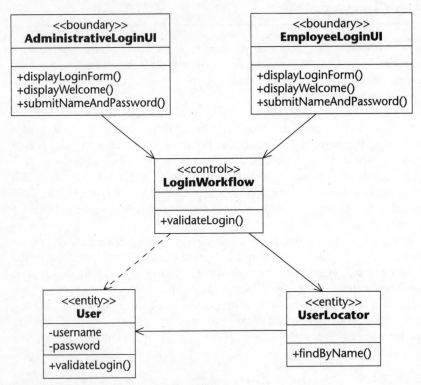

Figure 5.14   Participating classes for Login.

Find Relationships for Extract Time Entries

The BillingSystemInterface uses and reuses the ExtractTimeEntriesWorkflow object. The ExtractTimeEntriesWorkflow object uses the ExternalSystemLocator and External-System objects to validate the billing system's credentials. It does not reuse these two objects. The ExtractTimeEntriesWorkflow object also uses an ExtractRequest object to hold the selection criteria and an EntryLocator object to find the Entry objects that match the criteria.

Figure 5.15 shows these relationships.

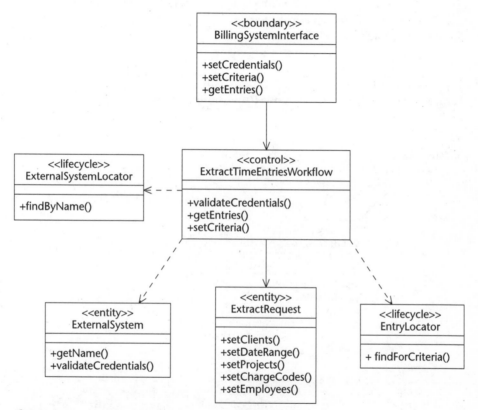

Figure 5.15   Participating classes for Extract Time Entries.

Find Relationships for Record Time

The RecordTimeUI object uses the RecordTimeWorkflow object, which in turn uses the User object and the Timecard object.

The RecordTimeUI object keeps a reference to the RecordTimeWorkflow object, and uses it to update the entries, so the relationship is an association.

The RecordTimeWorkflow object keeps a reference to the User object. This object is used when the RecordTimeWorkflow object submits the old timecard and replaces it with a new timecard, so the relationship is an association.

The RecordTimeWorkflow object keeps a reference to the Timecard object. This object is used when the RecordTimeWorkflow object sets the entries for the Timecard object, so the relationship is an association.

Figure 5.16 shows these relationships.

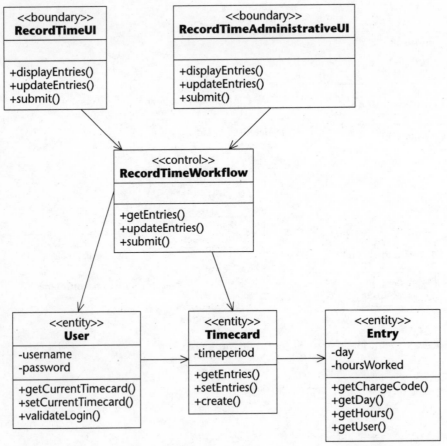

Figure 5.16   Participating classes for Record Time.

The Next Step

This chapter focused on some of the use cases, based on their risk, significance, and suitability. For each of these use cases, we used the flows of events to find some entity, control, and boundary objects. In the next step, we use sequence diagrams to describe the interactions between the objects. Finally, we use class diagrams to show the relationships between objects.

At this point, we have a good understanding of the system from the stakeholders' and the developers' point of view. This understanding provides a solid foundation as we invent the solution in the remaining processes.

Describing the System for Technology Selection

The previous chapters detailed how to use a consistent process and the UML to understand a system from the stakeholders' and developers' perspective. That effort leads to a very complete and detailed view of the problem. In this chapter, you'll learn how to describe and categorize the system so that technology experts can determine the most suitable technologies, without being overwhelmed by the intricacies of the problem.

In some cases, the developers who gather the requirements and develop the analysis model may also determine the best technologies. In other cases, the developers may use a variety of resources within and even outside of the organization. Having a higher-level description of the proposed system allows more and a wider variety of people to contribute to the technology selection process.

Perhaps a real-world example is in order. Architects can select materials and building technology for a proposed structure without understanding exactly how the building will be used. They do, however, need to know if the building is planned for residential, commercial, or industrial use, and they need a rough estimate of its size or capacity. They don't need to know what each room will be used for or who will occupy each space. Based on this limited and high-level view of the building, an architect can choose between wood, concrete, or steel for the building's skeleton. The same holds true for a computer system; the technology experts need to know only the basics about the system in order to choose the right technology to make the system work.

Are You Ready?

In order to describe the system for technology selection, you must have a clear understanding of the system. Without this understanding, developers are doomed to solve the wrong problem or to deliver unusable solutions. For example, a technology may meet all of the functional requirements but fail to function in the user's actual environment, due to hardware limitations, nonstandard operating systems, or network topology.

These misunderstandings can be avoided by gathering requirements, complete with deployment constraints and nonfunctional requirements for each use case. The analysis model helps developers identify common parts of the system that can be considered together during technology selection. In some cases, the developers must gather additional information, such as the expected number of concurrent users, the expected volume of data, and the deployment environment.

There are two significant steps to create a description of the problem for technology selection:

1. Group the analysis classes.

2. Describe each group.

Let's look at each of these.

Group the Analysis Classes

In the previous chapters, we developed an analysis model that identified entity, control, boundary, and lifecycle classes for each use case. Before performing technology selection, we will group similar analysis classes together. This allows developers to consolidate the decision-making process and helps ensure a coherent solution.

Different types of analysis classes connect in different ways, so you need to consider each of the following separately:

- Boundary classes between humans and the system
- Boundary classes between an external system and the system
- Control, entity, and lifecycle classes

Boundary (User Interface)

The boundary classes between humans and the system are more commonly known as the user interface. There are three main criteria for grouping user interface classes for technology selection:

- User group
- Deployment constraints
- Complexity of the user interface

Whenever possible, you should use a single technology for all user interface classes in the system. If this is impossible, all of the user interface classes for each group of users should use the same technology. Limiting and consolidating the user interface technologies greatly decreases deployment costs such as distribution, training, and support. Systems that depend on a patchwork quilt of different technologies tend to be difficult for new users to learn and for developers to maintain, extend, and support.

Unfortunately, varying deployment constraints and user interface complexity often complicate this goal. If the user interface classes in a group have radically different deployment constraints, then it may be necessary to split up the group. The same process must be followed for user interface complexity.

User Group

In the UML, actors in the use case model represent distinct user groups. This makes it very easy to identify a group of user interface classes: just group the boundary classes that are used by an actor.

For example, a banking system may use one presentation technology to allow customers to pay bills online, and another technology to allow bank tellers to manage new and existing accounts. This enables the developers to select one technology for the customers based on their needs for low deployment cost and universal access, while selecting the other technology based on the bank tellers' needs for ease of use and full functionality.

Deployment Constraints

When dividing the user interface classes into groups, it is important to consider deployment constraints. In order to be suitable for all of the user interface classes in a group, the technology must meet the most restrictive deployment constraint. If one class has more restrictive deployment constraints, it should be split out to a separate group.

The deployment constraints are found in the description of the use case that led to the creation of the user interface boundary class during analysis. For instance, a use case may specify that it must be accessible from behind a firewall or from any computer that is connected to the Internet.

User Interface Complexity

The complexity of the user interface must be considered when dividing the user interface classes into groups. If most of the user interface classes involve simple data entry, a sophisticated data visualization class may need to be considered separately when selecting technologies. Attempting to push a technology past its strengths often will cause headaches as the system evolves and expands. A technology that is just barely capable of supporting the current user interface may not support future desires for more user interface sophistication. Therefore, it is important to consider user interface complexity in grouping user interface classes.

User interface complexity can be derived from the flows of events for each use case and by examining the responsibilities of each user interface boundary class.

Boundary (System Interface)

Each boundary class that controls the system's interaction with another system must be considered separately. While it is desirable to use the same technology for all system interface classes, it may not be possible. In many cases, existing external systems dictate the interface. For example, a system may expose its functionality through CORBA or RMI, or support a standard protocol such as HTTP or FTP. External systems may require special formatting for the data, such as XML or a proprietary data structure.

It is easy to group the system interface classes, because each is its own group. Later, after technologies have been selected, it may be possible to combine system interface classes or share common functionality.

Remember, system interface classes encapsulate the interactions between your system and an external system. So, when describing a boundary class, use the flow of events and the responsibilities in the system interface class to derive the technology needs for the boundary class.

Control, Entity, and Lifecycle Classes

Recall the different responsibilities held by the control, entity, and lifecycle classes. Control objects convert high-level messages from the boundary objects into many simple messages to entity objects. This allows the entity objects to stay very focused and as simple as possible, while providing a convenient interface to the boundary objects.

Entity objects hold the persistent business data and business rules for the system. Lifecycle objects create, locate, and destroy entity objects. All control, entity, and lifecycle classes in a system should use the same technology or related technologies. After all, they are closely related, because control objects use lifecycle objects to obtain references to entity objects, then interact with those entity objects to fulfill the functionality for a use case. A lot of data and object references are passed about. In many cases, transactions must be started and completed. The alternative, a patchwork quilt of technologies, is often unpleasant to develop and extend. With these factors in mind, it is highly desirable to select a single technology or a closely related family of technologies for all of the control, lifecycle, and entity classes. There may be some esoteric exception to this rule, but I have never encountered it.

Describe Each Group

Once you have identified some groups of classes, you can describe each group's characteristics with respect to technology requirements. For example, you might categorize a group of user interface classes according to the complexity of the interface and according to its deployment constraints. Every user interface can be loosely located in a spectrum of complexity that ranges from simple data entry to slick interactive graphics. It can also be located in a spectrum for deployment constraints.

The real payoff comes when you use the same descriptive spectrums to describe the strengths and weaknesses of each technology. For instance, a user interface technology may be perfectly adequate for one level of complexity, but be inappropriate for a more complex level. Using the same descriptive spectrum to describe both the problem and the prospective solutions greatly simplifies the technology selection process and removes much of the uncertainty and guesswork.

I suggest a spectrum of descriptions for the following areas:

- User interface complexity
- Deployment constraints for user interfaces
- Number and type of users
- Available bandwidth
- Types of system interfaces
- Performance and scalability

Let's examine each of these aspects in detail.

User Interface Complexity

GUI complexity is the most important criterion to consider when selecting a technology for user interface classes. It is incredibly important to be clear on what your user wants and needs before making this decision. It would be horrible to be 80 percent done with a year's worth of tedious HTML and JavaScript generation only to find that you cannot satisfy your customer with an HTML-only solution. It would be equally painful to discover that you have completely overdesigned the interface, and that what they really need is tabular data that will load into their PalmPilot's Web browser. It is often difficult to extract such decisions from a user community that may not even know, collectively, what it wants. I empathize and offer the caveat that the following section is completely useless if you cannot establish solid requirements.

In describing the complexity of a user interface, it is helpful to have some descriptive categories to compare. With this goal in mind, consider a range of complexity from simple data entry to interactive graphics:

Simple data input.   A simple data input user interface allows a user to enter data into the system. It may help the user by presenting a list of choices or by performing simple field-level validation for dates or numbers. At the very least, the technology must allow text entry, as with a command prompt or text entry field. However, most users expect a little more; consequently, simple data input in our modern era often includes some not-so-simple widgets, such as drop-down selectors, selectable lists, radio buttons, check boxes, and scrollable text entry fields. Field-level validation, such as a check for valid dates or numeric data, may also be included.

Static view of data.   A static view of the data can be a table, tree, or graph that is unaffected by changes in the underlying system data. It is equally unresponsive to the user's desire to see more or less data or to change a sort order. The view is essentially a snapshot of some underlying data in the system. If users want to vary the presentation or see the latest data, they must have the system regenerate the entire view. For example, consider a list of books and prices from an online bookseller. The data is constant; customers must resubmit their request whenever they need the latest information. Also, if customers want to exclude some books, they must enter new search criteria.

Customizable views.   A customizable view allows a user to customize the presentation of static data without making a new request to the server. For example, given tabular data, the system user may filter the data, select the sort order, and hide particular columns. Given a graph, the system user may zoom in on one part of the graph or filter the data to create a new graph. The data is constant; only the presentation changes. For example, if you have a table of 50 used cars, a user can sort and re-sort by price, manufacturer, or cargo capacity, all without submitting a new request to the server.

Dynamic view of data.   A dynamic view of data is automatically refreshed to stay current as the underlying system data changes. There is no need for the user to request an updated view. Either the view is updated whenever the underlying data changes or the view is periodically updated. A news ticker is a good example. The user does not request the updated information. It simply appears unbidden and, often, unwanted.

Interactive graphics.   Interactive graphics are similar to dynamic views; the graphical view is automatically updated as the underlying system data changes. However, interactive graphics take this one step further. The user can update the underlying data by manipulating the graphics. This level of interaction can be very useful for visualizing resource allocation and interactive simulations, and developing collaborative designs.

A networked version of the game Doom is a good, if extreme, example. Each player uses interactive graphics to view and change the underlying data in the system. By keeping all of the remote views synchronized, the system allows the players to interact with one another and with the computer-generated players.

Other systems use interactive graphics to allow a user to change data visually, then see the effects as calculated by the system. Microsoft Project is an excellent example of this type of application. A user can change the scheduled end date for an activity by dragging it to the right on a timeline. The application determines if the change has a ripple effect on other activities. If so, it updates both the underlying data and the visual display. This gives the user access to an intuitive visual interface to evaluate complex project scheduling options.

These categories describe a spectrum of user complexity from very simple to very complex. A similar spectrum can be used to describe deployment constraints.

Deployment Constraints for User Interfaces

It is impossible to characterize a group of user interface classes without considering how the classes will be deployed. For most systems, the deployment constraints are as important as the complexity of the user interface. After all, great functionality does not help anyone if the intended audience cannot use the system.

When you describe the deployment constraints for a user interface, it is helpful to have some descriptive categories to which to compare. With this goal in mind, consider a range in deployment scenarios from a handheld device accessing the system over the Internet to a few dedicated workstations accessing the system on a high-speed LAN:

Handheld device.   This deployment constraint requires the user interface to work on a handheld device, such as a PalmPilot or perhaps even a cellular phone. While this requirement is quite rare today, it may become more and more common, as wireless technology improves and tiny user interfaces mature.

Any Web browser on the Internet.   This deployment constraint requires the user interface to perform acceptably on any browser, on any computer, over the slowest possible dial-up connection. Some browsers may not support images, much less dynamic HTML, so the user interface must be presented or at least presentable in a text-only form. While rare, this constraint is a reality, especially for government sites that provide access to people with disabilities. In other cases, the computer may be old, slow, and behind a corporate firewall, or old, slow, and connected to a painfully slow modem. In both cases, the system must perform adequately, despite the restrictions. There also is no limit to the number of concurrent users in this scenario.

Late-model Web browser on the Internet.   This deployment category relaxes the constraints a bit, by ensuring that each Web browser is no more than a few generations old. If this assumption is true, we know that the computer is also no more than one or two generations old, since significantly older computers cannot support resource-hungry late-model browsers. There is also no limit to the number of concurrent users in this scenario. This is the target deployment scenario for most commercial Web sites.

Late-model browser on a network.   This deployment category assumes a late-model Web browser and a reasonably late-model computer on the same network that contains the system. The number of concurrent users is certainly fewer than the total number of users on the network. This is a common deployment scenario for systems that are deployed on corporate intranets.

Specific browser on a network.   This deployment category restricts the users of a system to a single version of a specific browser. The number of concurrent users is certainly fewer than the total number of users on the network. This is a slightly less common deployment scenario for systems that are deployed on corporate intranets.

Dedicated workstations on a network.   In this scenario, users implement software installed on workstations to access the system. This allows the developers to completely control the software on both the server and the client. The number of clients that are installed limits the number of concurrent users. This is a traditional client/server approach.

These categories describe a spectrum of deployment constraints from very restrictive to completely under the control of the developers. A similar spectrum can be used to describe the number and type of users.

Number and Type of Users

The number of users influences technology selection in two ways. First and foremost, a high number of users forces the technology for the entity, control, and lifecycle classes to scale well. A high number of users also influences the selection of user interface technology. A larger audience makes ease of deployment and support costs major factors.

A system with many users must keep the incremental distribution, deployment, and support costs low. Distribution and deployment costs can be reduced, by allowing users to download the client software or by offering the entire service as a Web site. Support costs encourage simplicity over flash and extra functionality.

The type of users also influences the technology selection. An enthusiastic group of users who gain a lot by using the system will accept a slightly more difficult deployment process. Their vested interest in the system makes them more accommodating and flexible. On the other hand, users who have little to gain or who are forced to use a system to perform a nuisance task, such as filling in their timecard or paying personal property taxes, are less accommodating, in which case, the technology must be easy to use.

In describing the expected number and type of users for a system, it is helpful to have some descriptive categories to compare. With this goal in mind, consider a range from a few users within an organization to a mass market:

Small number of dedicated users.   This is a small group of users who help define the system and who directly benefit from the system. Distribution, installation, training, and support may be cost-effectively customized to fit their needs. Functionality is usually the priority, since these groups are often willing to invest their own time and energy as they learn the system. In many cases, the users spend much of each working day intertwined with the system.

While this seems like an esoteric category, examples can be found in many industries. Air traffic controllers use immensely complex systems to visualize the location and path of commercial air traffic. Stock traders use highly customized and proprietary systems to analyze risk and determine values for securities. Resource planners in the oil industry use complex systems to keep expensive refineries operating at high efficiencies, while keeping inventory costs low and fulfilling contracts. Call center systems allow people to handle huge volumes of calls for customer or technical support.

General use within an organization.   This is a much larger group of users, who are generally less motivated with respect to the system. In some cases, almost everyone in a company with tens of thousands of employees on three continents depends on a system. These systems tend to support the organization, rather than contributing directly to the core business. Examples include time tracking, benefits management, safety compliance, and information sharing.

Large audience with high interest.   In this scenario, a system must serve a large audience of very involved participants. The users may be geographically scattered and otherwise unconnected from one another. The users may log on to the system to exchange information or to collaborate. The Internet was actually started by one form of this audience, researchers who needed to share data and information in a loose collaborative environment.

This audience is generally willing to accept some inconvenience, because the system holds great value for them. For example, researchers may be willing to download and install fairly complex software if it will help them visualize mathematical models for weather or burning buildings, for example. An audiophile may be willing to do almost anything to hear his or her favorite recording artist's new track a week early.

In many cases, this audience is virtually self-supporting, because the community members help one another through the inevitable pitfalls of installing and using the software.

Huge audience with low interest.   In this scenario, a system must attract and serve a relatively fickle audience. This, of course, is the audience for most consumer Web sites. Visitors are alienated easily by systems that start slowly or that waste their time in any way. Both potential and existing customers want a very pleasant and efficient experience, and they are certainly not going to accommodate the system in any way.

These categories describe a spectrum of users from a small number of dedicated users to a large number of relatively disinterested users. A similar spectrum can be used to describe the available bandwidth.

Available Bandwidth

Available bandwidth is another key factor when selecting technologies. Some combinations of technologies allow the developers to meet low bandwidth restrictions, while other technologies exacerbate bandwidth constraints. The descriptive categories for bandwidth ranges from a dial-up connection to an Internet service provider at one end to a dedicated network at the other:

Dial-up Internet connection.   This is still the most common type of connection to the Internet. Supporting speeds from roughly 26 KBaud (thousand bits per second) to 56 KBaud, a dial-up connection is suitable for systems that let users view text and images, listen to streaming audio, and enter textual data. It is painfully slow for any sort of real-time video or other media.

Fast Internet connection.   Fast Internet connections consist of a variety of technologies, including digital data transmission over phone lines, cable and satellite transmission, and shared direct transmission lines to the Internet backbone. These connections allow users to view text, images, and even streaming video without significant discomfort.

Dedicated network between client and server.   A dedicated network allows the client and the server to exchange data at very high speeds. Even an inexpensive home network can easily support 100 million bits per second over relatively short distances.

These categories describe a spectrum of bandwidth from dial-up connections to a dedicated network. A similar spectrum can be used to describe different types of system interfaces.

Types of System Interfaces

In some cases, the technology for a system interface is determined by an existing external system. Otherwise, you must describe the system interface, then select an appropriate technology. Obviously, this process must be coordinated with the development team for the external system. System interfaces are divided into three categories:

Data transfer.   Many system interfaces exist solely to transfer large blocks of information from system to system. Such interfaces are traditionally referred to as electronic data interchange (EDI) interfaces. The exchange of data may be performed at preset intervals or it may be performed on demand. In any case, one system takes a snapshot of its internal data, formats it for the other system, and sends it to the other system. The receiving system must read the information and update its own internal information. Each interaction has its own agreed-upon data structure, so that both sides can read and write the records.

Data transfer interfaces are very common in business and financial systems. Semi-independent branch office systems retrieve the latest data from the home office. The home office collects the day's transactions from its satellite offices. Money flows from bank to bank. Business partners exchange data and make commitments.

Services through a protocol.   The next form of system interface allows a system to make requests through an agreed-upon protocol. A server allows a client system to authenticate itself and request data or services by sending predefined codes and values. This arrangement allows very structured access to the server, with substantially more flexibility than a simple data interchange.

Some protocols have been standardized for widespread use. For example, the File Transfer Protocol (FTP) allows clients to move files to and from the server. The HyperText Transfer Protocol (HTTP) allows a client to retrieve data from a Web server and to post requests to a Web server. Many organizations develop their own protocols to provide services and exchange more arbitrary information. Protocol-based interfaces use many of the same techniques as data interchange interfaces. It may even be difficult to distinguish between a simple protocol and a complex data interchange. However, protocol-based interfaces generally allow more flexibility and add behavior to the data. For instance, a data interchange interface sends a large block of data and lets the receiver determine the next step. A protocol-based interface might send a small block of data as part of a command, then wait for the response before deciding what to do next.

Direct access to system services.   This type of interface allows a client system to directly call designated methods in the server. The server exposes certain methods for remote access. The client passes the name of the method and any input arguments as a request to the server. The server calls the actual method and passes the result back to the client.

Procedural versions of this type of interface are called Remote Procedure Calls (RPCs), while object-oriented versions of this system use the open standard Common Object Request Broker Architecture (CORBA), Microsoft's Distributed Common Object Model (DCOM), or Sun's semi-open standard Remote Method Invocation (RMI).

This type of interface can provide a very flexible and intuitive interface between two systems. In many cases, it is infinitely easier to expose parts of an existing system in this manner than to implement an entire protocol between two systems.

These categories describe a spectrum of system interfaces from simple data transfer to remote access to the system's functionality. A similar spectrum can be used to describe the performance and scalability issues for a system.

Performance and Scalability

Performance and scalability requirements are increasingly important factors in the selection of technology for control, entity, and lifecycle classes. Performance must be balanced against data integrity in any multiuser system, and there aren't many single-user systems left. Also, as concurrent users and data are added to the system, the system must scale well so that the user experience stays tolerable.

Several factors complicate the development of high-performance and scalable systems. Certainly, the amount of data and the number of concurrent users affect the performance. However, high-performance databases can handle large amounts of data with ease, and high-speed networks minimize the impact of additional users. One factor that dramatically affects performance is concurrent access and updates of data. Some systems must contend with multiple users modifying the same data. In order to keep the data intact, while meeting performance requirements, these systems must use sophisticated locking strategies.

There are several descriptive categories that affect scalability and performance:

Read-only.   Some systems allow users to view the system data, but do not allow them to update it. While this sounds quite restrictive, many very important systems fit this description. For instance, a system may allow a stockbroker to analyze and visualize the risk in his or her portfolio, without allowing him or her to buy or sell securities. A safety compliance system may allow a user to search for safety regulations, without allowing that person to change the regulations. In fact, many systems allow a mass audience to view data, while narrowly restricting changes to the data.

Isolated updates.   In many systems, many users change the system's data, but the changes do not conflict with one another. An online store may have many customers, but they cannot change one another's billing or shipping preferences. Of course, this example falls apart if two people are allowed to log in as the same user, at the same time.

Concurrent updates.   In other systems, many users change the system's data, with some of the changes affecting the same data. An online airline reservation system allows many users to reserve a seat on a particular flight. Since a flight holds a limited number of passengers, each reservation affects a very important piece of data, the number of remaining seats on the flight.

These categories describe a spectrum of factors that affect the performance and scalability of a system. Now, we have several descriptive spectrums that allow us to describe a system's technology needs.

Technology Requirements for the Timecard Application

Now that we have the descriptive spectrums, let's apply them to our Timecard system. This section divides the analysis classes into groups and uses the descriptive categories to describe the technology requirements for each group. These descriptions will be used in subsequent chapters, when we select technologies for each group.

Find Groups of Analysis Classes

There are at least three distinct groups for the Timecard application: the user interface classes, the billing system interface, and the control, entity, and lifecycle classes.

While the deployment constraints for the employee's user interface classes are more restrictive than the administrative users' user interface classes, the user interface complexity is exactly the same. Therefore, any technology that satisfies the employees, with their additional requirements for remote access, will also satisfy the administrative users. Treating all of the user interface classes as a single group will greatly simplify the Timecard application.

There is only one external interface class, the BillingSystemInterface. It must be treated as a separate group.

Unless there is some compelling reason to do otherwise, the control, entity, and lifecycle classes should be treated as a single group. This group contains all of the application logic and business logic for the system.

These decisions leave us with the following groups of analysis classes:

- All user interface classes
- The system interface for the external billing system
- All application and business logic classes

Let's focus on the user interface classes first.

User Interface Complexity

To determine the complexity of the user interface, we need to consider each user interface class in turn. Since all of the user interface classes are grouped together, the selected technology must support the most complex user interface class.

The descriptive categories for user complexity are:

- Simple data input
- Static view of data
- Customizable views
- Dynamic view of data
- Interactive graphics

The group includes the following analysis classes we documented in Chapter 5, "Analysis Model for the Timecard Application":

AdministrativeLoginUI.   The AdministrativeLoginUI class allows the users to enter their username and password as proof that they are authorized to use the system. Examining the class and its methods, as shown in Figure 6.1, it is clear that the purpose of the AdministrativeLoginUI class is best described as simple data input.

EmployeeLoginUI.   Since the EmployeeLoginUI class provides functionality that is identical to that of the AdministrativeLoginUI class, it must have the same user interface complexity: simple data input. Figure 6.1 shows the methods for the class.

RecordTimeAdministrativeUI.   The RecordTimeAdministrativeUI class allows administrative users to enter hours for any employee. Examining the class and its methods, as shown in Figure 6.1, it is clear that the RecordTimeAdministrativeUI class displays existing time entries, and allows the user to enter new time entries and update existing time entries. We conclude that the purpose of the RecordTimeAdministrativeUI class is best described as simple data input and static view of data.

RecordTimeUI.   The RecordTimeUI class allows employees to enter their hours. Since the RecordTimeUI class provides less functionality than the Record-TimeAdministrativeUI class, we conclude that it has the same description, simple data input and static view of data. Figure 6.1 shows the methods for the class.

<<boundary>> **AdministrativeLoginUI**
+displayLoginForm() +displayWelcome() +submitNameandPassword()

<<boundary>> **EmployeeLoginUI**
+displayLoginForm() +displayWelcome() +submitNameandPassword()

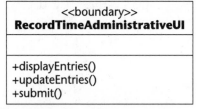

<<boundary>> **RecordTimeAdministrativeUI**
+displayEntries() +updateEntries() +submit()

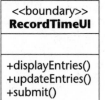

<<boundary>> **RecordTimeUI**
+displayEntries() +updateEntries() +submit()

Figure 6.1   User interface classes.

Deployment Constraints for User Interfaces

Examining the use case descriptions covered in Chapter 3, "Gathering Requirements for the Timecard Application," there seem to be two distinct sets of deployment constraints. The Login and Record Time use cases for the employee must be accessible from almost anywhere, while the use cases for the administrative user have no such restrictions.

Recall that all of the user interface classes have been grouped for technology selection. So, one user interface technology will be selected, and it must meet the most restrictive deployment constraints.

First, we survey the use case descriptions to determine the individual deployment constraints. Based on this information, we select a descriptive category that fits all of the use cases. Revisiting the use case descriptions in Chapter 3, we find the following deployment constraints:

Login use case. Employees must be able to log in from any computer, including those at home, at client sites, and on the road. This access may be from behind a client's firewall.

Record Time use case. The Record Time use case must be accessible from client sites and employees' homes. In the case of client sites, they will often be behind the client's firewall.

Next, we need to pick the descriptive category. The descriptive categories for deployment constraints are:

1. Handheld device
2. Any Web browser on the Internet
3. Late-model Web browser on the Internet
4. Late-model browser on a network
5. Specific browser on a network
6. Dedicated workstations on a network

Since the employee must be able to access the system from home and client sites, we can exclude categories 4, 5, and 6. There is no indication that handheld devices are used, so we can exclude category 1. This leaves us with option 2, "any Web browser on the Internet," and option 3, "late-model Web browser on the Internet." The deployment constraints in the use case descriptions do not determine which of these two options is most appropriate.

In this case, we might ask the stakeholders, or use a simple email survey to clarify the issue. For our example, let's assume that all of the employees already use late-model browsers, so we choose option 3, "late-model Web browser on the Internet."

Number and Type of Users

The number and type of users can usually be deduced from the use case model. Remember, each distinct group of users is represented by an actor in the use case documentation. In the Timecard application, there are only two actors, employee and administrative user. The employee actor represents all employees who use the system to record their time. The administrative actor represents people who administer the system.

The descriptive categories that describe users are:

1. Small number of dedicated users

2. General use within an organization

3. Large audience with high interest

4. Huge audience with low interest

Since all employees use the system to record their hours, category 2, "general use within an organization," seems very appropriate for the user interfaces that support the Login and Record Time use cases.

Available Bandwidth

Available bandwidth can usually be deduced from the deployment constraints on specific use cases and from the descriptions of the actors. For example, if all the actors use the system at a single facility, bandwidth may not be an issue. If some actors use the system from remote facilities, from home, or while traveling, bandwidth may be an important factor.

The descriptive categories for bandwidth are:

1. Dial-up Internet connection

2. Fast Internet connection

3. Dedicated network between client and server

From the deployment constraints in the use case descriptions, we see that the employee must be able to use the system from "any computer, including those at home, at client sites, and on the road." This clearly excludes the last two categories and leaves us with "dial-up Internet connection."

Types of System Interfaces

System interfaces are best described by examining the complexity of the interaction as documented in the flow of events for the use case(s) that use the external system. We must ask questions such as: What data is exchanged? Which services are obtained? How flexible is the interface?

The descriptive categories for system interfaces are:

1. Data transfer

2. Services through a protocol

3. Direct access to system services

The only system interface, the BillingSystemInterface, authenticates itself and extracts time entries from the Timecard system based on specified criteria. However, it does not have access to a full range of system functionality. So, category 2, "Services through a protocol" seems appropriate.

Performance and Scalability

The performance and scalability factors are generally found by examining the class diagrams and sequence diagrams from the analysis model. These diagrams describe the data access and update patterns that influence performance and scalability. Unfortunately, these diagrams cover a single use case at a time. It is up to the developers to consider the effects of several use cases occurring concurrently.

The descriptive categories for performance and scalability are:

1. Read-only

2. Isolated updates

3. Concurrent updates

To determine the most appropriate category, we must consider how multiple users performing the use cases simultaneously affects each entity object. In many cases, a cursory glance at the activity diagram and sequence diagrams for a use case is sufficient. In other cases, developers must examine the sequence diagrams to see exactly how the entity objects are used. It seems profitable to consider each use case in turn before considering the impact of users performing different use cases simultaneously on the categorization. The following sections each describe the performance and scalability factors for an individual use case.

Login use case.   In the Login use case, the system locates the user entity object that corresponds to the actual employee. Once the object is located, the system must determine if the password is valid. This requires the system to read the password from some sort of persistent store. No data is updated, so "read-only" is the appropriate description. The sequence diagram in Figure 6.2 shows this interaction between the objects.

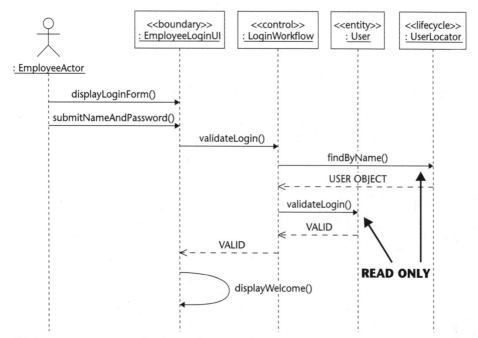

Figure 6.2 Data access for the Login use case.

Extract Time Entries use case.   In the Extract Time Entries use case, the system locates client, user, and time entry objects. It also retrieves the details for each time entry object. It does not update any system data, so "read-only" is the appropriate description. Figure 6.3 shows these interactions.

Record Time use case.   In the Record Time use case, the system retrieves and displays the time entry objects. After the user updates the entries, the system must update its data with the new data. Therefore, the use case must be described with either "isolated updates" or "concurrent updates."

Each employee can only record his or her own hours, so there is no danger of concurrent updates due to different employees using the system at the same time. We can easily preclude the same employee from logging in twice, so there is no danger of the same employee recording hours in multiple sessions. However, the administrative user can initiate the Record Time use case on behalf of any employee. So, two administrative users or one administrative user and the actual employee could record time for the same employee at the same time. The Record Time use case does introduce a risk of "concurrent updates." Figure 6.4 shows these interactions.

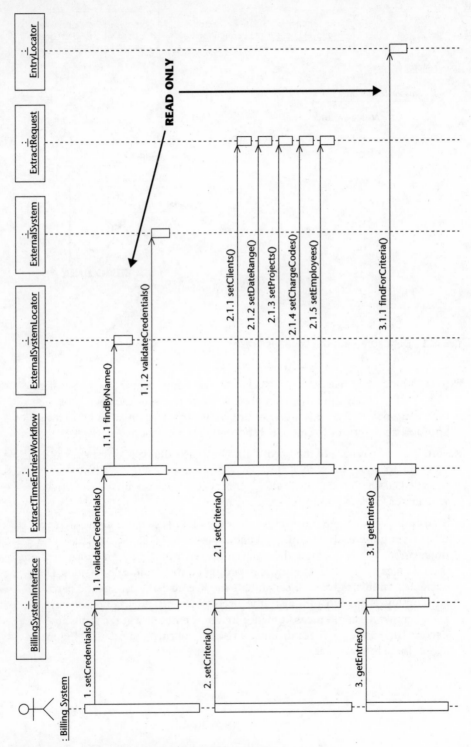

Figure 6.3   Data access for the Extract Time Entries use case.

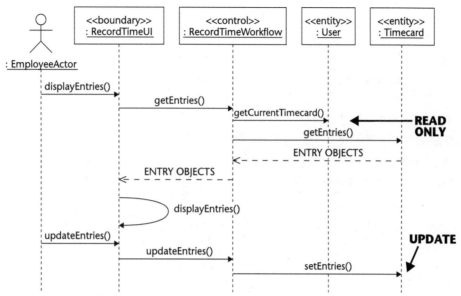

Figure 6.4 Data access for the Record Time use case.

The Next Step

Describing the technology requirements of a system forces you to carefully examine the requirements and analysis model for the system. For real-world systems, this is a very daunting prospect. Hundreds of pages of documentation must be read and understood as the system is gradually categorized. However, the result is well worth the effort, because the technology requirements for a complex system, with many interesting nuances and subtleties, can be summarized in a few paragraphs.

This summary is used to facilitate technology selection and to enable the participation of more people in the selection process. For instance, developers with experience in a given technology can easily use the summary to evaluate the suitability of that technology. They can share their expertise without spending countless hours learning the system. Summarizing the technology requirements for a system is also useful if you are *not* using outside expertise. By producing the summary before considering technology, developers avoid any urge to pick a technology and then justify its suitability for the system. It is very common for developers to semiconsciously select a technology before evaluating its suitability. This leads them to see the areas where the technology fits, while sometimes glossing over the areas where it does not.

The next two chapters use the following to describe and select technologies for the Timecard application:

- **User interface complexity.** Simple data input and static view of data.

- **Deployment constraints for user interfaces.** Late-model Web browser on the Internet.

- **Number and type of users.** General use within an organization.

- **Available bandwidth.** Dial-up Internet connection.

- **Types of system interfaces.** Data transfer.

- **Performance and scalability.** Concurrent updates.

CHAPTER

7

Evaluating Candidate Technologies for Shared Services

Shared services are technologies that can be used by several layers within a system or by different layers from system to system. Unlike most technologies, they do not serve one specific type of analysis class, such as boundary or entity. Instead they may be used to realize nonfunctional requirements, such as maintainability and reliability, or semifunctional requirements such as security. For example, most systems log error messages from each layer of the system. In fact, effective logging is extremely important to the system's long-term success. This chapter begins with an introduction of a standard template for describing technologies and then describes several shared services.

Technology Template

When learning a new technology, it is easy to become absorbed in the details and miss important information. Most developers, ourselves included, lose objectivity as they learn about the latest and slickest technology. Given a shiny new hammer, all we see are nails. The following template helps us focus our efforts and stay grounded as we assimilate a new technology. We suspect that, with some modifications, it may serve you in a similar way.

Each technology description contains the following elements:

Name and description.   This section provides the name, acronym, and origin of the technology, before briefly summarizing it. The emphasis is on the nature and purpose of the technology, rather than any of the details.

Gory details.   This section uses class diagrams, sequence diagrams, and code samples to describe how the technology works and how it is used. While full coverage of each technology is not possible, this section does capture the flavor and general use of each technology. For more information about specific technologies discussed here, refer to Appendix B, "Additional Resources."

Strengths.   This section describes areas and uses for which the technology excels.

Weaknesses.   This section describes any pitfalls or limitations of the technology.

Compatible technologies.   This section discusses common combinations of technologies that leverage the strengths of the candidate technology.

Cost of adoption.   This section quantifies the costs of adopting the technology. Special emphasis is given to the difficulty of acquiring expertise in the technology. It also mentions any product costs or licensing issues.

Suitability.   This section uses the descriptions established in Chapter 6, "Describing the System for Technology Selection," to describe the situations for which the technology is suitable.

With a reasonable template for describing technologies in hand, we can explore several technologies that can be used to implement shared services:

- The Java Logging classes are used to provide valuable insight into the behavior of the system at run time. Almost every layer of a system depends on Logging classes.

- Application exceptions are a simple technique for communicating different types of unexpected events to other affected parts of the system.

- The Java Cryptography Extension dramatically reduces the effort required to encrypt data for transition to a peer system or to protect persistent data.

- The Java Secure Sockets extension provides a very easy to use interface for creating secure connections with peer systems.

- The Java Management extension allows developers to expose different parts of a system for remote monitoring and configuration.

The following sections cover these technologies in some detail.

Java Logging Classes

Java Logging was added to the standard Java class libraries as Sun's answer to the age-old need for an easy-to-use, flexible, and configurable logging solution. It allows developers to easily add debugging messages for use during testing as well as warning, error, and status messages for use in the production system. As with most of their Java class libraries, Sun has created an immediately useful package by supplying reasonable implementation classes, while preserving unlimited flexibility for developers to write their own.

Java Logging clearly separates the generation of log messages from the processing of those messages. The applications developer is free to describe each system event without worrying about how it will be logged in test environments or in production. For example, the author of a class is not concerned with how the logger will process the log messages during integration testing, or when the system will be released to production. Instead, the developer stays focused on identifying important system events, such as unusual state changes, exceptions, the completion of a long task, the creation of an expensive resource, or user access to the system. Support for different output destinations, such as flat files, remote monitoring systems, and databases can be added at any time without revising the code that logs the messages. Additional output formats can be added with similar ease. These decisions on output format and destination can vary for different parts of the codebase.

This flexibility is very useful in real projects. For example, a system can easily be configured to output all log messages to the console during testing. Later, when the system is put into production, the system can be reconfigured to write error messages to a database, write warnings and errors to a log file, and suppress debugging messages entirely. Also, when resolving production issues, it is very useful to focus attention on one subsystem by logging all messages for that subsystem, while suppressing most messages for the rest of the system.

> **NOTE** As of J2SE 1.4, all of the classes needed for logging can be found in the java.util.logging package.

Gory Details

Now that you understand the purpose of the Logging package, let's explore how the classes work together to fulfill these goals and how logging for most systems can be implemented with minimal effort.

Each of the following class descriptions includes the objectives and responsibilities of the class and a description of its use. Where applicable, concrete implementations are described along with opportunities for extension and customization.

Level

The Level class describes seven different levels of logging detail, ranging from FINEST to SEVERE. The class developer uses these levels to describe the severity of each log message. Later, system-monitoring requirements determine which log messages are captured to an output destination and which are discarded. Obviously, these system-monitoring needs change over the life of the project. For instance, during development, programmers often want to see all messages. This is often bearable since developers control the number of concurrent users and performance is less of an issue. However, once the system is in production, including every message creates an overwhelming blizzard of messages that actually makes it more difficult to detect problems and greatly diminishes performance.

Levels are implemented in the Java Logging classes as enumerated types [Bloch 2001], with predefined Level instances created within the Level class. As shown in Figure 7.1, the constructor is protected. This means that the client code is limited to a set of predefined levels that are accessed as public final attributes of the Level class. Notice that the Level class is not final and that the constructor is protected rather than private. So, subclassing is certainly supported. However, in almost all cases, the seven predefined levels seem perfectly adequate. In fact, most projects should pick a subset of the seven levels, describe how each should be used, and then move on to more interesting topics. For example, the following descriptions might be incorporated into the coding standards for a project:

- **SEVERE.** This level is reserved for serious system errors that require immediate human intervention, such as the failure of a data source or a suspected security breach.

- **WARNING.** This level is reserved for significant errors that *do not* require immediate human intervention, such as intermittent timeouts by a data source.

- **INFO.** This level is used to track less important errors and state changes, such as completion of significant work or badly formed input data that does not indicate an attempted security breach. Info messages should *not* include code level details, such as entry into a method.

- **CONFIG.** This level is used to capture the initial configuration of the system and any changes to that configuration.

- **FINE.** Not used.

- **FINER.** This level is used to capture code level details, such as entry into a method and success or failure of assertions. The Logger will automatically use this level for method level convenience methods, such as entering and exiting.

- **FINEST.** Not used.

Once the usage of the different levels is determined, specifying the severity of a log message is quite simple. As you can see in the code sample below, Sun has graciously provided convenience methods that simplify the specification of the levels.

```
logger.log(Level.INFO, "FYI, the system is still going!");
```

or

```
logger.info("FYI, the system is still going!");
```

LogRecord

The LogRecord class defines a simple serializable data container. Each LogRecord object contains the message text, level, and surrounding context for a single logged message. Attributes that can be captured in a LogRecord object include the level of the message, the time the message was logged, any additional parameters, a unique sequence number, the class that logged the message, the method that logged the message, the thread ID, and any associated exception.

Level
+OFF:Level
+SEVERE:Level
+WARNING:Level
+INFO:Level
+CONFIG:Level
+FINE:Level
+FINER:Level
+FINEST:Level
+ALL:Level
#Level(par1:String,par2:int)
#Level(par1:String,par2:int,par3:String)
+getResourceBundleName():String
+getName():String
+getLocalizedName():String

Figure 7.1 Level enumerated type.

NOTE In some cases, a LogRecord will contain the Logger's best guess for the class and method that logged the message. Use this with caution.

There is no obvious reason to subclass the LogRecord class, and doing so would require changes throughout the logging package. For that matter, there is usually no need to directly create LogRecord objects. When a message is logged, the Logger creates a LogRecord object that is passed to the Handler, Filter, and Formatter objects.

Formatters

Formatter is an abstract class that defines the methods needed to convert a LogRecord object into a formatted String. Concrete implementations must override the format method, which accepts a LogRecord parameter and returns the formatted String. The getHead and getTail methods can be overridden to add a standard header to the top of a set of records and a standard footer to the bottom or tail of a set of records. The formatMessage method is a convenience method that uses the LogRecord's Resource-Bundle and parameters to build a formatted text message for inclusion in the overall formatted record.

Sun provides two implementations, one that produces simple text and another that produces XML. Alternate implementations can use a different subset of the information from the LogRecord or apply a different format. Figure 7.2 shows the abstract Formatter class and the two concrete implementations, SimpleFormatter and XMLFormatter.

As seen in the following code snippets, the output from the SimpleFormatter is much smaller and perfectly fine for human consumption, while the output from the XMLFormatter is much larger and suitable for use by humans or computers.

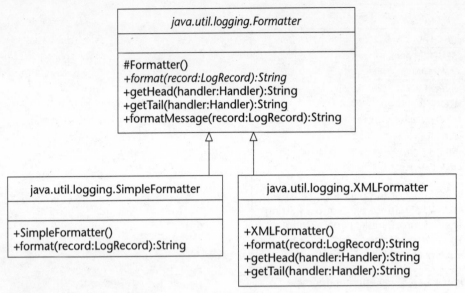

Figure 7.2   Formatter classes.

Output from SimpleFormatter:

```
Feb 13, 2002 12:11:26 AM
com.wiley.compBooks.EJwithUML.Samples.Logging.NoisyClient doNoisyStuff
FINE: A pretty fine message
```

Output from XMLFormatter:

```
<record>
  <date>2002-02-13T00:11:26</date>
  <millis>1013577086936</millis>
  <sequence>8</sequence>
  <logger>com.wiley.compBooks.EJwithUML.Samples.Logging</logger>
  <level>FINE</level>
  <class>com.wiley.compBooks.EJwithUML.Samples.Logging.NoisyClient
  </class>
  <method>doNoisyStuff</method>
  <thread>10</thread>
  <message>A pretty fine message</message>
</record>
```

TIP Formatters should not be used to filter records or to redirect output to different destinations. Instead, use the Filter and Handler classes as described in the following sections.

Filter

As shown in Figure 7.3, the Filter interface defines a single method, isLoggable, which determines if a LogRecord object merits logging. It is very easy to create powerful Filters, because LogRecord contains all of the information for a message. Filters are very useful during debugging, because they can zero in on specific classes or methods. A production snapshot filter might capture all messages for a brief period, such as for the first minute of each hour. This technique gathers detailed information about a system's behavior without completely destroying system performance or filling the filesystem with log messages. In many systems, Filters are not necessary once the system is deployed with the appropriate logging levels.

Handlers

The abstract Handler class defines the methods needed to configure a handler and to publish a LogRecord object to a destination, such as a set of rotated flat files, a socket, or a memory buffer. Each Handler object can be configured with a Filter object, a Formatter object, and a Level object. These should be used consistently by all Handler implementations. The Filter has a chance to reject each message before it is published. Each concrete implementation must override the publish, flush, and close methods for its specific destination. Figure 7.4 shows a few of the concrete implementation classes provided by Sun in the Logging package. The ConsoleHandler writes log messages to standard output, which is usually the console. FileHandlers can be configured to write log messages to a cycle of named log files. Developers can easily write their own handlers and integrate them with the existing Logging classes.

Logger

The Logger class associates output level, filters, and handlers together to capture the logging decisions of the system's designer. Each Logger object is associated with a Level object, an optional Filter object, and one or more Handler objects. As shown in Figure 7.5, each Handler object is also associated with a Level object, a formatter, and an optional Filter object.

Each Logger object can also have an optional parent logger. This allows the logger to use its parent's Level if does not have one and also allows the logger to forward log messages up to its parent.

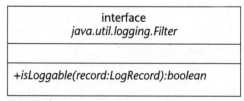

Figure 7.3   Filter interface.

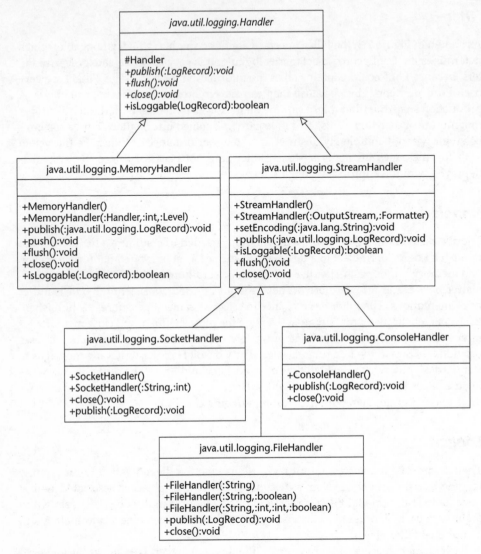

Figure 7.4 Handler classes.

In some cases, developers may want to easily vary the text of a log message to suit the needs of different audiences, such as customers with different native languages. To support this, the Logging API allows the user to pass a localization key in place of the log message. Assuming that the logger has been configured with a ResourceBundle, the logger searches the bundle for a matching key and uses the associated phrase as the message text. This allows developers to support a new audience by deploying a new ResourceBundle. However, the message parameter must exactly match a localization key. It cannot include a mix of plaintext or placeholders for parameters along with the localization key. However, the localized value may contain placeholders for parameters as shown below. The following line would appear in a properties file that corresponds to the ResourceBundle that is specified in the Logger's constructor.

```
BAD_NEWS=Local Version of Something Bad Happened In {0}!
```

The following code snippet will insert the first parameter into the localized string, as expected since the "{0}" in the localized value corresponds to the zero index of the params array.

```
Object[] params = {"The Place", new Integer(3)};
logger.log(Level.SEVERE, "BAD_NEWS", params);
```

LogManager

The Singleton LogManager initializes the Loggers for a system from a configuration file or from a set of startup configuration classes. As Loggers are added, the LogManager configures each Logger and organizes them into a hierarchy based on their name. So, a logger named "com.wiley.compBooks" would specify the default behavior for all loggers whose names match the pattern "com.wiley.compBooks.*". A more specific logger, such as "com.wiley.compBooks.Samples.Logging" can override the default behavior. There is also a logger, named "", at the root of the hierarchy. It provides default behavior for packages that do not have a specified logger, and default behavior that can be inherited by all loggers.

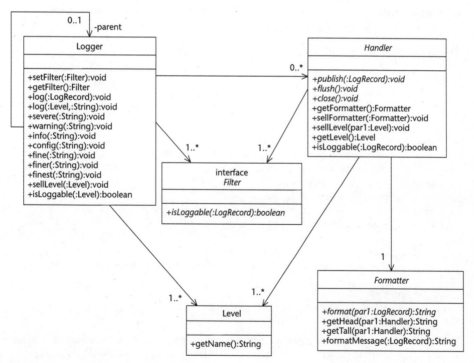

Figure 7.5 Logger and its associations.

On initialization, the LogManager first checks for a configuration file, as specified by the `java.util.logging.config.class` environment variable. If this variable is not set, the LogManager reads a configuration file, as specified by the `java.util.logging.config.file` environment variable or the default logging property file in the lib directory of the runtime environment. The configuration file may directly describe the desired logging configuration in a series of name-value pairs. The following sample configuration file causes the LogManager to create a FileHandler that uses an XMLFormatter and appends the log data to a file until 50KB is reached. At this point, the FileHandler opens a new file and continues the process. Note that both the handlers and the loggers have a specified level. The logger's level determines if a message is sent to any handlers. Each handler determines if it should actually output a message based on its level. In this configuration, the general-purpose logger will only log SEVERE messages. The com.wiley.compBooks.EJwithUML .Samples.Logging Logger will log all messages. The ConsoleHandler will only log messages that are FINE or more serious, so it will ignore any FINER or FINEST messages. The FileHandler will log all messages.

Let's look at all of these rules together:

- All messages that are logged to com.wiley.compBooks.EJwithUML.Samples .Logging will be logged by the Filehandler.

- All of these messages will also be sent to the ConsoleHandler, but it will only log messages that are FINE or more serious.

- Both handlers will log SEVERE messages for other packages. Less severe messages for other packages are dropped.

The following configuration file captures these decisions.

Configuration file:

```
handlers = java.util.logging.ConsoleHandler,java.util.logging.FileHandler

java.util.logging.FileHandler.pattern =
c:/EJwithUML2e/Code/com/wiley/compBooks/EJwithUML/Samples/Logging/java%g_%u.log
java.util.logging.FileHandler.limit = 50000
java.util.logging.FileHandler.count = 3
java.util.logging.FileHandler.append = TRUE
java.util.logging.FileHandler.formatter = java.util.logging.XMLFormatter
java.util.logging.FileHandler.level = ALL

java.util.logging.ConsoleHandler.level = FINE
java.util.logging.ConsoleHandler.formatter = java.util.logging.SimpleFormatter

.level = SEVERE
com.wiley.compBooks.EJwithUML.Samples.Logging.level = ALL
```

The configuration file may also specify one or more startup classes that configure Logger objects in their constructors. This allows developers to create arbitrarily complex logging configurations that might be difficult or impossible to obtain through the configuration file parameters. The name of the key in the parameter file is simply "config," and the value is a comma separated list of classes, as in config = com.wiley

.compBooks.EJwithUML.Samples.Logging.LogConfiguration. This startup class, shown below, creates two FileHandlers, one that writes ALL messages to a details file and another that writes WARNING and SEVERE messages to an errors file. However, the default Logger has a level of SEVERE, while the logger for the sample package has a level of ALL.

LogConfiguration

```
public class LogConfiguration
{
private static final String BASE_PATH = "C:\\EJwithUML2e\\Code\\com\\
wiley\\compBooks\\EJwithUML\\Samples\\Logging\\";
    public LogConfiguration()
    {
      try
      {
        Formatter simpleFormatter = new SimpleFormatter();
        Formatter xmlFormatter = new XMLFormatter();

        Handler detailFileHandler = new FileHandler(BASE_PATH +
        "LoggingSampleDetails%g.log", 50000, 5, true);
        detailFileHandler.setFormatter(simpleFormatter);
        detailFileHandler.setLevel(Level.ALL);

        Handler errorFileHandler = new FileHandler(BASE_PATH +
        "LoggingSampleErrors%g.log", 50000, 5, true);
        errorFileHandler.setFormatter(xmlFormatter);
        errorFileHandler.setLevel(Level.WARNING);

        Logger logger = Logger.getLogger("");
        logger.setLevel(Level.SEVERE);
        logger.addHandler(errorFileHandler);

        logger = Logger.getLogger("com.wiley.compBooks.
        EJwithUML.Samples.Logging", "com.wiley.compBooks.EJwithUML.
        Samples.Logging.LogMessagesLocalization");
        logger.setUseParentHandlers(false);
        logger.setLevel(Level.ALL);
        logger.addHandler(detailFileHandler);
        logger.addHandler(errorFileHandler);
      }
      catch (IOException e)
      {
        System.out.println("e: " +e);
      }
    }
}
```

Logging Hierarchies

As described earlier, the LogManager organizes loggers into hierarchies so that a call to the static method Logger.getLogger(String name) returns the closest match by name. However, your development team still has to determine what names will be passed to this method and configure matching loggers accordingly. For example, each call to getLogger might use the fully defined class name of the calling class, while the configuration file defines loggers for a few high-level packages. Following this practice removes all ambiguity when analyzing the logs, because most formatters include the name of the logger in the output. This approach does not require separate handlers and level decisions for each class, since the LogManager will find the closest match. It is easy for developers to configure the loggers to focus attention on an individual class during debugging or troubleshooting by specifying a specific logger in the configuration. A class-level hierarchy is very reasonable, since it provides excellent granularity without much effort and without any significant performance penalty. Common alternatives include using the fully defined package names or more arbitrary module names.

> **TIP** Decisions on the hierarchy must be made early and followed consistently, because any nontrivial application has countless calls to Logger.getLogger(). These decisions can easily be captured in the coding standards for your group or project.

Performance

With a little effort, the Logging API can be used without any noticeable penalty for log messages that are rejected by the loggers. The logger checks the level of each message before performing any expensive operations, such as formatting. However, it is still possible to waste a lot of time building a message that is never used. For example, the following innocuous looking code requires four String creations.

```
logger.log("Reached the " +ctr+ " record.", Level.FINE);
```

This wasteful practice can easily be avoided by using parameters, as shown here.

```
Object[] params = {new Integer(ctr)};
logger.log(Level.FINE, "Reached the {0} record.", params);
```

All Together Now

The following sequence diagrams show the initialization and use of the Logger objects that are constructed by the configuration class described in the LogManager section. A FileHandler with an XMLFormatter and a level of WARNING is used to capture error messages from all classes, including those from the sample package. In addition, messages from the sample package are also logged to a FileHandler with a SimpleFormatter and a level of ALL. Figure 7.6 shows how the objects are created, configured, and connected. The default logger is configured to have a level of SEVERE and to send its messages to the errorFileHandler. The logger for the detailFileHandler is configured with a level of ALL and sends its messages to both handlers.

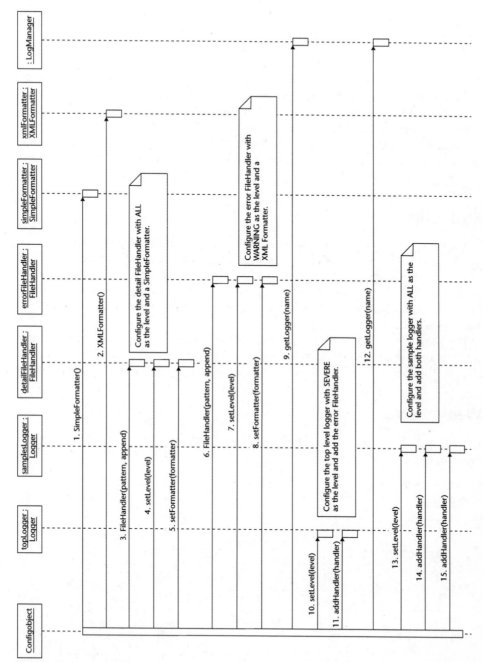

Figure 7.6 Initializing logging.

Next, consider how our default Logger object handles a log request for a message with a level of FINE. Figure 7.7 shows the topLogger object suppressing the log message based on a simple comparison to the logging level specified in the Level object.

In our sample, FINE messages from classes in the Logging sample package are not written by the errorFileHandler, but they are written by the detailFileHandler. Figure 7.8 shows how the sampleLogger passes the record to the errorFileHandler, which compares the record's level to its own level and rejects it. The sampleLogger then passes the record to the detailFileHandler, which verifies that the level of the record is acceptable. The detailFileHandler asks the simpleFormatter to build a string from the contents of the record. The fileHandler writes the response to the file and flushes politely.

Strengths

The Logging API is very flexible and extensible, thanks to its clear separation of responsibilities. Filters, handlers, and formatters can be combined and recombined in endless combinations. Many handlers can use a new formatter, and many loggers can use a new filter. Also, since each class does one and only one thing, they are remarkably easy to extend. Creating new filters and formatters is almost trivial, and adding new handlers is quite reasonable.

The Logging API is also extremely easy for application developers to use. Deciding when to log a message, what information to include, and what to say is the hard part. Obtaining the appropriate logger and writing log messages is extremely straightforward.

Weaknesses

The logging API has no real weaknesses that we are aware of.

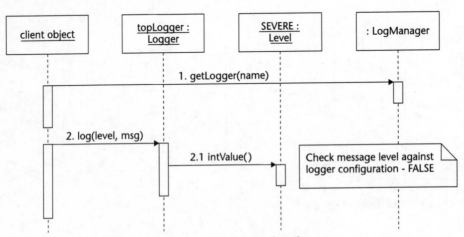

Figure 7.7 Log a FINE message from an uninteresting class.

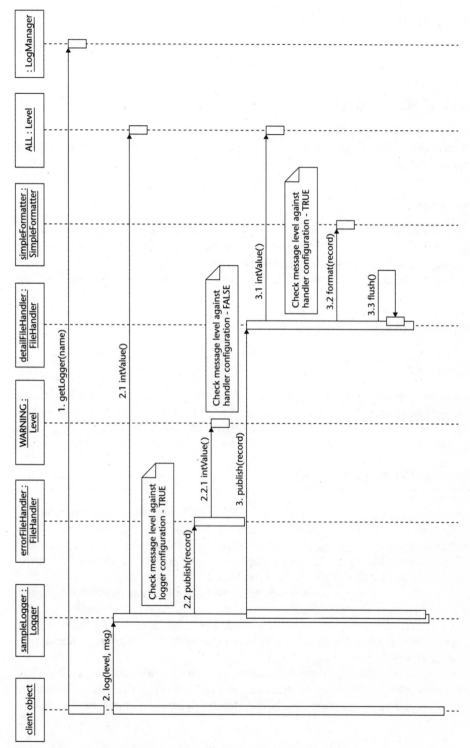

Figure 7.8   Logging a FINE message from Logging sample class.

Compatible Technologies

Any type of Java application can use the Logging API, including servlets, Swing, command-line applications, and Enterprise JavaBeans.

Cost of Adoption

The Logging API is provided free as part of the J2SE, and there is very little effort required to adopt it. To get full value from the API, your project must fill the roles of designer and developer.

Designer

A designer must develop standards for what system events will be logged, what levels will be used, and what information will be included. These decisions are best captured with guidelines in the coding standards and some illustrative examples. If Resource-Bundles will be used, the keys and parameters must be determined early and kept up to date.

The designer must also determine the Logging configuration for debugging, test, and different production environments.

Developer

Each developer is responsible for understanding the guidelines, following them, and participating in the code review process. With a little planning and coordination, logging can be a very effective tool during debugging and production support.

Application Exceptions

Every system design makes decisions about exception handling and propagation. What happens when an important data source is missing? Should the system retry every 30 seconds until the log file fills up? How does the user interface get the news that the database has crashed? What constitutes a fatal error? Can a system be recovered without restarting if it is only "mostly dead"?

It is probably impossible for a design to answer all of these questions for a moderately complex system until detailed design or perhaps even implementation. However, it is very important to establish a consistent application-level framework for exception handling so different designers and implementers make consistent and compatible decisions.

Unfortunately, there is no technology selection to be done, as there is no off-the-shelf solution for handling application exceptions. Instead, we will define what we mean by application exceptions, set some goals, and develop a solution of our own. However, before we move ahead in this manner, it is important to review some of the fundamental terminology and classes that are involved in error handling in Java.

Brief Review of Exceptions

In some languages, success or failure is indicated by numeric return codes. While simple and effective, this approach has several key weaknesses. First, the return value cannot be used to return a more intrinsically important value, because it is dedicated to the status. Also, the developer of the method and the developer of the calling code must agree on the meaning of each response value. Checking the status of the return codes tends to be a tedious process with error checking and error handling often dominating the resulting source code.

Fortunately, the original authors of Java were C programmers with years of frustrating experience in this area. So, they built a better form of error handling right into the Java Virtual Machine (JVM) and the core class libraries. The following section describes the classes that are used to represent nonrecoverable events, known as *Errors*, and recoverable events, known as *Exceptions*.

Java Classes for Exceptions and Errors

java.lang contains an Exception class that represents unexpected but recoverable events and an Error class for nonrecoverable errors. Both classes extend from the Throwable class, which includes a stack trace and a text description. These two classes are used extensively by the standard Java packages. Most Java developers have encountered IOExceptions and OutOfMemoryErrors. IOException extends from Exception, since in many cases the application can retry later or use an alternate data source. OutOfMemoryError makes similar sense as an Error, since there is usually nothing to be done when you run out of memory.

Developers are strongly encouraged to follow a similar pattern in their own classes, by capturing recoverable events as subclasses of Exception and by capturing nonrecoverable events as subclasses of Error. Figure 7.9 shows a small part of the gigantic exception and error hierarchy.

In some cases, the Java Virtual Machine detects a recoverable event or nonrecoverable error while it is executing statements, loading classes, or performing countless other thankless VM tasks. Exceptions that are generated by the Java Virtual Machine must extend RuntimeException, which extends Exception. RuntimeExceptions are never generated directly by Sun's class libraries. There is no such distinction for Errors; they may be used by code in class libraries or by the Java Virtual Machine. Non-runtime exceptions are often called checked exceptions.

NOTE RuntimeExceptions are intended for use by the JVM, so avoid extending RuntimeException when developing Exception classes for your own packages.

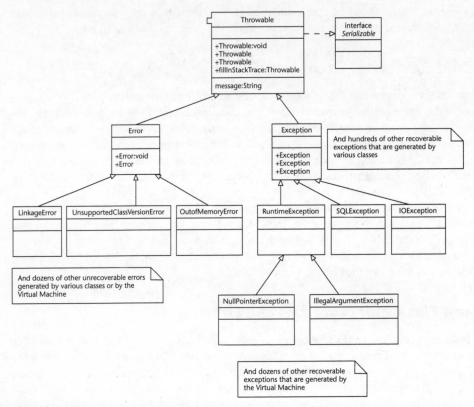

Figure 7.9   Errors and exceptions.

Exceptions and Flow Control

In Java, the reserved word throw is used to break out of the normal flow of execution when an error is detected. Blocks of code that can generate a checked exception must be enclosed within a try block or called from other code that is enclosed within a try block. The try block allows the developer to specify error-handling logic in a corresponding catch block. The last construct, a finally block, allows a developer to specify code that is executed no matter what the outcome is. For example, a FileReader throws a FileNotFoundException during construction if the named file does not exist. When an exception is thrown, the JVM searches up the call stack for a catch block that matches the thrown Exception or its superclass. When it finds a matching catch block, the JVM resumes statement execution inside the catch block. Once the catch block completes, the JVM jumps to the optional finally block, if any. After all of the exception-processing completes, the JVM resumes execution after the try catch block.

This behavior is seen in PropertyClient.java and PropertyReader.java which follow, as the second call to the PropertyReader's readProperties method throws a FileNot-FoundException, apparently due to a sticky "l" key while typing "sillllly". Since read-Properties does not catch the exception, it is required to list FileNotFoundException or a base class in its throw block. During execution, the exception propagates up to PropertyClient. The VM then finds the first catch block that has an identical Exception class or a base class, which in this case is FileNotFoundException. After the catch block is executed, the code inside the finally block is executed, before execution resumes below the finally block. This execution path is described by the comments at the end of each executed line in PropertyClient.java and is also reflected in the output file.

PropertyClient.java

```
package com.wiley.compBooks.EJwithUML.Samples.ApplicationExceptions;

import java.util.*;
import java.io.*;

public class PropertyClient
{
  public void doStuff()
  {
    System.out.println("Before try, catch block");     //3
    try
    {
      PropertyReader propertyReader = new PropertyReader();   // 4
      Properties props = propertyReader.readProperties("silly");// 5
      System.out.println("props = " +props);                   // 6

      props = propertyReader.readProperties("sillllllly");     // 7
      System.out.println("props = " +props);
    }
    catch (FileNotFoundException e)
    {
      System.out.println("FileNotFoundException e: " +e);     // 8
    }
    catch (IOException e)
    {
      System.out.println("IOException e: " +e);
    }
    finally
    {
      System.out.println("In finally");   // 9
    }
    System.out.println("After try, catch block"); // 10
  }
```

```
    public static void main(String[] args)
  {
    PropertyClient pc = new PropertyClient();    // 1
    pc.doStuff();                                 // 2
  }
}
```

PropertyReader.java

```
package com.wiley.compBooks.EJwithUML.Samples.ApplicationExceptions;

import java.util.*;
import java.io.*;

public class PropertyReader
{
  private static final String BASE_PATH = "C:/EJwithUML2e/Samples/com/
  wiley/compBooks/EJwithUML/Samples/ApplicationExceptions/";

  public Properties readProperties(String name) throws IOException
  {
    FileInputStream fis = new FileInputStream(BASE_PATH +name+ ".properties");
    Properties props = new Properties();
    props.load(fis);
    return props;
  }
}
```

Output

```
Before try, catch block
props = {name=fred flintstone, job=quarry worker}
FileNotFoundException e: java.io.FileNotFoundException:
C:/EJwithUML2e/Samples/com/wiley/compBooks/EJwithUML/Samples/
ApplicationExceptions/sillllllly.properties
(The system cannot find the file specified)
In finally
After try, catch block
```

This direct support for exception and error handling that is built into the Java Virtual Machine by the core classes provides a solid foundation for application-level error handling. The next section shows how a very simple design can allow different parts of an application to cooperate in their response to unexpected system events.

Goals for Application Exceptions

Most modern systems comprise distinct logical layers that may also be physically distinct. While an exception is thrown in one logical layer, it may affect other layers. This means that our framework must convert low-level exceptions into application-level exceptions that can carry useful information to other layers. For example, a user interface may obtain data from two databases to fulfill a user's request by making a high-level request to a dispatcher object, as shown in Figure 7.10. The dispatcher makes separate inquires to the billing database and the purchasing database. What information does the user interface need if one of the data access objects throws an exception? First, the user interface needs to know if the problem is transitory or if it needs to block user access during a long-term outage. Next, in order to provide a useful trail in the production support logs, the user interface must log the origin of the exception in clear terms.

It is also important to remember that most software is written and maintained by teams of developers over a period of years. With this in mind, our framework should be easy to learn and should make consistency simple.

Capturing the Origin

The simplest way to capture the origin of an application exception is to use a string, as in the following:

```
throw new ApplicationException("BillingDataAccess", "Database Is unavailable", sqe);
```

However, there is no support for consistency in this solution. Even well-intentioned developers would gradually accumulate a list of synonyms, such as "BillingDB" and "BillingDataaccess." Developers do not want to waste valuable time hunting for the right origin. Also, as synonyms accumulate, log analysis for production support and trend detection becomes increasingly difficult and less valuable. Imagine searching log files for every application exception that originated in the BillingDataAccess layer. The regular expression would be rather unwieldy and missing a synonym would be quite likely.

Instead of forcing developers to use a free-form string, our ApplicationException should limit developers to a finite set of origins. The best way to implement this in Java is an enumerated type (Bloch, 2001), which is a class that forces clients to use one of a pre-defined set of instances by limiting access to the constructor. In the Origin class below, the constructor is private and the class is final, so the only way to get an Origin object is through one of the publicly available static attributes. It is also important that the Origin objects be immutable once they are constructed, so that the name cannot change over time. In some cases, a system may need to compare an Origin object that was created on a remote VM with a local Origin object. The value attribute makes this easy.

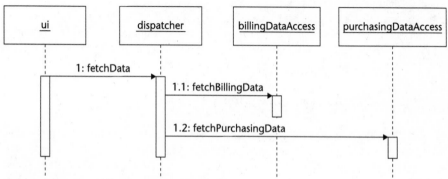

Figure 7.10 User interface and data access.

So the Origin class meets our design goal for ease of use, as the developer simply picks an Origin from a list. This is especially easy when using a modern IDE that actually displays attributes and methods in a pick list. It is also reasonably easy for a developer to add a new Origin by adding a new line to the Origin class. Consistency is enforced by the compiler, which will not allow a developer to create an Origin object outside of the Origin class.

Origin.java

```java
package com.wiley.compBooks.EJwithUML.Base.ApplicationExceptions;

import java.io.*;

public final class Origin implements Serializable
{
  public static final Origin BILLING_DATA_ACCESS = new Origin
  (0, "BillingDataAccess", "Data access layer for the billing system");
  public static final Origin PURCHASING_DATA_ACCESS = new Origin
  (1, "PurchasingDataAccess", "Data access layer for the purchasing system");
  public static final Origin USER_INTERFACE = new Origin(2, "UserInterface",
  "User Interface");

  private int value;
  private String name;
  private String description;

  private Origin(int value, String name, String description)
  {
    this.value = value;
    this.name = name;
    this.description = description;
  }

  public String getName()
  {
    return this.name;
  }

  public String getDescription()
  {
    return this.description;
  }

  public boolean equals(Object obj)
  {
    if (obj == null || !(obj instanceof Origin) )
    {
      return false;
    }
```

```
        Origin origin = (Origin) obj;
        return (this.value == origin.value);
    }
}
```

Capturing the Severity

When a layer receives an ApplicationException, it must determine the correct response based on the severity of the abnormality. The layer may need to shut down gracefully, wait for human intervention, or simply continue with normal processing. There are two obvious solutions. First, each ApplicationException object could have a status attribute that indicates if the exception is recoverable or not. When a layer catches the ApplicationException, it would check the status and determine the right course of action. However, if we use inheritance to describe recoverable and nonrecoverable exceptions, the catch blocks can support this exact need. If the receiving layer provides a separate catch block for each subclass of ApplicationException, then the VM will resume execution in the appropriate block. Figure 7.11 shows ApplicationException and its three subclasses, which do not add any data or behavior. Only the severity of an ApplicationException object is determined by its class. Each ApplicationException object has an association with an Origin object, so the receiver can determine which layer or subsystem threw the exception.

Chained Exceptions

Let us return to the earlier example of user interface logic and data access logic to see how the combination of the ApplicationException and Origin classes facilitates cooperation between different parts of the system. Message 1.2.1 in Figure 7.12 shows the data access subsystem for the purchasing database using a JDBC statement object to access the database. Unfortunately, rather than receiving data, a SQLException is caught from the execute call. After cleaning up and logging the event, the data access code throws a new RecoverableApplicationException that contains the SQLException. When the dispatcher catches this exception, it does not necessarily need to know why the exception was thrown. It trusts the data access subsystem's characterization of the exception as recoverable. The dispatcher takes any action that it deems necessary, logs the event, and then rethrows the RecoverableApplicationException. Finally, the user interface catches the exception, logs it, displays an error message to the user, and continues on with its work. It too trusts the data access layers characterization of the event as recoverable.

This technique is relatively simple to use, as the various subclasses of ApplicationException are easy to create and encapsulate all of the information that receiving code needs. Also, since this framework leverages Java's built-in support for exception handling, the code is compact and easy to read.

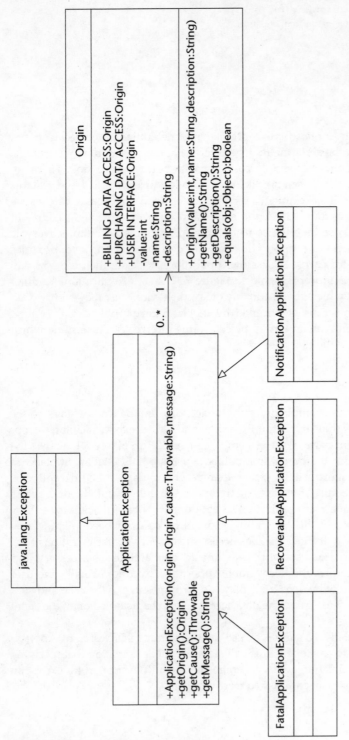

Figure 7.11 Application exceptions.

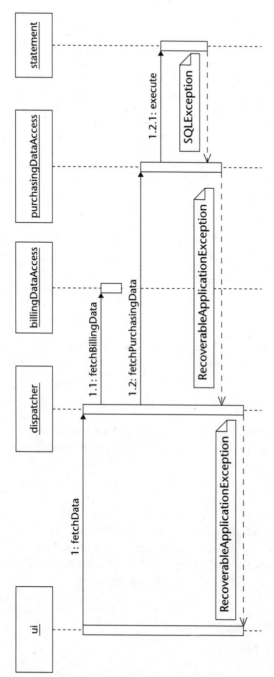

Figure 7.12 User interface and data access with exceptions.

Strengths

Application exceptions make it easier for developers to implement clear and consistent error handling in complex systems. By dividing unexpected events into discrete categories, the application exception class hierarchy makes it easier for the system to react appropriately to errors as they occur. Capturing the origin of the event as a member of an enumerated type makes it easier to troubleshoot production support issues and to detect trends over time.

Weaknesses

Application exceptions have no real weaknesses.

Compatible Technologies

Any type of Java application, including servlets, Swing, command-line applications, and Enterprise JavaBeans, can use application exceptions.

Cost of Adoption

There is virtually no development cost involved. To get full value from the classes, your project must fill the roles of designer and developer.

Designer

A designer must define the set of valid origins and may need to modify the class hierarchy to capture the severity needs of a specific system. Clear guidelines describing when to use each subclass of ApplicationException are key to consistent use.

Developer

Each developer is responsible for understanding the guidelines, following them, and participating in the code review process. Application exceptions should actually make the developer's life easier, while improving coordination between different parts of the system.

Data Protection with the Java Cryptography Extension (JCE)

JCE 1.2.1 is available as part of JDK 1.4 or separately for use with JDK 1.2 and 1.3. The SunJCE provider is also included and is automatically registered in the `java.security` security properties file.

Unless you keep your computer in a locked vault and cut all of your network cables, your data is accessible to an unknown number of people. Some people, such as the teenage hacker portrayed in the movies, may be blatantly destructive. Others, such as the guy in the cube upstairs who backs up your departmental servers, may be completely harmless. However, in both cases, they are not you, and they can see your data. Depending on the data, this may be an unacceptable risk. The systems that we develop may protect financial records, private customer data, medical records, or complex business deals. A security breach may result in corporate liability, financial losses, and real damage to real people.

People and companies also use computers to communicate with one another, so they can exchange information, buy and sell goods and services, and build profitable relationships. This communication is only valuable if the parties trust one another. In many industries, trust takes time and consistency to build. However, it only takes one incident to destroy that trust. So, organizations need to be able to communicate without fear that someone will impersonate them or impersonate their peers. They must be able to authenticate the source of a communication, be sure that the message was not tampered with, and prevent eavesdropping.

Fortunately, protecting data and verifying the authenticity of data in software applications has never been easier or cheaper. As we will see in the following sections, Sun's Java Cryptography Extension (JCE) class library provides a set of classes and interfaces that can be used to solve these core problems. The following section defines some cryptography terms before exploring the class library in more detail.

Terminology

Several terms are essential to understanding the JCE. These are:

Plaintext.   Plaintext is text that is readable by a general population, such as everyone who reads English or everyone who reads French. It may also be data in a commonly recognized format, such as an image stored as a .gif file. In the context of security and encryption, plaintext is something that we want to keep secret but that is currently exposed to anyone with access to a system. Plaintext is also called cleartext.

Encryption.   Encryption is a systematic conversion of plaintext into a sequence of bytes that appears to be random gibberish. Depending on the methods used, it may be difficult to nearly impossible for an untrusted party to deduce the plaintext. Depending on the purpose of the encryption, this random looking sequence of bytes may be reversible, so that trusted parties can recover the plaintext. Alternatively, the encrypted bytes may not be reversible, but they may enable a user to determine if a message has been tampered with during transmission. This is analogous to the tamper-proof plastic seals that are found on most over-the-counter medicines. They do not prevent tampering, as that would make the products hard to use. Instead, they make it hard to tamper with them without the buyer noticing.

Decryption.   Decryption is the conversion of encrypted bytes back into the original content. In decryption, the same algorithm that was used to encrypt the data is used to reverse the process and reveal the original bytes.

Cipher algorithm.   A cipher algorithm is a well-defined sequence of calculations and steps that are used for encryption and, where applicable, for decryption. In choosing an algorithm, you should consider its "strength," which is the security community's best guess as to the difficulty involved in cracking the algorithm. Depending on your application, you may also need to consider development complexity, cost of licenses, and, of course, the memory and CPU requirements.

Cipher block mode.   A cipher block mode can be used to modify the encryption from block to block. This helps hide patterns in the data and generally increases the effort required to deduce the plaintext without the key. Certain modes may also prevent an attacker from substituting blocks of encrypted data from previously intercepted messages. Over time, various cipher modes have been developed with different goals for speed, hiding patterns in the data, preventing substitution attacks, and reducing the impact of data corruption.

Key.   A key is a block of bytes or a sufficient set of parameters that determines the exact output of an algorithm for a given block of data.

Symmetric cipher algorithms.   With a symmetric algorithm, a single key can be used to encrypt plaintext and decrypt the resulting encrypted bytes back into the plaintext. A key for symmetric algorithms is often referred to as a secret key or a shared secret key, because two parties who share the key can enjoy secure communications as long as the key is kept secret.

Asymmetric algorithms.   With asymmetric algorithms, keys are generated in pairs, so that either key can encrypt plaintext, and then the other key is needed to decrypt the encrypted data back into plaintext. As we will see in more detail later in this chapter, the creative use of asymmetric algorithms makes secure communication between loosely related or unrelated organizations easy.

Provider.   As with JDBC drivers for databases, third-party data security providers can write their own cryptography implementations that fit seamlessly into the framework. Sun also provides default implementation classes for your convenience in the SunJCE provider package. Additional providers can be found at http://java.sun.com/products/jce/jce12_providers.html.

Gory Details: Protecting Data with Symmetric Ciphers

With symmetric key ciphers, a single key is used to encrypt and decrypt data. This allows an individual to protect data for future use or to exchange confidential data with another party who shares a key. Since the encrypted data's safety depends on the secrecy of the key, this type of encryption is often known as secret key or shared secret encryption.

Understanding the JCE classes for symmetric key encryption requires a little implementation-independent background information on encryption. The following sections cover some common algorithms and some common considerations when configuring a cipher before demonstrating JCE's support for symmetric key ciphers.

Symmetric Cipher Algorithms

A comprehensive description of encryption algorithms is well outside the scope of this book and well beyond this humble author's capability. With that caveat, the following descriptions provide some background for several common algorithms that are supported by the JCE.

Data Encryption Standard algorithm (DES).   DES was developed by IBM to fulfill a request by the National Bureau of Standards for a public standard encryption algorithm. It became a standard in the mid-seventies and has been very widely used since then. DES is still considered a valid defense unless the eavesdropper is willing to dedicate significant computing resources to a brute force attack. DES is probably completely vulnerable to the National Security Agency (NSA), as this organization contributed to its design, has high-speed computers, and employs quite a few very educated mathematicians.

Triple DES.   By using three keys to encrypt and reencrypt the plaintext, this variant of DES significantly impedes a brute force attack. It also increases the time needed to protect the data.

PBEWithMD5AndDES.   This variant of DES generally produces better keys for use with DES.

Blowfish.   This algorithm was put into the public domain by Bruce Schneier and has been exposed to extensive review within the cryptography community. It is generally faster than DES and allows the user to trade speed for security by adjusting the key length. It is intended for use in applications that use the same key for relatively large amounts of data.

Cipher Modes

By selecting a particular cipher mode, a user can decrease the chances of a successful attack against encrypted data. As with algorithms, a comprehensive discussion of cipher modes is out of this book's scope. With that caveat, the following descriptions provide some background for several common modes that are supported by the JCE. Each description will comment on the mode's ease of use, performance impact, ability to obfuscate patterns in the data, resistance to substitution attacks, and robustness in the face of data corruption. The SunJCE security provider includes implementations for the following modes:

Electronic Codebook (ECB) mode.   In ECB mode, the cipher treats each block exactly the same as any other block. This makes the mode fast and easy to use, while limiting the damage caused by data corruption in the encrypted data. However, it is perfectly consistent in its output for a given key and a given chunk of plaintext data. Encryption of text data with ECB mode is not recommended, because the patterns will also show up in the encrypted data. This may assist the eavesdropper greatly. ECB is also vulnerable to substitution attacks. ECB mode is suitable for encrypting keys and other binary data that do not have a pattern.

Cipher Block Chaining (CBC) mode.   In CBC mode, the encryption of a given block is determined by the key, the plaintext, and the previous block. This helps obfuscate any patterns without increasing processing time for each block. This mode does require the user to prime the cipher with a block of data known as an initialization vector. One corrupted bit in the encrypted data will affect the entire corresponding plaintext block and also one bit in the next block. CBC mode is less vulnerable to substitution attacks. If an extra bit is inserted in the encrypted data, then the rest of the plaintext will be unrecoverable.

Cipher Feedback (CFB) mode.   As with CBC, patterns in the plaintext are obfuscated without increasing processing time for each block. Ease-of-use is also similar, because CFB mode requires an initialization vector. CFB mode's vulnerability to substitution attacks is similar to CBC mode's. As for robustness, one corrupted bit in the encrypted data will affect the corresponding bit in the plaintext as well as the entire next block of plaintext. However, in the unlikely case that a bit is inserted in the encrypted text, only one block of plaintext will be affected.

Output Feedback (OFB) mode.   As with CBC mode and CFB mode, patterns in the plaintext are obfuscated without increasing processing time for each block. Ease-of-use is also similar, because OFB mode requires an initialization vector. OFB mode is more vulnerable to substitution attacks. Each corrupted bit in encrypted data affects only the corresponding bit in the plaintext. As with CBC, an inserted bit in the encrypted data makes the rest of the plaintext unrecoverable.

Padding

Ciphers in Java encrypt data one block at a time. If the plaintext data does not end on a block boundary, then the remaining space must be padded with additional bytes. The SunJCE security provider includes an implementation for PKCS5Padding, which fills the data out to a multiple of 8 bytes, and an implementation of NoPadding, which forces the user to provide data to the cipher in exact multiples of the block size.

TIP When configuring a cipher for decryption, the algorithm, mode, initialization vector, and padding must match exactly with the configuration that was used to encrypt the data.

Symmetric Keys

The Key interface is relatively simple, with methods that reveal the algorithm and format that the key supports and one method, getEncoded(), that returns the data bytes for the key. Keys are passive objects; they simply hold data rather than perform actions such as encrypting or decrypting data. The SecretKey interface does not have any

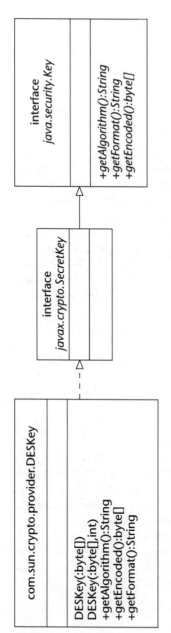

Figure 7.13   Symmetric keys.

methods and exists solely to differentiate symmetric keys from asymmetric keys. DESKey is a concrete implementation of the SecretKey interface. As seen in Figure 7.13, the constructors for DESKey are only visible to classes within the sun.crypto.provider package. As seen in the next section, this means that your application cannot directly construct concrete key implementation classes.

Symmetric Key Generation

In the JCE, Key objects are created by a KeyGenerator that is specific to a particular algorithm. As seen in Figure 7.14, the constructor for KeyGenerator is protected, while the constructor for specific key implementations is only accessible to classes within the provider package. This prevents users from directly constructing KeyGenerators or keys.

This protects users from the complexity of generating keys and forces them to use a set of convenient factory methods. If you know the name of an algorithm that is supported by your provider, then you can get a key in two easy steps. First, pass the name of the algorithm to KeyGenerator's static getInstance factory method. This returns a KeyGenerator object that has a reference to a concrete implementation of the KeyGeneratorSpi class. Next, use the generateKey method on the KeyGenerator object to obtain a concrete implementation of SecretKey. The code for key generation is remarkably simple:

```
KeyGenerator keygen = KeyGenerator.getInstance("DES");
SecretKey desKey = keygen.generateKey();
```

Using Symmetric Ciphers

As with KeyGenerator, the Cipher class provides a static factory method that returns an instance of the Cipher class configured for the specified cipher algorithm and mode. Once a concrete cipher is obtained, it must be initialized for encryption or for decryption by calling the init method with one of the public integer constants, such as ENCRYPT_MODE or DECRYPT_MODE. It must also be initialized with an instance of Key. After initialization, bytes are fed into the cipher through its update method, which returns the encrypted or decrypted bytes. The last group of bytes is fed into the cipher through the doFinal method, which completes the encryption or decryption. See Figure 7.15.

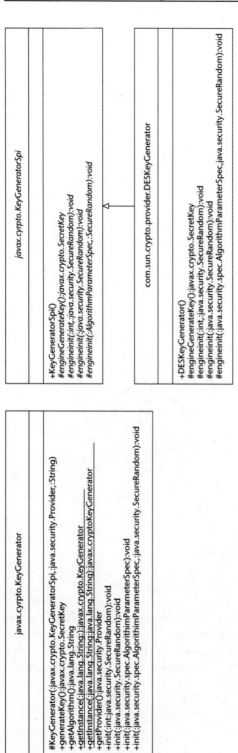

Figure 7.14 Generating symmetric keys.

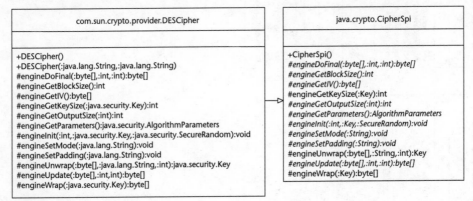

Figure 7.15 Symmetric ciphers.

Sample

The following code sample demonstrates how a DES symmetric key can be used to encrypt and decrypt a simple text string. Notice that the JCE provider is explicitly registered with the Security class before the key is generated and the cipher is obtained. Since there are only a few bytes, there is no need to use both update and doFinal methods when converting bytes through the cipher.

```
package com.wiley.compBooks.EJwithUML.Samples.Security;

import javax.crypto.*;
import java.security.*;
import com.sun.crypto.provider.*;
```

```java
public class EncryptAndDecrypt
{
  public static void main(String[] args)
  {
    try
    {
      // Initialize the provider.
      SunJCE jce = new SunJCE();
      Security.addProvider(jce);

      // Build the key.
      KeyGenerator keygen = KeyGenerator.getInstance("DES");
      SecretKey desKey = keygen.generateKey();

      // Build and initialize the cipher.
      Cipher desCipher = Cipher.getInstance("DES/ECB/PKCS5Padding");
      desCipher.init(Cipher.ENCRYPT_MODE, desKey);

      // Encrypt the cleartext.
      byte[] cleartext = "This is just an example".getBytes();
      byte[] ciphertext = desCipher.doFinal(cleartext);

      // Decrypt the ciphertext.
      desCipher.init(Cipher.DECRYPT_MODE, desKey);
      byte[] recoveredtext = desCipher.doFinal(ciphertext);
    }
    catch (GeneralSecurityException e)
    {
      System.out.println("e: " + e);
    }
  }
}
```

Data Exchange with Asymmetric Ciphers and Key Exchange

With asymmetric ciphers, a pair of keys is generated; each key can decrypt data that was encrypted by the other. Neither key can decrypt data that was encrypted by it. Due to this property, this method of encryption is called asymmetric key encryption. With pairs of asymmetric keys, a group of people can each publish one of their keys, known as the public key. They each guard the other key, known as the private key, quite carefully. A public key can be used by anyone else to send messages that only the owner of the corresponding private key can decrypt. An individual can use their private key to "sign" a message so that anyone with their public key can decrypt it and verify its authenticity.

Without any hyperbole, this technology completely revolutionized cryptology and is the foundation for large-scale electronic commerce, because it allows loosely connected individuals and organizations to communicate without fear of data tampering, eavesdropping, or impersonation. However, there is one drawback. Asymmetric key encryption is very slow compared to symmetric key encryption. So, it is generally used to exchange a symmetric key that is used for a particular communication and then discarded.

To solidify these concepts, let us consider a small circle of friends, Fred, Wilma, Barney, and Betty, who would like to send messages that cannot be read by anyone but the intended recipient. They also want to be able to verify the origin of each message. Each participant generates a pair of keys. They each pick one key as their public key and deliver that key to each of their friends over some arbitrary and unsecured channel, such as email. They each protect the other private key on their own personal and highly secure computer.

Now, when Betty wants to exchange information with Wilma, she follows a series of steps:

1. Betty generates a symmetric key and encrypts it with Wilma's public key. This ensures that only Wilma can read the key.

2. Betty also encrypts the already encrypted key with her own private key. This encryption with Betty's private key is the electronic equivalent of a verifiable signature.

3. When Wilma receives the message, she decrypts it with Betty's public key, thus verifying that Betty sent the message.

4. Wilma then uses her own private key to decrypt the message and recover the original plaintext, which happens to be a symmetric key. Once both parties have the symmetric key, they can communicate securely.

This approach allows secure and verifiable communications between any two people, without affecting the security of their other communications. Accomplishing a similar feat using symmetric ciphers would require a separate secret key for each pair of participants. In a circle of four friends, asymmetric keys are a nice convenience. However, when you consider the widespread secure communications that are required for e-commerce and data sharing over the Internet, it is clear that asymmetric ciphers are an essential enabling technology for the Internet.

Asymmetric Cipher Algorithms

A comprehensive description of encryption algorithms is well outside the scope of this book and well beyond this humble authors capability. The JCE provider includes the RSA and Diffie-Hellman algorithms. Other algorithms may be obtained from other providers.

Rivest, Shamir, and Adleman (RSA) Cipher Algorithm.   RSA is an acronym for its three inventors, Ron Rivest, Adi Shamir, and Leonard Adleman. After over 20 years of scrutiny by the cryptography community, it is widely considered to be quite secure and is the most widely used asymmetric key encryption algorithm. However, it is two to three orders of magnitude slower than DES, so large blocks of data should be encrypted with a symmetric key. This key can be encrypted with the intended recipient's public key and included in the message.

Diffie-Hellman Key Exchange Algorithm.   This algorithm allows parties to communicate securely based on a shared set of parameters and a shared set of public keys. Unlike RSA, the Diffie-Hellman algorithm does not require the parties to actually send a secret key. Instead, each party sends their public key, and one party determines and shares a set of parameters. Both parties use their own private key, the shared parameters, and their counterpart's public key to derive a shared secret key.

Core Classes

There are two new interfaces to support asymmetric keys, PublicKey and PrivateKey. Both extend the Key interface. As seen in Figure 7.16, these interfaces do not specify any methods. They simply differentiate public keys from private keys. For the Diffie-Hellman algorithm, the DHPublicKey and DHPrivateKey classes implement PublicKey and PrivateKey, respectively. While the constructor for DHPublicKey is public, there is no good reason for an application's developer to ever use it directly. As with symmetric keys, asymmetric keys are passive containers. They provide methods that describe their algorithm and parameters and allow a user to retrieve the raw data bytes for the key.

Key generation for asymmetric keys is similar to key generation for symmetric keys. The KeyPairGenerator class provides a factory method that creates algorithm-specific KeyPairGenerator objects based on the name of an algorithm. Once the concrete KeyPairGenerator object is obtained, it can be initialized and used to create KeyPair objects. Each KeyPair object is a simple collection of two keys, one public and one private. While the constructor for the DHKeyPairGenerator is public, there is no good reason for an application's developer to use it directly. Figure 7.17 shows the classes for key pair generation using the Diffie-Hellman algorithm.

The JCE also provides a very convenient class for exchanging shared secret keys among several individuals who know one another's public keys and wish to communicate securely as a group. They must also agree on a set of parameters, but there is no need to protect these parameters from eavesdroppers.

The KeyAgreement class, as seen in Figure 7.18, includes a factory method that constructs an algorithm-specific KeyAgreement object based on the specified algorithm name. As with the KeyPairGenerator, developers should ignore the public constructors for KeyAgreementSpi and DHKeyAgreement and instead use this getInstance factory method. Before use, this KeyAgreement object is initialized with the user's private key and any required parameters. The user can then use the doPhase method repeatedly to add public keys for the other people in the group. After all of the public keys have been incorporated, the user uses the generateSecret method to generate a shared secret key. Each member of the group repeats this process, initializing the KeyAgreement with their own private key and the parameters. They add the other participants' public key with the doPhase method. The key that they obtain through the generateSecret method will be identical to the secret key obtained by the other members of the group! They can communicate securely within their circle of friends as long as they protect their shared secret key.

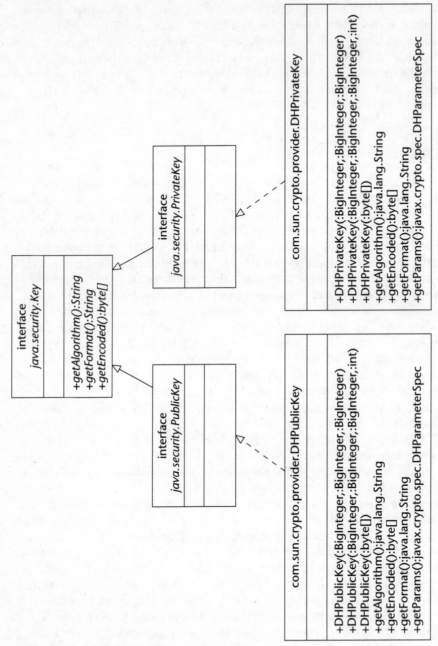

Figure 7.16   Asymmetric keys.

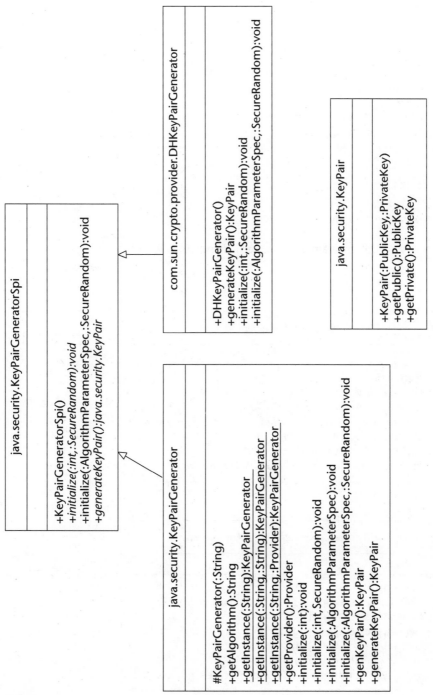

Figure 7.17   Asymmetric key generation.

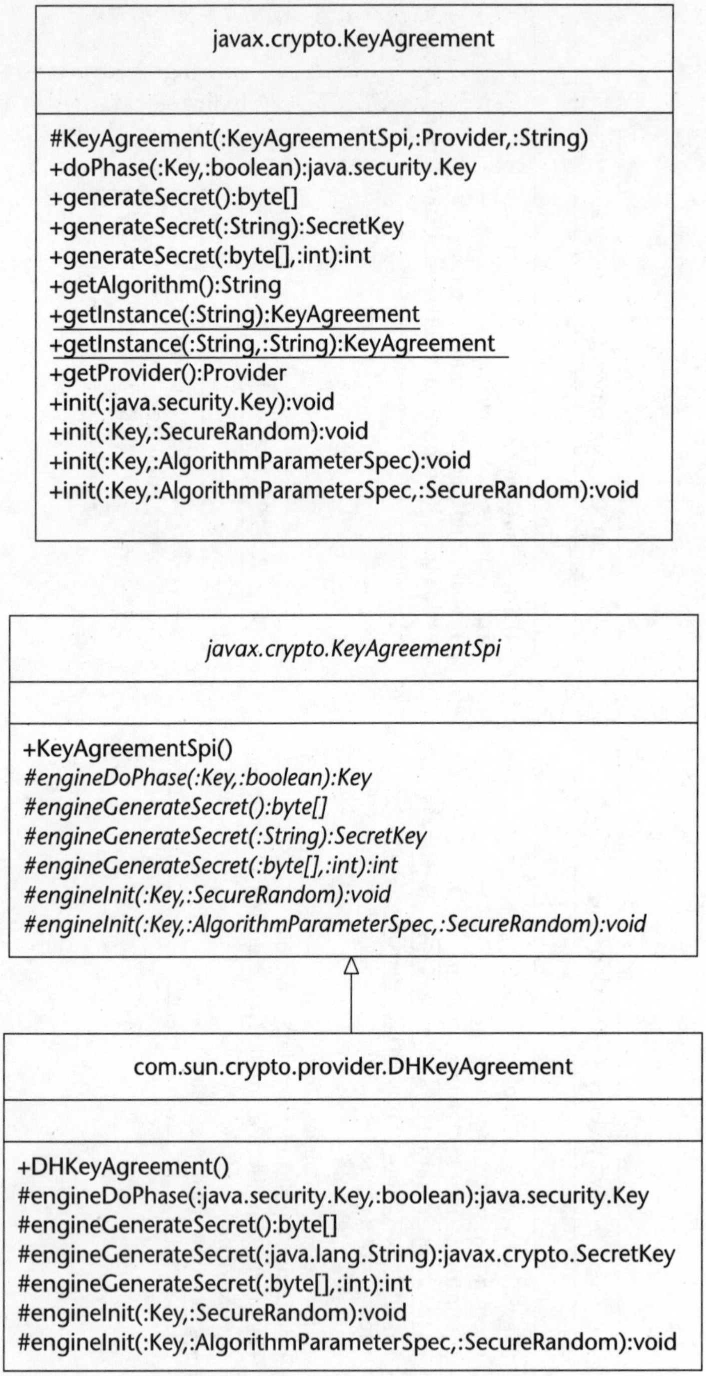

```
┌──────────────────────────────────────────────────────────────┐
│                  javax.crypto.KeyAgreement                     │
├──────────────────────────────────────────────────────────────┤
│                                                                │
├──────────────────────────────────────────────────────────────┤
│ #KeyAgreement(:KeyAgreementSpi,:Provider,:String)              │
│ +doPhase(:Key,:boolean):java.security.Key                      │
│ +generateSecret():byte[]                                       │
│ +generateSecret(:String):SecretKey                             │
│ +generateSecret(:byte[],:int):int                              │
│ +getAlgorithm():String                                         │
│ +getInstance(:String):KeyAgreement                             │
│ +getInstance(:String,:String):KeyAgreement                     │
│ +getProvider():Provider                                        │
│ +init(:java.security.Key):void                                 │
│ +init(:Key,:SecureRandom):void                                 │
│ +init(:Key,:AlgorithmParameterSpec):void                       │
│ +init(:Key,:AlgorithmParameterSpec,:SecureRandom):void         │
└──────────────────────────────────────────────────────────────┘
```

```
┌──────────────────────────────────────────────────────────────┐
│                 javax.crypto.KeyAgreementSpi                   │
├──────────────────────────────────────────────────────────────┤
│                                                                │
├──────────────────────────────────────────────────────────────┤
│ +KeyAgreementSpi()                                             │
│ #engineDoPhase(:Key,:boolean):Key                              │
│ #engineGenerateSecret():byte[]                                 │
│ #engineGenerateSecret(:String):SecretKey                       │
│ #engineGenerateSecret(:byte[],:int):int                        │
│ #engineInit(:Key,:SecureRandom):void                           │
│ #engineInit(:Key,:AlgorithmParameterSpec,:SecureRandom):void   │
└──────────────────────────────────────────────────────────────┘
                              △
                              │
┌──────────────────────────────────────────────────────────────┐
│             com.sun.crypto.provider.DHKeyAgreement             │
├──────────────────────────────────────────────────────────────┤
│                                                                │
├──────────────────────────────────────────────────────────────┤
│ +DHKeyAgreement()                                              │
│ #engineDoPhase(:java.security.Key,:boolean):java.security.Key  │
│ #engineGenerateSecret():byte[]                                 │
│ #engineGenerateSecret(:java.lang.String):javax.crypto.SecretKey│
│ #engineGenerateSecret(:byte[],:int):int                        │
│ #engineInit(:Key,:SecureRandom):void                           │
│ #engineInit(:Key,:AlgorithmParameterSpec,:SecureRandom):void   │
└──────────────────────────────────────────────────────────────┘
```

Figure 7.18   KeyAgreement.

Diffie-Hellman Key Exchange in Action

The following code sample demonstrates Diffie-Hellman key exchange between two parties who wish to communicate using a symmetric DES key. In this sample, a single AlgorithmParameters object is created and used by both Betty and Wilma. In real life, one party would generate the parameters and then share them with the other over any unsecured channel, such as email. The public keys can be exchanged with a similar disregard for the security of the delivery channel. Once the parameters and public keys have been exchanged, each person can construct a KeyAgreement object and generate the shared secret DES key.

DHEncryptAndDecrypt.java

```java
package com.wiley.compBooks.EJwithUML.Samples.Security;

import javax.crypto.*;
import javax.crypto.spec.*;
import java.security.*;
import com.sun.crypto.provider.*;

/**
 * The DHEncryptAndDecrypt class is a simple example of secure data exchange
 * using the Diffie-Hellman asymetric encryption algorithm to exchange a shared
 * secret key.
 *
 */
public class DHEncryptAndDecrypt
{
  public static void main(String[] args)
  {
    try
    {
      // Initialize the provider.
      SunJCE jce = new SunJCE();
      Security.addProvider(jce);

      // Betty and Wilma generate and share DH parameters.
      AlgorithmParameterGenerator paramGen =
      AlgorithmParameterGenerator.getInstance("DH");
          paramGen.init(512);
          AlgorithmParameters params = paramGen.generateParameters();
      DHParameterSpec sharedDhParams = (DHParameterSpec)
      params.getParameterSpec(DHParameterSpec.class);


      // Betty and Wilma build key pairs and exchange public keys.
      KeyPairGenerator pairGenerator = KeyPairGenerator.getInstance("DH");
      pairGenerator.initialize(sharedDhParams);
      KeyPair bettysPair = pairGenerator.generateKeyPair();
      KeyPair wilmasPair = pairGenerator.generateKeyPair();
```

```
        // Betty builds a KeyAgreement object and uses it to generate a secret key.
        KeyAgreement bettysKeyAgreement = KeyAgreement.getInstance("DH");
        bettysKeyAgreement.init(bettysPair.getPrivate());
        bettysKeyAgreement.doPhase(wilmasPair.getPublic(), true);
        SecretKey beetysSecretKey = bettysKeyAgreement.generateSecret("DES");


        // Wilma builds a KeyAgreement object and uses it to generate a secret key.
        KeyAgreement willmasKeyAgreement = KeyAgreement.getInstance("DH");
        willmasKeyAgreement.init(wilmasPair.getPrivate());
        willmasKeyAgreement.doPhase(bettysPair.getPublic(), true);
        SecretKey wilmasSecretKey = willmasKeyAgreement.generateSecret("DES");

        // Betty initializes the cipher and encrypts a message.
        String plaintext = "Hi Wilma, How are you and Fred?";
        Cipher desCipher = Cipher.getInstance("DES/ECB/PKCS5Padding");
        desCipher.init(Cipher.ENCRYPT_MODE, beetysSecretKey);
        byte[] encrypted_data = desCipher.doFinal(plaintext.getBytes());

        // Wilma decrypts the ciphertext.
        desCipher = Cipher.getInstance("DES/ECB/PKCS5Padding");  // parameters
        must match
        desCipher.init(Cipher.DECRYPT_MODE, wilmasSecretKey);
        byte[] recovered_data = desCipher.doFinal(encrypted_data);
        String recoveredtext = new String(recovered_data);

        System.out.println("plaintext = " +plaintext);
        System.out.println("encrypted_data = " +encrypted_data);
        System.out.println("recoveredtext = " +recoveredtext);
        System.out.println("Are they equal? " +plaintext.equals(recoveredtext));
      }
    catch (GeneralSecurityException e)
      {
        System.out.println("e: " + e);
      }
    }
  }
}
```

Key Management

So far, our examples for symmetric and asymmetric key encryption have been self-contained. Each example produces a key or keys, protects the plaintext, and then recovers it at the end. In real-world applications, the encryption and decryption are performed by separate parties or by the same party. So, for effective encryption, we need a way to store, protect, and recover keys. Fortunately, the JCE provides a class, KeyStore, that can be used to programmatically manage keys and a command-line utility, keytool, which provides a convenient text-based interface for managing key stores.

Core Classes

The KeyStore class, as seen in Figure 7.19, stores and retrieves keys along with their aliases. As usual, KeyStore objects are obtained through the getInstance factory method provided by the KeyStore class. Once a KeyStore object is obtained, it can be loaded from an InputStream, populated with keys, and saved to an OutputStream. A char array must be provided as a password when loading or storing the KeyStore. Keys are added by passing the key and a password to the setKeyEntry method.

> **NOTE** If you want to store symmetric keys, you must get a "JCEKS" KeyStore.

Keytool

The JCE also includes a command line utility that uses KeyStore objects and flat files to store, protect, and recover symmetric and asymmetric keys. Whenever a user interacts with a specific keystore, they must provide the location of the keystore file and the password that protects the keystore as a whole. When creating a key, the user must specify the alias by which the key will be known, the password that protects the specific key, and the encryption algorithm. If no password is specified on the command line, keytool will prompt the user. This key can then be accessed from within a Java application by constructing a KeyStore object and loading it from the designated file. When retrieving a key, the user must specify the alias of the key and provide passwords for the keystore and for the specified key.

> **NOTE** Including passwords in script files that manipulate keys is a potential security risk. Doing so forces users to protect the script file with the same care that they previously reserved for the keystore.

Keytool can also be used to create certificates, import certificates, and export certificates. More detail and some sample uses of keytool can be found in the following section on secure communication.

Strengths

The JCE is an easy to use, extensible, and low or no cost solution. Thanks to its consistent and relatively small API, developers can quickly learn everything they need to integrate encryption into their systems. Sun designed the library for extensibility and flexibility by allowing providers to build their own implementations. Perhaps best of all, the price is right!

Weaknesses

The JCE has no real weaknesses.

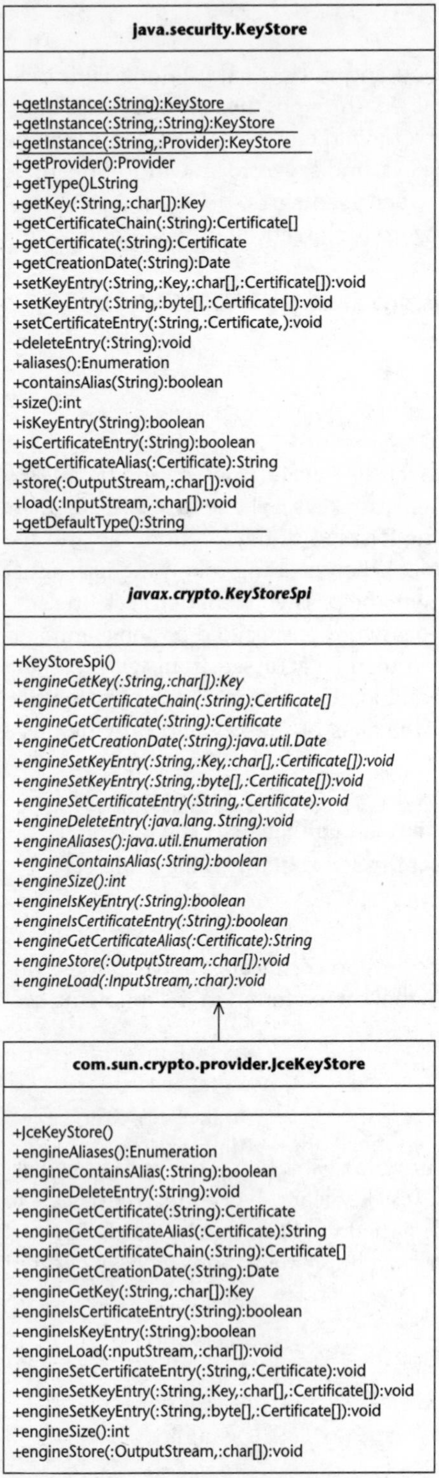

```
┌─────────────────────────────────────────────┐
│            java.security.KeyStore             │
├─────────────────────────────────────────────┤
│                                               │
├─────────────────────────────────────────────┤
│ +getInstance(:String):KeyStore                │
│ +getInstance(:String,:String):KeyStore        │
│ +getInstance(:String,:Provider):KeyStore      │
│ +getProvider():Provider                        │
│ +getType()LString                              │
│ +getKey(:String,:char[]):Key                   │
│ +getCertificateChain(:String):Certificate[]    │
│ +getCertificate(:String):Certificate           │
│ +getCreationDate(:String):Date                 │
│ +setKeyEntry(:String,:Key,:char[],:Certificate[]):void │
│ +setKeyEntry(:String,:byte[],:Certificate[]):void      │
│ +setCertificateEntry(:String,:Certificate,):void       │
│ +deleteEntry(:String):void                     │
│ +aliases():Enumeration                         │
│ +containsAlias(String):boolean                 │
│ +size():int                                    │
│ +isKeyEntry(String):boolean                    │
│ +isCertificateEntry(:String):boolean           │
│ +getCertificateAlias(:Certificate):String      │
│ +store(:OutputStream,:char[]):void             │
│ +load(:InputStream,:char[]):void               │
│ +getDefaultType():String                       │
└─────────────────────────────────────────────┘

┌─────────────────────────────────────────────┐
│            javax.crypto.KeyStoreSpi           │
├─────────────────────────────────────────────┤
│                                               │
├─────────────────────────────────────────────┤
│ +KeyStoreSpi()                                 │
│ +engineGetKey(:String,:char[]):Key             │
│ +engineGetCertificateChain(:String):Certificate[] │
│ +engineGetCertificate(:String):Certificate     │
│ +engineGetCreationDate(:String):java.util.Date │
│ +engineSetKeyEntry(:String,:Key,:char[],:Certificate[]):void │
│ +engineSetKeyEntry(:String,:byte[],:Certificate[]):void      │
│ +engineSetCertificateEntry(:String,:Certificate):void        │
│ +engineDeleteEntry(:java.lang.String):void     │
│ +engineAliases():java.util.Enumeration         │
│ +engineContainsAlias(:String):boolean          │
│ +engineSize():int                              │
│ +engineIsKeyEntry(:String):boolean             │
│ +engineIsCertificateEntry(:String):boolean     │
│ +engineGetCertificateAlias(:Certificate):String │
│ +engineStore(:OutputStream,:char[]):void       │
│ +engineLoad(:InputStream,:char):void           │
└─────────────────────────────────────────────┘
                       △
                       │
┌─────────────────────────────────────────────┐
│        com.sun.crypto.provider.JceKeyStore    │
├─────────────────────────────────────────────┤
│                                               │
├─────────────────────────────────────────────┤
│ +JceKeyStore()                                 │
│ +engineAliases():Enumeration                   │
│ +engineContainsAlias(:String):boolean          │
│ +engineDeleteEntry(:String):void               │
│ +engineGetCertificate(:String):Certificate     │
│ +engineGetCertificateAlias(:Certificate):String │
│ +engineGetCertificateChain(:String):Certificate[] │
│ +engineGetCreationDate(:String):Date           │
│ +engineGetKey(:String,:char[]):Key             │
│ +engineIsCertificateEntry(:String):boolean     │
│ +engineIsKeyEntry(:String):boolean             │
│ +engineLoad(:nputStream,:char[]):void          │
│ +engineSetCertificateEntry(:String,:Certificate):void │
│ +engineSetKeyEntry(:String,:Key,:char[],:Certificate[]):void │
│ +engineSetKeyEntry(:String,:byte[],:Certificate[]):void      │
│ +engineSize():int                              │
│ +engineStore(:OutputStream,:char[]):void       │
└─────────────────────────────────────────────┘
```

Figure 7.19 KeyStore.

Compatible Technologies

Any type of Java application, including servlets, Swing, command-line applications, and Enterprise JavaBeans, can use the JCE.

Cost of Adoption

The JCE and Sun's JCE provider are free from Sun. To get full value from the classes, your project must fill the roles of architect and developer.

Architect

The architect for a project must ensure that there is a coherent strategy for key management and that the JCE is used consistently throughout the system. He or she must select the provider, algorithm(s), and cipher modes that will be used. For most projects, this is a relatively small effort.

Developer

The developers must be familiar with the JCE classes and any project-specific guidelines. Despite the complexity of encryption, the API for JCE is very accessible, so this should not be a large burden.

Secure Communications with the Java Secure Socket Extension (JSSE)

So far, we have seen how developers can use the JCE to establish secure communications. However, in order to accomplish this feat, both parties to the communication must coordinate a large number of details. Obviously, the algorithm, cipher mode, and padding scheme must match. Moreover, the parties must somehow exchange keys, so they must either establish some secure meeting and exchange physical medium or use a key exchange protocol based on asymmetric keys. This requires a fairly large effort for development, testing, and coordination between parties. It also makes communication between new parties problematic. Creating a new and unique data exchange mechanism also introduces a lot of risk. Using the largest key size available may be completely ineffectual if one of the custom applications forgets to clean up a temp file of plaintext.

Fortunately, there is a well-proven standard solution for these problems. The Secure Sockets Layer is a widely accepted standard for secure socket-based communications between two parties. SSL defines a protocol for verification based on certificates, algorithm selection, key exchange, and the actual encryption and decryption of the data streams. The Java implementation of SSL is called the Java Secure Socket Extension (JSSE).

Using the JSSE is extremely simple. In fact, once the certificates for verification and key exchange are constructed, socket programming with SSL is almost identical to unsecured sockets.

Gory Details

There are two steps for establishing a secure connection with JSSE. First, the server must distribute its public key to the clients that need it, and the clients must determine which servers they trust. Next, the client must establish a socket connection with the server. Once the SSL protocol for verification and key exchange is completed, the client and server can use the connection in the same way they would use an unsecured connection. The following sections describe this process in more detail.

Establishing Trust

On the Internet, as in real life, we rarely have the luxury of a personal relationship with the organizations that provide services to us. In real life, consumers decide whom to trust with their homes, finances, and lives based on credentials such as diplomas, membership in a trade union, or the completion of residency at a major teaching hospital. If we are fortunate, we may be able to augment these impersonal criteria with a recommendation from a magazine or a friend. Once consumers determine the right provider, they establish communications by visiting a store, calling a toll-free number, or mailing their order to a designated address. They trust the contact information, perhaps because it was printed in a reputable newspaper, appeared in a thick phone book, or at least arrived in the mail in a nice glossy catalog.

The situation is surprisingly similar on the Internet. First, the process of selecting organizations is identical. Consumers still bear the burden of verifying the service provider's worth through conventional means. Once consumers select a service provider, they establish communications by visiting a Web URL, which they trust because it appeared in what they consider a reputable source. However, with the Internet, there is one extra step. Servers generally register themselves with a certificate authority, which, for a fee, will use their own private key to certify the server's credentials. When the browser receives credentials from a server, it verifies that a certificate authority signed them. It is left to the browser's manufacturer to determine which certificate authorities to use and to each certificate authority to validate the standing of the server's organization. If this process seems less than solid, consider the relatively low cost of procuring a print add in say the *Wall Street Journal* or the *Washington Post*. How carefully do these organizations check their advertisers?

Keystore

The server keeps its private key and a public key with its certificate in a keystore. When a client establishes a socket connection, the server retrieves its signed public key from the keystore and passes it to the client. If the client accepts the credentials, the server retrieves its private key from the keystore and uses it to share a secret key. For the JSSE, the keystore's location is contained in the javax.net.ssl.keyStore system property.

Truststore

In order to establish a secure connection, an SSL client validates the server's credentials against a list of trusted certificates. These certificates are kept in a dedicated keystore that is known as a truststore since it only holds the certificates of trusted certificate authorities and servers. Most clients trust a server if the server's certificate is in the truststore or if the server's certificate is signed by a certificate authority whose certificate is in the truststore. For the JSSE, the truststore's location is contained in the javax.net.ssl.trustStore system property.

NOTE A server may also maintain a truststore of clients with whom it is willing to establish secure connections.

SSLServerSocketFactory

The SSLServerSocketFactory extends the ServerSocketFactory class and provides the same behavior, just for secure sockets. SSLServerSocketFactory's static getDefault() factory method provides an instance of a concrete implementation of SSLServerSocketFactory. Once the factory is obtained, creating an server socket to listen for connection requests is easy. The createServerSocket() method of SSLServerSocketFactory creates a SSLServerSocket that can be used as easily as an unsecured ServerSocket. The accept method waits for a client socket to request a connection and then returns the SSLSocket for the actual connection. On the client, the SSLSocketFactory's static getDefault() method is used to obtain a SSLSocket. Once the SSLSocket is obtained, its use is identical to an unsecured socket.

The following example demonstrates these concepts in a simple client/server example.

A Simple Client/Server Sample

As previously described, the server needs a keystore, and the client needs a truststore. The following script cleans up any existing files, creates a pair of RSA keys, and stores them in a keystore file called .sslsample_keystore. This is the server's keystore for our sample. Next, the script exports the public key and associated certificate to a certificate file. This certificate is then imported into a keystore file named .sslsample_truststore. This is the client's truststore for our sample.

CreateKeysForSSL.bat

```
del .sslsample_keystore
del sslserver.cer
del .sslsample_truststore
keytool -keystore .sslsample_keystore -genkey -alias sslsample -keyalg RSA
keytool -keystore .sslsample_keystore -export -alias sslsample -file
sslserver.cer
keytool -keystore .sslsample_truststore -import -alias sslsample -file
sslserver.cer
```

Once the keys and credentials are created and stored appropriately, it is time to implement an SSL server. Each SecureEchoServerSocket object is constructed with a Socket object. The run method simply reads from the Socket's input stream and echoes back to the Socket's output stream. SecureEchoServerSocket implements Runnable so that our server can handle multiple concurrent requests. There is nothing SSL-specific about the SecureEchoServerSocket's instance methods or attributes. In fact, if the call to SSLServerSocketFactory's getDefault method in main is changed to a call to Server-SocketFactory's getDefault method, the sample will run perfectly well as an unsecured echo server.

Most of the interesting work happens in main. The keystore's location is set in a system property on the command line, as seen below in the runSecureEchoServer-Socket.bat script. However, revealing the password to the keystore in plaintext in a script is inadvisable. So, main reads the password from standard in and sets the javax.net.ssl.keyStorePassword system property. The rest of main is standard server socket fare. First, it creates a ServerSocket to listen on a specified port. Then it loops forever, blocking on the accept method inside of the loop. When a client establishes a connection, main creates a new SecureEchoServerSocket instance and uses it to create a new thread.

SecureEchoServerSocket.java

```
package com.wiley.compBooks.EJwithUML.Samples.Security;

import java.io.*;
import java.net.*;
import javax.net.*;
import javax.net.ssl.*;

/**
 * A SecureEchoServerSocket listens on a designated port for incoming client
 connections.
 * It handles each incoming connection on a separate thread. The
 javax.net.ssl.keyStore
 * property must be set to a keystore that contains a key pair for this server.
 */
public class SecureEchoServerSocket implements Runnable
{
  private Socket socket;
  private static boolean terminated;

  /** Construct a SecureEchoServerSocket to handle a connection on the
  specified socket. */
  public SecureEchoServerSocket(Socket socket)
  {
    this.socket = socket;
  }


  /** Processing logic for an individual connection*/
  public void run()
  {
    try
    {
      // Build a buffered reader around the socket's input stream.
      InputStream inputStream = this.socket.getInputStream();
      Reader reader = new InputStreamReader(inputStream);
```

```
      BufferedReader bufferedReader = new BufferedReader(reader);

      // Build a print writer around the socket's output stream.
      OutputStream outputStream = this.socket.getOutputStream();
      PrintWriter printWriter = new PrintWriter(outputStream);

      // Read a line at a time and write it back out.
      boolean done = false;
      System.out.println("Read from socket");
      while (!done)
      {
        String line = bufferedReader.readLine();
        System.out.println("line = " +line);
        printWriter.println(line);
        printWriter.flush();

        if ((line != null) && line.equals("Kill"))
        {
          System.exit(0);
        }
        done = ((line == null) || (line.equals("")) );
      }

      System.out.println("Connection complete");

      // flush and close
      bufferedReader.close();
      printWriter.flush();
      printWriter.close();
      this.socket.close();
    }
    catch (IOException e)
    {
      System.out.println("e: " +e);
      System.out.println("Usage SecureEchoServerSocket port");
    }
}

public static void main(String[] args)
{
  try
  {
    // read the keystore password from stdin
    System.out.println("Enter Password for keystore >");
    InputStreamReader stdinReader = new InputStreamReader(System.in);
    BufferedReader stdinBufferedReader = new BufferedReader(stdinReader);
    String keystorePassword = stdinBufferedReader.readLine();
    System.setProperty("javax.net.ssl.keyStorePassword", keystorePassword);

    // get a socket from the SSL socket factory
    ServerSocketFactory factory = SSLServerSocketFactory.getDefault();
    ServerSocket serverSocket = factory.createServerSocket
    (Integer.parseInt(args[0]));
```

```
            // loop forever and start a new thread for each connection
            System.out.println("Listening...");
            while (true)
            {
              Socket socket = serverSocket.accept();
              System.out.println("New connection.");

              SecureEchoServerSocket echoSocket = new SecureEchoServerSocket(socket);
              Thread runner = new Thread(echoSocket);
              runner.start();
            }
          }
          catch (IOException e)
          {
            System.out.println("e: " +e);
            System.out.println("Usage SecureEchoServerSocket port");
          }
        }
      }
```

runSecureEchoServerSocket.bat

```
java -Djavax.net.ssl.keyStore=.sslsample_keystore
com.wiley.compBooks.EJwithUML.Samples.Security.SecureEchoServerSocket 8787
```

SecureSocketClient objects are constructed based on the hostname and port of the desired server. Within the constructor, the SSLSocketFactory is used to get an instance of Socket. As with the server, this is the only SSL-specific line in the sample client. Once the client is constructed, its communicate method reads from standard in, writes to the socket's output stream, and reads the response from the socket's input stream. This continues until the user ends the session by entering either "Quit" or "Kill".

SecureSocketClient.java

```
package com.wiley.compBooks.EJwithUML.Samples.Security;

import java.io.*;
import java.net.*;
import javax.net.*;
import javax.net.ssl.*;

/**
 * A SecureSocketClient object reads from STDIN and writes to an SSL socket
connection,
 * one line at a time. The javax.net.ssl.trustStore property must be set to a
 * truststore that contains a trusted certificate for the designated server.
 *
 * When running, entering "Quit" exits the connection. Entering "Kill" will
cause the server to terminate.
 */
public class SecureSocketClient
{
```

```
  private Socket socket;

/** Construct a SecureSocketClient with the designated host and port
parameters for the server.*/
public SecureSocketClient(String host, int port) throws IOException
{
  // Get a socket from the SSL socket factory.
  SocketFactory factory = SSLSocketFactory.getDefault();
  this.socket = factory.createSocket(host, port);
}

/** Read lines from STDIN, write to the socket, read from socket */
public void communicate() throws IOException
{
  // Create a buffered reader around STDIN.
  InputStreamReader stdinReader = new InputStreamReader(System.in);
  BufferedReader stdinBufferedReader = new BufferedReader(stdinReader);

  // Create a buffered reader around the socket's input stream.
  InputStreamReader socketReader = new InputStreamReader
  (socket.getInputStream());
  BufferedReader socketBufferedReader = new BufferedReader(socketReader);

  // Create a print writer around the socket's output stream.
  PrintWriter socketPrintWriter = new PrintWriter
  (this.socket.getOutputStream());

  // Loop until the user quits.
  System.out.println("Enter Kill to kill the server");
  System.out.println("Enter Quit to end this connection");
  boolean done = false;
  while (!done)
  {
    // get user's input
    System.out.println("Enter text, Quit, or Kill >");
    String line = stdinBufferedReader.readLine();

    // send to server
    socketPrintWriter.println(line);
    socketPrintWriter.flush();

    // receive response
    String response = socketBufferedReader.readLine();
    System.out.println("response = " +response);

    done = (line == null || line.equals("Quit") || line.equals("Kill"));
  }

  // clean up, clean up, everybody do their share...
  socketBufferedReader.close();
  socketPrintWriter.close();
  socket.close();
}
```

```
      public static void main(String[] args)
      {
        try
        {
          String host = args[0];
          int port = Integer.parseInt(args[1]);
          SecureSocketClient client = new SecureSocketClient(host, port);
          client.communicate();
        }
        catch (Exception e)
        {
          System.out.println("e: " +e);
          System.out.println("Usage: SecureSocketClient host port");
        }
      }

    }
```

runSecureSocketClient.bat

```
java -Djavax.net.ssl.trustStore=.sslsample_truststore com.wiley.compBooks.    ⊃
EJwithUML.Samples.Security.SecureSocketClient localhost 8787
```

> **TIP** I recommend developing and unit testing your JSSE-based solution with unsecured sockets first. This will ferret out any errors in logic or configuration. Then, when you convert your solution to SSL sockets, any errors that arise will probably be due to the configuration of the keystore on the server and the truststore on the client.

Strengths

The JSSE is incredibly easy to use. Any developer who is familiar with unsecured sockets in Java can quickly adapt to use it. The only learning curve involves key management and determining which system properties must be set.

Weaknesses

The JSSE has no real weaknesses.

Compatible Technologies

Any type of Java application, including servlets, Swing, command-line applications, and Enterprise JavaBeans can use the JSSE.

Cost of Adoption

The JSSE and Sun's provider classes are free from Sun. To get full value from the classes, your project must fill the role of developer.

Developer

A JSSE developer must understand basic socket programming and pay careful attention to the relevant key management and certificate issues.

Java Management Extensions API—JMX 1.2

By definition, every successful system is eventually taken out of its comfortable development environment and exposed to unruly users who have endless expectations about availability, flexibility, and interoperability with other systems.

In order to accommodate the user's expectations for availability, developers and production support staff must be able to detect everything from catastrophic system failure to degradation of service, preferably before the customer realizes that anything is amiss. Many systems, such as credit authorization services, have a direct and dramatic impact on their owner's financial survival. In some cases, passive monitoring by tracking exceptions and response times is sufficient. In other cases, an external monitoring tool exercises the system and judges the result.

Flexibility is also important because real-world events may force the system to adapt in ways that were not anticipated during development. A critical database server may be moved after a system is deployed. Or perhaps the usage patterns that were used for performance tuning were incorrect and dozens of parameters for timeouts, thread counts, connection pool sizes, and cache schemes must be reworked. Our customers expect systems to adapt quickly and safely to a wide variety of changes, without needing to restart them.

Fortunately, Java Management Extensions (JMX) provide a framework for creating systems that are easy to monitor and configure.

> **NOTE** Of course, it helps if your users can agree on solid nonfunctional requirements that specify availability needs in measurable terms and indicate what system parameters are likely to change.

JMX Architecture

JMX has three layers, which are described as levels, as shown in Figure 7.20. The three layers are:

Instrumentation level. This layer defines how an application or its components are managed. It allows application developers to specify a set of attributes, and operations as well as a set of events for each managed resource, which can be any Java technology-based object.

Agent level. This layer controls the managed resources and exposes them to the management applications. An agent may group several components from the instrumentation layer together so they can be managed together.

Distributed services level. This layer allows management applications to communicate with agents to perform actual management tasks. The JMX 1.2 specification recognizes the need for this layer, but defers a true definition of this layer to a future release of the specification. In the interim, each vendor is free to fill this void as they wish.

The directions of each arrow from one layer to the next in Figure 7.20 show its dependency on the lower layer. Management applications in the distributed services layer are aware of the agents in the agent level. Similarly, agents in the agent level are dependent on the managed beans, also known as MBeans, in the instrumentation level.

JMX Terminology

Here is a brief introduction to JMX terminology:

MBean. An MBean, also known as Managed Bean, represents a unit of instrumentation implemented as a Java object.

JMX manageable resource. A JMX manageable resource is a Java application or a component represented as one or more MBeans. The MBean exposes all the necessary attributes and functions that are necessary to control the underlying resource that it represents.

JMX agent. A JMX agent is a management entity that directly controls one or more JMX manageable resources. It allows us to manage the resources from any management application without creating any direct coupling between the management application and the resources being managed.

JMX manager. A JMX manager is a management entity that allows the end user to manage the JMX manageable resources through one or more JMX agents.

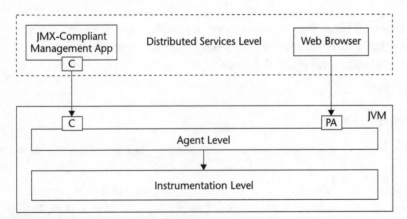

Figure 7.20 JMX layered architecture.

In JMX, application developers write MBeans that expose parts of the system to external scrutiny and control. The instrumentation level specification defines a set of naming rules, interfaces, and classes that are used when implementing MBeans. Using these interfaces and following the naming rules ensure that the system management agents can manage the MBeans. The instrumentation level also provides a notification framework that captures and propagates application events to management agents or to other MBeans.

Each JMX vendor provides an agent implementation that allows application developers to configure each agent with a set of MBeans. Agents reduce the complexity of the management application by isolating it from the actual MBeans. Any MBean registered with the agent becomes available for management from management applications. Agents also provide four types of services, Dynamic Class Loading (MLet Service), Monitors, Timers, and the Relation service.

JMX does not define how a managed application will register its MBeans with a remote agent. This is left to the vendors as they implement the specification. For that matter, JMX does not define how a remote management application will communicate with an agent. Vendors must provide protocol adaptors and connectors that expose their agents to management. Protocol adapters expose agents via a common protocol, such as HTTP. Connectors allow JMX clients or management applications to interact directly with agents. There are separate efforts under way to define standards for adapters and connectors.

NOTE In JMX 1.2, the MBeans and agents run in the same JVM.

Management applications access the managed resources through agents. Typically, these management applications provide consoles or user interfaces that allow users to perform the application management visually. A management application may be a JMX-compliant Java application, a proprietary management GUI, or a Web browser.

Gory Details

In JMX, a given resource is exposed for management by implementing one or more MBeans. An MBean is a Java class that implements a specific interface and conforms to certain naming rules. This interface is called the management interface of the resource that it represents. Managing a resource in JMX means:

- Manipulating the attributes of the MBean
- Invoking operations on the MBean
- Sending events to the MBean
- Receiving events from the MBean

A resource can represent a single Java class, a component, a subsystem, or even the entire application. It is the application developers' responsibility to define the granularity of each MBean as they see appropriate in a specific context. The four types of MBeans are:

- Standard MBean
- Dynamic MBean
- Model MBean
- Open MBean

Of these four types of MBeans, Open MBean is optional for JMX implementers to support. In the following sections, we describe Standard MBeans, Dynamic MBeans, the Notification Model, and Agents.

Standard MBean

Any Java object that statically defines and implements its own management interface following a set of naming rules is called Standard MBean. Typically, the management interface will include operations to access or modify attributes of the managed resource, operations to perform different management operations on the resource, and operations to propagate any event that it may emit. The naming rules to access and modify attributes are similar to those of the JavaBeans component model. However, MBeans use an inheritance scheme as well as naming rules.

In an MBean interface, the attributes are represented through getter and setter methods. An attribute with a name MyAttribute would have an accessor method named getMyAttribute() and a mutator method named setMyAttribute(). JMX recognizes the fact that there are three types of attributes, read-only, write-only, and read-write. Based on the type of access you want to provide to the attributes, you define an accessor, a mutator, or both. If an attribute has a Boolean value, you can define an accessor method as isAttributeName() instead of a getAttributeName() method, but not both. The MBean interface defines the attributes that are managed, regardless of which attributes are included in any classes that implement the MBean interface.

Additional rules for MBean with attributes include:

Management attributes are case sensitive. For example, getUserid() and setuserid() do not refer to the same attribute. getUserid() refers to an attribute with a name Userid whereas setuserid() refers to an attribute with a name userid. So, management applications will treat Userid as a read-only attribute and userid as a write-only attribute.

The accessor and mutator methods cannot be overloaded. In other words, defining setXxxx(int value) and setXxxx(String value) in the same MBean interface is prohibited.

JMX supports all data types. The only restriction is that array attributes must be handled as a whole. Attribute accessor and mutator methods cannot read or write an individual item in an array. However, the application developer is free to define an operation that accesses or sets an individual item in an array.

Any other methods defined in the management interface that do not follow the convention for defining attributes are called general management operations. These methods need not follow any specific naming pattern as long as they don't interfere with the attribute naming convention.

NOTE Do not confuse management attribute names with the actual data members of the resource class. The attribute name in the MBean interface is the name that is exposed to management applications. It may be different from the name of the attribute in the class that implements the MBean interface. Also, any methods that are not defined in the management interface are not accessible by management applications.

There is also a specific naming convention for the MBean interface itself. According to this convention, if the resource class name is MyResource, the MBean interface name must be MyResourceMBean. When a resource class extends from another resource, it may define its own interface. In this case, the parent's interface no longer applies. If a resource class does not define its own MBean interface, then the superclass's MBean interface applies. In order to include the superclass's MBean interface, its MBean interface will have to extend from the superclass's MBean interface.

As an example of these MBean rules, consider a simple application that maintains a pool of connections to a database. Our application will expose the following attributes as readable and writable by the management application:

- Connection name
- Database name
- Database location
- Minimum number of connections in pool
- Maximum number of connections in the pool
- User id

Our application also defines password as a write-only attribute and the number of open connections as a read-only attribute. In addition, two management operations allow a user to close all of the connections or to reinitialize the connection pool. As seen in the following listing, DBConnectionManager1MBean.java captures these decisions in an interface.

DBConnectionManager1MBean.java

```
package com.wiley.compBooks.EJwithUML.Samples.Jmx;

/**
 * This is a management interface for managing database connections.
 */
public interface DBConnectionManager1MBean
{
    // read-write attributes
    public String getConnectionName();
    public String getDatabaseName();
    public String getDatabaseLocation();
    public String getUserid();
    public int getMinConnection();
    public int getMaxConnection();
    public void setConnectionName(String name);
```

```
public void setDatabaseName(String name);
public void setDatabaseLocation(String name);
public void setUserid(String userid);
public void setMinConnection(int minConn);
public void setMaxConnection(int maxConn);

//read-only attributes
public int getOpenConnection();

//write-only attributes
public void setPassword(String password);

//management operations
public void closeAllConnections();
public void initializePool();

}
```

The following listing, DBConnectionManager1.java shows a concrete implementation of the DBConnectionManager1MBean interface. This example does not deal with real database connections. It only simulates the behavior of a pool of database connections in a very simplified manner. Notice that the MBean implementation defines an accessor method for the password attribute. Because it is not defined in the MBean interface, it is not available to the agent and hence not to any management application. Also, it implements methods, such as open(), close (), getConnection(), and takeConnection(), that are not exposed as management operations because they are not defined in the management interface. Another private data member, availableConnection, is also excluded from management because there is no corresponding accessor or mutator method in the MBean interface.

DBConnectionManager1.java

```java
package com.wiley.compBooks.EJwithUML.Samples.Jmx;

/**
 * This class mamanges a pool of database connections. It is
 * intrumented as an MBean. This is a simplified simulation class,
 * it does not deal with a real database connection. Hence, the
 * logic is simplified and does not account for different conditions
 * that may arise in real database pooling situations.
 */
public class DBConnectionManager1 implements DBConnectionManager1MBean
{

    // read-write attributes
    public String getDatabaseName()
    {
     return databaseName;
    }

    public String getDatabaseLocation()
    {
```

```
 return databaseLocation;
}


public String getUserid()
{
 return userid;
}

public int getMinConnection()
{
 return minConnection;
}

public int getMaxConnection()
{
 return maxConnection;
}

public void setDatabaseName(String name)
{
                                                    databaseName  = name;
 System.out.println("databse name = " + name);
}

public void setUserid(String userid)
{
 this.userid  = userid;
 System.out.println("userid = " + userid);
}

public void setDatabaseLocation(String location)
{
 databaseLocation = location;
 System.out.println("DB location = " + location);
}

public void setMinConnection(int count)
{
 minConnection = count;
 System.out.println("mas connection = " + count);
}

public void setMaxConnection(int count)
{
 maxConnection = count;
 System.out.println("mas connection = " + count);
}

//read-only attributes
public int getOpenConnection()
{
 return openConnection;
}
```

```java
//write-only attribute
public void setPassword(String password)
{
 this.password = password;
 System.out.println("password has been set.");
}

// a getter method for password field not available to MBean.
public String getPassword()
{
 return password;
}

//management operations
public void closeAllConnections()
{
   openConnection = 0;
   availableConnection = 0;
   System.out.println("all connections have closed.");

}

public void initializePool()
{
   openConnection = minConnection;
   availableConnection = minConnection;
   System.out.println("initial connections have been" +
                      "established.");

}

/*
 * nonmanangement operations - this is a simplified simulation.
 * Actual implementaion will return a connection object.
*/
public void getConnection()
{
 if (availableConnection > 0)
    {
            availableConnection-;
    }
    else
    {
     open();
    }
    System.out.println("connection taken from the pool.");
}

/*
 * nonmanangement operations - this is a simplified simulation.
 * Actual implementaion will receive a connection object.
 */
public void takeConnection()
{
```

```
            availableConnection++;
            System.out.println("connection returned to the pool.");
    }


    private void open()
    {
        if (openConnection < maxConnection)
        {
            openConnection++;
            availableConnection++;
            System.out.println("connection#" + openConnection +
                                "opned.");
        }
        else
        {
            //throw an exception;
        }
    }

    private void close()
    {
        openConnection--;
        availableConnection--;
        System.out.println("connection#" + openConnection +
                            "loseded.");
    }

    //private data members
    private String databaseName;
    private String databaseLocation;
    private String password;
    private String userid;
    private int maxConnection;
    private int minConnection;
    private int openConnection;
    private int availableConnection;


}
```

As you will see in the example, DBConnectionManager is implemented from scratch. However, many projects contain an existing class that needs to be exposed as an MBean. There are several ways to accomplish this. If the existing class already follows the naming conventions for attributes but cannot be renamed to fit the JMX rules for implementation class names, then a new class can implement the desired MBean interface by simply extending the existing class and following the naming rules. In many cases, the new subclass is empty. Alternatively, if the existing class's methods do not follow the naming convention, then a new class can implement the MBean interface by delegating each method call to the old class. The class diagram in Figure 7.21 illustrates these two techniques.

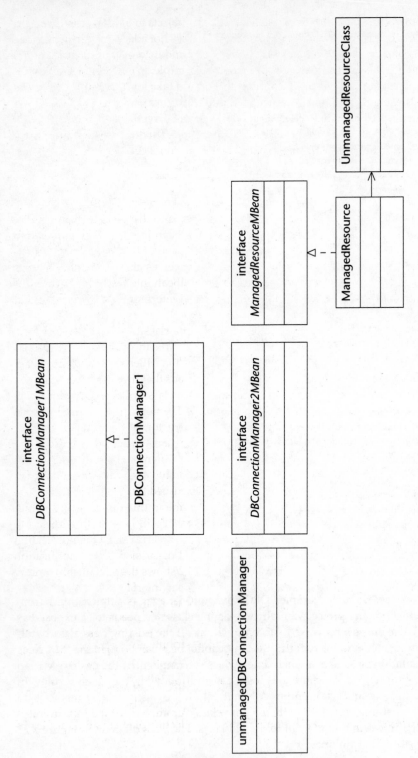

Figure 7.21   Exposing an existing class by inheritance or association.

In the real world, an MBean may delegate to many objects to fulfill its management interface. It is also important to remember that JMX does not address the synchronization issues explicitly. As a developer, you will have to understand your resource usage and implement synchronization appropriately. For example, in our previous example, the management operation closeAllConnection() should take into account the situation that some connections may still be in use by the application at the time of its execution by a management application. It needs to wait for all currently used connections to become available before it can close those connections. This will prevent any unexpected connection broken exception to occur while the connections are in use.

Dynamic MBean

As the name suggests, a Dynamic MBean allows agents to discover its management interface at run time by implementing the DynamicMBean interface. The application developer exposes attributes, operations, constructors, and notifications by constructing and configuring metadata objects. The agent accesses these metadata objects through the getMBeanInfo() method of the DynamicMBean interface. This is very different from Standard MBeans, where the management interface is statically bound at compile time.

MBeanInfo class is an aggregation of other metadata classes: MBeanAttributeInfo, MBeanConstructorInfo, MBeanOperationInfo, and MBeanNotificationInfo. Both MBeanConstructorInfo and MBeanOperationInfo use the MBeanParameterInfo class to describe the parameters and return type of the methods that they describe. All of the MBeanInfo classes extend from the MBeanFeatureInfo class. MBeanFeatureInfo provides two methods, getName() and getDescription(). The getName() method returns the name of the attribute, operation, parameter, constructor, or notification, and the getDescription() method returns a description of the same managed resource. The MBeanNotificationInfo class provides information on different types of notification that the MBean can transmit. The MBeanNotificationinfo class also extends from MBeanFeatureInfo like other classes. But, the name returned by getName() has different meaning than it does in the other classes. The name in this case must be a fully qualified class name of the actual notification object that will be sent. In addition to name and description, MBeanNotificationInfo provides an array of all the notification types through the getNotifTypes() method. A detailed discussion on the notification model in JMX is provided in a later section. Figure 7.22 shows the relationship among the metadata classes and their associated DynamicMBean interface.

DynamicMBean interface provides four methods to deal with the management attributes of the underlying MBean:

- **getAttribute().** Retrieves the value of a single attribute given its name.
- **setAttribute().** Writes the value of a single attribute identified by its name.
- **getAttributes().** Acts as a getter method for a collection of attributes. It returns a list of attributes whose values are successfully retrieved.
- **setAttributes().** Acts as a setter method for a collection of attributes. It returns a list of attributes whose values are successfully set.

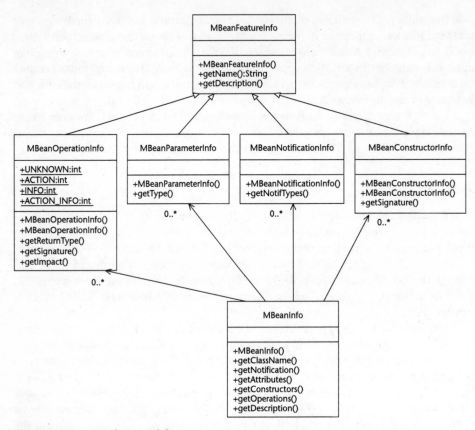

Figure 7.22   Metadata model.

These methods use the Attribute class as a wrapper class that represents a management attribute as a name-value pair. Also, AttributeList, which extends from ArrayList, represents a collection view of Attributes. Each value is represented as a Java object. This means that developers must wrap primitive data inside of the corresponding wrapper class. The DynamicMBean interface also provides a method called invoke() to perform management operations on the MBean. The caller of the invoke() method provides the name of the operation to perform, values for the parameters of the operation in an array as Java objects, and the types of the parameters as an array of strings. The order of the parameters must match the order in which they are defined in the corresponding MBeanOperationInfo object.

Some rules regarding Dynamic MBeans are:

■ An MBean can either be a Dynamic MBean or a Standard MBean, but not both.

■ The same inheritance rules apply on Dynamic MBean as Standard MBean. One interesting thing about the inheritance rules is that a class can inherit from a DynamicMBean, yet implements its own MBean interface and becomes a Standard MBean. The reverse is also possible.

Unlike Standard MBean, Dynamic MBean requires extra caution on the developer's part because the correctness of the mapping of names to attributes and their types, methods and their parameters and types are not checked at compile time or by agents during registration time. Any mismatch will manifest itself during run time. The following example shows a DBConnectionManager exposed as a Dynamic MBean. The class diagram is shown in Figure 7.23.

The class UmanagedDBConnectionManager is the same class as the DBConnectionManager1 except that it does not implement the Standard MBean interface. The DBConnectionManagerDynamicMBean class, as shown in the following listing, turns the UnmanagedDBConnectionManager class into a Dynamic MBean. A simple typo when referencing an attribute or operation by name can cause a lot of grief when it manifests itself at run time. Fortunately, a few simple practices remove a lot of this risk. Define all the operation and attribute names as string constants. This will save you from simple typing mistakes. Define all your MBeanAttributeInfo, MbeanConstructorInfo, MBeanOperationInfo, MBeanParameterInfo, and MBeanNotificationInfo objects as separate private members. Map only the attributes that you want to provide read-access in the getAttribute() method. For all other attributes, throw AttributeNotFoundException. This also safeguards your other attributes from accidental access—a simple security measure. Follow the same pattern in the setAttribute() method. Use getAttribute() in the getAttributes() method and setAttributes in the setAttributes() method.

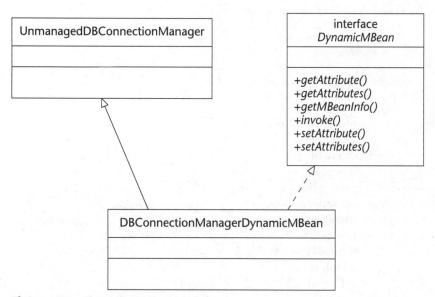

Figure 7.23   Dynamic MBean example.

DBConnectionManagerDynamicMBean.java

```java
package com.wiley.compBooks.EJwithUML.Samples.Jmx;

import java.util.Iterator;
import javax.management.*;

/**
 * This class provides instrumentation to
 * UnmanagedDBConnectionManager as a Dynamic MBean.
 */
public class DBConnectionManagerDynamicMBean extends
UnmanagedDBConnectionManager implements DynamicMBean
{

    // management attribute names as constants
    final static String DATABASE_NAME = "DatabaseName";
    final static String DATABASE_LOCATION = "DatabaseLocation";
    final static String USERID = "Userid";
    final static String PASSWORD = "Password";
    final static String MAX_CONNECTION = "MaxConnection";
    final static String MIN_CONNECTION = "MinConnection";
    final static String OPEN_CONNECTION = "OpenConnection";

    // management operation names as constants
    final static String CLOSE_ALL_CONNECTIONS =
                                "closeAllConnections";
    final static String INITIALIZE_POOL = "initializePool";

    // constants used in defining MBeanAttributeInfos
    final static boolean READABLE = true;
    final static boolean WRITABLE = true;
    final static boolean IS_GETTER = true;

    // constructor info

    // attribute infos - read-write type
    private MBeanAttributeInfo dbName = new
                MBeanAttributeInfo(DATABASE_NAME, // name
                            String.class.getName(), // type
                    "Database Name", // description
                READABLE, WRITABLE, !IS_GETTER /* flags */);

    private MBeanAttributeInfo dbLocation = new
                MBeanAttributeInfo(DATABASE_LOCATION,
                                String.class.getName(),
                                "Database Location",
                        READABLE, WRITABLE, !IS_GETTER);

    private MBeanAttributeInfo userid = new
                    MBeanAttributeInfo(USERID,
                            String.class.getName(),
                            "User Id",
                    READABLE, WRITABLE, !IS_GETTER);
```

```
private MBeanAttributeInfo maxConnection = new
                        MBeanAttributeInfo(MAX_CONNECTION,
                              int.class.getName(),
                           "Maximum Number of Connections",
                         READABLE, WRITABLE, !IS_GETTER);

private MBeanAttributeInfo minConnection = new
                        MBeanAttributeInfo(MIN_CONNECTION,
                                     int.class.getName(),
                             "Minimum Number of Connections",
                         READABLE, WRITABLE, !IS_GETTER);



// attribute infos - write-only type
private MBeanAttributeInfo password = new
                        MBeanAttributeInfo(PASSWORD,
                                  String.class.getName(),
                                      "Password",
                          !READABLE, WRITABLE, !IS_GETTER);

// attribute infos - read-only type
private MBeanAttributeInfo openConnection = new
                        MBeanAttributeInfo(OPEN_CONNECTION,
                                     int.class.getName(),
                      "Number of Currently Open Connections",
                        READABLE, !WRITABLE, !IS_GETTER);

private MBeanAttributeInfo[] attributes = new
                  MBeanAttributeInfo[]{ dbName, dbLocation,
userid, maxConnection, minConnection, password, openConnection};



// parameter infos for the operations


// operation infos
private MBeanOperationInfo closeAllConnections = new
                    MBeanOperationInfo(
                          CLOSE_ALL_CONNECTIONS, // name
                 "Closes all open connections", // description
                     null, //does not take any parameter
                     void.class.getName(), // return type
                  MBeanOperationInfo.ACTION /* impact type */);

private MBeanOperationInfo initializePool = new
                        MBeanOperationInfo(
                          INITIALIZE_POOL, // name
              "Opens minimum number of connections", // description
                     null, //does not take any parameter
                     void.class.getName(), // return type
                  MBeanOperationInfo.ACTION /* impact type */);

private MBeanOperationInfo[] operations = new
```

```
                                        MBeanOperationInfo[]{
                                                closeAllConnections,
                                        initializePool};


// constructor infos
private MBeanConstructorInfo defaultConstructor = new
                                MBeanConstructorInfo(
                                "Default Constructor",
                "Creates a new instance of ManagedDBManager",
                                null /* no parameters */);


private MBeanConstructorInfo[] constructors = new
                        MBeanConstructorInfo[]{
                                        defaultConstructor};




// MBeanInfo
private MBeanInfo dbManagerMBeanInfo = new
                MBeanInfo(this.getClass().getName(),
                "Managed Database Manager",
                attributes, // MBeanAttributeInfo[]
                constructors, // MBeanConstructorInfo[]
                operations, // MBeanOperationInfo[]
                null /* no MBeanNotificationInfo[] */);

//DynamicMBean interface implementation
public MBeanInfo getMBeanInfo()
{
  return dbManagerMBeanInfo;
}


public Object getAttribute(String attribute) throws
AttributeNotFoundException,MBeanException, ReflectionException
{
 if (attribute == null || attribute.trim().equals(""))
    {
        throw new AttributeNotFoundException(
                        "attribute name is null/empty");
    }


    if (attribute.equals(DATABASE_NAME))
    {
      return getDatabaseName();
    }
    else if (attribute.equals(DATABASE_LOCATION))
    {
      return getDatabaseLocation();
    }
    if (attribute.equals(USERID))
    {
      return getUserid();
    }
```

```
        else if (attribute.equals(MAX_CONNECTION))
        {
           return new Integer(getMaxConnection());
        }
        if (attribute.equals(MIN_CONNECTION))
        {
           return new Integer(getMinConnection());
        }
        else if (attribute.equals(OPEN_CONNECTION))
        {
           return new Integer(getOpenConnection());
        }
        else
        {
            throw new AttributeNotFoundException("attribute = " +
              attribute +" either not readable or does not exist.");
        }
    }


    // returns Attributes that are successfully retrieved
    public AttributeList getAttributes(String[] attributes)
    {

     if (attributes == null)
        {
           throw new IllegalArgumentException(
                            "empty attribute list");
        }

        AttributeList attrsWithValues = new AttributeList();

        //loop through the list and retrive values
        for(int i = 0; i < attributes.length; i++)
        {
           try
           {
             attrsWithValues.add(new Attribute(
                                 attributes[i], // name
                   getAttribute(attributes[i]) // value
                                       )
                          );
           }
           catch(JMException exception)
           {
              //ignore the exception - according to the spec
           }
         }

         return attrsWithValues;
    }

    public void setAttribute(Attribute attribute) throws
AttributeNotFoundException,InvalidAttributeValueException,
```

```
MBeanException, ReflectionException
{
   System.out.println("setting attribute " +
         attribute.getName() + " to " + attribute.getValue());
         System.out.println(attribute.getValue().getClass().getName());
if (attribute == null || attribute.getName() == null ||
         attribute.getName().equals(""))
   {
       throw new AttributeNotFoundException(
                     "attribute name is null/empty");
   }

   try
   {
      if (attribute.getName().equals(DATABASE_NAME))
      {
          setDatabaseName((String)attribute.getValue());
      }
      else if (attribute.getName().equals(DATABASE_LOCATION))
      {
          setDatabaseLocation((String)attribute.getValue());
      }
      else if (attribute.getName().equals(USERID))
      {
          setUserid((String)attribute.getValue());
      }
      else if (attribute.getName().equals(MAX_CONNECTION))
      {
          setMaxConnection(((Integer)attribute.getValue()).intValue());
      }
      else if (attribute.getName().equals(MIN_CONNECTION))
      {
          setMinConnection(((Integer)attribute.getValue()).intValue());
      }
      else if (attribute.getName().equals(PASSWORD))
      {
         setPassword((String)attribute.getValue());
      }
      else
      {
      System.out.println("attribute = " + attribute +
        " either not readable or does not exist.");
         throw new AttributeNotFoundException("attribute = " +
       attribute + " either not readable or does not exist.");
      }
   }
   catch(Exception exception)
   {
     System.out.println(exception);
     // we may get - ClassCastException, NumberFormatException,
     // NullPointerEcxeption ...
     throw new InvalidAttributeValueException(
     "invalid value of attribute " + attribute);
   }
```

```
    }

    // returns Attributes that are successfully set
    public AttributeList setAttributes(AttributeList inputList)
    {

     if (attributes == null)
        {
            throw new IllegalArgumentException(
                            "empty attribute list");
        }

        AttributeList resultList = new AttributeList();
        Iterator inputListIterator = inputList.iterator();

        //loop through the list and retrive values
        while(inputListIterator.hasNext())
        {
            try
            {
              Attribute attribute =
                  (Attribute)inputListIterator.next();
              setAttribute(attribute);
              resultList.add(attribute);
            }
            catch(JMException exception)
            {
                //ignore the exception - according to the spec
            }
        }

        return resultList;
    }

    public Object invoke(String operationName, Object[] parameters,
String[] parametertypes) throws MBeanException, ReflectionException
    {

        if (operationName == null || operationName.equals(" "))
        {
            throw new IllegalArgumentException(
                            "empty or null operation name!");
        }

        // map operation name to actual operation
        if (operationName.equals(CLOSE_ALL_CONNECTIONS))
        {
            closeAllConnections();
            return null;
        }
        else if (operationName.equals(INITIALIZE_POOL))
        {
            initializePool();
            return null;
```

```
            }
            else
            {
                throw new UnsupportedOperationException(
                                    "unknown operation!");
            }
        }
    }
```

Notification Model

JMX defines a notification model based on the Java event model defined in the "java.util" package. Sometimes, management applications need to react to different application events to prevent an unwanted situation. For example, a management application might notify production support personnel if a connection to a database goes down. An MBean captures management events and broadcasts them to all interested parties. The sender of the event is called a broadcaster and implements the NotificationBroadcaster interface. The receiver of the event is called a listener and implements the NotificationListener interface. Broadcasters and listeners can be either MBeans or a management application. MBeans that participate in event notification but do not implement the MBean interface are known as notification MBeans. The key classes and interfaces of this framework are:

Notification.   Extends from java.util.EventObject and represents any management event. The information propagated through this class includes notification type, a sequence number, time stamp, a message, and any user-defined data. The notification type is a string understood by the listeners. Notification may be subclassed if additional semantics are required.

NotificationBroadcaster.   An interface that defines methods to add and remove listeners. Additionally, it defines a method to allow listeners to retrieve the type of notification emitted by the broadcaster. An MBean can both be a listener and a broadcaster. Multiple listeners can register with a single broadcaster. A single listener can register with the same broadcaster multiple times.

NotificationListener.   An interface that defines the callback method handleNotification(). The broadcaster calls this method when an event that this listener is interested in occurs.

NotificationFilter.   An interface that defines a method called isNotificationEnabled() to filter events based on type and content. The listener provides a filter during the registration. If one is provided, the broadcaster invokes the method before transmitting an event to the listener.

NOTE Notification types with the prefix "jmx" are reserved for internal use by JMX. Listeners never directly register themselves with a broadcaster. They must go through an agent.

The class diagram in Figure 7.24 shows the relationships among these interfaces and class.

The association class between listener and broadcaster, as shown in Figure 7.25, is called a hand-back object. It can be any Java object. The listener provides a hand-back object when it registers itself with a broadcaster. The broadcaster passes the same hand-back object to the listener with every event notification. This hand-back object works as a context for the listener. If a listener wants to register more than once with the same broadcaster, it should use a different hand-back object.

> **NOTE** JMX defines two concrete classes for handling attribute changes as events. These classes are AttributeNotificationFilter and AttributeChangeNotification.

Typical interactions between a listener and a broadcaster are shown in Figure 7.25.

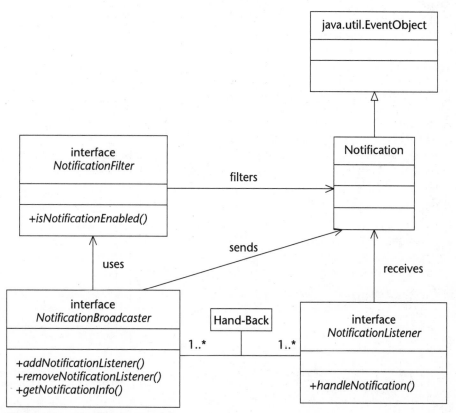

Figure 7.24   Notification model.

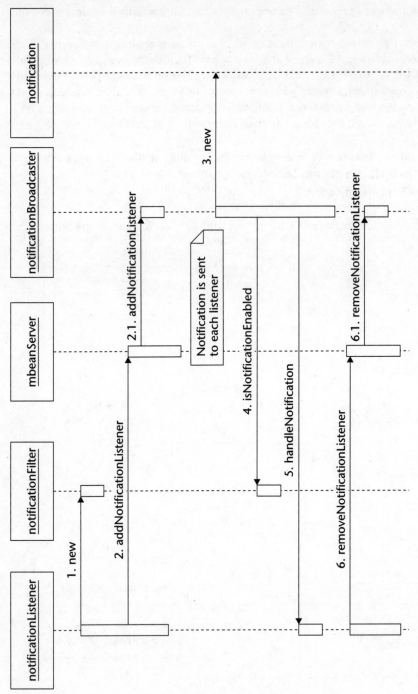

Figure 7.25   Interactions between a listener and a broadcaster.

One thing to note in the interaction diagram is that the listener does not interact directly with the broadcaster to register for notifications or to stop receiving notifications. Instead, the listener interacts with an MBeanServer object. An MBean server is the core interface that is implemented by agents. The MBeanServer interface defines two sets of methods to deal with listeners' registration with broadcasters, addNotificationListener() and removeNotificationListener(). As you can see, these methods are similar to the ones defined in the NotificationBroadcaster interface, with one difference. The listener identifies the broadcaster MBean that it wants to register with through these method calls to the MBean server.

So, you can see that a broadcaster needs to manage a triplet for each listener: a handback object, a filter, and the listener. This may become complex. The listener registration and delivery of notification are not tied to the type of listener and notification. Hence, JMX provides a helper class, NotificationBroadcasterSupport, which implements the NotificationBroadcaster interface to manage these common tasks on behalf of broadcast MBeans. The MBeans can either extend from this class or delegate calls to it for the actual handling of registration and transmission of notifications. The following code snippet shows how you can use delegation to take advantage of this support class.

```
import    javax.management.*;

public class SimpleEventBroadcasterMBean implements NotificationBroadcaster
{
    private NotificationBroadcasterSupport  broadcaster = new
    NotificationBroadcasterSupport();
    // code specific to this class
    .......
    // NotificationBroadcaster interface implementation
    public void addNotificationListener(NotificationListener listener,
    NotificationFilter filter, Object    handback)
    {
        broadcaster.addNotificationListener(listener, filter, handback);
    }
    public void removeNotificationListener(NotificationListener listener)
    throws ListenerNotFoundException
    {
        broadcaster.removeNotificationListener(listener);
    }
    public MBeanNotificationInfo[] getNotificationInfo()
    {
        // Return  an array of MBeanNotificationInfo for each type of event
        emitted by this MBean.
    }
}
```

Agent

Application developers must register all MBeans defined in the application with an agent before they can start managing the application from a management application. The management applications never directly interact with MBeans, they interact with MBeans through the agents. The core component of an agent is the MBeanServer class. Applications instantiate MBeanServers through a factory class called MBeanServerFactory.

For Java applications, the agents run in the same JVM as the application while the management applications generally reside in a separate process. The communication between an agent and a remote management application is done through either a connector or a protocol adaptor. The specification for protocol adaptors and connectors is not included in JMX 1.2. Most of the currently available implementations of JMX provide an HTTP protocol adaptor and an RMI connector. The following example shows how an application registers its MBeans and initializes the HTTP protocol adaptor. The example application uses the MBeans that we developed in the previous sections and uses TMX4J from IBM as a JMX provider. By default, the HTTP protocol adaptor provided with TMX4J listens on port 6969. You can connect to the application from your browser by pointing to http://localhost:6969 and then manage the running application.

SimpleMangedApplication.java

```
/*
 * SimpleManagedApplication.java
 *
 * Created on April 6, 2002, 11:02 AM
 */

package com.wiley.compBooks.EJwithUML.Samples.Jmx;

import javax.management.*;

/**
 * This class implements a simple managed application that can be
 * managed from a browser. It uses HTTP protocol Adapter for
 * interaction with a browser.
 */
public class SimpleManagedApplication
{

    /** Creates new SimpleManagedApplication */
    public SimpleManagedApplication()
    {
        // managed resources
        managerStandardMBean = new
                            DBConnectionManager1();
        managerDynamicMBean = new DBConnectionManagerDynamicMBean();
    }

    /**
     * @param args the command line arguments
     */
    public static void main (String args[])
    {
      try
      {
            SimpleManagedApplication application = new
                                SimpleManagedApplication();
            MBeanServer server =
```

```
                            MBeanServerFactory.createMBeanServer();
            server.registerMBean(application.managerStandardMBean,
               new ObjectName("example:name=DBManagerStandardMBean"));
            server.registerMBean(application.managerDynamicMBean,
               new ObjectName("example:name=DBManagerDynamicMBean"));
            com.tivoli.jmx.http_pa.Listener adaptor = new
                             com.tivoli.jmx.http_pa.Listener();
            server.registerMBean(adaptor, new
                    ObjectName("example:name=http_adaptor"));
            adaptor.startListener();
        }
      catch(Exception e)
         {
         System.out.println(e);
         }
      }


      private DBConnectionManagerStandardMBean managerStandardMBean;
      private DBConnectionManagerDynamicMBean managerDynamicMBean;
}
```

From the browser, you can select the standard MBean from the MBean query page by typing "example:name=DBManagerStandardMBean". This will take you to the MBean detail page where you can interact with MBean dynamically. Figure 7.26 shows the screen shot of the MBean Details page.

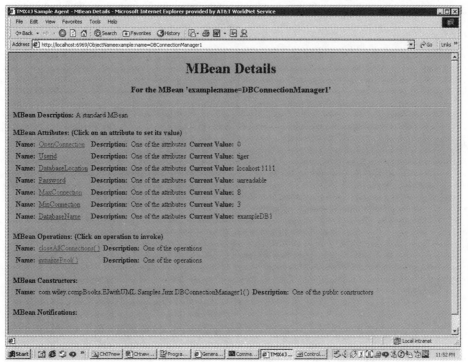

Figure 7.26   Management view of MBean using TMX4J's HTTP adaptor.

The previous example shows how MBeans can be registered with an agent programmatically. Agents also provide a service called M-Let service that allows an application to load Java classes from anywhere on the network. Like other agent services, M-Let is implemented as an MBean. The class MLet is the main class of this service. The getMBeansFromURL() method allows MBeans to be loaded and registered to the MBean Server. It uses a text file to determine which MBeans to load. The text file uses XML-like tagged data. The definition of the tag is as follows:

```
<MLET CODE = fully-qualified class name of MBean | OBJECT = ".ser" file -
serialized copy of an MBean
            ARCHIVE = "comma separated list of jar files containing MBean
            or .ser file"
            [CODEBASE ="URL of the jar files listed in ARCHIVE "]
            [NAME="name of the MBean as known to management applications"]
             [VERSION="a version of the MBean"] >
[<ARG TYPE="parameter type" VALUE="value of the parameter">
   .
   .
   .
]
</MLET>
```

The M-Let text file should not be confused as an XML file. It resembles XML, but is not well formed and does not follow all of the XML syntax rules. It also does not support XML-style comments. If the MBean has a parameterized constructor, the parameter values are passed through the ARG tags. The ARG tags must be in the same order as they are defined in the constructor of the MBean. Following is an example of such an M-Let text file:

conf.mlet

```
<MLET CODE = "com.wiley.compBooks.EJwithUML.Samples.Jmx.DBConnectionManager1"
      ARCHIVE = "mbeans.jar"
      CODEBASE =
"file:/e:/EJwithUML2e/Code/com/wiley/compBooks/EJwithUML/Samples/Jmx"
      NAME = "example:name=DBConnectionManager1"
      VERSION = 1.0>
</MLET>


<MLET CODE = "com.wiley.compBooks.EJwithUML.Samples.Jmx.DBConnectionManager2"
      ARCHIVE = "mbeans.jar"
      CODEBASE =
"file:/e:/EJwithUML2e/Code/com/wiley/compBooks/EJwithUML/Samples/Jmx"
      NAME = "example:name=DBConnectionManager2"
      VERSION = 1.0>
      <ARG  TYPE="java.lang.String" VALUE="exampleDB2">
      <ARG  TYPE="java.lang.String" VALUE="localhost:8888">
      <ARG  TYPE="java.lang.String" VALUE="lion">
      <ARG  TYPE="java.lang.String" VALUE="abc123">
      <ARG  TYPE="int" VALUE="10">
      <ARG  TYPE="int" VALUE="5">
</MLET>
```

The following code snippet shows how we can use the M-Let service to load our MBeans:

```
try
{
  SimpleManagedApplication2 application = new
      SimpleManagedApplication2();
  MBeanServer server = MBeanServerFactory.createMBeanServer();
  ObjectName name = new ObjectName("service:name=Mlet");
  server.registerMBean(new MLet(), name);
  server.invoke(name,"getMBeansFromURL", new Object[]{new
URL("file:/e:/EJwithUML2e/Code/com/wiley/compBooks/EJwithUML/Samples/Jmx/
conf.mlet")}, new String[]{URL.class.getName()});
  com.tivoli.jmx.http_pa.Listener adaptor = new
                              com.tivoli.jmx.http_pa.Listener();
  server.registerMBean(adaptor, new
                          ObjectName("example:name=http_adaptor"));
          adaptor.startListener();
}
catch(Exception e)
{
  System.out.println(e);
  e.printStackTrace();
}
```

Strengths

The programming model implemented by JMX 1.0 is simple yet powerful. In particular, standard MBeans are very easy to implement. There is virtually no learning curve for most Java developers. Standard MBeans are suitable for managing new resources. But, if the resource already exists and its methods and attributes do not follow the naming convention required for a Standard MBean, you can apply the adaptor pattern with a Standard MBean or use a Dynamic MBean. Dynamic MBeans allow the management interface to be defined declaratively. This allows changes to the management interface to be independent of the actual resource being managed. We can swap resources under the hood without forcing any recompilation of the Java classes. However, Dynamic MBeans are not as easy to learn or to implement.

Weaknesses

JMX is not usable without agents and managers. Unfortunately, JMX 1.0 does not define the interaction between agents and management applications. Connectors and protocol adaptors are left to the providers. However, most implementation providers offer an HTTP protocol adaptor and an RMI connector. But, if you are using any existing management application such as BMC Patrol or HP Openview, you may not be able to manage your application from these tools. Separate efforts are under way to define standard APIs for interaction with existing management environments, based on existing protocols such as SNMP.

Also, JMX 1.0 does not address the security of the MBeans. The application developers must implement their own security to protect the MBeans from unauthorized access.

Compatible Technologies

The JMX API can be used by any type of Java application, including servlets, Swing, command-line applications, and Enterprise JavaBeans.

Cost of Adoption

There are implementations of JMX available for free. Tivoli's TMX4J, developed by IBM, is a freely available JMX implementation and is now available from Apache. Sun also provides a reference implementation of JMX. It is available from Sun's Java site. To get the full value from the API, your project must fill the roles of architect and developer.

Architect

An architect will identify the resources to be managed. For these resources, he will identify the management attributes and operations. Also, he will determine the events that these resources may need to trap and broadcast. He will have to determine the listeners of these events—other MBeans and/or management applications—and what actions these listeners will take when the events are reported.

Developer

The developers should be familiar with the JMX programming model and be able to pick the right type of MBean for a given resource.

Suitability

JMX 1.0 is suitable for most intranet applications. If your applications run in a Weblogic environment, you can use Weblogic's implementation of JMX and use their Admin tool to manage your application along with Weblogic.

Conclusion

The Timecard application could reasonably use the Java Logging classes, application exceptions, and the Java Management extension. There is no obvious need for the Java Cryptography extension or the Java Secure extension. In order to keep the application simple and to make our code compatible with as many configurations as possible, we will only use application exceptions. In an actual production system, we would make very different decisions, based on the expected deployment scenario.

The Next Step

Now that we have considered technologies for shared services, we can turn our attention to producing the HTML that is so prevalent in modern user interfaces.

HTML Production

Many modern systems allow users to access the system from a conventional Web browser, either over the Internet or from an intranet with restricted access. As long as the complexity of the user interface is not too high, Web-based systems have some incredible advantages. For example, users can access the system from any system that has a Web browser. Also, changes to the system are made on the server and are seen by all users when they access the site.

NOTE **This chapter establishes a minimal HTML production class library to support the sample application and to quickly demonstrate the idea. For a far more complete exploration of these ideas and for a more useful library for use in actual projects, please visit the open source project page at http://htmlprod.sourceforge.net/.**

However, even a relatively simple Web-based system includes many pages of moderately complex and dynamically generated HTML. This can be a daunting task, as HTML and its surrounding technologies are often a capricious and unforgiving lot. There are details to learn for each browser, and a frighteningly large number of potential solutions for any problem. HTML documents can be both disturbingly large and incomprehensibly dense. Many large-scale Web-based systems are composed of hundreds of different pages, each sharing some common elements, and many with unique aspects. Keeping the pages consistent while providing flexibility and facilitating changes to the look and feel requires considerable effort and foresight. Also, dynamically generated Web content is notoriously difficult to develop and troubleshoot, with a tedious cycle: edit, redeploy, exercise the site, analyze the results, and repeat.

One effective approach to these issues is to develop a class library that is dedicated to the production of HTML. This chapter covers the design and implementation of a simple class library for HTML production. Servlet and JSP developers will use this framework as they build the user interface classes. Ideally, the servlet developers should not even need to directly produce any HTML. Instead, they will depend on HTML production classes to handle this tedious task. JSP developers can use the HTML production classes to create common dynamic elements, such as tables of data, lists of links, and data entry pages. Assuming that each class in the library is extensively unit tested, the time required to develop and test new pages should be dramatically reduced. Also, changing the look of a commonly occurring item for the entire site can be accomplished by changing a few classes, not every page!

Designing a class library is quite different from designing a package based on use cases; therefore, we will deviate a bit from the normal design steps. First, we will establish goals for the design. Next, we will attempt to design to one or more goals where it may help to consider existing design patterns or existing products as guides. Then, we will measure the resulting design against the goals.

Design Goals

Before we can design a clever solution to our problem, it is essential to formally determine the design goals for the HTML production framework. After all, how can we hit an undefined target? Think of the goals for a subsystem or framework as a technically oriented internal requirements document. The goals detail how other parts of the system will interact with the framework, and what these parts can expect from it.

You must establish concrete examples and very specific criteria for your goals before you begin to design. Clear and quantifiable goals can drive a design and provide a valuable measure of success. Vaguely defined goals do not provide direction for the design, and tend to frustrate developers more than they help. For example, consider a goal for our class library to support versions 4 and higher of Internet Explorer and Netscape Navigator. With some time and effort, we can verify that the HTML produced by the HTML production classes is rendered reasonably well in each browser.

Let's take a look at the design goals for the HTML production class library.

Goal 1: Support Modular Construction of Views

It can be useful to nest one HTML component inside another HTML component to form a more complex page. A page might contain a table, an input form, and some text. One cell in the table might contain an image, while another cell might contain another complete table. Component nesting allows a patient developer to assemble arbitrarily complex pages from a small number of relatively simple building blocks. We want our underlying HTML production classes to allow a presentation developer to easily nest and combine structures.

Consider a page that contains a table, which in turn contains an image and some text. This moderately complex view is built by combining these three simple elements. The pseudocode for this table might look like the following:

1. Construct a new table.
2. Construct a new image and set its source.
3. Add the image to the table.
4. Construct some text and add it to the table.
5. Construct a new page.
6. Add the table to the page.

Graphical interface programmers use this sort of bottom-up composition to stay sane while they create elaborate screens. Even the most complex screen is composed from a relatively small number of components, which are creatively combined. Our framework must provide the same capability.

Goal 2: Keep HTML Production Simple

We want the majority of our developers to remain focused on the intricacies of the business and to ignore the painful details that can be involved in generating the actual HTML. Presentation developers must be able to add data to views without worrying about differences between browsers or which arcane option on a particular HTML tag does what.

In short, we want to keep HTML production simple. To do this, there are three specific criteria:

Hide the actual tags and options.   Outside of the framework team, developers should not need more than a casual familiarity with HTML syntax.

Enable natural development of the user interface.   Adding content or data should be natural from the perspective of the view developer. It should not necessarily be dictated by the structure of the resulting HTML.

An example of how a view might use the class library might be helpful. Let's consider a view that extracts some data from the domain and displays it in a table. The pseudocode might look like the following:

1. Retrieve raw data from the domain.
2. Get a new page from the framework.
3. Set the title of the page.
4. Add some instructional text to the page.
5. Get a new data display table from the framework.
6. Set the column headings for the table.
7. Add the data to the data display table.
8. Add the table to the page.
9. Ask the page for its HTML.

Notice that the view does not know how the HTML is produced. It just wires the data into the elements that are provided by the framework.

By encapsulating the dirty details of HTML production, we allow staff specialization. Presentation developers can keep their data manipulation logic separate from the complexities of the actual HTML. This helps keep the code base smaller and easier to understand.

This is a very valuable form of reuse. It may not be as stunning or politically impressive as a cross-corporate domain infrastructure, but it is really nice when everyone can add data to a table and have it produce the same HTML. Without such a framework, developers must create their own unique, and often incompatible, solutions. When allowed to compound over time, this trend leads to chaos and terminal code bloat.

WARNING I have seen Web-based systems that required tens of thousands of lines of Java and JSP to produce a site of unremarkable size or complexity. In these systems, each page was produced by servlet or JSP code that extracted the data and formatted each HTML tag. Each page is similar to other pages that provide similar functionality, yet there is no way to make a change to the entire site without editing each and every page.

Goal 3: Extensibility and Independence

Class library developers must be able to extend the framework easily and without impacting existing views. The presentation logic will not change to accommodate each new version of Internet Explorer or Netscape Navigator. Instead, these changes must be isolated to the framework. Specifically, the framework must accommodate the following changes without impacting existing client code:

- New browsers
- Changes to the HTML specification for an element
- Changes to the preferred look of an HTML element

The HTML production classes must be protected from changes in the application or presentation layers. To ensure this, the HTML production classes should depend only on primitives and standard Java classes. For instance, the framework must not know anything about timecards or employees. The user interface developer would need to extract data from any domain-specific classes before using it to configure any HTML production classes.

Meeting these specific design goals will allow the framework developers to keep the presentation developers happy over time. The encapsulation also will make it easier for other projects to reuse the entire framework.

Design to Goals

Once we have developed specific goals, the next step is to develop high-level designs that meet them. It is difficult to design for all of the goals simultaneously. Instead, we will design for one goal at a time and periodically check for contradictions.

Design for Goal 1: Support Modular Construction of Views

Supporting modular construction of views captures the flavor of the HTML production classes. The class library exists because it lets developers build elaborate structures from simple primitives.

Goal 1 is also especially meaningful because it is a perfect fit for an existing design pattern. Gamma and his coauthors describe the Composite pattern's intent as follows: "Compose objects into tree structures to represent part-whole hierarchies. Composite lets clients treat individual objects and compositions of objects uniformly" [Gamma, et al. 1995].

A tree structure that represents a part-whole hierarchy sounds applicable. We can represent our page as the following tree:

- Page
- Table
- Image
- Text

The next part of the intent, "Composite lets clients treat individual objects and compositions of objects uniformly," is a bit more interesting. It implies that Composite objects implement the same interface as their children. So, the client does not care if it holds a reference to a Composite or an individual object. Similarly, a Composite does not care if a child is a Composite or an individual object.

Gamma and his colleagues demonstrate the pattern with graphical primitives, such as lines, rectangles, text, and pictures. These primitives can be combined to form elaborate pictures. As the intent states, the payoff comes when we draw the picture by asking the topmost container to draw itself. It in turn asks each of its children to draw itself. If it is a leaf, the child draws itself and is done. If it is a container, it draws itself then asks each of its children to draw itself. What a nice generic and recursive solution to a very common problem.

Consider the potential for using the Composite pattern for the HTML production class library. The Composite pattern can be used to construct very complex HTML pages by combining relatively simple HTML producers. For example, a table might contain text, images, forms, and other tables. A page might contain a table, a form, images, and some miscellaneous text. A form might contain input fields, descriptive text, and one or more submit buttons. Notice that some elements, such as forms and tables, can contain other elements. Other elements, such as text, cannot contain any other elements.

To access the elements, we need a common interface that the Composites and individual objects can implement. Since this is an HTML production framework, which will allow users to compose pages from simple or primitive building blocks, let's call the common interface IHtmlPrimitive. Each Composite will have methods that add IHtmlPrimitives. To keep names consistent, we'll name each class that implements IHtmlPrimitive with its type and the suffix Primitive. For the example, we invent PagePrimitive, TextPrimitive, ImagePrimitive, and TablePrimitive. As seen in Figure 8.1, each class overrides the buildContent method to build its own HTML content. The

PagePrimitive class allows us to add one primitive after another, while the Table-Primitive class allows control over the relative positioning of the primitives, by allowing us to add each primitive to a particular cell in the table.

The PagePrimitive class has a simple constructor, a method to add primitives to the body of the page, and a method to append the HTML for the page to a StringBuffer:

- public PagePrimitive(String title, String styleSheet)
- public void addToBody(IHtmlPrimitive primitive)
- public void buildContent(StringBuffer buffer)

TablePrimitive has a simple constructor and several methods that control the appearance of the table as a whole:

- public TablePrimitive()
- public void setStyle(Style style)
- public void setAlignment(HAlignment horizontalAlignment, VAlignment verticalAlignment)

It also has two methods that control the appearance of a specified row:

- public void setStyleForRow(int rowIndex, Style style)
- public void setAlignmentForRow(int rowIndex, HAlignment horizontalAlignment, VAlignment verticalAlignment)

The TablePrimitive class has several methods that control the appearance of all primitives that are added to the table after the methods have been called:

- public void setStyleForCells(Style style)
- public void setAlignmentForCells(HAlignment horizontalAlignment, VAlignment verticalAlignment)
- public void setColumnSpanForCells(int columnSpan)

Finally, the TablePrimitive class has a method to add a primitive to a specified cell and a method to append the HTML for the table to a StringBuffer:

- public void setPrimitiveAt(int rowIndex, int colIndex, IHtmlPrimitive primitive)
- public void buildContent(StringBuffer buffer)

So, our simple HTML page is composed by creating a PagePrimitive object then adding a TablePrimitive class to it. Next, we'll add an ImagePrimitive class and a Text-Primitive class to the TablePrimitive class, with the image in the top left and the text in the bottom right.

While each type of element needs different methods for adding data, all of them should support a simple way to retrieve the formatted HTML. Once the page has been constructed, getting the HTML is simple: The page asks each of its primitives to add its HTML to a buffer. Each primitive asks its primitives to add their HTML. Notice in Figure 8.2 that each enclosing primitive does not need to know much about its primitives. It just expects properly formatted HTML when it asks for it.

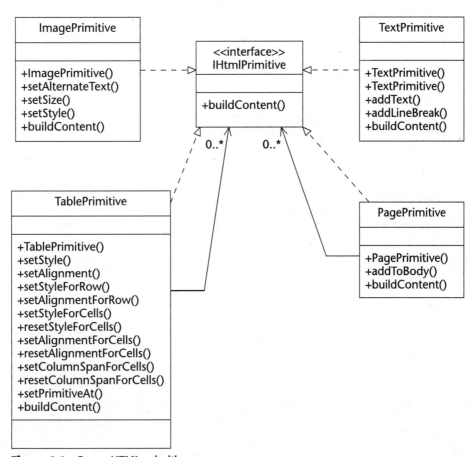

Figure 8.1   Some HTML primitives.

This pattern can be continued for increasingly complex and more application-specific constructs. For example, presentation developers can make a DataDisplay-Table class that implements IHtmlPrimitive and uses a variety of primitives to display a table of data in an attractive way. This application-specific construct can be added to a PagePrimitive class or even to a TablePrimitive class.

Let's express our design in terms of the Composite design pattern and evaluate our effectiveness. PagePrimitive and TablePrimitive are Composites since they implement the IHtmlPrimitive interface and contain objects that implement IHtmlPrimitive. This application of a time-tested pattern allows us to easily build complex HTML pages by combining IHtmlPrimitives. Also, when we add a new HTML primitive, existing HTML producers are not affected. We used the Composite pattern to build a very modular class library.

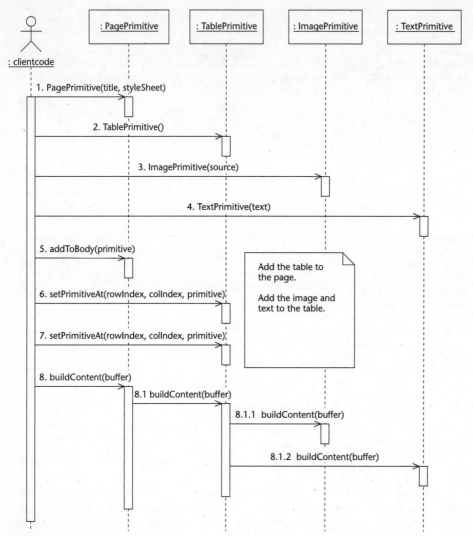

Figure 8.2   Creating a simple page.

Design for Goal 2: Keep HTML Production Simple

The second goal for the HTML production class library is to protect the view developers from HTML details and allow presentation developers to use the framework in a natural manner, without concern for the underlying HTML implementation. The first part of this goal can be met by dictating that all HTML tags are created inside of the buildContent method that each primitive implements. Encapsulation protects the user of the classes from the underlying complexity of the HTML.

Allowing the presentation developer to use the framework in a natural manner is a bit more complicated. The responsibility of each class and the methods for each primitive must be devised with the presentation developer in mind, not based on the HTML that they will produce. For example, an HTML input tag can be used for text input fields, check boxes, radio buttons, submit buttons, and reset buttons. So, a design that focuses on the HTML would have a class named InputPrimitive with methods for selecting the type, name, and value of the tag. This would be an improvement over hand-coding HTML, and it meets the encapsulation and modularity constraints on our design. However, it would only seem natural to developers who are already fluent in HTML!

Now, consider a design that focuses on the presentation developer. It should emphasize discrete user interface components without regard for the underlying HTML. So, it has more classes, since there are several distinct UI components involved. TextBox-Primitive encapsulates the details for building an HTML text entry box. It allows the user to specify a name, initial value, maximum length, width, and style class for the input box. It also allows the user to designate the text box as read-only. Similarly, the SubmitPrimitive class encapsulates the details of building the HTML for a submit button. It allows the user to specify a label and an internal name for the button. Behind the scenes, each class converts these attributes into tag-specific attributes. For example, both the initial value for the text box and the label for the submit button are used to populate the value attribute of an input tag. However, there is absolutely no reason why the user of either class should know or care about this bit of HTML trivia. Figure 8.3 shows several classes for producing HTML forms. Each of these primitives completely encapsulates the detailed logic that is required to build HTML for input forms. Perhaps a closer look at two of these classes will demonstrate the ease of use that comes from a focus on the user interface developer's needs.

TextBoxPrimitive contains a simple constructor, several configuration methods, and a method that adds the HTML for the input tag to the specified StringBuffer.

- public TextBoxPrimitive(String name)
- public void setMaximumLength(int maximumLength)
- public void setWidth(int width)
- public void setReadOnly()
- public void setHidden()
- public void setMasked()
- public void setStyle(Style style)
- public void buildContent(StringBuffer buffer)

SelectionPrimitive contains a simple constructor, a method that adds a value to the selection, and a method that adds the HTML for the select tag and enclosed option tags to the specified StringBuffer. An alternate implementation of SelectionPrimitive could easily use radio buttons instead of a pull-down selector without changing the public interface!

- public SelectionPrimitive(String name)
- public void setStyle(Style style)
- public void addValue(String displayValue, String dataValue, boolean selected)
- public void buildContent(StringBuffer buffer)

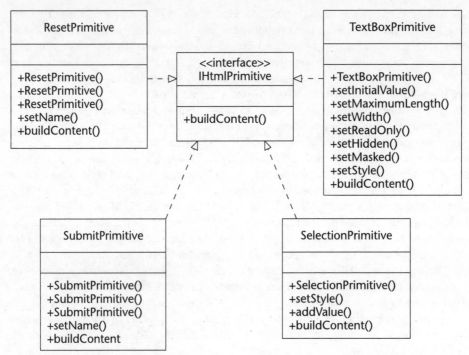

Figure 8.3   Primitives for HTML forms.

Let's evaluate our effectiveness. This design requires the class library developers to spend some time understanding how actual developers will use the class library and lots of time encapsulating the details of the HTML. However, this investment pays dramatic dividends when presentation developers actually start building the user interface for various use cases. Assuming that the developer knows Java and understands the requirements, they can be very successful without knowing any HTML!

Design for Goal 3: Extensibility and Independence

Over time, the implementation of the different primitives in the class library will change. They will be adapted to provide more features and to keep up with the evolution of HTML and the browser's implementation of the HTML specification. These changes must not affect the presentation logic that uses the HTML production class library. Also, the class library must not depend on any application-specific classes. Fortunately, the first goal is easily met by requiring classes that use the library to depend solely on the public interface, without making any assumptions about the HTML that is produced. The second goal simply requires that the classes in the framework depend only on one another and on the core Java libraries. Each application-specific presentation layer depends on a set of application-specific HTML producers that in turn depend on the HTML primitives. This allows presentation developers to leverage the class library to create their own unique and reusable HTML production components, such as navigation bars, data display tables, and lists of links.

Design for HTML Production

Now that we have an approach to meet the design goals, let's organize the different types of primitives into packages.

Core

There are some design elements that are used by all of the other HTML production classes. First, the IHtmlPrimitive interface defines the one method, buildContent, which every HTML primitive overrides to add its HTML to the collaborative effort of the composite. The Style class is a simple enumerated type that provides a list of style names for use with Cascading Style Sheets (CSS). Cascading Style Sheets, as defined by the World Wide Web Consortium (www.w3c.org), allow Web developers to define a single set of appearance rules that are used throughout a set of Web pages. Unlike most enumerated types [Bloch, 2001, p. 104], the Style class is not final and its constructor is protected rather than private. This allows application developers to define their own styles in an enumerated type that extends the Style class. Finally, the Formatting class provides some convenience methods for formatting attributes from different data types. Figure 8.4 shows these classes.

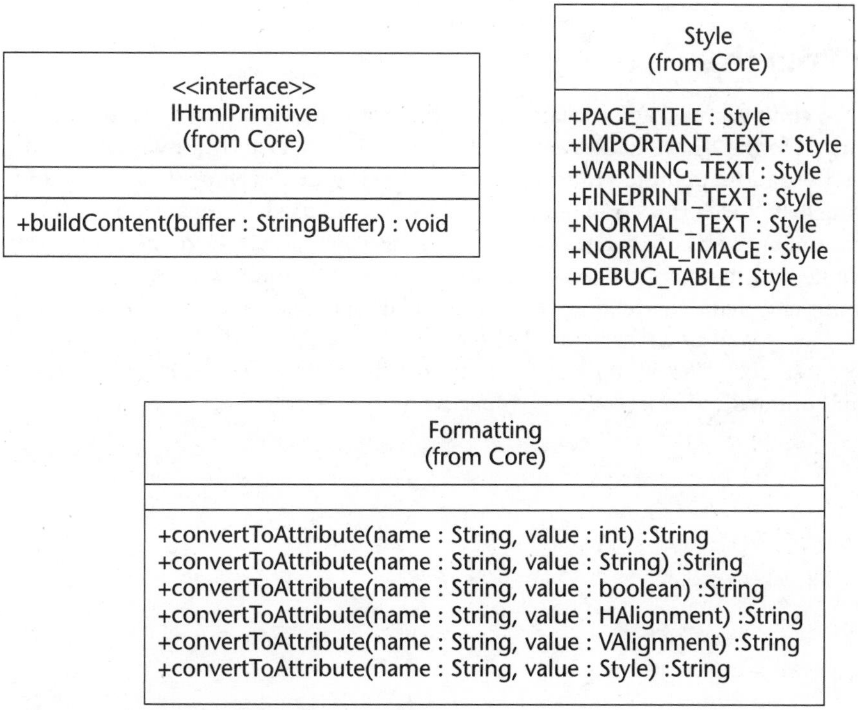

```
+--------------------------------------------+    +--------------------------------------+
|             <<interface>>                  |    |               Style                  |
|             IHtmlPrimitive                 |    |             (from Core)               |
|             (from Core)                    |    +--------------------------------------+
+--------------------------------------------+    | +PAGE_TITLE : Style                  |
+--------------------------------------------+    | +IMPORTANT_TEXT : Style              |
| +buildContent(buffer : StringBuffer) : void|    | +WARNING_TEXT : Style                |
+--------------------------------------------+    | +FINEPRINT_TEXT : Style              |
                                                  | +NORMAL _TEXT : Style                |
                                                  | +NORMAL_IMAGE : Style                |
                                                  | +DEBUG_TABLE : Style                 |
                                                  +--------------------------------------+
```

```
+------------------------------------------------------------------------+
|                              Formatting                                |
|                             (from Core)                                |
+------------------------------------------------------------------------+
+------------------------------------------------------------------------+
| +convertToAttribute(name : String, value : int) :String               |
| +convertToAttribute(name : String, value : String) :String            |
| +convertToAttribute(name : String, value : boolean) :String           |
| +convertToAttribute(name : String, value : HAlignment) :String        |
| +convertToAttribute(name : String, value : VAlignment) :String        |
| +convertToAttribute(name : String, value : Style) :String             |
+------------------------------------------------------------------------+
```

Figure 8.4   The HtmlPrimitives.Core classes.

Content Primitives

The Content package contains classes, as shown in Figure 8.5, for creating traditional HTML content, such as text, images, links to other resources, paragraphs, and spans. While far from complete, these classes will generate all of the HTML that we need for the sample application.

TextPrimitive is limited to plaintext and line breaks. TextPrimitives are ideal for use inside of primitives that restrict their content, such as LinkPrimitives that only allow plaintext and images. LinkPrimitive also allows the applications developer to pick a style from the Style enumerated type or from an application-specific extension of the Style enumerated type. ImagePrimitive allows the applications developer to specify the source of the image, provide descriptive text, and control the size. It also provides methods to select the style. It does not include any methods to control the spacing around the image or the background color, since those attributes are part of the style. This helps maintain a consistent look for similar images across the site. Paragraph-Primitive and SpanPrimitive apply styles to blocks of content. ParagraphPrimitives can contain any primitive, while SpanPrimitives are limited to text. In this case, Span-Primitive is more restrictive than the underlying HTML tag, which can contain many other tags. It is important to keep the interface for each primitive focused on the needs of the presentation developer and on the usability of the class library, rather than mirroring HTML.

Form Primitives

The FormPrimitives package contains all of the primitives that are needed to build HTML input forms. These classes are shown in Figure 8.6. FormPrimitive captures the URL that the data is submitted to and allows the application developer to add any arbitrary content to the form. For example, a table may be used to organize text boxes, selectors, and buttons into an orderly pattern. TextBoxPrimitive has methods to set the initial value and maximum size for text box entries. It also allows the developer to mask input and make the text box read-only or hidden. SelectionPrimitive produces the HTML for a pull-down selector. It allows the developer to add values for the end user to choose from. The SubmitPrimitive and ResetPrimitive classes create the HTML for submit buttons and reset buttons, respectively.

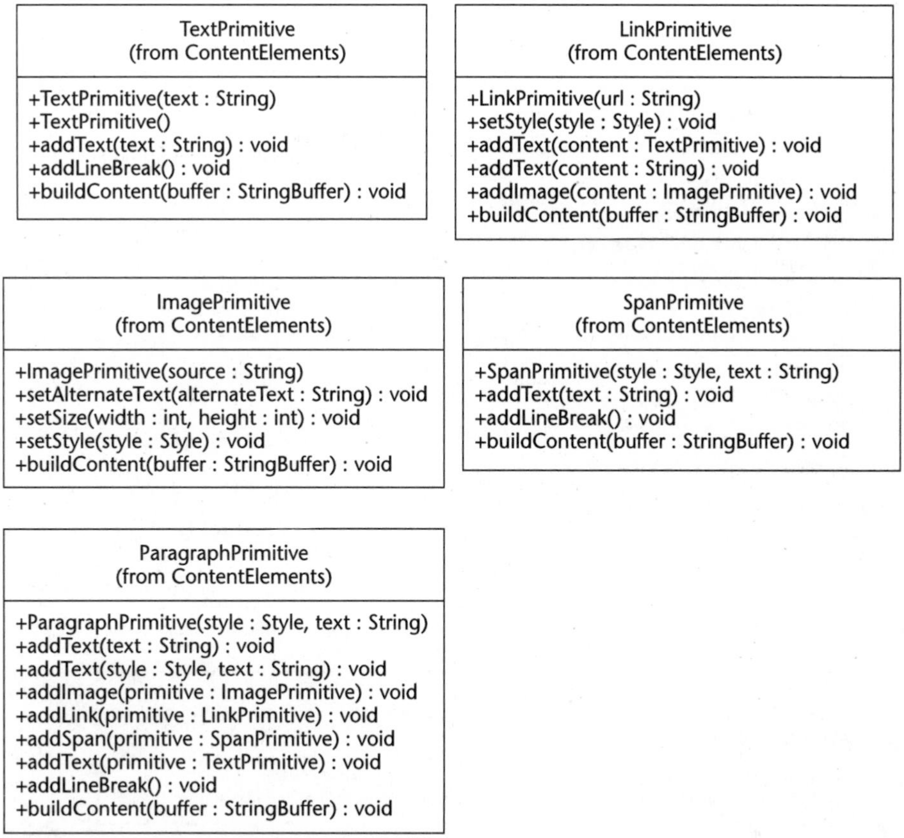

```
┌─────────────────────────────────────────┐   ┌─────────────────────────────────────────────┐
│             TextPrimitive                 │   │               LinkPrimitive                   │
│          (from ContentElements)           │   │           (from ContentElements)              │
├─────────────────────────────────────────┤   ├─────────────────────────────────────────────┤
│ +TextPrimitive(text : String)             │   │ +LinkPrimitive(url : String)                  │
│ +TextPrimitive()                          │   │ +setStyle(style : Style) : void               │
│ +addText(text : String) : void            │   │ +addText(content : TextPrimitive) : void      │
│ +addLineBreak() : void                    │   │ +addText(content : String) : void             │
│ +buildContent(buffer : StringBuffer) : void│  │ +addImage(content : ImagePrimitive) : void    │
│                                           │   │ +buildContent(buffer : StringBuffer) : void   │
└─────────────────────────────────────────┘   └─────────────────────────────────────────────┘

┌─────────────────────────────────────────────┐   ┌─────────────────────────────────────────────┐
│               ImagePrimitive                  │   │               SpanPrimitive                   │
│           (from ContentElements)              │   │           (from ContentElements)              │
├─────────────────────────────────────────────┤   ├─────────────────────────────────────────────┤
│ +ImagePrimitive(source : String)              │   │ +SpanPrimitive(style : Style, text : String)  │
│ +setAlternateText(alternateText : String) : void│ │ +addText(text : String) : void               │
│ +setSize(width : int, height : int) : void    │   │ +addLineBreak() : void                        │
│ +setStyle(style : Style) : void               │   │ +buildContent(buffer : StringBuffer) : void   │
│ +buildContent(buffer : StringBuffer) : void   │   │                                               │
└─────────────────────────────────────────────┘   └─────────────────────────────────────────────┘

┌─────────────────────────────────────────────┐
│             ParagraphPrimitive                │
│          (from ContentElements)               │
├─────────────────────────────────────────────┤
│ +ParagraphPrimitive(style : Style, text : String)│
│ +addText(text : String) : void               │
│ +addText(style : Style, text : String) : void │
│ +addImage(primitive : ImagePrimitive) : void  │
│ +addLink(primitive : LinkPrimitive) : void     │
│ +addSpan(primitive : SpanPrimitive) : void     │
│ +addText(primitive : TextPrimitive) : void     │
│ +addLineBreak() : void                        │
│ +buildContent(buffer : StringBuffer) : void   │
└─────────────────────────────────────────────┘
```

Figure 8.5   The HtmlPrimitives.Content classes.

Layout Primitives

The Layout package contains several classes for combining and controlling the relative positioning of HTML components. As seen in Figure 8.7, the simplest, Composite-Primitive, simply adds primitives sequentially to form a composite. TablePrimitive allows a developer to control the positioning of primitives down to the pixel. Other than table alignment and column span, HTML 4 allows a developer to capture all table-related appearance decisions in the style sheet. This implementation forces the application developer to follow this approach. TablePrimitive uses two classes with package visibility, RowPrimitive and CellPrimitive, as internal helper classes. HAlignment and VAlignment are enumerated types for aligning the table within its enclosing area and each cell within its enclosing row.

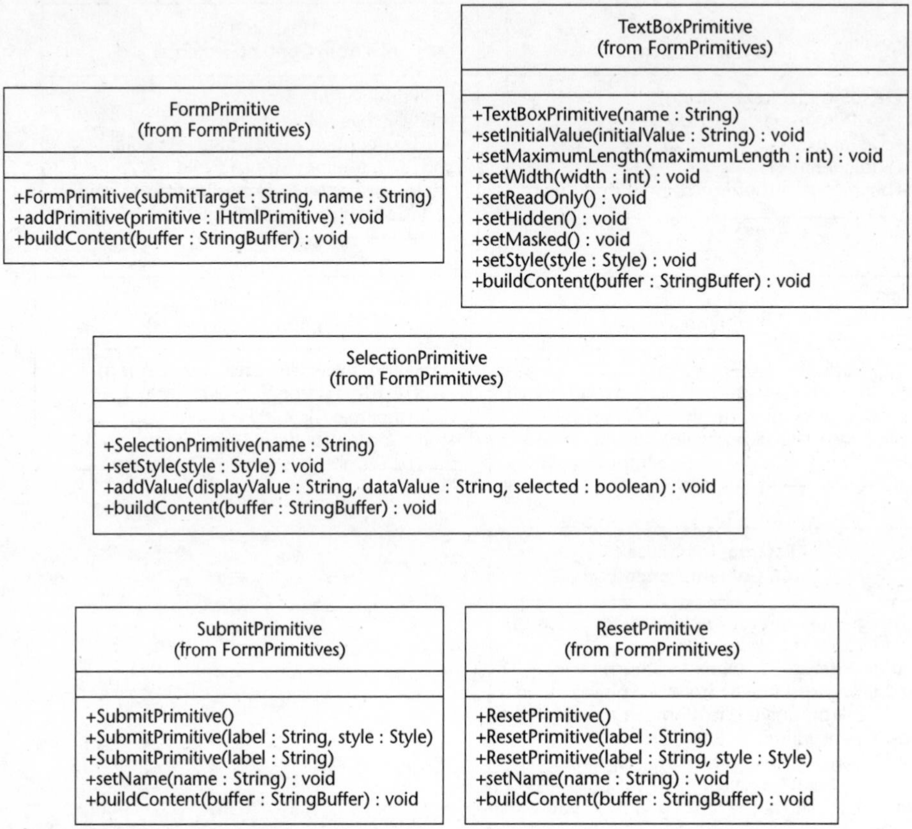

```
                                          ┌──────────────────────────────────────┐
                                          │          TextBoxPrimitive              │
                                          │        (from FormPrimitives)           │
                                          ├──────────────────────────────────────┤
                                          │                                        │
                                          ├──────────────────────────────────────┤
                                          │ +TextBoxPrimitive(name : String)       │
                                          │ +setInitialValue(initialValue : String) : void │
 ┌──────────────────────────────────────┐│ +setMaximumLength(maximumLength : int) : void │
 │            FormPrimitive              ││ +setWidth(width : int) : void          │
 │         (from FormPrimitives)         ││ +setReadOnly() : void                  │
 ├──────────────────────────────────────┤│ +setHidden() : void                    │
 │                                        │ +setMasked() : void                    │
 ├──────────────────────────────────────┤│ +setStyle(style : Style) : void        │
 │ +FormPrimitive(submitTarget : String, name : String) │ +buildContent(buffer : StringBuffer) : void │
 │ +addPrimitive(primitive : IHtmlPrimitive) : void │                               │
 │ +buildContent(buffer : StringBuffer) : void │
 └──────────────────────────────────────┘
```

```
         ┌──────────────────────────────────────────────────────────────┐
         │                      SelectionPrimitive                        │
         │                    (from FormPrimitives)                       │
         ├──────────────────────────────────────────────────────────────┤
         │                                                                │
         ├──────────────────────────────────────────────────────────────┤
         │ +SelectionPrimitive(name : String)                             │
         │ +setStyle(style : Style) : void                                │
         │ +addValue(displayValue : String, dataValue : String, selected : boolean) : void │
         │ +buildContent(buffer : StringBuffer) : void                    │
         └──────────────────────────────────────────────────────────────┘
```

```
 ┌──────────────────────────────────────┐  ┌──────────────────────────────────────┐
 │            SubmitPrimitive            │  │            ResetPrimitive             │
 │         (from FormPrimitives)         │  │         (from FormPrimitives)         │
 ├──────────────────────────────────────┤  ├──────────────────────────────────────┤
 │                                        │  │                                        │
 ├──────────────────────────────────────┤  ├──────────────────────────────────────┤
 │ +SubmitPrimitive()                     │  │ +ResetPrimitive()                      │
 │ +SubmitPrimitive(label : String, style : Style) │ +ResetPrimitive(label : String)        │
 │ +SubmitPrimitive(label : String)       │  │ +ResetPrimitive(label : String, style : Style) │
 │ +setName(name : String) : void         │  │ +setName(name : String) : void         │
 │ +buildContent(buffer : StringBuffer) : void │ +buildContent(buffer : StringBuffer) : void │
 └──────────────────────────────────────┘  └──────────────────────────────────────┘
```

Figure 8.6   The FormPrimitives classes.

TIP Cascading Style Sheets are the right place to capture appearance decisions! By their very nature, styles force developers to think in terms of common elements that should look the same. This encourages consistency across different pages of the site and allows enormous flexibility as developers move from functionality to aesthetics. Moving appearance-related decisions to style sheets also reduces clutter in the API of the primitives.

Implementation

The following sections show reasonable implementations for the HTML production design. These implementations are used in the servlet and JSP sections of this chapter and also in the Timecard sample.

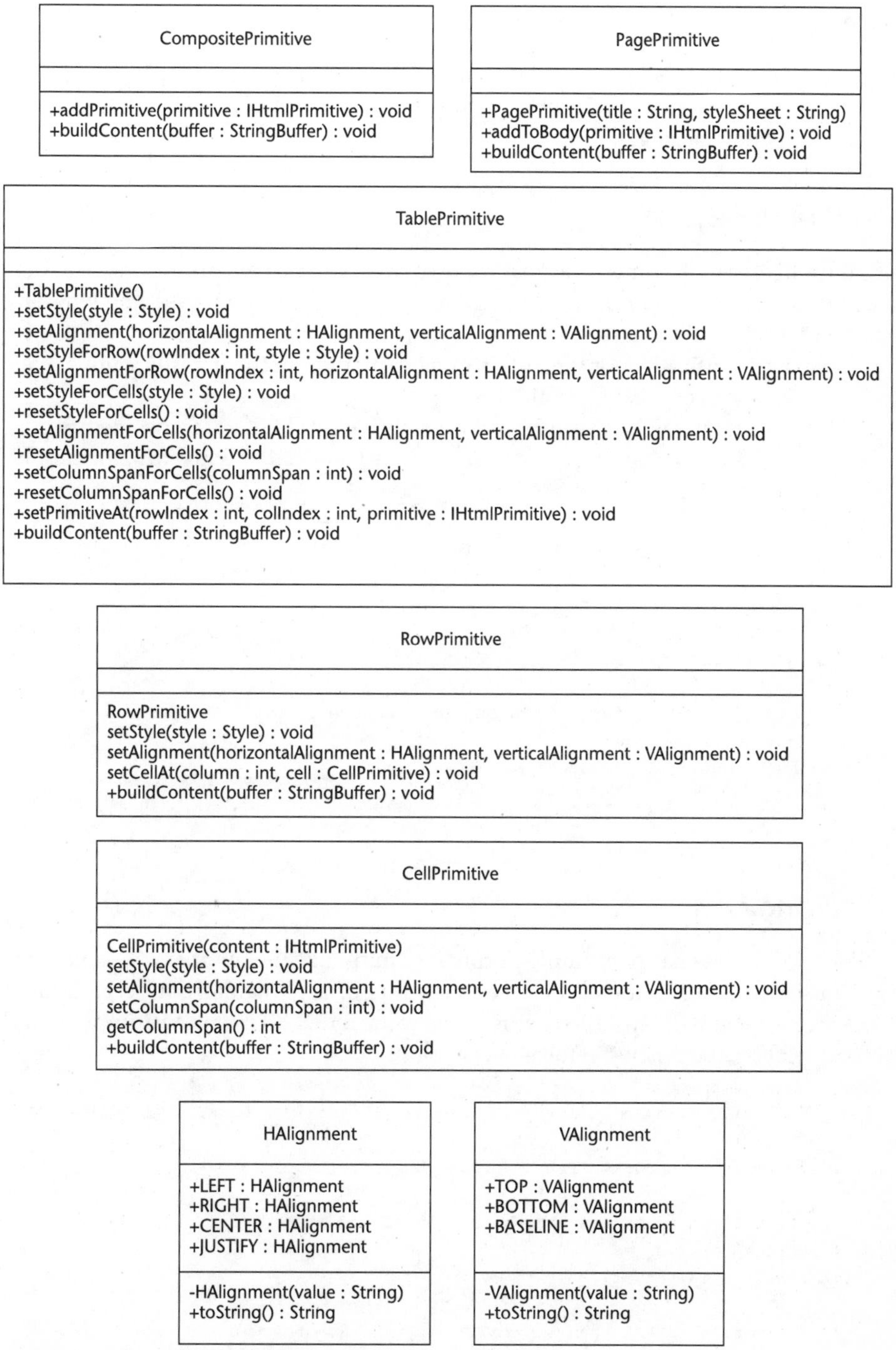

CompositePrimitive
+addPrimitive(primitive : IHtmlPrimitive) : void +buildContent(buffer : StringBuffer) : void

PagePrimitive
+PagePrimitive(title : String, styleSheet : String) +addToBody(primitive : IHtmlPrimitive) : void +buildContent(buffer : StringBuffer) : void

TablePrimitive
+TablePrimitive() +setStyle(style : Style) : void +setAlignment(horizontalAlignment : HAlignment, verticalAlignment : VAlignment) : void +setStyleForRow(rowIndex : int, style : Style) : void +setAlignmentForRow(rowIndex : int, horizontalAlignment : HAlignment, verticalAlignment : VAlignment) : void +setStyleForCells(style : Style) : void +resetStyleForCells() : void +setAlignmentForCells(horizontalAlignment : HAlignment, verticalAlignment : VAlignment) : void +resetAlignmentForCells() : void +setColumnSpanForCells(columnSpan : int) : void +resetColumnSpanForCells() : void +setPrimitiveAt(rowIndex : int, colIndex : int, primitive : IHtmlPrimitive) : void +buildContent(buffer : StringBuffer) : void

RowPrimitive
RowPrimitive setStyle(style : Style) : void setAlignment(horizontalAlignment : HAlignment, verticalAlignment : VAlignment) : void setCellAt(column : int, cell : CellPrimitive) : void +buildContent(buffer : StringBuffer) : void

CellPrimitive
CellPrimitive(content : IHtmlPrimitive) setStyle(style : Style) : void setAlignment(horizontalAlignment : HAlignment, verticalAlignment : VAlignment) : void setColumnSpan(columnSpan : int) : void getColumnSpan() : int +buildContent(buffer : StringBuffer) : void

HAlignment
+LEFT : HAlignment +RIGHT : HAlignment +CENTER : HAlignment +JUSTIFY : HAlignment
-HAlignment(value : String) +toString() : String

VAlignment
+TOP : VAlignment +BOTTOM : VAlignment +BASELINE : VAlignment
-VAlignment(value : String) +toString() : String

Figure 8.7   The HtmlPrimitives.Layout classes.

Core

The classes and interface in the HtmlPrimitive.Core package are relatively straightforward. They are also crucial to the utility and readability of all of the other classes in the HTML production packages.

IHtmlPrimitive.java

IHtmlPrimitive is the interface that allows the composite primitives, such as TablePrimitive and PagePrimitive to include other primitives without knowing any implementation details about them. Application developers can easily add any combination of existing primitives or their own implementations of the IHtmlPrimitive interface to any existing composite primitive.

The buildContent method appends the primitive's HTML to a specified String-Buffer. This reduces some of the performance impact associated with string manipulation and concatenation.

```
package com.wiley.compBooks.EJwithUML.Base.HtmlPrimitives.Core;

/** The IHtmlPrimitive interface defines the one method that
 *  all primitives must override.*/
public interface IHtmlPrimitive
{
  /** Build the content for this primitive and append it to
   *  the specified buffer.*/
  public void buildContent(StringBuffer buffer);
}
```

Formatting.java

The Formatting class has one simple purpose: to minimize the number of escape characters in the code. Each method converts a value of a particular data type into an HTML attribute with the specified name. If the value indicates that the attribute should not be displayed, the method returns "".

```
package com.wiley.compBooks.EJwithUML.Base.HtmlPrimitives.Core;

import com.wiley.compBooks.EJwithUML.Base.HtmlPrimitives.Layout.*;

/** The Formatting class contains some convenience methods for
 *  formatting attributes.*/
public class Formatting
{
  /** if the value is -1 then ignore the attribute. Otherwise
   *  include attribute name with value in quotes.*/
  public static String convertToAttribute(String name, int value)
  {
    return (value == -1) ? "" : " " +name+ "=\"" +value+ "\"";
  }
```

```java
/** Include attribute name with value in quotes*/
public static String convertToAttribute(String name, String value)
{
  return (value == null) ? "" : " " +name+ "=\"" +value+ "\"";
}


/** Include the attribute if the value is true.*/
public static String convertToAttribute(String name, boolean value)
{
  return (value == false) ? "" : " "+name;
}


/** Include attribute name with value in quotes*/
public static String convertToAttribute(String name, HAlignment value)
{
  return (value == null) ? "" : " " +name+ "=\"" +value+ "\"";
}


/** Include attribute name with value in quotes*/
public static String convertToAttribute(String name, VAlignment value)
{
  return (value == null) ? "" : " " +name+ "=\"" +value+ "\"";
}


/** Include attribute name with value in quotes */
public static String convertToAttribute(String name, Style value)
{
  return (value == null) ? "" : " " +name+ "=\"" +value+ "\"";
}
}
```

Style.java

The Style class is an enumerated type of style names for use with CSS. However, each application needs to define its own styles. So, Style is an extendable enumerated type. Its constructor is protected, rather than private as is the norm with enumerated types, and the class is not final. Style does offer a few relatively generic style names and a useful style for debugging layout tables.

```java
package com.wiley.compBooks.EJwithUML.Base.HtmlPrimitives.Core;

/**
 * Style is an extendable enumerated type that captures some
 * basic styles. Most applications should extend this class
 * with a set of application-specific styles.
 **/
public class Style
{
  private String value;

  /** Construct a Style object with the specified style class
   *  as its value. */
```

```
    protected Style(String style)
    {
      this.value = style;
    }

    public String toString()
    {
      return this.value;
    }

    public final static Style PAGE_TITLE = new Style("page_title");
    public final static Style IMPORTANT_TEXT = new Style("important_text");
    public final static Style WARNING_TEXT = new Style("warning_text");
    public final static Style NORMAL_TEXT = new Style("normal_text");
    public final static Style FINEPRINT_TEXT = new Style("fineprint_text");

    public final static Style NORMAL_IMAGE = new Style("normal_image");
    public final static Style DEBUG_TABLE = new Style("debug_table");


}
```

Content Elements

Content primitives create traditional HTML content, such as text, images, links to other resources, paragraphs, and spans. These primitives can be used inside of layout primitives to build complex HTML structures.

TextPrimitive.java

The TextPrimitive's sole purpose is to produce nothing but simple text. This plain-text can then be added to other style-aware primitives, such as SpanPrimitive or LinkPrimitive.

```
package com.wiley.compBooks.EJwithUML.Base.HtmlPrimitives.ContentElements;

import com.wiley.compBooks.EJwithUML.Base.HtmlPrimitives.Core.*;
import java.util.*;

/**
 * The TextPrimitive class encapsulates the details of building
 * simple text.
 * */
public class TextPrimitive implements IHtmlPrimitive
{
  private StringBuffer content = new StringBuffer();

  /** Construct a TextPrimitive object with the specified text
   *  as its initial content.*/
  public TextPrimitive(String text)
  {
    this.content.append(text);
```

```
  }

  /** Construct a TextPrimitive object with no initial content. */
  public TextPrimitive()
  {
  }

  /** Add the specified text to the cummulative content. */
  public void addText(String text)
  {
    this.content.append(text);
  }

  /** Add a line break to the cummulative content.*/
  public void addLineBreak()
  {
    this.content.append("</br>");
  }

  /** Build the content for this primitive and append it to the
   *  specified buffer.*/
  public void buildContent(StringBuffer buffer)
  {
    buffer.append(this.content.toString());
  }
}
```

ImagePrimitive.java

The ImagePrimitive class produces the HTML for an img tag. It allows the width and height of the image to be set directly through the setSize method. All other appearance choices are implemented by setting a style name for the ImagePrimitive and then defining the style in a style sheet. It uses the static attribute formatting methods from the Formatting class to build the attributes for the img tag.

```
package com.wiley.compBooks.EJwithUML.Base.HtmlPrimitives.ContentElements;

import com.wiley.compBooks.EJwithUML.Base.HtmlPrimitives.Core.*;
import java.util.*;

/**
 * The ImagePrimitive class encapsulates the details of building
 * the HTML for an img tag.
 */
public class ImagePrimitive implements IHtmlPrimitive
{
  private String source;
  private String alternateText;
  private Style style;
  private int width = -1;
  private int height = -1;
```

```
/** Construct an ImagePrimitive with the specified source URL. */
public ImagePrimitive(String source)
{
  this.source = source;
}

/** Specifies the text to use if the image is not displayed or
 *  to display to augment the image in a ToolTip.*/
public void setAlternateText(String alternateText)
{
  this.alternateText = alternateText;
}

/** Specifies the size in pixels of the image */
public void setSize(int width, int height)
{
  this.width = width;
  this.height = height;
}

/** Specify the style class that is applied to the image. */
public void setStyle(Style style)
{
  this.style = style;
}

/** Build the content for this primitive and append it to
 *  the specified buffer.*/
public void buildContent(StringBuffer buffer)
{
  String width_string = Formatting.convertToAttribute("width", width);
  String height_string = Formatting.convertToAttribute("height", height);
  String src_string = Formatting.convertToAttribute("src", source);
  String alt_string = Formatting.convertToAttribute("alt", alternateText);
  String class_string = Formatting.convertToAttribute("class", style);

  buffer.append("<img"
+src_string+width_string+height_string+alt_string+class_string+ "></img>");
  }
}
```

LinkPrimitive.java

The LinkPrimitive class is a very simple composite that only accepts ImagePrimitives, TextPrimitives, and simple text via its add methods. This restriction prevents developers from adding arbitrary primitives to a link. While most browsers will attempt to do something reasonable if arbitrary content is placed inside a link, the HTML 4 specification does limit the contents of an "a href" tag. From a purely practical perspective, it is difficult to imagine really needing to put anything else inside of a link; so following the specification does not seem particularly burdensome.

```java
package com.wiley.compBooks.EJwithUML.Base.HtmlPrimitives.ContentElements;

import com.wiley.compBooks.EJwithUML.Base.HtmlPrimitives.Core.*;
import java.util.*;

/**
 * The LinkPrimitive class encapsulates the details of building
 * an a href tag for a simple link. It limits the content to text
 * and images.
 * */
public class LinkPrimitive implements IHtmlPrimitive
{
  private String url;
  private Style style;
  private List producers = new ArrayList();

  /** Construct a LinkPrimitive instance with the specified URL. */
  public LinkPrimitive(String url)
  {
    this.url = url;
  }

  /** Set the style for this link. */
  public void setStyle(Style style)
  {
    this.style = style;
  }

  /** Add a TextPrimitive object to this link. */
  public void addText(TextPrimitive content)
  {
    producers.add(content);
  }

  /** Add some text to this link. */
  public void addText(String content)
  {
    producers.add(new TextPrimitive(content));
  }

  /** Add an ImagePrimitive object to this link. */
  public void addImage(ImagePrimitive content)
  {
    producers.add(content);
  }


  /** Build the content for this primitive and append it to
   *  the specified buffer.*/
  public void buildContent(StringBuffer buffer)
  {
    String href_string = Formatting.convertToAttribute("href", url);
    buffer.append("<a" +href_string+ ">");
```

```
        Iterator producers_iterator = producers.iterator();
        while (producers_iterator.hasNext())
        {
          IHtmlPrimitive content = (IHtmlPrimitive) producers_iterator.next();
          content.buildContent(buffer);
        }

        buffer.append("</a>");
    }


}
```

SpanPrimitive.java

The SpanPrimitive class is a very simple primitive that builds the HTML for a block of text that may have a single style. SpanPrimitives cannot contain any other primitives, just text and line breaks.

```
package com.wiley.compBooks.EJwithUML.Base.HtmlPrimitives.ContentElements;

import com.wiley.compBooks.EJwithUML.Base.HtmlPrimitives.Core.*;
import java.util.*;

/** The SpanPrimitive class encapsulates the logic for creating
 *  a span that encloses text. */
public class SpanPrimitive implements IHtmlPrimitive
{
  private StringBuffer content = new StringBuffer();

  /** Construct a SpanPrimitive with the specified style and text.*/
  public SpanPrimitive(Style style, String text)
  {
    String style_string = Formatting.convertToAttribute("class", style);
    content.append("<span " +style_string+ ">");
    if (text != null)
    {
      content.append(text);
    }
  }

  /** Add the specified text to this SpanPrimitive.*/
  public void addText(String text)
  {
    content.append(text);
  }

  /** Add a line break to this SpanPrimitive. */
  public void addLineBreak()
  {
    content.append("</br>");
  }
```

```
      /** Build the content for this primitive and append it to the
       *  specified buffer.*/
      public void buildContent(StringBuffer buffer)
      {
        content.append("</span>\n");
        buffer.append(content.toString());
      }
    }
```

ParagraphPrimitive.java

ParagraphPrimitives can contain styled text, images, links, and spans. They cannot contain arbitrary primitives. Like the rest of the classes in the ContentElements package, ParagraphPrimitives produce the HTML for the actual content that is generally text and images with different styles.

```
package com.wiley.compBooks.EJwithUML.Base.HtmlPrimitives.ContentElements;

import com.wiley.compBooks.EJwithUML.Base.HtmlPrimitives.Core.*;
import java.util.*;

/** The ParagraphPrimitive class encapsulates the logic for
 *  creating a paragraph that encloses text, links, spans,
 *  and images. */
public class ParagraphPrimitive implements IHtmlPrimitive
{
  private List primitives = new ArrayList();
  private Style style;

  /** Construct a ParagraphPrimitive with the specified style and text.*/
  public ParagraphPrimitive(Style style, String text)
  {
    this.style = style;
    addText(text);
  }

  /** Add the specified text to this ParagraphPrimitive.*/
  public void addText(String text)
  {
    primitives.add(new TextPrimitive(text));
  }

  /** Add the specified text with the specified style.*/
  public void addText(Style style, String text)
  {
    primitives.add(new SpanPrimitive(style, text));
  }

  /** Add the specified primitive to this ParagraphPrimitive. */
  public void addImage(ImagePrimitive primitive)
  {
    primitives.add(primitive);
```

```
   }

   /** Add the specified primitive to this ParagraphPrimitive. */
   public void addLink(LinkPrimitive primitive)
   {
     primitives.add(primitive);
   }

   /** Add the specified primitive to this ParagraphPrimitive. */
   public void addSpan(SpanPrimitive primitive)
   {
     primitives.add(primitive);
   }

   /** Add the specified primitive to this ParagraphPrimitive.*/
   public void addText(TextPrimitive primitive)
   {
     primitives.add(primitive);
   }

   /** Add the a line break to this ParagraphPrimitive. */
   public void addLineBreak()
   {
     TextPrimitive text = new TextPrimitive();
     text.addLineBreak();
     primitives.add(text);
   }

   /** Build the content for this primitive and append it to
    *  the specified buffer.*/
   public void buildContent(StringBuffer buffer)
   {
     String style_string = Formatting.convertToAttribute("class", style);
     buffer.append("<p " +style_string+ ">");

     Iterator it = primitives.iterator();
     while (it.hasNext())
     {
       IHtmlPrimitive primitive = (IHtmlPrimitive) it.next();
       primitive.buildContent(buffer);
     }

     buffer.append("</p>\n");
   }
}
```

Form Primitives

The FormPrimitives package contains all of the primitives that are needed to build the HTML input forms.FormPrimitive.java.

The FormPrimitive class allows a developer to configure a form and then add any primitives to it. For instance, TablePrimitive may be used to arrange TextPrimitives,

TextBoxPrimitives, SelectionPrimitives, and a SubmitPrimitive to create a pleasant appearance for a simple form.

```
package com.wiley.compBooks.EJwithUML.Base.HtmlPrimitives.FormPrimitives;

import com.wiley.compBooks.EJwithUML.Base.HtmlPrimitives.Core.*;
import java.util.*;

/** The FormPrimitive encapsulates the details of building the HTML
 *  for an input form. */
public class FormPrimitive implements IHtmlPrimitive
{
  private String submitTarget;
  private String name;
  private ArrayList primitives = new ArrayList();

  /** Construct a FormPrimitive with the specified submit target
   *  and form name. */
  public FormPrimitive(String submitTarget, String name)
  {
    this.submitTarget = submitTarget;
    this.name = name;
  }

  /** Add the producer to this form. */
  public void addPrimitive(IHtmlPrimitive primitive)
  {
    this.primitives.add(primitive);
  }

  /** Build the content for this primitive and append it to
   *  the specified buffer.*/
  public void buildContent(StringBuffer buffer)
  {
    String name_string = Formatting.convertToAttribute("name", name);
    String action_string = Formatting.convertToAttribute("action",
submitTarget);
    buffer.append("<form" +name_string+action_string+ " method=POST>");

    // Add the HTML from each producer to the HTML for this producer.
    Iterator producersIterator = primitives.iterator();
    while (producersIterator.hasNext())
    {
      IHtmlPrimitive producer = (IHtmlPrimitive) producersIterator.next();
      producer.buildContent(buffer);
    }

    // End the form tag.
    buffer.append("</form>\n");
  }
}
```

TextBoxPrimitive.java

The TextBoxPrimitive class produces the HTML for an HTML text input field. It is intended for use inside of FormPrimitives.

```java
package com.wiley.compBooks.EJwithUML.Base.HtmlPrimitives.FormPrimitives;

import com.wiley.compBooks.EJwithUML.Base.HtmlPrimitives.Core.*;

/**
 * The TextBoxPrimitive class encapsulates the details of
 * building the HTML for a text entry box.
 */
public class TextBoxPrimitive implements IHtmlPrimitive
{
  private String name;
  private String type = "text";
  private String initialValue;
  private int maximumLength = -1;
  private int width = -1;
  private boolean readOnly = false;
  private Style style;

  /** Construct a TextBoxPrimitive with the specified name
   *  for the form element.*/
  public TextBoxPrimitive(String name)
  {
    this.name = name;
  }

  /** Set the initial value that is displayed when this
   *  TextBoxPrimitive is rendered. */
  public void setInitialValue(String initialValue)
  {
    this.initialValue = initialValue;
  }

  /** Set the maximum number of characters to accept. */
  public void setMaximumLength(int maximumLength)
  {
    this.maximumLength = maximumLength;
  }

  /** Set the width of the text box in characters. */
  public void setWidth(int width)
  {
    this.width = width;
  }

  /** Set the text box to read-only. */
  public void setReadOnly()
  {
    this.readOnly = true;
```

```
    }

    /** Hide the text box so that it is not rendered by the browser. */
    public void setHidden()
    {
        this.type = "hidden";
    }

    /** Mask the input to the browser to protect it from prying eyes. */
    public void setMasked()
    {
        this.type = "password";
    }

    /** Specify the style class that is applied to the text box. */
    public void setStyle(Style style)
    {
        this.style = style;
    }

    /** Build the content for this primitive and append it to the
     *  specified buffer.*/
    public void buildContent(StringBuffer buffer)
    {
        String type_string = Formatting.convertToAttribute("type", type);
        String name_string = Formatting.convertToAttribute("name", name);
        String value_string = Formatting.convertToAttribute("value", initialValue);
        String maxlength_string = Formatting.convertToAttribute("maxlength",
maximumLength);
        String size_string = Formatting.convertToAttribute("size", width);
        String read_only_string = Formatting.convertToAttribute("readonly",
readOnly);
        String style_string = Formatting.convertToAttribute("class", style);

        buffer.append("<input" +type_string+name_string+value_string+
                maxlength_string+size_string+read_only_string+style_string+ ">");
        buffer.append("</input>");
    }
}
```

SelectionPrimitive.java

The SelectionPrimitive class produces the HTML for a select tag complete with
options. It is intended for use within a FormPrimitive.

```
package com.wiley.compBooks.EJwithUML.Base.HtmlPrimitives.FormPrimitives;

import com.wiley.compBooks.EJwithUML.Base.HtmlPrimitives.Core.*;
import java.util.*;

/**
```

```
 * The SelectionPrimitive class encapsulates the details of
 * building the HTML for a pull-down selector widget.
 *
 */
public class SelectionPrimitive implements IHtmlPrimitive
{
  private String name;
  private Style style;

  private StringBuffer optionsBuffer = new StringBuffer();

  /** Construct a SelectionPrimitive with the specified name
   *  of the form input element. */
  public SelectionPrimitive(String name)
  {
    this.name = name;
  }

  /** Specify the style class that is applied to the selection. */
  public void setStyle(Style style)
  {
    this.style = style;
  }

  /** Add a value to the selector. */
  public void addValue(String displayValue, String dataValue, boolean selected)
  {
    String class_string = Formatting.convertToAttribute("class", style);
    String data_value_string = Formatting.convertToAttribute("value",
dataValue);
    String selected_string = Formatting.convertToAttribute("selected",
selected);
    optionsBuffer.append("<option"
+data_value_string+selected_string+class_string+ ">" +displayValue+
"</option>\n");
  }

  /** Build the content for this primitive and append it to
   *  the specified buffer.*/
  public void buildContent(StringBuffer buffer)
  {
    String name_string = Formatting.convertToAttribute("name", this.name);
    buffer.append("<select" +name_string+ ">\n");
    buffer.append(this.optionsBuffer.toString());
    buffer.append("</select>");
  }
}
```

SubmitPrimitive.java

The SubmitPrimitive class builds the HTML for a submit button. It is intended for use inside of a FormPrimitive.

```
package com.wiley.compBooks.EJwithUML.Base.HtmlPrimitives.FormPrimitives;

import com.wiley.compBooks.EJwithUML.Base.HtmlPrimitives.Core.*;

/**
 * The SubmitPrimitive class encapsulates the details of building
 * the HTML for a submit button.
 */
public class SubmitPrimitive implements IHtmlPrimitive
{
  private String label;
  private String name;
  private Style style;

  /** Construct a simple submit button with the default label. */
  public SubmitPrimitive()
  {
  }

  /** Construct a submit input with the specified label and style.*/
  public SubmitPrimitive(String label, Style style)
  {
    this.label = label;
    this.style = style;
  }

  /** Construct a submit input with the specified label.*/
  public SubmitPrimitive(String label)
  {
    this.label = label;
  }

  /** Set the name of this submit button for internal use. */
  public void setName(String name)
  {
    this.name = name;
  }

  /** Build the content for this primitive and append it to
   *  the specified buffer.*/
  public void buildContent(StringBuffer buffer)
  {
    String type_string = Formatting.convertToAttribute("type", "submit");
    String value_string = Formatting.convertToAttribute("value", this.label);
    String name_string = Formatting.convertToAttribute("name", this.name);
    String class_string = Formatting.convertToAttribute("class", this.style);
    buffer.append("<input" +type_string+value_string+name_string+class_
string+ ">");
    buffer.append("</input>");
  }

}
```

ResetPrimitive.java

The ResetPrimitive class produces the HTML for a simple reset button that returns all
input fields to their original state. It is intended for use inside of a FormPrimitive.

```java
package com.wiley.compBooks.EJwithUML.Base.HtmlPrimitives.FormPrimitives;

import com.wiley.compBooks.EJwithUML.Base.HtmlPrimitives.Core.*;

/**
 * The ResetPrimitive class encapsulates the details of
 * building the HTML for a reset button.
 *
 */
public class ResetPrimitive implements IHtmlPrimitive
{
  private String label;
  private String name;
  private Style style;

  /** Construct a simple reset button with the default label. */
  public ResetPrimitive()
  {

  }

  /** Construct a reset button with the specified label. */
  public ResetPrimitive(String label)
  {
    this.label = label;
  }

  /** Construct a reset button with the specified label and style. */
  public ResetPrimitive(String label, Style style)
  {
    this.label = label;
    this.style = style;
  }

  /** Set the name of this reset button for internal use. */
  public void setName(String name)
  {
    this.name = name;
  }

  /** Build the content for this primitive and append it to
   *  the specified buffer.*/
  public void buildContent(StringBuffer buffer)
  {
    String type_string = Formatting.convertToAttribute("type", "reset");
    String value_string = Formatting.convertToAttribute("value", this.label);
    String name_string = Formatting.convertToAttribute("name", this.name);
    String class_string = Formatting.convertToAttribute("class", this.style);
```

```
      buffer.append("<input" +type_string+value_string+name_string+class_
string+ ">");
      buffer.append("</input>");
   }


 }
```

Layout Primitives

The layout primitives build HTML that defines the relative positioning for chunks of HTML. Each layout primitive has methods to add other primitives. Layout primitives may be nested to form intricate structures, such as content within a table that is also part of a table that is used to structure a page.

The PagePrimitive class allows users to set the title for the page, specify a style sheet, and add primitives to the body of the page. It can be used as the basis for more complex application-specific pages.

```
package com.wiley.compBooks.EJwithUML.Base.HtmlPrimitives.Layout;

import com.wiley.compBooks.EJwithUML.Base.HtmlPrimitives.Core.*;
import java.util.*;

/** The PagePrimitive class encapsulates the details of
 *  building the HTML for a page. */
public class PagePrimitive implements IHtmlPrimitive
{
  private String title;
  private String styleSheet;
  private ArrayList primitives = new ArrayList();

  /** Construct an instance of PagePrimitive with the specified title. */
  public PagePrimitive(String title, String styleSheet)
  {
    this.title = title;
    this.styleSheet = styleSheet;
  }

  /** Add primitives to the body. */
  public void addToBody(IHtmlPrimitive primitive)
  {
    primitives.add(primitive);
  }

  /** Build the content for this primitive and append it to
   *  the specified buffer.*/
  public void buildContent(StringBuffer buffer)
  {
    // Add the head.
    buffer.append("<html>\n");
```

```
        buffer.append("<head>");
        buffer.append("<title>" +title+ "</title>");

        // Add a link to the style sheet.
        if (this.styleSheet != null)
        {
            String href_string = Formatting.convertToAttribute("href", styleSheet);
            buffer.append("<link rel=\"stylesheet\" type=\"text/css\" " +href_
string+ "></link>\n");
        }

        buffer.append("</head>\n");

        buffer.append("<body>\n");

        // Ask each primitive to add its HTML to the buffer.
        Iterator primitives_iterator = primitives.iterator();
        while (primitives_iterator.hasNext())
        {
            IHtmlPrimitive primitive = (IHtmlPrimitive) primitives_iterator.next();
            primitive.buildContent(buffer);
            buffer.append("\n");
        }

        // Close out the body and HTML elements.
        buffer.append("</body>\n");
        buffer.append("</html>");
    }
}
```

TablePrimitive.java

TablePrimitive allows a user to add primitives with precise positioning by specifying
the row and column index, setting the table alignment, cell alignment, and column
span, and manipulating the attributes of the specified style. Once an attribute is set in
one of the setXXXForCells methods, it is applied to each primitive as it is added to a
cell. This allows a user to set the cell-level attributes before adding a similar set of
primitives, regardless of their proximity or lack of proximity. With a little patience and
a basic understanding of style sheets, you can achieve some fairly sophisticated effects.

```
package com.wiley.compBooks.EJwithUML.Base.HtmlPrimitives.Layout;

import com.wiley.compBooks.EJwithUML.Base.HtmlPrimitives.Core.*;
import java.util.*;

/** The TablePrimitive class encapsulates the details of building the HTML
  *  for a table. */
public class TablePrimitive implements IHtmlPrimitive
{
    private HAlignment tableHorizontalAlignment;
    private VAlignment tableVerticalAlignment;
```

```java
    private Style tableStyle;

    private Style cellStyle;
    private HAlignment cellHorizontalAlignment;
    private VAlignment cellVerticalAlignment;
    private int cellColumnSpan = -1;

    private HashMap rows = new HashMap();
    private int maxRow = -1;

    /** Construct an empty TablePrimitive.*/
    public TablePrimitive()
    {
    }

    /** Set the style for the entire table. */
    public void setStyle(Style style)
    {
      this.tableStyle = style;
    }

    /** Set the horizontal and vertical alignment of the table. */
    public void setAlignment(HAlignment horizontalAlignment, VAlignment
verticalAlignment)
    {
      this.tableHorizontalAlignment = horizontalAlignment;
      this.tableVerticalAlignment = verticalAlignment;
    }

    /** Specify the style class that is applied to the specified row. */
    public void setStyleForRow(int rowIndex, Style style)
    {
      getRow(rowIndex).setStyle(style);
    }

    /** Specify the alignment for the specified row. */
    public void setAlignmentForRow(int rowIndex, HAlignment
horizontalAlignment, VAlignment verticalAlignment)
    {
      getRow(rowIndex).setAlignment(horizontalAlignment, verticalAlignment);
    }

    /** Specify the style class that is applied to cells as primitives are
added to them. */
    public void setStyleForCells(Style style)
    {
      this.cellStyle = style;
    }

    /** Reset the style class that is applied to cells as primitives are
added to them. */
    public void resetStyleForCells()
    {
```

```
      this.cellStyle = null;
  }


  /** Specify the alignment that is applied to cells as primitives are
added to them. */
  public void setAlignmentForCells(HAlignment horizontalAlignment,
VAlignment verticalAlignment)
  {
     this.cellHorizontalAlignment = horizontalAlignment;
     this.cellVerticalAlignment = verticalAlignment;
  }


  /** Reset the alignment that is applied to cells as primitives are
added to them. */
  public void resetAlignmentForCells()
  {
     this.cellHorizontalAlignment = null;
     this.cellVerticalAlignment = null;
  }


  /** Specify the column span that is applied to cells as primitives are
added to them. */
  public void setColumnSpanForCells(int columnSpan)
  {
     this.cellColumnSpan = columnSpan;
  }


  /** Reset the column span that is applied to cells as primitives are
added to them. */
  public void resetColumnSpanForCells()
  {
     this.cellColumnSpan = -1;
  }


  /** Insert the specified primitive at the specified location. */
  public void setPrimitiveAt(int rowIndex, int colIndex, IHtmlPrimitive
primitive)
  {
     CellPrimitive cell = new CellPrimitive(primitive);
     cell.setAlignment(cellHorizontalAlignment, cellVerticalAlignment);
     cell.setColumnSpan(cellColumnSpan);
     cell.setStyle(cellStyle);

     RowPrimitive row = getRow(rowIndex);
     row.setCellAt(colIndex, cell);
  }


  /** Build the content for this primitive and append it to the specified
buffer.*/
  public void buildContent(StringBuffer buffer)
  {
     String class_string = Formatting.convertToAttribute("class", tableStyle);
```

```
        String align_string = Formatting.convertToAttribute("align",
    tableHorizontalAlignment);
        String valign_string = Formatting.convertToAttribute("valign",
    tableVerticalAlignment);
        buffer.append("<table" +class_string+align_string+valign_string+ ">\n");

        int ctr = 0;
        while (ctr <= maxRow)
        {
          RowPrimitive row = (RowPrimitive) rows.get(""+ctr);
          if (row != null)
          {
            row.buildContent(buffer);
            buffer.append("\n");
          }
          else
          {
            buffer.append("<tr></tr>\n");
          }
          ctr++;
        }

        buffer.append("</table>\n");
    }

    private RowPrimitive getRow(int row_index)
    {
      String key = ""+row_index;
      if (!rows.containsKey(key))
      {
        RowPrimitive row = new RowPrimitive();
        rows.put(key, row);
        maxRow = Math.max(maxRow, row_index);
      }

      return (RowPrimitive) rows.get(key);
    }
}
```

RowPrimitive.java

RowPrimitive is never accessed directly. It is a helper class for TablePrimitive and is only visible within the com.wiley.compBooks.EJwithUML.Base.HtmlPrimitives.Layout package. It stores CellPrimitives in a HashMap and renders the HTML for a <tr> tag in the buildContent method.

```
package com.wiley.compBooks.EJwithUML.Base.HtmlPrimitives.Layout;

import com.wiley.compBooks.EJwithUML.Base.HtmlPrimitives.Core.*;
import java.util.*;
```

```java
class RowPrimitive implements IHtmlPrimitive
{
  private Style style;
  private HAlignment horizontalAlignment;
  private VAlignment verticalAlignment;
  private HashMap cells = new HashMap();
  private int maxColumn = -1;

  RowPrimitive()
  {
  }

  /** Specify the style class that is applied to the cell. */
  void setStyle(Style style)
  {
    this.style = style;
  }

  void setAlignment(HAlignment horizontalAlignment, VAlignment
verticalAlignment)
  {
    this.horizontalAlignment = horizontalAlignment;
    this.verticalAlignment = verticalAlignment;
  }

  void setCellAt(int column, CellPrimitive cell)
  {
    cells.put(""+column, cell);
    maxColumn = Math.max(maxColumn, column);
  }

  /** Build the content for this primitive and append it to
   *  the specified buffer.*/
  public void buildContent(StringBuffer buffer)
  {
    String class_string = Formatting.convertToAttribute("class", style);
    String align_string = Formatting.convertToAttribute("align",
horizontalAlignment);
    String valign_string = Formatting.convertToAttribute("valign",
verticalAlignment);

    buffer.append("<tr" +class_string+align_string+valign_string+ ">");

    // Add cells.
    int ctr = 0;
    while (ctr <= maxColumn)
    {
      CellPrimitive cell = (CellPrimitive) cells.get(""+ctr);
      if (cell != null)
      {
        cell.buildContent(buffer);
        ctr += cell.getColumnSpan();
      }
```

```
      else
      {
        buffer.append("<td></td>");
        ctr++;
      }
    }

    buffer.append("</tr>");
  }
}
```

CellPrimitive.java

CellPrimitive is never accessed directly. It is a helper class for TablePrimitive and is only visible within the com.wiley.compBooks.EJwithUML.Base.HtmlPrimitives.Layout package. It stores a single primitive and renders the HTML for a <td> tag in the build-Content method.

```
package com.wiley.compBooks.EJwithUML.Base.HtmlPrimitives.Layout;

import com.wiley.compBooks.EJwithUML.Base.HtmlPrimitives.Core.*;

/** The CellPrimitive class encapsulates the logic for producing
 *  cells within a table.*/
class CellPrimitive implements IHtmlPrimitive
{
  private Style style;
  private HAlignment horizontalAlignment;
  private VAlignment verticalAlignment;
  private int columnSpan = -1;
  private IHtmlPrimitive content;

  /** Construct a cell primitive with the specified primitive
   *  as its content. */
  CellPrimitive(IHtmlPrimitive content)
  {
    this.content = content;
  }

  /** Specify the style class that is applied to the cell. */
  void setStyle(Style style)
  {
    this.style = style;
  }

  /** Set the horizontal and vertical alignment of the contents
   *  of the cell. */
  void setAlignment(HAlignment horizontalAlignment, VAlignment
verticalAlignment)
  {
    this.horizontalAlignment = horizontalAlignment;
```

```
          this.verticalAlignment = verticalAlignment;
      }


      /** Set the number of columns that this cell should span. */
      void setColumnSpan(int columnSpan)
      {
          this.columnSpan = columnSpan;
      }

      // return column span, but return 1 if it is not set.
      int getColumnSpan()
      {
          return Math.max(this.columnSpan, 1);
      }

      /** Build the content for this primitive and append it to
       *  the specified buffer.*/
      public void buildContent(StringBuffer buffer)
      {
          String class_string = Formatting.convertToAttribute("class", style);
          String align_string = Formatting.convertToAttribute("align",
      horizontalAlignment);
          String valign_string = Formatting.convertToAttribute("valign",
      verticalAlignment);
          String colspan_string = Formatting.convertToAttribute("colspan",
      columnSpan);

          buffer.append("<td" +class_string+align_string+valign_string+colspan_
      string+ ">");
          content.buildContent(buffer);
          buffer.append("</td>");
      }
  }
```

Unit Testing HTML Primitives

Unit testing HTML primitives is absolutely essential, because these primitives will be used by creative developers to obtain imaginative effects that the developer of the primitive cannot possibly anticipate. So, it is very important for the primitives to work well with a wide variety of configurations. Also, it is important to verify that the primitives are not compromised by related developments. Unfortunately, correctness for HTML primitives is somewhat subjective. The best we can do is assert that a primitive is still producing the same HTML that a knowledgeable person has previously verified as correct and aesthetically pleasing. The TestFileSet class allows primitives to be tested in this way as part of a regular JUnit testing discipline. The following snippet shows a PagePrimitive that contains an empty TablePrimitive. The resulting HTML is captured in a StringBuffer that is passed to the testFileSet for verification against an existing file named goldEmpty.html. If goldEmpty.html is not found, then the test will fail and the tester must manually examine the output file. However, if the gold file is present, then TestFileSet will compare each line until it detects a difference. If there are no differences, then the code will pass the test.

Snippet from Unit Test

```
StringBuffer buffer = new StringBuffer();
TablePrimitive table = new TablePrimitive();

PagePrimitive page = new PagePrimitive("test", "../../Default.css");
page.addToBody(table);
page.buildContent(buffer);

TestFileSet testFileSet = new TestFileSet("C:/UnitTestResults/TablePrimitive/");
boolean match =
    testFileSet.fileMatchesGold("Empty.html", buffer.toString());
assertEquals("Empty", match, true);
```

TestFileSet.java

TestFileSet represents a set of output files that correspond to a set of unit tests within a test case. Each output file is compared to a corresponding file that has been verified and renamed with the prefix "gold". As you develop a primitive, you can use a Test-FileSet to capture the output for review. Once the output is acceptable for all of the tests in the test case, simply rename the output files with the prefix "gold". Thereafter, if the output is unchanged, then the test will pass.

```
package com.wiley.compBooks.EJwithUML.Base.TestUtilities;

import java.io.*;

/**
 * A TestFileSet represents a set of output files from a set
 * of unit tests within a test case. Each output file is compared
 * to a coresponding file that has been verified and renamed
 * with the prefix "gold".
 *
 * As you develop a primitive, you can use a TestFileSet to
 * capture the output. Once the output is acceptable for all
 * of the tests in the test case, simply rename the output files
 * with the prefix "gold". Thereafter, if the output is unchanged,
 * the test will pass.
 * */
public class TestFileSet
{
  private String path;

  /** Construct a TestFileSet with the specified file path which
   *  should be unique for a particular test case.*/
  public TestFileSet(String path) throws IOException
```

```
    {
      this.path = path;
      File basePath = new File(path);
      basePath.mkdirs();
    }

    /** Answers true if the output matches a previously verified "gold" file.*/
    public boolean fileMatchesGold(String test, String output) throws IOException
    {
      File test_file = new File(path+test);
      File gold_file = new File(path+"gold"+test);

      BufferedWriter writer = new BufferedWriter(new FileWriter(test_file));
      writer.write(output);
      writer.flush();
      writer.close();

      if (!gold_file.exists())
      {
        System.out.println("gold file for " +test+ " does not exist");
        return false;
      }

      if (!test_file.exists())
      {
        System.out.println("test file for " +test+ " does not exist");
        return false;
      }

      BufferedReader test_reader = new BufferedReader(new FileReader(test_file));
      BufferedReader gold_reader = new BufferedReader(new FileReader(gold_file));

      boolean done = false;
      int line_ctr = 0;
      while (!done)
      {
        String test_line = test_reader.readLine();
        String gold_line = gold_reader.readLine();

        if (test_line == null && gold_line == null)
        {
          done = true;
          break;
        }

        if (test_line == null)
        {
          System.out.println("Test file for " +test+ " is shorter than the
    gold file");
          return false;
        }

        if (gold_line == null)
        {
```

```
            System.out.println("Test file for " +test+ " is longer than the
    gold file");
            return false;
        }

        if (!test_line.equals(gold_line))
        {
            System.out.println("Lines differ for = " +test+ ". line_ctr = "
    +line_ctr+ "\ntest: " +test_line+ "\ngold: " +gold_line);
            return false;
        }

        line_ctr++;
    }

    return true;
    }
}
```

An Application-Specific HTML Producer

An actual dynamic Web site or Web-based application consists of dozens of input screens and data display tables. End users expect your site to be easy to use, pleasant to look at, and consistent from page to page. Also, your marketing team probably expects to be able to change the look of the entire site solely for their post-lunch amusement. Common user interface elements can be factored out as application-specific HTML production classes that implement IHtmlPrimitive and use a variety of concrete primitives to accomplish their responsibilities. For example, an application-specific input form might add labels, instructions, required field indicators, TextBoxPrimitives, and SelectionPrimitives to a nice layout table. All decisions about appearance and relative positioning are captured in the application-specific HTML production class and a style sheet.

InputFormProducer.java

The InputFormProducer class uses an internal TablePrimitive to control the layout of the form elements. The title and instructions for the form are added across two columns with their own styles. Before each input row, an empty span with a style of FORM_SPACING is used to insert some vertical space. Each label is added to the leftmost cell in its row, followed by the input field and sometimes the word *(required)* together in one cell. The next row contains the instructions for the input field spread across two cells. The buildContent method adds another row of vertical space and the submit and reset buttons together in one cell in the last row. Figure 8.8 shows the results without any styles.

```
    package com.wiley.compBooks.EJwithUML.Samples.ApplicationSpecificHtml;

    import com.wiley.compBooks.EJwithUML.Base.HtmlPrimitives.Core.*;
    import com.wiley.compBooks.EJwithUML.Base.HtmlPrimitives.FormPrimitives.*;
```

```java
import com.wiley.compBooks.EJwithUML.Base.HtmlPrimitives.Layout.*;
import com.wiley.compBooks.EJwithUML.Base.HtmlPrimitives.ContentElements.*;

/** The InputFormProducer captures one way of formatting an input
 *  form. It implements the IHtmlPrimitive interface so that
 *  it can be combined with existing primitives or other application
 *  specific producers. */
public class InputFormProducer implements IHtmlPrimitive
{
  private FormPrimitive form;
  private TablePrimitive layoutTable;
  private int rowCtr = 0;

  /** Construct an InputFormProducer with the specified submit
   *  target and form name. */
  public InputFormProducer(String title, String instructions, String
submitTarget, String name)
  {
    form = new FormPrimitive(submitTarget, name);
    layoutTable = new TablePrimitive();
    layoutTable.setStyle(AppStyle.FORM_LAYOUT_TABLE);
    form.addPrimitive(layoutTable);

    layoutTable.setColumnSpanForCells(2);
    layoutTable.setPrimitiveAt(rowCtr++, 0, new
SpanPrimitive(AppStyle.FORM_TITLE, title));
    layoutTable.setPrimitiveAt(rowCtr++, 0, new ParagraphPrimitive(null, " "));

    layoutTable.setPrimitiveAt(rowCtr++, 0, new
SpanPrimitive(AppStyle.FORM_INSTRUCTIONS, instructions));
    layoutTable.setPrimitiveAt(rowCtr++, 0, new ParagraphPrimitive(null, " "));
    layoutTable.resetColumnSpanForCells();
  }

  /** Add a primitive as an input field.*/
  public void addPrimitive(String label, String fieldTip, IHtmlPrimitive
primitive, boolean required)
  {
    layoutTable.setPrimitiveAt(rowCtr++, 0, new SpanPrimitive(AppStyle.
FORM_SPACING, " "));

    // add label, but make sure it doesn't take up too much room
    layoutTable.setStyleForCells(AppStyle.FORM_FIELD_LABEL_CELL);
    layoutTable.setPrimitiveAt(rowCtr, 0, new
SpanPrimitive(AppStyle.FORM_FIELD_LABEL, label+ ":"));

    // Build a composite of the input field and the required marker.
    CompositePrimitive field = new CompositePrimitive();
    field.addPrimitive(primitive);
    if (required)
    {
      field.addPrimitive(new SpanPrimitive(AppStyle.FORM_REQUIRED,
"(required)"));
    }
```

```
        layoutTable.setStyleForCells(AppStyle.FORM_FIELD_INPUT_CELL);
        layoutTable.setPrimitiveAt(rowCtr++,1, field);

        layoutTable.setColumnSpanForCells(2);
        layoutTable.setPrimitiveAt(rowCtr++,0, new
    SpanPrimitive(AppStyle.FORM_FIELD_TIP, fieldTip));
        layoutTable.resetColumnSpanForCells();
        layoutTable.setPrimitiveAt(rowCtr++, 0, new SpanPrimitive(null, " "));
    }


    /** Create the HTML for this field. */
    public void buildContent(StringBuffer buffer)
    {
        /* The rowCtr is intentionally not incremented. If an ingenious
           developer reuses a InputFormProducer and adds more primitives
           for the second use, the new primitives will replace the buttons. */
        layoutTable.setPrimitiveAt(rowCtr, 0, new SpanPrimitive(AppStyle.
    FORM_SPACING, " "));

        CompositePrimitive buttons = new CompositePrimitive();
        buttons.addPrimitive(new SubmitPrimitive("Submit Data", AppStyle.FORM_
    BUTTON));
        buttons.addPrimitive(new ResetPrimitive("Clear Data", AppStyle.FORM_
    BUTTON));

        layoutTable.setColumnSpanForCells(2);
        layoutTable.setPrimitiveAt(rowCtr+1, 0, buttons);
        layoutTable.resetColumnSpanForCells();

        this.form.buildContent(buffer);
    }
}
```

The following code snippets show the creation and configuration of the TextBox-
Primitives and the SelectionPrimitive followed by the creation of the application-
specific input form. There are only 10 lines of code for this moderately complex form
and every line describes the content of the form, not its appearance. All of the appearance decisions are captured in the InputFormProducer, as described above and in a
style sheet.

```
// Build the form input fields.
TextBoxPrimitive name = new TextBoxPrimitive("name");
TextBoxPrimitive band = new TextBoxPrimitive("band");
SelectionPrimitive flavor = new SelectionPrimitive("flavor");
flavor.addValue("Vanilla Bean", "vanilla", false);
flavor.addValue("Fudge Ripple", "fudge", false);
flavor.addValue("Mint Chocolate Chip", "mintChocolateChip", true);

// Add the fields to the form.
InputFormProducer form = new InputFormProducer("Important Personal
Information","Please divulge your personal information. We won't give it to
anyone. We promise. Really... Trust us, we have honest faces... Please! Is
this line long enough to demonstrate a little wrapping?",
```

```
"http://sillyservlet/", "daForm");
form.addPrimitive("Name", "Enter your first and last name.", name, true);
form.addPrimitive("Favorite Band", "Enter the name of your favorite band.", ⮐
band, false);
form.addPrimitive("Favorite Flavor", "Select your favorite flavor.", flavor, ⮐
true);

StringBuffer buffer = new StringBuffer();
PagePrimitive page = new PagePrimitive("SimpleForm", "../../HtmlPrimitives/ ⮐
Default.css");
page.addToBody(form);
page.buildContent(buffer);
form.addPrimitive("Favorite Flavor", "Select your favorite flavor.",
   flavor, true);
```

Without any style sheets, this results in the semitolerable output in Figure 8.8.

A little effort in the style sheet can greatly enhance the appearance and usability of the form. First, styles for the form title, form instructions, field labels, and field tip use font color and size to help differentiate them. The following snippet from the style sheet shows that all of the form text is blue and uses the same font family as the rest of the page. It also shows that the title is displayed in a 14-point font, while the rest of the form text is displayed at the default size for the page. So, the title is shown as 14-point blue Arial text. The form's instructions, labels, and tips are shown as 10-point blue Arial text. The actual contents of the text input fields and selectors use the page defaults of 10-point black Arial text. The required text shows up as 10-point red Arial text.

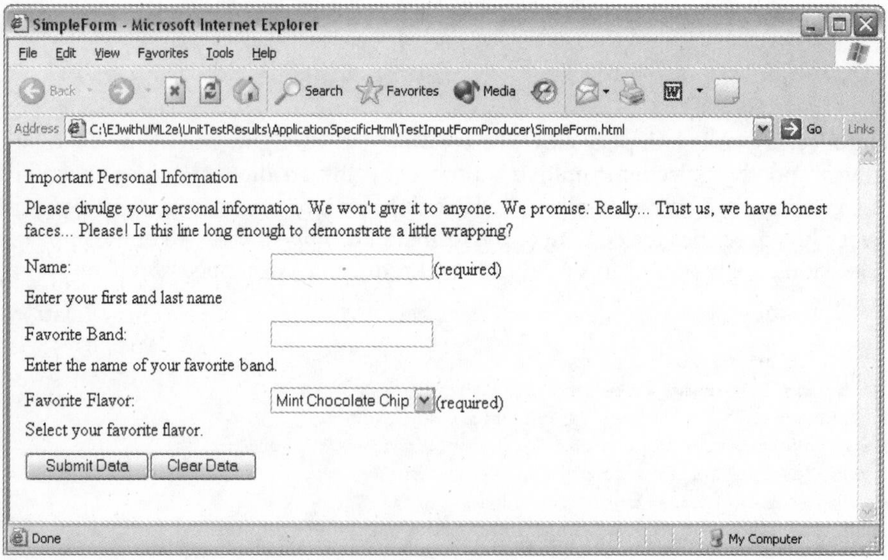

Figure 8.8 Input form without a style sheet.

Snippet from Style Sheet

```
* {font: 10pt Arial,sans-serif; color: black}
.form_title {font-size: 14pt; font-weight: bold; color:blue}
.form_instructions {color:blue}
.form_field_label {font-weight: bold; color:blue}
.form_field_tip {font-size: 10pt; color:blue}
.form_required {padding-left: 10; font-size: 10pt; color:red}
```

The form in Figure 8.8 allowed the input fields to float too far to the left. Fortunately, we can use the width attribute of the label's style to limit the space it uses. The padding and margin attributes allow us to separate the text and input elements as they flow across the page.

```
.form_field_label_cell {padding: 2; margin:5; width: 10%}
.form_field_input_cell {padding: 2; margin:5}
```

Finally, the vertical space and the space between the buttons are controlled by the last two styles.

```
.form_spacing {height: 20}
.form_button {margin-left: 30; font-size: 10pt; color:black}
```

Figure 8.9 shows the aggregate result of these styles as applied by Internet Explorer. The combination of an application-level input form producer and styles yields a very convenient way to customize the look of all of the input forms for the site. Cosmetic changes are made by altering the styles, while fundamental changes to the layout are made in a single class.

Strengths

The HTML production framework protects most developers from the intricacies of HTML and JavaScript. A few brave souls spend most of their time finding the right way to produce HTML and then encapsulate it for easy use. This allows the bulk of the team to focus their energies on the core functionality of the system. This encapsulation also encourages consistency from page to page. As long as each developer uses the same HTML producers and the same style sheet, the site's pages will evolve together as changes affect the system as a whole.

For most systems, this is a correct balance. Very few systems really require that every page is a work of art. Quite the contrary, most systems benefit if each page incorporates the same visual cues and allows the user to move from page to page in a consistent manner.

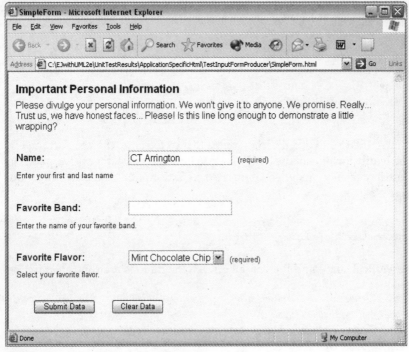

Figure 8.9   Input form with style sheet.

Weaknesses

Sites that really do require different pages to evolve independently should not use an HTML production framework. Creating new variations of different components will result in an incomprehensible tangle of classes.

Compatible Technologies

HTML production classes can easily be used with Java servlets and JavaServer pages.

Cost of Adoption

In order to create an HTML production framework, your project must fill the roles of UI designer and Java developer.

UI Designer

It is always good to have a user interface designer who can address usability and human factors. A UI designer devises alternate interface strategies that meet the requirements, and works with the stakeholders and the developers to determine which approach is most suitable for the project. Deliverables range from screen shots in a drawing program to thin prototypes.

This is especially important in Web-based development, where user interfaces are limited by the capabilities and idiosyncrasies of the users' browsers. Creativity and persistence are definitely required. Also, the user interface designer for a Web-based interface must constantly refresh his or her skills, as browsers and Web technologies evolve and mutate at a disturbingly quick pace. At the very least, designers must know or be on a sharp learning curve for HTML and JavaScript.

Java Developer

A Java developer for HTML production must have a clear grasp of OO design fundamentals and a good understanding of Web technologies such as HTML and JavaScript. They must also be able to work with the UI designer to understand and convert their static designs into HTML primitives and application-specific producers.

On a positive note, HTML production does not require a deep understanding of the Java class libraries. The developer does need to understand string manipulation and the collections classes. In my experience, HTML production can be a great first exposure to Java for developers with a background in Web technologies, because it does not force them to learn all of Java at once and it leverages their existing skills. It also has a very satisfying code and unit testing cycle because you actually see the results of your labor in a browser!

Suitability

HTML production classes are typically used by servlets or Java Server Pages. So, rather than considering HTML production classes in isolation, we will defer the question of suitability until Chapter 9, "Evaluating Candidate Technologies for User Interface Classes," which describes a variety of user interface technologies.

The Next Step

Now that we have a class library that facilitates the production of HTML, we can consider several user interface technologies.

CHAPTER

9

Evaluating Candidate Technologies for User Interface Classes

Now that we've grouped our classes and described each group, we're ready to examine the classes and select the technologies that will achieve our system requirements.

This chapter describes and evaluates candidate technologies for user interface (UI) classes. We'll apply the template from Chapter 7, "Evaluating Candidate Technologies for Shared Services," to several technologies. Once this is done, we'll use the technology requirements from Chapter 6, "Describing the System for Technology Selection," and the technology descriptions to find the right technologies for the UI classes in the Timecard system.

Swing

Swing is Sun's framework for GUI development. It continues to receive well-deserved accolades for fulfilling Sun's "write once, run anywhere" philosophy for user interface development and for its object-oriented design. A Swing application, or applet, looks and behaves the same on any compliant Java Virtual Machine (JVM). Since JVMs exist for Microsoft Windows, most flavors of Unix, and Linux, developers have a lot of freedom in developing and deploying Swing-based products. I continue to be impressed when the code I write at night on my PC runs fine under Solaris the next morning. While far from perfect, Swing is a solid implementation of a great vision.

Another, less-hyped, characteristic of Swing is its clear separation of model and view classes. Swing provides many valuable model classes that can be used with Swing view components, with other presentation implementations, or as independent data structures in a model. Once a model object is constructed, it can be wired to one or more view objects. The view objects are kept in sync with the model by an event model. For example, consider a list component that is wired to an underlying list model object. Updates to the model are automatically reflected in the list component. Similar model and view pairs are available for pull-down lists, trees, and tables, to name a few.

In an effort to make the view and model separation even more flexible and powerful, Swing's architects made each model an interface, and provided a default implementation. Custom implementations of the model interface work seamlessly with the corresponding view objects. For example, a developer could provide a fancy implementation of ComboBoxModel that keeps the elements in alphabetical order.

Many of Swing's early weaknesses, such as poor IDE support, poor performance, and unsettling instability in the API, have been resolved. Undoubtedly, it will continue to improve incrementally; it is now a stable and legitimate alternative for GUI development. I predict that Swing will complete its move from a leading-edge technology to a mainstream technology over the next few years.

Gory Details

Swing is an incredibly large and rich class library. It is impossible to do it justice here. However, I can cover some important facets of Swing that, hopefully, will capture its elegance and its versatility.

Separation of Model and View

In our analysis model, user interface classes are carefully separated from entity classes, because they have very different responsibilities. Encapsulation is the key goal. Business data and business logic are encapsulated in the entity classes so that they are easy to find, easy to extend, and easy to reuse. Presentation logic and user interaction logic are encapsulated in the UI class, so that they are easy to find, and can be extended without affecting other classes. Also, this separation allows developers to specialize; one set of developers acquires knowledge of the business, while another focuses on user interface design and the details of the presentation technology.

Swing has built-in support for this separation. Like all user interface class libraries, Swing comes with a rich array of widgets, including everything from text entry to progress bars to tree controls. However, Swing also includes classes that represent the data in a view-independent way. These classes are called *model classes*, a name derived from the common synonym for entity classes. Swing model classes organize data into lists, trees, and tables, just to name a few. These models are completely independent of the view, and may be useful even if no view is involved. This is especially true of

DefaultTreeModel, which provides methods for adding nodes to a tree, removing nodes from a tree, traversing a tree, and generating a list of nodes from a leaf node to the root node.

By design, Swing model classes are highly extensible. In each case, Swing provides an interface that defines the behavior for the model, as well as a default implementation. This approach allows developers to solve straightforward problems with little effort, while allowing developers to handle more complex modeling problems with proportionally more effort.

Consider a list of objects and the corresponding graphical widget for displaying the objects in a pull-down combo box. In Swing, all concrete combo box model classes must implement the ComboBoxModel interface if they intend to be used by graphical combo box components. The JComboBox class contains all of the presentation and user interaction logic for producing combo box widgets. Each JComboBox object has a unidirectional association with exactly one object, whose class implements the ComboBoxModel interface. The JComboBox object is completely protected from the implementation details of the model; as long as the object supports all of the methods in the ComboBoxModel interface, the JComboBox object's needs are satisfied. Notice that one ComboBoxModel interface can support many JComboBox objects. Figure 9.1 shows these relationships. Sun provides the DefaultComboBoxModel as a quite reasonable implementation of the ComboBoxModel interface. More complex implementations, such as a list model that sorts its contents, must implement the ComboBoxModel interface.

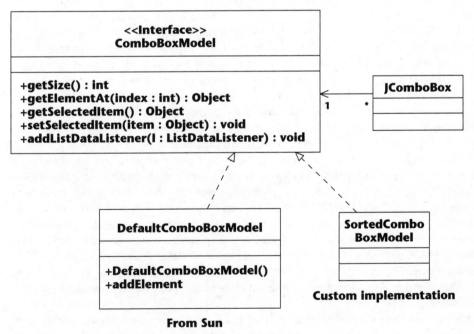

Figure 9.1 ComboBoxModel and implementations.

Event Model

In many applications, each graphical view object must stay up to date with its underlying model object. The most obvious approach is to have the model object notify each view object when a change occurs. However, this introduces a dangerous mutual association between the model object and the view objects, as shown in Figure 9.2, for the JComboBox and its associated model class. The JComboBox object calls the getSize and getElementAt methods on the ComboBoxModel object, and the model object calls the intervalAdded notification method on the view object whenever an object is added to the model. This mutual association makes it impossible to reuse the model class without also reusing the view class, which is often inappropriate. Also, allowing a model class to access one method in the view class may lead developers to use other methods, until the two classes are tightly coupled.

The architects of the Swing class libraries needed a way to update view objects to reflect changes to the model objects' state, without introducing direct dependencies from the model classes to the view classes. Fortunately, there is a well-defined and well-respected design pattern that solves this exact problem, called Observer (Gamma 1995). In this pattern, the observer class implements an interface that contains all of the notification methods. An observer object is registered with the observed object. When a change occurs, the observed object must notify each registered observer. However, the observed object does not depend directly on the observers; it just knows that they implement the observer interface.

In Swing, this pattern is implemented by requiring the view objects to register themselves as listeners on the model objects. Swing adds an additional twist, because the JComboBox does not know the specific implementation of ComboBoxModel. It only knows that the model object implements the ComboBoxModel interface. Since JComboBox implements ListDataListener, it is able to add itself as a listener to the model object. Once the model object has a reference to the listener, it can use the intervalAdded or contentsChanged method to notify the listener of changes. The bidirectional association is avoided, because the model object does not know about JComboBox objects, just ListDataListeners. Figure 9.3 shows the way in which Swing's event model works for JComboBox objects and the underlying model.

The Observer pattern allows the objects to communicate with one another while keeping the model independent of the view and providing an amazing amount of flexibility. An application can create a particular type of ComboBoxModel, such as a DefaultComboBoxModel. The application can then create a JComboBox object that receives a reference to the model object in its constructor. However, the JComboBox object does not know or care which concrete implementation of ComboBoxModel it receives. JComboBox's constructor calls the addListDataListener method on the ComboBoxModel object. This registers the JComboBox as a listener on the model. Finally, the JComboBox object extracts the current state of the ComboBoxModel and uses the information to populate itself.

When the DefaultComboBoxModel object receives new elements, it notifies each registered ListDataListener object by calling its intervalAdded method. In the case of the JComboBox object, it knows to repopulate itself to reflect the model. Figure 9.4 shows the interaction between objects, while ignoring the interfaces.

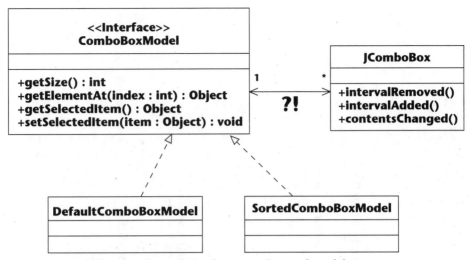

Figure 9.2 A bidirectional association between view and model.

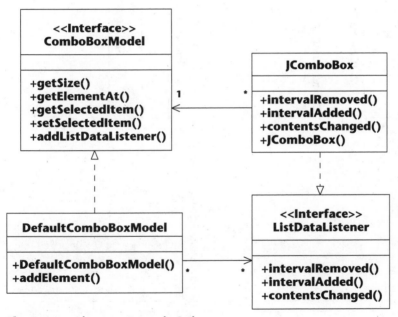

Figure 9.3 Observer pattern in Swing.

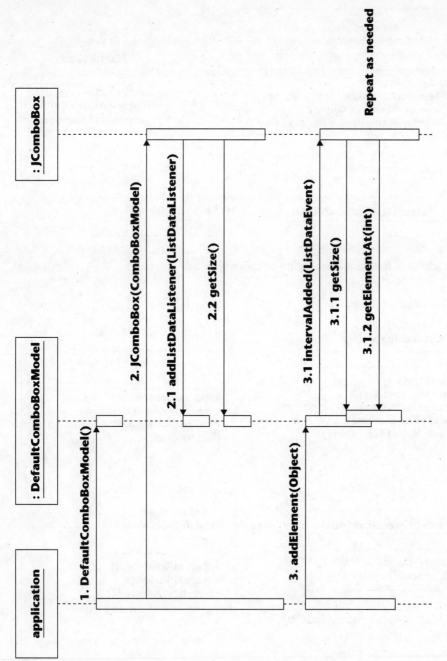

Figure 9.4 Object interactions for the observer pattern in Swing.

Combining User Interface Components

Swing includes almost 50 user interface classes, from entire tables to tiny ToolTips and everything in between. While many of these classes are independently impressive, any real user interface requires developers to connect user interface objects in sophisticated combinations. A user interface might include a tree control and a detail editor that allows the user to view and update the data for the item that is selected in the tree control. This navigation and editing tool might live inside of a larger user interface that includes a menu bar and a toolbar with icons.

The key to Swing's power and flexibility lies in the breadth and sophistication of the user interface classes themselves and in the ease with which developers can assemble a complicated whole from relatively simple parts. In providing this functionality, the Swing classes make excellent use of the Composite design pattern (Gamma 1995). A JPanel is a Swing class that extends JComponent. Figure 9.5 shows how a JPanel object can hold any number of other JComponent objects, including other JPanels. This gives Swing developers full freedom to compose several components into a group, then use several groups to build a still larger user interface.

Layout Managers

Combining many components to form a coherent user interface requires the developer to determine how the components will be organized relative to one another, and how each component handles changes to the size of the enclosing window. Swing provides several classes, known as *layout managers*, that allow developers to control the layout of components within a container. Each JPanel object has exactly one layout manager object, which is an instance of a class that implements the LayoutManager interface. As shown in the one-to-one relationship between JPanel and LayoutManager in Figure 9.6, each LayoutManager object is dedicated to a single JPanel. Since the JPanel has a reference to the LayoutManager interface, it can use any concrete implementation of LayoutManager without modification.

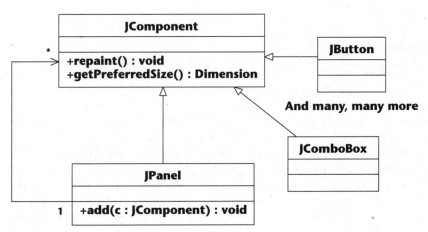

Figure 9.5 Use of the Composite design pattern.

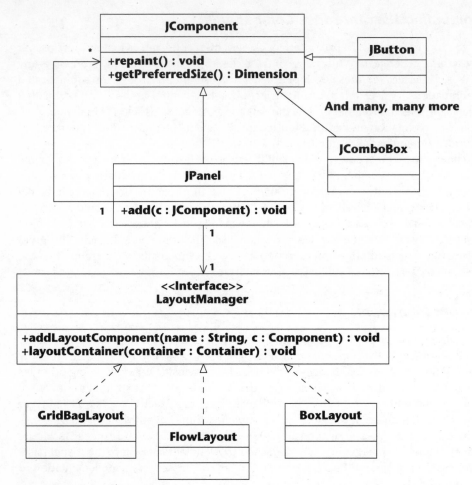

Figure 9.6   Layout managers.

Putting It Together

Swing makes excellent use of the Observer pattern to keep the model and presentation classes separate, while keeping the views in sync with the model. It also uses the Composite pattern to allow the incremental construction of arbitrarily complex user interfaces. Flexibility is constantly increased through the creative use of interfaces. In fact, as you can see in Figure 9.7, every single association relationship is to an interface or to a base class, rather than directly to a concrete implementation class. This means that any JPanel can contain any number of different components, and use any layout manager. A JComboBox can use any model that implements the ComboBoxModel interface, and a DefaultComboBoxModel object can keep any object up to date, as long as the object's class implements the ListDataListener interface. Swing's developers clearly designed with flexibility and extensibility in mind.

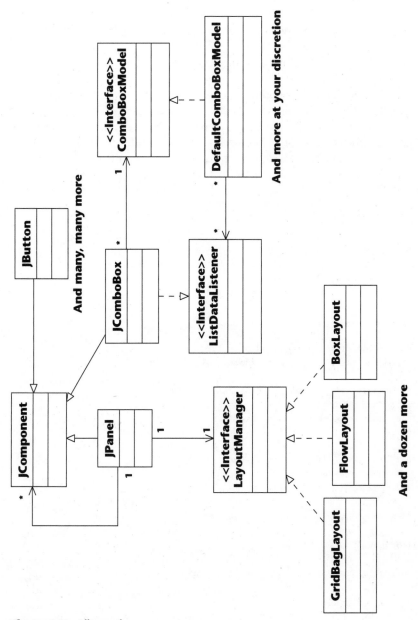

Figure 9.7   All together now.

A Small Sample

The following sample application shows how several JComboBox objects can present the elements of the same ComboBoxModel object. A separate text entry frame is used to add items to the model. Each time an object is added as an item in the ComboBox-Model object, it is immediately available in all of the JComboBox objects.

Let's take a look at the files that produce the combo boxes and the entry widget. The UpdatedChooser's constructor receives a reference to an object that realizes the ComboBoxModel interface. This UpdatedChooser's only job is to pass the model object along to the JComboBox and display the JComboBox inside of a frame. It is not at all involved in the Observer pattern.

The main method of UpdatedChooser, which as you know serves as a static entry point into this little application, constructs a new DefaultComboBoxModel and passes it to the constructor of a few UpdatedChooser objects. Notice that the constructor for the UpdatedChooser objects only knows that the parameter is an object whose class implements the ComboBoxModel interface. The main method could use any other implementation of ComboBoxModel, without affecting the code for the UpdatedChooser.

UpdatedChooser.java

```
package com.wiley.compBooks.EJwithUML.SwingExamples;

import javax.swing.*;

/**
 *
 * Each instance of UpdatedChooser consists of a JFrame with a
 * JComboBox inside of it. The JComboBox allows the user to
 * select from the items in a ComboBoxModel.
 *
 * The ComboBoxModel is passed in as a parameter to the
 * constructor and is used to construct the JComboBox. This
 * allows the JComboBox to register itself as a listener on
 * the model.
 *
 *
 */
public class UpdatedChooser extends JFrame
{
  public UpdatedChooser(ComboBoxModel model)
  {
    super("Updated Chooser Exampple");

    // Construct a JComboBox that displays the model.
    JComboBox chooser = new JComboBox(model);

    // Add the JComboBox to the main container for this Jframe.
    this.getContentPane().add(chooser);
    this.pack();

    this.addWindowListener(new ExitListener());
    this.setVisible(true);

  }
```

```java
public static void main(String[] args)
{
  /* Create a combo box model and pass it along to a few
     presentation and update objects. */
  DefaultComboBoxModel model = new DefaultComboBoxModel();
  new UpdatedChooser(model);
  new UpdatedChooser(model);
  new TextEntryFrame(model);
  new TextEntryFrame(model);
}

}
```

The TextEntryFrame keeps a reference to the DefaultComboBoxModel object, which it receives in its constructor. The constructor also adds a text field and an OK button to the frame, and registers the TextEntryFrame object as an action listener on the button. When the OK button is pressed, Swing's framework calls the TextEntryFrame object's actionPerformed method, which reads the text field and adds the resulting string to the model.

TextEntryFrame.java

```java
package com.wiley.compBooks.EJwithUML.SwingExamples;

import javax.swing.*;
import java.awt.event.*;
import java.awt.*;

/**
 * Each instance of the TextEntryFrame class contains a text
 * field and an "OK" button. Each instance also receives a
 * DefaultComboBoxModel object as a parameter to its
 * constructor.
 *
 * Whenever the user presses OK, the TextEntryFrame reads
 * the text field and adds the contents to the
 * DefaultComboBoxModel.
 *
 */
public class TextEntryFrame extends JFrame implements
                                      ActionListener
{
  private JTextField field;
  private JButton button;
  private DefaultComboBoxModel model;

  public TextEntryFrame(DefaultComboBoxModel model)
  {
    super("Entry Frame");
```

```java
      // Initialize instance variables.
      this.model = model;
      field = new JTextField(15);
      button = new JButton("OK");
      button.addActionListener(this);

      // Get a new box container.
      Box box = Box.createVerticalBox();
      box.add(field);
      box.add(button);

      // Add the box container to the main container of this Jframe.
      this.getContentPane().add(box);
      this.pack();
      this.addWindowListener(new ExitListener());
      this.setVisible(true);
   }

   /** Implement behavior for ActionListener interface */
   public void actionPerformed(ActionEvent ae)
   {
      // Read the text field and add it to the model.
      String text = this.field.getText().trim();
      model.addElement(text);

      this.field.setText("");
   }
}
```

This fairly small sample shows how the Observer design pattern works behind the scenes in Swing. All the developer has to do is wire the right objects together using the addXXXListener methods.

Now that we have explored some of the inner workings of the Swing classes, let's continue to discuss the strengths and weaknesses more specifically.

Strengths

Swing's strengths lie in its limitless flexibility and richness, its cross-platform nature, and in the clear separation of model classes from view classes. The first two strengths allow developers to create incredibly slick user interfaces that look and behave the same on dozens of platforms, from Microsoft Windows to Linux to high-end Unix workstations. Used effectively, the clear separation of model classes from view classes allows developers to write extremely extensible and readable code.

Swing has very reasonable performance and usability characteristics. Certainly, no one is writing the next commercial 3-D point-and-shoot game in Swing and Java 3D, but Swing is quite suitable for business applications or even interactive data visualization. In fact, several popular arcade games from the 1980s have found new life as Swing applets.

Weaknesses

Swing is not a low-end GUI solution. Some organizations buy an IDE, send their PowerBuilder and COBOL programmers to a week of Java training and a week of Swing training, and expect to be up and running the next week. It is not possible. Learning to develop Swing applications takes time, and is easier with a strong background in object-oriented user interface development. Consequently, the use of Swing may be precluded due to a lack of expertise.

Compatible Technologies

Swing applications, or applets, integrate well with all server-side Java technologies, such as RMI, JDBC, and EJB. For example, a UI object that is implemented in Swing can interact with remotely deployed control or entity objects that are implemented with RMI or Enterprise JavaBeans. It is also possible to locate the UI, control, and entity objects in the same virtual machine. For example, a Swing UI object may talk directly to control and entity objects that use JDBC to retrieve information from a relational database.

Cost of Adoption

Swing is provided free as part of the standard JDK, but there are costs of adoption. First and foremost, to be successful with Swing, your project must fill the roles of *UI designer*, *architect*, and *Swing developer.*

UI Designer

It is always good to have a user interface designer who can address usability and human factors. A UI designer devises alternate interface strategies that meet the requirements, and works with the stakeholders and the developers to determine which approach is most suitable for the project. Deliverables range from screen shots in a drawing program to thin prototypes.

Architect

Swing user interfaces can degenerate into a series of unconnected works, with no two screens following the same format or using the same components. An architect can reduce this effect by establishing reusable components, such as button panels, layouts for input forms, and default windows. This allows developers to easily change the look of the entire application by altering the reusable components. The alternative requires each screen to be laboriously edited, perhaps for something as trivial as the background color or the space between buttons.

The architect can also keep the code base sane and avoid costly rework by establishing standards for exception handling, error logging, and the use of layout managers.

The architect for a Swing-based user interface must have a strong knowledge of object-oriented principles, extensive design experience, and a clear grasp of the Swing architecture and event model.

Developer

At minimum, a Swing developer needs a solid understanding of the event model, layout managers, and some basic components. However, every Swing project needs at least one developer who knows the full breadth of classes that make up Swing. Almost any GUI component you can dream up can be built from Swing's classes. The trick is knowing where to start.

Developers who have solid object-oriented skills and a strong background in user interface development can migrate to Java and Swing without too much difficulty. However, it does take time and practice. A C++ developer with Motif experience would need a few months before he or she was truly comfortable with Java and the Swing class libraries. An experienced Java developer with GUI development experience in some other language might take considerably less time.

Developers who are migrating from a procedural background to Java and Swing may be overwhelmed by the challenge of learning object-oriented development, Java, and the intricacies of Swing. Most developers in this situation should gain experience with Java before tackling Swing.

Suitability

In Chapter 6, "Describing the System for Technology Selection," we discovered the following descriptive categories:

- User interface complexity
- Deployment constraints for user interfaces
- Number and type of users
- Available bandwidth

Let's evaluate Swing to see if it is a suitable choice for our system.

User Interface Complexity

Swing is certainly capable of handling simple data input and static data presentation tasks. It comes with a full array of input widgets, including text entry fields, pull-down selectors, radio buttons, scrollable lists, and nifty sliders. Presentation classes include tables, tree controls, and image maps. In addition:

- Swing also easily supports customizable views, such as sorted tables and filtered tables.

- Dynamic views of data are incredibly easy to implement in Swing, because its architecture has built-in support for change propagation, and stresses a clear separation between the data and the presentation of the data. Once a view object is connected to an underlying data or model object, any changes to the model object automatically cause changes to the view object.

■ Swing can be combined with the Java 2D or Java 3D graphics frameworks to produce some very impressive interactive graphics. By manipulating the view, a user can update the underlying data.

In summary, Swing supports the entire spectrum of user interface complexity, from simple data input to interactive graphics.

Deployment Constraints for User Interfaces

The first two deployment constraints, handheld devices and any Web browser, clearly are not supported by Swing. However, most late-model Web browsers do include support for Swing applets, either directly or through the Java plug-in. Almost every workstation, from Unix to Linux to Microsoft Windows, has a JVM, and therefore supports Swing applications.

Number and Type of Users

Swing is easily appropriate for a small number of dedicated users. Deployment and support of a Swing applet or dedicated application may easily be justified for low numbers of users.

Swing may also be appropriate for general use within an organization, if the complexity of the user interface makes Swing a desirable choice. However, Swing does have some incremental support costs. Swing applications must be installed on each user's workstation, complete with the appropriate JVM. Swing applets do not need to be individually installed, but an appropriate browser or Java plug-in must be present.

Similar considerations apply to using Swing for a large audience with high interest. If the complexity of the user interface and the system is sufficiently compelling, users will install the JVM, Java plug-in, and appropriate browser.

Swing is completely inappropriate for huge audiences with low interest. Any users who do not have a suitable configuration will not take time out of their day to install new software.

Available Bandwidth

Swing can be a very attractive option even for low-bandwidth scenarios. Swing applets do require the client browser to download the class files before running the application. However, the class files for a reasonably complex application are still smaller than three large images.

Once it starts running, a Swing applet can actually use less bandwidth than other user interface technologies. The server does not need to control the presentation; instead, the server can send the smallest possible amount of data or even compressed data.

With a little creativity, Swing is appropriate for all bandwidth categories, from dial-up connections to dedicated networks.

Java Servlets

The Servlet API is Sun's flexible and extensible framework for server-side development. Within the Servlet API, the HTTP package protects developers from tiresome HTTP protocol details and allows them to focus on their own unique data presentation problems. Servlets are used in conjunction with a Web server to create dynamic content based on the user's input.

There are several key terms that are critical to an understanding of servlets. These are:

HyperText Transfer Protocol (HTTP).   Specifies a communication protocol between Web clients and Web servers. It specifies valid request and response formats, error codes, and datatypes. By complying with HTTP, a Web browser is able to communicate with millions of Web servers, regardless of their hardware, operating system, or Web server vendor.

HTTP is a *connectionless protocol*, in that the browser does not keep a connection open nor send multiple requests across it. Instead, each request requires a new socket connection to the Web server. The connection is closed as soon as the request is complete.

HTTP request.   A group of data sent from the browser to the Web server. An HTTP request includes the name of the requested page, descriptive information about the browser, acceptable datatypes for the response, any cookies that were dropped by the target server, and any data as entered by the user. In a nutshell, each HTTP request packages a request from the user into a format that any Web server can understand.

There are two types of HTTP requests, GET and POST. GET requests are simple requests for a particular resource. For example, everytime you type a URL into your browser's location or address field and hit return, the browser makes a GET request to the specified Web server. POST requests allow the browser to include data within the request itself. So, when you enter data on a Web page and hit the "submit" button, the browser makes a POST request to the specified Web server.

HTTP response.   A group of data sent from the Web server to the Web browser in response to a request. An HTTP response includes descriptive information about the server, an expiration date for the response, and formatted data. The formatted data might be plaintext, formatted HTML, an image, or even binary data. The browser is responsible for displaying the formatted data.

Form data.   HTTP allows Web browsers to collect data from the user and pass it along to the Web server as a list of strings. The user fills in an HTML form in his or her browser and submits the data. The browser packages the form data as part of the HTTP request and passes it to the Web server as part of an HTTP request.

Cookie.   When a browser loads a page, the page may ask the browser to save a relatively small chunk of data on the client machine. This chunk of data is called a cookie. If the browser accepts the cookie, then the browser stores the data and the name of the site that "dropped" the cookie.

When a browser sends a request to a Web server, it appends all of the cookies previously dropped by that site. This allows the Web server to keep track of each user so it can simulate a continuous interactive session.

HTTP servlet.   A Java class that accepts an HTTP request and fills in an HTTP response. Servlets extend javax.servlet.http.HttpServlet, which protects them from the messy details of parsing HTTP headers, retrieving form data, and formatting HTTP data for the response.

The actual processing occurs inside of the servlet's doGet or doPost method, which accepts the HTTP request and HTTP response objects as method parameters. The doGet or doPost method uses the HTTP request object to retrieve any form data, then builds the formatted response data.

Servlet engine or servlet container.   Allows a Web server to redirect incoming requests to a deployed servlet. The Web server must be configured to associate certain relative URLs with servlets. When the Web server receives an HTTP request for one of these URLs, it captures the request and passes it along to the servlet engine. If the servlet is not already active, the servlet engine loads the servlet class and instantiates it. Next, the servlet engine creates a response object and wraps the request data in a request object. These well-encapsulated and easy-to-use objects are gift-wrapped and presented to the servlet's doGet or doPost method. The servlet uses the request and any other resources at its disposal, including database connections, Enterprise JavaBeans, and HTML formatting code to fill in the response. The response from the servlet can be an HTML page, an image, or a file.

Relative URL specifications.   Also known as a URI path, relative URLs specify a path relative to the Web application or current page. So, a URI that begins with a "/" is relative to the Web application, while a URI that begins with anything else is relative to the page.

For more detailed information about any of these technologies, refer to the additional resources in Appendix B.

Gory Details

Servlets make life easier for developers by retrieving form data in a convenient form and by managing sessions and session data. However, a lot of work remains for the developer, who must build huge quantities of HTML and keep the system safe despite concurrent access from the Web server.

Retrieving Form Data

When a request is received from the Web server, the servlet engine creates the HttpServletRequest object, parses the form data out of the raw request, and adds the form data to the HttpServletRequest object. This encapsulates the logic for reading HTTP in the servlet engine. The doPost or doGet methods of the processing servlet can use the getParameterNames and getParameter methods of HttpServletRequest to extract each piece of form data.

Sessions

Servlet engines use cookies or URL rewriting to keep track of different users by unique identifiers and to simulate a continuous session. Remember that each request is a distinct connection, so the servlet container needs the unique identifier to match each request to the right session.

With cookies, the unique identifier is passed along as part of the HTTP request. With URL rewriting, the servlet container appends a unique identifier to each link that is included in the content, so the identifier becomes part of the URL. If there is no unique identifier accompanying the request, then the servlet engine creates a new session. If a unique identifier exists, the servlet engine verifies that the session is still active. If so, it treats the request as part of a continuing session.

Consider a real-world analogy. When you make a flight reservation with an airline by phone, the booking agent gives you a confirmation number at the end of the call. It is up to you to write this number down and make sure that you do not confuse it with the confirmation number for your rental car. If you need to make changes to your flight, you simply call the airline and provide the confirmation number. This enables the booking agent to easily find the relevant transaction out of tens of thousands of similar transactions. To complete the analogy: You are the Web browser, the booking agent is the servlet engine, and the confirmation number is the cookie.

When the servlet engine receives a request from the Web server, it constructs an HttpServletRequest object that encapsulates the request information. The servlet engine also attaches the HttpSession object to the HttpServletRequest. This session object is especially valuable to servlet developers, because it allows them to store references to any object in a map of name and value pairs. This makes it really easy to associate different useful objects with a user and to retrieve them by name when processing subsequent requests.

Configuring a Servlet within a Web Application

The Servlet Specification defines an XML schema that allows developers to configure a servlet as part of a Web-based application. Developers can define a servlet, map the servlet to particular URLs, set configuration parameters for an individual servlet, set configuration parameters for the entire Web application, and set error pages for particular types of exceptions.

The specification defines the following elements for each servlet element within the Web application:

servlet-name. Specifies the internal name of the servlet.

display-name. Optional name for display in an administration tool.

description. Optional description of the servlet for display in an administration tool.

servlet-class. Specifies a class that extends HttpServlet.

init-param. Zero or more initialization parameter elements for the servlet.

load-on-startup. Optional indicator that the servlet should load when the servlet container starts.

run-as. Optional directive for the servlet container to run the servlet with the specified identity.

security-role-ref. Optional reference for the servlet container to run the servlet with the specified security role. The security role must also exist in the Web application.

The following elements are a few of the servlet-related elements that may be used inside of the web-app element:

name. Specifies the internal name of the Web application.

display-name. Optional name for display in an administration tool.

description. Optional description of the Web application for display in an administration tool.

context-param. Zero or more initialization parameter elements for the Web application.

servlet. Each servlet element defines a servlet that can be used as part of the Web application.

servlet-mapping. Each servlet mapping element binds a URL pattern to a servlet as defined in a separate servlet element. A servlet may be bound to more than one URL pattern.

session-config. Optional specification of how the servlet container should manage sessions, including timeout interval.

error-page. Each error-page element binds a type of exception or error code to a resource within the Web application.

For more information, refer to the Java Servlet Specification version 2.3, which covers the configuration of servlets and Web applications in exquisite detail.

Life Cycle Events

Previous versions of the servlet specification allow servlet developers to override the init and destroy methods, which are called when the servlet container places the servlet into service or removes it from service. This allows the developer to explicitly allocate resources that are required to support the servlet as a whole. It is important to note that these methods are called when the container creates or destroys instances of the servlet. They do not help the developer effectively reclaim resources or manage resources that are specific to individual sessions, since an instantiated servlet may service an unlimited number of sessions before it is destroyed.

Life is better with version 2.3 of the servlet specification, which introduces event notification for servlets and sessions. The following callback interfaces allow registered objects to receive notification for lifecycle and data modification events. Each callback passes an event object that encapsulates the information about the change and its source.

ServletContextListener. The container calls the contextInitialized and contextDestroyed methods when the entire context is initialized and destroyed. This allows explicit management of resources at the servlet context level. For example, when the context is initialized, a listener might establish a shared database connection and add it to the context for use by any servlet in the Web application.

ServletContextAttributeListener.   The container calls the attributeAdded, attributeRemoved, and attributeReplaced methods when attributes in the servlet context are changed. This allows different registered listener objects to update their state based on the changes.

HttpSessionActivationListener.   The container calls the sessionDidActivate and sessionWillPassivate methods when a session is activated and immediately before it is passivated. This allows explicit management of session specific resources. It can also be used to persist changes to a user's preferences or progress through a use case for use in subsequent sessions.

HttpSessionAttributeListener.   The container calls the attributeAdded, attributeRemoved, and attributeReplaced methods when session attributes are changed. This allows different registered listener objects to update their state based on the changes.

Configuration of listeners is fairly simple, with listeners of different types added to the web-app element by their class. The container constructs the actual listener objects and calls the appropriate event notification methods as needed. However, in order to provide any real value, the listener object must interact with the servlets or sessions. For example, a Web application might have a SessionSpecificResourceManager class as a HttpSessionActivationListener. When the SessionSpecificResourceManager object receives a sessionDidActivate event, it can create a new SessionSpecificResource object and add it to the session. When the SessionSpecificResourceManager object receives a sessionWillPassivate event, it can remove the SessionSpecificResource from the session and reclaim the resources.

The following snippet from a deployment descriptor shows how the SessionSpecificResourceManager is registered as a listener.

```
<web-app>
...
  <listener>
    <listener-class>
Samples.Servlets.SessionSpecificResourceManager
    </listener-class>
  </listener>


    ...
</web-app>
```

Filters

New in the 2.3 servlet specification, Filters can intercept and transform both requests and responses. Filters treat all content equally, so it doesn't matter if the content is a static HTML file or dynamic content created by a servlet or JSP. Filters allow you to impose your will on parts of a site or the entire site with ease. The following ideas can all be implemented with Filters on the outgoing response:

- Transform every image to grayscale.
- Replace every occurrence of a word or phrase with another word or phrase.
- Capture metrics on the system's use.
- Compress data.
- Encrypt data.
- Include marketing banners.
- Exclude content based on the user's identity.

The following ideas can be implemented with Filters on the incoming request:

- Parse a request into a common format.
- Capture metrics on the system's use.
- Uncompress data.
- Decrypt data.
- Authenticate a user.

Custom filter classes implement the Filter interface and override the init, doFilter, and destroy methods. The init method allows the Filter to initialize itself from configuration parameters as specified in the Web application deployment descriptor and access the ServletContext. The doFilter method allows the Filter to modify or replace the request or response objects. It may then pass the request or response to the next filter in the FilterChain or decide to break the chain. The destroy method is called just before the container takes the Filter out of service. The following code shows the methods from the Filter interface.

```
public void init(FilterConfig filterConfig) throws ServletException

public void doFilter(ServletRequest request, ServletResponse response,
FilterChain chain) throws java.io.IOException, ServletException

public void destroy()
```

The deployment descriptor for Web applications allows you to configure a Filter and associate it with one or more URL patterns. The XML element <filter> contains the name, full class, and any initialization parameters. The following snippet shows a debug filter that is applied to all requests and responses for the entire application.

```
<web-app>
  ...
  <filter>
    <filter-name>DebugFilter</filter-name>
    <filter-class> Samples.Servlets.DebugFilter</filter-class>
  </filter>
```

```
<filter-mapping>
  <filter-name>DebugFilter</filter-name>
  <url-pattern>/*</url-pattern>
</filter-mapping>
  ...
</web-app>
```

TIP Limit each filter class to a single purpose and name it clearly. If used as part of a coherent and documented layered approach, filters should improve the flexibility and elegance of your system!

Concurrency Issues

Servlets are remarkably easy to learn and use. However, there are a few critical steps that must be followed to ensure that the dynamic data generated by your system is correct. This section explains the interactions between the Web server, servlet container, and your servlet, and describes some simple guidelines for creating safe servlets.

Web servers are inherently multithreaded. A typical Web server listens on port 80 and uses a separate thread each time a new request is received. If the Web application matches the request to a servlet, then the thread will forward the request to the servlet container. The servlet container subsequently calls the appropriate servicing method on your servlet. So, at any point in time, your servlet may be servicing 0, 100, or 500 requests.

Consider a servlet that displays recent transactions for an online brokerage. What will happen if the servlet uses an instance variable to hold the display table that is built in the doGet method? Consider a scenario where the servlet is adding data to the display table for Jane when the operating system gives control to another thread that is processing the same request for Bob. Bob's data will show up in Jane's Web page!

The following types of data are shared and must be immutable or thread safe:

- Any static variables
- A servlet's instance variables
- Objects stored in the servlet context's attributes

The following types of data are not shared and do not require protection:

- Objects that are created, used, and fall out of scope inside of the doPost or doGet method.
- Objects that are created inside of the doPost or doGet method and kept in the session object are usually safe. If a request takes enough time, then a user could open a new window and submit a competing request or use the back button to resubmit the request.

Survey Sample

The following sample shows how servlets are coded and configured, while solving a problem that seems common to many organizations. Many groups spend a surprising amount of time and effort surveying members for input on enumerable topics from "Where should we have the holiday party?" to "Do you have enough RAM?" So, this set of sample servlets implements a simple survey system. The following sections show how servlets are configured and implemented.

Configuration

The deployment descriptor for our survey servlet is used to define everything from the output path for survey results to the questions and permissible answers for each survey. The deployment descriptor for a Web application allows you to specify parameters for the entire Web application or for an individual servlet. The following snippet from our deployment descriptor shows a parameter named OutputPath that is available to all servlets and JSPs that are deployed within the Web application.

```
<context-param>
    <param-name>OutputPath</param-name>
    <param-value>c:/EJwithUML2e/OutputFiles/</param-value>
</context-param>
```

Other parameters are defined within an individual servlet's XML element in the deployment descriptor. The following snippet configures the SurveyServlet0 servlet with an output filename of favorites.dat and a variety of personal questions. It also restricts the user's choice of favorite color to red, blue, green, or purple.

```
<servlet>
    <servlet-name>SurveyServlet0</servlet-name>
    <servlet-class>
        com.wiley.compBooks.EJwithUML.Samples.Servlets.SurveyServlet
    </servlet-class>
    <init-param>
      <param-name>SurveyFile</param-name>
      <param-value>favorites.dat</param-value>
    </init-param>
    <init-param>
      <param-name>Question0</param-name>
      <param-value>What is your favorite flavor?</param-value>
    </init-param>
    <init-param>
      <param-name>Question1</param-name>
      <param-value>What is your favorite color?</param-value>
    </init-param>
    <init-param>
      <param-name>Question2</param-name>
      <param-value>What is your favorite band?</param-value>
    </init-param>
```

```
      <init-param>
        <param-name>ValidAnswers1</param-name>
        <param-value>red,blue, green, purple</param-value>
      </init-param>
   </servlet>
```

WARNING This sample is intentionally limited to use servlet configuration parameters and basic IO for data storage and retrieval. Real applications should generally use other technologies to capture even moderately complex data. For example, each survey could be defined in an XML file rather than laboriously captured in name-value pairs in the deployment descriptor.

A similar mechanism is used to configure a SurveyList servlet with a description of each survey.

```
<servlet>
  <servlet-name>SurveyListServlet</servlet-name>
  <servlet-class>
    com.wiley.compBooks.EJwithUML.Samples.Servlets.SurveyListServlet
  </servlet-class>
  <init-param>
    <param-name>SurveyServlet0</param-name>
    <param-value>Describe your favorite things!</param-value>
  </init-param>
  <init-param>
    <param-name>SurveyServlet1</param-name>
    <param-value>Feedback on your development team.</param-value>
  </init-param>
</servlet>
```

Classes

There are two classes that capture the essence of a survey: Survey and Question. A Question class consists of the text for the question and an optional list of allowed values. A Survey class consists of a text description and a list of questions. It is also responsible for formatting the header and the user's responses. Each SurveyServlet object builds its Survey object based on its configuration parameters and uses the HtmlPrimitives package to create the HTML to solicit responses via HTML input forms. It also writes the actual output file that holds the responses. The SurveyList also reads the parameters from the deployment descriptor and uses the HtmlPrimitives package to build links to each survey. Figure 9.8 shows how the servlets depend on the HtmlPrimitives package and the entity classes.

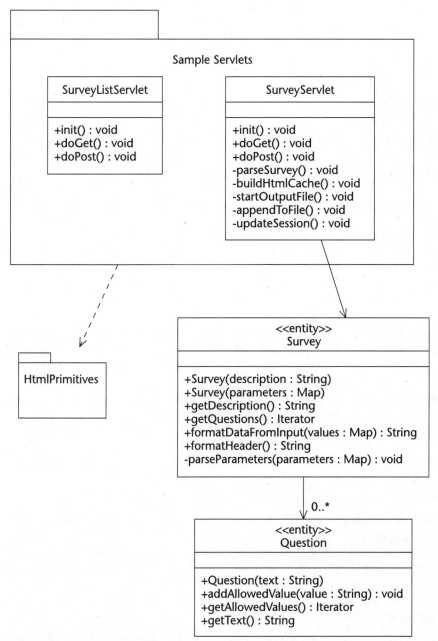

Figure 9.8   Survey servlet classes.

Question.java

The Question class captures the description and allowed values for a survey question.

```
package com.wiley.compBooks.EJwithUML.Samples.Servlets;

import java.util.*;

/**
 * The Question class represents an individual question in a survey.
 * @stereotype entity
 */
public class Question
{
  private String text;
  private ArrayList allowedValues = new ArrayList();

  /** Create the specified question. */
  public Question(String text)
  {
    this.text = text;
  }

  /** Add an allowed value to this question. */
  public void addAllowedValue(String value)
  {
    this.allowedValues.add(value);
  }

  /** Answers all allowed values for this question */
  public Iterator getAllowedValues()
  {
    return this.allowedValues.iterator();
  }

  /** Answers the text of this question */
  public String getText()
  {
    return this.text;
  }
}
```

Survey.java

The Survey class aggregates questions together to form a survey. It also builds a formatted string that contains the question descriptions and another formatted string based on the user's input values. These formatted strings are suitable for export to other applications, such as Excel, that can be used to analyze the raw data.

```
package com.wiley.compBooks.EJwithUML.Samples.Servlets;

import java.util.*;
import javax.servlet.http.*;
```

```java
/**
 * The Survey class represents a survey of questions.
 */
public class Survey
{
  private static final String DELIMITER = "|";
  private String description;
  private ArrayList questions;


  /** Construct a survey with the specified description. */
  public Survey(String description)
  {
    this.description = description;
  }

  /** Construct a survey with the specified parameters. */
  public Survey(Map parameters)
  {
    this.parseParameters(parameters);
  }

  /** Returns the description of this survey. */
  public String getDescription()
  {
    return this.description;
  }

  /** Answers all questions for this survey. */
  public Iterator getQuestions()
  {
    return this.questions.iterator();
  }

  /** Format output data from user input. */
  public String formatDataFromInput(Map inputValues)
  {
    StringBuffer formatted_data = new StringBuffer();
    int num_of_questions = this.questions.size();
    for (int ctr = 0; ctr < num_of_questions; ctr++)
    {
      String question_key = "Question" + ctr;
      Object response = inputValues.get(question_key);

      String response_value = "";
      if (response != null)
      {
        response_value = ((String[]) response) [0];
      }

      formatted_data.append(response_value + DELIMITER);
    }
```

```java
      return formatted_data.toString();
  }

  public String formatHeader()
  {
    StringBuffer header = new StringBuffer();
    Iterator qs = this.questions.iterator();

    while (qs.hasNext())
    {
      Question question = (Question)qs.next();
      header.append(question.getText() + DELIMITER);
    }

    return header.toString();
  }

  private void parseParameters(Map parameterMap)
  {
    this.questions = new ArrayList();
    boolean done = false;
    int ctr = 0;
    while (!done)
    {
      String question_text = (String)parameterMap.get("Question" +
                                                      ctr);
      String valid_answers = (String)parameterMap.get("ValidAnswers"
                                                      + ctr);

      if (question_text == null)
      {
        done = true;
        continue;
      }

      Question question = new Question(question_text);

      if (valid_answers != null)
      {
        StringTokenizer tokenizer =
          new StringTokenizer(valid_answers, ",");
        while (tokenizer.hasMoreTokens())
        {
          String token = tokenizer.nextToken();
          question.addAllowedValue(token);
        }
      }
      this.questions.add(question);
      ctr++;
    }
  }
}
```

SurveyServlet.java

Each SurveyServlet constructs a Survey object based on its configuration parameters and uses a variety of HTML producers and primitives to build the HTML for the form. It uses the Survey to format the data that it writes to the output file.

```java
package com.wiley.compBooks.EJwithUML.Samples.Servlets;

import javax.servlet.http.*;
import javax.servlet.*;
import java.io.*;
import java.util.*;

import com.wiley.compBooks.EJwithUML.Base.HtmlPrimitives.Core.*;
import com.wiley.compBooks.EJwithUML.Base.HtmlPrimitives.ContentElements.*;
import com.wiley.compBooks.EJwithUML.Base.HtmlPrimitives.FormPrimitives.*;
import com.wiley.compBooks.EJwithUML.Base.HtmlPrimitives.Layout.*;

import com.wiley.compBooks.EJwithUML.Samples.ApplicationSpecificHtml.*;

/**
 * Each instance of the SurveyServlet class builds the HTML
 * input form for a particular survey and stores the user's
 * input in a flat file. Each servlet uses the initialization
 * parameters, as specified in the Web application, to determine
 * the name of the output file, the questions, and the allowable
 * answers for each question. This allows the same class to be
 * used to create many different surveys, since each instance
 * has different questions and a different output file.
 *
 */
public class SurveyServlet extends HttpServlet
{
  private ServletContext context;
  private String outputPath;
  private String filename;
  private StringBuffer htmlCache = new StringBuffer();
  private Survey survey;

  /** Read the configuration parameters, build the HTML for
   *  the form, and establish the output file. */
  public void init() throws ServletException
  {
    this.context = getServletContext();
    this.outputPath = context.getInitParameter("OutputPath");
    this.filename = getInitParameter("SurveyFile");

    parseSurvey();
    buildHtmlCache();
    startOutputFile();
  }
```

```
/** Process data submitted for the survey by writing the user's
 *  answers to a file and producing a thank you page. */
public void doPost(HttpServletRequest request, HttpServletResponse
                   response) throws ServletException, IOException
{
  appendToFile(request);
  updateSession(request.getSession(true));

  PagePrimitive page = new PagePrimitive("Thanks!",
      "http://localhost:8080/EJwithUML2e/Default.css");


  ParagraphPrimitive paragraph = new
      ParagraphPrimitive(Style.PAGE_TITLE, "Thanks!");
  paragraph.addLineBreak();
  paragraph.addText(Style.NORMAL_TEXT, "Thanks for completing the survey. " +
  " Your input has been captured for data analysis...");

  LinkPrimitive listLink =
      new LinkPrimitive("./SurveyListServlet");
  listLink.addText("List of Surveys");

  paragraph.addLineBreak();
  paragraph.addLink(listLink);

  // Add the verbiage and link producers to the page.
  page.addToBody(paragraph);

  // Get the HTML from the page and write it to the response's
  // PrintWriter.
  StringBuffer content = new StringBuffer();
  page.buildContent(content);

  PrintWriter pw = response.getWriter();
  pw.print(content.toString());
  pw.flush();
  pw.close();
}

/** Send the HTML for the form. */
public void doGet(HttpServletRequest request, HttpServletResponse response)
throws IOException
{
  PrintWriter pw = response.getWriter();
  pw.print(this.htmlCache.toString());
  pw.flush();
  pw.close();
}

/** Parse the survey from the intialization parameters that
 *  follow the format of question0, question1, ... */
private void parseSurvey()
{
  HashMap parameter_map = new HashMap();
```

```java
  Enumeration keys = this.getInitParameterNames();
  while (keys.hasMoreElements())
  {
    String key = (String)keys.nextElement();
    String value = (String)this.getInitParameter(key);
    parameter_map.put(key, value);
  }

  this.survey = new Survey(parameter_map);
}

/** Build the HTML for the input form, based on the questions
 *  and valid answers. */
private void buildHtmlCache()
{
  // Determine name.
  String servlet_name = this.getServletName();

  InputFormProducer form = new InputFormProducer("Survey",
      "Please complete the following survey. All results are anonymous
       and confidential.",
      "http://localhost:8080/EJwithUML2e/servlet/" + servlet_name,
      servlet_name);

  Iterator questions = this.survey.getQuestions();
  int ctr = 0;
  while (questions.hasNext())
  {
    Question question = (Question)questions.next();
    String label = question.getText();
    String name = "Question" + ctr;

    IHtmlPrimitive input = new TextBoxPrimitive(name);

    // If there are valid answers, then this is a selection
    // rather than free-form text entry.
    Iterator valid_answers = question.getAllowedValues();
    if (valid_answers.hasNext())
    {
      SelectionPrimitive choice = new SelectionPrimitive(name);
      while (valid_answers.hasNext())
      {
        String valid_answer = (String)valid_answers.next();
        choice.addValue(valid_answer, valid_answer, false);
      }
      input = choice;
    }

    form.addPrimitive(label, "", input, false);
    ctr++;
  }

  PagePrimitive page = new PagePrimitive("Survey",
      "http://localhost:8080/EJwithUML2e/Default.css");
  page.addToBody(form);
```

```java
      this.htmlCache = new StringBuffer();
      page.buildContent(htmlCache);
  }


  /** If the file does not exist, create it and write the
   *  questions to the header. */
  private void startOutputFile() throws ServletException
  {
    try
    {
      File file = new File(this.outputPath + this.filename);

      if (file.exists())
      {
        return;
      }

      FileWriter fw = new FileWriter(file);
      BufferedWriter bw = new BufferedWriter(fw);

      String header = this.survey.formatHeader();
      bw.write(header);
      bw.newLine();
      bw.flush();
      bw.close();
    }
    catch (IOException e)
    {
      throw new ServletException(e);
    }
  }


  /** Append the user's answers to the file. */
  private void appendToFile(HttpServletRequest request) throws ServletException
  {
    try
    {
      FileWriter fw = new FileWriter(this.outputPath + this.filename, true);
      BufferedWriter bw = new BufferedWriter(fw);

      Map parameters = request.getParameterMap();

      String data = this.survey.formatDataFromInput(parameters);
      bw.write(data);
      bw.newLine();
      bw.flush();
      bw.close();
    }
    catch (IOException e)
    {
      throw new ServletException(e);
    }
  }
```

```
/** Add this survey to the list of completed surveys. */
private void updateSession(HttpSession session)
{
  String completedSurveys = (String)session.getAttribute
  (SessionKeys.COMPLETED_SURVEYS.toString());
  String servletName = this.getServletName();
  completedSurveys = completedSurveys + " " + servletName;
  session.setAttribute(SessionKeys.COMPLETED_SURVEYS.toString(),
  completedSurveys);
}

}
```

SurveyListServlet.java

The SurveyListServlet produces an HTML page with links to the surveys that the user has not yet completed.

```
package com.wiley.compBooks.EJwithUML.Samples.Servlets;

import javax.servlet.http.*;
import javax.servlet.*;
import java.util.*;
import java.io.*;

import com.wiley.compBooks.EJwithUML.Base.HtmlPrimitives.Core.*;
import com.wiley.compBooks.EJwithUML.Base.HtmlPrimitives.ContentElements.*;
import com.wiley.compBooks.EJwithUML.Base.HtmlPrimitives.FormPrimitives.*;
import com.wiley.compBooks.EJwithUML.Base.HtmlPrimitives.Layout.*;

/**
 * The SurveyListServlet builds a list of surveys that have not been
 completed by the requestor.

 */
public class SurveyListServlet extends HttpServlet
{
  private ServletContext context;
  private ArrayList surveys = new ArrayList();

  public void init() throws ServletException
  {
    this.context = getServletContext();
    this.parseSurveys();
  }


  public void doGet(HttpServletRequest request, HttpServletResponse response)
  throws IOException
  {
    ParagraphPrimitive list_of_links = new ParagraphPrimitive(Style.
    NORMAL_TEXT, "");
```

```
String completed_surveys = (String)request.getSession(true).getAttribute
(SessionKeys.COMPLETED_SURVEYS.toString());

boolean empty_list = true;
Iterator survey_iterator = this.surveys.iterator();

int ctr = 0;
while (survey_iterator.hasNext())
{
  Survey survey = (Survey)survey_iterator.next();
  String servletName = "SurveyServlet" + ctr;
  String description = survey.getDescription();


  if (completed_surveys == null || completed_surveys.indexOf
  (servletName) == -1)
  {
    TextPrimitive description_p = new TextPrimitive(description);
    LinkPrimitive link = new LinkPrimitive("./" + servletName);
    link.addText(description_p);

    list_of_links.addLink(link);
    list_of_links.addLineBreak();
    list_of_links.addLineBreak();
    empty_list = false;
  }

  ctr++;
}

if (empty_list)
{
  list_of_links = new ParagraphPrimitive(Style.NORMAL_TEXT, "Thank you!
  You have completed all of the surveys!");
}

PagePrimitive page = new PagePrimitive("List of Surveys",
"http://localhost:8080/EJwithUML2e/Default.css");
ParagraphPrimitive paragraph = new ParagraphPrimitive
(Style.NORMAL_TEXT, "");
paragraph.addText(Style.PAGE_TITLE, "List of Surveys");
paragraph.addLineBreak();

page.addToBody(paragraph);
page.addToBody(list_of_links);
StringBuffer buffer = new StringBuffer();
page.buildContent(buffer);

PrintWriter pw = response.getWriter();
pw.print(buffer.toString());
pw.flush();
pw.close();
}
```

```
private void parseSurveys()
{
  int ctr = 0;
  boolean done = false;

  while (!done)
  {
    String key = "SurveyServlet" + ctr;
    String description = getInitParameter(key);

    if (description == null)
    {
      done = true;
    }
    else
    {
      Survey survey = new Survey(description);
      this.surveys.add(survey);
    }

    ctr++;
  }
}
```

SessionKeys.java

The sessionKeys class is a simple enumerated type for session keys. Holding session keys in an enumerated type allows the compiler to verify that each key used to add or retrieve data from the session is a valid key. This greatly simplifies the development process and reduces errors.

```
package com.wiley.compBooks.EJwithUML.Samples.Servlets;

/**
 *  The SessionKeys class provides an enumerated type of keys for
 *  storing and retreiving data in the HttpSession. */
public final class SessionKeys
{
  private String key;

  /** The constructor is private so that all instances of the class
   *  come from the list below.*/
  private SessionKeys(String key)
  {
    this.key = key;
  }

  public String toString()
  {
    return this.key;
  }
```

```
/* Add keys below as needed! */
public static final SessionKeys COMPLETED_SURVEYS = new SessionKeys
("completed surveys");
}
```

Strengths

Servlets are incredibly simple to learn. A simple "hello world" servlet takes only a few lines, and once developers understand the session management logic, a shopping cart servlet is quite trivial.

Servlets protect developers from the HTTP's complexity, since all of the nasty details of parsing and building HTTP headers and payloads are hidden within the HTTP servlet classes.

Weaknesses

Though servlets are technically very sound and very easy to learn, by having a separate servlet for each dynamically generated page, and by lumping data access and HTML production into the doGet or doPost method, it is also very easy to create a maintenance and extensibility nightmare. Despite the simplicity of the servlet classes, servlet-based systems must still be designed with extensibility and flexibility in mind.

Compatible Technologies

Servlets are very compatible with Web technologies, such as HTML, DHTML, JavaScript, and XML. Servlets are often used to create elaborate, dynamically generated Web pages that produce content in these forms.

Servlets are also quite compatible with server-side technologies, such as JDBC, RMI, and EJB. A servlet can easily access a remote control or entity object using RMI or EJB. As with Swing, the variations are limited only by your architectural imagination.

Cost of Adoption

The servlet classes are provided free as part of the enterprise edition of Java, and most commercial quality Web servers include a servlet engine. However, there are other costs of adoption. First and foremost, to be successful with servlets, your project must fill the roles of UI designer, architect, and servlet developer.

UI Designer

It is always good to have a user interface designer who can address usability and human factors. A UI designer devises alternate interface strategies that meet the requirements, and works with the stakeholders and the developers to determine which approach is most suitable for the project. Deliverables range from screen shots in a drawing program to thin prototypes.

This is especially important in servlet development, where user interfaces are limited by the capabilities and idiosyncrasies of the users' browsers. Creativity and persistence are definitely required. Also, the user interface designer for a servlet-based interface must constantly refresh his or her skills, because browsers and Web technologies evolve and mutate at a disturbingly quick pace. At the very least, designers must know or be on a sharp learning curve for HTML, DHTML, JavaScript, XML, and XSL.

Architect

Servlet-based user interfaces can degenerate into a series of unconnected works, with no two following the same format or producing HTML in the same way. An architect can reduce this effect by establishing reusable HTML production classes to produce everything from tables and trees to frames and the enclosing page. This allows developers to easily change the look of the entire application by altering the reusable HTML production classes. The alternative requires each servlet to be laboriously edited, perhaps for something as trivial as the background color or the space between buttons.

The architect can also keep the code base sane and avoid costly rework by establishing standards for exception handling, concurrency, error logging, and the use of session data.

The architect for a servlet-based user interface must have a strong knowledge of object-oriented principles, extensive design experience, an understanding of Web technologies, and a clear grasp of the servlet architecture.

Servlet Developer

Compared to Swing, servlets require substantially less object-oriented sophistication, and frequently have a significantly shorter learning curve. This is especially true when the architect or other senior developer defines the intent of each servlet, and the UI designer prototypes the HTML and associated Web scripting. Given these assumptions, servlet development may serve as an excellent first project for a budding Java developer.

If the architect and user interface designer roles are not filled, then the servlet developer is forced to know everything from object-oriented design to DHTML to JavaScript. This requires a strong object-oriented Java developer who understands Web technologies and who can visualize usable interfaces.

Suitability

In Chapter 6, "Describing the System for Technology Selection," we identified the following descriptive categories:

- User interface complexity
- Deployment constraints for user interfaces
- Number and type of users
- Available bandwidth

Let's see how suitable servlets are for each of these requirements.

User Interface Complexity

Servlets, in combination with HTML, can easily support simple data input and static views of data. First, a servlet formats the HTML for a customized form. When the user submits the form, the form data is sent to a servlet for processing. The servlet can use any other data sources, such as database connections, Enterprise JavaBeans, or external systems, to create a response. The response is usually formatted HTML, although it could be a file or an image.

Customizable views, in which the user can manipulate the view without making a separate request to the server, are more difficult. Remember, the servlet responds to each request with a single block of data that is interpreted by the browser. So, the formatted response must include some combination of more complicated Web technologies, such as JavaScript or DHTML. These solutions depend on the browser to correctly render them, and they must be customized for each browser vendor and browser version. Therefore, creating customizable views using servlets is a complex undertaking that requires patience and a sophisticated understanding of Web technologies.

Dynamic views of the data are equally problematic. Remember, a dynamic view keeps current with the underlying model, either by receiving notification when a change occurs or by periodically retrieving the new data. With servlets and Web browsers, the first option is impossible; the server does not maintain a connection to the Web browser and therefore cannot notify it when the data changes. The second option can be achieved by using JavaScript to reload the entire page or a frame at suitable intervals. Of course, this is not very efficient, as all of the data, not just the updates, must be retrieved. As with customizable views, creating dynamic views using servlets is a complex undertaking that requires patience and a sophisticated understanding of Web technologies.

Interactive graphics, in which the user sees changes as they occur and updates the underlying data by interacting with the graphics, are not possible with servlets and an unmodified Web browser. Just rendering the graphics requires some form of plug-in, such as a VRML or ActiveX viewer. Propagating changes back to the server is even more problematic.

Servlets are most appropriate for simple data input and static views of data. Customizable views and dynamic views of data are quite possible, but depend on browser-specific Web technologies, such as JavaScript and DHTML. Interactive graphics are not possible with servlets and standard Web browsers.

Deployment Constraints for User Interfaces

Servlets can support the entire range of deployment scenarios; the hard part is to generate HTML that presents well for the different users. For instance, a micro-Web browser on a handheld device will not present large images very well, so the HTML produced by the servlet must include an alternate textual description in place of the image.

Number and Type of Users

Servlets are very appropriate for all user communities. The users should not even notice that servlets are being used. They will know that they requested information from a Web server and that they received information in response. They do not need to alter the configuration of their Web browser or accommodate the system in any way.

Available Bandwidth

Servlets are generally appropriate for all bandwidth levels. However, there are some limitations when attempting to stretch the capabilities of the browsers while constrained by low bandwidths. Remember, the browser simply renders the formatted HTML as sent by the Web server and servlet engine. This HTML contains data, presentation instructions, and any special processing logic, all in a form that the browser can interpret. In some cases, this may lead to an amazingly large quantity of HTML. For instance, implementing a customizable view by making each option a separate layer may replicate most or all of the data for each layer. Similarly, implementing a dynamically updated view by reloading the page periodically forces the servlet to send all of the data and presentation instructions each time.

JavaServer Pages

Javaserver Pages (JSP) version 1.2 allows Java developers and Web content developers to collaborate together to create dynamic Web content. JSPs are basically inside-out servlets! The HTML and other content forms the body of the JSP file with Java code embedded in strategic locations. This allows JSP developers to access enterprise resources, such as databases or application servers, while allowing Web content developers to directly manipulate the file's appearance and static content. JSP pages can also easily create and use HTML producers for components that are common from page to page.

This is an extremely powerful development model. Developers can build JSP pages that meet the business requirements, by building the right dynamic data, but look horrible. (We have decades of experience with this approach!) This JSP can then be turned over to the Web content developers who can alter the appearance of the page until it actually provides a pleasant user experience. Alternatively, the Web content developers can create an attractive set of JSP pages with fake data. The Java developers can add the dynamic parts until it actually delivers the right business logic. This shared responsibility continues throughout the project, as Web content developers and JSP developers collaborate closely as the JSP pages evolve. As the appearance of the site solidifies, it is wise to encapsulate common components as described in the HTML production section. JSP development allows Java developers and Web content developers to specialize and cooperate to build fully functional Web-based systems that attract and keep users.

Gory Details

The following sections discuss the details for using JSP to create dynamic content.

While JSP can be used to create almost any type of content, including HTML, XML, and plaintext, this discussion is limited to HTML for simplicity.

JSP Page Translation

Sun provides a tool that translates JSP pages into servlets, either as the last manual step in development or within the servlet container before the page is put in service. This tool walks through the JSP and builds a class that extends a specified class or HttpServlet. If a base class is specified, it must extend HttpServlet. The tool adds a variety of instance variables to the class, method variables to the service methods, methods to the class, and code to the service methods.

JSP pages do not require a well-defined structure. In fact, you can simply rename an existing HTML file to a JSP file and the servlet container will translate it into a servlet. In practice, most JSP pages contain a mixture of content and JSP elements. JSP derives much of its power and flexibility from its ability to mix content and JSP elements.

While JSP pages are lenient in structure, they can be difficult to debug. Errors can be introduced at several levels; since the JSP tags themselves must be well formed, the resulting servlet code must compile. Finally, the actual logic must be correct. I recommend developing JSP pages in tight iterations; code a little, then test a little. Using helper classes is also very helpful, because helper classes can be independently tested.

Directives

Directives are elements that are used to specify independent attributes for the page. For example, the page may need to include classes from a class library, set the content type, include another file, or specify an error page. The form of each directive is <%@ directiveName attribute1="value" attribute2="value" %>. There is no need to explicitly include the end tag, and all attributes must be quoted. There are three directive names and many attributes for each directive:

Page.   The attributes of this directive enable auto flushing, control the buffer size, set the content type, set the scripting language, enable sessions, specify an error page, specify a base class for the generated servlet, import Java classes, provide descriptive information about the page, indicate that the page is an error page, and indicate the thread safety of the page.

Include.   This directive includes the specified file just before the JSP is translated into a servlet. The file attribute uses a URI to specify a fragment of text, HTML, or JSP to include.

Taglib.   This directive includes the specified tag library.

Basic Scripting Elements

There are several scripting elements that embed Java code inside of a page. They allow you to process arbitrary Java code, declare instance variables and methods, and evaluate expressions.

Blocks of arbitrary Java code, known as scriptlets, are contained inside of a <% %> tag. So, the following scriptlet initializes a local variable called favoriteColor that is available to subsequent scriptlets in the page. During the translation phase, this script-let becomes a line inside the doPost or doGet method.

```
<% String favoriteColor = "Blue" %>
```

Declarations of instance variables and methods are contained inside of a <%! %> tag. So, the following declaration is translated into a private instance variable.

```
<%! String outputPath = "c:\EJwithUML\outputfiles\" %>
```

WARNING The little "!" in the declaration element also means "danger," because the resulting instance variable is not thread safe! Accidentally including a "!" can lead to some rather interesting system behavior that doesn't show up until the system is under load.

JSP also includes a neat little trick that takes the value of an expression and adds it to the surrounding content. The content of the <%= %> tag, which is known as an expression, is evaluated and converted to a string. So, the following expression would produce a link with "Blue" as its text:

```
<a href="./mycolor.html"> <%= favoriteColor %> </a>
```

Implicit Objects

JSP also provides an extensive list of predefined objects that can be accessed from any declaration, scriptlet, or expression. They include:

request.   The HttpServletRequest object that is passed to the doPost or doGet method

response.   The HttpServletResponse object that is passed to the doPost or doGet method

session.   The HttpSession object that is bound to the request

application.   The ServletContext object that exposes the configuration and information of the entire Web application

out.   An instance of JspWriter that is equivilent to response.getWriter() in servlets

exception.   An instance of Exception that is only available to error pages

config.   An instance of ServletConfig that exposes the configuration and information of the JSP page

page.   An actual reference to the object that is processing the request

These objects allow you to do everything that you would ordinarily do in servlets.

Action Elements

An action element encapsulates some functionality and exposes it for use within JSP pages. An action element may contain attributes and may be nested inside of another action element. An action element's tag looks like <prefix:action attribute1="value"> where the prefix indicates which tag library to use, and the action indicates which action within the tag library to use.

Sun provides several action elements that greatly simplify JSP pages by streamlining some common tasks. Some of these actions are:

jsp:forward.   Causes the JSP to stop processing the request and forward the request to the specified URI. The content from the initial page is lost.

jsp:include page.   Pulls the content from the specified JSP page, servlet, or static page and includes it in the current page.

jsp:useBean.   Finds or creates a JavaBean for use in one or more JSP pages. The scope of the bean can be set to page, request, session, or application. This provides a convenient way to exchange information among pages and requests.

jsp:setProperty.   Sets a property in a JavaBean that has been identified in a useBean action.

jsp:getproperty.   Adds the value of the specified property of the specified JavaBean to the current content.

Actions encapsulate complexity and expose it in a form that is comfortable for non-coders. Action elements allow you to reuse code and keep your JSP pages readable for both Web content developers and Java developers.

Custom action elements are created by implementing the javax.servlet.jsp.tagext .Tag interface. This interface defines methods for setting attributes, building content when the start tag is processed, and building content when the end tag is processed.

Groups of related custom action elements should be bundled together to form a tag library. The Web application's deployment descriptor uses a taglib element to reference a tag library descriptor. The tag library descriptor maps each tag to a class and lists the attributes that are supported by the tag.

Strengths

JSP allows Java developers and Web content developers to focus on their core competencies, while collaborating to create JSP pages. This clear division of labor can be leveraged to obtain sites that function well and provide a positive user experience.

Weaknesses

The simplicity and quick development cycle of JSP pages can lead developers to create new pages by copying and modifying existing pages. Each new variation is easy and, factoring out common components, seems like a bother. However, over time, a system based on this sort of "cut-and-paste reuse" can become difficult to understand and to modify. Even simple changes to the entire site become problematic. Creating reusable components and tag libraries can prevent this degradation.

JSP requires Java developers to learn a new syntax and a new mechanism for encapsulating functionality. Assuming that the developers are already familiar with servlets, this learning curve is generally manageable.

JSP is also more difficult to debug and unit test than Java servlets. This can be mitigated by keeping as much code as possible out of the JSP pages. Rather than including a lot of code in a scriptlet, consider using a helper class that can be independently unit tested and verified.

Compatible Technologies

Like Java servlets, JSPs are very compatible with Web technologies, such as HTML, DHTML, JavaScript, and XML. JSP is often used to create elaborate, dynamically generated Web pages that produce content in these forms.

JSP pages are also quite compatible with server-side technologies, such as JDBC, RMI, and EJB. A JSP can easily access a remote control or entity object using RMI or EJB. As with Swing and Java servlets, the variations are limited only by your architectural imagination.

Cost of Adoption

The servlet and JSP classes are provided free as part of the enterprise edition of Java, and most commercial-quality Web servers include a servlet engine. However, there are other costs of adoption. First and foremost, to be successful with JSP, your project must fill the roles of UI designer, architect, and servlet developer.

UI Designer

It is always good to have a user interface designer who can address usability and human factors. A UI designer devises alternate interface strategies that meet the requirements, and works with the stakeholders and the developers to determine which approach is most suitable for the project. Deliverables range from screen shots in a drawing program to thin prototypes.

This is especially important in JSP development, where user interfaces are limited by the capabilities and idiosyncrasies of the users' browsers. Creativity and persistence are definitely required. Also, the user interface designer for a servlet-based interface must constantly refresh his or her skills, because browsers and Web technologies evolve and mutate at a disturbingly quick pace. At the very least, designers must know or be on a sharp learning curve for HTML, DHTML, JavaScript, and XML.

Architect

JSP-based user interfaces can degenerate into a series of unconnected works, with no two following the same format or producing HTML in the same way. An architect can reduce this effect by establishing reusable HTML production classes to produce everything from tables and trees to the enclosing page. This allows developers to easily change the look of the entire application by altering the reusable HTML production classes. The alternative requires each JSP to be laboriously edited, perhaps for something as trivial as the background color or the space between buttons.

The architect can also keep the code base sane and avoid costly rework by establishing standards for exception handling, concurrency, error logging, and the use of session data.

The architect for a JSP-based user interface must have a strong knowledge of object-oriented principles, extensive design experience, an understanding of Web technologies, and a clear grasp of the servlet architecture.

JSP Developer

Compared to Swing, JSP requires substantially less object-oriented sophistication, and frequently has a significantly shorter learning curve. This is especially true when the architect or other senior developer defines the intent of each JSP, and the UI designer prototypes the HTML and associated Web scripting. Given these assumptions, JSP development may serve as an excellent first project for a budding Java developer.

If the architect and user interface designer roles are not filled, then the JSP developer is forced to know everything from user interface design to object-oriented design to HTML to JavaScript. This requires a strong object-oriented Java developer who understands Web technologies and who can visualize usable interfaces.

Suitability

The suitability criteria for JavaServer Pages are virtually identical to the criteria for servlets as described in the previous section.

JavaServer Pages and Servlets

This section considers the similarities and differences between JavaServer Pages and Java servlets and suggests some basic criteria for choosing between them for different parts of your system.

Depending on your perspective, JSPs are either virtually identical to Java servlets or completely opposite! First, let's discuss their similarities. JSPs have the same purpose, to process HTTP requests and produce HTTP responses. They also have very similar capabilities. Anything you can do with a servlet can be done with a creatively written JSP. The reverse is also true; anything you can do with a JSP can be done with a creatively written servlet. In fact, every JSP is converted into a servlet by the servlet engine before it begins servicing requests. So, they have similar capabilities, and there is clearly an algorithmic transform from JSPs to servlets. From a technical and capability perspective, they are the same!

However, from an actual practitioner's perspective, JSPs are completely different from Java servlets. Most servlets consist of Java code with HTML inside. Most JSPs consist of HTML with Java inside. JSPs allow developers to quickly create distinct dynamic pages that use Java to leverage enterprise resources and common components. In general, JSPs have a faster code, deploy, and test cycle for appearance changes, while servlets have a faster code, deploy, and test cycle for business logic and system changes. JSPs can also be refined and redeployed by nonprogrammers.

There are several choices for producing Web-based systems with Java:

- Use only servlets.
- Use servlets for complex business logic and system interface logic. Use JSPs for HTML creation.
- Use servlets for complex business logic and system interface logic. Use a mix of servlets and JSPs for HTML creation.
- Use only JSPs

In practice, the last solution is fairly unlikely. Business logic with servlets is just too easy, and redirecting to the JSP page is straightforward. The third solution is interesting but will generally make your system significantly more difficult for new developers to learn. So, the following selection criteria will focus on the first two solutions:

Consistency of page structure.   Some sites have a very consistent and unchanging page structure, perhaps with a logo at the top and a navigational aid on the left and some fine print at the bottom. Other sites vary the structure from page to page in different ways or evolve the structure rapidly.

If most of the pages for a system are well defined and similar to one another, then the common look and feel should be encapsulated into an HTML page producer class, and servlets make slightly more sense. If JSP is indicated by other criteria, you can always use includes, tag libraries, and HTML production components from the JSP pages.

On the other hand, if there is a lot of variation between pages or rapid evolution of the page structure, then encapsulation is impossible, and JSPs definitely make more sense.

Expertise of staff.   Some development teams have a wide spectrum of Java developers, content developers, OO architects, and usability experts. Other teams draw from a less diverse talent pool. Also, some teams have a lot of experienced members who are ready to branch out, while other teams have novices.

If your development team is fairly new to Java and mostly from a development background, then I strongly encourage you to minimize their learning curve by limiting the number of technologies in the system. So, if they already need Java to access the database, then they also use servlets and an HTML production framework for the presentation classes.

On the other hand, if most of your development team come from an HTML and JavaScript background, then use JSP and encourage one or two fast learners to master the Java and OO principles required to implement the data access and business logic for the system.

Complex system interfaces.   Some systems have very complex interfaces with existing systems of records, databases, and even systems owned by other companies. This should not affect your decision when choosing between servlets and JSP! As long as the system interfaces are well encapsulated, they can be independently developed and unit tested.

Emphasis on business logic.   Some systems have very complex business logic. Again, this should not affect your decision when choosing between servlets and JSP! As long as the business logic is well encapsulated, it can be independently developed and unit tested.

It can be difficult to choose between servlets and JSP. However, you are in luck because, with a little planning and discipline, either decision can yield excellent results. If neither option seems a clear win, I suggest that you base the decision on the team's skills and comfort level. If you have access to creative Web content developers who can independently develop static content in JSP pages, then by all means use them. Otherwise, I suspect that most Java developers are more productive using Java servlets and a reasonable HTML production framework.

Technology Selections for the Timecard System

Now that you have an understanding of the different technologies available for user interface classes, let's use the technology requirements from Chapter 6, "Describing the System for Technology Selection," and the technology descriptions from this chapter to select technologies for the timecard system's user interface classes. We'll also need to consider the cost of adopting the technology. Based on our team's composition, we will favor servlets over JSP, so the remaining technology selection will decide between Swing and servlets.

Recall from Chapter 6 that we lumped all of the user interface classes for the system into a single group for technology selection. Also, we characterized those user interface classes in several areas:

User interface complexity.   Simple data input and static view of data.

Deployment constraints for user interfaces.   Late-model Web browser on the Internet.

Number and type of users.   General use within an organization.

Available bandwidth.   Dial-up Internet connection.

Based on these descriptions, we must choose between servlets, JSP, and Swing. Let's examine them individually.

User Interface Complexity

Both technologies are perfectly capable of supporting simple data input and static views of data. Neither technology has an advantage. We will have to base our decision on other criteria.

Deployment Constraints for User Interfaces

Servlets can be used to produce dynamic Web pages for display in any late model browser. Swing is also appropriate for deployment as an applet under these same circumstances, since all late model browsers either have a built-in Java Virtual Machine or support the Java plug-in. This may require the users to install the Java plug-in or change the configuration of their browser.

While these accommodations seem trivial to developers and other power users, some users may resist making them, due to security concerns, lack of time, or for sheer perverse pleasure. Making any additional demands on the user results in extra demands on the development or deployment staff for the system, so servlets have a slight advantage over Swing.

Number and Type of Users

Servlets are appropriate for any number of users. Swing applets are appropriate for general use within an organization. However, there must be some advantage to using Swing, to offset the incremental support costs that result from deploying an applet to a large and often unmotivated audience. In this case, there does not seem to be any advantage to using Swing, since the user interface seems straightforward. Therefore, the advantage is to servlets.

Available Bandwidth

The Timecard system must support low-bandwidth scenarios, such as traveling employees using a slow dial-up connection. On the other hand, updating a timecard does not require much data. Either Swing or servlets are perfectly appropriate. There's no advantage to either technology. We will have to base our decision on other criteria.

Cost of Adoption

The cost of adopting servlets for this application is quite low, as the user interface is fairly straightforward. The UI designer and servlet developers should have a reasonably easy time. As far as user interface classes go, this project is appropriate for developers with low to moderate experience in Web technologies and Java development.

The cost of adopting Swing for this application could be a bit higher, due to the complexity of Swing development. Unless the developers already know Swing, and do not know any Web technologies, the cost of adoption is clearly higher for Swing. Servlets, therefore, have the advantage.

Conclusion

The Timecard application could reasonably be implemented with either Swing or servlets. However, there are no indications for choosing Swing over servlets. In the absence of any strong preference on the part of the development staff or the users, we will use servlets.

The Next Step

UML provides package dependency diagrams that show the relationships between large parts of the system. In this case, we can show that the user interface classes depend on the servlet classes and the HTML primitives. Figure 9.9 shows these relationships.

Now that we have decided to use servlets to implement the user interface classes, we can turn our attention to boundary classes.

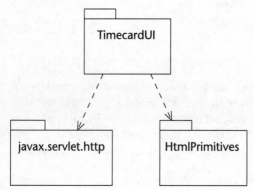

Figure 9.9 Package dependencies and technology selection.

CHAPTER 10

Evaluating Candidate Technologies for the System Interface

Between layers in an *n*-tier application, or between applications in an application integration scenario, the system interfaces are not always graphical in nature. The technologies used to realize these non-GUI boundary classes are very different from technologies (JSP, Swing) used for traditional boundary classes. XML has become the de facto standard for representing data across these boundaries. While data are represented in XML, they are exchanged using message-oriented middleware such as MQSeries or Tibco. This chapter covers these technologies that are used to implement system interfaces:

- XML has become the technology of choice in representing data across system boundaries.

- Simple API for XML or SAX is a lightweight XML parser that helps parse XML data exchanged across system boundaries.

- Document Object Model or DOM API provides another way to handle XML data.

- Java Messaging Service, or JMS, allows Java applications to use message-oriented middleware (MOM) to integrate with each other in a loosely coupled and flexible manner.

The following sections consider these technologies in some detail.

XML

The Extensible Markup Language (XML) is a rare example of an extremely hyped technology that really is worth the hoopla. Since its specification by the World Wide Web Consortium (W3C) in 1998, XML has become the standard mechanism for storing and exchanging descriptive data via electronic data interchange (EDI). Industry groups and government agencies are establishing XML document formats to describe everything from astronomical data to job descriptions to workflow management. Other common uses include configuration files, flexible data storage, and language-independent object serialization.

XML documents are valuable for people as well as computers. XML documents are precise enough for computers to create, read, and update them. Most people find them fairly easy to work with, especially with the aid of an XML authoring tool. For example, authors might use XML to divide a document into sections and to describe the suitability of the document for various audiences, based on their language and organizational role. An XML-based document management system can tailor each user's view of the documents based on the user's profile and the suitability description.

Before continuing this discussion in more depth, there are a few key terms that must be defined:

Element. XML divides a document into elements. Each element may contain data, attributes, and other elements. Conceptually, elements are rather like nodes in a tree.

Document type definition (DTD). This defines the structure of a set of documents. Specifically, a DTD defines which elements can be part of each element, how many elements can be used, and in what order. The notation is reasonably simple and consistent with other pattern definitions, such as regular expressions.

XML Schema. This defines the structure of an XML document. It is an alternative to DTD and a preferred approach. The difference between DTD and XML Schema is that DTD has its own notation, which is different from XML's, whereas XML Schema is expressed in XML. Also, it is much more flexible and expressive than DTD.

Namespace. This is a mechanism used to associate elements of a document with a particular context within which the name of an element is unique. This helps to avoid name collision.

Parser. This breaks a document into a tree of elements, and validates the document's structure against the DTD. Note that the validation tests for the presence of the correct elements, attributes, and data within defined elements. It does not test data against an allowable range, or even differentiate between letters and numbers.

Authoring tool. This helps a human being read and write XML documents that are valid for a particular DTD. Authoring tools reduce typing and save your sanity, so you want one of these.

Now, we can plunge into the details of XML.

Gory Details

XML allows people and computers to create and read documents that present data and describe themselves. This section discusses the structure of XML documents and the technology for creating and parsing XML documents.

Self-Describing Documents

Every piece of data in an XML document is inside of an element or is a named attribute of an element. As long as the author of the DTD/XML Schema picks explanatory names for elements and attributes, the XML document is self-describing. This eliminates an entire class of errors that have plagued EDI developers for decades. Traditionally, a protocol or data interchange format described the meaning and allowable values for each position in each record. Imagine the resulting chaos if a program reads field 11, which is Social Security number, as field 12, which is age in seconds since 1970. Also, changing the interchange format may ruin existing documents; you certainly cannot safely delete a field or insert one in the middle.

Now, consider a self-describing document format, such as XML. There is never any argument over the identity of a piece of data. The name literally surrounds the data. Of course, there may be arguments over the associated units or how to interpret the data, but this is hardly the technology's fault. Also, a new element can be added anywhere in the document. As long as it is optional, no existing documents break. This really helps when different organizations create documents that are similar but not identical in structure.

For example, XML can be used to describe a transaction in a form that is easy to read and unambiguous for both human beings and computers. Consider the following brief snippet of XML that describes a single transaction in which someone gets very lucky on February 1, 1999.

```
<transaction>
  <date>
    <day>1</day>
    <month>Febuary</month>
    <year>1999</month>
  </date>
  <amount>
    <value>1000000</value>
    <units>USD</units>
  </amount>
</transaction>
```

Consider the alternate approach of simply allocating a particular number of bytes for each field. Tiny disagreements in the size or starting index of a field can lead to strange and sometimes difficult-to-diagnose problems. The following densely packed line shows the same data as in the preceding XML sample; however, the meaning of each byte is left to the human being or computer that reads the line.

```
01Febuary   19991000000USD
```

Parsers

Parsers come in two flavors and use two parsing methods. First, parsers either validate the document against the DTD or they don't. Thus, parsers are often described as validating or nonvalidating. The first parsing method, the Simple API for XML (SAX), is an event-based parser that deserves recognition for its elegance and the fact that its acronym encapsulates two other acronyms. The second parsing method, the Document Object Model (DOM), builds a tree of elements in memory. Let's look at these two parsing technologies briefly. Later in this chapter we describe each of these technologies in greater detail from the application development perspective.

SAX

As a SAX parser works its way through an XML document, it notifies the registered document handler whenever an element begins and ends. This allows the handler to react to the content a piece at a time, so it can build objects or perform any required actions. Any extraneous information is discarded, with no wasted memory. Also, it is easy to stop parsing at any point. For instance, an application might parse through a document looking for the first valid record. With a SAX parser, it is easy to stop because it is processing one record at a time.

Writing applications that use a SAX parser can be somewhat tedious, however, because each event must be caught, identified, and processed. This is especially painful when the processing depends on where the element occurs in the tree.

DOM

DOM parsers are generally built on top of a SAX parser; they provide an extra level of convenience. A DOM parser builds a tree structure from the document. Once the entire document has been parsed, this tree structure can be navigated and explored at length. Also, an application can modify the DOM tree and save it as a new XML document. So, for many applications, a DOM parser is the clear choice.

Unfortunately, this convenience may come at a price. The entire document is parsed and held in memory before the tree of elements is returned to the application. DOM parsers are notoriously wasteful if the document is large and the application needs only a fraction of the data. Or are they? Some DOM parsers accept event handler objects and notify them when certain events occur. For instance, IBM's venerable, and horribly named, xml4j parser allows an application to register element event handler objects with the parser. These handlers are notified when matching elements are completely parsed. In this scheme, the element handler can do nothing, can replace the element with another element, or can consume the element completely. If the parser supports this sort of scheme, then developers get the convenience of a nice DOM tree without the wasted space.

NOTE IBM's xml4j has been integrated into Apache's open source toolkit for XML. It is now called Xerces. While the name is undeniably cool, it is even less explanatory.

Strengths

XML greatly improves data interchange between peer systems and between people and systems. It dramatically decreases development time and minimizes the risk of translation errors. In short, it actually deserves its hype.

Weaknesses

If network bandwidth is a very high priority, then an XML document with more bytes spent on element names than on the actual data values may be a foolish luxury. Otherwise, it is a great way to exchange data.

Another less obvious weakness of XML is its natural hierarchical structure. While XML is perfect for treelike data, it is not such a natural fit for webs of interconnected nodes. Relationships must be stored as data. This may seem awkward, and prove to be error-prone, because deleting a data element requires the deletion of the associated relationships.

Compatible Technologies

XML can be used by any Java application, applet, or servlet. It is used to store information on both clients and servers, and to communicate between different parts of the same system and between different systems. It truly is well on its way to ubiquity.

Cost of Adoption

Use of XML requires several, some, or all of the following roles.

DTD Author

DTD authors determine the structure of XML documents. At a minimum, they need a mastery of the data that is described in the document, and a facility with the syntax and idioms of DTDs. Fortunately, DTDs are fairly straightforward, and there are many excellent texts on the pragmatics and theory of DTD construction. Also, an effective DTD author needs a strong vision for the future of the document.

In some cases, the DTD author may not have sole control over the document's structure. In many cases, XML documents help diverse organizations exchange information. Each organization promotes certain perspectives and interests as the document structure evolves by consensus. A DTD author in such a situation needs patience and persistence in unusually large quantities, as well as skills in negotiation and compromise.

Document Author

Once the DTD solidifies, actually authoring XML documents is fairly straightforward. Tools automate much of the drudgery, and prevent invalid XML based on a particular DTD. This frees the document author to concentrate on the actual data.

In some cases, humans do not create XML documents. Instead, XML documents are generated by a system. For instance, a system may extract data from a database and convert it into XML. In this case, there is no need for a human document author.

Developer

XML development requires developers to learn at least one parser technology. Fortunately, documentation and sample code for XML parsers is readily available. XML development does not generally require extensive knowledge of the Java class libraries.

Suitability

Recall from Chapter 6, "Describing the System for Technology Selection," that system interfaces can be divided into three categories: data transfer, services through a protocol, and direct access to system services. This section explores XML applicability for these three categories.

Data Transfer

XML is very useful for data transfer between systems. XML was created in part as a more flexible and easy-to-use alternative for electronic data interchange. One system may extract data from a database or two, use an XML parser to build an XML document, and send the document across to the other system. The receiving system can use a parser to recover the document. Once a system has recovered a document, it can process each element individually or build a set of interrelated objects.

XML is an excellent choice for system interfaces that emphasize data transfer.

Services through a Protocol

XML is also very useful for system interfaces that allow one system to receive services through a series of requests and responses. One system builds an XML document and sends it over a socket connection to the server system. The server parses the request, performs any required actions, builds a response document with XML, and sends it back to the client system. The same flexibility and extensibility characteristics that make XML an ideal EDI technology are assets in this situation. Also, the readability of XML is very helpful when debugging the interactions between the client and server.

Direct Access to System Services

This type of system interface exposes some of its methods for remote access. XML is gaining acceptance as an object serialization mechanism for use with language-independent remote method invocation. Hopefully, this will allow greater interoperability between EJB and CORBA systems in the near future.

SAX

SAX, Simple API for XML, uses event models for parsing XML documents. SAX parsers report contents of XML documents as parsing events. Examples of such events are the start of a document, the end of a document, the start of an element, the end of an element, and so on. Applications selectively capture these events and take appropriate actions. While the SAX API originally targeted the Java platform, ports to other language platforms have emerged.

The development of SAX started on the XM-DEV mailing list under David Magginson's coordination. The SAX 1.0 specification was released in 1998. Since its first release, it gained popularity and is now in release 2.0. Recently, it has been institutionalized under the Source Forge project infrastructure and has found an official Web site: www.saxproject.org.

SAX 1 defines an API for parsing XML 1.0 documents without a namespace. SAX 2 adds support for namespaces, filters, and properties, while modifying some interfaces from SAX 1 in non-backward-compatible fashion. Earlier in this chapter, we briefly described the SAX parser. In this section, we will discuss SAX 2.0 in greater detail.

Gory Details

Applications using a SAX parser register their interests in specific events through handlers. As the parser works its way through an XML document, it notifies the application of the requested events through the registered handlers. It is the responsibility of the applications to track and decide what to do with the contents as they are reported as events. Typically, applications store the data in an application-specific format or take some actions based on the content and forget about it. The data not stored by the applications are lost.

In the following sections, we will look at some of the key interfaces and classes of SAX and how they work together to accomplish parsing. All the interfaces needed for parsing can be found in the org.xml.sax package. The parser provider implements some of these interfaces, while the others are there for the applications to implement as deemed necessary. Default implementations of some of these interfaces are provided in the org.xml.sax.helpers package.

NOTE To ensure the portability of your application to SAX parsers from different vendors, you should not refer to the driver-specific implementation classes explicitly. Rather, you should only use the interfaces defined in the org.xml.sax package. This will allow you to swap drivers without any code change. One such widely used implementation is available from Apache and is known as Xerces.

XMLReader

XMLReader is the interface that represents the SAX parser. It is a new interface added in SAX 2 and replaces the Parser interface defined in SAX 1. A parser provider implements this interface. An application developer instantiates a parser through a factory class: XMLReaderFactory. Before you can use the parser, you would need to provide Handler objects to the parser. At a minimum, you would need to provide a ContentHandler and an ErrorHandler. XMLReader defines a setter method for registering each type of handler. For example, the setContentHandler method is used to provide the ContentHandler object to the parser.

XMLReader defines methods to set and query different features and properties of the underlying parser. Features and properties allow applications to customize the behavior of the parsers. The distinction between features and properties is that features will always have Boolean values, whereas properties can have any types of values. Both feature and property names are fully qualified URIs. All SAX parsers must support two features: "http://xml.org/sax/features/namespace" with true value and "http://xml.org/sax/features/namespace-prefix" with false value. This is to ensure that parsers can support all emerging higher-level specifications such as RDF, XSL, XML Schemas, and Xlink. SAX also defines standard IDs or names for some optional features such as validation. As shown in the code sample below, you can query the parser whether or not validation is supported, or you can turn the validation on before parsing a document. If the parser does not understand a feature or a property name, the setter or getter methods throw SAXNotRecognizedException. But if a parser does not support a feature or a property, the setter or getter methods throw SAXNotSupportedException.

```
boolean isValidating =
parser.getFeature("http://xml.org/sax/features/validation");
```

or

```
parser.setFeature("http://xml.org/sax/features/validation", true);
```

Parser providers can define new features and properties specific for their parser implementations. But they must use their own URIs to name these features and properties.

Once the application configures the parser, it calls the parse() method by passing the XML document to be parsed as an argument. There are two overloaded parse methods. One takes an XML document as an InputSource, and the other takes the URI of the XML document.

ContentHandler

ContentHandler is the main interface that all applications should implement. It is a new interface added in SAX 2 and replaces the DocumentHandler interface in SAX 1. Applications interested in the basic parsing events implement this interface and provide application-specific logic to handle different events. The events supported by this interface include the start of a document, the end of a document, the start of an element, the content of the element (character data), and the end of an element. An understanding of the order of the events is very important because the parser will report these events in the order in which they occur. Typically, applications do not directly implement this interface. Rather, they extend a default implementation of this interface, DefaultHandler, which is provided in the org.xml.sax.helpers package.

The application creates an instance of the concrete handler and registers it with the parser through the setContentHandler() method of the XMLReader interface. The parser uses this handler object to communicate parsing events back to the application. Hence the methods on this interface are called callback methods. Each type of event has a corresponding callback method. The following are the important callback methods:

startDocument.   This signals the occurrence of the start tag of the root element of the XML document.

startElement.   This signals the occurrence of the start tag of any subsequent element of the XML document.

characters.   This signals an occurrence of a text value of an element preceding this event.

endElement.   This signals the occurrence of the end tag of the element corresponding to the latest startElement event.

endDocument.   This signals the occurrence of the end tag of the root element.

ErrorHandler

ErrorHandler is an interface that allows a parser to communicate different error conditions that it encounters during the parsing of XML documents. SAX parsers do not throw exceptions to report errors related to parsing XML documents. Instead they use callbacks through error handlers. Parsers pass instances of SAXParseException as arguments to these methods. SAXParseException contains the detail of the exception, including the location of the error in the XML documents. Applications can simply throw a SAXParseException as is, or throw application-specific exceptions derived from SAXException. Alternatively, applications can choose to take some action based on the information in the SAXParseException, or ignore the errors and proceed with the parsing of the rest of the document. SAX classifies errors into three categories, and ErrorHandler defines one method for each of these types:

Error.   Errors that are recoverable from as defined in XML 1.0 specification. The callback method to report this type of errors is error().

Fatal Errors.   Errors that are nonrecoverable from as defined in XML 1.0 specification. The callback method to report this type of errors is fatalError().

Warnings.   All other errors. The callback method to report this type of errors is warning().

If an application does not register an error handler with the parser, the parser ignores all the errors except fatal errors, in which case it throws SAXParserException.

The parser may behave erratically if errors or warnings are ignored. So, it is recommended that applications provide error handlers. A default implementation of this interface is DefaultHandler provided in the org.xml.sax.helpers package. Instead of directly implementing the ErrorHandler interface, you can extend your own error handler from DefaultHandler and just override the methods that you need to override.

NOTE The SAX parser always throws exceptions for non-XML errors.

Attributes

The Attributes interface allows applications to access individual attributes of an element by index or by name. It also allows applications to query the types of the attributes. A concrete implementation of this interface is provided in the org.xml.sax.helpers package as the AttributeImpl class. It is a new class defined in SAX 2 and replaces the class AttributeList in SAX 1.

The attributes of an element are reported as an instance of Attributes with the startElement() callback method in ContentHandler. Applications then can access the attributes from the Attributes object. This interface defines methods to access the values of an attribute by index, by XML 1.0 qualified name, or by Namespace name. It also defines methods to look up the index, given the name of an attribute.

Locator

The Locator interface allows the parser to provide the location of the element being parsed as an approximate line number. This information can be used for debugging purposes. Applications can access the location of the current event from the ContentHandler. The information is only valid for the current event.

InputSource

InputSource is a wrapper class that encapsulates an XML document independent of its actual type. An input source can be a Java byte stream, a character stream, or an URI. The parser uses InputSource to determine how to read the document.

XMLReaderFactory

The XMLReaderFactory class, defined in the org.xml.sax.helpers package, provides static factory methods to create SAX 2 parser—an instance of the XMLReader class. It decouples the application from directly referencing the actual parser class.

It can create a parser from a concrete XMLReader class name provided explicitly by the caller. Alternatively, it can create a parser by looking up a class name from either a system property, "org.xml.sax.driver," or in the META-INF/services/org.xml.sax. driver file in JAR files on the CLASSPATH. The latter approach is preferred over explicitly providing the parser class name, because it allows applications to use different drivers without modifying any code.

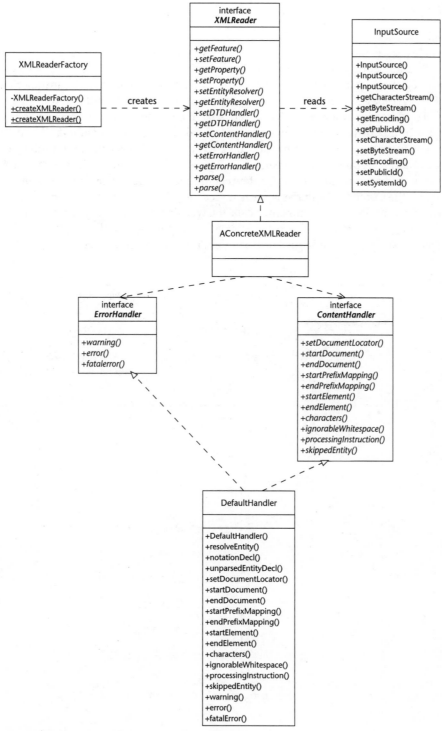

Figure 10.1   XMLReader and its associations.

All Together

The relationships among all the key interfaces and classes discussed in the previous sections are shown in Figure 10.1. The sequence diagram shown in Figure 10.2 depicts the key interactions among different objects participating in a hypothetical scenario of parsing an XML document. First, the application creates an instance of XMLReader—the SAX2 parser. It then creates instances of ErrorHandler and Content-Handler and registers them with the parser. Next, it creates an InputSource by passing the name of the XML document to be parsed. Finally, it initiates parsing on the XML document by calling the parse method on the parser and passing the InputSource object to it as an argument. As the parser starts parsing the document, it calls the start-Document callback method on the ContentHandler. The parser calls the startElement method on the ContentHandler as soon as it sees the first element. When it encounters a warning condition in the document, it calls the warning method on the ErrorHandler. The ErrorHandler ignores the warning. The parser continues with the parsing. Finally, it wraps up parsing by calling the endDocument method on ContentHandler.

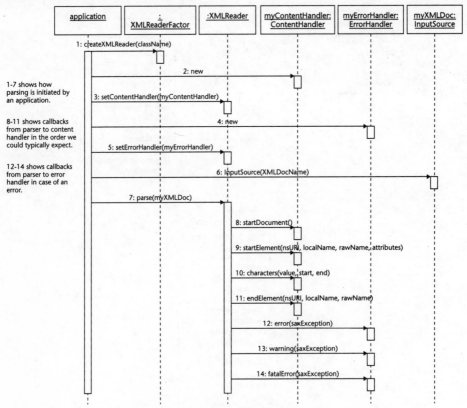

Figure 10.2 A sequence diagram—parsing an XML document.

TIP XMLReader and Handler objects should be created on a per thread basis. Since SAX does not explicitly deal with concurrency, you should consult your driver documentation for reusing an XMLReader object. An easier solution is to create them for each parsing and throw them away at the end of each parsing.

An Example

The following sample application shows how to implement a content handler and error handler as well as how to parse an XML document using these custom handlers. The handlers are derived from the DefaultHandler provided in the org.xml.sax.helpers package. Implementing handlers using DefaultHandler is quicker and easier than directly implementing the ContentHandler and ErrorHandler interfaces. Default-Handler allows us to override only the methods that we are interested in.

Let's consider an XML document as shown here:

```
<transaction>
    <date>
            <day>1</day>
            <month>2</month>
            <year>1999</year>
    </date>
    <amount value="1000000" unit="USD"/>
</transaction>
```

As shown in the following example, we define a content handler that tracks the transaction attributes and provides a method to return the date of the transaction as a Java Date object. We could similarly provide a method to return a transaction object. We would like to leave that as a fun-to-do task for you.

XMLTransactionHandler.java

```
package com.wiley.compBooks.EJwithUML.Samples.Sax;

import java.util.*;
import java.io.*;
import org.xml.sax.*;
import org.xml.sax.helpers.*;

/**
 * A custom implementation of ContentHandler. This shows
 * the order of the main parsing events as they occur.It also
 * shows how we can track data and map them onto
 * application-specific aggregate data.
 */
public class XMLTransactionHandler extends DefaultHandler
{
    HashMap transaction = new HashMap();
```

```java
    String currentElement;

    public void startDocument()throws SAXException
    {
        System.out.println("event - startDocument");
    }

    public void startElement(String namespaceURI, String localName, String
qName, Attributes atts) throws SAXException
    {
        System.out.println("event - startElement(" + qName + ")");
        currentElement = localName;
    }

    public void characters(char[] ch, int start, int end) throws SAXException
    {
        String value = new String(ch, start, end).trim();
        System.out.println("event - elementValue(" + value + ")");
        if (!value.equals(""))
        {
        transaction.put(currentElement, value);
        }
    }

    public void endElement(String namespaceURI, String localName, String
qName) throws SAXException
    {
        System.out.println("event - endElement(" + qName + ")");
      currentElement = null;
    }

    public void endDocument() throws SAXException
    {
        System.out.println("event - endDocument");
    }

    public Date getTransactionDate() throws IOException
    {
     int month = Integer.parseInt((String)transaction.get("month"));
     int day = Integer.parseInt((String)transaction.get("day"));
     int year = Integer.parseInt((String)transaction.get("year"));
     Calendar calendar = Calendar.getInstance();
     /*
      * months are numbered from 0-11 internally in Java, but month
      * in printed format ranges from 1-12. It clears the hour,
      * minute, and seconds.
      */
     calendar.set(year, month-1, day, 0, 0, 0);
      return calendar.getTime();
      }

}
```

We define a custom error handler from DefaultHandler as shown in the following example. In DefaultHandler, the error() and warning() methods ignore the errors. In our implementation, we override the default behavior of these methods to throw exceptions.

XMLTransactionErrorHandler.java

```
package com.wiley.compBooks.EJwithUML.Samples.Sax;

import org.xml.sax.*;
import org.xml.sax.helpers.*;

/**
 * A custom implementation of ErrorHanlder. This shows
 * what can be done in the event of an error. It overrides
 * the default behavior provided in DefaultHandler.
 */
public class XMLTransactionErrorHandler extends DefaultHandler
{
    public void warning(SAXParseException exception)
                        throws SAXException
    {
      System.out.println("event - warning");
      /*
       * any other application specific error handling
       * code could go here.
        */
      throw exception;
    }


    public void error(SAXParseException exception)
           throws SAXException
    {
      System.out.println("event - error");
      /*
       * any other application specific error handling
       * code could go here.
       */
      throw exception;
    }


    public void fatalError(SAXParseException exception)
                  throws SAXException
    {
      System.out.println("event - fatal error");
      /*
       * any other application specific error handling
       * code could go here.
       */
       throw exception;
    }
}
```

Now, we write the main application that reads the transaction information as an XML document and parses it to get the transaction date as a Java Date object. The example uses the Xerces SAX parser available from Apache. This parser supports the validation feature.

XMLTransactionApplication.java

```java
package com.wiley.compBooks.EJwithUML.Samples.Sax;

import java.io.*;
import org.xml.sax.*;
import org.xml.sax.helpers.*;

/**
 * This is an application that parses an XML transaction
 * document using SAX parser.
 */
public class XMLTransactionApplication
{
    public static void main(String[] args)
    {
        if (args.length != 1)
        {
            System.out.println("usage: java com.wiley.compBooks.EJwithUML.
Samples.Sax.XMLTransactionApplication <xmlDataFile>");
        }
        else
        {
          InputSource xmlTransaction = new InputSource(args[0]);
          ContentHandler contentHandler = new XMLTransactionHandler();
          ErrorHandler errorHandler = new
XMLTransactionErrorHandler();
            try
            {
             XMLReader parser = XMLReaderFactory.createXMLReader(
             "org.apache.xerces.parsers.SAXParser");
            parser.setContentHandler(contentHandler);
            parser.setErrorHandler(errorHandler);
                parser.parse(xmlTransaction);
                System.out.println("transaction date: " +
        ((XMLTransactionHandler)contentHandler).getTransactionDate());
            }
            catch (IOException e)
            {
                System.out.println("invalid date - " + e.getMessage());
            }
            catch (SAXException e)
            {
                System.out.println("invalid transaction - " +
        e.getMessage());
            }
```

```
            }
         }
      }
```

Strengths

The SAX parser can be very efficient and fast because it does not store the XML document in memory. Hence, it is best suited for systems with memory constraints like hand-held devices. It is also suitable for applications that need to perform some actions based on the values of certain elements of the XML document, or for applications that need to map the data to strongly typed data objects.

Weaknesses

When applications require using the knowledge of the structure of the original XML document, or need to manipulate the XML document in its original structure, the SAX parser is not a good choice. If applications need to keep track of the data as well as their locations, the SAX parser provides little or no help. In those cases, the burden falls squarely on the shoulders of the application developer, which can become quite tedious.

Compatible Technologies

The SAX API can be used by any type of Java application, including servlets, Swing, command-line applications, and Enterprise Java Beans.

Cost of Adoption

The SAX API is available for free as part of the Xerces XML toolkit from Apache. There are two forces that can influence the decision of whether to adopt a SAX parser for your project. On one hand, the SAX API is a relatively small library to learn. A developer with some experience with the Java language should be able to use SAX in a short period of time. On the other hand, the event model of the SAX parsers may pose some challenges to using it effectively. To get the full value from the API, your project must fill the roles of designer and developer.

Designer

A designer must develop standards for what SAX events will be logged, and what the default actions will be for error, fatal error, and warning events. The designer must also make sure the handlers are implemented in a thread-safe way.

Developer

Each developer is responsible for understanding the SAX event model, XML syntax, associated rules and concepts, and concurrency issues.

DOM

Document Object Model, or DOM for short, is a platform- and language-neutral interface that allows applications to process XML and HTML documents. With DOM, an XML document is represented as a tree (hierarchy of nodes as elements) in memory. A tree view fits naturally with an XML document and so is easier to understand from the user's perspective.

Activity on DOM was initiated by the DOM working group at the World Wide Web Consortium in August 1997. The first specification on DOM came out in October 1998. This specification is called DOM Level 1. W3C has broken down the DOM architecture into modules. Examples of such modules are DOM core, DOM XML, DOM HTML, DOM events, and so on. W3C is addressing all these modules of the DOM architecture in phases or levels. In the Level 1 specification, they addressed XML 1.0 and HTML. The Level 2 specification was introduced in November 2000 and extended Level 1 with support for XML 1.0 with namespaces, CSS (Cascading Style Sheets), events, and tree manipulations through range and traversal. Currently, W3C is working on the Level 3 specification. Earlier in this chapter, we briefly described the DOM parser. In this section, we will look at DOM level 2 implementation in greater detail.

Gory Details

The parser that returns XML documents as DOM objects is called a DOM parser. However, the DOM specification does not provide any parser-specific interface like the XMLReader in SAX. The driver provider is free to choose any parser under the hood. The widely used XML toolkit from Apache called Xerces implements the DOM parser on top of Apache's SAX parser.

Once an application initiates parsing using a DOM parser, the parser creates a corresponding tree view of the XML document in memory and hands it over to the application as a Document object. The application can then explore and modify this Document object as needed.

Let's look at the key interfaces and classes that are needed at a minimum to parse an XML document as a DOM object and access its different parts. The core interfaces required to represent a document in a treelike structure can be found in the org.w3c.dom package.

Node

Node is the basic interface of the DOM API. It is intended to be the base interface for all other components of a document tree. It represents a single node in the tree. A Node object cannot exist outside a document. Hence, all nodes are always associated with a Document object called Owner Document. A node is associated with an owner document at the time of its creation. This association cannot be altered later, as it does not provide any setter method for this. This establishes a strong aggregation type relationship between a Document and a Node where the Document is the whole and the Node is the part. You can always get the owner document of a Node by calling getOwnerDocument.

There can be three types of nodes based on their relationships to each other: sibling nodes, parent nodes, and child nodes. A sibling node is a node with the same parent node. A parent node is the immediate node at one level up. A child node is an immediate node at one level down. A root node does not have a parent node or a sibling node. DOM does not define interfaces to represent these types of nodes. Instead, the Node interface defines a set of methods to deal with these relationships. Thanks to people who worked on DOM, the names of these methods are pretty self-explanatory. For example, you can get to the parent node by calling getParentNode, or you can get to all the child nodes by calling getChildNodes, or you can get to the next sibling node by calling getNextSibling.

Nodes are also classified according to the types of their contents. These types are defined as constants in the Node interface, as shown in Figure 10.3. DOM also defines specific interfaces to represent most of these types of nodes. All of these interfaces extend from Node. If the methods of Node interface are not meaningful to a specific type of node, the concrete implementation of that type of node must throw DOMException. For example, a Text node cannot have child nodes, and hence the implementation of the getChildNodes() of a concrete Text class throws DOMException.

The Node interface also defines methods to deal with a node in a generic fashion without having to typecast a Node object to its more specific type. These methods are getNodeType, getNodeName, and getNodeValue. These methods return null for nodes that have no values.

To handle child nodes in a group, DOM defines two interfaces representing a collection of nodes. One is NamedNodeMap. It allows applications to access nodes by names or by index. However, the order of the nodes is not indicative of how they are defined in the actual document. The other is NodeList. It represents an ordered list of nodes accessed by index. The order of the nodes is defined by the implementor.

Document

The Document interface represents the entire XML or HTML document. It extends the Node interface. A DOM parser creates a Document object representing the XML document passed to it. Then an application can get to any element in the document by following the link starting at the root element. The method getDocumentElement returns the root element. The root element holds all other elements in the document as a hierarchy of nodes using the Composite pattern [Gamma 1995].

Node
+ELEMENT_NODE:short +ATTRIBUTE_NODE:short +TEXT_NODE:short +CDATA_SECTION_NODE:short +ENTITY_REFERENCE_NODE:short +ENTITY_NODE:short +PROCESSING_INSTRUCTION_NODE:short +COMMENT_NODE:short +DOCUMENT_NODE:short +DOCUMENT_TYPE_NODE:short +DOCUMENT_FRAGMENT_NODE:short +NOTATION_NODE:short
+getNodeName():String +getNodeValue():String +setNodeValue(:java.lang.String):void +getNodeType():short +getParentNode():Node +getChildNodes():NodeList +getFirstChild():Node +getLastChild():Node +getPreviousSibling():Node +getNextSibling():Node +getAttributes():NamedNodeMap +getOwnerDocument():Document +insertBefore(:Node,:Node):Node +replaceChild(:Node,:Node):Node +removeChild(:Node):Node +appendChild(:Node):Node +hasChildNodes():boolean +cloneNode(:boolean):Node +normalize():void +isSupported(:String,:String):boolean +getNamespaceURI():String +getPrefix():String +setPrefix(:String):void +getLocalName():String +hasAttributes():boolean

Figure 10.3   The Node interface.

As shown in Figure 10.4, the methods of this interface can be grouped into two sets. The first set of methods allows applications to create different types of nodes in the context of a document. These methods are called factory methods. An example of such a method is createElement(). The second set of methods provides access to different information associated with the document such as the root document and the document type.

Element

This interface represents an element in an XML document. It extends the Node interface. It provides methods to manipulate attributes of an element. Attributes can be accessed as Attr objects or as values by name.

Document
+getDoctype():DocumentType
+getImplementation():DOMImplementation
+getDocumentElement():Element
+createElement(:String):Element
+createDocumentFragment():DocumentFragment
+createTextNode(:String):Text
+createComment(:String):Comment
+create CDATASection(:String):CDATASection
+creatProcessingInstruction(:String,:String):ProcessingInstruction
+createAttribute(:String):Attr
+createEntityReference(:String):EntityReference
+getElementsByTagName(:String):NodeList
+importNode(:Node,:boolean):Node
+createElementNS(:String,:String):Element
+createAttributeNS(:String,:String):Attr
+getElementsByTagNameNS(:String,:String):NodeList
+getElementsById(:java.lang.String):org.w3c.dom.Element

Figure 10.4 The Document interface.

Attr

This interface represents an attribute of an element. Even though it extends the Node interface, it is not treated as a real node. This is because in DOM, attributes are not treated as child nodes of the elements they qualify. Rather, the DOM considers attributes as properties of elements and does not allow them to have separate identities from the elements they describe. Hence, the DOM does not implement them as a part of the document tree. They are treated separately from other nodes. The Node interface defines a special method, getAttributes, to access attributes associated with a node, if any. For the same reason, the parent node, previous sibling, and next sibling for Attr objects are always null values.

Attr defines methods to access its name, its value, and the element it describes. Although the value of an attribute can be a reference to another element, core DOM does not support this. So, the getValue method always returns the value as a string.

CharacterData

This interface defines methods to manipulate character data and is treated as a node. It is not meant to be used directly from an application. It is used as a base interface for all other interfaces that represent different types of character data in an XML document, such as CDATA, comment, and text.

Text

This is an interface representing the textual content of an element or an attribute. It extends the CharacterData interface and is treated as a type of node.

All Together

The class diagram in Figure 10.5 puts all these interfaces together to show their relationships to each other and their concrete classes. The DOM specification does not provide any concrete classes for any of these interfaces. The driver provider implements these interfaces. The concrete classes shown in the diagram are intended for illustration purposes only. They do not represent any concrete implementation available today.

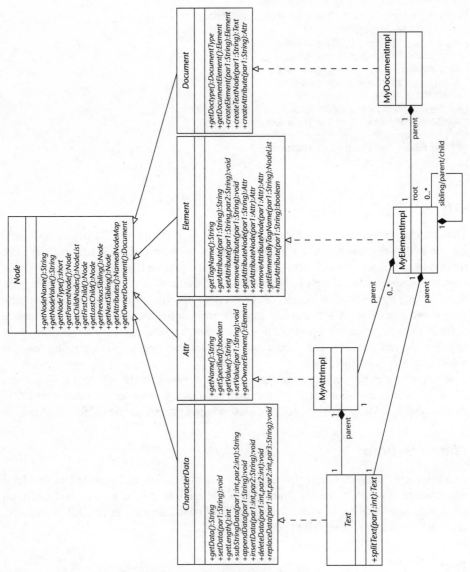

Figure 10.5 Document interface and its association.

Let's consider the following XML document:

```
<person marital_status="married">
    <age>32</age>
   <name>
            <first>Mike</first>
            <middle_initial>Q</middle_initial>
            <last>Jones</last>
    </name>
</person>
```

If we parse this document using a DOM parser, the corresponding DOM tree would look like the tree in Figure 10.6.

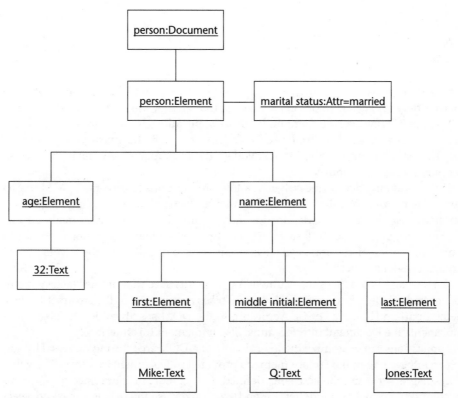

Figure 10.6   A collaboration diagram of DOM objects.

Traversing a DOM Tree

The package org.w3c.dom.traversal defines two interfaces that allow applications to traverse a DOM tree. The order of the traversal supported by these interfaces is called document order. Document order is defined as the order in which the start tags appear in a document. This is established by a depth first, preordered traversal of a tree. This can be explained using the DOM tree shown in Figure 10.6. If we start traversing the document from the root node, `person`, the order that the nodes will appear is:

```
person
age
32
name
first
Mike
middle
Q
last
Jones
```

Note that we have not shown `marital_status` as a node, because attributes are not considered first class nodes in DOM, even though they are implemented as nodes.

The first interface is NodeIterator. It allows applications to traverse a tree or a segment of a tree as a set of nodes. It uses a NodeList to create this linear view of a DOM tree. The main traversal method is nextNode(). It also supports traversal in the reverse direction through previousNode().

The second interface is TreeWalker. It allows applications to traverse a DOM tree as a tree. The main traversal method of this interface is nextNode(). Calling nextNode() repeatedly would return nodes in document order. It also provides methods like nextSibling(), parentNode(), lastChild(), and firstChild() that applications can use to control the order of the traversal. It also supports navigation in the reverse order through previousNode().

The package also defines a DocumentTraversal interface that defines factory methods for both NodeIterator and TreeWalker. This is an example of the Abstract Factory Method pattern [Gamma, 1995]. According to the DOM specification, the object that implements the Document interface must also implement this interface.

Applications can customize the logical view of a DOM tree during traversal by setting an integer flag in the factory methods provided in DocumentTraversal. The value of this flag is set using the constants defined in the NodeFilter interface to represent different types of nodes. NodeIterator and TreeWalker use the flag as a mask to select nodes. Multiple node types can be combined together using the OR operator. The following example shows how to set the value of this flag:

```
int whatToShow = NodeFilter.ELEMENT_NODE|NodeFilter.TEXT_NODE;
```

Also, DOM defines an interface, NodeFilter, which allows applications to define criteria to include or exclude nodes during traversal. Applications can define complicated node selection logic that cannot be expressed just by using Node types. When a Node-Filter object is provided, NodeIterator and TreeWalker call the acceptNode() method on the filter object before they return a node to the application. Filter objects can signal one of three things: ACCEPT, REJECT, or SKIP. A node is returned on ACCEPT. A node and all its children are excluded on REJECT. A node is excluded but not all its children on SKIP. DOM does not provide any implementation of this interface. The driver provider may provide some concrete implementations. In most cases, applications implement their own filters as deemed necessary.

The following program shows how we can use these interfaces to navigate a DOM tree.

DOMApplication.java

```
package com.wiley.compBooks.EJwithUML.Samples.Dom;


import java.io.*;
import org.w3c.dom.*;
import org.w3c.dom.traversal.*;
import org.xml.sax.*;
import org.apache.xerces.parsers.*;


/**
 * This is a sample DOM application that uses the Xerces DOM parser
 * to parse an XML document,and shows how to traverse a DOM tree
 * using both NodeIterator and TreeWalker.
 */
public class DOMApplication extends java.lang.Object
{
    public static void main (String args[]) throws DOMException, SAXException,
        IOException
    {
      DOMApplication application = new DOMApplication();
      if (args.length != 1)
      {
          System.out.println("usage: java
com.wiley.compBooks.EJwithUML.Samples.Dom.DOMApplication <xmlDataFile>");
      }
      else
      {
        InputSource xmlSource = new InputSource(args[0]);
        DOMParser parser = new DOMParser();
        parser.setFeature("http://xml.org/sax/features/validation", false);
        parser.setFeature("http://apache.org/xml/features/dom/include-
ignorable-whitespace", false);
        parser.parse(xmlSource);
        Document xmlDocument = parser.getDocument();
        Node root = xmlDocument.getDocumentElement();
        System.out.println("***Start:traversing DOM using Iterator ***");
        application.iterateWithoutFilter(root, xmlDocument);
        System.out.println("***End:traversing DOM using Iterator ***\n");
        System.out.println("***Start:traversing DOM using TreeWalker ***");
        application.traverseTreeWithoutFilter(root, xmlDocument);
        System.out.println("***End:traversing DOM using TreeWalker ***");
```

```
        }
    }

    public DOMApplication ()
    {
    }

    public void iterateWithoutFilter(Node node, Document doc)
    {
        NodeIterator iterator =
((DocumentTraversal)doc).createNodeIterator(node,
                                    NodeFilter.SHOW_ALL, /*
whatToShow flag */
            null, /* no filter */
            false /* flag for entity reference expansion */);
        Node currentNode = null;
        while((currentNode = iterator.nextNode())!= null)
        {
            if(currentNode.getNodeType() == Node.ELEMENT_NODE)
            {
                System.out.println(currentNode.getNodeName());
            }
            else if (currentNode.getNodeType() == Node.TEXT_NODE)
            {
                System.out.println("value - " +
currentNode.getNodeValue());
            }
        }
    }

    public void traverseTreeWithoutFilter(Node node, Document doc)
    {
        TreeWalker walker =
((DocumentTraversal)doc).createTreeWalker(node,
    NodeFilter.SHOW_TEXT, /* whatToShow flag */
                null, /* no filter */
                false /* flag for entity reference expansion */);
        Node currentNode = null;
        while((currentNode = walker.nextNode())!= null)
        {
            System.out.println("value - " +
currentNode.getNodeValue());
        }
    }
}
```

Strengths

When applications require the knowledge of the structure of the original XML document, or need all the data but need not map them to internal data objects, the DOM parser is a very good choice. Also, if applications need to keep track of the data as well as their locations, DOM can come in handy without much effort.

Weaknesses

DOM parsers are very memory-intensive. Handling large documents using DOM parsers can become challenging if not impossible on platforms with memory constraints such as hand-held devices. It can easily slow down applications and bring systems with low memory to their knees. It is also wasteful in applications where the whole document is not needed, or where applications need to perform some actions based on the values of only a few elements of the XML document. It can also be wasteful when applications need to map data to internal data objects. In this case, the application creates a DOM object only to unnecessarily map the data to another strongly typed object.

Compatible Technologies

DOM can be used by any type of Java application, including servlets, Swing, command-line applications, and Enterprise JavaBeans.

Cost of Adoption

The DOM API is available free as part of the Xerces XML toolkit from Apache. Because DOM is a natural fit for XML documents, newcomers can quickly put it to use. To get full value from the API, your project must fill the roles of designer and developer.

Designer

Unlike using SAX, you do not need to implement any interface to use DOM in your project. Hence, the involvement of a designer is considerably reduced. A designer needs to make sure that the DOM APIs are used in a thread-safe manner, especially when traversing a DOM tree, as well as when modifying it.

Developer

Each developer is responsible for understanding the basic concepts behind the data structure, the Tree, because it is the basis of the DOM API. The developer must also know the XML syntax and associated rules and concepts.

JMS

In traditional client/server applications, the client and server communicate with each other using technologies like remote procedure calls (RPC) or Remote Method Invocation (RMI). The server publishes the protocol of interaction as a remote API. A remote

API has two parts—a client part that works as a proxy for the server code that the client wants to run, and a server part that invokes the actual server code. It is this API that establishes a tight coupling between the server and client. Whenever the API changes, the client has to be recompiled. Additionally, since these technologies are synchronous in nature, applications communicating using these technologies have to be up during the communication and the client blocks on the call. This may not be acceptable in some situations where response time is critical. Consider another situation: What if the network connection breaks down while the server is processing a request? The client will see the problem immediately and will try to reestablish the connection and resend the request. If the server completes the transaction before it sees the network problem, we may end up with duplicate transactions.

All these problems mentioned above can be addressed if we use a technology called message-oriented middleware, or MOM. Applications using MOM communicate indirectly with each other through a broker. The broker plays a key role here. It breaks the dependencies among the systems by facilitating asynchronous communication using messages. A message is self-contained data that consists of two parts: the header and the payload. The header contains the information required by the broker to manage and distribute the message to its intended destination. The payload contains application-specific information. As a result, systems can perform tasks in parallel, perform other tasks while waiting for a result from another system, or communicate in a time-independent fashion. The whole notion of this indirect interaction may not be intuitive at first. MOM can be compared to the traditional postal system. With the postal system, people communicate with each other through letters. The postman delivers the letter to an address stated on the envelope. The address is associated with a mailbox that holds the letter for the receiver. The receiver need not be present at the time of the delivery. He or she can get the letter from the mailbox at a suitable time.

Let's consider a hypothetical scenario where we have two systems, A and B, deployed at two different companies. Let's also assume that both systems use two different technologies and run on two different platforms. If these two systems were ever to be integrated with each other, because of a merger or a partnership between the two companies, we would have quite an interesting challenge in hand. With RPC or RMI-based technologies, we would have to build adapter layers on both sides to encapsulate the interactions. If either of the systems moved to another host without any explicit coordination with the other, the communication would break down. If either of the applications changed its API, the adapter layer would need to be modified and the other application would need to be recompiled. Things could get even more interesting if either of the systems were not always guaranteed to be available when the other needed to send data. But, none of these issues will be a problem, or at least they will be insignificant, if both the applications communicate using asynchronous messaging facilitated by the MOM systems. How can the MOM solution address all the issues mentioned with using RPC or RMI? With the MOM solution, both the applications agree upon a standard format and well-known destinations for messages. A destination is a temporary storage place for the messages, and the MOM server maintains these storage locations. Applications interact with these storage locations through the MOM instead of directly interacting with each other. They refer to these destinations by name. With this setup, we have a very loose coupling between the two applications.

Even if the server moves physically, the client can still get the service as long as the name of the destination remains the same. For the same reason, the client can request service while the server is down because the MOM server holds the message in storage until the server retrieves them. The server can send the response back at some later time.

Sun, in their effort to incorporate messaging capability into the J2EE platform, has created a vendor-neutral abstraction layer called Java Messaging Service, or in short JMS, to access MOM. They achieved this through the participation of leading MOM vendors in the industry. JMS allows a Java application to access any MOM system in a standard way without any direct dependence on the underlying MOM implementation.

The following section introduces some JMS terms before exploring the class library in detail.

Terminology

Several terms are essential to understanding the JMS. These are:

- JMS clients
- JMS provider
- Destination
- Message
- Administered objects
- Messaging domain
- Asynchronous messaging
- Synchronous messaging

JMS Client

A JMS client is a Java program or component that uses the JMS API to produce messages, or consume messages, or both.

JMS Provider

A JMS provider is a messaging system that implements the JMS API.

Destination

A destination is the address that the JMS clients send messages to or receive messages from. It can be thought of as a temporary storage place for messages. However, it should not be used as an alternative to a database.

Message

A message is the data produced and consumed by the JMS clients. The JMS provider uses these messages to manage the interactions among the JMS clients.

Administered Objects

JMS administered objects are those objects that are created and configured by administrators outside JMS clients and usually bound in a JNDI namespace with simple names. The JMS clients look these objects up in the JNDI namespace using those bound names. The reason for doing this is these objects are better maintained externally because they depend on configuration parameters that are JMS provider-specific. Therefore this process eliminates any dependency of JMS clients on a specific JMS provider. Typically, JMS providers implement administrative tools to perform these tasks. Two such administered objects are destinations and connection factories.

Messaging Domain

The messaging style or model is referred to as a messaging domain in the JMS specification. There are two such styles defined in JMS. One is the point-to-point, or PTP, and the other is the publish-and-subscribe, or Pub/Sub, style of messaging. These two styles are described in detail in the "Gory Details" section. An application can use both the styles as deemed necessary. JMS providers are not required to support both messaging domains.

Asynchronous Messaging

JMS is inherently asynchronous in nature, that is, there is no timing dependency between producing and consuming a message. However, asynchronous messaging is used in a more strict sense in JMS. A JMS client is said to implement asynchronous messaging if it consumes messages using a message listener. A message listener waits for messages on behalf of the JMS client while the JMS client is free to do other things.

Synchronous Messaging

How JMS supports synchronous messaging may seem confusing at first, because it is inherently asynchronous. It depends on how a JMS client is using the JMS API. You can simulate the traditional synchronous request/reply messaging if you produce a request message and immediately wait for a reply message. However, the JMS specification defines this term more strictly in that a JMS client is said to use synchronous messaging when it explicitly requests a message from a destination and blocks on the call (receive method of a MessageConsumer object).

Let us look at the JMS API in detail.

Gory Details

With point-to-point messaging, messages flow between two applications. The application that sends a message is called sender. The application that reads the message is called receiver. Because each message is delivered to only one receiver, it is called point-to-point messaging. The communicating applications do not interact with each other directly. Instead, the sender sends a message to a destination called queue. This queue is identified by a name. The receiver reads the message from the same queue. The JMS provider works as a broker to manage this queue and the interactions of the applications with the queue. The JMS server holds the message in the queue until the receiver application reads it. The only dependency that the two applications have on each other is that they expect to use the same queue. With publish-and-subscribe messaging, messages flow from one application to multiple applications. The application that sends a message is called publisher. The publisher knows nothing about who is receiving its messages. The application that reads these messages is called subscriber. The subscriber also knows nothing about who is sending the messages. The messages are not directly delivered to all the subscribers. The destination that holds the message is called topic. The JMS provider manages the topic as well as the interactions of the publisher and the subscriber with the topic. One subscriber can subscribe to multiple topics. Similarly, a publisher can publish to multiple topics.

All the interfaces and classes in the JMS API library are defined in the javax.jms package. The core interfaces in this package can be grouped into three categories: common interfaces, PTP specific interfaces, and Pub/Sub specific interfaces. Both of the domain-specific interfaces inherit from the common interfaces. Before JMS 1.1, the common interfaces did not contain the domain-specific behavior. Hence, JMS clients had to explicitly refer to the domain-specific interfaces. This strong distinction between the two domains at the JMS client level had one major drawback. That is, JMS clients could not mix and match the two domains in the same transaction. To address this limitation in JMS 1.1, the two domains have been unified in the common interfaces. Now, JMS clients using JMS 1.1 can use these common interfaces to use either domain and hence mix and match the two domains in the same transaction as deemed necessary. In fact, it is recommended that applications use these common interfaces instead of using the domain-specific interface. However, this unification resulted in a rather minor inconvenience, that is, some methods in the common interfaces may only be applicable to one domain, but not both. In those cases, those domain-specific methods throw IllegalStateException.

In the following sections, we will discuss the common interfaces and refer to the domain-specific interfaces as necessary.

NOTE Even though JMS is an integral part of the J2EE platform from release 1.3, the reference implementation of J2EE supported JMS 1.0.2 at the time of this writing. The reference implementation of JMS 1.1 is separately available from the Sun Web site.

Message

Message is an important interface of JMS. It represents data that is exchanged by the JMS clients. A JMS message consists of the following parts:

Header. It contains fields used by both clients and provider to determine how to handle messages. A pair of setter and getter methods is provided for each field. Even though the Message interface defines a setter method for each header field, a JMS provider may override the values of some of the header fields set by a JMS client. This behavior is specific to a JMS provider. You need to consult the documents of your JMS provider to find out which headers can be set by applications and which cannot. Some of the important header fields are:

JMSDeliveryMode. This can be persistent or nonpersistent. These modes are defined as constants in the DeliveryMode interface: PERSISTENT and NON_PERSISTENT. You can specify this in two ways, either at the time of sending a message, or by configuring the message producer with a default value by calling the setDeliveryMode() method. The JMS provider uses the store-and-forward mechanism to handle persistent messages, and hence they are expensive compared to nonpersistent messages. However, for reliable messaging, you need to use persistent messages because they survive the JMS client and provider crashes.

JMSExpiration. This specifies how long a message is valid. JMS clients do not set this field directly. Instead, they specify the time-to-live parameter, and the JMS provider computes the expiration value and sets this field. You can specify the time-to-live parameter in two ways. You can do this at the time of a message delivery or you can configure a message producer with a default value by calling the setTimeToLive() method. The JMS provider does not deliver a message after it has expired. If it is set to zero, the message never expires, which is the default behavior.

JMSPriority. This indicates the level of importance of a message to the JMSProvider. JMS defines priority on a scale of 0 to 9, 0 being the lowest and 9 being the highest. The default is 4. A JMS provider tries to deliver higher-priority messages before lower-priority ones, but it may not be in the exact order of priority.

JMSMessageID. This uniquely identifies a message. Typically, the JMS provider sets its value after the JMS client sends the message. This value is accessible from the copy of the message, which is available after it is sent.

JMSCorrelationID. This is used by the JMS clients to link a message with some other previous message. Typical use of this field is in request/reply type interactions between two JMS clients in a client-server environment. The server sets this field of a response message with the value of the JMSMessageID of the request message. The client looks for a response message with a correlation ID equal to the message ID of its request message.

JMSReplyTo.   This is typically used in a request/reply type interaction between two JMS clients in a client-server environment. The client can set this field with a destination that it wants the server to send the reply to instead of predefining a destination for all clients. This allows the server to be flexible and generic, that is, new clients can be added or existing clients can move easily. Also, the clients do not have to compete for the same resources.

Properties.   These are name-value pairs that act as additional headers to further qualify a message. The value of a property can be of type boolean, byte, int, long, float, double, or String. The Message interface defines a pair of setter and getter methods for each specific Java primitive type. For example, if a property has an integer type value, we can use the getIntProperty() and setIntProperty() methods. Additionally, there is a getter method and a setter method to handle property values as corresponding wrapper objects—getObjectProperty() and setObjectProperty().The properties of a message control the behavior of the message. Properties are classified into three categories:

Application-specific.   The application can define any properties to help select or filter messages.

JMS-defined.   JMS defines a set of properties that are optional. JMS providers can choose to support them. The names of these properties have the prefix "JMSX."

Provider-Specific.   A JMS provider can define its own set of properties. The name of these properties must have the prefix "JMS."

Body.   Application-specific data content.

NOTE You should always set the time-to-live property of your message. This will help maintain your disk space, because the JMS provider will automatically delete all expired messages. You should use either the JMSReplyTo or JMSCorrelationID to link a request with its reply, but not both. You should not set the JMSMessageID yourself. Let the JMS provider take care of it. Messages may be lost if the IDs are not unique across the system. Consult your JMS provider documents to find out how the Header fields are interpreted and what their recommended use is.

A message is classified based on the type of data it contains. JMS supports five types of messages. There is an interface defined for each type, as shown in Figure 10.7. All of them derive from Message interface.

TextMessage.   A message that contains String data. XML data can also be used.

StreamMessage.   A message that contains a stream of data of Java primitive types. They are accessed sequentially.

MapMessage.   A set of name-value pairs, where names are strings and values are Java primitive types.

ObjectMessage.   A message that contains a Serializable Java object.

BytesMessage.   A message that contains an array of bytes.

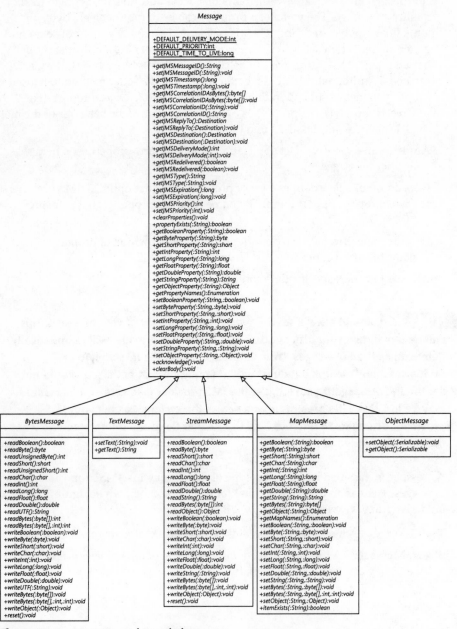

Figure 10.7   Message and Its subclasses.

Destination

The Destination interface represents an address of a message and encapsulates the provider-specific syntax of the address. It works as a tagging interface (a tagging interface is an interface that is used to associate a type, that is, a Serializable interface in the java.lang package) and hence does not define any method. There are two types of destinations, as shown in Figure 10.8, queue and topic. A destination in the PTP domain is called queue and is represented by the Queue interface. A destination in the Pub/Sub domain is called topic and is represented by the Topic interface. The whole JMS API library is organized into two major groups based on these two types of destinations. One group deals with queues and supports the PTP messaging domain, and the other deals with topics and supports the Pub/Sub messaging domain.

Since applications only refer to destinations by their names, both topic and queue define a single method to retrieve the name of the underlying destination as a string. These methods are getQueueName() and getTopicName().

Usually topics and queues are JMS administered objects. That is, a JMS administrator creates and maintains topics and queues using tools provided by the JMS provider. Applications access them by performing a JNDI lookup, as shown here.

```
Queue requestQueue = (Queue) jndiContext.lookup("TestRequestQueue");
```

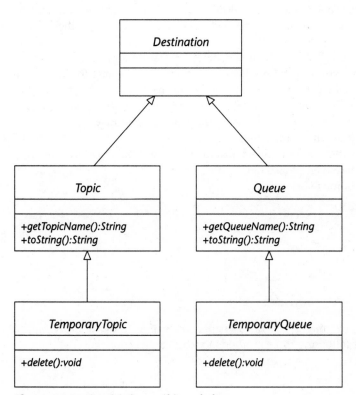

Figure 10.8   Destination and its subclasses.

There are special types of topics and queues called TemporaryTopic and TemporaryQueue. Unlike normal topics and queues, these are created by the application at run time. These destinations only exist for the duration of the connection of the application to the JMS provider. As soon as the connection is closed, all the temporary queues and topics belonging to the connection are deleted, along with their contents. Typically a TemporaryQueue or TemporaryTopic is used to implement a request/reply type interaction in a client-server environment. A TemporaryQueue can be used for a simple request/reply where the interaction occurs between a client and a server. If a client needs to interact with more than one server for the same request, a TemporaryTopic is used. The JMS client that plays the role of a client creates a TempraryQueue/TemporaryTopic and sets it to the JMSReplyTo header field of the request message. The server retrieves the Destination from the request message and sends the response to this Destination.

ConnectionFactory

A ConnectionFactory is an interface that encapsulates the JMS provider-specific parameters required to create a connection. It defines two overloaded factory methods to create connections—one without any arguments, which creates a connection using a default user and password, and the other that takes a specific username and a password. There are two types of ConnectionFactory based on the type of destination, QueueConnectionFactory and TopicConnectionFactory, as shown in Figure 10.9. Each of these interfaces defines two overloaded factory methods similar to their parent interface.

ConnectionFactories are JMS administered objects because connection configuration parameters are different for different JMS providers. So, it is easier to define them outside the applications than have applications define them programmatically. This also decouples applications from a specific JMS provider and allows the changing of a JMS provider without changing applications. Usually a JMS administrator creates the ConnectionFactory objects and binds them with names in a JNDI namespace. This process is different for different JMS providers. However, applications look them up in the same JNDI namespace using those names the same way. The following code snippet shows how this lookup is performed:

```
Context jndiContext = new InitialContext();
QueueConnectionFactory aTestConnectionfactory =
jndiContext.lookup("TestQueueFactory");
```

Connection

Connection is an interface that represents a virtual connection to the underlying JMS provider. It defines the following three methods to manage the connection:

start(). This starts the delivery of incoming messages. The applications must call start() before they can receive messages.

stop(). This temporarily halts all delivery of incoming messages to all the associated message consumers and listeners. The applications can still send messages over this connection.

close(). This closes the connection and releases the underlying resources of the JMS provider. Applications must call this method after they are done using the connection objects.

The Connection interface also defines a factory method to create Session objects. As shown in Figure 10.10, the first parameter of this factory method specifies whether the session supports transactions or not. If the value is true, it creates a session of type XASession and is called a transacted session. The second parameter of the factory method specifies the message acknowledgment mode. JMS providers use acknowledgment of the receipt of messages as part of reliable messaging. The acknowledgment mode specifies to the JMS provider when it should consider a message has been delivered successfully. In a transacted session, acknowledgment occurs automatically when a transaction is committed. In a nontransacted session, JMS allows three types of acknowledgment:

AUTO_ACKNOWLEDGE. The session automatically acknowledges a client's receipt of a message.

CLIENT_ACKOWLEDGE. The client acknowledges the receipt of a message explicitly by calling the acknowledge() method on any received message. It automatically acknowledges the receipt of all the messages received by the session so far.

DUPS_OK_ACKNOWLEDGE. The session performs the acknowledgment in time-deferred fashion. As this may result in the delivery of duplicate messages, this should only be used by JMS clients that can handle duplicate messages.

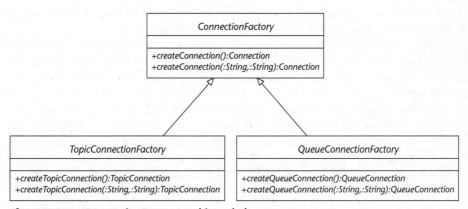

Figure 10.9 ConnectionFactory and its subclasses.

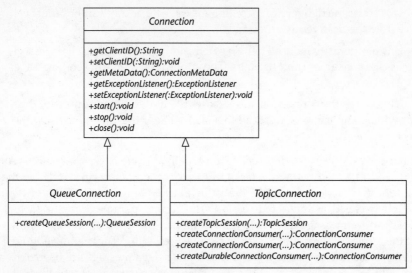

Figure 10.10 Connection and its subclasses.

Session

A Session represents a single-threaded execution context for a JMS client. It defines a set of factory methods to create each type of message, as shown in Figure 10.11. It also defines a set of overloaded factory methods to create a MessageProducer and Message-Consumer. All of these factory methods take a destination object as their first parameter. The destination can be either a topic or a queue. If you provide one, the Producer/Consumer object becomes associated with that destination. Alternatively, you can defer the association of a producer with a specific destination until later by specifying null as the value of the destination. This type of producer is known as an undefined producer. With undefined producers, the destination can be specified at the time of message delivery. This is typically done with a request/reply type of messaging, where the destination of the reply is provided in the JMSReplyTo header field of the request.

Session also defines a set of methods to handle messages in a transaction. These methods are commit() and rollback(). The transaction is enabled at the time of the session creation. In a transacted session, all the messages produced and received are automatically grouped under a unit of work. A transaction is completed by a call to either the commit() or rollback() method. If the transaction is rolled back, all the sent messages are destroyed, and all the received messages are prepared for redelivery. The completion of the current transaction automatically starts the next. JMS supports distributed transactions through JTA, which is X/Open-standard-compliant. The support for JTA is optional for a JMS provider. In a distributed transactional environment like an application server environment, the JMS client must not use the local transaction feature of the Session object. In a nontransacted session, a receive or send operation on a message takes effect immediately.

Figure 10.11   Sessions.

MessageProducer

A MessageProducer interface represents the sender of a message. It defines setter methods to define default values for three JMS message header fields: JMSTimeToLive, JMSPriority, and JMSDeliveryMode. All messages get these default values if not explicitly provided at the time of message delivery. It also defines corresponding getter methods to retrieve the default values associated with a producer object for these header fields.

This interface also defines four overloaded send() methods to send messages to any destination, two of the methods additionally take a Destination object as the first parameter. Usually a MessageProducer is associated with a destination at the time of its creation. However, for undefined MessageProducers, the send methods with the Queue parameter are used.

There are two types of MessageProducer based on the Destination types, as shown in the Figure 10.12. One is QueueSender and the other is TopicPublisher.

MessageConsumer

A MessageConsumer interface represents the receiver of a message. As shown in Figure 10.13, it defines three overloaded receive methods to receive messages synchronously, meaning that the caller blocks until the call returns:

receive().   The caller waits forever for a message. You should not use this because it may cause your application to become unavailable while it waits patiently.

receive(long timeout).   The caller blocks for the next message up to the timeout in milliseconds. If a message is available, the call returns the message; otherwise, the call returns null after the timeout expires. This is the preferred method over the previous receive() method.

receiveNoWait().   As its name suggests, the call returns immediately with the next message if available, otherwise it returns null.

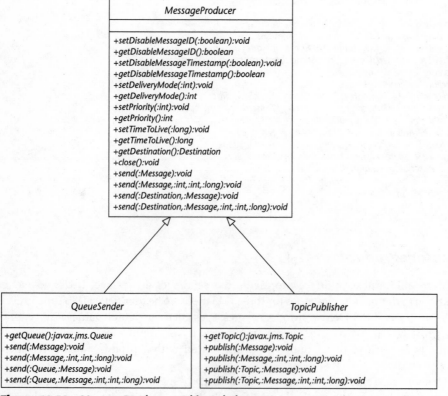

Figure 10.12   MessageProducer and its subclasses.

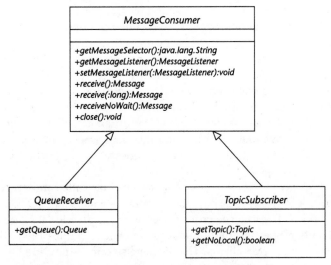

Figure 10.13 MessageConsumer and its subclasses.

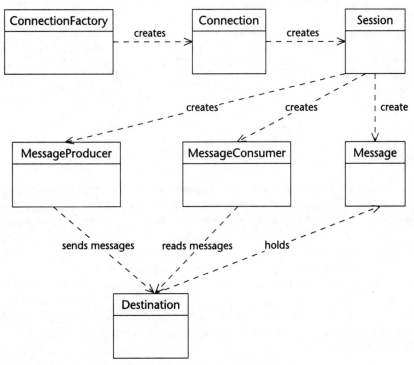

Figure 10.14 Associations of the common interfaces.

The MessageConsumer interface also defines a method to register a MessageListener object—setMessageListener(). The MessageListener interface defines a single method—onMessage(). A MessageListener object allows JMS clients to receive messages asynchronously. The JMS client will provide an implementation of this interface where the onMessage() method will contain the business logic of processing the incoming message. Once the MessageListener is registered with the MessageConsumer and the connection is started, the MessageListener starts to receive messages from the JMS provider as they arrive at the destination. The difference between the receive() method of the MessageConsumer interface and the onMessage() method is that receive() pulls messages from the destination, whereas messages are pushed to onMessage().

MessageConsumer can selectively receive messages using a filter called message selector. A message selector is a String expression whose syntax is a subset of SQL 92 conditional expressions (WHERE clauses). The criteria used in the expression include the Message header fields and properties. Only messages for which the expression evaluates to true are delivered to the JMS clients. The message selector is provided to the MessageConsumer at the time of its creation. In a simple request/reply, the request can be linked with the reply using a selector shown in the following code snippet. The selector uses the JMSCorrelationID of the response message to equal the JMSMessageID of the request message. Of course, the replier has to put the message ID of the request in the correlation ID of the response.

```
// message id of the request is used as a message selector for the response
message
String responseSelector = "JMSCorrelationID = '" + request.
getJMSMessageID() + "'";
MessageConsumer qReceiver = qSession.createConsumer(respQueue,
responseSelector);
```

All Together

All the interfaces described in the previous sections are implemented by the JMS providers, except MessageListener and ExceptionListener. These listener interfaces are implemented by the JMS clients to hold the business logic to process messages asynchronously.

The object diagram in Figure 10.14 shows the static relationship among the objects implementing the common interfaces described in the previous sections.

The typical interactions among a JMS client, a JMS provider, and the objects implementing these interfaces are captured in the interaction diagram shown in Figure 10.15. The diagram is depicted from a generic JMS client's perspective. However, based on the context of the application, the order of producing and consuming messages may be different for different JMS clients.

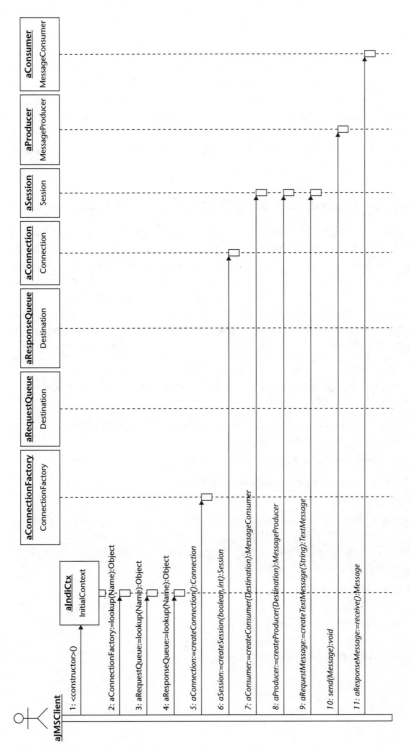

Figure 10.15   A simple interaction by a JMS client.

A JMS client first looks up a ConnectionFactory object and a Destination object by name from a JNDI namespace. It creates a Connection object from the ConnectionFactory by calling the createConnection method. From the Connection object, it creates a Session by calling the createSession method. From the Session object, it creates a MessageProducer object. It then creates a message from the session object by calling the appropriate factory method corresponding to the type of message it wants to create. It sends the message by calling the send method on the MessageProducer object. It creates a MessageConsumer object from Session by calling the createConsumer method. Then it waits for a response message by calling the receive method on the MessageConsumer object.

A Client/Server Application Using Point-to-Point Messaging

The following sample programs show you how to implement a simple client/server application using the PTP messaging domain. In this example, we have a client that can inquiry or update an employee record through a server. The client is implemented in JmsP2Pclient.java, and the server is implemented in JmsP2Pserver.java. The server waits in an infinite loop for client requests in a well-known request queue named "test.request.queue." For each request, it determines the type of request—GET(inquiry) or SET (Update)—and performs the corresponding task on an employee database. The database is simulated using a Java properties file. Some of the design choices made for this example are:

- Client uses synchronous messaging (it uses the receive method of the MessageConsumer).
- Server uses asynchronous messaging by implementing its own MessageListener—SampleMessageListener.java.
- The client uses a temporary queue for the response.
- The request and response data are exchanged as name-value pairs, so MapMessage is used.
- Messages are nonpersistent and have a time-to-live value of 2 seconds. This is because we assume that the client program is used by a live user. In which case, an immediate response is meaningful. Hence, the client waits for a response message for 2 seconds on a receive call.
- Auto acknowledgment is used.

JmsP2PClient.java

```
package com.wiley.compBooks.EJwithUML.Samples.Jms;

import javax.jms.*;
import java.util.*;
import javax.naming.*;

/**
```

```
 * This program retrieves employee information from a server. It
 * uses P2P messaging model to communicate with the server. The
 * request and response data is formatted as name-value pairs.
 */
public class JmsP2PClient
{
  public static final String REQUEST_NAME = "REQUEST_NAME";
  public static final String ATTRIBUTE_NAME = "ATTRIBUTE_NAME";
  public static final String GET_REQUEST = "GET";
  public static final String SET_REQUEST = "SET";
  public static final String EMPLOYEE_ID = "id";
  public static final String STATUS = "STATUS";
  public static final boolean SUCCESS = true;
  public static final boolean FAILED = false;

  public static void main(String[] args)
  {
    Connection qConnection = null;
    try
    {
      if (args.length < 3)
      {
        System.out.println("Usage: java
com.wiley.compBooks.EJwithUML.Samples.Jms.JmsP2PClient <GET|SET>
<attribute_name> <employeed_id>");
        System.exit(1);
      }
      String requestName = args[0].toUpperCase().trim();
      String attributeName = args[1].toLowerCase().trim();
      String employeeId  = args[2].trim();
      java.util.Properties env = new Properties();
      env.put(Context.PROVIDER_URL, "jndi://localhost:7002");
      javax.naming.Context jndiContext = new InitialContext(env);
      ConnectionFactory qFactory = (ConnectionFactory)
      jndiContext.lookup("QueueConnectionFactory");
      qConnection = qFactory.createConnection();
      qConnection.start();
      Session qSession = qConnection.createSession(false,
                              Session.AUTO_ACKNOWLEDGE);
      Destination reqQueue = (Destination)jndiContext.lookup(
                              "test.request.queue");
      MessageProducer qSender = qSession.createProducer(reqQueue);
      TemporaryQueue respQueue = qSession.createTemporaryQueue();
      /*
       * configures the time-to-live feature of the sender with a
       * default value of 2 seconds. This means all the messages sent
       * by this sender will expire in 2 second after the messagess
       * have been sent.
       */
      qSender.setTimeToLive(20000);
      // get / set an attribute of an employee record
      MapMessage request = qSession.createMapMessage();
      request.setString(REQUEST_NAME, requestName);
      request.setString(EMPLOYEE_ID, employeeId);
      request.setString(ATTRIBUTE_NAME, attributeName);
```

```
          // tells the server where to send the response to
          request.setJMSReplyTo(respQueue);
          qSender.send(request,DeliveryMode.NON_PERSISTENT,
                      Message.DEFAULT_PRIORITY,20000);
          System.out.println(attributeName + " " + requestName +
                  " =  resquest sent for employee " + employeeId);
          MessageConsumer qReceiver = qSession.createConsumer(
                                                      respQueue);
          MapMessage response = (MapMessage) qReceiver.receive(10000);
          if (response == null)
          {
            System.out.println(" request timed out!");
          }
          else
          {
            System.out.println("request processing status - " +
                            response.getBoolean(STATUS));
          System.out.println("response received - " + attributeName +
            "=" + response.getString(attributeName) +
            " of employee= " + response.getString(EMPLOYEE_ID));
          }
        }
        catch(Exception e)
        {
          System.out.println(e);

        }
        finally
        {
          if (qConnection != null)
          {
          try
          {
            qConnection.close();
          }
          catch(Exception e)
          {
              System.out.println("error closing queue connection -" +
              e);
          }
          }
        }
      }
    }
```

SampleMessageListener.java

```
package com.wiley.compBooks.EJwithUML.Samples.Jms;

import javax.jms.*;
import java.util.*;
import javax.naming.*;
import java.io.*;
```

```java
/**
 *       This is an asynchronous request handler for JmsP2PServer.java.
 */
public class SampleMessageListener implements MessageListener
{
  public static final String REQUEST_NAME = "REQUEST_NAME";
  public static final String ATTRIBUTE_NAME = "ATTRIBUTE_NAME";
  public static final String GET_REQUEST = "GET";
  public static final String SET_REQUEST = "SET";
  public static final String EMPLOYEE_ID = "id";
  public static final String STATUS = "STATUS";
  public static final boolean SUCCESS = true;
  public static final boolean FAILED = false;

  private Properties employeeDatabase;
  private Session qSession;
  private MessageProducer responseSender;

  public SampleMessageListener(Properties database, Session
                               session) throws JMSException
  {
    employeeDatabase = database;
    qSession = session;
    /*
     * creates an undefined sender, that is, the sender is not
     * associated with any queue yet. Later it will be associated
     * with the ReplyTo Queue specified by the client.
     */
    responseSender = session.createProducer(null);
  }

  public void onMessage(Message message)
  {
    try
    {
      MapMessage request = null;
      if (message instanceof MapMessage)
      {
          request = (MapMessage) message;
          String requestName = request.getString(REQUEST_NAME);
          Destination respQueue = (Destination)
                                    request.getJMSReplyTo();
          MapMessage response = qSession.createMapMessage();
          if (requestName.equals(GET_REQUEST))
          {
            int employeeId = request.getInt(EMPLOYEE_ID);
            String attributeName = request.getString(ATTRIBUTE_NAME);
            System.out.println("==>" + attributeName +
            " get request received for employee - " + employeeId);
            String dataKey = employeeId + "." +  attributeName;
            String requestedData = (String)
                              employeeDatabase.get(dataKey);
            if (requestedData != null)
```

```
            {
               System.out.println("==>requested data found - " +
               requestedData);
               response.setBoolean(STATUS, SUCCESS);
               response.setInt(EMPLOYEE_ID, employeeId);
               response.setString(attributeName, requestedData);
            }
            else
            {
               System.out.println("==>requested data not found!");
               response.setBoolean(STATUS, FAILED);
               response.setInt(EMPLOYEE_ID, 1234);
               response.setString(ATTRIBUTE_NAME, attributeName);
            }
         }
         else if (requestName.equals(SET_REQUEST))
         {
            String employeeId = request.getString(EMPLOYEE_ID);
            String attributeName = request.getString(ATTRIBUTE_NAME);
            System.out.println("==>" + attributeName +
            " set request received for employee - " + employeeId);
            String dataKey = employeeId + "." + attributeName;
            String newData = request.getString(attributeName);
            employeeDatabase.put(dataKey, newData);
            response.setBoolean(STATUS, SUCCESS);
          } // end of else - SET_REQUEST
         else
         {
            System.out.println("unknown request type - " +
                                requestName);
            response.setBoolean(STATUS, SUCCESS);
          }
      responseSender.send(respQueue, response,
        DeliveryMode.PERSISTENT,Message.DEFAULT_PRIORITY,20000);
        System.out.println("==>response sent.");
      } // end of if MapMessage
      else
      {
        /*
         * request message is not of type MapMessage. Cannot
         * process this request. Something is very wrong.
         * Sending a response as MapMessage may throw the client
         * off! It is better to ignore the request.
         */
        System.out.println("unsupported message format - " +
        request.getClass().getName());
        System.out.println("request is ignored!");
      }
    }
catch(Exception e)
{
  System.out.println(e);
```

```
      }
   }
}
```

You can run this example using the reference implementation of JMS that comes with J2EE 1.3.1 SDK from Sun. You have to define the request queue using the admin tool that comes with the SDK. Before you can create the queue, you have to have the J2EE server up by executing the j2ee command at the command line. To create the queue, run the following command at the command line:

```
j2eeadmin -addJmsDestination test.request.queue queue
```

A Publish-and-Subscribe Application

The following sample programs show you how to implement an application that uses the pub/sub messaging domain. In this example, we have a publisher that publishes sports news to any sports channel. The client subscribes to any of these news channels and reads the news. The publisher is implemented in JmsSportsNewsPublisher.java, and the subscriber is implemented in JmsSportsNewsSubscriber.java. The channel is implemented as a topic. The publisher takes single news and a channel name to publish the news to the command line. The subscriber takes a channel name to read news from the command line. The topic name is computed from the channel name by concatenating "news.channel." before it. Some of the design choices that we made are:

- Both the Publisher and Subscriber programs use synchronous messaging (use receive method of MessageConsumer).
- The Subscriber program uses regular subscription (not durable), so it receives news only when it is up. We assume that our subscribers do not care about news published while they are not up. Otherwise, we have to use durable subscription.
- Messages are persistent and have a time-to-live value of 180 seconds. This is because we do not want to lose the published news, should the JMS provider crash or stop. Also, we do not want to have the old news lying around when no one cares about it any more. This would eat up our valuable disk space.
- Auto acknowledgment is used.

JmsSportsNewsPublisher.java

```
package com.wiley.compBooks.EJwithUML.Samples.Jms;

import javax.jms.*;
import java.util.*;
import javax.naming.*;

/**
 * This program publishes sports news using JMS pub/sub domain. It
```

```
 * publishes news on any sports. Each type of sports news is called
 * a channel. Each channel is Implemented as a JMS Topic. The
 * program assumes that a Topic already exists with a name
 * "news.sports.<channel_name>". The program
 * expects a channel name and the news on the command line.
 */
public class JmsSportsNewsPublisher
{
  public static void main(String[] args)
  {
    Connection tConnection = null;
    try
    {
      if (args.length < 2)
      {
        System.out.println("Usage: java
com.wiley.compBooks.EJwithUML.Samples.Jms.JmsSportsNewsPublisher
<NBA|NFL|MLS> <news>");
        System.exit(1);
      }
      String newsChannelName = "news.sports." +
                              args[0].toUpperCase().trim();
      String newsContent = args[1].toUpperCase().trim();

      java.util.Properties env = new Properties();
      env.put(Context.PROVIDER_URL, "jndi://localhost:7002");
      javax.naming.Context jndiContext = new InitialContext(env);
      ConnectionFactory tFactory = (ConnectionFactory)
                  jndiContext.lookup("TopicConnectionFactory");
      tConnection = tFactory.createConnection();
      tConnection.start();
      Session tSession = tConnection.createSession(false,
                          Session.AUTO_ACKNOWLEDGE);
      Destination currentTopic = (Destination)
                          jndiContext.lookup(newsChannelName);

      MessageProducer tPublisher =
                          tSession.createProducer(currentTopic);

      // publishes news as a text message
      TextMessage news = tSession.createTextMessage();
      news.setText(newsContent);
      tPublisher.send(news,DeliveryMode.PERSISTENT,
                      Message.DEFAULT_PRIORITY,180000);

      System.out.println("published the following news over " +
                      newsChannelName + " sports channel:");
      System.out.println("********" + newsContent + "********");
    }
    catch(Exception e)
    {
      System.out.println(e);
    }
```

```
    finally
    {
      if (tConnection != null)
      {
        try
        {
          tConnection.close();
        }
        catch(Exception e)
        {

        }
      }
    }
  }
}
```

JmsSportsNewsSubscriber.java

```
package com.wiley.compBooks.EJwithUML.Samples.Jms;

import javax.jms.*;
import java.util.*;
import javax.naming.*;
import java.io.*;



/**
 * This program subscribes to a sports news channel using JMS
 * pub/sub domain. It takes the channel name and the news on the
 * command line. The program assumes that a Topic already exists
 * with a name "news.sports.<channel_name>".
 */
public class JmsSportsNewsSubscriber
{
  public static void main(String[] args)
  {
    Connection tConnection = null;
    try
    {
      if (args.length < 1)
      {
        System.out.println("Usage: java
com.wiley.compBooks.EJwithUML.Samples.Jms.JmsSportsNewsSubscriber
<NBA|NFL|MLS>");
        System.exit(1);
      }
      String newsChannelName = "news.sports." +
                              args[0].toUpperCase().trim();
```

```
        java.util.Properties env = new Properties();

        env.put(Context.PROVIDER_URL, "jndi://localhost:7000");
        javax.naming.Context jndiContext = new InitialContext(env);
        ConnectionFactory tFactory = (ConnectionFactory)
                jndiContext.lookup("TopicConnectionFactory");
        tConnection = tFactory.createTopicConnection();
        Session tSession = tConnection.createSession(false,
                              Session.AUTO_ACKNOWLEDGE);
        Destination newsChannel = (Destination)
                            jndiContext.lookup(newsChannelName);
        MessageConsumer tSubscriber =  tSession.createConsumer(
                                    newsChannel);
        tConnection.start();

        while(true)
        {
          System.out.println("*********waiting for news on channel- "
            + newsChannelName + "*********");
          TextMessage request = (TextMessage) tSubscriber.receive();

          String news = request.getText();
          String messageIdOfReq = request.getJMSMessageID();

          System.out.println("news received==>" + news);
        }
      }
      catch(Exception e)
      {
        System.out.println(e);
      }
      finally
      {
        if (tConnection != null)
        {
          try
          {
      tConnection.close();
    }
    catch(Exception e)
    {

    }
        }
      }
    }
  }
```

You can run this example using the reference implementation of JMS that comes with J2EE 1.3.1 SDK from Sun. You have to define the topic (news channel) using the admin tool that comes with the SDK. Before you can create the topic, you have to bring the J2EE server up by executing the j2ee command at the command line. To create the topic, run the following command at the command line:

```
j2eeadmin -addJmsDestination news.sports.NBA queue
```

Strengths

The JMS API with the consolidation of the two messaging domains in the 1.1 specification has become really simple and easy to use. With a handful of classes to learn, anyone with the basic knowledge of Java can quickly come up to speed and effectively use them in any project without knowing any detail about the underlying MOM system.

Weaknesses

While JMS provides a common interface to the existing MOM systems, you still have to be familiar with all the features supported by your JMS provider. Writing applications may be easy using JMS, but it can be quite challenging to support a JMS application in a production environment. Unlike applications using RPC or RMI, an error in a JMS application does not immediately point to the actual problem. It requires further investigation to determine the actual cause of the problem.

Compatible Technologies

The JMS can be used by any type of Java application, including servlets, Swing, command-line applications, and Enterprise JavaBeans.

Cost of Adoption

The JMS API comes with the MOM free. However, the MOM itself has a licensing cost associated with it like any other commercial server product. The only known JMS provider freely available is called JBossMQ, and it comes bundled with the open-source application server JBoss. It can be downloaded from JBoss's official Web site: http://www.jboss.org. To get the full value from the API, your project must fill the roles of architect, developer, and administrator.

Architect

Since the JMS API provides a common interface to existing MOM products, a successful adoption of MOM through JMS requires an intimate knowledge of both. The appropriate person to provide that expertise on a project is the architect. He not only has to be familiar with the programming model but also has to be familiar with the system. He will have to interact with the administrator to communicate the application requirements, so that the administrator can set up the JMS provider environment appropriately.

Developer

With a handful of common JMS classes to learn, developers need to know the high-level concepts of the messaging domains.

Administrator

Since queues, topics, and connection factories are administered objects, your project will need an administrator who will define these objects according to the requirements provided by the architect and maintain them as necessary. He will also have to perform other maintenance activities as required by the JMS provider.

Conclusion

The Timecard application could reasonably use either SAX or DOM. However, there are no indications for choosing DOM over SAX. In the absence of any strong preference on the part of the development staff or the users, we will use SAX.

System Interface with the Billing System

Recall from Chapter 6, "Describing the System for Technology Selection," that the interface with the billing system is simple data transfer. XML lets us create a flexible data interchange format; and it comes with free tools and parsers. We happily follow the rest of the industry and select XML.

The Next Step

Now that we have selected technologies for the boundary classes, we can turn our attention to the control and entity classes.

Evaluating Web Services Technologies for the System Interface

The past few years, the software development community has begun to agree on some technologies that simplify system-to-system interfaces. These advances leverage the interface technologies described in Chapter 10, while adding common mechanisms to discover system functionality, to invoke these discovered functionalities remotely, and to format and propagate application data in a platform-independent way. Collectively, these advances are frequently referred to as Web services. While the specifications defining these technologies and their implementations are still changing rapidly, their promise for the future of system interface development is enormous. This chapter describes several Web services technologies in some detail:

- SOAP is a language-neutral specification for a communication protocol used by Web services.

- UDDI is a language-neutral specification for publishing and discovering business information. It is one of the standards used for publishing and discovering Web services.

- WSDL is an XML-based language used to describe Web services.

- JAXP is a Java API for XML processing. It works as a façade layer to both SAX and DOM API, creating a seamless view of the applications.

- JAXR is a Java API for XML registry that allows companies to publish their applications in a standard way as well as allows others to discover and use those published applications dynamically.

- JAX-RPC is a Java API to invoke remote services synchronously in a protocol-independent way.

The following sections consider these technologies in some detail.

Demystifying Web Services

Over the last year or so, Web services have generated a considerable amount of interest in the industry. With XML being at the core of the Web services, they promise to integrate and use applications written in different languages and running on different platforms in an ad hoc fashion with ease. In this section, we will take a look at the core technologies that make up the Web services. However, it is not the intent to explore them in detail because each of these technologies deserves a whole book.

What are Web services? In simple words, Web services are a new application model that allows companies to make their applications available over the Internet or an intranet as services; hence the name Web services. These published Web services can then be mixed and matched to create business applications or composite Web services. Where is the value proposition in all these? Unlike the traditional client/server model, client/server programming using Web services effectively eliminates the code dependencies (in the form of client libraries) between thick client and server, and hence greatly simplifies the development process. This dynamic nature of interaction and integration represents a fundamental paradigm shift in client/server programming.

For example, let us consider an online shopping application that we all are familiar with and use every day for buying things from books to plane tickets to anything else over the Internet. There are two crucial components of an online shopping application. One is the component that processes payments, and the other is the component that processes shipping. For each type of payment method, the application uses a corresponding component that understands that particular payment method and knows how to process it. If you choose to pay your bill using your PayPal account, the application will use the component (client library) that knows how to communicate with the system (server) used by the PayPal company. The reason for using different components for handling different methods of payment is that all these payment-processing systems use different technologies and run on different platforms. In addition, it is most likely that the protocols they use are also proprietary. The same is true for the module that handles shipping of the purchased item. The online retailer (aptly know as an etailer) offers different carriers to ship your item. If you choose to use FedEx as the carrier, the system will use a client component provided by FedEx to communicate with the Fedex order-processing system to fulfill the purchase request. This is shown in Figure 11.1.

The problem with this architecture is that it becomes a daunting task to integrate with all these disparate systems explicitly, not to mention that it becomes a maintenance nightmare for both the online retailer and their business partners. If PayPal or FedEx wants to change its system, it has to modify its client components and distribute the client components to all its business partners (etailers). As for the online retailers,

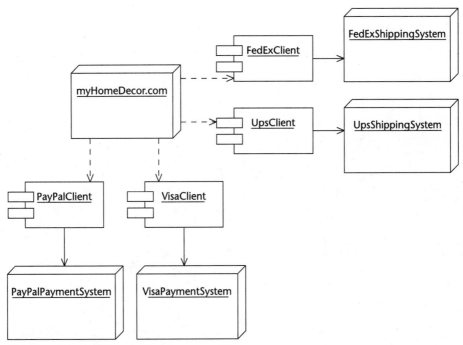

Figure 11.1   Traditional client/server architecture.

this would mean a rollout of their systems with the new client components at a minimum, and, quite possibly, code changes to some extent. Think about a shopping application that supports a number of different methods of payment. Suddenly system maintenance becomes quite a task. This is where a Web service is going to make a huge difference. Let's look at the system that we have described and see how we can simplify a seemingly involved integration task using the Web services architecture. The first step in using the Web services model is to publish the applications of all the business partners of our online retailer as Web services. Once those systems are converted to Web services, the task of integrating the shopping application with these Web services becomes very easy. The shipping companies and the payment-processing companies, on one hand, would no longer need to maintain and provide client components to the online retailer. The online retailer, on the other hand, could use generic components that would look up the required services from some business registry and use them in an ad hoc manner. The whole integration process happens at run time, rather than at compile time like that in a traditional integration environment. The same system using Web services is shown in Figure 11.2.

In any client/server environment, there are three distinct tasks involved in implementing a meaningful communication between the client and the server.

- First, determining how to locate the server over a network

- Second, determining how to send and receive data over the network

- Third, determining how to publish what functionality the server provides to the client

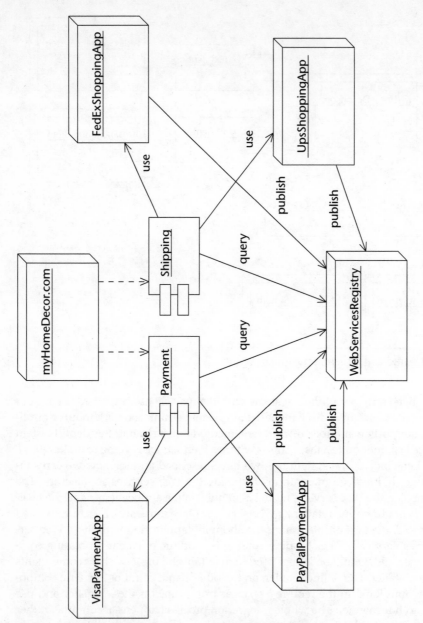

Figure 11.2   Client/server architecture using Web services.

Over the years, different paradigms have emerged, providing different solutions around these three basic steps of a client/server communication. Some of these solutions are completely proprietary to the application, while others are semiproprietary in that they may use some standard architecture such as RPC, RMI, CORBA, or even EJB, but the clients still have to know about the locations of the servers and the operations supported by the servers as well as the format and structure of the data used in the requests and responses during the implementation in some form of client library. The different technologies have tried to minimize these issues in their own ways with varying degrees of success. However, these technologies have not been able to completely eliminate the code dependencies between client and server nor to facilitate communication between applications using different languages running on different platforms. The concept of Web services has emerged with the lofty goal of eliminating all these issues once and for all.

The architecture on which Web services are based is the well-known concept of protocol layering found in networking protocols like TCP/IP. While XML is the basic ingredient of the whole Web services architecture, at its core is the wire protocol called SOAP (Simple Object Access Protocol) that keeps everything connected in the Web services world.

HISTORY In the beginning, companies like Microsoft and IBM started working on defining the architecture of Web services individually. As a result, several variations of the Web services architecture emerged, as each company introduced their own extensions (protocol layers) to the core architecture, threatening the very fundamental premise of Web services—a universal client/server architecture. Realizing the potential problem, Microsoft and IBM copresented their vision of the Web services architecture to the W3C Workshop on Web services held in April 2001. Following that workshop, the W3C created the Web Services Activity in January 2002 to bring all the activities around Web services under a single organizational umbrella to ensure that a standard architecture for Web services emerges from all the separate activities on different technologies that support Web services.

The architecture of the Web services is a work in progress by the Web Services Architecture Working Group, a part of the Web Services Activity. We will see this architecture evolve in the coming years as it matures. However, the architecture group has identified a core architecture that consists of three protocol layers to address all three fundamental tasks mentioned earlier in a client/server communication. These protocols are:

Simple Object Access Protocol (SOAP).   It defines how an application can invoke operations on a server or send messages to another application. The XML Protocol Working Group is responsible for defining this protocol.

Universal Description, Discovery, and Integration (UDDI).   It defines how a client can locate a server dynamically and how a server can publish its capabilities to the world. UDDI.org is a cross-industry effort that maintains and defines this protocol.

Web Services Definition Language (WSDL). It defines how to describe what a Web service can do and how to request that service. The description includes the definition of the format and structure of the data or message supported by the Web services as well as a mapping to the underlying network protocol. The Web Services Description Working Group of the W3C is responsible for defining this protocol.

The interactions between a Web services client and provider are shown in Figure 11.3. A Web services client sends a query to a UDDI registry server for a specific type of service. The registry looks up a service that matches the criteria and sends the WSDL information associated with the service back to the client. The client using the WSDL data establishes a connection with the targeted service. Once a connection is established, the Web services client and provider carry on a conversation using SOAP messages. Note that the client does not know anything about the provider before it finds the service from the registry. It is this runtime discovery and binding with the service that makes Web services so exciting.

In the following sections, we will explore each of these specifications in some detail to get a working knowledge of the Web services model.

SOAP

SOAP, the Simple Object Access Protocol, is an XML-based lightweight protocol used by applications to communicate in a language- and platform-neutral way. It defines a framework to construct messages containing application data in XML format and to exchange these XML messages over different transport protocols in a distributed environment. SOAP itself does not define any application semantics such as a programming model or implementation-specific semantics; rather, it defines a simple mechanism for expressing application semantics by providing a modular packaging model and encoding mechanisms for encoding data within modules.

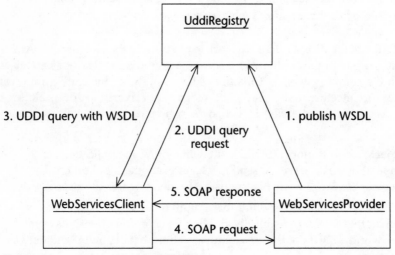

Figure 11.3 Web services collaboration.

HISTORY After SOAP was first introduced, the industry quickly realized the potential of SOAP and started to experiment with it. As a result, different implementations of SOAP started to emerge for different platforms. The companies like IBM and Microsoft jointly submitted the SOAP 1.1 specification to W3C in May 2000 with a proposal to form a working group for advancing the standard. This eventually led to the formation of the XML Protocol Working Group in September 2000. The submission (SOAP 1.1) became a W3C note and served as a reference for the group's activity. At the time of this writing, a working draft of SOAP 1.2 was available from the W3C.

In this section, we will discuss the basic concepts of SOAP, and we will use the SOAP 1.2 specification in its current state. Even though the specification may change before it becomes a final public release, the core concepts should not change.

SOAP messages are at the heart of a SOAP system. It is a unit of information exchanged between two systems. The systems involved in transmitting, relaying, receiving, and/or processing a SOAP message are known as SOAP nodes. A SOAP node can be one of three types: the initial SOAP sender, an ultimate SOAP receiver, or a SOAP intermediary. A SOAP message originates at an initial SOAP sender and moves through zero or more SOAP intermediaries until it reaches the ultimate SOAP receiver. Usually, SOAP intermediaries perform as proxies, caches, store-and-forward hops, or gateways. The functions that the SOAP nodes perform in processing a message are identified by a SOAP role. A SOAP role can be defined in the context of an application. The SOAP distributed communication model can support many different styles of messaging known as Message Exchange Patterns, or MEPs. Examples of MEPs are one-way messaging, request/reply messaging, point-to-point messaging, and so on. SOAP is designed to be used with a variety of transport protocols such as HTTP, SMTP, and RPC. This is achieved through SOAP binding that defines how to wrap SOAP messages within or on top of the underlying transport protocols. HTTP is the default SOAP binding because SOAP messages are intended to be exchanged over the Internet. SOAP messaging may support additional functionality known as SOAP features. Examples of such features are reliability, security, routing, and correlation.

A SOAP message is an XML document that consists of three parts:

Envelope.   This is the root element of the message that encapsulates everything related to the message and hence the name Envelope. The Envelope defines various namespaces that are used by the rest of the SOAP message, typically including xmlns:env (SOAP Envelope namespace), xmlns:xsi (XML Schema for Instances), and xmlns:xsd (XML Schema for DataTypes). It usually contains two child elements: Header, and Body. Figure 11.4 shows the structure of a SOAP message.

Header.   The Header is an optional element for carrying auxiliary information such as authentication information and transactions. Any element in a SOAP processing chain can add or delete items to or from the Header; elements can also choose to ignore items if they are unknown. If a Header is present, it must be the first child of the Envelope. It may define optional attributes such as encodingStyle, namespace definitions, and role. A role attribute is defined to associate a Header with a particular SOAP node. If a role is not defined, then the Header is targeted for the ultimate SOAP receiver node. A Header provides a modular way to extend SOAP functionality. This is achieved through the addition of child elements that are application-specific. You should define elements in the Header that are common to all messages. Each Header element carries a specific meaning in the context of an application to a specific SOAP node. The SOAP node will take a certain action based on the value of this Header element. For example, you can use elements to carry username and password in the Header, and the receiver SOAP node can use these data to authenticate the requester before it services the request. Thus, you augment the basic SOAP system with a security feature. A header element may optionally define an attribute called mustUnderstand with a value of true that indicates that the SOAP node processing the Header must know how to process this Header element. If it does not recognize the Header element, then it must generate an error message.

Body.   The Body is the main payload of the message. If a Header is present, the Body must be its immediate sibling, otherwise it must be the first child of the Envelope. It may define optional attributes like namespace and encodingStyle. It can contain any number of application-specific elements representing the actual data content of the message. SOAP defines one particular child element called Fault for reporting errors in processing SOAP messages.

Fault.   The SOAP Fault element is used to carry error and/or status information within a SOAP message. If a Fault element is present, it must appear as the only child of the Body element and must not appear more than once. It defines the following five child elements:

Code.   The Code element is intended for use by applications to provide an algorithmic mechanism for identifying the fault. It may optionally define the namespace attribute and contain two child elements: Value and Subcode. The Code must contain the Value element and the value of the Value element can be one of the following enumerated types already defined by SOAP:

- env:Sender (incorrectly formed message)
- env:Receiver (delivery problem)
- env:VersionMismatch (invalid namespace for the Envelope element)
- env:MustUnderstand (error processing header content)
- env:DataEncodingUnknown (unsupported data encoding)

The Subcode element is a recursive structure of the Code element. You can have any number of Subcode elements embedded in it. Each Subcode element must have a Value child element, which contains an application-defined more-specific error code.

Reason.   The Reason element is intended to provide a human-readable description of the error and is not intended for algorithmic processing. It must be present in a SOAP Fault element and should provide at least some information explaining the nature of the fault.

Node.   The Node element is intended to identify the SOAP node where the fault occurred on the SOAP message path. It indicates the source of the fault. The value of the Node attribute is a URI identifying the source. Applications that do not act as the ultimate destination of the SOAP message must include the Node element in a SOAP Fault element. The ultimate destination of a message may use the Node element to indicate explicitly that it generated the fault.

Role.   This is an optional element that can be used to indicate the role the node was playing at the time the error occurred.

Detail.   The Detail element is an optional element intended for carrying application-specific error information related to the Body element. It must be present if the contents of the Body element could not be processed successfully.

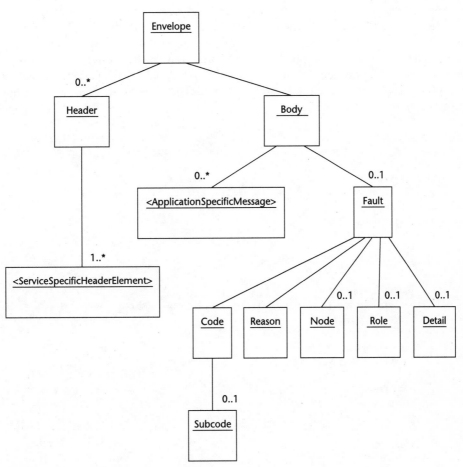

Figure 11.4   SOAP Message structure.

> **NOTE** The detailed error message related to Header processing must not be embedded in the Fault element. Instead, detailed error messages for SOAP header blocks must be carried within SOAP header blocks themselves.

Example of a SOAP Request

A complete SOAP request, with the data content, is shown below. The example shows SOAP encoding for request/reply type Message Exchange Pattern (MEP) and is simplified for illustration purposes. In this example, we build a request that invokes a method to retrieve a rate for a particular shipping type to a particular destination on a shipping rate query system. The shipping system is a SOAP node that is identified by an URI in the SOAP binding. If we use the HTTP protocol, the request URI indicates the application that we invoke the method on. The method and associated parameters are encoded as an XML document embedded within the SOAP Body element. The name of the root element is the same as the method name, and all the parameters are encoded as child elements. In the example, the method is GetShippingRate, and the input parameters of the method are shippingType and destination. We also added two elements in the header block specific to this application. The Requester element identifies who is making the request to the shipping system, and the Transaction element provides a way to track the total number of transactions/requests made to the shipping system from the same client.

```
<env:Envelope
  xmlns:env="http://www.w3c.org/2002/06/soap-envelope">
  <env:Header
    xmlns:eju="http://com.wiley.compBooks/EJwithUML">
    <eju:Requester env:mustUnderstand="1">
      myHomeDecor.com
    </eju:Requester>
    <eju:Transaction>
      1
    </eju:Transaction>
  </env:Header>
  <env:Body
    xmlns:exp="http://com.wiley.compBooks.EJwithUML.Samples/Soap">
    <exp:GetShippingRate>
      <exp:shippingType>
        2-3-day-ground
      </exp:shippingType>
      <exp:city>
        Dhaka
      </exp:city>
      <exp:country>
        Bangladesh
      </exp:country>
    </exp:GetShippingRate>
  </env:Body>
</env:Envelope>
```

> **NOTE** SOAP can ride on any other transport protocol. You can use SMTP, the Internet email protocol, for example, to deliver SOAP messages. The header differs between transport layers, but the XML payload remains the same.

Example of a SOAP Response

A complete SOAP response with the data content is shown below. This is a response message corresponding to the request shown in the previous section, when the method invocation is successful. It is shown for illustration purposes only and hence is simplified. The response message follows the same encoding rules as the request message. The response data is embedded in the SOAP Body element. The return data is encoded as an element with the same name as the parameter.

```
<env:Envelope
    xmlns:env="http://www.w3c.org/2002/06/soap-envelope">
    <env:Header
      xmlns:eju="http://com.wiley.compBooks/EJwithUML">
      <eju:Responder
        env:mustUnderstand="true">
        myWorldWideShipping.com
      </eju:Responder>
      <eju:Transaction>
        1
      </eju:Transaction>
    </env:Header>
    <env:Body
      xmlns:exp=
      "http://com.wiley.compBooks.EJwithUML.Samples/Soap">
        <exp:rate>
          33.25
        </exp:rate>
    </env:Body>
  </env:Envelope>
```

If the shipping system fails to process the request, it returns a response with a Fault element embedded in the Body element. In this example, the shipping system could not process the request because of an invalid value provided by the client for the input parameter shippingType. The Fault element appropriately indicates the situation. The high-level Code is set to Sender, which indicates that the reason for failure is that the request does not contain the appropriate value. It also provides an application-specific error code in the Subcode element of the Code block. Finally, it also provides a Detail element with a more specific description of the problem in the context of the request. This is shown in the following listing:

```
<env:Envelope
    xmlns:env="http://www.w3c.org/2002/06/soap-envelope">
    <env:Header
      xmlns:eju="http://com.wiley.compBooks/EJwithUML">
      <eju:Responder
        env:mustUnderstand="true">
        myWorldWideShipping.com
      </eju:Responder>
      <eju:Transaction>
        1
      </eju:Transaction>
    </env:Header>
    <env:Body
      xmlns:exp=
      "http://com.wiley.compBooks.EJwithUML.Samples/Soap">
        <env:Fault>
          <env:Code>
            <env:Value>
              env:Sender
            </env:Value>
            <env:Subcode>
              <env:Value>
                soapExample:InvalidShippingType
              </env:Value>
            </env:Subcode>
          </env:Code>
          <env:Reason>
            One or more Input parameter values not understood
          </env:Reason>
          <env:Detail>
            shippingType 2-3-day is not a valid value.
          </env:Detail>
        </env:Fault>
    </env:Body>
</env:Envelope>
```

UDDI

UDDI, Universal Description, Discovery, and Integration, is designed to provide a directory service that all businesses can use to advertise their products and services (a.k.a Web services) to their customers and partners and conduct business over the Internet. It allows companies to publish their Web services so that other companies can perform queries against the directory, locate the desired service, and use it in a truly dynamic fashion.

HISTORY The UDDI standard was put together by a collaborative effort of most software and hardware vendors as well as marketplace operators and e-business companies. The standard is maintained and actively developed by the UDDI Specification Technical Committee (www.uddi.org), a part of the Organization for the Advancement of Structured Information Standards (OASIS), a nonprofit global consortium to drive e-business standards. The committee published UDDI version 3 in July 2002. This has a variety of enhancements and additions to provide better support for the Web services architecture. An implementation of the specification, known as the UDDI Business Registry, is operated as a distributed service. Currently, IBM, Microsoft, and SAP each operate a registry node. In this section, we will discuss the basic concepts of UDDI.

The idea behind this UDDI directory is similar to that of the yellow pages. We all are familiar with the yellow pages and use it regularly. They contain a list of business names categorized by business type and sorted in alphabetical order to help us locate a particular business. When we are not sure of a business's name but we know what kind of product or service we want, all we have to do is to look up the businesses listed in the directory that offer our intended service or product, choose one of them, and contact that particular business by using the phone number or address provided in the listing. It is that simple. With the UDDI registry, the idea is the same, except the registry is an electronic service and the query is performed over the Internet by business applications, instead of by human beings.

UDDI is designed to run in a truly distributed environment. The UDDI registries can be organized in a hierarchical fashion where subtrees can be physically located in different hosts. These registries can share data among themselves. In fact, the registries can be interrelated in a complex way, creating a network of registries that is transparent to the clients.

UDDI defines standard API sets to perform actions such as inquires, publication, and subscription. These APIs standardize the behavior and interaction between a client and a UDDI registry as well as among the registries. It also defines a data model that helps organize the information published in the registry in a standard way so that later the same information can be retrieved using standard queries also defined in the specification. To facilitate complex queries, UDDI supports complex categorization of the published information based on different data points such as geographic location or business type.

Each type of data structure in UDDI is known as an entity. Entities are represented in XML and persisted in a UDDI registry. The data can be published in multiple languages to support global business interactions. The following are the key entities of a UDDI information model:

businessEntity. This is a top-level entity that represents a business or a company. It captures information such as name, description, and contact information about the business. The information related to a business is represented as other entities at the appropriate level of abstraction and stored within the business-Entity. Even though the word *business* appears in the name of this entity, it can be used to model any service provider, such as a department, a team, or even an application or a server. The modeling decision depends on the context of the data represented in the registry.

businessService. This represents a group of related Web services that a businessEntity provides. Hence it is contained within a businessEntity. It contains name, description, and classification information about the Web service that it represents.

bindingTemplate. This represents the technical information about a Web service. Hence it is associated with a corresponding businessService entity. The information includes all the necessary data that may be necessary for an application to establish a connection with the Web service and interact with it.

tModel. This stands for technical model, and it is used in UDDI to represent technical concepts that are not specific to any particular application but may be common to more than one application. Examples of such common concepts are Web Services Definition Language (WSDL) and XML Schema Definition Language (XSD). tModel represents each distinct specification, transport, and protocol used by many applications or Web services. This way, the tModels are reused by multiple bindingTemplates. Each bindingTemplate makes references to all the tModels that outline and specify the contract and behavior that the associated Web service supports.

The relationship among the entities described above is shown in Figure 11.5.

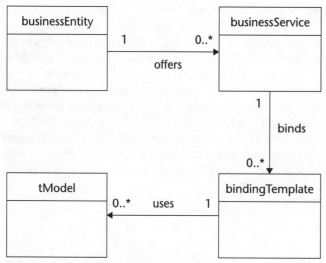

Figure 11.5 UDDI information model.

WSDL

Web Services Description Language (WSDL) is a language defined in XML for describing a Web service. Using this description, an application can establish a connection with the Web service and request its services without any implementation knowledge. The information required to describe a Web service would include a description of the name of the operations supported by the Web service (the interface), a description of the name and type of the data used by each operation, and a description of the mapping of the data to an actual type system and to the underlying transport protocol, known as binding, required to communicate with the service.

HISTORY The Web Services Description Working Group, a part of the Web Services Activity of W3C, was formed in January 2002 with the responsibility of defining this standard based on the suggestions submitted by companies like Microsoft and IBM in a W3C note in March 2001. The note represented the WSDL 1.1 specification. Recently, the group has published the first working draft of WSDL 1.2.

In this section, we will look at the basic concepts behind WSDL, based on its 1.2 working draft. Please understand that this standard may evolve considerably before it becomes a final public release. However, the core concepts should remain the same.

WSDL identifies six logical entities that can completely describe any Web service. These logical entities are called description components of a Web service. Each description component represents some aspect of a Web service. These six description components are:

- type description component
- message description component
- portType description component
- messageType description component
- binding description component
- service description component

A collection of description components is called a definition group. Definition groups serve as reusable modules for describing Web services that can be shared. A complete description of a Web service may require one or more of these definition groups.

The main XML elements of a WSDL document are described below. All these elements are defined in the http://www.w3.org/2002/07/wsdl namespace, and their relationship with each other is shown in Figure 11.6.

Definitions.   This is the root element of a WSDL document. It contains one optional documentation element, zero or more import elements, at most one type element, zero or more message elements, zero or more portType elements, zero or more serviceType elements, zero or more binding elements, and zero or more service elements. It has an attribute called targetNamespace that defines the namespace in which all other definition components are described in the document.

documentation. This can contain an optional description of the element it is part of. Any WSDL element can have this documentation element as an optional child element.

import. This provides an inclusion mechanism for WSDL. Any WSDL document can include other WSDL documents by defining one or more import elements. This allows the document writer to write cleaner WSDL documents by separating definitions based on different levels of abstraction. Thus, it promotes better reusability.

types. This contains type definitions of the data used in the messages exchanged during any interaction with Web services. WSDL does not define its own datatyping language. Instead, it supports the use of any existing type system such as the XML Schema Document (XSD). The types element can have zero or more child elements that describe the type system used by the Web service. For the XSD type system, this child element is called a schema. The schema element can have zero or more child elements, each called *element*, that define an application-specific data type.

message. It defines a message by defining all its constituent parts. A message part is the atomic entity as perceived by a WSDL. Such a description of a message has two aspects— the abstract definition, and the message binding—the mapping of data from abstract definition to a concrete representation of some type system. The message element captures the abstract definition of a message. It has one or more child elements, called part. A part element describes a logical data unit of the message and is associated with a type by the type attribute. The type attribute can directly refer to a data type of a type system or can refer to a type definition in the types element.

portType. This defines one or more operations that Web services offer using child elements, called operation. It is the interface of the Web service it is associated with. Each operation can have zero or more input messages described using an element called input, and output messages described using an element called output. Each of these messages refers to a message element.

serviceType. This groups a set of portType elements.

binding. This defines the message format mapping as well as the transport protocol. For most type systems, the mapping of data from the abstract definition to a concrete format is minimal, and hence the need for a mapping definition is minimal or nonexistent. However, for some other systems, there may be extensive mapping information required. The binding element has a required attribute called type that refers to a portType that it qualifies. It contains one or more binding detail elements. The scope of a binding detail element can be a portType, operation, or messages input, output, or fault. There may be more than one binding for a given portType.

service. This describes an actual Web service by associating it with a serviceType element through an attribute called serviceType. It contains one or more port elements, each of which defines an endpoint for the Web service by specifying a single address for a specific binding. Each port refers to a binding through an attribute called binding. In case of a single port Web service, the serviceType need not be defined. Figure 11.6 shows the relationship among all the elements mentioned here.

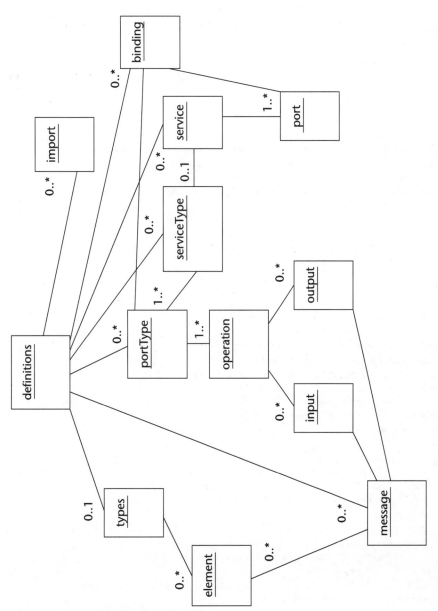

Figure 11.6 WSDL document structure.

NOTE The current release of WSDL 1.2 specification defines binding to SOAP 1.1 instead of SOAP 1.2.

The following is an example of a WSDL document describing a shipping system defined in the SOAP section. It uses SOAP 1.1 binding.

```xml
<?xml version="1.0">
<definitions name="ShippingSystem"
  targetNameSpace="http://com.wiley.compBooks/shippingsystem.wsdl"
  xmlns:eju="http://com.wiley.compBooks/EJwithUML"
  xmlnx:xsd="http://www.w3.org/2000/10/XMlSchema"
  xmlns:soap="http://www.w3c.org/2002/4/wsdl/soap"
  xmlns="http://www.w3.org/2002/04/wsdl">

  <message name="GetShippingRateRequestHeader">
    <part name="Requester" type="xsd:string"/>
    <part name="Transaction" type="xsd:int"/>
  </message>
  <message name="GetShippingRateResponseHeader">
    <part name="Responder" type="xsd:string"/>
    <part name="Transaction" type="xsd:int"/>
  </message>
  <message name="GetShippingRateInput">
    <part name="shippingType" type="xsd:string"/>
    <part name="destination" type="xsd:string"/>
  </message>
  <message name="GetShippingRateOutput">
    <part name="rate" type="xsd:float"/>
  </message>

  <portType name="ShippingSystemPortType">
    <operation name="GetShippingRate">
      <input message="eju:GetShippingRateInput"/>
      <output message="eju:GetShippingRateOutput"/>
    </operation>
  </portType>

  <binding name="ShippingSystemSoapBinding"
           type="eju:ShippingSystemPortType>
    <soap:binding style="rpc"
      transport="http://schemas.xmlsoap.org/soap/http"/>
    <operation name="GetShippingRate">
      <soap:operation
        soapAction="http://myWorldWideShipping.com/GetShippingRate">
        <input>
          <soap:header message="eju:GetShippingRateRequestHeader"/>
          <soap:body use="encoded"
namespace="http://com.wiley.compBooks.EJwithUML.Samples/Soap"
encodingStyle="http://schemas.xmlssoap.org/soap/encoding"/>
        </input>
        <output>
          <soap:header message="eju:GetShippingRateResponseHeader"/>
```

```
        <soap:body use="encoded"    namespace="http://com.wiley.compBooks.
EJwithUML.Samples/Soap"
encodingStyle="http://schemas.xmlssoap.org/soap/encoding"/>
      </output>
    </operation>
  </binding>

  <service name="ShippingSystemService">
    <documentation>A Reliable Shipping Service</documentation>
    <port name="ShippingSytemPort"
        binding="eju:ShippingSystemSoapBinding">
      <soap:address
          location="http://myWorldWideShipping.com/shippig"/>
    </port>
  </service>
</definitions>
```

Web Services in Java

XML has already become an integral part of the Java platform as Java is a natural fit for XML. Java provides platform neutrality, and XML provides the data neutrality. Combine these two technologies together, and you get a virtual universal platform for computing that essentially eliminates all your worries about whether your applications will be compatible with different hardware and operating systems. Now, the introduction of Web services to the Java platform takes Java one step closer to being the most coveted universal platform. Web services in Java will allow Java applications to talk not only with other Java applications in an ad hoc manner, but also with any applications implemented using other languages.

Sun, in its efforts to provide support for Web services in Java, has defined a set of XML-based APIs that, when combined, allow developers to implement Java Web services. These API sets are:

- Java API for XML Processing (JAXP)
- Java API for XML Registry (JAXR)
- Java API for XML-based RPC (JAX-RPC)
- Java API for XML Messaging (JAXM)
- SOAP with Attachments API for Java (SAAJ)
- Java Architecture for XML Binding (JAXB)

A reference implementation of these API sets along with supporting tools is available as a package called Java WSDP (Web Services Development Pack) from Sun. The latest release of this package at the time of this writing is 1.0. In this section, we will take a look at some of these APIs and show a client/server application based on the Web services programming model using Java WSDP.

JAXP

JAXP is a Java API for XML processing. It brings two popular APIs for processing XML data, DOM and SAX, under one umbrella and allows a Java application to seamlessly use either of the API sets under the hood without explicitly referencing them. It also includes support for the XML Schema and XML Stylesheet Language Transformations (XSLT) standards. So, JAXP library has become a self-sufficient tool that allows XML document parsing and transformation in an implementation-independent way.

The current version of JAXP is 1.2, which includes SAX 2.0, DOM level 2, and XSLT 1.0. The reference implementation of JAXP included in WSDP 1.0 uses Xerces 2 as the default XML parser and Xalan as the default XSLT engine. Xerces is an XML parser implementation that supports both SAX and DOM from Apache. Xalan is also an implementation of XSLT specification by Apache. However, any conforming implementation can be plugged in through its pluggable layer. The javax.xml.parser package provides an abstraction layer for XML parsing, and javax.xml.transform provides an abstraction layer for XSLT processing. Together these two packages create the JAXP pluggable architecture.

XSLT, defined by the W3C XSL working group, defines an XML-based language for transforming XML documents into other XML documents or into non-XML formats. Because XSLT may not be used directly in the context of Web services, we will skip the discussion of XSLT language. In this section, we will take a look at some of the classes defined in javax.xml.parser and javax.xml.transform. The SAX- and DOM-specific APIs were already covered in detail in Chapter 9, "Evaluating Candidate Technologies for User Interface Classes."

DocumentBuilderFactory

As the name suggests, it allows applications to create parsers that build DOM objects in a parser-independent way. It defines two factory methods:

- newDocumentBuilder(), which returns an instance of DocumentBuilder that builds DOM objects.

- newInstance(), which returns an instance of the DocumentBuilderFactory class. This method reads the name of the actual implementation class from the javax.xml.parser.DocumentBuilderFactory property found in the environment, or in the jaxp.properties file located under JRE lib directory, or in the META-INF/services/javax.xml.parsers.DocumentBuilderFactory file located in any JAR file on the classpath. It uses the platform default if the javax.xml.parser.DocumentBuilderFactory property is not defined.

This class also defines a pair of getter and setter methods to get and set parser attributes such as validation, entity reference expansion, and namespace awareness. It also defines generic setter and getter methods to get or set parser features by name.

DocumentBuilder

DocumentBuilder defines a set of overloaded parse() methods to create Document object (DOM) from different types of sources of XML documents. These sources are files, URLs, InputStreams, and SAX InputSources. It also defines a factory method, newDocument(), to create an empty Document object.

SaxParserFactory

Like DocumentBuilderFactory, this also defines two factory methods:

- newSaxParser(), which returns an instance of SaxParser that builds DOM objects.
- newInstance(), which returns an instance of the DocumentBuilderFactory class. This method ,like the newInstance() method of DocumentBuilderFactory, reads the name of the actual implementation class from the javax.xml.parser .SaxParserFactory property found in the environment, or in the jaxp.properties file located under the JRE lib directory, or in the META-INF/services/javax.xml .parsers.SaxParserFactory file located in any JAR file on the classpath. It uses the platform default if the javax.xml.parser.SaxParserFactory property is not defined.

This class also defines a set of getter and setter methods to set parser attributes like validation, entity reference expansion, namespace awareness, and so on. It also defines generic setter and getter methods to get or set parser features by name.

SaxParser

This is a wrapper class that wraps an XMLReader implementation. Like Document-Builder, it defines a set of overloaded parse() methods to create DOM document objects from different types of source XML documents. These sources are files, URLs, Input-Streams, and SAX InputSources. It also defines a factory method, newDocument(), to create an empty document object. Additionally, it provides a set of generic methods to set and get parser properties by name.

TransformerFactory

This defines three factory methods:

- newInstance(), which returns an instance of this factory class. This method reads the name of the actual implementation class from the javax.xml. transform.TransformerFactory property found in the environment, or in the jaxp.properties file located under the JRE lib directory, or in the META-INF/ services/javax.xml.transform.TransformerFactory file located in any JAR file on the classpath. It uses the platform default if the javax.xml.transform. TransformerFactory property is not defined.

- newTransformer(), which returns an instance of Transformer that can be used to transform an XML document into different formats.

- newTemplates(), which returns a Templates object that a transformer can use to transform a document into a target document. It loads XSLT instructions as an XML document and compiles them into optimized Templates objects. It improves the performance of the transformer. Templates objects are thread-safe, that is, multiple threads can concurrently use the same Templates object. The Templates interface defines a factory method, newTransformer(), to create a Transformer object for this Templates object.

It also defines methods to get and set attributes of a transformer by name.

Transformer

It defines the transform() method that takes as input an XML document and an empty target XML document and then applies the XSLT rules associated with the transformer to the input to create the output. The input XML document is represented by the interface called Source and the output document is represented by the interface called Result. Both the interfaces are defined in the javax.xml.transform package. The corresponding implementation classes for these interfaces are defined in the javax.xml.transform.dom, javax.xml.transform.sax, and javax.xml.transform.stream packages. The following code snippet shows how a transformer is used to apply XSLT on an XML document to convert it into an HTML document.

```
TransformerFactory xformerFactory =
                              TransformerFactory.newInstance();
Source xsltSource = new StreamSource("xml2html.xslt");
Templates xformationRules = formerfactory.newTemplates(xsltSource);
Transformer xformer = xformationRules.newTransformer();
Source inputData = new StreamSource("input.xml");
Result outputData = new StreamResult("output.html");
xformer.transform(inputData, outputData);
```

Input.xml

```
<?xml version="1.0"?>
<shippingRatesFromMyWorldWideShipping>
  <origination>Richmond, VA, US</origination>
  <shippingType>2-3-day-Air</shippingType>
  <shippingRate>
    <destination>Bangladesh, Dhaka</destination>
    <rate>$32/lb</rate>
  </shippingRate>
  <shippingRate>
    <destination>Manhattan,NY, US</destination>
    <rate>$12/lb</rate>
  </shippingRate>
  <shippingRate>
    <destination>Austin, TX, US</destination>
```

```
      <rate>$18/lb</rate>
    </shippingRate>
</shippingRatesFromMyWorldWideShipping>
```

xml2html.xslt

```
<xsl:stylesheet xmlns:xsl="http://www.w3.org/1999/XSL/Transform" version="1.0">
  <xsl:output method="html"/>
  <xsl:template match="/">
    <html>
    <head>
      Shipping Rate from myWorldWideShipping.com
    </head>
      <body>
        <p>The rates are valid when sent from
        <xsl:value-of select="//origination"/>
      </p>
      <p>shipping type:
        <xsl:value-of select="//shippingType"/>
      </p>
    <table>
    <xsl:for-each select="//shippingRate">
      <tr><td>
        <xsl:value-of select="destination"/>
      </td></tr>
      <tr><td>
        <xsl:value-of select="rate"/>
      </td></tr>
    </xsl:for-each>
    </table>
        </body>
      </html>
  </xsl:template>
</xsl:stylesheet>
```

output.html

```
<html>
<head>
<META http-equiv="Content-Type" content="text/html; charset=UTF-8">
      Shipping Rate from myWorldWideShipping.com
    </head>
<body>
<p>The rates are valid when sent from
      Richmond, VA, US</p>
<p>shipping type:
      2-3-day-Air</p>
<table>
<tr>
<td>Bangladesh, Dhaka</td>
</tr>
<tr>
```

```
<td>$32/lb</td>
</tr>
<tr>
<td>Manhattan,NY, US</td>
</tr>
<tr>
<td>$12/lb</td>
</tr>
<tr>
<td>Austin, TX, US</td>
</tr>
<tr>
<td>$18/lb</td>
</tr>
</table>
</body>
</html>
```

NOTE The classes DocumentbuilderFactory, DocumentBuilder, SAXParserFactory, SAXParser, TransformerFactory, and Transformer are not guaranteed to be thread-safe. A good way to ensure thread-safety while keeping it simple is to allocate instances of these classes per thread.

JAXR

JAXR, the Java API for XML Registries, defines a standard set of API for publication and discovery of Web services. It provides a pluggable architecture that consists of three layers: JAXR client, JAXR provider, and registry provider. This is shown in Figure 11.7. A JAXR client depends on a JAXR provider and thus is isolated from the actual underlying registry implementation. You can swap registries without needing to change anything in the client. A JAXR provider can be implemented as a full-fledged registry provider of its own, in which case, there will not be any registry provider layer. However, it is usually implemented as a façade to an existing industry standard registry provider such as a UDDI or ebXML. The motivation for this architecture is to shield Java clients from the differences among the existing Web services registries and provide a common registry information model and a common set of APIs to interact with the registries.

JAXR defines an information model that is a superset of other registry models and not every registry need to support all the features defined in the JAXR specification. In order to address the differences in the support for JAXR by the registry providers, JAXR defines a concept called capability profile. It currently defines two levels of capability profile—level 0 and level 1—and models this capability as CapabilityProfile. Each method of JAXR interface is assigned a capability level, and all the methods with the same capability level define the capability profile of the underlying JAXR provider. At a minimum, all JAXR providers must be capability level 0 compliant. UDDI registries are level 0 and ebXML registries are level 1 providers.

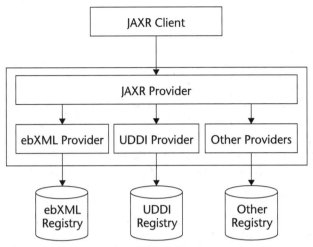

Figure 11.7   JAXR pluggable architecture.

There are two parts to a JAXR specification: APIs to perform registry operations, and the information model. The APIs allow applications to interact with registries for performing different tasks like adding, editing, removing Web services, as well as querying registries for a specific Web service. The API used for adding, editing, and deleting information is called the lifecycle management API, and the API used for querying information is called the query management API. Again, each type of API is organized by the capability level. All the interfaces related to the level 0 profile are prefixed with the term Business and known as business-focused APIs, whereas all the interfaces without the Business prefix represent the level 1 profile and are known as generic APIs. These APIs are defined in the javax.xml.registry package.

The information model represents the data stored in the registries. It defines the structure of the data and their relationship with each other so that it is easy to perform the tasks supported by the APIs. All the interfaces representing these data models are defined in the javax.xml.registry.infomodel package. The JAXR information model closely resembles the ebXML registry information model. However, it defines mappings to the data types defined in the UDDI information model.

In this section, we will look at some of the key interfaces from both the packages.

RegistryService

This is the key interface of a JAXR registry provider. It defines methods to access other interfaces. It defines a getter method for accessing task-specific interfaces—Business LifeCycleManager, BusinessQueryManager, and DeclarativeQueryManager. It provides a getCapabilityProfile() method that returns the CapablityProfile of the underlying provider. It should be called first to determine the capability of the registry before proceeding with any other operations.

LifeCycleManager

It defines methods for performance, addition, deletion, modification, association, and classification of data. LifeCycleManager, as shown in Figure 11.8, defines low-level methods to perform the same tasks as mentioned above as well as a set of factory methods to create the data objects that are stored in the registry. The factory methods are prefixed with the word create to distinguish them from lifecycle management methods. The lifecycle management methods in the LifeCycleManager interface deal with generic data represented by the RegistryObject interface, which is the base interface of most of the interfaces in the javax.xml.registry.infomodel package.

There is a derived interface called BusinesLifeCycleManager that defines a set of methods at a higher level of abstraction know as business-focused methods. Each of these methods deals with a specific data type. It defines a set of save methods to add a new data in the registry or modify the data if it already exists in the registry. It also defines a set of delete methods to delete data from the registry.

The LifeCycleManager interface is a level 1 API, whereas BusinessLifeCycleManager is a level 0 API.

QueryManager

It defines a set of getter methods to retrieve data stored in the registry by unique ID and type. The ID is provided as a String object. It has methods that return a single data object of the RegistryObject type, which is the base type of all the data in a JAXR registry. It also has methods that return a collection of RegistryObjects.

There are two derived interfaces, as shown in Figure 11.9, called BusinessQueryManager and DeclarativeQueryManager. BusinessQueryManager is a level 0 API, whereas QueryManager and DeclarativeQueryManager are level 1 APIs.

DeclarativeQueryManager defines the createQuery() factory method to create a declarative Query object from a string. It also defines an executeQuery() method to actually run the query in the registry. Currently, JAXR supports SQL-92 and OASIS/ebXML registry filter queries.

BusinessQueryManager defines a set of find methods that supports high-level business-style queries. There are find methods for retrieving different types of the RegistryObject based on different types of qualifiers, as defined in the FindQualifier interface and based on classification.

ConnectionFactory

It defines three factory methods:

- newInstance(), which creates an instance of ConnectionFactory.
- createConnection(), which creates an instance of Connection that represents a physical connection to the underlying registry provider.
- createFederatedConnection(), which creates a virtual connection to a group of registries. The connection is called federated connection. This type of connection supports distributed queries.

```
┌─────────────────────────────────────────────────────────────────────────────┐
│                            LifeCycleManager                                   │
├─────────────────────────────────────────────────────────────────────────────┤
│                                                                               │
├─────────────────────────────────────────────────────────────────────────────┤
│ +createObject(:String):Object                                                 │
│ +createAssociation(:RegistryObject,:Concept):Association                       │
│ +createClassification(:ClassificationScheme,:String,:String):Classification    │
│ +createClassification(:ClassificationScheme,:InternationalString,:String):Classification │
│ +createClassification(:Concept):Classification                                 │
│ +createClassificationScheme(:String,:String):ClassificationScheme              │
│ +createClassificationScheme(:InternationalString,:InternationalString):ClassificationScheme │
│ +createClassificationScheme(:Concept):ClassificationScheme                     │
│ +createConcept(:RegistryObject,:String,:String):Concept                        │
│ +createConcept(:RegistryObject,:InternationalString,:String):Concept           │
│ +createEmailAddress(:String):EmailAddress                                      │
│ +createEmailAddress(:String,:String):EmailAddress                              │
│ +createExternalIdentifier(:ClassificationScheme,:String,:String):ExternalIdentifier │
│ +createExternalIdentifier(:ClassificationScheme,:InternationalString,:String):ExternalIdentifier │
│ +createExternalLink(:String,:String):ExternalLink                              │
│ +createExternalLink(:String,:InternationalString):ExternalLink                 │
│ +createExtrinsicObject():ExtrinsicObject                                        │
│ +createInternationalString():InternationalString                               │
│ +createInternationalString(:String):InternationalString                        │
│ +createInternationalString(:Locale,:String):InternationalString                │
│ +createKey(:String):Key                                                        │
│ +createLocalizedString(:Locale,:String):LocalizedString                        │
│ +createLocalizedString(:Locale,:String,:String):LocalizedString                │
│ +createOrganization(:String):Organization                                      │
│ +createOrganization(:InternationalString):Organization                         │
│ +createPersonName(:String,:String,:String):PersonName                          │
│ +createPersonName(:String):PersonName                                          │
│ +createPostalAddress(:String,:String,:String,:String,:String,:String,:String):PostalAddress │
│ +createRegistryPackage(:String):RegistryPackage                                │
│ +createRegistryPackage(:InternationalString):RegistryPackage                   │
│ +createService(:String)Service                                                 │
│ +createService(:InternationalString):Service                                   │
│ +createServiceBinding():ServiceBinding                                          │
│ +createSlot(:String,:String,:String):Slot                                      │
│ +createSlot(:String,:Collection,:String):Slot                                  │
│ +createSpecificationLink():SpecificationLink                                    │
│ +createTelephoneNumber():TelephoneNumber                                        │
│ +createUser()User                                                              │
│ +saveObjects(:Collection):BulkResponse                                         │
│ +deprecateObjects(:Collection):BulkResponse                                    │
│ +unDeprecateObjects(:Collection):BulkResponse                                  │
│ +deleteObjects(:Collection):BulkResponse                                       │
│ +createConceptEquivalence(:Concept,:Concept):void                              │
│ +deleteConceptEquivalence(:Concept,:Concept):void                              │
└─────────────────────────────────────────────────────────────────────────────┘
                                    △
                                    │
           ┌────────────────────────────────────────────────┐
           │              BusinessLifeCycleManager           │
           ├────────────────────────────────────────────────┤
           │                                                 │
           ├────────────────────────────────────────────────┤
           │ +saveOrganizations(:Collection):BulkResponse    │
           │ +saveServices(:Collection):BulkResponse         │
           │ +saveServiceBindings(:Collection):BulkResponse  │
           │ +saveConcepts(:Collection):BulkResponse         │
           │ +saveClassificationSchemes(:Collection):BulkResponse │
           │ +saveAssociations(:Collection,:boolean):BulkResponse │
           │ +deleteOrganizations(:Collection):BulkResponse  │
           │ +deleteServices(:Collection):BulkResponse       │
           │ +deleteServiceBindings(:Collection):BulkResponse │
           │ +deleteConcepts(:Collection):BulkResponse       │
           │ +deleteClassificationSchemes(:Collection):BulkResponse │
           │ +deleteAssociations(:Collection):BulkResponse   │
           └────────────────────────────────────────────────┘
```

Figure 11.8   LifeCycleManager and related classes.

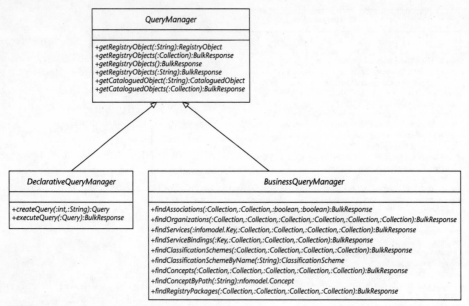

Figure 11.9 QueryManager and related classes.

ConnectionFactory uses properties to establish a connection. Some properties are defined as standard JAXR properties such as javax.xml.registry.queryManagerURL, javax.xml.registry.lifeCycleManagerURL, and javax.xml.registry.security.authentication Method. There are properties that are implementation-specific. Examples of such properties for Sun's reference implementation provided with WSDP are com.sun .xml.registry.http.proxyUsername and com.sun.xml.registry.http.proxyPassword.

Connection

This represents a connection between a JAXR client and a JAXR provider. JAXR clients call the getRegistryService() method on a connection object to access a RegistryService object associated with the connection. There is a derived interface called Federated-Connection that represents a logical connection to a group of JAXR registry providers to support distributed queries.

RegistryObject

This is the base interface for most of the data models defined in the JAXR specification. It defines getter and setter methods for a set of attributes common to all the data models. These common attributes include name, description, and key. The key is a Universal Unique ID (UUID) and is represented by the interface key.

RegistryObject extends the ExtensibleObject interface that allows RegistryObjects to be extended by adding arbitrary attributes on a per instance basis. The dynamic attributes are represented by the interface called Slot. A slot has a name, a type, and a collection of values. An attribute represented as a slot can have a single value or a collection of values.

Organization

As the name suggests, it represents a logical organization that may correspond to a real-world organization or a logical body that offers some kind of Web services. An organization can be logically defined in a hierarchical structure through a parent/child relationship, as shown in Figure 11.10. Hence it defines a set of methods to add, remove, or get child organizations. Also, it defines methods to get the parent organization as well as the root organization.

An organization can offer a host of Web services, and hence it defines methods to add, remove, and get services. It also defines methods to add, remove, and get users affiliated with the organization. The users are represented by the interface user that defines getter and setter methods for attributes like name, address, telephone number, email address, and type.

It maps to a BusinessEntity of the UDDI information model.

Service

This represents a logical service offered by an organization and defines methods to get, add, and remove information such as ServiceBinding about the service it represents. It maps to a BusinessService of the UDDI information model.

ServiceBinding

This represents the technical information to invoke the service it is associated with. It defines getter and setter methods for a URL by which the service can be accessed. It defines methods to add, remove, and get the external specification as a Specification-Link. This specification contains the technical information that describes how to use the service. For Web services, this information is represented as a WSDL document. A service may have one or more specifications and hence one or more SpecificationLink. It maps to a tModel in the UDDI information model.

Association

It represents a relationship between two RegistryObjects. The two objects involved in an Association are called a source object and a target object. Based on the type of objects involved in an association, it is important to correctly identify the source and target object because this determines the direction of the association. There are two types of associations based on who creates an association: intramural association and extramural association. In an intramural association, the user who defines the association is the same user who created the objects of the association. In extramural association, the user who creates the association is different from the user who created the objects in the association.

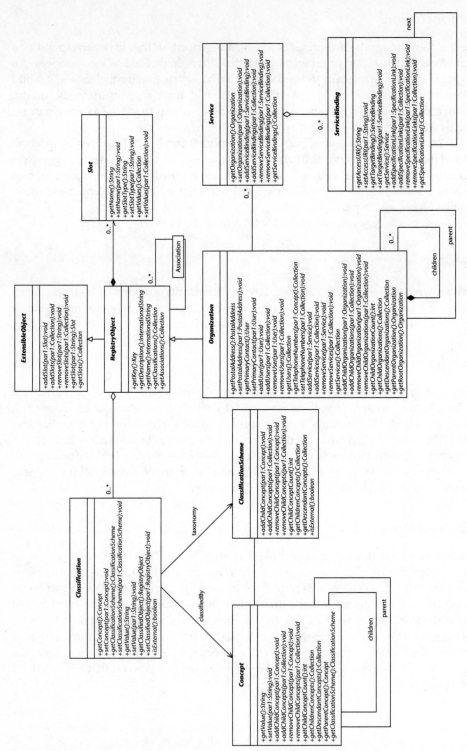

Figure 11.10 JAXR information model.

An association needs to be confirmed by all parties involved before it can be visible to the external world. The process of accepting an association is known as confirmation. In the case of an intramural association, because all objects are created by the same user, there is no need for an explicit confirmation of the association. In the case of an extramural association, the users who created the objects in the association have to explicitly confirm the association through the BusinessLifeCycleManager object before the association becomes visible to the third parties.

An association must have a type associated with it. The type is defined as an enumerated type represented by the Concept interface. This type is used for classification purposes. A concept can have a hierarchical structure with a parent/child relationship. This is explained in detail in the next section.

JAXR Taxonomy

JAXR represents a taxonomy as a ClassificationScheme. Each ClassificationScheme represents a way to classify or organize a group of related information stored in a registry. For example, businesses can be classified by their geographic location. The same information can be classified in multiple ways. For example, we can also classify businesses by the industry they belong to. When a JAXR registry uses a ClassificationScheme according to an industry-standard taxonomy, it is known as external classification. The North American Industry Classification System (NAICS) is an example of external taxonomy that classifies businesses by the industry. When a JAXR registry uses a ClassificationScheme implemented by the registry itself, it is known as internal classification. The internal classification is represented as a hierarchy of Concepts with the ClassificationScheme at the root of the tree. The external classification is represented by the name and the value of the taxonomy it refers to. Each Registry Object is then associated with a Classification object that refers to either a Concept object in case of internal classification or the ClassificationScheme directly with a name and value that identifies a particular taxonomy element within the external ClassificationScheme. The same RegistryObject is classified in different ways by associating it with multiple Classification objects. An example of both external and internal classification is shown in Figure 11.11.

An Example of Publishing a Web Service

An important step in implementing any Web service is the publication of the service in a standard registry like UDDI or ebXML. In this section, we implement a tool that registers our Web service with a UDDI registry using the JAXR APIs discussed in the previous section. The Java WSDP (Web Services Development Pack) provides a UDDI registry that supports the UDDI 2.0 specification and JAXR APIs with a level 0 capability profile.

The following code shows how to connect to the UDDI registry, and how to create an organization and populate all the information associated with the organization, including the Web service that the organization provides. The organization is classified using the well-known taxonomy—NAICS. The client can look up this organization and retrieve its service information using the same classification scheme. After the organization is received for publication, the registry updates the organization with the modified data if it already exists; otherwise it creates a new entry for the organization.

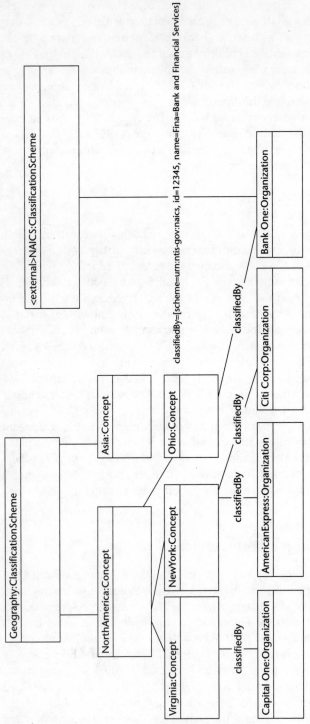

Figure 11.11   An example of the JAXR taxonomy.

WebServicesPublisher.java

```
package com.wiley.compBooks.EJwithUML.Samples.WebServices;

/**
 * This class publishes a Web service in the UDDI registry that
 * comes with the Java WSDP using the JAXR API.
 */
import javax.xml.registry.*;
import javax.xml.registry.infomodel.*;
import java.util.*;
//import java.security.*;
import java.net.PasswordAuthentication;

public class WebServicesPublisher
{
  public static final String DEFAULT_REG_SERVER =
  "http://localhost:8080/registry-server/RegistryServerServlet";
  public static final void  main(String[] args)
  {
    if (args.length < 2)
    {
      System.out.println(
       "Usage: java
       com.wiley.compBooks.EJwithUML.Samples.WebServicesPublisher
       <username> <password> <server URL>");
      System.out.println("<server URL> is optional. Default URL is
       http://localhost:8080/registry-server/RegistryServerServlet");
      return;
    }
    String username = args[0];
    String password = args[1];
    String server = DEFAULT_REG_SERVER;
    if (args.length >= 3)
    {
      server = args[2];
    }
    Properties jaxrProps = new Properties();
    jaxrProps.setProperty("javax.xml.registry.queryManagerURL",
     "http://localhost:8080/registry-server/RegistryServerServlet");
    jaxrProps.setProperty("javax.xml.registry.lifeCycleManagerURL",
     "http://localhost:8080/registry-server/RegistryServerServlet");
    Connection jaxrConn = null;
    try
    {
      //establishes a connection to the registry
      ConnectionFactory jaxrConFactory =
                              ConnectionFactory.newInstance();
      jaxrConFactory.setProperties(jaxrProps);
      jaxrConn = jaxrConFactory.createConnection();
      RegistryService regSrvc = jaxrConn.getRegistryService();
      BusinessLifeCycleManager blcMgr =
```

```
                              regSrvc.getBusinessLifeCycleManager();
        BusinessQueryManager bqMgr =
                              regSrvc.getBusinessQueryManager();


        // Credential is required to publish information in a JAXR
        //registry.
        jaxrConFactory.setProperties(jaxrProps);
        PasswordAuthentication passwdAuth = new
        PasswordAuthentication(username,password.toCharArray());
        Set creds = new HashSet();
        creds.add(passwdAuth);
        jaxrConn.setCredentials(creds);


        //creates an organization and poulates the basic information
        Organization org = blcMgr.createOrganization(
                              "myWorldWideShipping.com");
        InternationalString description = blcMgr.createInternationalString("a
reliable efficient carrier for your business.");
        User primaryContact = blcMgr.createUser();
        PersonName pName = blcMgr.createPersonName(
                              "Syed Humayun Rayhan");
        primaryContact.setPersonName(pName);
        TelephoneNumber telNum = blcMgr.createTelephoneNumber();
        telNum.setNumber("123-456-7890");
        Collection telNumbers = new ArrayList();
        telNumbers.add(telNum);
        primaryContact.setTelephoneNumbers(telNumbers);
        EmailAddress emailAddr= blcMgr.createEmailAddress(
                              "syed@hotmail.com");
        Collection emails = new ArrayList();
        emails.add(emailAddr);
        primaryContact.setEmailAddresses(emails);
        org.setPrimaryContact(primaryContact);


        //clasifies the roganization using NAICS taxonomy
        ClassificationScheme cScheme =
bqMgr.findClassificationSchemeByName(null,"ntis-gov:naics");
        // concept code = 481112, concept name = Scheduled Freight Air
        // Transportation
        Classification classification = (Classification)
                blcMgr.createClassification(cScheme,
              "Scheduled Freight Air Transportation", "481112" );
        Collection classifications = new ArrayList();
        classifications.add(classification);
        org.addClassifications(classifications);


        //adds a service
        Collection services = new ArrayList();
        Service service = blcMgr.createService("Shipping System");
        InternationalString svcDescrpt =
blcMgr.createInternationalString("Shipping Rate Query Service");
        service.setDescription(svcDescrpt);
        Collection serviceBindings = new ArrayList();
```

```
      ServiceBinding binding = blcMgr.createServiceBinding();
      InternationalString svcBindDescrpt =
blcMgr.createInternationalString("WSDL Soap Binding");
      binding.setDescription(svcBindDescrpt);
      //By default JAXR checks the validity of a URI.
      binding.setValidateURI(false);
      binding.setAccessURI("http://localhost:8080/ShippingSystem/");
      serviceBindings.add(binding);
      service.addServiceBindings(serviceBindings);
      services.add(service);
      org.addServices(services);
      Collection orgs = new ArrayList();
      orgs.add(org);

      // registers the oganization in the Java WSDP UDDI registry
      BulkResponse response = blcMgr.saveOrganizations(orgs);
      Collection exceptions = response.getExceptions();
      if (exceptions == null)
      {
        System.out.println("organization was added successfully.");
        Collection keys = response.getCollection();
        Iterator keyItr = keys.iterator();
        //retrieves the key assigned to the organization by the
        //registry
        while(keyItr.hasNext())
        {
          Key orgKey = (Key) keyItr.next();
          String id = orgKey.getId();
          System.out.println("Organization key is " + id);
          org.setKey(orgKey);
        }
      }
      else
      {
        System.out.println("failed to add organization.");
        Iterator excpItr = exceptions.iterator();
        while(excpItr.hasNext())
        {
          Exception exception = (Exception)excpItr.next();
          exception.printStackTrace(System.out);
        }
      }
    }
    catch(JAXRException ex)
    {
      ex.printStackTrace(System.out);
    }
    finally
    {
      if (jaxrConn != null)
      {
        try
        {
```

```
        jaxrConn.close();
      }
      catch(JAXRException e)
      {
        //Not much can be done!
      }
    }
  }


  }
}
```

The following code snippet shows how a Web services client can look up a Web service. You would need to establish a connection with the registry, as shown in the previous example, before you could perform the following query. The query in this example uses the classification used in the previous example so that we can retrieve the organization that we added in the previous example. We can iterate through the organizations returned from the query and pick the one that offers the service that we are looking for by digging through the service and its bindings of each organization. To get a better result from a query, you should add other additional search attributes like search qualifiers and names.

```
RegistryService regSrvc = jaxrConn.getRegistryService();
BusinessLifeCycleManager blcMgr =
                    regSrvc.getBusinessLifeCycleManager();
BusinessQueryManager bqMgr = regSrvc.getBusinessQueryManager();
ClassificationScheme cScheme = bqMgr.findClassificationSchemeByName(null,
"ntis-gov:naics");
// concept code = 481112, concept name = Scheduled Freight Air
// Transportation
Classification classification = (Classification)
blcMgr.createClassification(cScheme, "Scheduled Freight Air Transportation",
"481112" );
Collection classifications = new ArrayList();
classifications.add(classification);
//makes a query
BulkResponse response = bqMgr.findOrganizations(null, null, classifications,
null, null, null);
Collection orgs = response.getCollection();
```

JAX-RPC

Java API for XML-based RPC (JAX-RPC) is an adoption of the SOAP 1.1 specification for the Java platform. Remote procedure calls, or RPC, are a form of synchronous request/reply type messaging that is traditionally used for the client/server application model. JAX-RPC, through the use of XML for data encoding and HTTP for a transport protocol, not only facilitates communication among Java-only applications, but also enables Java and non-Java applications to talk seamlessly for the first time.

Java Web services can easily publish all their services as a collection of procedures that any remote SOAP clients can invoke. The current reference implementation of JAX_RPC 1.0 is available with WSDP 1.0_01. The APIs can be categorized in two groups—one that supports SOAP and the other that supports WSDL and provides a framework to implement the Web services client and provider. The javax.xml.soap package defines interfaces and classes that directly support SOAP. The APIs in this package are defined in the SOAP with Attachment API for Java (SAAJ) 1.1 specification. These APIs can be used for creating and editing SOAP messages. The packages—javax.xml.rpc, javax.xml.rpc.handler, and java.xml.rpc.server—define various interfaces that are used to implement the Web services client and provider applications and are defined in the JAX-RPC 1.0 specification.

Call

This interface, defined in the javax.xml.rpc package, allows client applications of Web services to dynamically invoke services as remote operations. It defines setter methods to configure the invocation for the targeted operation. This includes setting the operation name, name of the portType, and address of the target endpoint. It also defines methods to add parameters for the operation to be invoked. It defines two overloaded invoke() methods to actually invoke an operation synchronously on the service endpoint. The return values from an invocation of an operation can be retrieved either as a List by calling getOutputValues() or as a Map (a list of name-value pairs) by calling getOutputParams(). It defines a variation of the invoke() method called invokeOneWay() that supports the one-way invocation of an operation, where the call returns immediately without waiting for a response from the service endpoint.

Service

This interface, defined in javax.xml.rpc, defines a set of factory methods that create a dynamic invocation object of a given service endpoint. It has two types of factory methods:

Instance of the Call interface.   There are four overloaded createCall() methods that return an object of type Call that a service client can use to invoke operations on the target service endpoint.

Instance of the Stub interface or a dynamic proxy.   There are two overloaded getPort() methods that return objects of type Stub or dynamic proxy objects based on the service endpoint interface class provided as an argument.

Handler

This interface, defined in the javax.xml.rpc.handler package, defines methods to handle SOAP messages. There is one handler method for each type of message: handleRequest(), handleResponse(), and handleFault(). Additionally, it defines methods to manage the life cycle of a Handler: init() and destroy(). The init() method initializes a handler based on the HandlerInfo object provided as an argument to it. HandlerInfo is a class defined in the same package to provide handler-specific initialization parameters as name-value pairs.

HandlerChain

This interface, defined in the javax.xml.rpc.handler package, represents a list of handlers that share a common policy and mechanism for their invocation. It defines the same handler and life cycle management methods as the Handler interface.

HandlerRegistry

This interface, defined in the javax.xml.rpc.handler package, represents a registry of handlers. Handlers are registered as HandlerChain per service endpoint represented as a port in WSDL. It provides methods to register (set) and look up (get) Handler-Chain by port names.

MessageContext

This interface, defined in javax.xml.rpc.handler package, represents a context of a SOAP message. The context is represented as a set of properties. The interface defines methods to manage these properties. This allows handlers to share processing state of messages.

SOAPHeader

This interface represents the header element of a SOAP message. It defines methods to add, examine, and extract SOAPHeaderElement, an interface representing the contents in a header part of a SOAP message. It can contain one or more objects of type SOAP-HeaderElement.

SOAPFault

This interface represents a fault element of a SOAP message. It defines getter and setter methods for the contents of a fault element such as code, actor, and detail.

SOAPBody

This interface represents the body part of a SOAP message. It can contain one or more objects of type SOAPBodyElement, an interface that represents application-specific data contents. In the event of an error, a SOAPBody object may have one object of type

SOAPFault, an interface representing SOAPBody that defines methods to add SOAP-BodyElement objects as well as to add and retrieve (get) a SOAPFault object.

SOAPEnvelope

This interface represents the Envelope element of a SOAP message. It works as a container for a SOAPHeader object and a SOAPBody object. It defines methods to set and retrieve (get) these objects.

SOAPMessage

This class represents a SOAP message. It contains a SOAPPart object, which is a container for the SOAP-specific contents of a SOAP message. It also contains zero or more AttachmentParts that represent the attachments of a SOAP message. The contents of an AttachmentPart can be any type of application-specific data. It defines getter methods for AttachmentPart and SOAPPart. It also defines a number of overloaded factory methods to create AttachmentPart. Figure 11.12 shows the relationship of a SOAPMesssage class with its constituent classes.

An Example of a SOAP Client/Server Application

In this section, we will implement a client/server application using SAAJ 1.1, which supports the SOAP 1.1 specification. The server is a shipping system that allows its clients to perform a query about shipping rates to different cities and countries. We use the SAAJ 1.1 implementation of the Java WSDP 1.0.01. When directly using SOAP APIs, the clients have to be intimately aware of the request and response message formats supported by the server as well as the location of the server. You can see it takes a lot of processing just to create and extract data from SOAP messages.

In the example, the server is implemented as a servlet and uses SOAP APIs directly. However, most of the Web services development kits, including the Java WSDP, provide tools that automate most of the steps involved in implementing Web services, and provide frameworks that allow you to implement the business logic of the service as simple Java classes. Apache SOAP and Axis are examples of such development kits. When the SOAP server in the example receives a request from a client inquiring about a shipping rate to a specific city and a country, it looks up the rate using the city and country as a key and returns the rate as a SOAP response. If it cannot find a rate for a specific city and country combination, it returns a SOAP fault response with an appropriate error description.

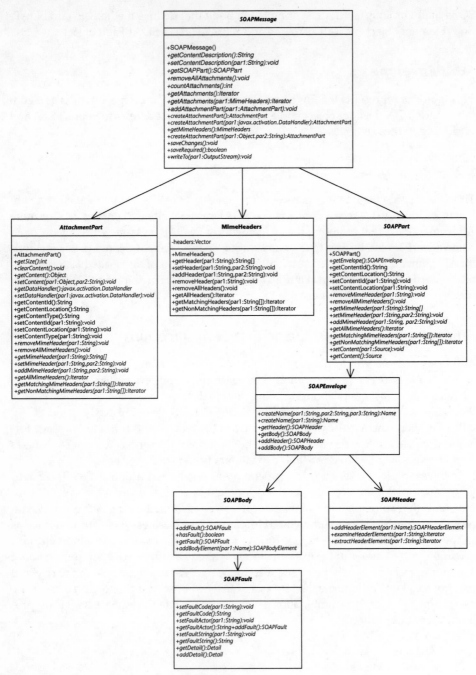

Figure 11.12 SOAPMessage and related classes.

SoapClient.java

```java
package com.wiley.compBooks.EJwithUML.Samples.WebServices;

/**
 * This is a SOAP client that perform queries on shipping rates to
 * different countries and cities. It uses SOAP APIs (SAAJ 1.1)
 * provided with JWSDP 1.0.01. The SAAJ 1.1 supports the SOAP 1.1
 * specification.
 */
import javax.xml.soap.*;
import java.io.IOException;
import java.net.URL;

public class SoapClient {

  public static final String DEFAULT_SERVER =
"http://localhost:8080/ShippingSystem";

  public static final void main(String[] args)throws SOAPException, IOException
  {
    if (args.length < 2)
    {
      System.out.println(
        "Usage: java com.wiley.compBooks.EJwithUML.Samples.WebServices <city>
<country> <server URL>");
      System.out.println("<server URL> is optional. Default URL is
http://localhost/ShippingSystem");
      return;
    }
    String city = args[0];
    String country = args[1];
    String server = DEFAULT_SERVER;
    if (args.length >= 2)
    {
      server = args[2];
    }
    SoapClient client = new SoapClient();
SOAPConnectionFactory factory = SOAPConnectionFactory.newInstance();
    SOAPConnection connection = factory.createConnection();
    SOAPMessage request = client.createShippingRateRequest(city,
                                country);
    System.out.println("\nsending request:");
    request.writeTo(System.out);
    java.net.URL serviceEndpoint = new URL(server);
    SOAPMessage response = connection.call(request,serviceEndpoint);
    System.out.println("\nreceived response:");
    response.writeTo(System.out);
    SOAPBody body = response.getSOAPPart().getEnvelope().getBody();
    if (body.hasFault())
    {
      System.out.println("\nrequest failed.");
```

```
      }
      else
      {
        System.out.println("\nrequest successful.");
      }
   }

   private SOAPMessage createShippingRateRequest(String city, String
                       country)throws SOAPException
   {
      MessageFactory msgFactory = MessageFactory.newInstance();
      SOAPMessage request = msgFactory.createMessage();
      SOAPPart sp = request.getSOAPPart();
      SOAPEnvelope envelope = sp.getEnvelope();
      SOAPHeader header = envelope.getHeader();
header.addNamespaceDeclaration(
                       "eju","http://com.wiley.compBooks/EJwithUML");
      SOAPHeaderElement hdElement = header.addHeaderElement(envelope.createName(
          "eju:Requester"));
      hdElement.setMustUnderstand(true);
      hdElement.addTextNode("myHomeDecor.com");
      hdElement = header.addHeaderElement(envelope.createName("eju:Transaction"));
      hdElement.setMustUnderstand(true);
      hdElement.addTextNode("1");
      SOAPBody body = envelope.getBody();
      body.addNamespaceDeclaration("exp",
            "http://com.wiley.compBooks.EJwithUML.Samples/Soap");
      SOAPBodyElement bdElement =
body.addBodyElement(envelope.createName("GetShippingRate"));
      SOAPElement dataElement = bdElement.addChildElement("shippingType", "exp");
      dataElement.addTextNode("2-3-day-Shipping");
      dataElement = bdElement.addChildElement("city", "exp");
      dataElement.addTextNode(city);
      dataElement = bdElement.addChildElement("country", "exp");
      dataElement.addTextNode(country);
      return request;
   }
}
```

ShippingSystemSoapServlet.java

```
package com.wiley.compBooks.EJwithUML.Samples.WebServices;

/**
 * This is a SOAP server implemented as a servlet. It supports
 * clients' requests about shipping rates to different cities and
 * countries. The shipping rates are provided through a properties
 * file called database.properties. The key is a concatenation of
 * country and city. The format of the key is:
 *              <country>.<city>
 * This properties file simulates a database in the real world.
 */
```

```java
import javax.servlet.http.*;
import javax.servlet.*;
import java.util.*;
import javax.xml.soap.*;
import java.io.*;

public class ShippingSystemSoapServlet extends HttpServlet {

  private static Properties database = new Properties();

  public void init(ServletConfig config)throws ServletException
  {
    try
    {
      super.init(config);
      String dbName = config.getInitParameter("database");
      System.out.println("\ndatabase = " + dbName);
      database.load(this.getClass().getResourceAsStream(dbName));
      database.list(System.out);
    }
    catch (Exception e)
    {
      throw new ServletException(e.getMessage());
    }
  }

  public void doPost(HttpServletRequest request, HttpServletResponse
                response)throws IOException
  {
    try
    {
    MimeHeaders headers = new MimeHeaders();
    Enumeration hdNames = request.getHeaderNames();
    while(hdNames.hasMoreElements())
    {
      String name = (String)hdNames.nextElement();
      headers.addHeader(name,request.getHeader(name));
    }
    MessageFactory msgFactory = MessageFactory.newInstance();
    SOAPMessage soapRequest = msgFactory.createMessage(headers,
                                  request.getInputStream());
    System.out.println("\nreceived request:");
    soapRequest.writeTo(System.out);
    SOAPPart sp = soapRequest.getSOAPPart();
    SOAPEnvelope envelope = sp.getEnvelope();
    SOAPHeader header = envelope.getHeader();
    SOAPBody body = envelope.getBody();
    Iterator it = body.getChildElements();
    SOAPBodyElement getRateRequestData = (SOAPBodyElement)it.next();
    it = getRateRequestData.getChildElements();
    Map reqParameters = new HashMap();
    while (it.hasNext())
    {
```

```
      SOAPElement dataElement = (SOAPElement) it.next();
      reqParameters.put(dataElement.getElementName().getLocalName(),
                      dataElement.getValue());
    }
  String databaseKey = reqParameters.get("country")+ "." +
                      reqParameters.get("city");
  String rate = (String)database.get(databaseKey);
  SOAPMessage soapResponse = null;
  if (rate == null)
  {
    soapResponse = createErrorResponse(header, "Client",
      "service to " + databaseKey + " not available!");
  }
  else
  {
    soapResponse = createResponse(header, rate);
  }
  OutputStream os = response.getOutputStream();
  soapResponse.writeTo(os);
  response.addHeader("Content-Type", "text/xml");
  os.flush();
  }
  catch(SOAPException e)
  {

  }
}

private SOAPMessage createResponse(SOAPHeader reqHeader, String
      rate) throws SOAPException, IOException
{
  SOAPMessage response = createSoapMessage(reqHeader);
   //creates the body part and inserts the response data
  SOAPBody body = response.getSOAPPart().getEnvelope().getBody();
  body.addNamespaceDeclaration("exp",
    "http://com.wiley.compBooks.EJwithUML.Samples/Soap");
  SOAPBodyElement bdElement = body.addBodyElement(
      response.getSOAPPart().getEnvelope().createName("rate"));
  bdElement.addTextNode(rate);
  return response;
}

private SOAPMessage createErrorResponse(SOAPHeader reqHeader, String
faultCode,String errorMsg)throws SOAPException, IOException
{
  SOAPMessage response = createSoapMessage(reqHeader);
  //creates the body part and inserts the response data
  SOAPBody body = response.getSOAPPart().getEnvelope().getBody();
  body.addNamespaceDeclaration("exp",
```

```
                    "http://com.wiley.compBooks.EJwithUML.Samples/Soap");
        SOAPFault fault = body.addFault();
        fault.setFaultCode(faultCode);
        fault.setFaultString(errorMsg);
        return response;
    }


    private SOAPMessage createSoapMessage(SOAPHeader reqHeader)throws SOAPException
    {
        MessageFactory msgFactory = MessageFactory.newInstance();
        SOAPMessage response = msgFactory.createMessage();
        SOAPPart sp = response.getSOAPPart();
        SOAPEnvelope envelope = sp.getEnvelope();
        SOAPHeader header = envelope.getHeader();

header.addNamespaceDeclaration("eju","http://com.wiley.compBooks/EJwithUML");
        SOAPHeaderElement hdElement = header.addHeaderElement(envelope.createName(
            "eju:Responder"));
        hdElement.addTextNode("myWorldWideShipping.com");
        //sets the value of the Transaction headerelement from
        //the request
        hdElement = header.addHeaderElement(envelope.createName(
                            "eju:Transaction"));
        Iterator it = reqHeader.getChildElements();
        while(it.hasNext())
        {
            SOAPHeaderElement nextElement = (SOAPHeaderElement)it.next();
            if (nextElement.getElementName().getLocalName().equals(
                                "Transaction"))
            {
                hdElement.addTextNode(nextElement.getValue());
            }
        }
        return response;
    }
}
```

Conclusion

Web services promise a world where smart applications carry out complicated business processes through dynamic integration of components deployed over the Internet as individual services. Has that day arrived yet? With all the core specifications—SOAP, WSDL, UDDI—supporting the Web services programming model changing every day, it will be some time before it is ready for serious use. There are also gray areas in the architecture that prevent Web services from being deployed in the real world today. Such gray areas include security, subscription (license), service negotiation, and so on that are required for creating a true environment for real business integration. Until such a time arrives, Web services will continue to be a technology for experimentation with limited use in a restricted environment like the intranet of an organization, where the gray areas of the technology do not come into play.

The Next Step

Now that we have evaluated technologies for boundary classes, we can turn our attention to control and entity classes.

CHAPTER

12

Evaluating Candidate Technologies for Control and Entity Classes

The control and entity classes constitute the second group of analysis classes we identified in Chapter 6, "Describing the System for Technology Selection." In this chapter, we'll use the template we introduced in Chapter 7, "Evaluating Candidate Technologies for Shared Services," to describe and evaluate the candidate technologies for implementing this group of classes. The first step is to apply the simple descriptive template to several technologies, before using the technology requirements descriptions from Chapter 6, to find the right combination of technologies for the control and entity classes in the Timecard application.

The technologies we'll evaluate are Remote Method Invocation (RMI), Java Data-Base Connectivity (JDBC), and Enterprise JavaBeans (EJB). However, we evaluate the suitability of RMI and JDBC together, since they are often used together.

RMI

Remote Method Invocation (RMI) was added to version 1.1 of the Java Development Kit (JDK) to allow remote access to objects. It is important to understand RMI both as an alternative to EJB for simple applications and as a technology that directly supports EJB.

RMI has a simple and wonderful purpose. It allows a client object on one host to call methods on an object that resides on another host. The client objects use a *stub object* to communicate with a *skeleton object* on the server. Fortunately, RMI and its tools provide the stub and skeleton objects, which do all of the hard work. Figure 12.1 shows communication between a client and an RMI server. While the client thinks it is calling a method on a remote object, it is actually calling a method on a stub object in the same virtual machine (VM). The client stub converts the method parameters into data and sends them across to the waiting server skeleton. (Note: The client stub and the server skeleton live in different virtual machines and may even be located on different continents, so the communication between the stub and the skeleton is over a network connection.) The client stub then waits for a response. Once the skeleton receives the data, it converts the data back into parameter objects and calls the same method on the implementation object. The return value, if any, is converted into data and sent back across the socket connection to the waiting client stub that converts it back into an object and passes it along to the client.

Gory Details

RMI consists of a handful of classes and interfaces and a few simple tools. Thanks to this simplicity, a reasonably experienced Java developer can learn enough to have a remote HelloWorld server up in a few hours. However, designing an efficient and effective RMI server is a bit more challenging. RMI developers must consider what data is passed for each remote method, and protect against concurrent access to their RMI server's objects. As explained in the next section, RMI is both very simple and very complex.

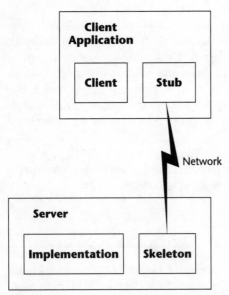

Figure 12.1 RMI communications between clients and servers.

Classes and Interfaces

Consider a user interface that uses RMI to access some functionality on a remote server. Each ClientView object has a reference to an object that implements the SomeRemote Interface interface. For the client, the object that implements the SomeRemoteInterface interface is an instance of ClientStub. When one of the interface methods is called, the ClientStub object converts each parameter and sends it over the socket to the server. It then waits for a response. The response is either a return type or an error. If it is an error, then the ClientStub converts the raw data into a RemoteException and throws the RemoteException to the calling client. Otherwise, it converts the returned data and returns it to the calling client. Figure 12.2 shows the classes and interfaces for this simple scenario.

On the server, the SomeImplementation class extends UnicastRemoteObject and implements the SomeRemoteInterface. A ServerSkeleton that has a socket connection to the ClientStub has a reference to the actual implementation. When the ServerSkeleton receives data from the socket, it converts the data to parameters and calls the correct method on the SomeImplementation object. If any RemoteExceptions are thrown, they are converted to data, and the data is sent back across the socket. Otherwise, the return value is converted to data and sent back across the socket.

Fortunately, developers do not need to write the complex code that dwells inside of the stubs and skeletons. Sun Microsystems provides a tool, called rmic, as part of the JDK, which produces the stub class files based on your class files. It is up to you to bundle the class files so that the client and server applications can find them.

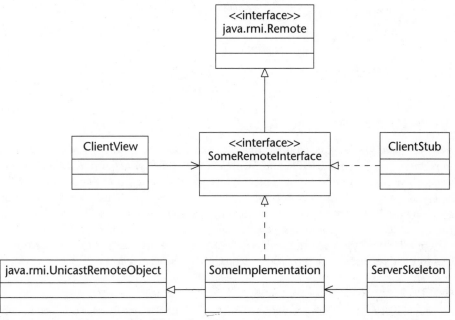

Figure 12.2 Classes and interfaces for RMI.

> **NOTE** In JDK 1.1, rmic also produced custom skeleton class files. As of JDK 1.2, the skeleton is part of the RMI server.

Remote Object Registration

Before a client can reference a remote object, the RMI registry must be running on the server, and the remote object must be registered with the RMI registry. The RMI registry is simply a Java application that listens on a port for incoming requests. When it receives a request for a particular object, it tries to match the request against all of the implementation objects that have registered. A remote object is instantiated by a Java application, which then uses the static bind or rebind method in the Naming class to register the object with the RMI registry.

The following code snippet shows how a remote object for the example in Figure 12.2 is instantiated and registered.

```
public static void main(String[] args)
{
    try
    {
      System.setSecurityManager(new RMISecurityManager());

      SomeImplementation remoteObject = new SomeImplementation();
      Naming.rebind("SomeServer", remoteObject);
    }
    catch(Exception e)
    {
      e.printStackTrace();
    }
}
```

Parameter Passing

So far, we have glossed over a great deal of complexity by ignoring how parameters and return types are converted to and from data. Consider what happens when a client object calls a method on a remote object reference. Before the client stub can pass the request to the server, it must convert the parameters into data. This is known as *serialization*. When the response is received, the client stub must convert the data back into a return value. This is known as *deserialization*.

There are three types of serializable data that can be used as parameters or return types in RMI: *primitive data, serializable objects,* and *remote references*.

Primitives

Primitive data types are very convenient for use with RMI, since there is no need to convert primitive data types to data; they are already simple data. They allow remote clients to configure the remotely accessible object and to request data from the remotely accessible object.

Serializable Objects

The client stub must convert each parameter object into data. If the object contains primitive data, then this process is fairly straightforward. The stub simply serializes the object by sending the name of the object's class and all of the object's data. However, if the object contains other objects, then they must be serialized also. So, serializing a single object can lead to the serialization of an entire network of connected objects.

Java provides two mechanisms that help developers manage the serialization process. First, an attribute can be marked as *transient* in the class. Transient data is ignored during serialization. Also, in order for an object to be serialized, the class must implement the Serializable interface, which has no methods. By allowing a class to implement Serializable, a developer is stating that objects of that type are reasonable for serialization.

Each object that is serialized on the client was instantiated from a particular class. When the skeleton on the server receives the serialized data, it instantiates an object of the same class and loads the data into it. This requires that the same version of the class exist on both the client and the server.

In remote method calls, a serialized copy of the object is passed to the server, so any changes to the passed object's state on the server do not affect the original object on the client.

Remote References as Parameters

When the stub is converting the parameters, it checks for objects that implement java.rmi.RemoteObject. These parameters are not serialized. Instead, their stubs are serialized and sent in their place. Thus, the server receives as a parameter a stub object that connects back to the remote object on the client machine.

Thread Safety

When an object is registered with the RMI registry, it is open for access by concurrent threads. RMI, like most distributed architectures, allows more than one client to access the server at the same time. So, the remote object and every object that the remote object has a reference to must be designed with thread safety in mind. It is up to the developer to make sure that any resources that are shared among client requests are thread-safe, by synchronizing the appropriate methods or code blocks.

Development and Deployment

Applications based on RMI have a reasonable, if somewhat tedious, development and deployment cycle. In order to develop and deploy an RMI-based system, you need to follow these steps:

1. Write remote interfaces and implementations for the server.

2. Use the rmic command to generate stub classes.

3. Write client applications.

4. Distribute stub classes and any common domain classes to the client.

5. Start the RMI registry.

6. Run the main application to register the remote objects with the registry.

7. Start the clients.

Most of these steps can be automated in a build or make file.

Common Uses of RMI

RMI is a fairly simple and very flexible technology. There are three ways in which RMI can expose business logic to clients:

- Remote object that hides entity objects
- Direct access to entity objects
- Direct access to entity objects with event notification

The following sections describe these common uses in more detail.

Remote Object That Hides Entity Objects (Strict Layering)

In many cases, it is possible to completely isolate the user interface objects from the entity objects. As discussed in Chapter 3, "Gathering Requirements for the Timecard Application," this separation helps simplify the user interface, while keeping the entities well focused. When the user interface objects are distributed, the control object may expose its methods through RMI. Figure 12.3 shows the UpdateTimecardControl as a remote interface that is implemented by the UpdateTimecardControlImpl class. The UpdateTimecardControl object keeps track of the employees and receives the employee ID as the first argument of each method. This allows the UpdateTimecard-Control object to get the current timecard from the correct employee and call the appropriate method on that timecard.

There is only one remote object, the UpdateTimecardControl. None of the entity objects are exposed as remote objects. All of the parameters and return types are simple objects, primitives, or enumerations of simple objects.

Hiding the entity objects keeps the remote client isolated from the remote objects. All interactions funnel through a very straightforward interface. This reduces the deployment burden, because as long as the UpdateTimecardControl interface remains the same, the domain objects can be altered without affecting the clients.

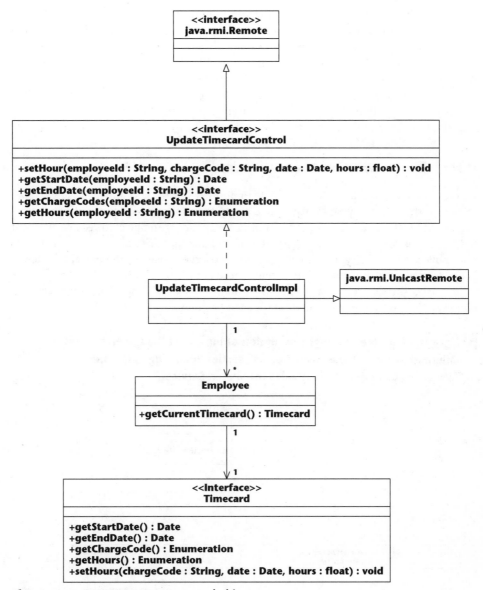

Figure 12.3   Remote access to control object.

Direct Access to Entity Objects (Relaxed Layering)

An alternate design allows the user interface to directly access the entity objects. Since the user interface and entity objects are on different hosts, RMI is used to expose the entity objects as remote objects. A locator object is registered as a remote object. The locator object's methods allow the user interface to find Timecard objects. Rather than receiving a serialized copy of the timecard object, the user interface receives a remote object reference to the specified timecard object. Thereafter, the user interface communicates with the timecard object via RMI. Figure 12.4 shows the classes and interfaces for this alternative.

Notice that each change to the Timecard interface requires a new deployment. It is important to note that changes to the internal implementation of the Timecard class may not require redeployment.

Direct Access with Event Notification

It is common for objects to track the state of another object. This allows a view to stay in sync with an underlying entity, or one entity to monitor a group of entities. Fortunately, the Observer design pattern [Gamma 1995] allows an object to receive an event notification whenever the state of another object changes. The object of interest does not know the specific type of each registered observer. Instead, the object of interest keeps references to any object that implements a simple notification interface.

Java uses the Observer pattern both in JavaBeans with PropertyChangeListeners and in AWT and Swing with different types of listeners for different events.

NOTE For a more thorough description of the use of the Observer design pattern in Swing, see the "Gory Details" section for Swing in Chapter 7, "Evaluating Candidate Technologies for Shared Services."

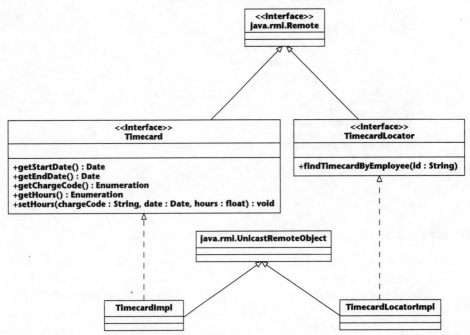

Figure 12.4   Remote access to entity objects.

In some cases, the observer object and the observed object may reside in different virtual machines, perhaps on different continents. One solution to this scenario extends the JavaBeans event model to notify remote clients of changes in an entity object's state. For example, an object might provide a remote method to register remote property change listeners. The property change listener must also be remotely accessible, so that the object of interest can notify it of changes. Figure 12.5 shows some classes and interfaces that illustrate this scenario. An InterestingThing object is registered with the RMI registry. Once a client gets a reference to the InterestingThing, it can register a listener object. Whenever a client changes the state of the InterestingThing by calling its changeSomething method, the InterestingThing must call the propertyChanged method on each registered listener.

Strengths

RMI is a great starting point for distributed applications. It makes distributed computing palatable to developers by hiding the nasty details of serializing and deserializing parameters and return values. There are not many classes or interfaces to learn, and the rmic and rmiregistry tools are very easy to use. Also, the error handling is fairly straightforward, assuming a basic knowledge of exception handling in Java. It is a very elegant and easy-to-assimilate technology. Moreover, it works between any hosts that have a compliant virtual machine. For example, a client on a PC can easily access a remote object on a Unix server.

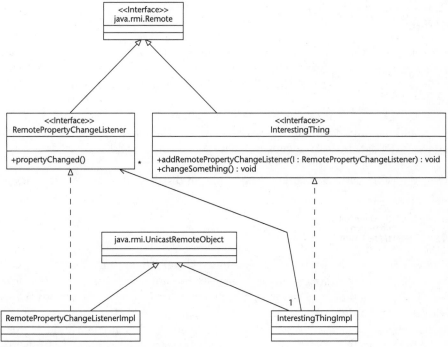

Figure 12.5 Remote event notification.

Weaknesses

RMI leaves scalability, fault tolerance, load balancing, and data integrity concerns up to the developers. This is an intentional limitation in Sun's vision for RMI, not a weakness in the execution of the vision. In any case, using RMI for an enterprise class system requires developers to consider a host of issues, from object and resource pooling to redundancy to thread safety. In many cases, designing and implementing simple solutions for these issues may be reasonable. Otherwise, the architecture must include more sophisticated technology that leverages RMI, such as Enterprise JavaBeans.

Compatible Technologies

RMI and JDBC are often combined to form a remotely accessible and persistent control and entity layer. This allows a central repository of application, business logic, and business data to support a variety of user interfaces and peer systems.

Methods that are exposed through RMI can be called from any Java code, including servlets, applications, and applets.

Cost of Adoption

While RMI is provided free as part of the standard JDK, there are other costs of adoption. In order to be successful with RMI, your project must fill the roles of architect and RMI developer.

Architect

The architect for an RMI-based system needs a clear understanding of the performance and scalability issues involved with different design choices. Choices between strict and relaxed layering and for event notification need to be made early in the development cycle.

Also, the architect must establish clear guidelines for exception handling, error logging, and naming for different types of common RMI classes and interfaces. This upfront effort yields huge dividends in the form of a smaller and more readable code base.

The architect must have a strong background in distributed object-oriented development and in Java.

RMI Developer

RMI developers need to understand distributed development, threads, and concurrency. A clear understanding of these issues is more important than the actual Java classes and programming techniques, which are actually fairly straightforward. A developer with the right experience can easily pick up the RMI specifics from a few examples. So, a system or subsystem that is dominated by domain data and RMI may serve as an excellent entry point for a developer who is transitioning to Java from, say, C++ and CORBA.

RMI developers do need a strong understanding of synchronization, exceptions, serialization from the java.io package, and, of course, the java.rmi package.

JDBC

Java DataBase Connectivity (JDBC) was introduced in JDK 1.1. JDBC is a thin, object-oriented wrapper around the full functionality of SQL. You can create, read, update, and delete the schema and the data, execute stored procedures, commit or roll back transactions, and even fiddle with isolation levels. If you can do it in SQL, you can do it with JDBC.

Using JDBC to save a few objects to a database is very easy. You just figure out the mapping from the object's data to the table's fields, and the rest is straightforward drudgery.

Real systems tend to be a bit more complex. Problems begin to crop up when you have different flows through the system that all update an object but that all have different transaction boundaries. Where do transactions originate? Where is each transaction committed? Who creates database connections, and can they be reused? Also, no useful object is an island. How do you store the relationships between objects? When you load an object, do you load all of the objects that the object knows about, or do you wait until they are needed? How many objects can you store in memory?

Fortunately, a lot of very smart people have dedicated their careers to solving the puzzles inherent in object-to-relational persistence. This body of work can be consumed and leveraged by absorbing the theory and by using commercial object-to-relational mapping products. Also, EJB servers are becoming increasingly sophisticated in this area.

Gory Details

JDBC allows developers to write database-independent code, while still getting the performance of database specific drivers, which are written and tuned by the vendor.

As you explore the technology in this section, be alert for creative uses of object-oriented principles, such as encapsulation, interfaces, and polymorphism. In addition to its technical merits, JDBC is a valuable and accessible example of object-oriented theory as applied to a very real problem.

Drivers, Connections, and Statements

JDBC derives much of its appeal from the freedom it gives developers to almost completely ignore the differences between databases. JDBC requires the code to load one or more drivers and to request a specific connection from the DriverManager. After that, the rest of the code is entirely generic. Many projects use a configuration file to hold the connection information and the driver class names that must be registered. This means all of the code can be blissfully unaware of the database specifics. Let's examine some of the classes and interfaces that perform this rather impressive feat.

The Driver interface defines the methods that are required to determine if a driver is suitable and to open a connection. If it is, database vendors must provide a specific implementation class for the Driver interface, which encapsulates the details of opening a connection to their specific type of database, and provides information about the supported features for their database and their driver.

The thoughtful developers at Sun also protect developers from worrying about the individual drivers by supplying a class, DriverManager, that collects drivers and determines which one fits a particular situation. When a concrete implementation of the Driver interface is loaded, it must register with the DriverManager class by calling the static registerDriver method. Later, when an object needs a connection to a database, it calls the static getConnection method on the DriverManager class. This method searches the DriverManager's list of drivers until it finds one that matches the requested database type. It then asks the driver to open a connection to the database by calling the connect method on the driver. Assuming that all goes well, this connection is returned to the requesting object. Figure 12.6 shows the sequence diagram as an application first registers two drivers and then obtains a connection that fits the second driver.

Notice that this connection is really a vendor-specific implementation of the Connection interface. Connection objects allow full control over the current transaction, through the commit and rollback methods. If the database allows it, they also allow configuration of the isolation level for subsequent transactions on the connection.

Consequently, the code that we write deals solely with the DriverManager and the Connection and Statement interfaces. We are protected from all of the database-dependent variations that are hidden inside of the vendor-supplied implementation classes. Figure 12.7 shows the classes and interfaces required to obtain a Connection object and a Statement object. The vendor must supply a chain of database-dependent implementation classes, as shown on the right, that implement the chain of interfaces shown on the left. This elegant scheme simplifies development for application developers, as well as driver writers.

New and Improved Result Sets

In JDBC 2.0, the createStatement method in the Connection interface accepts two new integer parameters. The first determines how the result set can be traversed. In previous versions of JDBC, the result set is traversed from beginning to end, with each row seen exactly once. This is one option for the first parameter. Another option allows the result set to be traversed in any order, and for multiple visits for each row. The next parameter determines if the result set can be updated.

The result set contains several distinct types of methods. These methods traverse the result set, retrieve data from the result set, update data in the result set, and refresh the result set from the database.

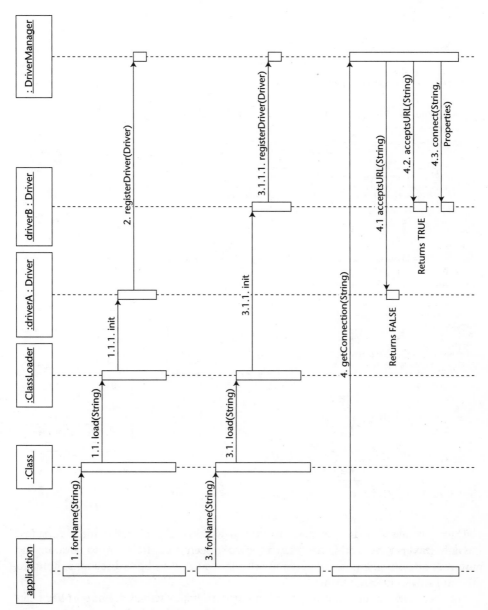

Figure 12.6   Register and use drivers.

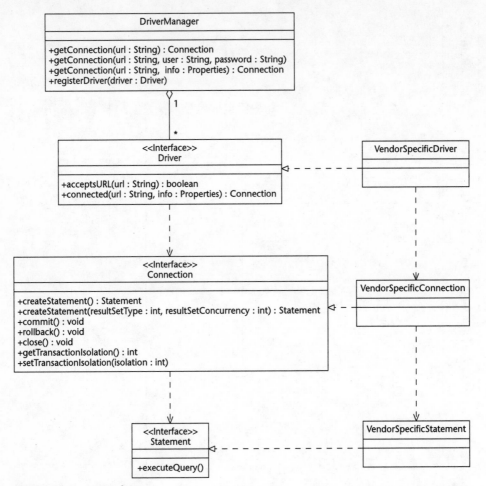

Figure 12.7   JDBC classes.

The traversal methods move the current row within the result set. In older versions, the only traversal method is next. Each record is seen once, from top to bottom. The new version adds methods to move about the result set in both directions, jump to arbitrary rows, and revisit rows.

The data retrieval methods are very similar to previous versions. Support has been added for additional data types, but the pattern is the same.

An entirely new set of methods has been added to update the data. The current row can be deleted or have its data changed. A new row can be added by moving to the insert row, which serves as a buffer, and by updating each column for the new row. After changes have been made, the updateRow method submits the changes to the database.

Another completely new method, refreshRow, has been added to reread the current row from the database.

Figure 12.8 shows the classes for retrieving and using a result set. As before, the vendor must supply a chain of database-dependent implementation classes, as shown on the right. These classes implement the chain of interfaces on the left.

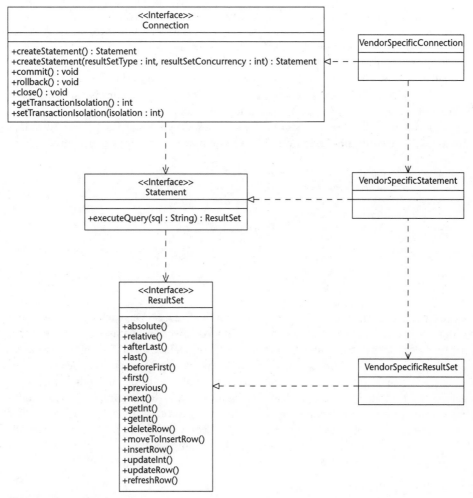

Figure 12.8   Result sets.

DataSources

The javax.sql package, which is included with JDK 1.4, provides the DataSource interface as a compelling alternative to the Driver registration process provided in java.sql. With Drivers, the database client must know where to find the database and what protocol will be used to reach it, as well as the username and password. Many developers have the JDBC database client read this information from a configuration file. This speeds up changes and is a reasonable solution if the number of independent clients is small and changes are rare. However, Sun has created a significantly more flexible solution with the introduction of DataSources to the JDBC extensions in JDBC 2.0.

DataSource objects are created and configured before the clients are started. Each DataSource is configured with a database server, a database instance, and any other implementation-specific details. Only the user name and password are excluded. The DataSource is then registered with a naming service for use by any number of clients. A database or middleware vendor that provides a concrete implementation of Data-Source can allow developers to configure DataSources in a variety of ways. For instance, the vendor might supply an administration tool that stores configuration data as serialized JavaBeans or in an XML file. The following sample shows how a data source might be configured and bound to a JNDI name from a Java program.

```
// construct and configure DataSource
DataSource ds = MyBasicDataSource();
ds.setServerName("myslowserver");
ds.setDatabaseName("TIMECARD");
ds.setDescription("Sample timecard database");

// Bind DataSource to name
Context ctx = new InitialContext();
ctx.bind("jdbc/TimecardDB", ds);
```

Once the DataSource is bound to the name in the JNDI server, each client uses JNDI to find a specific DataSource object and obtains a connection by passing the username and password to the getConnection method of the DataSource. As long as the username and password are consistent, the underlying database can be switched or reconfigured without requiring any changes to the client's code or configuration. If the clients are written to reacquire the DataSource after errors, this indirection allows database administrators to move a database for maintenance, failover, or load balancing without reconfiguring or restarting the clients. They would, of course, need to reconfigure and replace the DataSource's entry in the naming service.

The following sample shows the simplicity from the client's perspective.

```
// Find DataSource
Context ctx = new InitialContext();
DataSource ds = (DataSource)ctx.lookup("jdbc/TimecardDB");

// Get connection
Connection con = ds.getConnection("scott", "tiger");
```

Connection Pooling

JDBC Drivers force the database client to manage its own pools of database connections or live with the performance implications of creating many new connections. This is also true of basic DataSources as described above. However, the JDBC extensions introduced in JDBC 2.0 also include support for reusing database connections without adding any complexity to the database client.

There are several steps before the database client can obtain a reusable connection from a DataSource. First, your middleware vendor must provide a connection manager, implementations for the ConnectionPoolDataSource and PooledConnection interfaces and a tool for configuring DataSources. Next, a ConnectionPoolDataSource object is configured with specific database connectivity information and registered with a naming service. Then, a DataSource object is configured to use the ConnectionPoolDataSource and is also registered with the naming service. The rest is simple; the client just:

1. Uses the JNDI naming service to obtain the DataSource
2. Obtains a connection from the DataSource
3. Uses the connection
4. Closes the connection

From the client's perspective, the DataSource for a pool of reusable connections behaves exactly as a non-pooled DataSource. Once the connection is closed, the connection manager is free to hand the connection to the next client that calls getConnection on the DataSource. The connection pooling is completely hidden from the database clients.

Behind the scenes, the vendor's connection manager, DataSource, and PooledConnection must cooperate to provide this appearance of simplicity. Specifically, the vendor's ConnectionPoolDataSource must delegate connection requests to the connection manager. When a new PooledConnection is requested, the connection manager registers itself with the PooledConnection as a ConnectionEventListener. This allows the PooledConnection object to notify the connection manager when it is closed or when an error occurs. This allows the connection manager to reclaim connections when they are closed and to destroy them on errors.

Strengths

Like RMI, JDBC is a great starting point; database-independent code is easier than ever. As long as there is a JDBC driver for your favorite databases, and as long as you stick to SQL-compliant data types and syntax, you can change databases with ease. The class libraries are easy to understand, and behave as expected.

Weaknesses

Like RMI, JDBC leaves many issues to the developer. Larger datasets and more complex transactions require caching, transaction management, and connection pooling. In many cases, designing and implementing simple solutions for these issues may be reasonable. Otherwise, the architecture must include more sophisticated technology that leverages JDBC, such as a commercial object-to-relational framework or Enterprise JavaBeans.

Compatible Technologies

RMI and JDBC are often combined to form a remotely accessible and persistent control and entity layer. This allows a central repository of application, business logic, and business data to support a variety of user interfaces and peer systems.

JDBC can be used to access a database from any Java code, including servlets, applications, and applets.

Cost of Adoption

JDBC is provided free as part of the standard JDK, but there are other costs of adopting it. In order to be successful with JDBC, your project must fill the roles of architect and JDBC developer.

Architect

Architects for JDBC-based systems must be familiar with many performance, scalability, and data integrity issues. Database connections, which are fairly expensive to establish, must be used efficiently. Transactions must be started and completed. Mappings from objects to database tables must be established in a flexible and extensible manner. The simple class library makes JDBC development look easy, but there are many subtleties that, if ignored, can cripple a project.

The architect must have a solid object-oriented background and some experience with object-to-relational persistence.

JDBC Developer

Developing JDBC-based applications is generally straightforward. The class library is extremely clear and easy to use. A basic understanding of transactions and SQL is needed. Developers who are migrating to Java may find JDBC to be a comfortable starting point.

Suitability of RMI and JDBC

In Chapter 6, "Describing the System for Technology Selection,"we identified two descriptive categories:

- Number and type of users
- Performance and scalability

Let's evaluate how RMI and JDBC perform in these categories.

Number and Type of Users

RMI and JDBC are certainly a valid choice for the first three audiences: a small number of dedicated users, general use within an organization, and a large audience with high interest. As the number of users and the data accessed grows, developers will need to cache objects and pool resources, but these are common problems in large-scale development.

This combination is less applicable for huge audiences. At some point, the performance characteristics of RMI, like any distributed technology, will be overwhelmed by the demands of a mass audience. Unfortunately, RMI does not support any form of load balancing across servers. In some cases, it may be possible to create a simple architecture that spreads the load across several hosts. However, this is not an easy task. Really large audiences usually require a more formal and scalable solution, such as EJB, which leverages both RMI and JDBC.

Performance and Scalability

A combination of RMI and JDBC is certainly a reasonable choice for read-only systems and for systems that allow isolated updates. These systems do not require any special design for transaction management or data integrity. The combination is also appropriate for systems that allow concurrent updates of data. However, in this case, the developers must supply their own architecture for coordinated transaction management on top of the simple control provided by JDBC.

EJB 2.0

The Enterprise JavaBeans specification, which is part of the Java 2 Enterprise Edition, completely specifies a framework that exposes business objects to remote clients. It builds heavily on the lessons and innovations of CORBA, while defining a more comprehensive suite of services, including object caching, transaction management, object-to-relational persistence, and security. Any developer who has struggled to implement these services for his or her own distributed application knows that doing so is both painful and risky.

EJB implementations tend to depend heavily on the technologies described so far. They use RMI to provide distributed access, JDBC as a basis for persistence, and XML to describe the deployment decisions.

Several terms are essential to the understanding of EJB. These are:

- Entity bean
- Session bean
- Container
- Home interface
- Remote interface

- Local interface
- Local home interface
- Message-driven bean
- Implementation
- Deployment descriptor
- Bean-managed persistence
- Container-managed persistence
- Transaction boundaries

The following sections give a general overview of these terms. Resources for more information on these topics can be found in Appendix B.

Entity Bean

Entity beans are remotely accessible components that encapsulate business data and business logic for an EJB system. Each entity bean represents a single independent and persistent entity in the domain. An individual employee and an employee's timecard are both examples of appropriate entity beans.

Individual pieces of data, such as a name or contact information, may be contained within entity beans, but they are not good candidates for separate entity beans.

Entity beans generally evolve very cleanly from entity objects in the analysis model.

Session Bean

Session beans are remotely accessible components that expose high-level business logic and workflow logic that may use multiple entity beans. Session beans simplify and support access to entity beans in several ways. A session bean translates an individual high-level request into many requests to many entity beans. In translating the request, the session bean may protect the caller from knowledge of the entity beans by returning simple data or collections of simple data.

Session beans should not generally update domain data directly. Instead, they should call methods on entity beans that change the persistent state of the entity bean. I realize that many developers use session beans as thin wrappers around JDBC code and few of them have come to any serious harm as a result. That said, adhering to the EJB specification's vision for the role of each type of bean makes a system easier to comprehend and allows developers to leverage the full capabilities of the container.

Despite the superficial similarity in names, EJB session beans are completely distinct from HTTP sessions. A single HTTP session may use many session beans to accomplish many subtasks during a single login.

Session beans typically evolve fairly cleanly from control objects in the analysis model.

Container

An EJB container holds entity and session beans. It is responsible for a variety of house-keeping activities, from object caching to transaction management to managing resource pools. The interactions between beans and their enclosing container are tightly defined in the EJB specification. The following are some interesting aspects to the relationship between beans and their enclosing container.

Object caching.   A large-scale enterprise system may hold data for thousands or even millions of entity beans. However, at any point in time, most entity beans are not being accessed. It is up to the container to determine which entity beans need to be active due to current or recent usage. When the container takes beans in or out of service, it notifies the bean via callback methods, such as ejbPassivate and ejbActivate.

Concurrent access.   In order to preserve data integrity, the container controls access to each entity bean. Many clients or session beans may have access to the same bean, but each method call must be completed before another method call can start on that bean. Notice that a series of calls from different clients may be interleaved. Also, calls to different beans of the same type may be executed simultaneously.

> **WARNING** The EJB specification precludes developers from using the synchronized keyword in beans or code that is called from beans.

Transaction management.   The container also enforces any transaction require-ments specified in the deployment descriptor. By moving the decisions out of the developer's code and requiring the container to enforce it, the EJB specifica-tion gives the developer a lot of flexibility and opportunity to procrastinate or experiment. For example, developers can defer any serious thoughts on transac-tion boundaries until late in a project without disturbing existing code.

Persistence.   The container also determines when each entity bean needs to be saved, and in the case of container-managed persistence, uses the mapping in the deployment descriptor to save the data.

Home Interface

Entity and session beans are only useful if remote clients can create, locate, and destroy them. This is the role of the home interface. Each home interface specifies remotely accessible methods for the creation, location, and destruction of one type of entity bean. For example, if a system has entity beans for employees and for timecards, then the system has separate home interfaces for employees and for timecards. Home interfaces generally evolve nicely from the object life cycle analysis objects.

Remote Interface

Each entity and session bean has an interface that defines its remotely accessible methods. When a call to a bean's home interface returns an object, it is actually returning a reference to a client-side object that implements the corresponding remote interface. All remote access to the entity bean is accomplished through this reference. The concrete implementations of the remote interface are responsible for data serialization and network connectivity.

Local Interface

Entity and session beans frequently need to call methods on an entity bean or session bean in the same container. These local method calls can be made by obtaining and using a remote reference, just as if the caller was a remote client. However, this forces the container to serialize and deserialize the arguments and return values despite the fact that the caller resides in the same virtual machine.

EJB 2.0 provides local interfaces for this exact situation. An entity or session bean may provide a local interface that can be used by other beans within the same container. This allows local clients to avoid the performance penalties that are introduced when data is serialized and deserialized for remote access. A bean may expose one set of methods in its local interface and another set in its remote interface. A bean, such as a session bean that is exclusively used by remote clients, may have a remote interface and not need a local interface. On the other hand, an entity bean that is only used by session beans may not even need a remote interface.

Local methods behave a bit differently from the corresponding remote methods. Local methods pass each argument by reference rather than passing a serialized copy of each argument. So, if a bean is altering the arguments for any reason, the remote client will not receive the changes but a local client will!

Consistent use of local and remote interfaces can minimize this confusion. For example, it frequently makes sense for entity beans to only have a local interface, while session beans only have remote interfaces. Under this approach, remote clients cannot directly access the entity beans. This strict layering also makes the system easier to understand and generally easier to optimize for performance and transactional integrity.

Local Home Interface

Local client beans need the capability to find, create, and destroy beans. Each locally accessible bean must provide a local home interface for this purpose. Each local home interface specifies locally accessible methods for the creation, location, and destruction of one type of bean. For example, if a system has locally accessible entity beans for employees and for timecards, then the system has separate local home interfaces for employees and for timecards. Local home interfaces generally evolve nicely from the object life cycle analysis objects.

Message-Driven Bean

Message-driven beans receive asynchronous messages from a wide variety of Message Oriented Middleware (MOM) implementations. Each message-driven bean is configured to consume messages sent to a particular message destination. The sender simply sends the message and goes on about its business. Once a message-driven bean receives a message, it can use low-level APIs, such as JDBC, to accomplish its goals or interact with session and entity beans. As with session beans, using JDBC to directly interact with the database is perfectly feasible but fails to leverage the strengths of the EJB container. A message-driven bean can also use JMS to send a response message to the sender or to another interested party.

Message-driven beans are quite different from entity and session beans. Message-driven beans receive simple text or data messages rather than strongly typed data. Message-driven beans cannot directly respond to the sender. So, message-driven beans do not return any result or throw any exceptions to the sender. Also, there is no other way to interact with a message-driven bean, so they do not need local, home, or remote interfaces. As a general rule, message-driven beans should serve as simple entry points into the system by parsing each message and then calling a session bean to perform the remaining processing.

NOTE For more details on MOM and the Java Message Service, refer to the JMS section in Chapter 9, "Evaluating Candidate Technologies for User Interface Classes."

Implementation

Each bean has a concrete implementation class that implements an EntityBean, SessionBean, or MessageDrivenBean interface. The implementation contains the Java code for the business logic for entity beans, the workflow logic for session beans, or the message processing logic for message-driven beans.

Deployment Descriptor

The deployment descriptor is an XML document that describes how beans are deployed and how the container treats them at run time. It describes everything from the location of class files to decisions about persistence, transactions, and security.

Bean-Managed Persistence

In bean-managed persistence (BMP), the entity bean loads and saves its own data. The entity bean does not need to determine when it is time to load or save. Bean-managed persistence requires developers to embed JDBC code within the bean's implementation.

Container-Managed Persistence

In container-managed persistence (CMP), the developer specifies a mapping between each piece of persistent data and a field in a table in the database. This mapping is stored in the deployment descriptor.

Transaction Boundaries

The container determines transaction boundaries based on decisions that are recorded in the deployment descriptor. For each remotely available method, developers specify if the method should join an existing transaction, start its own transaction, or execute outside of any transaction.

Gory Details

Enterprise JavaBeans is a fairly complex technology, with lots of terms, concepts, rules, classes, and interfaces to learn. However, one thing is certain: Using EJB is infinitely better than trying to produce your own scalable remote object framework.

Session Beans

In order to gain all of the benefits of an EJB system, the developer must create classes and interfaces that fit within the specification. Specifically, for each session bean, the developer provides either a remote interface, a local interface, or both so that the session bean can be used either by remote clients, other beans in the container, or both. The developer also provides a home interface, a local home interface, or both so that the session bean can be located by remote clients, other beans in the container, or both. Finally, the developer provides an implementation class. Figure 12.9 shows a sample session bean that exposes some workflow for access by external clients. The remote interface, which defines the public face of the bean, extends the EJBObject interface as provided by Sun. The home interface extends the EJBHome interface, also provided by Sun. Finally, the implementation class realizes the SessionBean interface.

Notice that the implementation class does not implement the home and remote interfaces. This is a good thing, as you really do not want to write code for some of the methods in EJBObject and EJBHome. These tasks are left to the container vendor, who supplies a proxy class that implements your remote and home interfaces. Since these interfaces extend Sun's interfaces, the proxy must provide behavior for your business behavior, as described in your remote interface, the bean life cycle behavior, as described in your home interface, and the behavior defined by Sun in the EJBObject and EJBHome interfaces.

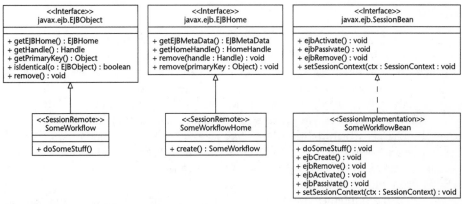

Figure 12.9   A workflow session bean.

Stateful Session Beans

Session beans are divided into two distinct categories, *stateless* and *stateful*. A stateful session bean maintains a dialogue with the client application, in which the session bean remembers past requests, and uses them to simplify subsequent requests. For example, a stateful session bean for an online store might allow the customers to select a product, enter their billing information, then enter their shipping information, and finally confirm the purchase. This allows each interaction to stay simple, while useful information builds up in the session bean.

This convenience comes with a price. The stateful session object takes up memory, and must be managed by the container until the session is completed by the client application. If the container runs low on memory, it must serialize the bean and recover it when the client makes another request. Also, there is no guarantee that the client will gracefully end the session. This forces the container to worry about timeouts and cleanup for orphaned stateful session beans.

Control objects that provide a conversational workflow for the client are generally very appropriate as stateful session beans.

Stateless Session Beans

A stateless session bean is not required to remember any conversational state from request to request. In fact, the same client making multiple requests to the same stateless session bean may actually receive a different instantiation each time.

This is very efficient, as the container can keep a small pool of stateless session beans for use by many clients. There is no need for the container to manage relationships between the session beans and the client application.

Stateless session beans often evolve from control objects, which convert a single method into a series of smaller requests, and consolidate the results.

Entity Beans

For each entity bean, the developer provides a remote interface, a local interface, or both so that the entity bean can be used either by remote clients, other beans in the container, or both. The developer also provides a home interface, a local home interface, or both so that the entity bean can be located by remote clients, other beans in the container, or both. Finally, the developer provides an implementation class. Figure 12.10 shows a sample entity bean that exposes some business logic for access by other beans. The local interface, which defines the public face of the bean, extends the EJBLocal Object interface as provided by Sun. The local home interface extends the EJBLocal Home interface, also provided by Sun. Finally, the implementation class implements the EntityBean interface.

Notice that the implementation class does not implement the home and remote interfaces. This is a good thing, because you really do not want to write code for some of the methods in EJBLocalObject and EJBLocalHome. These tasks are left to the container vendor, who supplies a proxy class that implements your local and local home interfaces. Since these interfaces extend Sun's interfaces, the proxy must provide behavior for your business behavior, as described in your local interface, the bean life cycle behavior, as described in your local home interface, and the behavior defined by Sun in the EJBLocalObject and EJBLocalHome interfaces.

Message-Driven Beans

Message-driven beans do not provide business or workflow methods. They are limited to a single method, onMessage, which is called when a text or data message is sent to the appropriate destination. So, message-driven beans do not have remote, home, local, or local home interfaces. The developer simply provides a single implementation class that implements the MessageDrivenBean and MessageListener interfaces, both of which are provided by Sun.

Figure 12.11 shows a message-driven bean that provides a simple entry point to an EJB-based system.

BMP Relationships

BMP relationships are fairly tedious to develop, since each entity bean's ejbLoad method contains JDBC code to retrieve any foreign keys from the database, obtain a home interface, and use its finder methods to retrieve references to the entity beans that are part of the relationship. Also, each entity bean's ejbStore method contains JDBC code to store identifying information for each relationship. This type of JDBC code tends to be extremely repetitive, time consuming, and tedious to test and debug.

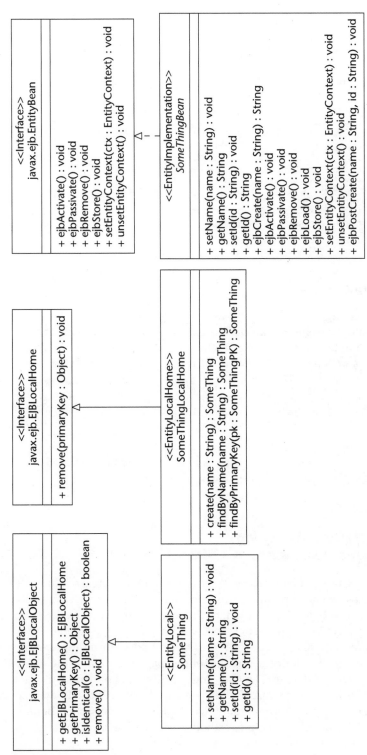

Figure 12.10   An entity bean.

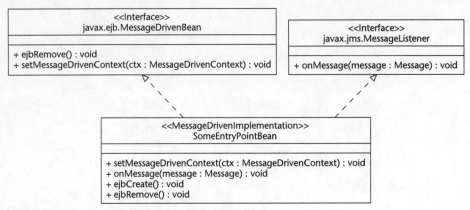

Figure 12.11   An entry point message-driven bean.

CMP Relationships

With EJB 2.0, implementing relationships between entity beans is easier than ever before. Each relationship is specified by an ejb-relation element within the deployment descriptor and by including getter and setter methods in the entity beans. All of the monotonous code to populate each entity bean with local references to other entity beans is handled by the container. The persistence mapping is declarative and as minimal as possible. For more information on this topic, refer to Chapter 15, "Design for the TimecardDomain and TimecardWorkflow," which uses CMP to implement the Timecard example.

> **TIP** The bulk of the deployment descriptors and methods can be generated directly from your UML diagrams by the modeling tool.

Development Workflow, Assuming Container-Managed Persistence

As a system is designed and implemented with EJB, development breaks into fairly distinct pieces. First, developers determine the business data that resides in each entity bean, along with the remotely accessible interface that exposes the data. At the same time, session beans are identified from control objects in the analysis model. They encapsulate the high-level business logic and workflows that span multiple entity beans. After these two efforts solidify, a separate effort maps the data in the entity beans to fields in a relational database. The mapping is held in a deployment file, not in the code itself. As these efforts mature and are exercised against actual data and usage scenarios, developers can determine the most appropriate transaction boundaries and permissions for remotely accessible methods. Again, these decisions are kept in a deployment file, not in the code.

So, development of an EJB system breaks into the following primary steps:

1. Allocation of business data, business logic, and control logic to entity and session beans

2. Mapping entity data to persistent data store

3. Determining transaction boundaries and security

The key is that each step does not affect the previous steps. For instance, the code for the entity beans and session beans is completely unaffected by the mapping from the data to the database. Even the data mappings are independent of the decisions regarding transaction boundaries and security.

This clear division between software development activities may be EJB's greatest contribution to enterprise development. By allowing developers to defer and revisit different steps without destroying the existing work, use of EJB technology can dramatically decrease project risk.

Strengths

By providing a coherent framework of services and standards, EJB greatly simplifies the development of enterprise systems. EJB allows developers to leverage several decades of research and innovation in transaction management, object-to-relational persistence, object caching, and resource management. Standing on the backs of giants allows us to approach formidable projects with confidence. The following section discusses some specific advantages of EJB.

Object Life Cycle Management

Object life cycle management includes creating, locating, caching, and deleting objects. In EJB, the methods for performing these tasks are defined in the home interface. In most cases, no code is written by the developer to realize these methods. Instead, the container uses SQL statements and database mappings as defined in the deployment descriptor to realize them at run time.

This approach has two tremendous advantages. First, developers save a great deal of effort that would otherwise be spent writing tedious JDBC code to load and save objects, as well as complex and error-prone code for caching objects. Also, entity beans can easily be reused in other systems, since developers follow standard conventions.

Transaction Management

In EJB development, transaction boundaries may be handled within the code or described in the deployment descriptor. The first approach gives developers limitless flexibility, while the latter approach is incredibly easy to use and allows developers to revisit their decisions without disturbing the existing code base.

Security

EJBs provide security by allowing developers to specify which users can access each method. This approach allows developers to control system access with a great deal of precision and at a fine granularity. Of course, the user interface must handle invalid requests gracefully or prevent users from attempting to access forbidden functionality.

Persistence

As with transaction management, EJB development offers limitless flexibility for beans that require custom persistence code or easy point-and-click descriptions of the mapping from entity bean data to database fields. While this is certainly not unique to EJB, it is still a huge advantage.

Vendor Neutrality

Since the relationship between the container and the enclosed beans is very well determined by the EJB specification, a set of beans can be redeployed within a different compliant container with proportionally little effort. This allows developers to scale their system by changing the container, not the code. For instance, a system might be developed within a free or cheap container, initially deployed inside of a midrange container, and then redeployed to a fancy cluster of high-performance EJB servers. Also, containers may be selected based on particular strengths, such as superior transaction management or scalability.

Portability and Reuse

By definition, every EJB developer follows the same specification. This greatly increases reuse potential. There is no worry that a bean will not fit the persistence or security scheme of the new system. So, a bean that fits nicely with the new system's domain can never be excluded due to implementation decisions.

Weaknesses

While EJB development has many advantages, it is not without a price. Application servers that provide substantial value come with substantial price tags. Also, Enterprise JavaBeans require developers to comply with the EJB specification, master the application server's deployment tool, and endure painful code-deploy-test cycles.

Compatible Technologies

Enterprise JavaBeans can be accessed from any kind of application, applet, or servlet. They can be used to create entity and control objects that are accessed from almost any sort of boundary objects.

Cost of Adoption

Commercial application servers with EJB support are quite expensive. You pay the vendor so that you will not have to solve the rather nasty problems associated with enterprise development. If your project really needs the strengths of EJB, the costs of not using it may be incredibly high. Your development team must provide solutions for the object caching, persistence mapping, and transaction control needs of a scalable enterprise system. On the other hand, using EJB should decrease risk and speed up the development cycle.

The financial cost of adoption may be decreased dramatically if your organization is comfortable using open source free software. At least one free open application server, JBoss, seems poised to compete as a viable alternative to the leading commercial application servers.

TIP If you worry that finding or cultivating EJB developers is difficult and expensive, consider the option: finding the developers who are qualified to develop an alternate solution to each of the problems that EJB solves.

In order to be successful with EJB, your project must fill the roles of architect, bean developer, and deployer.

Architect

Architects for EJB systems need knowledge of the EJB specification, the J2EE platform, distributed computing, object-to-relational persistence issues, transaction management, concurrency, exception handling, and architectural patterns. Experience with CORBA or another distributed computing technology may be helpful. This role requires a wide breadth of knowledge, as well as practical low-level experience.

Bean Developer

In many cases, bean development is fairly straightforward. Knowledge of transaction basics, exceptions, and the Java language is essential. No particular breadth of knowledge of the Java class libraries is required.

Deployer

A bean deployer needs a basic understanding of transactions, concurrency, resource pools, and security. A deployer does not need to implement any of these areas in code; instead, he or she must make deployment decisions that maximize performance while protecting data integrity.

In-depth knowledge of the application server and its associated deployment tool is also essential. Expertise in the Java programming language is not necessary.

Bean deployment is not like other design and code activities. It is closer to system administration or database administration.

Suitability

In Chapter 6, "Describing the System for Technology Selection," we identified two descriptive categories:

- Number and type of users
- Performance and scalability

Let's take a look at how EJB meets these criteria.

Number and Type of Users

EJB is certainly a valid choice for all four types of audience: a small number of dedicated users, general use within an organization, a large audience with high interest, and a huge audience with low interest. As the number of users and the amount of data accessed grows, the capability of an EJB server to cache objects and pool resources becomes increasingly important.

While load balancing and clustering will never be easy, vendors of commercial application servers are already focusing on this challenge. It is important to note that several of the application server vendors, including BEA, IBM, and Sun, have extensive experience with enterprise system development and clustering technology.

Performance and Scalability

EJB is not always a reasonable choice for read-only systems and systems that allow isolated updates. These systems make use of a small set of EJB's strengths, such as object caching. And if the system has demanding performance requirements, using EJB may actually increase overall project risk.

EJB really starts to show its value when faced with concurrent updates of the system data. The combination of object caching and transaction management is more efficient than 99 percent of all in-house efforts. Also, EJB developers and deployers can manipulate the transaction boundaries without altering a single line of code. This is invaluable when attempting to achieve just the right balance between data integrity and performance.

Sample Technology Selection

This section uses the technology requirements from Chapter 6, "Describing the System for Technology Selection," and the technology descriptions from this chapter to select technologies for the Timecard system's control and entity classes. It also considers the cost of adopting the technology.

One choice is a custom implementation based on RMI and JDBC. The other choice is an EJB implementation.

Let's review the Timecard application's technology requirements as developed in Chapter 6 and proceed from there.

Technology Requirements

The relevant areas for control and entity classes are number and type of users and performance and scalability. The results were:

- Number and type of users: General use within an organization
- Performance and scalability: Concurrent updates

Based on these descriptions, we must choose between the custom combination and EJB.

Number and Type of Users

RMI and JDBC certainly make a valid combination for general use within an organization. As the number of users and the data accessed grows, developers will need to cache objects and pool resources, but these are common problems in large-scale development.

Recall that RMI and JDBC do not provide any clustering or load-balancing framework. However, it seems unlikely that any one company's Timecard application will require a cluster of servers to meet demand, so this is not a factor.

EJB is certainly appropriate for general use within an organization. It has the object-caching and resource-pooling capabilities that greatly simplify system development. Conclusion: EJB has a slight advantage.

Performance and Scalability

A combination of RMI and JDBC is appropriate for systems that allow concurrent updates of data. However, in this case, the developers must supply their own architecture for coordinated transaction management on top of the simple control provided by JDBC.

EJB is designed with concurrent updates in mind. Supporting them in this case should not require any great effort or creativity. EJB has the advantage.

Cost of Adoption

This category is more difficult and subjective to assess. First, for most systems, the licensing cost is not financially significant when compared to payroll. Certainly, application servers are expensive. However, reducing the project staff by one person over a year or reducing the schedule by a month or two is worth a lot of money. Such modest reductions in effort are very reasonable when comparing EJB with RMI/JDBC for a challenging project.

Now, let us consider the remaining cost of adoption: assembling a team. EJB has one huge advantage over RMI/JDBC in this area. With EJB, you must acquire one or two experts who understand the technology and the application servers. With RMI/JDBC, you must acquire one or two experts who must develop a framework and usage guidelines for persistence, resource pooling, and object caching. Either way, to avoid chaos, you must allow most developers to work within a fairly narrow and well-documented framework. However, with EJB, the framework and guidelines already exist, along with books, seminars, and online tutorials. Even the best in-house solutions cannot reach this level of sophistication. Therefore, EJB reduces the workload on the architect, while making all of the developers more productive.

If EJB is technically suitable for an application, it seems wise to use it. While it is difficult to balance salaries against licenses, the advantages of EJB seem fairly clear.

Conclusion

The Timecard system could clearly be implemented with RMI/JDBC or EJB. However, given the slight advantage for EJB in each category, it seems prudent to select EJB.

> **WARNING** Some companies are selecting EJB as an implementation technology even before they establish their requirements. Unfortunately, not all systems are appropriate for EJB, and choosing EJB when the technical requirements do not indicate it may be very risky. For instance, some systems place a high premium on speed, but do not have data integrity issues. Using EJB for such a system may decrease development time but fail to meet the performance requirements.

The Next Step

We selected technologies for the boundary classes in Chapter 9, and for the control and entity classes in this chapter. We are ready to move forward with our understanding of the solution. Next, in architecture, we elaborate and structure our growing understanding of the solution.

Software Architecture

In previous chapters, we discussed techniques for understanding a problem from the users' and developer's perspective. In Chapters 6, "Describing the System for Technology Selection", 7, "Evaluating Candidate Technologies for Shared Services," 8, "HTML Production," 9, "Evaluating Candidate Technologies for User Interface Classes," 10, "Evaluating Candidate Technologies for the System Interface," 11, "Evaluating Web Service Technologies for the System Interface," and 12, "Evaluating Candidate Technologies for Control and Entity Classes," we discussed a disciplined approach to technology selection and selected technologies for each group of analysis classes. Finally, we have the information we need to describe a viable solution to the system problem. The software architecture is exactly that: It is a high-level structural description of the solution for the system.

A software architecture composes groups of classes into a coherent solution, and shows how the pieces are structured with respect to one another. The emphasis is on the structure and relationships, not on the details of each piece. This is similar to a blueprint for a building, which shows the dimensions of the building and indicates the building materials, while omitting details about the interior of the building and the actual construction techniques.

A software architecture allows a variety of participants to understand the entire system as a coherent whole. More people can understand and review the solution before it is implemented, and this helps to minimize confusion and facilitates a more orderly development process. A solid architecture reduces confusion and creates a clearly defined goal. This has a significant effect on developers' morale and productivity. Just as a blueprint helps separate teams of carpenters, electricians, and masons to contribute efficiently to a greater goal, a software architecture helps developers coordinate their efforts around a common and consensual understanding of the solution.

We are continually shocked at how little emphasis is placed on architecture in our industry, especially compared to other industries. No home builder would commit to a project without reviewing detailed plans, yet even sophisticated software companies often spend more money on catering than on the software architecture. The result is all too common and all too predictable: Developers flounder about, unsure how their efforts contribute to the whole system. Periodically, the code from different developers and from different teams is merged and tested. At this point, a host of incompatible interfaces and inconsistencies brings the entire process to a halt. After the finger-pointing subsides, the developers resolve their integration issues as quickly as possible and describe the changes as "bug fixes." Not a pretty sight.

Are You Ready?

Before you can create a software architecture for your system, you must have a clear understanding of the problem and a clear understanding of the technologies that will be used.

Clear Understanding of the Problem

You need solid requirements, analysis classes, and sequence diagrams for a representative subset of the use case model. This model of the system forms and documents your understanding of the problem that will be solved. Failing to understand the problem from the users' perspective leads to the dreaded, "That's nice, but . . . " reaction at the first large-scale demonstration. Failing to understand the problem from the developers' perspective often leads to a brittle architecture that cannot easily meet the functional requirements of the system.

Clear Understanding of the Technology

You need a clear understanding of the technologies, including their strengths, weaknesses, and compatibilities. This information is invaluable as you organize the solution. In some cases, technologies may not be directly compatible. For example, you may create an additional piece of the system solely to adapt a commercially available class library for use in your system. In other cases, the technology may not support a desired relationship. Time spent upfront understanding the technologies prevents a wide array of difficulties, and greatly lowers your risk of spectacular failure.

You should also consider the difficulties in adopting a technology when dividing a system into parts. After all, actual human beings, who may not know all of the technologies involved, must implement each part. You must ensure that each part is sufficiently limited in the technology it uses, so that a reasonably small group of your organization's developers can master the required technologies.

TIP Never forget the developers. At first, it seems that architecture is all about technology and object-oriented theory. Certainly these factors are important, but an elegant and technologically impressive solution may still fail if your organization is not prepared to implement it. As a professional, with obligations to customers and to your peers, it is better to succeed quietly than to fail spectacularly.

Goals for Software Architecture

A good software architecture is also the result of an endless series of compromises and trade-offs. Moving closer to one goal may inadvertently move the architecture away from another goal. For example, increasing the scalability of a system usually makes the system more complex and more difficult to maintain. Using a new technology may reduce technical risk, but increase schedule risk as developers scramble to adopt the technology. In short, perfect architectures are sought, but are never found.

TIP Architecture, like politics, is the art of the possible.

Most software architectures have some or all of the following goals, either implicitly or explicitly, but it is better to spell out the goals explicitly, so that they can be prioritized and monitored. This does not need to be an elaborate process; it can even be a simple list for internal use.

We will refer back to these goals as we discuss various techniques for creating a high-quality software architecture.

Extensibility

Enterprise systems are expected to provide value over many years. Over time, a successful system evolves to meet the changing needs of the customer. Completely new functionality may be added, or existing functionality may change radically. A good system architecture must easily assimilate small changes, gracefully adapt to large changes, and survive radical changes. In order to produce an architecture that handles change well, the architect must have a solid vision about what can change and what is truly fixed.

Maintainability

Over a decade, a large enterprise system may be developed and maintained by 50 or even 100 different people. The original developers often leave the project to create the next big thing, perhaps with an entirely different organization. Even stalwart maintenance developers are promoted or retire. Therefore, bug fixes and requirements may have to be made with little or no help from the original system architect and developers.

This means that the system architecture must be accessible to an entirely new group of developers. Simplicity and clarity may need to be balanced against extensibility or performance goals.

Reliability

Many systems have nonfunctional requirements that specify the reliability of the system. These requirements may limit system downtime or prohibit any downtime. Reliability certainly constrains hardware selection, network topology, technology selection, and software architecture for the system.

Scalability

Many systems have goals for the number of concurrent users and the amount of data that the system will contain. These scalability goals must be considered when developing the system architecture. Otherwise, the system may meet the functional requirements but fail to scale as the business it serves grows. This often leads to a series of desperate attempts to improve performance, followed by unchecked finger-pointing, and finally to a complete redesign of the system.

With these goals in mind, we can consider some theory and pragmatic techniques that will help you develop strong software architectures.

UML and Architecture

Architecture is all about managing complexity by dividing the solution into small pieces, then combining the small pieces into larger, more coherent structures. Fortunately, there are several object-oriented principles that assist us in this endeavor. As always, UML is used to visualize and communicate our decisions.

The following concepts are especially helpful:

- Packages
- Package dependency diagrams
- Subsystems
- Layers

The following sections examine each concept in detail, and provide the applicable UML notation.

Packages

In UML, a group of classes is known as a *package*. A package may also contain other packages, so that developers can construct arbitrarily complex groupings and subgroupings.

Packages are valuable for several reasons. First, when classes are organized in logical groups, it is far easier to find classes and understand the system. Packages serve the same purpose as folders in an email system or directories in a file system; they help keep us sane.

There are two distinct approaches to grouping classes. Classes can be grouped according to similar responsibilities, even if they do not collaborate. Classes can be grouped because they collaborate to fulfill a larger responsibility, even if each of the classes has very different individual responsibilities.

Similar Responsibilities

It makes sense to group classes that have the same responsibility, but vary in their implementation. The classes form a group of alternatives, not a group of collaborators. For example, there are several implementations of the Border interface in Java's javax.swing.border package. Each implementation has a different way of drawing a border around a component. Figure 13.1 shows several of the alternative border classes and the interface that they all realize. Packaging the different borders together makes it easy for developers to find the right alternative for their needs.

In this case, all of the classes realize the same interface. While this is desirable in many cases, it is far from essential. A package may hold classes that have very similar responsibilities, but do not realize the same interface.

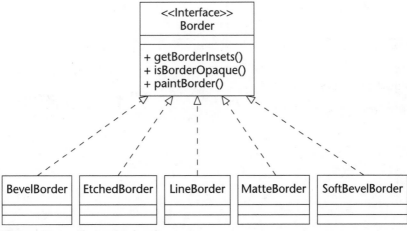

Figure 13.1   Alternative borders.

Collaborations

Another package may group more diverse classes because the classes collaborate to fulfill a significant responsibility. For example, all of the classes for compressing and uncompressing data are held in the java.util.zip package. The classes have quite different responsibilities. The ZipOutputStream writes compressed data to an arbitrary output stream. It allows client objects to start a new entry, write data, and close the entry when they are done writing. This process may be repeated for any number of entries. A ZipInputStream object reads compressed data from an arbitrary input stream and uncompresses it, one entry at a time. A ZipFile uses a ZipInputStream to provide convenient functionality for reading compressed data from a file. Figure 13.2 shows the classes for compressing and uncompressing data using the Zip format. Each class has a separate responsibility, and collaborates with the others to meet a larger goal.

Notice that changes to the implementation of one class in this package may ripple to the other classes in the package. For example, any change to the compression logic in the ZipOutputStream causes a corresponding change in the uncompression logic in the ZipInputStream. However, no class outside of this package should need to depend on the implementation of any of these classes. Together, these classes fully encapsulate compression and uncompression within the package.

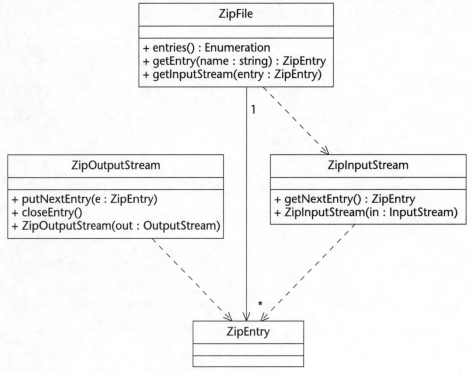

Figure 13.2 Collaborating classes.

Packages are also a useful unit of work that can be assigned to a small team. If a team takes responsibility for a package, that package must be sized appropriately, and all of the implementation technology must fall within the team's expertise. In order to divide up the effort in this way, each package must be fairly independent, so that it can be developed and tested separately.

Package Dependency

Package dependencies show how changes to classes can ripple throughout the system. A dashed dependency arrow from package A to package B indicates that there is at least one class in package A that uses at least one class in package B. This means that some changes to the classes in package B will ripple to affect the classes in package A. Other changes to package B may not affect package A at all. The absence of a dependency arrow from package B to package A would indicate that the classes in package A may change as much as you wish, with no effect on the classes in package B. Figure 13.3 shows package A depending on package B.

Package dependencies may be direct, as in Figure 13.3, or indirect. If package A depends on package B, and package B depends on package C, then it is possible for a change to a class in package C to require a change to a class in package B, which requires a change to a class in package A. Package A indirectly depends on package C. This has tremendous implications when attempting to reuse a package in a new system. Trying to extract the desired package may require radical surgery, as each of its dependencies must be extracted, along with each of the dependency's dependencies. With this in mind, examining the package dependencies helps developers gauge the difficulty of reusing a package or a class from a package.

Package dependencies are often shown in high-level views, called *package dependency diagrams*, which ignore the individual classes and show all of the packages and their dependencies. These diagrams allow developers to measure the complexity of a system in a high-level view and help them evaluate the effects of a proposed change to the system.

TIP A package dependency diagram is like a road map. It only helps you if it is up-to-date.

Figure 13.3 Package A depends on package B.

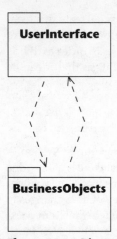

Figure 13.4 Direct mutual dependency.

Avoiding Mutual Dependency

We refer to packages that depend on one another, either directly or indirectly, as *mutually dependent*. Figure 13.4 shows the UserInterface package and the BusinessObjects package depending directly on one another. Figure 13.5 shows the UserInterface package depending directly on the SessionManagement package, which depends on the BusinessObjects package, which completes the cycle by depending on the UserInterface package.

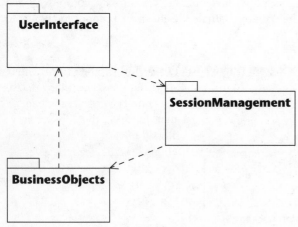

Figure 13.5 Indirect mutual dependency.

Mutual dependencies are definitely worth avoiding. Their presence dramatically decreases your ability to predict the effects of changes to the system, because a change in one package can ripple throughout the dependency cycle.

Mutual dependencies also reduce the architect's ability to limit and control the complexity of the system. Packages tend to intertwine over time, as the challenges and pressures of detailed design and code lead developers to discover ways in which the packages can cooperate to meet the needs of the system. A mutual dependency between packages gives free rein to this tendency. If the packages are already dependent on one another, it is difficult to fight the urge to add one more dependency. This process gradually increases complexity, while decreasing extensibility and reusability.

TIP When creating package dependency diagrams, organize the packages so that the dependency arrows all point horizontally, down, or diagonally down. Following this convention makes it very easy to spot dependency cycles, as they will require an upward arrow.

Once you accept that mutual dependency is dangerous, you must break the cycle by reorganizing the classes within the packages or splitting some classes into new packages. The example in Figure 13.5 is a mutual dependency because the BusinessObjects package depends on the UserInterface package. This may seem necessary for some applications, because the user interface may demand notification whenever the business objects change. However, we can use the event model from JavaBeans to achieve this effect while removing the mutual dependency cycle. The user interface classes can implement the PropertyChangeListener interface as found in java.beans. The user interface objects can then be registered as listeners on the business objects. This allows business objects to notify registered listeners of changes without knowing their specific class. Figure 13.6 shows the new package dependency diagram without the mutual dependency cycle.

Subsystems

A *subsystem* is a package that completely encapsulates its implementation. Client objects access the subsystem's functionality through a narrowly defined interface. As long as the interface does not change, the dependent classes do not need to change.

For example, a project may need a logging subsystem. In UML, the subsystem is shown as a stereotyped package, and the subsystem directly realizes the interface. Of course, we know that there must be some implementation class hidden inside of the subsystem and that the running system needs an instance of the implementation class. We need to expose this instance to the objects that need it, without having them depend on its constructor or its specific type.

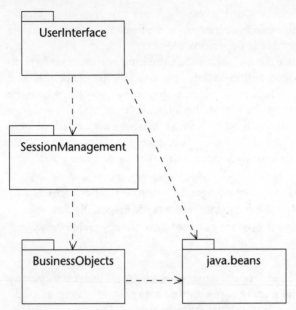

Figure 13.6   Breaking the dependency cycle.

Fortunately, the Singleton design pattern [Gamma 1995] is a perfect match for this problem. We introduce a new class, LoggerSingleton, which has a public static method, called getLogger, that returns an ILogger reference. The LoggerSingleton instantiates the LoggerImplementation once, and passes that single instance to each caller.

Figure 13.7 shows the LoggingSubsystem and the ILogger interface in a class diagram. A more concise view of the same scenario is shown in Figure 13.8.

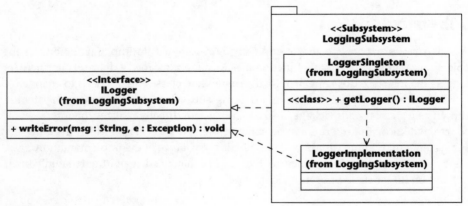

Figure 13.7   A logging subsystem.

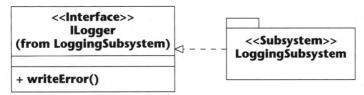

Figure 13.8 A logging subsystem with no details shown.

To summarize, a subsystem hides functionality that can change—the implementation— behind something that will not change—the interface. Subsystems facilitate efficient development, support system configuration, and allow the system to evolve as requirements change.

Efficient Development

Subsystems with well-established and consensual interfaces allow developers to work in parallel. The developers whose code depends on the subsystem do not actually need a fully functional version of the subsystem. All they need is a stub or trivial implementation of the subsystem and confidence that their code will integrate seamlessly with the real subsystem. This enables one set of developers to work on the subsystem without impeding the progress of the other developers.

To continue our logging subsystem example, the initial version of the subsystem simply writes the formatted messages to standard out. A subsequent version will write messages to a recycled error log file.

Variability and Configuration

Multiple subsystems may implement the same interface in very different ways. Once an implementation is selected, the rest of the system ignores the choice. This allows a development team to easily configure and deploy variations of a system.

For example, some clients for a system may want to log to an error file, while others want to log to a database. One approach is to use a configuration file to tell the LoggerSingleton which implementation class to instantiate. This provides a lot of flexibility without breaking any existing code.

Extensibility

A subsystem's implementation is hidden. As long as the interface does not change, the implementation of the subsystem can freely evolve to meet new or expanding requirements.

For example, a requirement to add a timestamp to the formatted errors produced by our logging subsystem can be accommodated by changing the implementation class. There is no need to change the interface or alter the code that calls the logger's writeError method.

NOTE The previous example of a logging subsystem is *not* a description of Sun's Java Logging package as provided in J2SE 1.4. For more information on that package, see Chapter 7.

Guidelines for Software Architecture

As you develop a software architecture, you must keep some guiding principles in mind. The first, cohesion, helps you organize parts of the system into logical groups. The second, coupling, helps you keep groups independent and understandable.

Cohesion

Cohesion describes how members of the same group are related to one another. Strong cohesion indicates that the members of the group belong together. Weak cohesion indicates that the grouping is arbitrary or even illogical.

Cohesion can be applied to a group of methods inside a class, a group of classes inside a package, and a group of packages. Given the members of the group, an outsider should be able to deduce the overall responsibility of a cohesive group. For instance, what is the responsibility of a class that has these methods: makeEggs, makeToast, makeHashBrowns, and makeJuice? The responsibility, make breakfast, is fairly clear, so these methods have strong cohesion within a class called Cook.

A similar level of cohesion should be demanded of classes within a package and packages in a layer. Groups with weak cohesion are hard to understand and to remember. They make a system more difficult to maintain and to extend.

Coupling

Coupling describes the level of dependence between different groups. Tight coupling indicates that the groups are very interdependent and that changes to one group may require a complex ripple of changes to the other groups. Loose coupling indicates that the groups are relatively independent. Loose coupling invariably makes the groups and their relationships easier to understand, maintain, and extend.

Coupling can be determined for a group of methods inside a class, a group of classes inside a package, and a group of packages. However, the amount of permissible coupling varies greatly between the different types of groups. For instance, the methods in a class may be tightly coupled, as they interact with the same instance variables and frequently call one another. At the next level up, classes within a package should be less interdependent. They should not depend at all on one another's implementation, and they should depend on a fairly narrowly defined set of methods. The coupling between packages should be even looser. Whenever possible, they should depend on one another through interfaces rather than implementation.

Creating a Software Architecture

Creating a solid architecture requires a dedicated effort within the project. Choosing an architect and committing to a reasonably disciplined process for creating an architecture pays immense dividends throughout the life of the project.

The Architect

The software architect works with other senior developers to determine the architecture of the system, including technology selection and subsystem design. Architectural mechanisms, such as error-handling and caching strategies, must be defined before developers need them. Subsequent responsibilities include evaluating detailed designs for conformance with the architecture, revisiting the architecture, and encouraging developers to use good OO and software engineering practices. These practices include the use of the UML, solid OO design principles, the educated use of design patterns, iterative development, and design and code reviews.

A software architect needs extensive experience developing object-oriented systems and mentoring technical people. Language and technology expertise are also required. It is impossible to select technology and decompose a solution into the right pieces without getting your hands dirtied in the details.

Strong communication and people skills are equally important. An architect must be able to hold and defend strong opinions, or the project will lack technical vision. On the other hand, architects must build consensus and mentor developers. They are obligated to push back against excessive and destructive schedule pressure, yet they must work closely with project managers to manage risks and ensure the project's timely success.

Architecture also requires an odd mix of personality characteristics. To be successful in the short term, architects design a high-level solution with incomplete information while under schedule pressure. This requires them to be decisive, knowledgeable, and persuasive. To be successful over the life of the project, they must accept and improve their inevitably flawed ideas. They must be humble enough to admit their own failings in full view. They must also work with project management and highly technical people to resolve issues that range from risk mitigation and iteration planning to mechanisms and subsystem interfaces.

In our experience, this responsibility cannot be distributed among multiple architects for a system. Certainly, a good architect gathers input from many participants, and builds consensus among the senior technical people. However, the final responsibility cannot be shared. Cohesive and coherent solutions are not made by committee. Once the overall solution has been developed, individual parts can be delegated to designers, but there must be one coherent vision and one accountable person.

A Process

Creating a solid architecture involves several steps:

1. Set goals.
2. Group classes.
3. Show technologies.
4. Extract subsystems.
5. Evaluate the architecture against guidelines and goals.

The following sections discuss each step in detail.

Set Goals

Earlier in this chapter, we discussed goals for extensibility, maintainability, reliability, and scalability. Your system may have some of these, and perhaps other, goals. In any case, you must establish the goals and have some idea of their relative importance. Remember, architecture requires you to make a series of decisions based on incomplete information, and almost every decision has some unintended side effect.

Setting clear priorities is also a nice counterpoint to risk management. Risk management tracks all of the outcomes that you want to avoid. Goals are all of the outcomes that you want to foster. Either way, establishing priorities does not need to be an exhaustive process. Most projects need only a page or two of very informal text to get a huge benefit. Just discussing goals or risks on a regular basis is a healthy exercise, because it encourages people to think about the project as a whole.

Group Classes

Classes can be grouped into packages to keep collaborators together or to keep similar classes together. This choice is not easy. You must consider coupling and cohesion as well as the potential for variability and reuse. In general, classes that may be reused in different situations should be organized together by responsibility. Grouping them by responsibility rather than by collaboration helps to keep them independent of any one type of use. Classes that are dedicated to a single collaboration must be packaged with the other classes that they support.

We tend to group different types of analysis classes into layers by responsibility. For example, more than one control class can use each entity class, so the entity classes belong in a layer. The same is true for the control classes, because each control class can interact with different versions of the same boundary class.

Within each layer, the classes often divide into packages. For example, the entity layer may contain several packages or even subsystems with clearly defined responsibilities. The control layer may be divided into groups of control classes that interact as part of a larger workflow for a particular type of user.

The layers and the packages within each layer must be shown in one or more package dependency diagrams.

Show Technologies

We selected technologies in Chapters 7 to 12, so this step is fairly mechanical. Each use of a technology must be added to the package dependency diagram(s) that shows the appropriate package.

Extract Subsystems

Remember that subsystems facilitate efficient development, support system configuration, and allow parts of the system to evolve independently as requirements change. Candidate subsystems can be found by looking for packages that have a clearly defined interface and loose coupling with the rest of the system. Within the candidates, look for packages that can be developed independently and/or that encapsulate volatile requirements.

Evaluate against Guidelines and Goals

You must periodically evaluate the architecture against the goals and against the guidelines of high cohesion and loose coupling. UML and modeling tools allow you to review and revise a model with little waste. UML also allows you to efficiently communicate the structure of the system to other developers. Given these advantages, there is no reason not to review, collaborate, and revise the architecture.

TIP You must accept the simple fact that, initially, all architectures are flawed. Software systems are horribly complex, and we have a finite capacity to manage complexity. You will not get it right the first time. You can fix it in a high-level tool immediately after architecture and design reviews or you can fix it in code later. The cost, in terms of time, wasted effort, diminished credibility, and lost business opportunities, goes up dramatically if you wait and catch architectural flaws during code reviews, during testing, or after the code goes into production.

Sample Architecture for the Timecard System

Now that we have discussed the theory and process for creating a software architecture, let's create the architecture for the example Timecard system. We'll walk through each of the steps:

1. Set goals.
2. Group classes.
3. Show technologies.
4. Extract subsystems.
5. Evaluate the architecture against guidelines and goals.

Set Goals

The first step is to set goals for the system. In some cases, a goal is given weight by an explicit requirement. For example, reliability and scalability requirements are often plainly stated in the supplementary requirements. Developers usually determine maintainability and extensibility goals. This makes sense, because the developers know how the system will be developed and can estimate the stability of the requirements.

Extensibility.   While all systems change, the Timecard application seems fairly well focused. It gathers timecard data from the user. It does not analyze that data, bill clients, or calculate the pay for each employee. If I ever see such a well-defined system outside of a book, I may just dance a little jig. Caveats aside, we conclude that extensibility is not a huge priority.

Maintainability.   The Timecard system must be easy to comprehend and to maintain. The company has separate teams for maintenance and for new projects, so the system will be transitioned to a new group.

Reliability.   As part of the infrastructure of a company, the Timecard system must be reliable. However, it is not responsible for credit card processing or life support. Scheduled downtime is perfectly acceptable. Unanticipated downtime is not.

Scalability.   The Timecard system must scale to accommodate more data and more users, because the company plans to grow rapidly.

Explicitly defining these goals and their relative importance helps shape subsequent architectural and design decisions. In this case, it is useful to know that we can sacrifice some extensibility to increase scalability, if the opportunity arises.

Group and Evaluate Classes

The next step is to group our classes into candidate packages and evaluate their cohesion. To do this, we'll identify some groups of classes from the analysis model and examine their responsibilities. We want each group of classes to be closely related, so that the resulting package has a clear and well-defined purpose.

Grouping Classes

In Chapter 5, "Analysis Model for the Timecard Application," we were able to identify five distinct groups of classes:

- Entity classes
- User interface classes
- Control classes
- System interface classes
- Locator classes

We will consider these groups as candidate packages and evaluate them for strong cohesion. If the packages exhibit strong cohesion, we will use the class diagrams created in analysis to evaluate them for loose coupling. In some cases, this simplistic layering approach will fail because the collaborations between classes of different types are stronger than the collaborations between classes of the same type. However, it is by far the easiest approach, and it is often sufficient.

Let's consider each candidate package separately.

Entity classes.   This is our first group of classes, which were identified in Figure 5.2. Most of the classes describe a tightly related set of business concepts that are core to our understanding of a timecard. The only class that does not fit is ExtractRequest, which has nothing to do with timecards in general. We decide to exclude ExtractRequest from the package and look for a better fit.

We also need a name for this group of packages, as entity classes is simply too vague. Since all of the classes are part of our model of a timecard, the package name becomes TimecardDomain. Figure 13.9 shows the classes for the package.

User interface classes.   This is our second set of classes, shown in Figure 5.3. These classes all encapsulate the logic needed to present data and interact with the user for time entry. In Chapter 8, "HTML Production," we decided to use one user interface technology, servlets, for all user interface classes. Based on this decision, there is no reason to keep separate classes for the AdministrativeLoginUI and the RecordTimeAdministrativeUI.

The name for this package should reflect the application and the technology, so it becomes TimecardUI. Figure 13.10 shows the classes for the package.

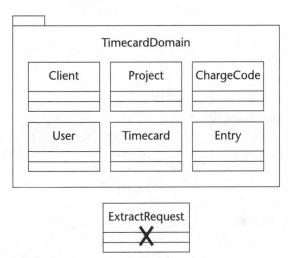

Figure 13.9   The TimecardDomain package.

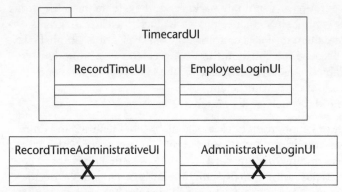

Figure 13.10   The TimecardUI package.

Control classes.   The third group of classes we identified in Chapter 5 was control classes, shown in Figure 5.4. These all encapsulate various parts of the timecard entry or timecard processing workflow. All of these workflows seem to use the same entity classes and are reasonably cohesive.

Since each of the classes contains a workflow for the timecard system, the name of the package becomes TimecardWorkflow. Figure 13.11 shows the classes for the package.

Billing system interface.   The BillingSystemInterface class was the fourth group of classes, shown in Figure 5.3. This also seems like a good home for the Extract-Request class, which was excluded from the TimecardDomain package. The package encapsulates the logic for generating the extracted data and also contains the extract request. This seems to be reasonably strong cohesion.

Since the class is a system interface to the billing system, the package becomes the BillingSystemInterface. Figure 13.12 shows the classes for the package.

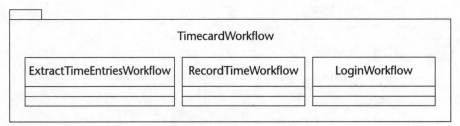

Figure 13.11   The TimecardWorkflow package.

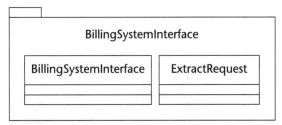

Figure 13.12   The BillingSystemInterface package.

Locator classes.   Because we are using EJB to implement our entity classes, we will not need separate locator classes. The functionality is provided by the Home interface for each entity bean.

As described, each package has a clear purpose and strong cohesion between its classes. Next, we need to see if the packages are tightly or loosely coupled.

Describe Coupling between Packages

In the next step, we use a package dependency diagram to evaluate the coupling between packages. Recall that package A depends on package B if there is a class in A that has a relationship with a class in B.

Fortunately, we collected a lot of information about the dependencies between classes during analysis. Figures 5.14 to 5.16 showed the dependencies between classes for each use case. We must merge these three diagrams into one class diagram, then summarize that diagram in a package dependency diagram.

Figures 13.13 to 13.15 show the diagrams exactly as they appeared in Chapter 5.

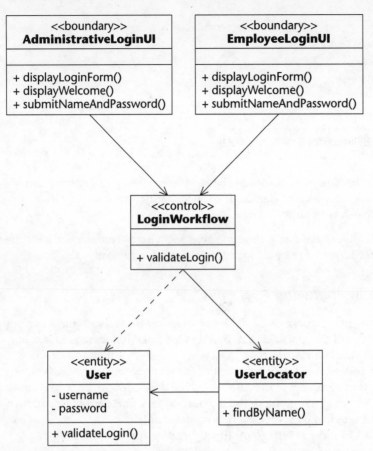

Figure 13.13   Participating classes for Login.

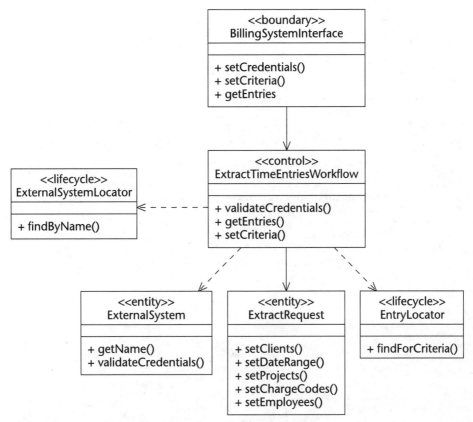

Figure 13.14   Participating classes for Extract Time Entries.

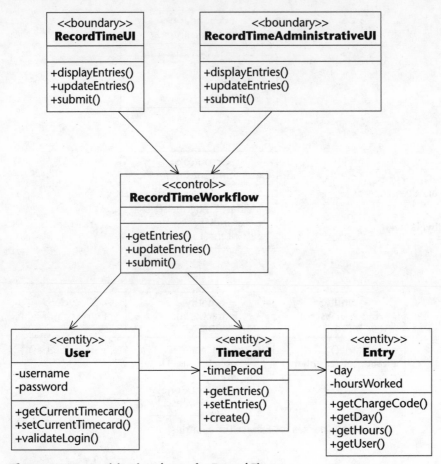

Figure 13.15   Participating classes for Record Time.

From these class diagrams, we can produce a single class diagram that shows all of the dependencies between all of the classes. This is a highly mechanical process, in which each relationship in each of the participating class diagrams is added to a single diagram. Figure 13.16 shows the classes and their dependencies.

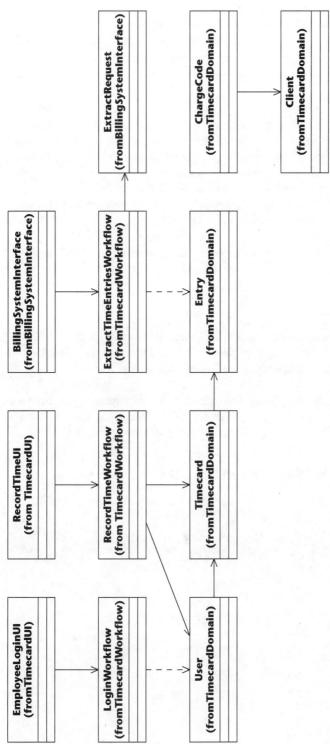

Figure 13.16 Classes and relationships.

TIP In real life, you need automated tool support to find dependencies. You just can't spend several days finding each relationship in a large model. Fortunately, this is exactly the sort of mindless drudgery that these tools were created to do.

The next step is to produce a package dependency diagram from the class relationships. Each relationship from a class to another class in a different package leads to a package dependency. For example, the relationship from RecordTimeUI (in the TimecardUI package) to the RecordTimeWorkflow (in the TimecardWorkflow package) leads to a dependency from the TimecardUI package to the TimecardWorkflow package. Again, this is a highly mechanical process, best left to a tool.

The package dependencies seem fairly reasonable. There are no circular dependencies. Also, the packages that we might expect to be reusable, such as TimecardDomain do not have any dependencies.

There is strong cohesion between the classes in each package, and loose coupling between the packages. We have a preliminary structure for our system.

Show Technologies

Fortunately, all of the technology selections for our Timecard system were made in Chapters 7 to 11. Recall that the entity and control classes will use Enterprise JavaBeans, while the user interface classes will become servlets. Also, the BillingSystemInterface class will use XML. All we have to do is add a package for each technology to the package dependency diagram. Use of a technology is shown by drawing a dependency line from the original package to the technology package that it uses. For example, the TimecardUI package depends on the Servlets package. Figure 13.17 shows the updated diagram.

Evaluate against Guidelines and Goals

Now that we have a reasonable draft architecture, we must evaluate it against our guidelines and our goals.

Recall that the goals for the Timecard system emphasized maintainability, reliability, and scalability. Extensibility was less significant, because the system has a very stable vision.

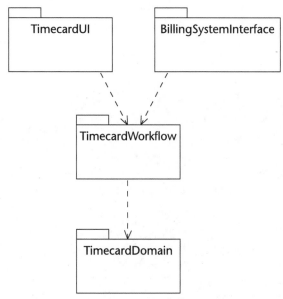

Figure 13.17   Package dependencies.

Maintainability and Extensibility

Each package has a very well-defined set of responsibilities, and the packages are well encapsulated. These factors are quite encouraging when planning for an easy-to-understand and easy-to-maintain system. Also, the system is based on reasonably standard technology, so the future developers will have a wealth of resources outside of the system documentation.

Reliability and Scalability

Most of the system's reliability and scalability concerns can be isolated to the Timecard-Domain and TimecardWorkflow packages, which will be implemented as Enterprise JavaBeans. Picking the right application server and allocating plenty of time for design and prototyping with the selected application server should address these concerns. These are tactical efforts within the development process; the architectural choice of EJB for these components is very sound.

The updated package dependency diagram in Figure 13.18 shows the TimecardUI package using the TimecardWorkflow package as well as the HTMLProduction package.

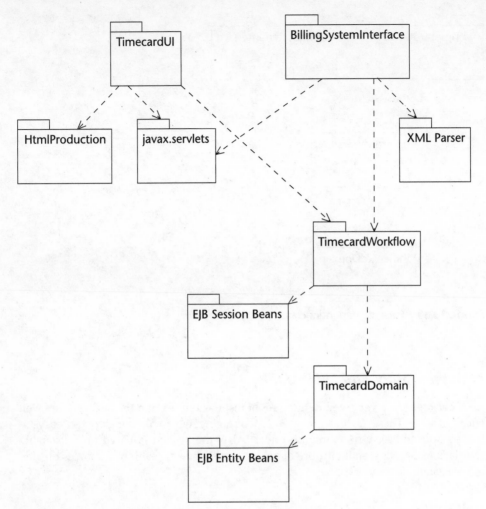

Figure 13.18   Package dependencies with technology.

The Next Step

This chapter identified architectural goals, determined the structure of the system, and defined the relationships between the packages. These elements provide context and a solid foundation as we fill in the details of the solution during design. As we make decisions during design, we can evaluate them against the package dependency relationships that we have established.

CHAPTER

14

Introduction to Design

Design builds on the understanding of the problem as developed during requirements gathering and analysis. It is an attempt to fully understand the solution as constrained by the structure developed during architecture. The goal of design is to make the next step, implementation, as simple and efficient as possible. It is your last chance to make changes quickly and efficiently in a tool and a notation method, rather than in code and other deliverables.

What Is Design?

An object-oriented design is a detailed description of the objects that work together to fulfill the system's requirements. Design describes the solution, in great detail. It specifies instance variables, method parameters, return types, and technology details.

Design uses the same diagrams as analysis, and for the same purposes. Sequence diagrams show interactions between objects. Class diagrams show the structure, behavior, and relationships that objects of particular types have in common. With the added level of detail, the diagrams in design are much larger and more intricate.

Are You Ready?

Good designs are built on a solid foundation, including a clear vision of the system, a solid use case model, a fairly complete analysis model, careful and appropriate technology selection, and a resilient architecture.

If you engage in design prematurely, you risk project failure in several ways. If the system vision or use case model is incomplete or inaccurate, then even a brilliant design may solve the wrong problem. Omissions and inaccuracies in the analysis model lead to an incomplete architecture and poor technology selections, which in turn lead to a flawed design. If the analysis model is incomplete or inconsistent, the design model will probably perpetuate these omissions or errors.

Each step in the development process feeds the next, so that a good design is not possible unless the preceding steps are complete and of high quality.

The Need for Design

Omitting or neglecting design is prohibitively expensive and insanely risky. Without a good design, developer productivity and morale suffer. Inconsistent code and incompatible modules are a certainty. Discovery of deficiencies in the architecture is delayed because there is no way to see the larger picture. Accurate scheduling is impossible, since the problems are not well understood before coding begins. Flawed ideas and incompatible implementations that are not caught until integration or system test are incredibly expensive to fix.

My grandfather, who built residential and commercial buildings back in the days when craftsmen still laid bricks and cut lumber to fit, used to say, "Measure twice, cut once." This captures the essence of design for me. You are about to write code, which tends to resist change. A little extra effort in design often prevents painful reworking later.

On the other hand, it is far cheaper and less time-consuming to make decisions in the design than in code. Also, a clear design model enables more developers to understand and review more of the system, which makes it possible for them to understand their own responsibilities and contribute to the overall success of the project through design discussions and reviews. Moreover, project managers and senior developers can estimate effort more accurately if their estimates are based on a clear and concrete design.

Productivity and Morale

Implementing high-quality systems is a complicated process. New technology, complex requirements, and extreme schedule pressure create challenging and oftentimes frustrating puzzles for developers. Complex code must be developed, tested, and integrated with other developers' equally complex code. Anyone who has tried it knows that design and implementation are by turns daunting, exhilarating, frustrating, and at times addictive.

Momentum is an important key to thriving in this environment. Small successes lead to more successes and help the entire team build confidence and credibility. On the other hand, failure and wasted efforts destroy momentum. In order to gain and maintain momentum, developers must have a realistic and complete architecture and design for the system. This facilitates realistic expectations, partitions the project into reasonable and achievable parts, and avoids incompatibilities between different developers' modules.

Design helps developers succeed, and incremental success motivates developers more than any other stimulus. Okay, high salaries help, but a chance to produce high-quality work in a sane effort is a major motivator for most of us.

A Malleable Medium

UML in a modern tool can be shaped and reshaped very easily. It is a very malleable medium. Code is not so easy to work with. Code is dispersed over hundreds of files, with a very low level of detail obscuring the larger patterns. A UML model in a modern design tool is infinitely easier to assimilate, change, and extend.

Remember, the step after design is implementation. Mistakes that are not caught before implementation are often very expensive to fix. Fixing incompatible interfaces can take weeks, with developers alternating between coding, testing, and blaming. A poor architecture that survives into implementation often leads to months of rework or even to project failure.

Even radical surgery on a fairly large UML model can be completed in a hundred person-hours. Relationships between classes can be changed with a click of a mouse. Responsibilities easily migrate from class to class. A class becomes an interface with several concrete alternate implementations. Classes and packages are split or merged with relative ease.

Moreover, a developer who knows UML can review the design for a large subsystem in a short day. Compare this to the weeks consumed developing a serious understanding of the code for a large subsystem. Consistent and thorough review of design artifacts is far more economically feasible than a similar review of code.

Scheduling and Delegation

A sound design makes estimation, scheduling, and delegation possible. Given a thorough design, a developer estimates the effort required for each class. The sum of these estimates is invariably more accurate than a rough guess based on the requirements. This gives the project manager something solid to work with. A solid design also allows developers to develop a few classes or a package and then integrate their code with the rest of the project. Delegation without a design is far less efficient, and generally requires a significant effort during integration.

Design Patterns

A *design pattern* is a well-defined, well-documented, and time-tested solution to a common problem in software design. Each pattern has a name, a problem description, a solution, a discussion of the consequences, a sample implementation, and a list of related patterns [Gamma 1995].

Problem description.   This describes the specific problem that the pattern is intended to solve. This allows developers to quickly search through a catalog of patterns and extract the one or two that seem appropriate for more careful consideration.

Solution.   This describes the objects and their interactions in a fairly abstract way, so that the pattern can be applied to a variety of designs. In most cases, a more concrete example is used to clarify and explain this generic solution.

Consequences.   Discuss the positive and negative impact of using the pattern to achieve common design goals. This helps developers to determine which candidate pattern is best for their situation, and may lead them to modify the pattern when applying it to their own design.

Sample implementation.   This shows how the solution can be implemented in at least one object-oriented language. This makes the solution more concrete for developers, and provides a solid proof of concept for cynical practitioners.

Related patterns section.   This shows how other patterns can support or extend the pattern in question. In many cases, patterns can be combined to form very resilient and elegant designs.

Benefits

Without getting too mushy, we must say that learning and using design patterns radically changed the way we design software, and solidified our grasp of object-oriented theory more than any other experience.

Design patterns help developers design better software in two very significant ways:

- They provide a common language for collaboration and documentation.
- They reinforce object-oriented theory.

Common Language

Learning design patterns takes patience and effort. Each pattern takes time to assimilate, and there are a lot of patterns. However, the effort only adds to the incredible rush you get when you realize that the developer across the table shares a common language and that you just compressed 3 hours worth of design discussion into 15 incredibly productive minutes. A group of developers who all understand design patterns can communicate in a common language that is both expressive and compressed.

Design patterns help developers communicate their designs quickly and efficiently. Any uncertainty can be resolved by consulting a widely accepted source. This works in design meetings, design documents, and code comments.

WARNING In the same way a well-understood pattern enables you to communicate effectively, a misunderstood design pattern will confuse people just as effectively. You must know the patterns that you use.

Reinforces OO Theory

Object-oriented theory and practices are not intuitive for most people. They require us to think abstractly, analytically, and creatively—all at the same time. In our experience, exposure to good object-oriented design is the best way to refine your own understanding and to improve your own habits. Design patterns apply object-oriented practices to a clearly defined problem. This makes them excellent case studies for object-oriented design. It is interesting to see the consequences of different decisions and to see how the same techniques can be used in radically different ways.

Use

Fortunately for us, many design patterns have been captured in books, articles, and online repositories. An entire community of developers donates an enormous amount of time, effort, and expertise as they revise and extend a collective catalog of design patterns. The best single source for design patterns is the seminal book *Design Patterns: Elements of Reusable Object-Oriented Software*, by Erich Gamma, Richard Helm, Ralph Johnson, and John Vlissides (Addison-Wesley-Longman, 1995). These authors are often referred to as the Gang of Four; thus, their book is often referred to as the GoF book.

Design patterns are best applied to a well-defined problem. Fortunately, analysis and architecture identify lots of problems for us to solve. In many cases, you can apply a series of design patterns to a package or small group of packages. Each pattern helps provide some functionality or helps you reach a design goal.

Planning for Design

To be successful, design must be a coherent and unified effort. Unfortunately, design is naturally a divisive process. Design breaks people into small teams or even isolates people by themselves. Each team or person is then immersed in the details of new technologies and the challenges of object-oriented design. Becoming absorbed in the design of his or her piece, to the exclusion of all other interests, is a natural part of the process, as the designer struggles to make sense out of complexity.

Once design begins, each design effort will go its own way for a while. Failure to accept this reality often leads to slow, painful progress, as developers are constantly expected to see the whole picture and ensure that their work fits with everyone else's work. In order to simulate a coherent and unified effort, we establish clear goals for the entire design before giving developers the freedom to work on their separate efforts. The following steps summarize this process:

1. Establish goals for the entire design.

2. Establish design guidelines.

3. Find independent design efforts.

Each of these steps is described in detail in the subsections that follow.

Establish Goals for the Entire Design

Every system contains a million decisions. Many of these decisions are more compromise than brilliant discovery of perfect truth. This is as true for design as it is for requirements and architecture. Establishing design goals before making decisions helps us maintain the consistency of the system, and makes each decision easier.

One person's well-focused system is another person's overly restricted disappointment. An architecture or technology selection may trade performance for functionality and extensibility. Or it may partition subsystems to accommodate the development team's available skill set or to maximize the reuse potential of a subsystem. Design decisions often balance clarity, performance, reliability, extensibility, and reuse potential. We will refer back to these common goals as we discuss various techniques for creating a high-quality software design.

Clarity

Clarity and understandability is a key goal for every design. Developers cannot review or implement something that they cannot understand. Faced with an unclear design, most developers either attempt to follow the design and develop confusing code or simply ignore the design entirely. Clear and unambiguous designs often lead to code that is easy to maintain and to extend.

Clarity is increased by keeping strong cohesion for methods in classes and for classes in packages. Loose coupling makes the interfaces between packages tight and easy to understand. Encapsulation improves readability by limiting what you need to know to use a class.

Performance and Reliability

Many systems have demanding performance and reliability requirements. In most cases, performance and reliability goals can be reached by picking the right technology, then designing to the technology's strengths. Developers must understand how the technology exchanges data between different tiers and how the technology ensures data integrity. Establishing performance and reliability goals early in the design process encourages developers to consider these issues, rather than procrastinating and hoping for the best.

Extensibility

Extensibility is almost always a priority, even if the customer does not realize it. As the needs of the organization change, the system must be able to accommodate the new reality.

As a rule, loose coupling and strong cohesion make it more likely that the classes that need to change will reside in the same package and that the package will be loosely coupled with the rest of the system. This limits the ripple effect of each change.

If you can identify areas that are very likely to change, you may be able to design the variability into the system, by encapsulating the variability inside of a swappable subsystem or by designing the system to use configuration data. Of course, this requires a very clear vision of the future of the system; and if you are wrong, you have wasted time and increased the complexity of the system.

Reuse Potential

The reuse of classes, both within a project and between projects, is a tremendous selling point for object-oriented technology. Reusable classes must have a generically useful abstraction and well-encapsulated data. When aiming for reuse, keep classes small and well focused. Also, in order to reduce the burden on the person who wants to adopt or adapt your class or package, keep the dependencies to a minimum and make the abstraction easy to use and understand.

TIP Despite the hype, reuse never comes for free. You must design with reuse in mind, or be willing to clean up an existing design to gain reusability.

Establish Design Guidelines

It is important to have projectwide guidelines during design. This unifies the efforts of the different designers or teams of designers. Each design effort should use the same diagrams, describe the solution at the same level of detail, and follow the same naming conventions. The following guidelines form a reasonable starting point for most projects.

Diagrams for Each Use Case

Use several sequence diagrams to describe each use case, one for each significant flow of events. Also, a single class diagram should be used to capture the relationships between all of the classes that participate in the different sequence diagrams. In some cases, state diagrams can be used to show state-dependent behavior for a particular class.

Level of Detail

The level of detail for design is far lower than for analysis. Each method must be fully specified, complete with arguments and return types.

Also, any object that is used in a sequence diagram must be located or created, either in the same sequence diagram or in a supporting sequence. In analysis, sequences are often supported by a series of minor miracles, with objects simply appearing when needed. In design, objects are created, kept for future use, located, and finally destroyed.

Naming Conventions

Name each method with a well-selected verb or a combination of a verb and a noun; paint and open are good examples from the Java class libraries. The name of the method should match the return type, if any. For instance, a method that returns a reference to a Timecard object might be called getTimecard or getCurrentTimecard.

Each class should be named with a noun, a combination of nouns, or a combination of adjectives and nouns. String, MenuItem, and OutputStream are good examples from the Java class libraries.

The purpose of each class and each method must be clear and unambiguous to other developers. This usually precludes the use of filler class names, such as manager. Whenever possible, clearly defined terms from design patterns, such as Factory or Singleton, should be used as part of applicable class names.

Cohesion

Each set of methods within a class must form a cohesive whole. This requires them to have a common goal or responsibility. Similarly, the classes inside of each package must have a unifying purpose or nature. Classes and methods must not be grouped, arbitrarily or simply for convenience.

Find Independent Design Efforts

In order to divide up the design effort, you must identify packages or groups of packages that are loosely coupled with the rest of the system. This allows developers from different efforts to agree on the interfaces before starting independent design activities.

Packages that are tightly coupled must be designed together. Packages that are loosely coupled and well encapsulated are good candidates for independent development. Subsystems are perfect for independent development. By their very definition, they are independent and well encapsulated.

Each independent design effort must fit the technical abilities of a single team. This may require an otherwise coherent design effort to be divided into smaller efforts that more closely match the skill sets of existing teams. Otherwise, this may require reorganization and the training of team members to improve their skill sets.

Designing Packages or Subsystems

The design for a package or subsystem builds on the analysis model, including class diagrams and sequence diagrams. While each package is designed and implemented as a separate deliverable, all of the packages cooperate to realize the use cases. As part of the initial design of the package, developers must identify the use cases that include the package. This process highlights the interactions between the package and the other packages that are involved in the use case. At this point, the developers must cooperate with the developers of the other involved packages to finalize the interfaces between the packages.

A package or subsystem design is also constrained by the architecture and the overall goals for the system. Specifically, the architecture determines the permissible relationships between the system's packages. Each time a class in the package uses a class outside of the package, it establishes a dependency between these packages. These new relationships must be evaluated for compliance with the architecture.

Each package or subsystem may have its own goals. For instance, a package of user interface classes may need to be highly flexible and extensible, while a package of entity classes may need to be well encapsulated and meet demanding performance goals.

The following steps must be followed for each design effort:

1. **Identify goals and priorities.** While goals are established for the entire design, not every design effort can influence each goal. Each design effort must identify the goals and priorities that it can and cannot affect. This is usually clear from the technology involved and from the purpose of the package or subsystem. For instance, the design effort for the TimecardDomain and TimecardWorkflow packages will undoubtedly have a most noticeable effect on performance, because it controls persistence and the flow of data. On the other hand, the design efforts for the HtmlProduction framework and the TimecardUI package will have a greater effect on extensibility, since user interfaces are notoriously vulnerable to requirements changes.

2. **Review prior steps.** Previous steps created an analysis model, selected technologies, and established structural constraints for the design of the Timecard system. Those involved in each design effort must review, then follow these inputs and constraints. The analysis model describes the problem from the developer's perspective. Thus, it is the best resource when designing packages and subsystems. In many cases, the responsibilities of a class or package can be directly extrapolated from the responsibilities of analysis classes.

3. **Design to goals.** In some cases, the high-level design is almost completely determined by the technology. For instance, Enterprise JavaBeans development completely determines much of your design. Decisions must be made for each use case to meet goals, but there are no sweeping design decisions left to the developer. In other cases, it is up to the developers to design the package or subsystem to meet the goals. Design patterns may serve as a valuable resource in this highly creative and iterative process.

4. **Apply the design to use cases.** Applying the high-level design to the use cases validates and invariably improves the design. In this process, the high-level design developed in the previous step is applied to each use case in turn, until the design is fully fleshed out and all the applicable use cases are met or the design is proven intractable.

Design Efforts for the Timecard Application

The Timecard application seems to naturally break into four design efforts:

- TimecardDomain and TimecardWorkflow packages
- HtmlProduction framework
- TimecardUI package
- BillingSystemInterface subsystem

The TimecardDomain and TimecardWorkflow packages should be designed together, because they are so closely related. They depend on the same technologies, and are very tightly coupled.

The HtmlProduction framework should be designed as a separate package from the TimecardUI. It is the only package that produces the actual HTML for the system. The TimecardUI package clearly uses it and should drive its development, but the HtmlProduction framework should be able to evolve independently. One approach is to build a minimum set of functionality for the HtmlProduction framework before starting the design and implementation of the TimecardUI package. With this minimum functionality established, the HtmlProduction can grow in sophistication while the TimecardUI is designed and implemented.

The BillingSystemInterface subsystem is a naturally independent design activity. Since the rest of the system does not depend on it, it can be developed concurrently or deferred until development resources are available.

The Next Step

We have spent the last 14 chapters building up to this point, improving our understanding of the problem, selecting technology, and structuring the solution. Now, it is time to use UML to build a design model for the Timecard application.

Each of the following chapters shows how UML can be used to design a package or subsystem. The analysis model is used to determine each package's functionality and interfaces with other packages. Well-defined goals are met by applying object-oriented principles and design patterns. Finally, the design is evaluated for compliance with the architecture and the overall goals of the system.

In Chapters 15 through 17, the design is used as a basis for actual Java code. This is intended to reinforce the basic principles and to show how modeling in UML simplifies the coding process.

CHAPTER 15

Design for the TimecardDomain and TimecardWorkflow

The design for the TimecardDomain and TimecardWorkflow packages builds heavily on the analysis model, technology selection, and architecture we developed in Chapter 5, "Analysis Model for the Timecard Application," Chapter 12, "Evaluating Candidate Technologies for Control and Entity Classes," and Chapter 13, "Software Architecture." The analysis model in Chapter 5 showed how the boundary, control, and entity classes collaborate to fulfill the system's requirements. Chapter 12 described Enterprise JavaBeans and some of the decisions that must be made when developing with EJBs. Chapter 13 showed how to constrain the relationships between packages.

This chapter builds a sample design and implementation for the TimecardDomain and TimecardWorkflow packages. It follows the steps described in Chapter 14, "Introduction to Design":

1. Identify goals and priorities for the effort.

2. Review prior steps.

3. Design to goals.

4. Apply design to use cases.

The following sections apply each step to the TimecardDomain and TimecardWorkflow packages.

Establish Goals for the Effort

Establishing goals upfront makes it easier to make consistent decisions during design. This is important, because design is all about making an endless series of decisions, generally under fairly strong schedule pressure.

The most important goals for the TimecardDomain and TimecardWorkflow packages are performance, reliability, and reuse potential. Extensibility is less of a priority, since the system is very well understood and has a narrow focus.

Performance and Reliability

Performance and reliability are important goals for the entire Timecard system. After all, a lot of people depend on a corporate Timecard system, and they do not have time to wait.

The classes in the TimecardDomain package contribute greatly to the performance and reliability of the entire system. The classes that reside in the TimecardDomain package are responsible for the availability and integrity of the timecard data itself. Design decisions for the TimecardDomain package dramatically affect the time required for data access and data updates. For instance, decisions on how the data is represented in the database and how the data maps to entity beans greatly impact the speed and efficiency of the EJB container as it services requests for data.

The classes of the TimecardWorkflow package have a different but equally significant impact on performance and reliability. The TimecardWorkflow classes contain the methods that client objects use to get access to the data and services provided by the TimecardDomain objects. The Workflow object may require the client object to make several requests, one large request, or some variation in between. Remember that the Client and TimecardWorkflow classes are invariably in separate virtual machines and are often on separate hosts. This makes the efficiency of the data flow very important, since even a fast network is far slower than the host's internal data bus, and the data must be serialized and deserialized at every turn.

Reuse

Reuse is another important goal for the TimecardDomain and TimecardWorkflow packages. To reach this goal, each entity bean in the TimecardDomain package should be useful in a wide variety of workflows within the Timecard application, and most of the session beans in the TimecardWorkflow package should be able to support new user interface classes as new views of the system evolve.

Extensibility

While extensibility is less of a priority, experience indicates that there are no static systems. Extensibility is improved by encapsulating potential variability and by keeping the classes small and narrowly focused.

Now that we have established some goals, we must review the prior decisions that affect the design effort.

Review Prior Steps

Several prior steps drive design. The analysis model describes exactly what the system will do, from a developer's perspective. The architecture describes the structural and technology decisions that constrain the design. In this section, we review the analysis model and the architectural decisions.

Review of the Analysis Model

Our first task requires us to work through each analysis diagram, first to refresh our understanding of the sequence of interactions between the objects and then to identify any important characteristics. We'll consider the Login, Record Time, and Extract Time Entries use cases.

The Login Use Case

The Login use case contains several flows. First, there is the normal flow in which everything proceeds according to plan. Next, there are alternate flows for invalid passwords and unknown users.

Normal Flow for Login (Analysis)

The actor asks the boundary EmployeeLoginUI object to display the login form, as shown in Figure 15.1. The actor then fills in username and password and submits them to the system. The EmployeeLoginUI object asks the control LoginWorkflow object to validate the login. In order to satisfy this request, the LoginWorkflow object asks the UserLocator object to find the User object that corresponds to the name. Once the LoginWorkflow object gets the correct User object, it asks it to validate the password. Once the LoginWorkflow object receives a response, it passes it back to the EmployeeLoginUI object. When the EmployeeLoginUI object receives the valid response, it displays a welcome message and the flow is complete.

The only object in this sequence that is outside of our current design effort is EmployeeLoginUI. There is only one request from the EmployeeLoginUI object to the LoginWorkflow object, validateLogin. This request includes very simple data and receives a simple yes/no response.

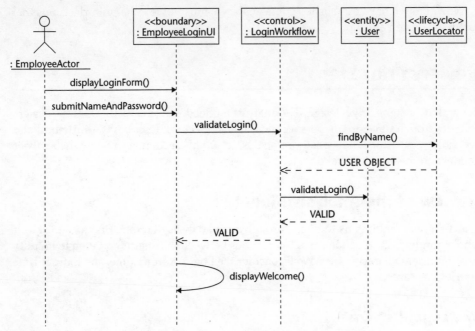

Figure 15.1   Sequence diagram for the normal flow for Login (analysis).

Alternate Flow for Invalid Password (Analysis)

The sequence for an invalid password proceeds exactly as in the normal flow, until the User object responds with INVALID to the validateLogin method. This response is propagated up to the EmployeeLoginUI, which must display an invalid password message to the actor. Figure 15.2 shows this sequence.

This sequence is incredibly similar to the normal flow. Within the TimecardDomain and TimecardWorkflow packages, there is no difference in what is done, only in the response values, so we will not need to develop a separate design sequence diagram for this flow of events.

Alternate Flow for Unknown User (Analysis)

The sequence for an unknown user proceeds exactly as in the normal flow, until the UserLocator responds with a NULL when asked to locate the User object by name. Obviously, the LoginWorkflow cannot ask an unknown User object to validate the password, so it returns INVALID to the EmployeeLoginUI object. As in the sequence for the invalid password, the EmployeeLoginUI calls its own displayErrorMessage method. Figure 15.3 shows this sequence.

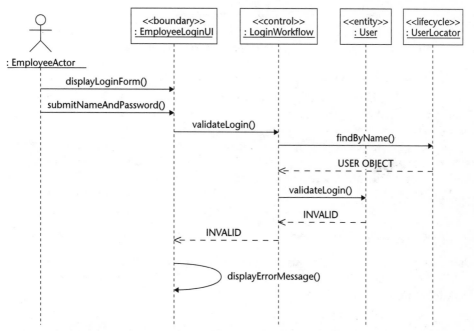

Figure 15.2 Sequence diagram for invalid password (analysis).

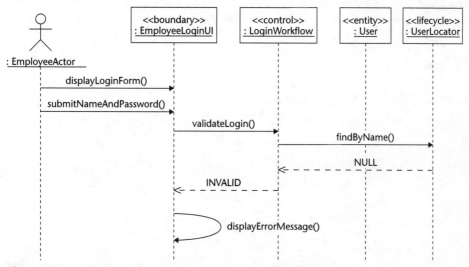

Figure 15.3 Sequence diagram for unknown user (analysis).

Again, the sequence is incredibly similar to the normal flow. However, it does high-light the reaction of the LoginWorkflow object when the User object cannot be located. It is not an error or exception case, but rather a reasonable outcome.

Participating Classes (Analysis)

The user interface objects use LoginWorkflow objects to validate the user's login data. The resulting relationship needs to be an association, so that the user interface objects can reuse the same LoginWorkflow object for login retries.

The LoginWorkflow object finds and uses a User object, but does not need to remember it for future use. So, the resulting relationship is a dependency. The Login-Workflow object uses a UserLocator object, and does keep it for future use, so the resulting relationship is an association. These relationships are shown in Figure 15.4.

The Record Time Use Case

The Record Time use case contains two flows of events. First, there is the normal flow in which everything proceeds according to plan. Next, there is an alternate flow for Submit Timecard.

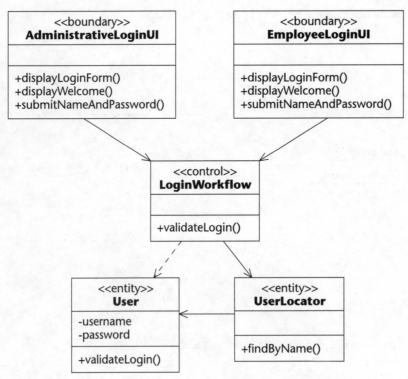

Figure 15.4 Participating classes for the Login use case (analysis).

Normal Flow (Analysis)

The normal flow for the Record Time use case begins when the actor requests the current entries. The RecordTimeUI object calls the RecordTimeWorkflow object's getEntries method, which magically has a reference to the correct User object. Given the User object, the RecordTimeWorkflow object asks it for its current Timecard object. The RecordTime-Workflow object can then ask the Timecard object for its entries and return them to the RecordTimeUI. After the Employee actor updates the time entries, the RecordTimeUI object uses the updateEntries method on the RecordTimeWorkflow to propagate the changes to the system. The RecordTimeWorkflow object calls the setEntries method on the previously stored reference to the Timecard object. These interactions are shown in Figure 15.5.

Submit Timecard (Analysis)

The submit timecard flow of events describes how the actor marks his or her current timecard as submitted and gets a new current timecard. Once the actor decides to submit his or her current timecard, the RecordTimeUI object calls the submit method on its RecordTimeWorkflow object, which knows the User and the Timecard objects. The RecordTimeWorkflow creates a new Timecard object and sets it as the current Timecard object for the user. The old Timecard object still exists, but it is not a current Timecard, so it cannot be edited by the user. These interactions are shown in Figure 15.6.

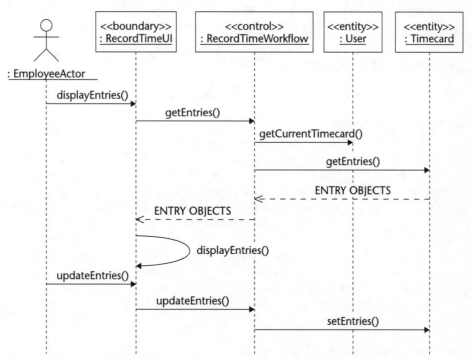

Figure 15.5 Sequence diagram for the normal flow of Record Time (analysis).

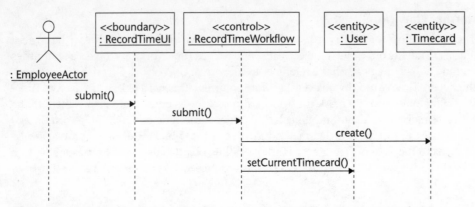

Figure 15.6 Sequence diagram for the submit Timecard flow of events (analysis).

Participating Classes (Analysis)

Each method in the sequence diagrams requires some sort of relationship between the object calling the method and the object that contains the method. Each RecordTimeUI object is associated with an undetermined number of RecordTimeWorkflow objects. The undetermined multiplicity indicates that during analysis we did not know whether RecordTimeUI objects would have dedicated RecordTimeWorkflow objects or would share them. Each RecordTimeWorkflow object is associated with the User and Timecard objects. These relationships are shown in Figure 15.7.

The Extract Time Entries Use Case

The Extract Time Entries use case contains a single flow of events, the normal flow.

Normal Flow (Analysis)

The normal flow for the Extract Time Entries use case begins when the external billing system sends a request for time entry information of users to BillingSystemInterface based on some criteria. The criteria include the billing period as the date range for which the time entries have to be pulled from the database. The BillingSystemInterface object invokes the extractForCriteria method on the ExtractTimeEntriesWorkflow object. The ExtractTimeEntriesWorkflow object finds the client from ClientLocator and asks the UserLocator a list of employees. The ExtractTimeEntriesWorkflow object then uses the EntryLocator's findForCriteria method to get a list of time entries that match the criteria. The ExtractTimeEntriesWorkflow object extracts the relevant information from each entry object and sends the information back to the billing system. Because the billing system is outside the boundary of the Timecard application, it is treated as an Actor. This sequence is shown in Figure 15.8.

Participating Classes (Analysis)

Each method call in the sequence diagram requires a dependency or association in the participating classes diagram. A fairly mechanical process yields the relationships, as shown in Figure 15.9.

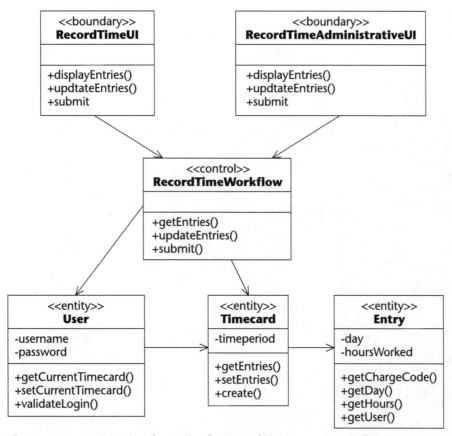

Figure 15.7 Participating classes for the Record Time use case (analysis).

Review Architectural Constraints

For the Timecard application example, the server-side entity and control classes are implemented in Enterprise JavaBeans. The TimecardWorkflow package, which contains the control classes, depends on EJB session beans. The TimecardDomain package, which contains the entity classes, depends on EJB entity beans.

The architecture also precludes classes in the TimecardUI package from having direct relationships with classes in the TimeCardDomain package. Instead, they must delegate any requests for information or services to a control class in the TimeCardWorkflow. This is shown in the lack of a dependency from the TimecardUI directly to the TimeCardDomain. Figure 15.10 shows these dependency relationships in a package diagram.

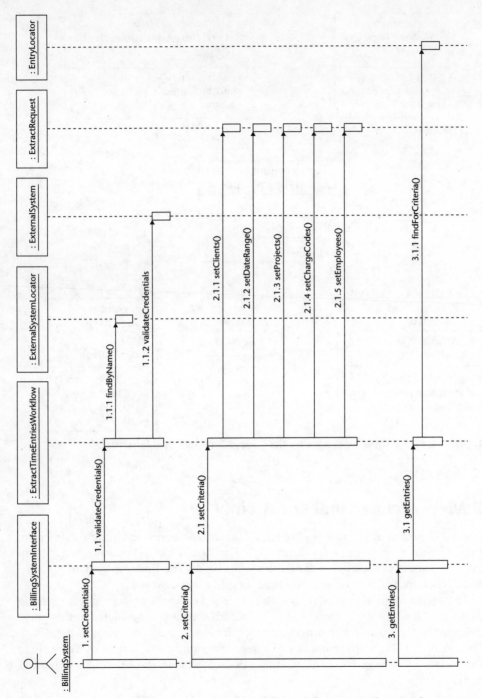

Figure 15.8 Sequence diagram for the normal flow of the Extract Time Entries use case (analysis).

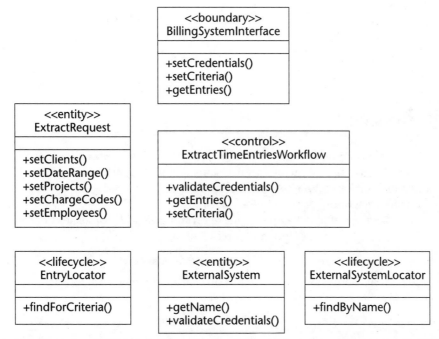

Figure 15.9 Participating classes for the Extract Time Entries use case (analysis).

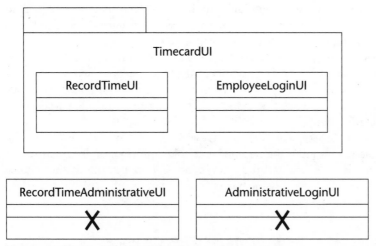

Figure 15.10 Architectural decisions and constraints.

WARNING If you are not familiar with Enterprise JavaBeans, review the technology description for EJB in Chapter 12, "Evaluating Candidate Technologies for Control and Entity Classes."

Design for Goals

Enterprise JavaBeans constrain the developer to a fairly small number of decisions. In this section, we discuss some of the design decisions that are important in EJB development. In the next major section, "Apply Design for Each Use Case," we will make these decisions for each bean involved in the use case.

Every technology forces the developer to make certain design decisions in order to meet his or her goals. EJB is no exception. It forces you to:

1. Choose between each session bean's being stateful or stateless.

2. Choose between container-managed or bean-managed persistence for each entity bean.

3. Choose between a Local or Remote interface for each bean.

Stateless or Stateful Session Beans

Recall from Chapter 11, "Evaluating Web Service Technologies for the System Interface," that stateless session beans do not hold any conversational state from request to request. This makes them very efficient, but decreases their usefulness as session beans that must moderate a series of requests from the same client object. Stateful session beans are far more appropriate when the session bean must maintain a conversational state with the client object, since it can remember information from previous requests that were made by the client object. This allows it to accumulate information for a consolidated transaction, such as a shopping cart, or remember previous results so that it does not need to rebuild them.

For each session bean, the sequence diagrams reveal the pattern of requests from the client object to the session bean. If the session bean holds information from request to request, it is best modeled as a stateful session bean. Otherwise, the default choice should be stateless, since stateless session beans are much more efficient and place less of a burden on the bean container.

Container-Managed or Bean-Managed Persistence

Each entity bean has data that must be persisted to the database. Container-managed persistence allows the developer to isolate the persistence information in the deployment descriptor. This allows the developer or deployer to specify the object-to-relational mapping and the transaction boundaries in a very concise form, without modifying any code. This is the default choice.

Bean-managed persistence forces you to write database access and transaction management code directly in the entity beans. However, it also provides unlimited flexibility. The most common reason to use bean-managed persistence is to achieve a tricky object-to-relational mapping that is not supported by the deployment tool. This is less preferable, but still fairly common.

Local or Remote Interface for EJBs

As mentioned in Chapter 11, "Evaluating Web Service Technologies for the System Interface," EJB 2.0 allows EJBs to make its business interface as well as its home interface either locally or remotely accessible. The recommended practice is to implement session beans as a façade to the underlying entity beans. Exposing entity beans directly to the remote clients may result in a performance problem. This is because the entity beans usually provide granular methods, and hence the client may need to use multiple calls to perform a single business operation. Alternatively, the client can delegate the request to session beans that can manipulate the local entity beans on behalf of the client. These session beans are known as a session façade. In our application, we will follow this design strategy and implement session beans using the EJB remote interface (EJBObject). Since the entity beans are not accessed by the remote clients directly, we can implement our entity beans using the EJB local interface (EJBLocalObject). This will further improve the performance because marshaling/demarshaling does not take place with local beans.

Application Exception

Application exceptions are a great way to communicate problems associated with performing business operations back to the clients. The process of identifying the exceptions starts with a careful review of the sequence diagrams of the use cases. The identified exceptions are declared with the methods in the EJB interface. The custom exception classes help distinguish between a problem in the application and a problem in other parts of the system. We define the following exception classes to communicate application-level error conditions:

DataNotFoundException.   This is thrown when any required data is not found in the database.

InvalidDataException.   This is thrown when the client provides incorrect data/omits required data.

DataUpdateException.   This is thrown when modifying data in the database fails.

DataCreateException.   This is thrown when data insertion into the database fails.

Apply Design for Each Use Case

Remember, a design model is one step away from implementation. So, we need to carefully build a model that applies all of these decisions to all of the use cases in the requirements model. This model will provide a solid foundation for a clean and consistent implementation. As in analysis, the domain model includes sequence diagrams and a view of the participating classes for each use case. Unlike analysis, the design model is extremely detailed and thorough. Each return type and parameter must be shown. Each object must be created or retrieved before it is used. Significant mysteries and ambiguity in the design model lead to problems and poor solutions during implementation.

In designing an EJB-based solution for each use case, we follow these steps:

1. Consider each of the key design decisions for EJB development, as well as the goals for the package.

2. Build sequence diagrams for the normal and alternate flow of events as identified in the use case model.

3. Build a class diagram that shows all of the classes that participate in the use case.

We'll follow these steps for the Login, Record Time, and Extract Time Entries use cases in the Timecard application.

Design for the Login Use Case

We are finally ready to start our design based on the first use case, Login. Let's walk through each of the steps.

Key Design Decisions for Login

We need to make two key design decisions for the Login use case.

- Is the LoginWorkflow object a stateless session bean or a stateful session bean?
- Is there any indication that bean-managed persistence is required for the User entity bean?

There is no indication in the sequence diagrams that the LoginWorkflow object needs any data from or about previous attempts. A quick glance at the system's requirements reveals that there is no limit on the number of login attempts, so there is no need for a counter of login attempts. For performance reasons, we use stateless session beans by default. There is no reason not to follow that rule of thumb in this case.

The data for each User entity bean consists of a username and a password. Both fields are strings. There is no indication for bean-managed persistence, since the data is incredibly simple and the database schema is controlled by the development team.

Create Sequence Diagrams and Participating Classes for the Login Use Case

Now that we have refreshed our memory of the analysis model and made some design decisions based on the architecture and on the analysis model, it is time to do the actual design for the Login use case. We will create sequence diagrams for the normal flow and for the alternate flow for an unknown user. Working from the analysis sequence diagram, we can simply apply the technology selections to each object. The messages are basically the same, just with more details.

Normal Flow

In the first part of the sequence diagram, shown in Figure 15.11, the login servlet asks the LoginWorkflow session bean to validate the user. The LoginWorkflow session bean calls the findByUserName method on the UserHome, which returns a local reference to the appropriate User entity bean. The LoginWorkflow calls the isPasswordValid method on the User entity bean and returns the result.

Notice that this diagram does not attempt to show any behavior within the user interface object. For this design effort, we are mostly concerned with the interactions with the objects from the LoginWorkflow and TimeCardDomain packages.

Our earlier decision to make the LoginWorkflow a stateless session bean is validated by this sequence. There is no need for the LoginWorkflow to keep any information between method calls. It receives both the username and the password each time, and it uses the UserHome to find the right User entity bean each time.

NOTE The Java Naming and Directory Interface (JNDI) lookups of the LoginWorkflow and the UserHome are not shown. This seems appropriate, since they are so incredibly repetitious and common.

Alternate Flow for Unknown User

Similar to the normal flow, the login servlet in the alternate flow asks the LoginWorkflow session bean to validate the user. The LoginWorkflow session bean calls the findByUsername method on the UserHome. Since the User object does not exist in the system, the UserHome returns null. The LoginWorkflow session bean throws DataNotFoundException, because the user's login information is clearly not valid. Figure 15.12 shows this sequence.

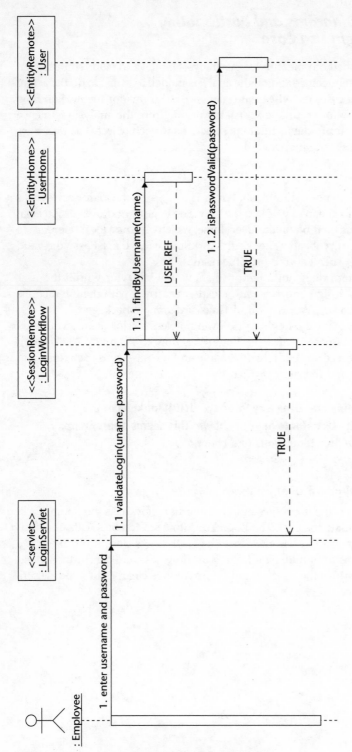

Figure 15.11   Sequence diagram for normal flow.

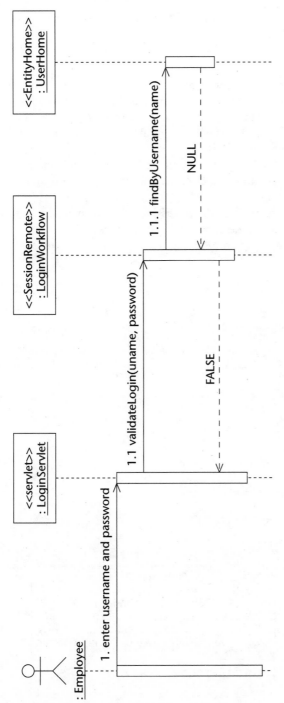

Figure 15.12   Sequence diagram for unknown user.

This sequence is very similar to the normal flow. Other than some internal logic within the LoginWorkflow session bean, there is no new information here.

Participating Classes

The validateLogin message from the LoginServlet to the LoginWorkflow requires a dependency relationship between the LoginServlet class and the LoginWorkflow class. The other messages in the sequence diagram lead to the dependency relationships shown in Figure 15.13. Notice that none of the objects retains any information between messages, so all of the relationships are dependencies.

It is always wise to verify that none of the relationships between the classes violates the structural decisions that were made during architecture. In this case, you can see that the dependencies exactly match the package dependencies specified in architecture. The user interface class depends on the Workflow class, which in turn depends on the user entity bean class, which resides in the TimeCardDomain package.

Now that we have a fairly complete design for the Login use case, the next step is to design the Record Time use case.

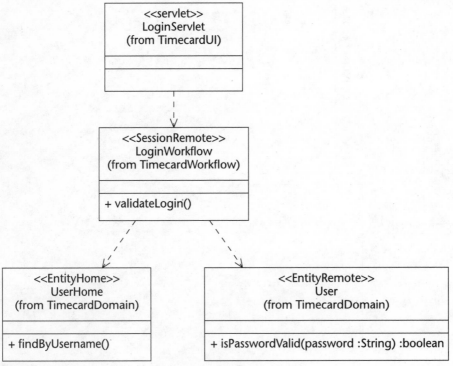

Figure 15.13   Participating classes for the Login use case.

Design for the Record Time Use Case

To design the Record Time use case, we follow the same steps as those used for the Login use case design. First we consider the key design decisions, then create sequence diagrams and a class diagram.

Key Design Decisions for Record Time

We need to make three key design decisions for the Record Time use case:

- Is the RecordTimeWorkflow object a stateless session bean or a stateful session bean?

- How should data be returned from the session beans to the UI: as remote references or simple data?

- How should the persistent data be stored and mapped to entity beans?

Stateless or Stateful Session Bean?

In the analysis model, the RecordTimeWorkflow object appears to hold a reference to the Timecard object. If we carry this approach over to design, the RecordTimeWorkflow session bean must keep a reference to the Timecard entity bean, which means that it must be a stateful session bean.

Holding a reference to the User entity bean that has a reference to the user's current Timecard entity bean would save the RecordTimeWorkflow from having to find the right User entity bean each time it needs to get the current Timecard bean. It almost certainly makes sense to avoid the extra database access and make RecordTimeWorkflow a stateful session bean.

Remote References or Simple Data?

RecordTimeWorkflow objects allow RecordTimeUI objects to obtain a lot of information about the current Timecard object. There are two fundamental ways that this goal can be accomplished. First, the RecordTimeWorkflow object can return remote references to any entity beans that the RecordTimeUI needs; alternatively, the RecordTimeWorkflow can return simple data.

Returning remote references allows the receiving object a lot of flexibility, because it can call any available method on the remote reference. For timecard data, this sort of flexibility seems excessive. The RecordTimeUI has very narrow needs. Also, allowing the RecordTimeUI object to have direct access to an entity bean violates the structural constraints established during architecture, because it introduces a direct dependency between the TimecardUI package and the TimecardDomain package. So, in our application, we will return simple data that contains only the data that is required by the client. These types of simple data objects are also know as data transfer objects (DTOs) [EJB Design Patterns, Marinescu, 2002].

TIP In EJB development, it is usually better to have the session beans return simple data or a collection of simple data. The client already has a remote reference to the session bean, and every remote reference introduces overhead on the client and, more importantly, on the server.

Create Sequence Diagrams and Participating Classes for Record Time Use Case

Now that we have refreshed our memory of the analysis model, and made some design decisions based on the architecture and on the analysis model, it is time to do the actual design for the Record Time use case. We will create sequence diagrams for the normal flow and the Submit Timecard alternate flow.

Normal Flow

The normal flow begins when the actor requests the current entries. The RecordTime-Servlet asks the RecordTimeWorkflow's home interface for a remote reference to a RecordTimeWorkflow session bean. The RecordTimeServlet can then ask the Record-TimeWorkflow session bean for the current timecard. The RecordTimeWorkflow returns the timecard information as a data transfer object instead of returning a reference to the Timecard entity bean. This design complies with the architectural decision of package dependencies that we established earlier. Notice that the first request for information requires the RecordTimeWorkflow to find the User object and stores the local reference to this User entity bean. This requires the RecordTimeWorkflow to be implemented as a stateful session bean. Subsequent requests use the reference to the User entity bean as held by RecordTimeWorkflow.

The interaction between the RecordTimeWorkflow session bean and the Timecard entity bean is quite straightforward. Each time the RecordTimeWorkflow receives a request for information, it passes the request on to the Timecard entity bean, and returns the result. Each time the RecordTimeWorkflow receives an update command, it passes it along to the Timecard entity bean. Figure 15.14 shows this sequence.

Submit Timecard

The Submit Timecard flow begins when the actor sends the submit command to the servlet. The RecordTimeServlet asks the RecordTimeWorkflow session bean to submit the timecard. No information is passed as part of this request. The RecordTimeWork-flow session bean uses a previously established reference to the User object to ask it to submit the current timecard. The User object uses the Timecard entity bean's home interface to create a new Timecard. It keeps this as the new current timecard. Figure 15.15 shows this sequence.

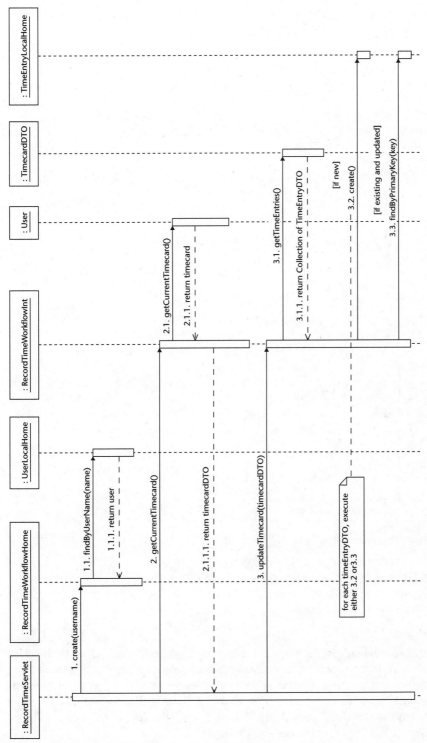

Figure 15.14 Sequence diagram for normal flow.

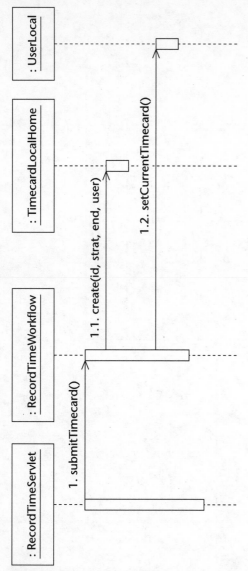

Figure 15.15   Sequence diagram for submit timecard flow.

Participating Classes

As always, each message in the sequence diagram requires a relationship in the class diagram. Notice that the structural constraints established in architecture have been met, as the classes in the TimecardUI package depend on classes in the Timecard-Workflow package, which depend on classes in the TimeCardDomain package. These exactly match the structural constraints that were introduced in architecture. Figure 15.16 shows the participating classes and their relationships.

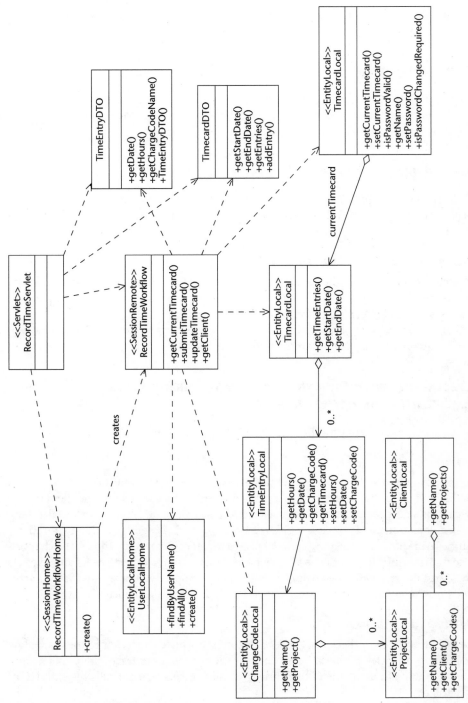

Figure 15.16   Participating classes for the Record Time use case.

Now that we have a fairly complete design for the Record Time use case, we turn our attention to the Extract Time Entries use case.

Design for the Extract Time Entries Use Case

To design the Extract Time Entries use case, we follow the same steps we used for the Login use case design. First, we consider the key design decisions, then create sequence diagrams and a class diagram.

Key Design Decisions for Extract Time Entries

Only one key design decision remains: whether to use a stateless or a stateful session bean. The design for the other use cases has determined the design for all of the entity beans.

Stateless or Stateful Session Bean?

There is no indication in the sequence diagrams that the ExtractTimeEntriesWorkflow needs any data from or about previous attempts. In fact, we expect extract requests to be few and far between compared to other system functionality.

For performance reasons, we use stateless session beans by default. There is no reason not to follow that rule of thumb in this case.

Create Sequence Diagrams and Participating Classes for Extract Time Entries Use Case

There is only one significant flow of events, the normal flow.

Normal Flow

In the normal flow, the ExtractTimeEntriesServlet receives a request from the external billing system for time entry data of a list of users or all users for a specific client so that it can bill the client. The Servlet uses the criteria provided by the external billing system to build an ExtractCriteriaDTO object, which it sends to the ExportTimeEntriesWorkflow as an argument to the extractForCriteria method. The ExportTimeEntriesWorkflow retrieves all the specified users in the criteria users and extracts the time entries for the specified client using their respective home interfaces to actually find the relevant entity beans. Figure 15.17 shows this sequence.

Participating Classes

Each ExtractTimeEntriesServlet object depends on an ExtractTimeEntriesWorkflow object and an ExtractCriteria object, because it creates an ExtractCriteria object and passes it along to the ExtractTimeEntriesWorkflow object when it calls the extractForCriteria object.

Notice in the sequence diagram that the ExtractTimeEntriesWorkflow depends on many entity beans, but does not keep any references to any of them. This indicates that the ExtractTimeEntriesWorkflow is perfectly acceptable as a stateless session bean, as we planned. Figure 15.18 shows the participating classes and their relationships.

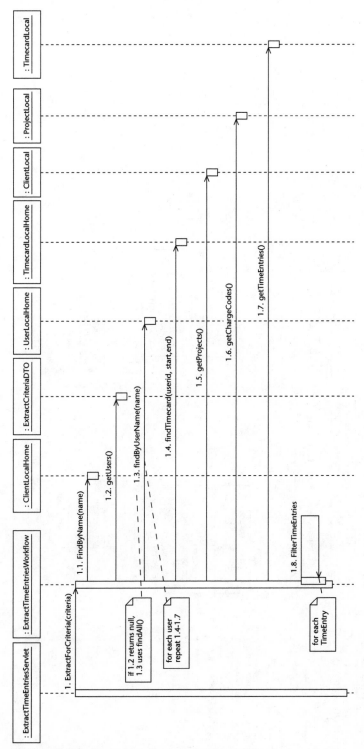

Figure 15.17 Sequence diagram for normal flow.

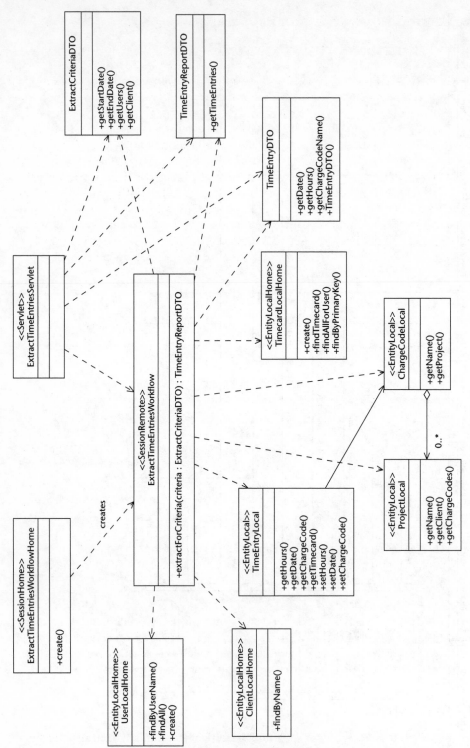

Figure 15.18   Participating classes for the Extract Time Entries use case.

Persistent Data and Design Implications

In the analysis model, each Timecard object contains many TimeEntry objects, one for each date/charge code combination. This is a reasonable way to express the relationship between hours, charge codes, and dates for an employee in the analysis model. However, it may not be an optimum design strategy.

A separate TimeEntry entity bean for each employee, charge code, and date combination can lead to an explosion of entity beans. Consider a typical employee, with four charge codes in each 7-day timecard. That employee's timecard is associated with 28 TimeEntry beans. As the system scales, to, say, 1,000 employees updating their timecards each hour on Friday morning, the application server must load 1,000 employee entity beans, 28,000 TimeEntry entity beans, and many charge code entity beans. Current experience with EJB systems indicates that creating tens of thousands of fine-grained entity beans has an adverse affect on performance and scalability. Each time an entity bean is loaded, a record must be read from the database, and a pooled object must be initialized with the data. This takes time, and forces the container to do more work tracking the objects and maintaining a pool of available entity objects.

There are three choices for persisting Timecard entity beans:

Use many fine-grained TimeEntry entity beans.   This allows us to use CMP and keep the database in first normal form. However, it undoubtedly affects the scalability of the system, since the system will require approximately 28 timecard entries per employee per week.

Normalize the database and use BMP to keep all of the data for a timecard within the Timecard entity bean.   Keep the persistent data in well-normalized tables with a separate row for each time entry. BMP allows us to write the SQL to join the timecard and time entry data to build the consolidated Timecard entity bean. This is a bit harder to implement, but makes the database more useful for reporting and enables flexible queries against the time entry data.

Keep the data for a timecard within the Timecard entity bean.   Keep the persistent data in one table that stores all of the hours in a single field and all of the charge codes in another field. This violation of first normal form allows us to use CMP, but it also reduces the database to a simple data store. Generating reports from the database becomes very painful. For example, if we want a list of all time entries for a particular client, we would have to extract the charge codes list out of every timecard and parse for the client.

Since we desire the convenience of CMP, and also do not want to violate the database normal form, the first option seems to be the most viable solution. In fact, CMP can perform better compared to BMP, as the current application servers can apply advanced optimization techniques implemented by the experts in the relevant fields. It is always better to let the expert take care of things as much as possible.

Domain Data Model

It is important to model the static relationship among the domain data, also known as the business entity. There are two different data models that the designers consider— the application data model and the underlying database data model. The two can be quite different, depending on the type of modeling used—object-oriented vs. relational. After reviewing all the use cases, we can identify the following application domain data:

Client.   A client represents an organization that hires the company to perform some task or tasks.

User.   This is a person (employee) who enters a timecard.

Project.   A project represents a large-scale task or deliverable that may contain many charge codes for a client.

Timecard.   A set of time entries for a week—Monday through Sunday.

TimeEntry.   This is time spent on a particular day for a particular type of work.

ChargeCode.   A charge code is a billable unit of work.

The relationships among these objects are shown in Figure 15.19. These data objects are implemented as entity beans, and their relationship is implemented using a container-managed relationship (CMR). One interesting thing to note here is that there are two relationships between a User and a Timecard. The first one is the 1-to-1 relationship that a User has with his or her current Timecard. The application is interested in this relationship. The second one is the 1-to-many relationship that a User has with all Timecards, and it is the same relationship that exists in the underlying relational data model. This is what is captured as a CMR.

NOTE CMR fields are those that capture the relationship between the objects at the database level. There may be relationships between objects at the application level that are not CMRs. This distinction is important because the container generates codes that apply constraints on the persistent data based on the CMR definitions.

This design decision is based on the fact that a User object, in the application, is only interested in the current Timecard object. There is no particular requirement/use case to provide the ability to move from a User to all of his or her timecards. Besides, there is a performance repercussion associated with implementing this relationship. If implemented, each time we look up a User, all of his or her Timecards, and hence all the TimeEntries, will be loaded into the memory. This can quickly bring the machine to its knees. If we need to retrieve all the Timecards of a User, we can certainly do that by providing a finder method in the Timecard Home object instead.

It is important to understand the subtle difference between object-oriented data modeling and relational data modeling in order to define the correct CMR. In object-oriented modeling, there are two dimensions to capturing the relationship—the first is called cardinality (or multiplicity), and the second is called directionality (navigability). In relational data modeling, only multiplicity is important in capturing the relationship; navigability is moot since it is easy to traverse a relationship in any direction using SQL.

The data objects identified earlier for the Timecard application are persisted in a relational database. Because the relational data model and application object data model are quite different in their approach, the mapping between them has always been a challenge. There are several different strategies for mapping objects to a relational table:

One object to one table. Each persistent field in the object maps to a column in the table.

One object to multiple tables. Persistent fields in the object map to columns from more than one table.

Multiple objects to one table. Persistent fields from multiple objects map to columns in a single table.

Mixed approach. Any combination of the above approaches can also be applied.

So, as you can see, this could quickly become complex for a complex domain model. Hence, over the years, different O/R mapping tools have emerged in the market just to make this mapping a bit easier for the application developers. An example of such a tool is TopLink. With the introduction of CMP/CMR in EJB2.0, now the application server/container provider allows developers to define these mappings declaratively. The container-provided tools generate the required code from these definitions. This greatly reduces the code size of the entity beans and allows the developers to concentrate more on the business logic. The tools can optionally generate the database schema if one is not already present. We are lucky enough to have the option of creating a database from scratch in our Timecard application. In most of the real-world application development projects, however, you may have to go through the analysis of mapping the CMP fields of the application data object to the already existing legacy database tables.

CMR is defined through fields in the objects participating in the relationship that reflects the relationship at the database level. Each end of the relationship is represented as a field. Then the container uses this CMR definition to map data between the application and the underlying database. The type of the field represents the multiplicity: A Collection field is used to represent the plurality (many) of a relationship, and a non-Collection field is used to represent the singularity (one) of a relationship. The directionality is captured by whether or not the endpoint (field) of the relationship is defined. When both of the ends of a relationship are defined, we establish a bidirectional relationship. In the Timecard application, we define a bidirectional relationship between a Client and a Project. That is, we can get all Projects from a given Client object through the projects field and from a Project to its Client through the client field. When one endpoint is omitted, the application loses the ability to traverse from a given object to the object at the other end of the relationship, and we have a unidirectional relationship. In the Timecard application, the relationship between the User and Timecard is implemented as unidirectional from Timecard to User by omitting the CMR field in the User. That is, we can get to a User object from a Timecard object through the user field in the Timecard, but not the other way around. Now, what about the second relationship that we have implemented between a timecard and a user, as shown in Figure 15.19? This is an example of a non-CMR relationship, specific to the object-oriented modeling. The relationship is a bidirectional, 1-to-1 type. That is, there is one current Timecard for each User. It is established through a currentTimecard field in the User object and a user field in the Timecard object. It is important to understand that currentTimecard is not a CMR field. From a Timecard's perspective, it is really the same as the CMR relationship since the same relationship field (user) participates in both the cases.

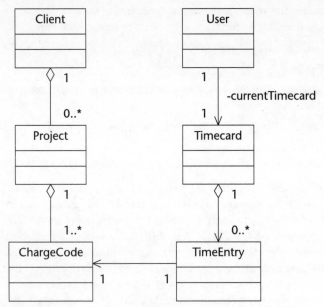

Figure 15.19 Timecard application domain data model.

With CMP, the primary key of an entity bean can either be a data type defined in the java.lang package or can be a user-defined class that implements Serializable. The field(s) must be public and should have the same name as the corresponding CMP field(s) in the bean. It is a good design strategy to define a primary key class even if the primary key is a single field of basic data type. This gives you the flexibility to change the key in the future easily without requiring any widespread code change.

This concludes the design for the Login, Record Time, and Extract Time Entries use cases. The next, and last, step before implementation is to evaluate our design.

Evaluate the Design

Now that we have completed the exhausting and exhaustive design for each use case, we must evaluate the design against our goals and for compliance with the structural constraints from architecture. Recall that the primary goals for this design effort are reuse, performance, and reliability.

Performance and reliability. The design works toward our performance and reliability goals by leveraging EJB's strengths and by staying away from its weaknesses. Reviewing the sequence diagrams, we can see that remote connections are kept to a minimum and that the data access emphasizes speed for the Record Time use case, which is the most demanding of the common use cases.

Reuse.   We have achieved a fairly high level of reuse within the system. The same entity beans, such as Timecard, are used by several session beans. Examining the methods for each bean, we can see that the methods are closely related and fulfill a clear responsibility. Based on these observations, we can use formal OO terminology and say that each bean is well encapsulated and has strong cohesion. Thus, there may be reuse opportunities with new systems within the organization.

The participating class diagrams show that the design fits the structural constraints in almost every case. The ExtractTimeEntryServlet, from the TimecardServlet package, depends on the ExtractCriteriaDTO, which resides in the Dtos package. This requires an updated package dependency diagram, as shown in Figure 15.20, but does not introduce any major issues, such as cyclical dependencies or tight coupling.

Finally, we are ready for implementation.

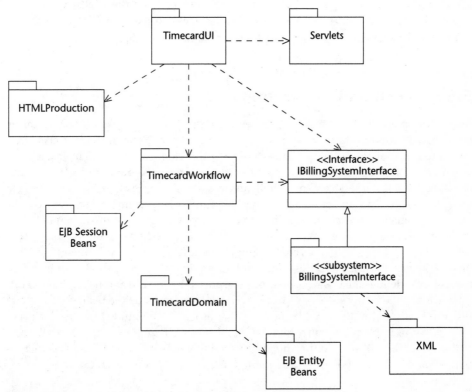

Figure 15.20   Revised package dependencies diagram.

Implementation

Now that the design is complete, and we have evaluated it, we have a solid foundation for implementation. We will make some important decisions during implementation, but we made most or all of the major structural decisions during analysis, architecture, and design. For example, we know each significant class, its responsibilities, and its relationships with other classes. We know how each entity bean holds data and how the session beans package that data for consumption by the user interface classes.

The implementation will be split into two parts. First, there are core classes, which are directly derived from the design model and play a significant role in the use cases. Each section will show the derivation and code for the different parts of each bean. Second, described in the last section, are some helper classes. These classes are not in the design; they will be discovered as part of the implementation process.

> **NOTE** All of the code for this book, and additional code for the interfaces described in this chapter, can be found at www.wiley.com/compbooks/arrington. The package names in the book match the packages on the site.

EJB Implementation Strategy

Any EJB implementation by definition requires three files: an EJB interface (local or remote), a Home interface (local or remote), and a Bean (Session, Entity) class that implements the methods defined in both the EJB and Home interfaces. The implementation Bean class provides the implementation of the business methods defined in the (local/remote) EJB interface. Since the Bean class and the corresponding EJB interface are not tied directly together through inheritance, there is no compile-time type checking. One problem with this approach is that if there is a signature mismatch between the Bean class and the interface, it cannot be caught until the time of deployment. This can be very annoying as well as challenging, depending on the development environment. We can easily address this problem by defining another normal Java interface that actually defines the business methods supported by the EJB and have both the EJB interface and the Bean class derive from it. This interface will tie the Bean class with its EJB interface and thus allow the compiler to perform a compile-time type checking. We will apply this implementation technique for all of our EJB implementations. In the rest of this book, we will refer to this interface as the Business interface. This implementation scheme is shown in Figure 15.21 using the User entity bean as an example.

User Entity Bean

The User entity bean, as mentioned in the implementation strategy section, requires five files:

- **UserInt.** The Business interface
- **UserLocal.** The local EJB interface

- **UserLocalHome.** The EJB Home interface
- **UserBean.** The Bean implementation class
- **UserPK.** The primary key class

UserInt.java

UserInt.java is the local Business interface for the User entity bean. It defines all of the locally accessible business methods for the bean, as shown in Figure 15.21. This class consolidates behavior discovered in the Record Time and Login use cases.

Methods in UserInt.java need not throw RemoteException, since the User bean is not remotely accessible. Each method returns either void, a primitive, or a local reference to other entity beans.

```java
package com.wiley.compBooks.EJwithUML.TimeCardDomain;

/**
 * The UserInt is the interface that ties the Bean with the Remote interface
 * to provide compile time type checking.
 */
public interface UserInt
{
  /** Answers the name of this User bean. */
  public String getName();

  /** Answers true if the entered password matches this User's password */
  public boolean isPasswordValid(String entered);

  /** Answers true if the password should be changed */
  public boolean isPasswordChangeRequired();

  /** Set the password of this User bean. */
  public void setPassword(String password);

  /** Set the password change flag of this User bean. */
  public void setPasswordChangeFlag(boolean flag);

  /** Answers the current timecard of this User bean */
  public TimecardLocal getCurrentTimecard();

  /** Sets the current timecard */
  public void setCurrentTimecard(TimecardLocal timecard);

}
```

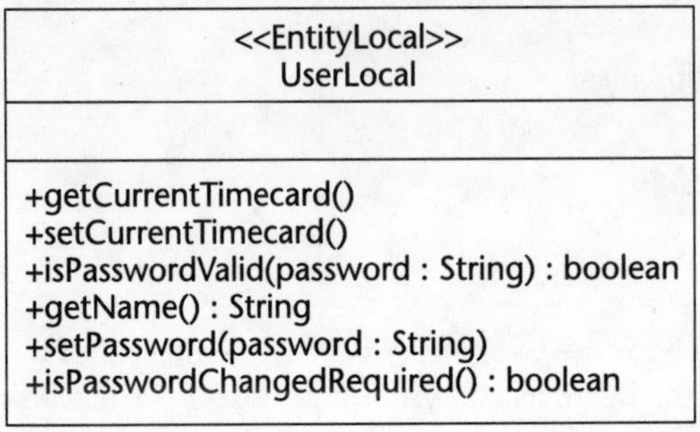

```
        ┌─────────────────────────────────────────────┐
        │              <<EntityLocal>>                  │
        │                 UserLocal                     │
        ├─────────────────────────────────────────────┤
        │                                               │
        ├─────────────────────────────────────────────┤
        │ +getCurrentTimecard()                         │
        │ +setCurrentTimecard()                         │
        │ +isPasswordValid(password : String) : boolean │
        │ +getName() : String                           │
        │ +setPassword(password : String)               │
        │ +isPasswordChangedRequired() : boolean        │
        └─────────────────────────────────────────────┘
```

Figure 15.21   Local interface of the User entity bean.

UserLocal.java

UserLocal.java is the local EJB interface that inherits from UserInt and hence has an empty body. This is in line with what we have set as our implementation strategy for all of our EJBs.

```
package com.wiley.compBooks.EJwithUML.TimeCardDomain;

import javax.ejb.*;
import java.rmi.*;

/**
 * The User bean holds descriptive information about a User.
 * UserLocal is the local interface through which local clients access the
 * underlying entity bean.
 */
public interface UserLocal extends EJBLocalObject, UserInt
{
}
```

UserLocalHome.java

UserLocalHome.java is the local Home interface for the User entity bean. It defines all of the methods needed to find, create, or destroy User entity beans, as shown in Figure 15.22.

Each of the methods in UserHome.java throws either CreateException or FinderException. CreateExceptions and FinderExceptions indicate logic errors or data errors in the implementation.

Initially, it is quite surprising to see the findByUserName method returning a Collection. After all, logically, there should be only one User entity bean for each username. The Enterprise JavaBeans specification mandates that primary keys are unique. Any other criteria for a find method could yield more than one entity bean. So, the findByPrimaryKey method is the only find method that is permitted to return a single remote reference. It is up to the developers to verify that other criteria are unique when creating entity beans and to extract the entity bean's reference from the Collection returned by the find method.

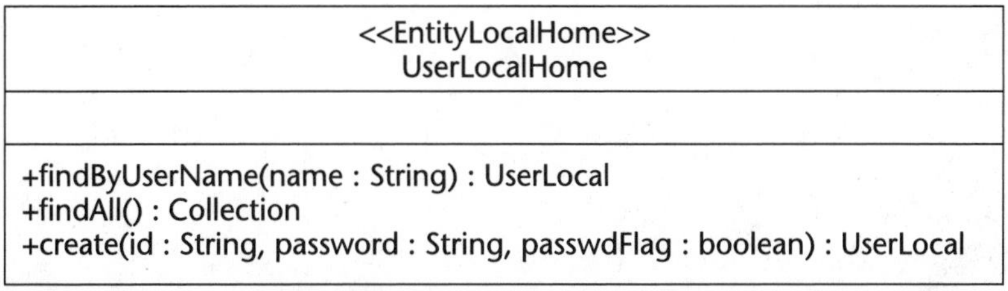

```
┌─────────────────────────────────────────────────────────────┐
│                     <<EntityLocalHome>>                       │
│                       UserLocalHome                           │
├─────────────────────────────────────────────────────────────┤
│                                                               │
├─────────────────────────────────────────────────────────────┤
│ +findByUserName(name : String) : UserLocal                    │
│ +findAll() : Collection                                       │
│ +create(id : String, password : String, passwdFlag : boolean) : UserLocal │
└─────────────────────────────────────────────────────────────┘
```

Figure 15.22   Local Home interface of the User entity bean.

```
package com.wiley.compBooks.EJwithUML.TimeCardDomain;

import java.util.*;
import javax.ejb.*;

/**
 * The User bean holds descriptive information about a User.
 * UserLocalHome is the local interface through which local clients find and
 * create the underlying entity beans.
 */

public interface UserLocalHome extends EJBLocalHome
{
  /**
   * Answers a Collection that contains references to User beans that
   * match the username. Should be unique.
   */
  public Collection findByUserName(String name) throws FinderException;

  /** Answers a Collection that contains references to all User beans */
  public Collection findAll() throws FinderException;

  /** Answers a local reference to the User bean, if it exists */
  public UserLocal findByPrimaryKey(UserPK key) throws FinderException;

  /** Answers a local reference to the newly created User bean */
  public UserLocal create(String id, String name, String password,
                          boolean passwordFlag) throws CreateException;
}
```

UserPK.java

UserPK.java represents the primary key class of the User entity bean. It is important to note here that it implements the hashCode() and equals() methods and implements the Serializable interface.

```
package com.wiley.compBooks.EJwithUML.TimeCardDomain;

import java.io.Serializable;
```

```
/**
 * UserPK is the primary key class for the User entity bean.
 */
public class UserPK implements Serializable
{
  public String id;

  public UserPK()
  {
  }

  public UserPK(String id)
  {
     this.id = id;
  }

  public String toString()
  {
    return id;
  }

  public  int hashCode()
  {
    return id.hashCode();
  }

  public boolean equals(Object key)
  {
    if (key == null)
    {
      return false;
    }
    else
    {
      if (!key.getClass().equals(this.getClass()))
      {
        return false;
      }
      else
      {
        return ((UserPK)key).id.equals(this.id);
      }
    }
  }
}
```

UserBean.java

UserBean.java is the implementation for the User entity bean. It provides implementations for the methods in the Home and local EJB interfaces.

WARNING Enterprise JavaBeans should never be reused outside of an EJB context. Without the context, Enterprise JavaBeans are not even thread-safe, because the data is public, and the use of the synchronized keyword is precluded by the specification.

One thing to note here is that the UserBean class is implemented as an abstract class. The CMP and CMR fields are defined using getter/setter methods. The only methods implemented are the business methods. The business methods can access the data members only through the getter/setter methods. With CMP in EJB 2.0, the container generates the actual implementation class from this abstract class.

```java
package com.wiley.compBooks.EJwithUML.TimeCardDomain;

import com.wiley.compBooks.EJwithUML.Base.EjbUtil.*;
import java.util.*;
import javax.ejb.*;
import javax.naming.*;

/**
 * The User bean holds descriptive information about a User.
 * UserBean is the actual entity bean implementation.
 */
public abstract class UserBean extends BasicEntityBean  implements UserInt
{
   private TimecardLocal currentTimecard;

   /** CMP fields */
   public abstract String getId();
   public abstract void setId(String id);
   public abstract String getName();
   public abstract void setName(String name);
   public abstract String getPassword();
   public abstract void setPassword(String password);
   public abstract boolean getPasswordChangeFlag();
   public abstract void setPasswordChangeFlag(boolean flag);


   public TimecardLocal getCurrentTimecard()
   {
     return currentTimecard;
   }

   public void setCurrentTimecard(TimecardLocal currentTimecard)
   {
     this.currentTimecard=currentTimecard;
   }


   /** Create an EmployeeBean with the specified parameters. This is never called
directly. */
   public UserPK ejbCreate(String id, String name, String password,
                       boolean passwordFlag) throws CreateException
```

```
    {
      try
      {
        setId(id);
        setName(name);
        setPassword(password);
        setPasswordChangeFlag(passwordFlag);
        Context initialContext = new InitialContext();
        TimecardLocalHome thome = (TimecardLocalHome) initialContext.lookup(
                           EjbReferenceNames.TIMECARD_HOME);
        Collection tcards = thome.findCurrentTimecardForUser(id);
        //There should be at most one timecard marked as current.
        if (tcards.size() == 1)
        {
          this.currentTimecard = (TimecardLocal)tcards.iterator().next();
        }
        else if(tcards.size()>1)
        {
          throw new CreateException("more than one timecard are marked as
current.");
        }
        return null;
      }
      catch(Exception exp)
      {
        throw new CreateException("failed to lookup current timecard-" +
exp.toString());
      }
    }

  /** Actions performed after creation. This is never called directly. */
  public void ejbPostCreate(String id, String name, String password, boolean
passwordFlag)
  {
  }

  /** Answers true if the entered password matches this Employee's password */
  public boolean isPasswordValid(String entered)
  {
    return getPassword().equals(entered);
  }

  /** Answers true if the password should be changed */
  public boolean isPasswordChangeRequired()
  {
    return getPasswordChangeFlag();
  }
}
```

Timecard Entity Bean

The Timecard entity bean, like the User entity bean, has five files:

- **TimecardInt.** The Business interface
- **TimecardLocal.** The local EJB interface
- **TimecardLocalHome.** The EJB Home interface
- **TimecardBean.** The Bean implementation class
- **TimecardPK.** The primary key class

TimecardInt.java

TimecardInt.java is the local Business interface for the Timecard entity bean. It defines all of the locally accessible business methods for the bean, as shown in Figure 15.23. This class consolidates behavior discovered in the Record Time, Extract Time Entries, and Login use cases.

```
package com.wiley.compBooks.EJwithUML.TimeCardDomain;

import java.util.*;
import javax.ejb.*;

/**
 * The TimecardInt is the interface that ties the Bean with the Remote interface
 * to provide compile-time type checking.
 */
public interface TimecardInt
{
  /** Answers all TimeEntries as a Collection for this Timecard */
  public Collection getTimeEntries();

  /** Answers the start date of the timecard */
  public long getStartDate();

  /** Answers the end date of the timecard */
  public long getEndDate();

  /** Answers whether or not the Timecard is a current timecard */
  public boolean getIsCurrent();

  /** Sets the isCurrent flag */
  public void setIsCurrent(boolean isCurrent);
}
```

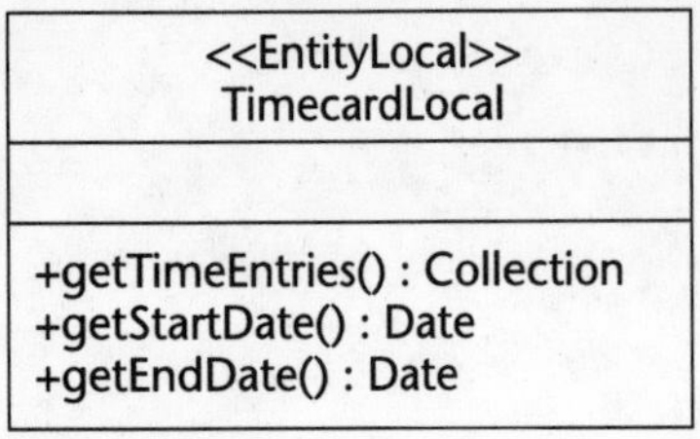

Figure 15.23   Local interface of the Timecard entity bean.

TimecardLocal.java

TimecardLocal.java is the local EJB interface that inherits from TimecardInt and hence has an empty body. This is in line with what we have set as our implementation strategy for all of our EJBs.

```
package com.wiley.compBooks.EJwithUML.TimeCardDomain;

import java.util.*;
import javax.ejb.*;

/**
 * The Timecard bean holds time entries for a date range.
 * TimecardLocal is the local interface through which local clients access the
 * underlying entity bean.
 */
public interface TimecardLocal extends EJBLocalObject, TimecardInt
{
}
```


TimecardLocalHome.java

TimecardLocalHome.java is the Home interface for the Timecard entity bean. It contains all of the methods for creating and finding Timecard entity beans, as shown in Figure 15.24.

Note the variety of find methods that can be used for an entity bean. In more traditional Java development, each one-to-many relationship is kept in the containing object. In EJB development, this is accomplished by providing suitable finder methods on the Home interface of the corresponding entity bean. For example, each User entity bean only contains a reference to the current Timecard entity bean. However, if the User entity bean needs to find all of its timecards, it can use a find method on Timecard's Home interface.

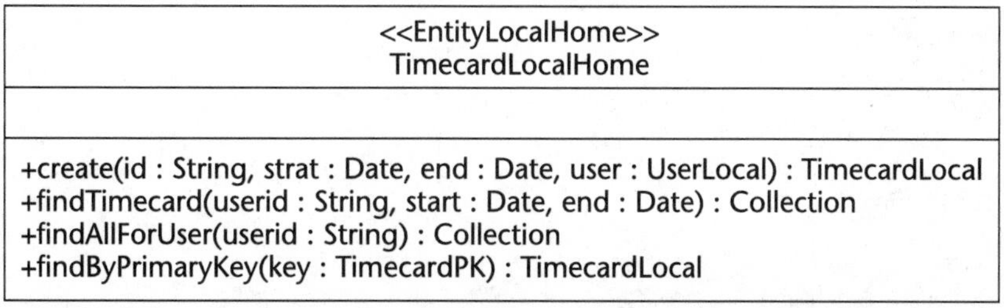

| <<EntityLocalHome>> |
| TimecardLocalHome |
| |
| +create(id : String, strat : Date, end : Date, user : UserLocal) : TimecardLocal
+findTimecard(userid : String, start : Date, end : Date) : Collection
+findAllForUser(userid : String) : Collection
+findByPrimaryKey(key : TimecardPK) : TimecardLocal |

Figure 15.24   Local Home interface of the Timecard entity bean.

This has a huge advantage, since relationships are kept in the data and are not realized unless they are needed. However, it also breaks the encapsulation of the containing entity bean. Any object can ask the Timecard's Home interface for a list of all timecards for a given username. The User bean is not even involved.

```
package com.wiley.compBooks.EJwithUML.TimeCardDomain;

import java.util.*;
import javax.ejb.*;

/**
 * The Timecard bean holds time entries for a date range.
 * TimecardLocalHome is the local interface through which clients
 * find and create the underlying entity beans.
 */
public interface TimecardLocalHome extends EJBLocalHome
{
    /**
     * Answers a local reference to the newly created Timecard bean
     */
    public TimecardLocal create(String userId, Date start, Date end,
            boolean isCurrent, UserLocal user) throws CreateException;

    /**
     * Answers a Collection that contains references to all Timecards
     * for the specified Use
     */
    public Collection findAllForUser(String userId) throws
                                            FinderException;

    /**
     * Answers the current Timecard
     */
    public Collection findCurrentTimecardForUser(String userId) throws
                                            FinderException;

    /**
     * Answers a Collection of Timecards that matches the user and
     * has a start date that falls within the date range, inclusive
     */
```

```
        public Collection findTimecard(String userId, long start,
                                  long end) throws FinderException;


     /**
      * Answers a local reference to the specified Timecard, if it
      * exists
      */
     public TimecardLocal findByPrimaryKey(TimecardPK key) throws
                                               FinderException;

   }
```

TimecardPK.java

TimecardPK.java represents the primary key class of the Timecard entity bean. It is important to note here that it implements the hashCode() and equals() methods and implements the Serializable interface.

```
   package com.wiley.compBooks.EJwithUML.TimeCardDomain;

   import java.io.Serializable;

   /**
    * TimecardPK is the primary key class for the Timecard entity bean.
    * It is,
    *                 timecard id = userid + "-"+ year+ "-"+ "week";
    */
   public class TimecardPK implements Serializable
   {

     public String id;

     public TimecardPK()
     {
     }

     public TimecardPK(String id)
     {
       this.id = id;
     }

     public String toString()
     {
       return id;
     }

     public int hashCode()
     {
       return id.hashCode();
     }

     public boolean equals(Object key)
     {
```

```
        if (key == null)
        {
          return false;
        }
        else
        {
          if (!key.getClass().equals(this.getClass()))
          {
            return false;
          }
          else
          {
            return ((TimecardPK)key).id.equals(id);
          }
        }
      }
    }
  }
```

TimecardBean.java

TimecardBean.java is the implementation class for the Timecard entity bean. It holds a list of TimeEntry entity beans and a reference to a User entity bean.

```java
package com.wiley.compBooks.EJwithUML.TimeCardDomain;

import com.wiley.compBooks.EJwithUML.Base.EjbUtil.*;
import java.util.*;
import java.rmi.*;
import javax.ejb.*;
import javax.naming.*;

/**
 * The Timecard bean holds time entries for a date range.
 * TimecardBean is the actual entity bean implementation using CMP.
 */

public abstract class TimecardBean extends BasicEntityBean implements
TimecardInt
{
 /** CMP fields */
  public abstract String getId();  // PK
  public abstract void setId(String id);  // PK
  public abstract long getStartDate(); // time in milliseconds
  public abstract void setStartDate(long start);
  public abstract long getEndDate();
  public abstract void setEndDate(long end);
  public abstract boolean getIsCurrent();
  public abstract void setIsCurrent(boolean isCurrent);

  /** CMR fields */
  public abstract UserLocal getUser();
  public abstract void setUser(UserLocal user);
```

```
    public abstract Collection getTimeEntries();
    public abstract void setTimeEntries(Collection entries);

    public TimecardBean()
    {
    }

    /**
     * Create a TimecardBean with the specified parameters. This is never called
     * directly.
     */
    public TimecardPK ejbCreate(String id, Date start, Date end, boolean
isCurrent,
                        UserLocal user) throws CreateException
    {
      System.out.println("in ejbCreate() of TimecardBean!");
      setId(id);
      setStartDate(start.getTime());
      setEndDate(end.getTime());
      setIsCurrent(isCurrent);
      return null;
    }

    /** Actions performed after creation. This is never called directly. */
    public void ejbPostCreate(String id, Date start, Date end, boolean isCurrent,
                        UserLocal user)
    {
      System.out.println("in ejbPostCreate() of TimecardBean!");
      // set the CMR fields
      setUser(user);
    }
}
```

TimeEntry Entity Bean

The TimeEntry entity bean is a simple data repository with no behavior. A TimeEntry entity holds the data for a single entry in a Timecard. It contains the hours worked on a particular task represented by a ChargeCode on a particular day. The TimeEntry entity bean, like the Timecard entity bean, has five files:

- **TimeEntrydInt.** The Business interface
- **TimeEntryLocal.** The local EJB interface
- **TimeEntryLocalHome.** The EJB Home interface
- **TimeEntryBean.** The Bean implementation class
- **TimeEntryPK.** The primary key class

NOTE The code for these files can be found on the Web site for this book (www.wiley.com/compbooks/arrington).

LoginWorkflow Stateless Session Bean

The LoginWorkflow stateless session bean consists of four files:

- **LoginWorkflowInt.** The Business interface
- **LoginWorkflowLocal.** The remote EJB interface
- **LoginWorkflowLocalHome.** The EJB Home interface
- **LoginWorkflowBean.** The Bean implementation class

LoginWorkflowInt.java

LoginWorkflowInt.java is the local interface for the LoginWorkflow entity bean. It defines the remotely accessible methods for the LoginWorkflow entity bean. Since LoginWorkflow is a stateless session bean, each method includes all of the information needed to perform the request. For example, setPassword must specify the user, since the LoginWorkflow session bean does not remember who is logged in. In fact, consecutive calls to a stateless session bean are frequently received by different bean implementations. The container pools implementations and can do as it pleases with stateless session beans between method invocations.

```java
package com.wiley.compBooks.EJwithUML.TimeCardWorkflow;

import java.rmi.*;
import javax.ejb.*;
import com.wiley.compBooks.EJwithUML.Base.ApplicationExceptions.*;

/**
 * The LoginWorkflowInt is the interface that ties the Bean with the Remote
interface
 * to provide compile-time type checking.
 */
public interface LoginWorkflowInt
{
  /** Answers true if the password is correct for the specified user */
  public boolean isUserValid(String username, String password) throws
                                 DataNotFoundException, RemoteException;

  /** Answers true if the password is due to be changed */
  public boolean isPasswordChangeRequired(String username) throws
                                 DataNotFoundException, RemoteException;

  /** Sets the password, if the old password is valid */
  public void setPassword(String username, String oldPassword, String
newPassword)
          throws InvalidDataException, DataNotFoundException, RemoteException;
}
```

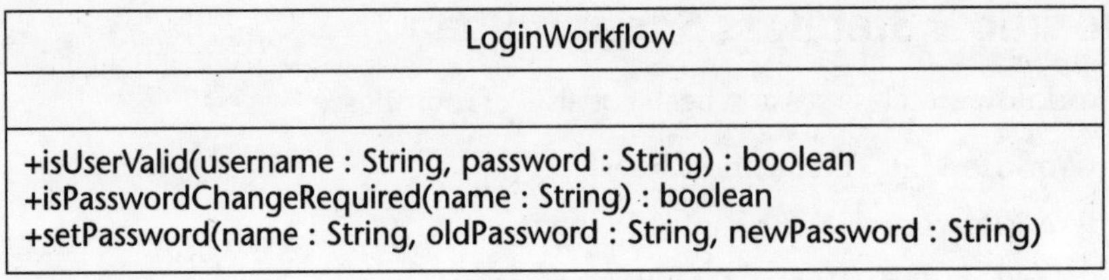

LoginWorkflow
+isUserValid(username : String, password : String) : boolean +isPasswordChangeRequired(name : String) : boolean +setPassword(name : String, oldPassword : String, newPassword : String)

Figure 15.25   Remote interface of the LoginWorkflow session bean.

LoginWorkflow.java

LoginWorkflow.java is the remote EJB interface that inherits from LoginWorkflowInt and hence it has an empty body. This is in line with what we have set as our implementation strategy for all of our EJBs. This is shown in Figure 15.25.

```
package com.wiley.compBooks.EJwithUML.TimeCardWorkflow;

import javax.ejb.*;
import com.wiley.compBooks.EJwithUML.Base.ApplicationExceptions.*;

/**
 * The LoginWorkflow allows client objects to validate users and update their
 * passwords. LoginWorkflow is the remote interface through which clients access
 * the underlying session bean.
 */
public interface LoginWorkflow extends EJBObject, LoginWorkflowInt
{
}
```

LoginWorkflowHome.java

LoginWorkflowHome.java is the Home interface for the LoginWorkflow session bean. It contains the method by which LoginWorkflow session beans are created.

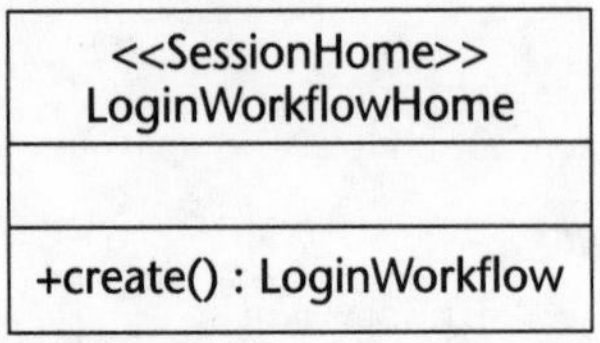

<<SessionHome>> LoginWorkflowHome
+create() : LoginWorkflow

Figure 15.26   Home interface of the LoginWorkflow session bean.

Since LoginWorkflow is a stateless session bean, there would not be much point to including parameters in the create method, as shown in Figure 15.26. Nevertheless, we must specify the method.

```
package com.wiley.compBooks.EJwithUML.TimeCardWorkflow;

import java.util.*;
import java.rmi.*;
import javax.ejb.*;

/**
 * The LoginWorkflow allows client objects to validate users and update their
 * passwords.
 * LoginWorkflowHome is the remote interface through which clients find and
create
 * the underlying session beans.
 */
public interface LoginWorkflowHome extends EJBHome
{
    /** Answers a reference to the newly created LoginWorkflow bean */
    public LoginWorkflow create() throws CreateException,RemoteException;
}
```

LoginWorkflowBean.java

LoginWorkflowBean.java is the implementation class for the LoginWorkflow session bean.

As you can see in the code here for the isPasswordValid method, LoginWorkflow-Bean obtains and uses local references to entity beans as it needs them. There is no way for one entity or session bean to directly get at an implementation bean. Instead, the entity or session bean must obtain an EJB remote or local reference. Performance between two local beans is dramatically better than the performance between a client object in a different VM and a bean in an application server, even if both VMs are on the same host.

```
package com.wiley.compBooks.EJwithUML.TimeCardWorkflow;

import com.wiley.compBooks.EJwithUML.Base.EjbUtil.*;
import com.wiley.compBooks.EJwithUML.TimeCardDomain.*;
import com.wiley.compBooks.EJwithUML.Base.ApplicationExceptions.*;
import java.util.*;
import java.rmi.*;
import javax.ejb.*;
import javax.naming.*;

/**
 * The LoginWorkflow allows client objects to validate users and update their
 * passwords. LoginWorkflowBean is the actual session bean implementation.
```

```
 */
public class LoginWorkflowBean extends BasicSessionBean
{
  public void ejbCreate() throws CreateException
  {
    System.out.println("in ejbCreate() of LoginWorkflowBean!");
  }

  public void ejbPostCreate()
  {
    System.out.println("in ejbPostCreate() of LoginWorkflowBean!");
  }

  /** Answers true if the password is correct for the specified user */
  public boolean isUserValid(String username, String password) throws
DataNotFoundException
  {
    UserLocal user = findUser(username);
    return user.isPasswordValid(password);
  }

  /** Answers true if the password is due to be changed */
  public boolean isPasswordChangeRequired(String username) throws
DataNotFoundException
  {
    UserLocal user = findUser(username);
    return user.isPasswordChangeRequired();
  }

  /** Sets the password, if the old password is valid. */
  public void setPassword(String username, String oldPassword, String
newPassword)
        throws InvalidDataException, DataNotFoundException
  {
    UserLocal user = findUser(username);
    if (!user.isPasswordValid(oldPassword))
    {
      throw new InvalidDataException(Origin.LOGIN_WORKFLOW, "Old password is
invalid.");
    }
    user.setPassword(newPassword);
  }

  private UserLocal findUser(String username) throws DataNotFoundException
  {
    try
    {
      Context initialContext = getInitialContext();
      UserLocalHome uhome = (UserLocalHome)initialContext.lookup(

EjbReferenceNames.USER_HOME);
      Collection users = uhome.findByUserName(username);
      UserLocal user = null;
```

```
        if (users.isEmpty())
        {
          throw new DataNotFoundException(Origin.LOGIN_WORKFLOW, "User(" +
username +

") Not Found");
        }
        else
        {
          user = (UserLocal) users.iterator().next();
        }
        return user;
      }
      catch (NamingException e)
      {
        throw new DataNotFoundException(Origin.LOGIN_WORKFLOW, e, "User Bean Not
Found");
      }
      catch (FinderException e)
      {
        throw new DataNotFoundException(Origin.LOGIN_WORKFLOW, e, "User(" +
username +
                                                            ") Not
Found");
      }
  }
}
```

RecordTimeWorkflow Stateful Session Bean

The RecordTimeWorkflow stateless session bean consists of four files:

- **RecordTimeWorkflowInt.** The Business interface
- **RecordTimeWorkflowLocal.** The remote EJB interface
- **RecordTimeWorkflowLocalHome.** The EJB Home interface
- **RecordTimeWorkflowBean.** The Bean implementation class

NOTE The code for these files can be found on the Web site for this book (www.wiley.com/compbooks/arrington).

Supporting Classes

The rest of the classes for this chapter support the classes that were found in the design. While implementing a design, developers often discover classes that capture common functionality or provide significant functionality. As long as these new classes do not significantly affect the architecture by introducing new dependencies between packages, this discovery process is a healthy refinement of the design.

NOTE The code for all of these supporting classes can be found on the Web site for this book (www.wiley.com/compbooks/arrington).

BasicSessionBean.java

The BasicSessionBean class removes some of the drudgery from creating implementation classes for session beans. It provides default implementations for all of the required EJB methods. Except for the initial context, all of the methods are empty.

```java
package com.wiley.compBooks.EJwithUML.Base.EjbUtil;

import java.rmi.*;
import javax.ejb.*;
import javax.naming.*;

/**
 * An adapter base class for all session beans. It provides default
 * implementations for all the required methods of the SessionBean
 * interface.
 */
public class BasicSessionBean implements SessionBean
{
  protected SessionContext context;

  public void ejbRemove() throws RemoteException
  {
  }

  public void ejbPassivate() throws RemoteException
  {
  }

  public void ejbActivate() throws RemoteException
  {
  }

  public void setSessionContext(SessionContext context)
  {
    this.context = context;
  }

  protected Context getInitialContext() throws NamingException
  {
    return new InitialContext();
  }
}
```

BasicEntityBean.java

The BasicEntityBean.java class removes some of the drudgery from creating implementation classes for entity beans. It provides default implementations for all of the required methods. Except for the initial context, all of the required methods are empty.

```java
package com.wiley.compBooks.EJwithUML.Base.EjbUtil;

import java.rmi.*;
import javax.ejb.*;
import javax.naming.*;

/**
 * An adapter base class for all entity beans. It provides default
 * implementations for all the required methods of the EntityBean
 * interface.
 */
public class BasicEntityBean implements EntityBean
{
  protected EntityContext context;

  public BasicEntityBean()
  {
  }

  public void setEntityContext(EntityContext context) throws
                          RemoteException
  {
    this.context = context;
  }

  public void unsetEntityContext() throws RemoteException
  {
    this.context = null;
  }

  public void ejbPassivate() throws RemoteException
  {
  }

  public void ejbRemove() throws RemoteException
  {
  }

  public void ejbLoad() throws RemoteException
  {
  }

  public void ejbStore() throws RemoteException
  {
```

```
      }

      public void ejbActivate() throws RemoteException
      {
      }
   }
```

ChargeCode Entity Bean

The ChargeCode entity bean is a simple data repository with no behavior. A charge code is a billable unit of work.

Client Entity Bean

The Client entity bean is a simple data repository with no behavior. A client represents an organization that hires the company to perform some task or tasks.

Project Entity Bean

The Project entity bean is a simple data repository with no behavior beyond a simple check for uniqueness. A project represents a large-scale task or deliverable that may contain many charge codes for a client.

TimecardDTO.java

TimecardDTO.java is a simple Java class that merely holds the data pertaining to a timecard. It is used to transfer data efficiently across application layers—in this case, between Servlet and EJB layers. This type of object is also known as a data transfer object (DTO) [EJB Design Patterns, 2002].

```java
package com.wiley.compBooks.EJwithUML.Dtos;

import java.util.*;
import java.io.*;
import com.wiley.compBooks.EJwithUML.Base.DateUtil;
import
com.wiley.compBooks.EJwithUML.Base.ApplicationExceptions.InvalidDataException;
import com.wiley.compBooks.EJwithUML.Base.ApplicationExceptions.Origin;

public class TimecardDTO implements Serializable
{
   private Date startDate;
   private Date endDate;
   private ArrayList entries = new ArrayList();

   public TimecardDTO(Date start, Date end)
   {
```

```java
    this.startDate = start;
    this.endDate = end;
  }

  public int getTotalEntries()
  {
    return this.entries.size();
  }

  public Date getStartDate()
  {
    return this.startDate;
  }

  public void setStartDate(Date date)
  {
    this.endDate = date;
  }

public Date getEndDate()
{
  return this.endDate;
}

public void setEndDate(Date date)
{
  this.endDate = date;
}

  public int getTotalHoursWorked()
  {
    int total = 0;
    Iterator entryIterator = entries.iterator();
    while(entryIterator.hasNext())
    {
      TimeEntryDTO entry = (TimeEntryDTO) entryIterator.next();
      total = total + entry.getHours();
    }
    return total;
  }

  public Iterator getEntries()
  {
    return this.entries.iterator();
  }

  public void addEntry(TimeEntryDTO entry) throws
                            InvalidDataException
  {
    if (DateUtil.isWithinDateRangeInclusive(startDate, endDate,
        entry.getDate()))
    {
      this.entries.add(entry);
```

```
              //Sets the ID to an incomplete value. TimecardWorkflowBean adds
              //the timecard
              // ID to it before actual insertion into the database.
              if (entry.isNew())
              {
                entry.setId((getTotalEntries())+"");
              }
          }
          else
          {
            throw new InvalidDataException(Origin.DTO,
            "timeentry date is outside the timecard date range.");
          }
      }

    public String toString()
    {
      StringBuffer buffer = new StringBuffer();
      Iterator entryIterator = entries.iterator();
      int count = 0;
      buffer.append("Timecard[start date ="+
    DateUtil.toDateString(startDate) +
                      ",end date = " + DateUtil.toDateString(endDate));
      while(entryIterator.hasNext())
      {
        count++;
        TimeEntryDTO entry = (TimeEntryDTO) entryIterator.next();
        buffer.append( ",#"+count+"{" + entry + "}");
      }
      buffer.append("]");
      return buffer.toString();
    }

    public  int hashCode()
    {
      return (startDate.hashCode() ^ endDate.hashCode() ^
              entries.hashCode());
    }

    public boolean equals(Object obj)
    {
      if (obj == null)
      {
        return false;
      }
      else
      {
        if (!obj.getClass().equals(this.getClass()))
        {
          return false;
        }
        else
        {
```

```
        TimecardDTO entry = (TimecardDTO)obj;
        return ((entry.startDate.equals(this.startDate)) &&
                (entry.endDate.equals(this.endDate)) &&
                (entry.entries.equals(this.entries)));
    }
  }
 }
}
```

Unit Testing with JUnit

The importance of testing cannot be stressed enough. The quality of software is ensured through thorough testing. The process starts at the developers end. The type of testing that the developers are expected to do on the codes they write is unit testing. For Java developers, JUnit has become the most popular unit-testing framework. The framework allows developers to concentrate on their test cases and not worry about how to drive all the test cases.

Testing a simple Java class is easy. However, it gets a little complicated when we move to J2EE classes like EJBs and Servlets. Because these classes are designed to run within a container and the container is provided by the container provider (Application Server), you would need to deploy the code in the application server before you can test. If you treat the bean class as a simple Java class and just test that directly, your test may not be valid since the methods in the Bean class may require the transactional as well as the security context that is provided by the container. Additionally, if your bean accesses resources, such as the database connection and other beans, through the JNDI lookup, your test will not even work outside the application server.

In our Timecard application, all our entity beans are local by our design choice that we made. The local entity beans are not accessible from outside the application server. So, how do we test our entity beans? The are two ways to get around this problem: Either make the local beans (entity beans) remotely accessible for our testing purposes and, once tested, deploy them as local beans for actual use, or write a remote stateless session bean to drive each entity bean from the test programs. Because all our entity beans do not implement any significant business methods, we decided not to test them separately. Instead, we wrote our test programs to test the session beans (Workflow beans), which in turn use the entity beans. But, this may not be a good strategy for other applications. You may always want to test your entity beans separately. This is because you may be working on just entity beans and someone else may be working on other beans that use your beans. You do not want to make your beans available without testing. This brings up the need for another type of testing that developers should perform, called integration testing. Integration testing refers to the testing that is designed to test two or more classes together. These classes are designed to work together to perform certain tasks and are usually coded by two different developers. Both the developers test their own code separately and later collaborate to test the classes together. The integration testing can be applied at different levels of abstraction. For our Timecard application, we unit tested our EJBs and servlets separately, and then performed integration testing between servlets and EJBs.

The following code shows how a unit test can be implemented using the JUnit framework. It shows the unit test code to test our LoginWorkflow session bean. Each test case is implemented as a separate method and the name of each method is prefixed with the word"test." This naming convention allows the JUnit framework to load all the test cases and execute them all with a single invocation. Thus, you can automate all your test cases and later run them as your regression test suite. Also, notice that the name of each test method clearly depicts the test condition that it tests. All the test cases are defined in a single test class that is also named after the class under test, with the word Test as the prefix.

TIP It is sometimes helpful to not only run your test cases individually, but also to run them repeatedly, and if need be, in a loop. Some bugs do not manifest when you run the test just once or when you run disconnected.

TestLoginWorkflow.java

```java
package com.wiley.compBooks.EJwithUML.Clients;

import javax.naming.*;
import javax.ejb.*;
import java.rmi.*;
import javax.rmi.PortableRemoteObject;
import java.util.*;
import com.wiley.compBooks.EJwithUML.TimeCardDomain.*;
import com.wiley.compBooks.EJwithUML.Dtos.*;
import com.wiley.compBooks.EJwithUML.TimeCardWorkflow.*;
import com.wiley.compBooks.EJwithUML.Base.ApplicationExceptions.*;
import com.wiley.compBooks.EJwithUML.Base.EjbUtil.*;
import junit.framework.*;

/**
 * This is JUint test class for testing LoginWorkflow EJB. This
 * test assumes that the EJB is running and accessible.
 */
public class TestLoginWorkflow extends TestCase
{
  private static LoginWorkflow lwf;

  public TestLoginWorkflow(String name)
  {
    super(name);
  }

  /** Executes all the test case */
  public static void main(String[] args)throws CreateException,
                            NamingException,RemoteException
  {
    Context initial = new InitialContext();
    Object objref = initial.lookup(
                    EjbReferenceNames.LOGIN_WORKFLOW_HOME);
    LoginWorkflowHome lwhome = (LoginWorkflowHome)
                    PortableRemoteObject.narrow(
```

```
                      objref,LoginWorkflowHome.class);
  lwf = lwhome.create();
  junit.textui.TestRunner.run(TestLoginWorkflow.class);
}


public void testLoginWithInvalidName()throws RemoteException
{
  try
  {
    boolean valid = lwf.isUserValid("syed", "abc123");
    fail("did not receive expected exception!");
  }
  catch(DataNotFoundException e)
  {
    System.out.println("received expected exception-" + " " + e);
  }
}


public void testLoginWithInvalidPassword()throws
                  DataNotFoundException, RemoteException
{
  boolean valid = lwf.isUserValid("fred", "a123");
  assertTrue("expected login failure.", !valid);
}


public static void testValidLogin()throws RemoteException
{
  try
  {
    boolean valid = lwf.isUserValid("fred", "abc123");
    assertTrue("login falied.", valid);
  }
  catch(ApplicationException e)
  {
    fail("received unexpected exception-" + " " + e);
  }
}


public void testSetPasswordSuccess()throws RemoteException
{
  try
  {
    lwf.setPassword("fred","abc123", "newp");
    boolean valid = lwf.isUserValid("fred", "newp");
    lwf.setPassword("fred","newp", "abc123");
  }
  catch(ApplicationException e)
  {
    fail("received unexpected exception-" + " " + e);
  }
}


public void testSetPasswordWithInvalidOldPassword() throws
DataNotFoundException, RemoteException
{
```

```
      try
      {
        lwf.setPassword("fred","ab123", "newp");
        fail("did not receive expected exception!");
      }
      catch(InvalidDataException e)
      {
        System.out.println("received expected exception-" + " " + e);
      }
    }

    public void testSetPasswordWithInvalidUser()throws RemoteException
    {
      try
      {
        lwf.setPassword("Syed","abc123", "newp");
        fail("did not receive expected exception!");
      }
      catch(DataNotFoundException e)
      {
        System.out.println("received expected exception-" + " " + e);
      }
      catch(InvalidDataException e)
      {
        fail("received unexpected exception-" + " " + e);
      }
    }

    public void testIsPasswordChangeRequiredWith()throws
                          RemoteException
  {
    try
    {
      boolean isRequired = lwf.isPasswordChangeRequired("fred");
      assertTrue("expected fred's password to be not temporary.",
                !isRequired);
    }
    catch(DataNotFoundException e)
    {
      System.out.println("received expected exception-" + " " + e);
    }
  }
}
```

The Next Step

The design and implementation for the TimecardDomain and TimecardWorkflow packages are now complete. Now, we move on to the next design effort: the TimecardUI package.

CHAPTER

16

Design for the TimecardUI Package

The TimecardUI package contains the servlets that provide a Web front end to the Login and Record Time use cases of the Timecard application. These servlets obtain and update system data by using the session beans in the TimecardWorkflow package and use the HTML production framework from the HtmlPrimitives packages to format the results into HTML. The Sun Microsystems servlet class library is used to interpret the HTTP request and to build the HTTP response.

As in earlier design efforts, we must identify goals and priorities, review prior steps, design to goals, and apply design to use cases.

Establish Design Goals

To develop a solid design, we need clear goals. Establishing clear goals before you begin to design helps designers avoid hasty decisions. After all, design forces a developer to compromise or pick between competing goals. Establishing clear goals upfront makes this easier and less arbitrary.

Extensibility

User interfaces always evolve over time, as users' needs mature. At times, users may desire different appearances for particular screens or for the system as a whole. In some cases, the customer might want to update the look of the entire site to emphasize a brand or to produce a fresh look. To keep the code base small, each new feature should reuse existing components or introduce new modular components that can be used on other features.

Because of these factors, the servlets in our system should never produce their own HTML. Instead, this tedious activity is always delegated to the classes of the HtmlProduction framework. If a new feature cannot be created by combining existing HTML producers, then a new HTML producer must be added to the framework. Once in the framework, the new producer becomes available for use in other servlets. Achieving a new look for the entire site should be accomplished by changing the style sheet and a few key producers, without altering the servlets themselves. Preventing the servlets from producing their own HTML, and forcing them to depend on the HTML production framework, keeps the system smaller and easier to understand and to extend.

Testability

The servlets tie together much of the system to provide direct benefit to the customer, so they are a logical place to start system and integration testing. While final testing involves Web browsers going against the Web server and the application server, it is useful to test the servlets inside an integrated development environment. This allows quick edit and rebuild cycles, and the use of a debugger. The alternative, whereby developers recompile classes and restart or notify the servlet engine after each change, is demoralizing and time-consuming. If the servlets are testable outside of the servlet engine, developers can perform independent and isolated load testing, which is useful to determine scalability and to locate performance bottlenecks.

Review Prior Steps

Before proceeding, we must review the architectural constraints as well as the analysis model.

Review Architectural Constraints

At the end of Chapter 13, "Software Architecture," we determined that the TimecardUI package depends directly on the HtmlProduction package and on the TimecardWorkflow package. It must not directly depend on any other package in the system. Specifically, TimecardUI classes must never directly access any entity beans. In addition, no other package depends on the TimecardUI package. Together, these restrictions help make the system more extensible and easier to understand and to maintain. For example, even radical changes in the way data is stored or in the business logic for validating timecards will not affect the servlets, as long as they do not affect the public interface of the TimecardWorkflow session beans. Figure 16.1 shows the architecture as it affects the TimecardUI package.

Review Analysis Model

In this step, we review the analysis model for the Login and Record Time use cases.

Review Analysis Model for Login Use Case

The Login use case allows users to validate themselves to the system as a precursor to any use of the system. The Login use case has one normal flow and two alternate flows. The alternate flows show different ways that the user's information can be invalid.

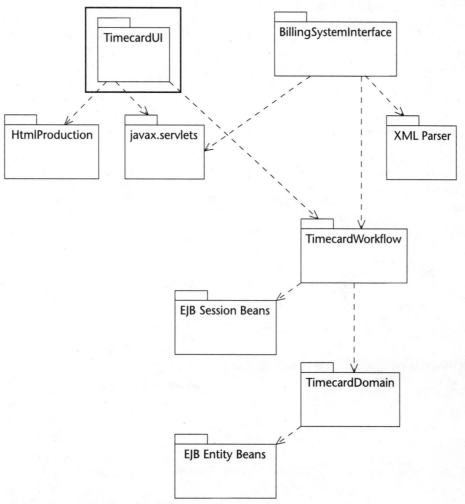

Figure 16.1   Architectural constraints.

Normal Flow (Analysis)

The sequence begins when the employee asks the EmployeeLoginUI to display the login form. The employee then uses the form to submit his or her username and password. The EmployeeLoginUI asks the LoginWorkflow to validate the login information. Since the LoginWorkflow does not have the information needed to perform the validation, it uses the UserLocator to find the User object, and the resulting User object to finally validate the login information. Figure 16.2 shows the sequence diagram from the analysis model.

Alternate Flow for Invalid Password (Analysis)

The sequence for the alternate flow for an invalid password begins when the employee asks the EmployeeLoginUI to display the login form. The employee then uses the form to submit his or her username and password. The EmployeeLoginUI asks the Login-Workflow to validate the login information. Since the LoginWorkflow does not have the information needed to perform the validation, it uses the UserLocator to find the User object, and the resulting User object to finally validate the login information. In this case, the User object responds that the user's information is invalid; the EmployeeLoginUI displays an error message, and the sequence is complete. Figure 16.3 shows the sequence diagram from the analysis model.

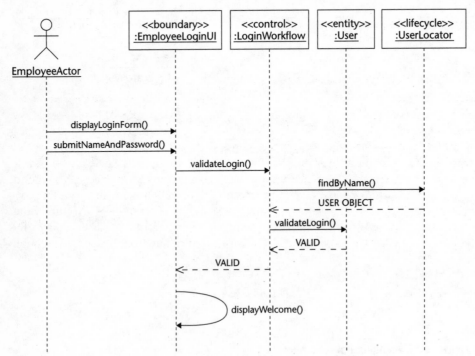

Figure 16.2 Sequence diagram for normal flow of Login (analysis).

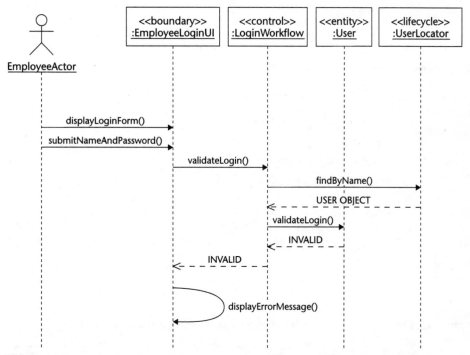

Figure 16.3 Sequence diagram for invalid password for Login use case (analysis).

Alternate Flow for Unknown User (Analysis)

When the user is unknown, the sequence for the alternate flow begins when the employee asks the EmployeeLoginUI to display the login form. The employee then uses the form to submit his or her username and password. The EmployeeLoginUI asks the LoginWorkflow to validate the login information. Since the LoginWorkflow does not have the information needed to perform the validation, it uses the UserLocator to find the User object. In this flow of events, no matching User object can be found, so the LoginWorkflow responds that the user's information is invalid. The EmployeeLoginUI displays an error message, and the sequence is complete. The return value of invalid does not convey the reason why the login information is invalid to the EmployeeLoginUI. Figure 16.4 shows the sequence diagram from the analysis model.

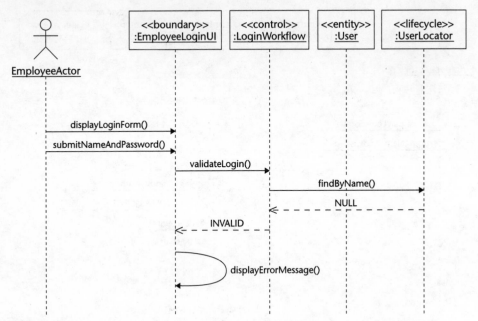

Figure 16.4   Sequence diagram for unknown user for Login use case (analysis).

Participating Classes for the Login Use Case (Analysis)

The user interface objects use LoginWorkflow objects. The resulting relationship needs to be an association, so that the user interface objects can reuse the same LoginWorkflow object for login retries. The LoginWorkflow object uses a User object, but does not need to remember it for future use; therefore, the resulting relationship is a dependency. The LoginWorkflow object uses a UserLocator object and keeps it for future use, so the resulting relationship is an association. These relationships are shown in Figure 16.5.

Review Analysis Model for Record Time Use Case

In the Record Time use case, an employee views his or her current hours, edits existing hours, adds new hours, and optionally submits the timecard. The normal flow is the only significant flow of events from a user interface based on user interface complexity and processing.

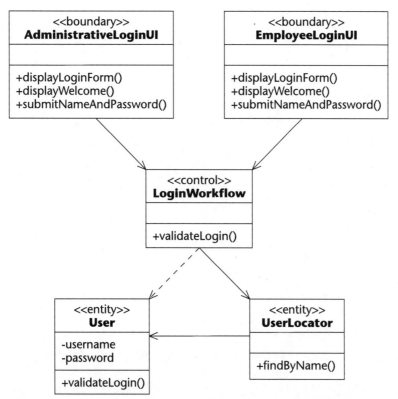

Figure 16.5   Participating classes for the Login use case (analysis).

Normal Flow for Record Time Use Case (Analysis)

The sequence for the normal flow of events begins when the employee actor asks the RecordTimeUI object to display his or her current timecard. The RecordTimeUI object passes the request along to the RecordTimeWorkflow object, which finds the user's current timecard and extracts the current timecard data. The RecordTimeUI uses this raw data to build a display. The employee actor uses the display to update the entries. The RecordTimeUI sends the updated entries back to the RecordTimeWorkflow, which applies them to the current timecard. Figure 16.6 shows this sequence.

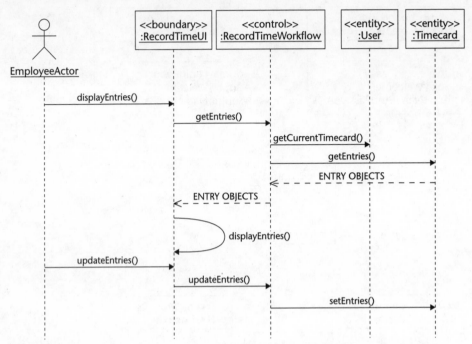

Figure 16.6   Sequence diagram for normal flow for Record Time use case (analysis).

Design to Goals

Our design is fairly constrained, since we know that we will use servlets and the HTML production classes. However, we must still consider our two goals: extensibility and testability.

Extensibility can be achieved by keeping each servlet well focused and by always depending on the HTML production classes. If the desired functionality does not exist within the HTML production class library, we must either create a new HTML producer that can live within the library or wait for an HTML production developer to do so. Creating our own custom HTML production code that lives within a servlet is not acceptable, because this gradually leads away from standardization and reusable HTML production code.

Stressing testability leads to several useful utility classes. Fully testing a servlet-based application requires us to simulate requests, capture the responses, and validate them. For example, a JUnit test case might include a test method that builds a request, submits it to the servlet, and saves the response bytes to a file. The test method asserts that the response bytes match a previously validated file. For our purposes, we will refer to this file as a "gold" file, as in "good as gold" or "gold standard." If the gold file doesn't exist or if the gold file differs from the results, the assertion fails. When the developer decides that the output is okay, they rename it so that it has the prefix "gold" and subsequent tests will pass as long as the output matches. This approach requires the unit test to simulate the HttpServletRequest, HttpServletResponse, and HttpSession objects. It also requires a file comparison utility to save each response and verify it against the gold file. This allows us to test the bulk of the servlet's functionality from a static main entry point, perhaps even from the debugger of our choice. The code, compile, and test cycle is significantly easier in an integrated development environment (IDE). It pays to minimize the amount of time spent testing servlet code in an actual servlet container.

> **NOTE** A reasonable implementation of this scheme can be found in the com.wiley.compBooks.EJwithUML.Base.TestUtilities package on the accompanying Web site (www.wiley.com/compbooks/arrington).

Design for Each Use Case

We need to create a design for both the Login and the Record Time use cases. Each use case dynamically builds several HTML pages and processes the data that the user enters, for one or more HTML forms. Since page production and form processing are tightly intertwined, it seems logical to encapsulate those tasks for each set of closely related forms in a single servlet. This results in three servlets: LoginServlet, SelectChargeCodeServlet, and RecordTimeServlet. The decision to split the Record Time use case into two servlets rather than one is based on our personal preferences for class size. It is fairly common for one boundary class in the analysis model to evolve into multiple user interface classes in the actual design.

Create Design for the Login Use Case

Our design for the Login use case considers three major flows: building the empty form, processing valid login data, and processing invalid login data.

Build the Login Form

The first step is to build an empty login form in HTML. While it is certainly possible to use a static HTML page for this purpose, producing dynamic HTML for static pages helps ensure the same look for all of the pages.

The LoginServlet knows to produce the empty form because the username parameter is not set in the HttpRequest object.

Next, a SimpleInputFormProducer is created with a title, instructions, a label for the Submit button, and a target URL that links back to the LoginServlet.

Fields for the name and password are added to the SimpleInputFormProducer before the SimpleInputFormProducer is added to the TimecardPageProducer. Finally, formatted HTML is extracted from the TimecardPageProducer and written to the HttpServletResponse's output stream. Figure 16.7 shows the sequence of messages that produces an empty login form.

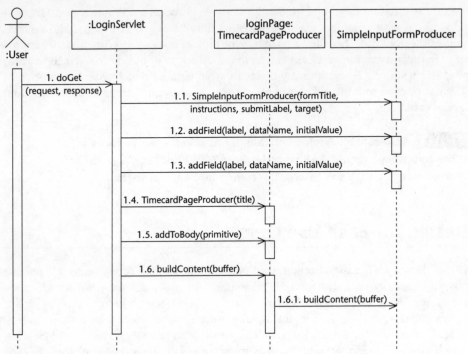

Figure 16.7   Sequence to build Login form.

Process Valid Login Data

In the sequence for processing valid login data, the username and password parameters exist in the HttpServletRequest. The LoginServlet asks the LoginWorkflow to validate the username and password combination. When the true response is received, the LoginServlet stores the username in the HttpSession.

Next, the LoginServlet builds a page with links to the user's options. For now, there is only one option, record time. In any case, the link is built by creating a LinkPrimitive. As we might expect, the target for the LinkPrimitive is set to the URL of the Record-TimeServlet.

The LoginServlet adds the LinkPrimitive to the TimecardPageProducer and extracts the formatted HTML from the PageProducer. This sequence is shown in Figure 16.8.

Process Invalid Login Data

As in the sequence for valid data, the username and password parameters exist in the HttpServletRequest. However, in this scenario, the isUserValid method in the LoginWorkflow returns false, so the LoginServlet builds a page with a SimpleInput-FormProducer, as in the build empty form, and adds a SpanPrimitive with some explanatory error text. Figure 16.9 shows this sequence.

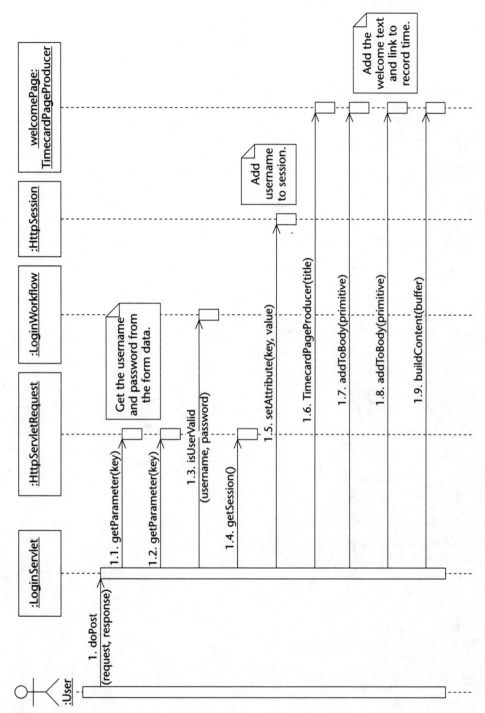

Figure 16.8   Sequence for a valid user.

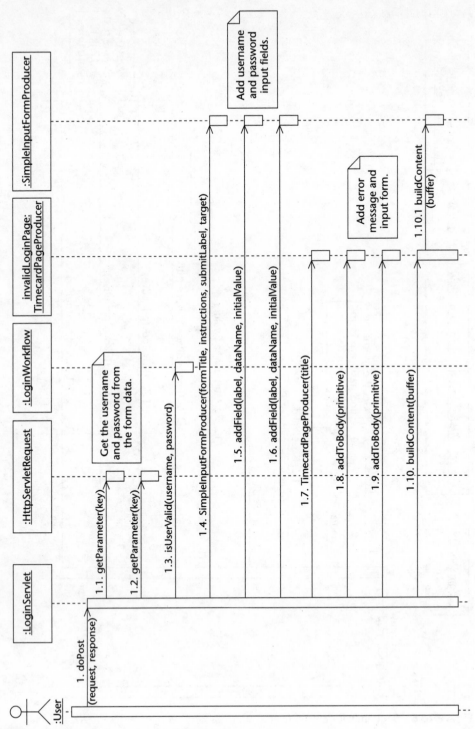

Figure 16.9 Sequence for invalid login data.

Participating Classes for the Login Use Case

LoginServlet sits in the middle of the action, like a frantic Hollywood agent, knowing all of the players but unable to accomplish anything on its own. This is a very common and powerful concept: One thin class combines the talents of many other classes to form a new and interesting whole. Luckily, classes and objects are truly egoless, so the HTML producers do not mind the servlets' time in the limelight while they perform the tedious HTML formatting.

Notice the complete lack of association relationships in the class diagram. Remember, each sequence begins when the servlet engine calls the doPost method of the LoginServlet, and the same LoginServlet object is used to validate any number of users. Everything that the LoginServlet needs to produce the HTML is passed into the doPost method inside of the HttpServletRequest object. Figure 16.10 shows the classes for the Login use case.

Create Design for the Record Time Use Case

Based on our recently refreshed memory of the analysis model for the Record Time use case and our knowledge of the Servlet class library and the HTML production classes, we can develop a design for the Record Time user interface. There are two main sequences: building the Record Time form and updating the timecard based on a submitted form.

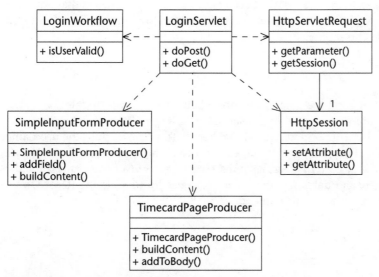

Figure 16.10   Participating classes for the Login use case.

Build the Record Time Form

The sequence begins when the employee actor asks the RecordTimeServlet to build the time entry form. The RecordTimeServlet extracts the username from the HttpSession, and uses it to create a RecordTimeWorkflow object for the specified employee. The RecordTimeServlet asks the RecordTimeWorkflow for the charge codes, dates, and hours for the current timecard. With the raw data in hand, the RecordTimeServlet creates a FormPrimitive and a TablePrimitive. The TablePrimitive will hold the data and the input text fields, so it must be added to the FormPrimitive. Each SpanPrimitive holds the charge codes, and the dates must be created, configured with the correct text and style, and added to the correct cell in the TablePrimitive. A similar process populates the table with TextBoxPrimitives for the hours. Next, the FormPrimitive is configured with the appropriate submit target and is added to the TimecardPageProducer. A welcome message and a LinkPrimitive configured with SelectChargeCodeServlet as its target complete the page. Figure 16.11 shows this sequence.

Build the Select Charge Code Form

The sequence begins when the employee clicks on the Add Charge Code link on the Record Time page, which results in a GET request being sent to the SelectChargeCode-Servlet. The SelectChargeCodeServlet creates a RecordTimeWorkflow session bean and calls its getAllClients method. It then iterates through the resulting collection of charge codes, adding text and an Add link for each charge code to a TablePrimitive. Each Add link points to the RecordTimeServlet and contains parameters that uniquely identify the charge code. The TablePrimitive is then added to a TimecardPageProducer. Figure 16.12 shows this sequence.

Update the Timecard

The sequence for updating the timecard begins when the employee updates his or her time entries and submits the form to the servlet. The RecordTimeServlet extracts the HttpSession from the HttpServletRequest. The RecordTimeServlet pulls the username out of the session and uses it to get a remote reference to the appropriate RecordTime-Workflow. Next, the RecordTimeServlet pulls parameters out of the request for the hours, charge codes, and dates. The hours are then used to update the RecordTime-Workflow. Figure 16.13 shows this sequence.

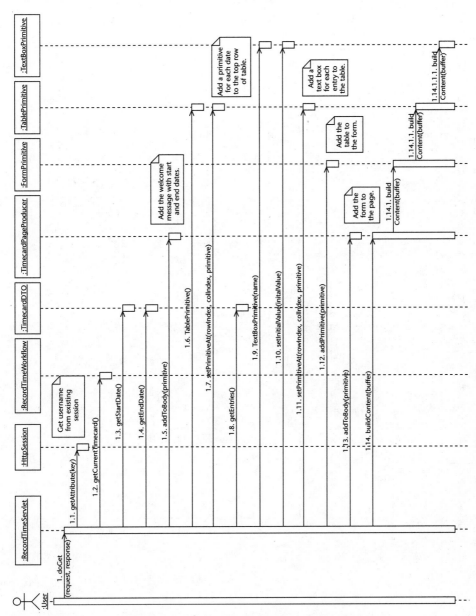

Figure 16.11 Sequence diagram for building the Record Time form.

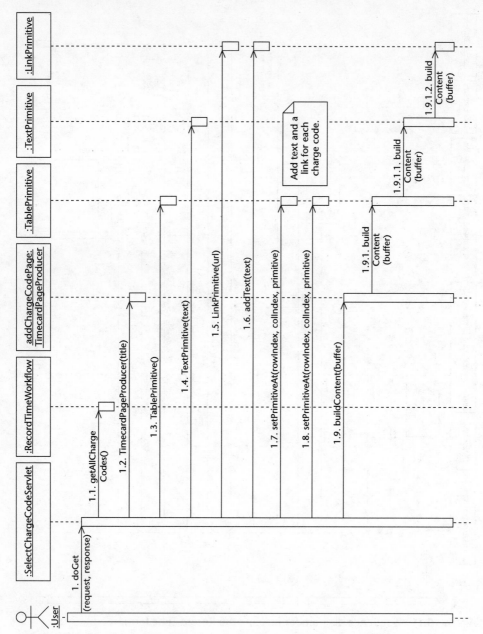

Figure 16.12 Sequence diagram for building the Add a Charge Code page.

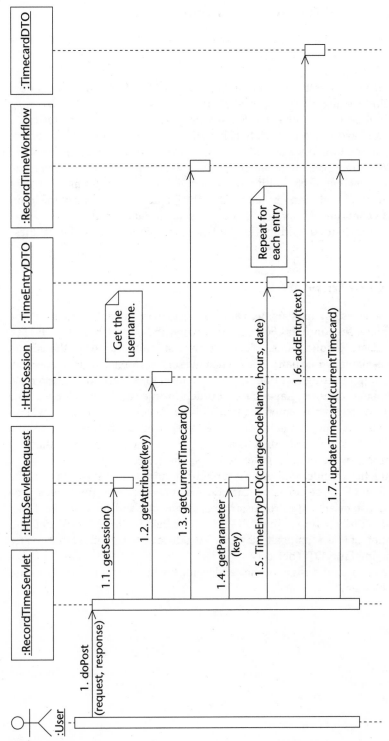

Figure 16.13 Sequence diagram for updating the timecard.

Participating Classes for the Record Time Use Case

Many classes help realize the Record Time use case, but most are independent of the others. As in the Login use case, the servlet ties the disparate objects together. Again, it is worth noting that the RecordTimeServlet does not do any real work: It does not retrieve any data from the database, it does not format any HTML, and it certainly does not hold any business logic. It just knows where to go to ask.

At first glance, it seems odd that the RecordTimeServlet class depends on many classes, yet does not have any lasting relationship with any classes. For instance, where is the one-to-one or one-to-many association between the RecordTimeServlet class and the RecordTimeWorkflow class? Remember that all of the work done by a servlet is initiated when the servlet engine calls either the servlet's doPost or doGet method. Also recall that many users may share a servlet. So, the HttpRequest contains all of the information that the RecordTimeServlet needs, including form data and the RecordTime-Workflow that is embedded within the HttpSession. Figure 16.14 shows these relationships.

Keeping the Data Straight

Every servlet-based system uses name/value pairs to pass data to and from the browser and to track session data. For example, when the servlet builds an HTML form, each field has a unique name. When the user submits the form, the servlet receives the data as name/value pairs. Also, when the servlet stores data in the session, it must provide a unique string identifier that can be used to retrieve the session data. Managing these names does not have to be a burden for the servlet developers. One simple solution is to create an enumerated type of keys. As long as all of the developers use this enumerated type, retrieving data is easy—just select the right key from a list of values. This saves time and prevents a multitude of errors due to variations in spelling. For example, without an enumerated type, one piece of code might build a form with a uname field, while another servlet might attempt to retrieve data from the username field. To avoid these issues, we introduce a TimecardKeys enumerated type and add public constant attributes for username, password, and other fields. Timecards also include entries whose names should reflect the charge code and date. To simplify the creation of these composite keys, we introduce a static method that creates a key based on a TimeEntryDTO object.

Now that we have a solid design for the servlets for the Login and Record Time use cases, we can implement them in Java.

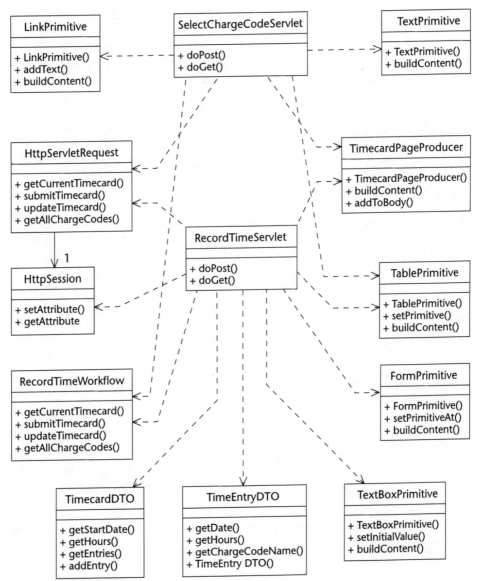

Figure 16.14   Participating classes for Record Time use case.

Implementation

The following sections show the implementation for the TimecardKeys, the Timecard-specific producers, the TimecardStyle, the stylesheet, the LoginServlet, the Record-TimeServlet, and the AddChargeCodeServlet.

TimecardKey.java

The TimecardKey class is a simple enumerated type that captures all of the keys that are used to store and retrieve values in the HTTP session and in the HTTP form data. This prevents confusion due to different spelling practices. For example, similarly to the situation mentioned in the *Keeping the Data Straight* section, left to their own devices, one developer might capture a username in a parameter named "uname," while another developer might spell out the parameter as "username." Using an enumerated type to hold the keys eliminates these potential errors and, in conjunction with a modern IDE, allows developers to pick the appropriate key from a list.

```java
package com.wiley.compBooks.EJwithUML.TimecardUI;
public class TimecardKey
{
  public static final TimecardKey USERNAME = new TimecardKey("username");
  public static final TimecardKey PASSWORD = new TimecardKey("password");
  public static final TimecardKey CLIENT = new TimecardKey("client");
  public static final TimecardKey PROJECT = new TimecardKey("project");
  public static final TimecardKey CODE = new TimecardKey("code");
  public static final TimecardKey SAVE_CODE = new TimecardKey("save_code");
  public static final TimecardKey SAVE_TIMECARD = new
TimecardKey("save_timecard");
  public static final TimecardKey SUBMIT_TIMECARD =  new
TimecardKey("submit_timecard");

  private String keyText;

  private TimecardKey(String keyText)
  {
    this.keyText = keyText;
  }

  public String getKeyText()
  {
    return this.keyText;
  }

  public boolean equals(Object o)
  {
    if (!o.getClass().getName().equals(TimecardKey.class.getName()))
    {
      return false;
    }

    TimecardKey other = (TimecardKey) o;
```

```
        return other.getKeyText().equals(this.getKeyText());
    }
}
```

TimecardPageProducer.java

The TimecardPageProducer class captures the common appearance of all Timecard pages. Specifically, each page has a header at the top and a footer at the bottom. Since TimecardPageProducer does not override addToBody, client objects are actually adding their content directly to the superclass, PagePrimitive. TimecardPageProducer simply adds its own header content through its constructor. It also adds its footer to the superclass's content as part of its buildContent method. It is important to note that the TimecardPageProducer determines the gross structure of every page in the Timecard application, while leaving details such as colors, fonts, and spacing to a common Timecard stylesheet.

```java
package com.wiley.compBooks.EJwithUML.TimecardProducers;

import com.wiley.compBooks.EJwithUML.Base.HtmlPrimitives.*;
import com.wiley.compBooks.EJwithUML.Base.HtmlPrimitives.Core.*;
import com.wiley.compBooks.EJwithUML.Base.HtmlPrimitives.Layout.*;
import com.wiley.compBooks.EJwithUML.Base.HtmlPrimitives.FormPrimitives.*;
import com.wiley.compBooks.EJwithUML.Base.HtmlPrimitives.ContentElements.*;


public class TimecardPageProducer extends PagePrimitive
{
    public TimecardPageProducer(String title)
    {
        super(title, "./Timecard.css");
        super.addToBody(new ParagraphPrimitive(TimecardStyle.TOP_OF_PAGE, "Timecard
Sample Application"));
    }

    /** Adds the HTML for this TimecardPageProducer to the specified buffer */
    public void buildContent(StringBuffer buffer)
    {
        ParagraphPrimitive bottom =new
ParagraphPrimitive(TimecardStyle.BOTTOM_OF_PAGE, "Just a sample application");
        bottom.addLineBreak();
        bottom.addText("Part of Enterprise Java with UML");
        bottom.addLineBreak();
        bottom.addText("By CT Arrington and Syed Rayhan");
        bottom.addLineBreak();
        bottom.addText("Definitely NOT for commercial use ;)");

        super.addToBody(bottom);
        super.buildContent(buffer);
    }
}
```

SimpleInputFormProducer.java

The SimpleInputFormProducer class defines the main structure for simple input forms. It also greatly simplifies form production for client objects. As with the Time-cardPageProducer, the details of colors, fonts, and spacing are left to the stylesheet.

```java
package com.wiley.compBooks.EJwithUML.TimecardProducers;

import com.wiley.compBooks.EJwithUML.Base.HtmlPrimitives.*;
import com.wiley.compBooks.EJwithUML.Base.HtmlPrimitives.Core.*;
import com.wiley.compBooks.EJwithUML.Base.HtmlPrimitives.Layout.*;
import com.wiley.compBooks.EJwithUML.Base.HtmlPrimitives.FormPrimitives.*;
import com.wiley.compBooks.EJwithUML.Base.HtmlPrimitives.ContentElements.*;

import java.util.*;

/** The SimpleInputFormProducer class encapsulates the details of building the HTML
  *  for a simple input form. */
public class SimpleInputFormProducer implements IHtmlPrimitive
{
  private FormPrimitive form;
  private TablePrimitive table;
  private SubmitPrimitive submit;
  private String instructions;
  private int rowCtr = 0;


  /** Construct a SimpleInputFormProducer with the specified submit button label
and target.*/
  public SimpleInputFormProducer(String formTitle, String instructions, String
submitLabel, String target)
  {
    submit = new SubmitPrimitive(submitLabel);

    SpanPrimitive titleSpan = new SpanPrimitive(TimecardStyle.FORM_TITLE,
formTitle);
    titleSpan.addLineBreak();

    SpanPrimitive instructionsSpan = new
SpanPrimitive(TimecardStyle.FORM_INSTRUCTIONS, instructions);
    instructionsSpan.addLineBreak();
    instructionsSpan.addLineBreak();

    form = new FormPrimitive(target,"sip");
    form.addPrimitive(titleSpan);
    form.addPrimitive(instructionsSpan);

    table = new TablePrimitive();
    table.setStyle(TimecardStyle.FORM_LAYOUT_TABLE);
    form.addPrimitive(table);
  }

  /** Adds the HTML for this SimpleInputFormProducer to the specified buffer */
```

```
    public void buildContent(StringBuffer buffer)
    {
      table.setPrimitiveAt(rowCtr,1,submit);
      form.buildContent(buffer);
    }

    public void addField(String label, String dataName, String initialValue)
    {
      this.addField(label, dataName, initialValue, false);
    }

    public void addMaskedField(String label, String dataName, String initialValue)
    {
      this.addField(label, dataName, initialValue, true);
    }

    /** Add a labeled input field to this SimpleInputFormProducer. */
    private void addField(String label, String dataName, String initialValue,
  boolean masked)
    {
      TextBoxPrimitive textBox = new TextBoxPrimitive(dataName);
      if (masked)
      {
        textBox.setMasked();
      }
      textBox.setInitialValue(initialValue);

      table.setStyleForCells(TimecardStyle.FORM_FIELD_LABEL_CELL);
      table.setPrimitiveAt(rowCtr, 0, new
  SpanPrimitive(TimecardStyle.FORM_FIELD_LABEL,label));
      table.setStyleForCells(TimecardStyle.FORM_FIELD_INPUT_CELL);
      table.setPrimitiveAt(rowCtr++, 1, textBox);
    }

}
```

TimecardStyle.java

The TimecardStyle is an extension of the Style enumerated type, which defines the styles that may be used throughout the HTML production framework. The Timecard-Style adds styles that are referenced by the TimecardPageProducer, the SimpleInput-FormProducer, and the various Timecard servlets.

```
package com.wiley.compBooks.EJwithUML.TimecardProducers;

import com.wiley.compBooks.EJwithUML.Base.HtmlPrimitives.Core.Style;

/** The TimecardStyle class is an application-specific extension of the Style
  *  enumerated type.*/
public class TimecardStyle extends Style
{
  /** Construct a TimecardStyle object with the specified style class as its
```

```
value. */
  protected TimecardStyle(String style)
  {
    super(style);
  }


  public final static TimecardStyle FORM_LAYOUT_TABLE = new
TimecardStyle("form_layout_table");
  public final static TimecardStyle FORM_TITLE = new
TimecardStyle("form_title");
  public final static TimecardStyle FORM_INSTRUCTIONS = new
TimecardStyle("form_instructions");
  public final static TimecardStyle FORM_FIELD_LABEL = new
TimecardStyle("form_field_label");
  public final static TimecardStyle FORM_FIELD_LABEL_CELL = new
TimecardStyle("form_field_label_cell");
  public final static TimecardStyle FORM_FIELD_INPUT_CELL = new
TimecardStyle("form_field_input_cell");
  public final static TimecardStyle FORM_FIELD_TIP = new
TimecardStyle("form_field_tip");
  public final static TimecardStyle FORM_REQUIRED = new
TimecardStyle("form_required");
  public final static TimecardStyle FORM_SPACING = new
TimecardStyle("form_spacing");
  public final static TimecardStyle FORM_BUTTON = new
TimecardStyle("form_button");


  public final static TimecardStyle TOP_OF_PAGE = new
TimecardStyle("top_of_page");
  public final static TimecardStyle BOTTOM_OF_PAGE = new
TimecardStyle("bottom_of_page");
  public final static TimecardStyle CHARGE_CODE_SELECTION_TABLE = new
TimecardStyle("charge_code_selection_table");
  public final static TimecardStyle CHARGE_CODE_SELECTION_CELLS = new
TimecardStyle("charge_code_selection_cells");


}
```

Timecard.css

The Timecard stylesheet captures the low-level color, font, and spacing decisions for the style classes that are used in the application.

```
<style>
<!--
* {font: 12pt sans-serif; color: black}

body {background-color: ivory}

.page_title {color: blue; font-size: 16pt}
.important_text {font-weight: bold}
.warning_text {font-weight: bold;color: red}
```

```
.normal_text {color: black}
.fineprint_text {font-size: 8pt}

.data_table_header {font-weight: bold;color:blue}
.data_table_dark_row {background-color: lightgray}
.data_table_light_row {background-color: aliceblue}
.data_table_normal_row {}

.form_layout_table {}
.form_title {font-size: 14pt; font-weight: bold; color:blue}
.form_instructions {color:blue}
.form_field_label_cell {padding: 5; margin:5; width: 30%}
.form_field_input_cell {padding: 3; margin:5}
.form_field_label {font-weight: bold; color:blue}
.form_field_tip {font-size: 10pt; color:blue}
.form_required {padding-left: 10; font-size: 10pt; color:red}
.form_spacing {height: 20}
.form_button {margin-left: 30; font-size: 10pt; color:black}

.charge_code_selection_table {border-color: blue; border-style: solid; border-
width: 2px}
.charge_code_selection_cells {padding: 5;font-weight: bold;color:blue;border-
color: blue; border-style: solid; border-width: 1px}

.normal_image {padding: 0.5cm; background-color: gray}
.normal_textbox {}
.debug_table {border-color: blue; border-style: solid; border-width: 2px; width:
600; height: 600}

.top_of_page {padding: 5; text-align: center; font-size: 20pt; font-weight:
bold; color: Black; background-color: lightgrey; border: medium solid black}
.bottom_of_page {padding: 5; text-align: center; font-size: 8pt; font-weight:
bold; color: Black; background-color: lightgrey; border: medium solid black}
-->
</style>
```

LoginServlet.java

The LoginServlet does not directly format any HTML. Instead, it extracts information from the LoginWorkflow class and uses the HTML Production packages to format all of the HTML.

If the username parameter is not set, then the LoginServlet knows that the user needs to enter his or her information in an HTML form.

```
package com.wiley.compBooks.EJwithUML.TimecardUI;

import javax.servlet.http.*;
import javax.servlet.*;

import javax.naming.*;
import javax.ejb.*;
import java.rmi.*;
```

```java
import javax.rmi.PortableRemoteObject;

import java.io.*;

import com.wiley.compBooks.EJwithUML.Base.HtmlPrimitives.Core.*;
import com.wiley.compBooks.EJwithUML.Base.HtmlPrimitives.Layout.*;
import com.wiley.compBooks.EJwithUML.Base.HtmlPrimitives.ContentElements.*;
import com.wiley.compBooks.EJwithUML.Base.EjbUtil.*;
import com.wiley.compBooks.EJwithUML.Base.ApplicationExceptions.*;
import com.wiley.compBooks.EJwithUML.TimeCardWorkflow.*;
import com.wiley.compBooks.EJwithUML.TimecardProducers.*;


/**
 *
 * The LoginServlet class uses the TimecardWorkflow and
 * HtmlPrimitives packages to create the formatted HTML
 * for the Login form and to validate the user.
 *
 */
public class LoginServlet extends BasicTimecardServlet
{
  private LoginWorkflowHome lwfHome = null;

  public void doGet(HttpServletRequest request, HttpServletResponse response)
throws ServletException, IOException
  {
    doPost(request, response);
  }

  /** Overrides method from HttpServlet.
      doPost is called by the servlet engine. */
  public void doPost(HttpServletRequest request, HttpServletResponse response)
throws ServletException, IOException
  {
    System.out.println("LoginServlet: doPost");
    PagePrimitive pagePrimitive = null;

    try
    {
      // Extract username and password.
      String username = request.getParameter(TimecardKey.USERNAME.getKeyText());
      String password = request.getParameter(TimecardKey.PASSWORD.getKeyText());

      if (username == null)
      {
        pagePrimitive = buildLoginPage();
      }
      else
      {
        if (this.isLoginValid(username, password))
        {
          HttpSession session = request.getSession(true);
```

```
                session.setAttribute(TimecardKey.USERNAME.getKeyText(), username);

                pagePrimitive = buildWelcomePage(username);
            }
            else
            {
                pagePrimitive = buildLoginInvalidPage();
            }
        }
    }
    catch (NamingException e)
    {
      pagePrimitive = this.getErrorPage("Error During Login\n", e);
    }
    catch (CreateException e)
    {
      pagePrimitive = this.getErrorPage("Error During Login\n", e);
    }

    StringBuffer buffer = new StringBuffer();
    pagePrimitive.buildContent(buffer);
    response.getWriter().println(buffer);
    response.getWriter().flush();
    response.getWriter().close();
  }

  /** Build the page to display for a successful login.*/
  private PagePrimitive buildWelcomePage(String username)
  {
    PagePrimitive page = new TimecardPageProducer("Welcome");
    ParagraphPrimitive welcome = new
ParagraphPrimitive(TimecardStyle.PAGE_TITLE, "Welcome, " +username);
    page.addToBody(welcome);
    LinkPrimitive link = new LinkPrimitive("/Timecard/RecordTimeServlet");
    link.addText("Enter Hours");
    page.addToBody(link);
    return page;
  }

  /** Build the page for user input */
  private PagePrimitive buildLoginPage()
  {
    SimpleInputFormProducer form = new SimpleInputFormProducer("Login", "Please
enter your username and password.","Login", "./LoginServlet");
    form.addField("User Name", TimecardKey.USERNAME.getKeyText(), "");
    form.addMaskedField("Password", TimecardKey.PASSWORD.getKeyText(), "");

    PagePrimitive page = new TimecardPageProducer("Login");
    page.addToBody(form);
    return page;
  }

  /** Build the page with an error message for when login fails. */
```

```
      private PagePrimitive buildLoginInvalidPage()
      {
         PagePrimitive page = buildLoginPage();

         SpanPrimitive errorMessage = new SpanPrimitive(Style.WARNING_TEXT, "Invalid
username or password. Remember, case matters.");
         page.addToBody(errorMessage);
         return page;
      }

      /** Answer true if the login data matches the database.*/
      private boolean isLoginValid(String username, String password) throws
NamingException, RemoteException, CreateException
      {
         boolean valid = false;

         try
         {
            createLoginWorkflowHome();
            LoginWorkflow lwf = lwfHome.create();
            valid = lwf.isUserValid(username, password);
         }
         catch (DataNotFoundException e)
         {
            valid = false;
         }

         return valid;
      }

      private void createLoginWorkflowHome() throws NamingException
      {
         if (lwfHome == null)
         {
            Context initial = new InitialContext();
            Object objref = initial.lookup(EjbReferenceNames.LOGIN_WORKFLOW_HOME);
            lwfHome =
(LoginWorkflowHome)PortableRemoteObject.narrow(objref,LoginWorkflowHome.class);
         }
      }
}
```

RecordTimeServlet.java

The RecordTimeServlet uses the RecordTimeWorkflow to retrieve and update time-cards. If no entry or new charge code is specified, the RecordTimeServlet retrieves the current timecard and builds an entry form. If an entry is submitted, the RecordTime-Servlet first updates the timecard through the RecordTimeWorkflow and then builds an entry form. If a new charge code is specified, then the RecordTimeServlet creates new zero hour entries for the charge code, updates the timecard, and then builds an entry form.

NOTE To see a sample of this code, please visit the Web site at
www.wiley.com/compbooks/arrington.

SelectChargeCodeServlet.java

The SelectChargeCodeServlet uses the RecordTimeWorkflow to get a collection of
charge codes that are valid for the system. It uses TablePrimitive, TextPrimitive, and
LinkPrimitive to build a list of charge codes with an associated "Add" link for each
charge code. When the user clicks on an "Add" link, RecordTimeServlet uses the
request parameters to identify the correct charge code to add to the timecard.

NOTE To see a sample of this code, please visit the Web site at
www.wiley.com/compbooks/arrington.

The Next Step

In this chapter, we used session beans, as designed in Chapter 15, "Design for the
Timecard Domain and TimecardWorkflow," and the HTML production classes, as
designed in Chapter 8, "HTML Production," to produce the dynamically generated
HTML for the Timecard system. At this point, we have completed the core functionality for the Timecard system. The last step is the interface with the billing system, which
we cover in Chapter 17, "Design for the BillingSystemInterface."

Design for the BillingSystemInterface

The design for the BillingSystemInterface subsystem builds heavily on the analysis model, architecture, and technology selection, and the design for the TimecardWorkflow packages, as developed in Chapter 5, "Analysis Model for the Timecard Application," Chapter 11, "Evaluating Web Service Technologies for the System Interface," Chapter 12, "Evaluating Candidate Technologies for Control and Entity Classes," Chapter 13, "Software Architecture," and Chapter 15, "Design for the Timecard-Domain and TimecardWorkflow." The analysis model developed in Chapter 5 will help us to determine the behavior of the BillingSystemInterface subsystem, while the content in Chapters 11, 12, and 13 will help us to determine the technologies, and Chapter 15 will help us to implement the subsystem using the existing packages defined for the other use cases.

As in the preceding design chapters, the goal here is to develop a design that is quite close to code and that is also constrained by the functional, architectural, and technological decisions made in those chapters. In this chapter, we will establish design goals, review the analysis model to recall the required functionality, then review the architecture to remind us of the architectural constraints. Based on this foundation, we will build a design that fits the use case.

Identify Goals

The design for the BillingSystemInterface should support the goals established for the entire system in Chapter 14, "Introduction to Design." Clarity, performance, reliability, extensibility, and reuse potential are all considered goals for the BillingSystemInterface.

Clarity

Clarity is always an important goal, and the BillingSystemInterface is no exception. Both the design and the code must be understood by a wide variety of developers, from reviewers to maintenance developers. Adherence to design guidelines and code standards is very important.

Performance and Reliability

Performance and reliability are less important for the BillingSystemInterface than for the system in general. The BillingSystemInterface is intended for occasional use, and can be limited to off-peak hours if necessary.

Extensibility

Extensibility is fairly important for the BillingSystemInterface, since the billing system itself is outside of our control and subject to change. The BillingSystemInterface must be able to evolve to meet different requirements for the format or content of the interchange data. Also, the BillingSystemInterface must be flexible in the criteria used to include or exclude time entries.

At the very least, these two areas must be kept well encapsulated, so that any changes are confined to a few closely related classes.

Reuse Potential

Reuse potential is relatively unimportant. No other part of the Timecard system needs any of this logic, and the BillingSystemInterface is not solving a generally applicable problem that might be shared by other systems.

Review of Analysis Model

There is only one use case that uses the BillingSystemInterface subsystem, Extract Time Entries. The sequence begins when the BillingSystem sends a request to the Extract-TimeEntriesServlet, the boundary object, for time entry data based on some criteria. The ExtractTimeEntriesServlet parses this request and forwards the request on to the control object, ExportTimeEntriesWorkflow. The ExportTimeEntriesWorkflow uses the criteria to filter the time entries using the locator objects and the corresponding entity objects. Figure 17.1 shows this sequence.

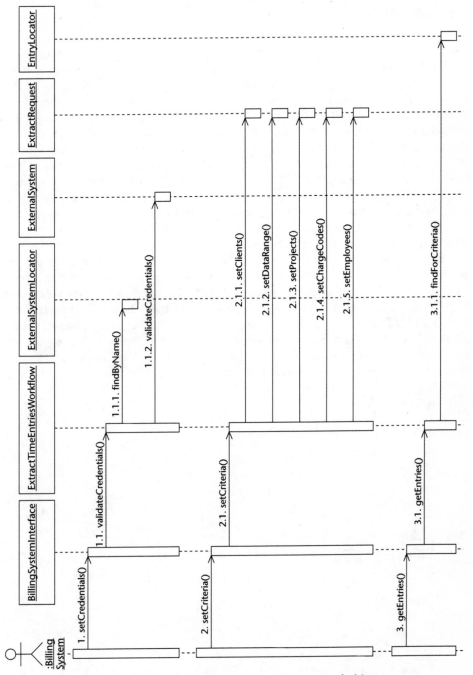

Figure 17.1 Sequence diagram for the Extract Time Entries (analysis) use case.

Review of Architecture

Based on the architecture developed in Chapters 12 and 13, the BillingSystem could potentially connect with the Timecard application at one of the two entry points—either the presentation layer (servlet) or the business logic layer (EJB). In other words, the BillingSystemInterface can either be an EJB or a servlet. If we choose to have the Billing SystemInterface be an EJB, the billing system needs to be able to speak RMI (the billing system is a pure Java application), or IIOP (the billing system is CORBA-compliant). This choice will lead us to a much tighter coupling between the two systems. On the other hand, if we use a servlet to implement the BillingSystemInterface, the BillingSystem needs to be able to speak HTTP. HTTP is a fairly lightweight protocol that can support different data formats, and hence provides the flexibility that we are looking for. Since the BillingSystem is an external system that we do not control, it is reasonable to expect that it may change and evolve independently of our Timecard application. If we create a tight coupling between the two systems, it would restrict the ability of both the systems to evolve independently. As described in Chapter 11, "Evaluating Web Service Technologies for the System Interface," XML is the best technology for achieving a loose coupling between two independent systems. And XML is a complementary technology to HTTP. So, our decision is that the BillingSystem and the BillingSystemInterface use XML over HTTP to communicate with each other. The BillingSystemInterface uses a class or classes in the TimecardWorkflow package, shown in Figure 17.2. This does not introduce any new dependencies among the packages defined in Chapter 15, "Design for the TimecardDomain and TimecardWorkflow."

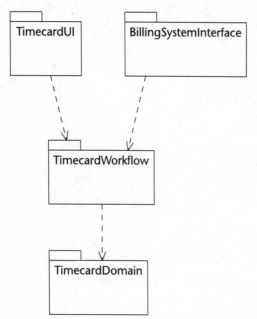

Figure 17.2   Package view of the Timecard application architecture.

Design

The architecture and analysis diagrams indicate that the billing system and the BillingSystemInterface subsystem encode request and response data in XML. The first step in using XML to encode data is to define the schema of the XML request and response. Basically there are two options for defining the schema—one, to come up with our own proprietary format, or two, to use some industry-standard format such as SOAP. It is always better to go with the industry standard over any proprietary solution. In the following sections, we will define the XML schema of the request and response data.

Extract Time Entry SOAP/XML Request

Since we have decided to use SOAP as the packaging standard, we only need to define the application-specific content of the Body and the Header part of the SOAP request. For a detailed description of SOAP, please see Chapter 10, "Evaluating Candidate Technologies for the System Interface." The following schema defines the Extract Time Entries request message:

```
<xsd:schema xmlns:xsd="http://www.w3.org/2001/XMLSchema"
targetNamespace="http://www.wiley.com/CompBooks/EJwithUML2e"
xmlns:soap="http://www.w3.org/2002/06/soap-envelope"
xmlns:tcapp="http://www.wiley.com/CompBooks/EJwithUML2e">
  <xsd:import namespace="http://www.w3.org/2002/06/soap-envelope"
      schemaLocation="http://www.w3.org/SOAP"/>
  <xsd:complexType name="GetTimeEntryReportType"/>
    <xsd:element name="ClientName" type="xsd:string"
             use="required"/>
    <xsd:element name="StartDate" type="xsd:date" use="required"/>
    <xsd:element name="EndDate" type="xsd:date" use="required"/>
    <xsd:choice>
      <xsd:element name="AllUsers" type="xsd:empty"/>
      <xsd:element name="Users" type="tcapp:UsersType"/>
    </xsd:choice>
  </xsd:complexType>
  <xsd:complexType name="UserType">
    <xsd:element name="UserName" type="xsd:string" minOccurs="1"
             maxOccurs="unbounded"/>
  </xsd:complexType>
  <xsd:complexType name="RequesterType" type="xsd:string">
    <xsd:attribute ref="soap:mustUnderstand" fixed="1"/>
  </xsd:complexType>
  <xsd:element ref="soap:Header">
    <xsd:restriction>
      <xsd:element name="Requester" type="tcapp:RequesterType"/>
    </xsd:restriction>
  </xsd:element>
  <xsd:element ref="soap:Body">
    <xsd:restriction>
      <xsd:element name="GetTimeEntryReport"
             type="tcapp:GetTimeEntryReportType"/>
```

```
    </xsd:restriction>
  </xsd:element>
</xsd:schema>
```

At a first glance, the schema may seem to be overwhelming. However, with a careful review, you will realize that it is in fact self-explanatory. It is simply extending the definition of the generic SOAP message for the Timecard application. The import tag specifies that the definitions provided in the SOAP specification are used in the current schema. The Header element defined in the generic SOAP message is extended by including a new element called Requester. The Body element defined in the generic SOAP message is extended to contain the GetTimeEntryReport element. The GetTimeEntryReport contains other elements: ClientName, StartDate, EndDate, and either AllUsers or Users. The AllUsers element is used when the BillingSystem wants to retrieve data from all users. To retrieve data for a list of users, the Users element is applied instead. The following is an example of a request for time entry data for all users:

```
<env:Envelope xmlns:env="http://www.w3c.org/2002/06/soap-envelope"
              xmlns:tcapp="http://www.wiley.com/CompBooks/EJwithUML2e">
  <env:Header>
    <tcapp:Requester env:mustUnderstand="1">
      "http://www.wiley.com/CompBooks/EJwithUML2e/BillingSystemSimulator"
    </tcapp:Requester>
  </env:Header>
  <env:Body>
    <tcapp:GetTimeEntryReport>
      <tcapp:ClientName>GM</tcapp:ClientName>
      <tcapp:StartDate>10/4/2002</tcapp:StartDate>
      <tcapp:EndDate>11/28/2002</tcapp:EndDate>
      <tcapp:AllUsers/>
    </tcapp:GetTimeEntryReport>
  </env:Body>
</env:Envelope>
```

The above example shows a complete SOAP request. The application-specific elements are defined in the namespace http://www.wiley.com/CompBooks/EJwithUML2e to avoid namespace collision, and the elements in this namespace are prefixed with tcapp (timecard application). This is a request for time entry data for all users as indicated by the tag AllUsers. Note that it is an empty element and hence does not require an end tag. The next example shows a request for a list of users. For purposes of clarity, we will not include the SOAP-specific parts of the request in the rest of this chapter.

```
  ...
<tcapp:GetTimeEntryReport>
  <tcapp:ClientName>ford</tcapp:ClientName>
  <tcapp:StartDate>10/4/2002</tcapp:StartDate>
  <tcapp:EndDate>11/28/2002</tcapp:EndDate>
  <tcapp:Users>
    <tcapp:UserName>fred</tcapp:UserName>
    <tcapp:UserName>CT</tcapp:UserName>
    <tcapp:UserName>syed</tcapp:UserName>
```

```
     </tcapp:Users>
</tcapp:GetTimeEntryReport>
 ...
```

In this request we replace the AllUsers tag with the Users tag, which contains a list consisting of each UserName.

NOTE The process of defining the application-specific request response data is a collaborative effort between the client (BillingSystem) and the server (Timecard Application/BillingSystemInterface). Both the parties need to agree upon the schema definition. Once this is defined, neither party can change the format without prior notice to the other.

Extract Time Entries SOAP/XML Response

Like the request message, the response message extends the generic SOAP message to add elements to the Body and the Header parts. The following schema defines the Extract Time Entries response message:

```
<xsd:schema xmlns:xsd="http://www.w3.org/2001/XMLSchema"
targetNamespace="http://www.wiley.com/CompBooks/EJwithUML2e"
xmlns:soap="http://www.w3.org/2002/06/soap-envelope"
xmlns:tcapp="http://www.wiley.com/CompBooks/EJwithUML2e">
  <xsd:import namespace="http://www.w3.org/2002/06/soap-envelope"
      schemaLocation="http://www.w3.org/2002/06/soap-envelope"/>
  <xsd:complexType name="TimeEntriesType"/>
    <xsd:element name="User" type="tcapp:UserType"
    minOccurs="0" maxOccurs="unbounded"/>
    <xsd:element name="UserNotInDatabase"
    type="tcapp:UserNotInDatabaseType" minOccurs="0" maxOccurs="1"/>
  </xsd:complexType>
  <xsd:complexType name="UserType">
    <xsd:element name="Name" type="xsd:string"/>
    <xsd:element name="TimeEntry" type="tcapp:TimeEntryType"
      minOccurs="0" maxOccurs="unbounded"/>
  </xsd:complexType>
  <xsd:complexType name="TimeEntryType">
    <xsd:element name="Project" type="xsd:string"/>
    <xsd:element name="ChargeCode" type="xsd:string"/>
    <xsd:element name="Date" type="xsd:date">
    <xsd:element name="Hours" type="xsd:positiveInteger"/>
  </xsd:complexType>
  <xsd:complexType name="UserNotInDatabaseType">
    <xsd:element name="UserName" type="xsd:string"
      minOccurs="1" maxOccurs="unbounded"/>
  </xsd:complexType>
  <xsd:complexType name="ResponderType" type="xsd:string">
    <xsd:attribute ref="soap:mustUnderstand" fixed="1"/>
  </xsd:complexType>
  <xsd:element ref="soap:Header">
```

```
            <xsd:restriction>
              <xsd:element name="Responder" type="tcapp:ResponderType"/>
            </xsd:restriction>
          </xsd:element>
          <xsd:element ref="soap:Body">
            <xsd:restriction>
              <xsd:element name="TimeEntries"
                        type="tcapp:TimeEntriesType"/>
            </xsd:restriction>
          </xsd:element>
        </xsd:schema>
```

By now, you already have gotten acquainted with the XML schema. This schema definition of the Extract Time Entries response message is conceptually similar to that of the corresponding request message. The Header contains an element called Responder that identifies who is sending the response to the requester. The Body contains the actual time entry data.

An important thing to note here is that the response data optionally contains a data block represented by the element UserNotInDatabase, which lists the users not found in the database. When the billing system requests data for a list of users, it is possible that some users in the list will not exist. One reason may be that the Timecard application and the billing system are out of sync. No matter what the reason is, the Timecard application should be able to identify those nonexistent users in the response, and still provide data for all other users. An example of a response to a request for the time entry data for all users follows:

```
...
<tcapp:TimeEntries>
  <tcapp:User>
    <tcapp:Name>fred</tcapp:Name>
    <tcapp:TimeEntry>
      <tcapp:Project>Mustang</tcapp:Project>
      <tcapp:ChargeCode>Paint</tcapp:ChargeCode>
      <tcapp:Date>10/04/2002</tcapp:Date>
      <tcapp:Hours>5</tcapp:Hours>
    </tcapp:TimeEntry>
    <tcapp:TimeEntry>
      <tcapp:Project>Mustang</tcapp:Project>
      <tcapp:ChargeCode>Paint</tcapp:ChargeCode>
      <tcapp:Date>10/05/2002</tcapp:Date>
      <tcapp:Hours>8</tcapp:Hours>
    </tcapp:TimeEntry>
  </tcapp:User>
  <tcapp:User>
    <tcapp:Name>CT</tcapp:Name>
    <tcapp:TimeEntry>
      <tcapp:Project>Mustang</tcapp:Project>
      <tcapp:ChargeCode>Paint</tcapp:ChargeCode>
      <tcapp:Date>10/04/2002</tcapp:Date>
      <tcapp:Hours>5</tcapp:Hours>
    </tcapp:TimeEntry>
    <tcapp:TimeEntry>
```

```
        <tcapp:Project>Explorer</tcapp:Project>
        <tcapp:ChargeCode>Paint</tcapp:ChargeCode>
        <tcapp:Date>10/05/2002</tcapp:Date>
        <tcapp:Hours>8</tcapp:Hours>
      </tcapp:TimeEntry>
    </tcapp:User>
  </tcapp:TimeEntries>
  ...
```

The data for each user is contained within each corresponding User tag block. The next example shows a response to a request for time entry data for a list of users. Here, it is the same as the response for all users, except that it also lists the users who are not in the database.

```
  ...
  <tcapp:TimeEntries>
    <tcapp:User>
      <tcapp:Name>fred</tcapp:Name>
      <tcapp:TimeEntry>
        <tcapp:Project>Mustang</tcapp:Project>
        <tcapp:ChargeCode>Paint</tcapp:ChargeCode>
        <tcapp:Date>10/04/2002</tcapp:Date>
        <tcapp:Hours>5</tcapp:Hours>
      </tcapp:TimeEntry>
      <tcapp:TimeEntry>
        <tcapp:Project>Mustang</tcapp:Project>
        <tcapp:ChargeCode>Paint</tcapp:ChargeCode>
        <tcapp:Date>10/05/2002</tcapp:Date>
        <tcapp:Hours>8</tcapp:Hours>
      </tcapp:TimeEntry>
    </tcapp:User>
    <tcapp:User>
      <tcapp:Name>CT</tcapp:Name>
      <tcapp:TimeEntry>
        <tcapp:Project>Mustang</tcapp:Project>
        <tcapp:ChargeCode>Paint</tcapp:ChargeCode>
        <tcapp:Date>10/04/2002</tcapp:Date>
        <tcapp:Hours>5</tcapp:Hours>
      </tcapp:TimeEntry>
      <tcapp:TimeEntry>
        <tcapp:Project>Explorer</tcapp:Project>
        <tcapp:ChargeCode>Paint</tcapp:ChargeCode>
        <tcapp:Date>10/05/2002</tcapp:Date>
        <tcapp:Hours>8</tcapp:Hours>
      </tcapp:TimeEntry>
    </tcapp:User>
  </tcapp:TimeEntries>
  <tcapp:UsersNotInDatabase>
    <tcapp:UserName>syed</tcapp:UserName>
  </tcapp:UsersNotInDatabase>
  ...
```

The next example shows a response in the event of an error in which the Timecard application cannot return any time entry data at all. SOAP allows applications to communicate error conditions through its Fault tag. For detailed information on Fault tags, please refer to Chapter 11, "Evaluating Web Service Technologies for the System Interface." The only thing that both the parties need to agree on is the definitions of the application-specific error conditions and their encoded form.

```
...
<env:Fault>
  <env:Code>
    <env:Value>
      env:Receiver
    </env:Value>
    <env:Subcode>
      <env:Value>
        "published error code"
      </env:Value>
    </env:Subcode>
  </env:Code>
  <env:Reason>
  com.wiley.compBooks.EJwithUML.Base.ApplicationException.DataNotFoundException
  </env:Reason>
  <env:Detail>
    client(totyto)not found.
  </env:Detail>
</env:Fault>
...
```

The Code tag contains the values specified by the SOAP specification. However, the Subcode tag captures the application-specific error code as mutually agreed on by the billing system and the Timecard application. In the event of an error, the billing system can take actions based on the value of the Subcode. The Reason tag contains the exception class name and the Detail tag contains the exception message. The data that goes into these two tags are defined by the application. In the Timecard application, we have decided to communicate the actual exception through these tags.

NOTE Any changes to the architecture must be reviewed by the architects who are responsible for the architecture. However, in many cases, the developers who create the detailed design for a package or subsystem gain a more thorough understanding of the problem and of the solution. They must be allowed to apply this deeper understanding as they create the solution. Judicious changes to the architecture are an inevitable and healthy part of the design process.

Design for the Extract Time Entries Use Case

From the analysis of the Extract Time Entries use case in Chapter 5, "Analysis Model for the Timecard Application," and in Chapter 15, "Design for the TimecardDomain and TimecardWorkflow," we can say that if the users are specified in the criteria, the time entries for those users can be retrieved and the data extracted for comparison with the other criteria. If the criteria include all users, then the UserHome interface can be used to obtain a list of all users. The rest of the process is the same.

We will develop two sequence diagrams, one for each variation.

Sequence Diagram for Extract Time Entries for Specific Users

The sequence to extract specific users begins when the external BillingSystem sends a request for time entry data for a list of users to the ExtractTimeEntriesServlet. The ExtractTimeEntriesServlet creates the ExtractCriteria object from the request and forwards the request to the ExtractTimeEntriesWorkflow. The ExtractTimeEntries Workflow obtains the list of users from the ExtractCriteria object. The ExtractTimeEntries Application at this point could go to either TimecardHome or to TimeEntryHome to retrieve all TimeEntries for the given date range provided in the ExtractCriteria. Going through the Timecard adds unnecessary overhead to the whole process. So, the Extract-TimeEntriesWorkflow uses TimeEntryHome to obtain local references to all of the Time Entry entity beans for each user. The entries that match the criteria are added to the TimeEntryReport, which works as a container for data exchanged between ExtractTime EntriesServlet and ExtractTimeEntriesWorkflow.

Sequence Diagram for Extract Time Entries for All Users

As in the sequence for Extract Time Entries for Specific Users, the sequence to extract all users begins when the external BillingSystem sends a request for time entry data to the ExtractTimeEntriesServlet. The request in this case is for all users. The Extract-TimeEntriesServlet creates the ExtractCriteria from the request and forwards the request to the ExtractTimeEntriesWorkflow. However, in this sequence, the Extract-TimeEntriesWorkflow gets an empty list of users from ExtractCriteria by calling the getUsers method. This leads the ExtractTimeEntriesWorkflow to ask the UserHome for a list of all users. The remainder of the sequence is the same as before, with the Extract-TimeEntriesWorkflow object using the ExtractCriteria object to determine if each entry meets the criteria, and adding the matching entries to the TimeEntryReport object. Figure 17.3 shows the sequence diagram for Extract Time Entries.

Participating Classes

Each ExtractTimeEntriesWorkflow depends on many entity beans, but does not need to keep any reference to any of them to perform its task. None of these dependencies violate the structural constraints established in the architecture we defined earlier. Figure 17.4 shows the participating classes for Extract Time Entries.

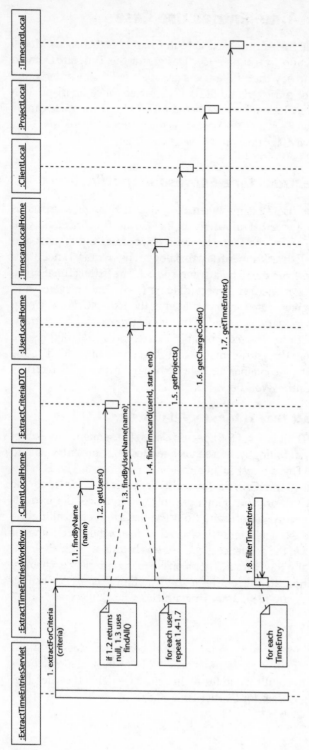

Figure 17.3 Sequence diagram of normal flow for Extract Time Entries.

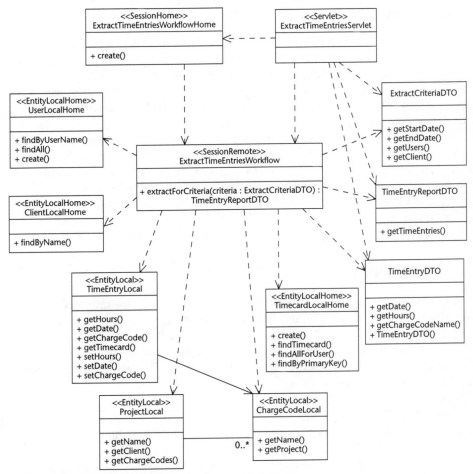

Figure 17.4   Participating classes for Extract Time Entries.

Stateless or Stateful Session Bean

The ExtractTimeEntriesServlet cannot use the existing beans from the TimecardWork-flow since the Extract Time Entry use case involves all time entries instead of just the time entries in the current timecard. Also, it cannot directly manipulate TimecardDo-main packages to gather the raw data that it needs since, in Chapter 15, "Design for the TimecardDomain and TimecardWorkflow," we made a design choice to make all our entity beans locally accessible. We need to provide a session façade EJB that will manipulate the entity beans on behalf of the ExtractTimeEntriesServlet. Since the inter-action between the ExtractTimeEntriesServlet and the ExtractTimeEntriesWorkflow bean is not a conversational type that spans multiple calls, ExtractTimeEntriesWorkflow can be a stateless session bean.

Implementation

Now that the design is complete, we have a solid foundation for implementation. We will make some important decisions during implementation, but we made most or all of the major structural decisions during analysis, architecture, and design. For example, we know each significant class, its responsibilities, and its relationships with other classes. We know how each entity bean holds data and how the session beans package that data for consumption by the user interface classes.

The implementation will be split into two parts. First, there are core classes, which are directly derived from the design model and play a significant role in the use case. Second, in the last section, we described some helper classes. These classes are not in the design; they will be discovered as part of the implementation process.

The implementation of these classes is fairly straightforward. We begin with the ExtractTimeEntriesServlet and ExtractTimeEntriesWorkflow, then proceed to the helper classes that use them: ExtractCriteriaDTO and TimeEntryReportDTO.

ExtractTimeEntriesServlet

ExtractTimeEntriesServlet receives an XML request containing the criteria for retrieving time entry data from the billing system. During design, we decided to use SOAP, so we have two choices to parse the data in the request: (1) use the SOAP library (SAAJ), or (2) use the XML parser directly. Since SOAP is a specification that is still in development and SAAJ is based on the older version of SOAP, we decided to use the XML SAX parser to parse the data.

ExtractTimeEntriesServlet.java

The ExtractTimeEntriesServlet supports both POST and GET methods.

```
package com.wiley.compBooks.EJwithUML.BillingSystemInterface;

import javax.servlet.http.*;
import javax.servlet.*;
import javax.naming.*;
import javax.ejb.*;
import java.rmi.*;
import javax.rmi.PortableRemoteObject;
import java.io.IOException;
import java.util.*;
import org.xml.sax.SAXException;
import com.wiley.compBooks.EJwithUML.TimeCardWorkflow.ExtractTimeEntriesWorkflow;
import com.wiley.compBooks.EJwithUML.TimeCardWorkflow.
ExtractTimeEntriesWorkflowHome;
import com.wiley.compBooks.EJwithUML.Dtos.ExtractCriteriaDTO;
import com.wiley.compBooks.EJwithUML.Dtos.TimeEntryReportDTO;
import com.wiley.compBooks.EJwithUML.Dtos.TimeEntryDTO;
import com.wiley.compBooks.EJwithUML.Base.DateUtil;
import com.wiley.compBooks.EJwithUML.Base.ApplicationExceptions.
ApplicationException;
```

```
import com.wiley.compBooks.EJwithUML.Base.EjbUtil.EjbReferenceNames;

/**
 * The ExtractTimeEntryServlet uses the ExtractTimeEntriesWorkflow to service
 * the external client, the billing system. It accepts SOAP/XML request and
 * returns a SOAP/XML response.
 */
public class ExtractTimeEntryServlet extends HttpServlet
{
  private XMLRequestFilter filter = new XMLRequestFilter();
  public void doGet(HttpServletRequest request, HttpServletResponse response)
      throws ServletException, IOException
  {
    doPost(request, response);
  }

  /**
   * Overrides the method from the HttpServlet.  doPost is called by the
servlet engine.
   */
  public void doPost(HttpServletRequest request, HttpServletResponse response)
                                    throws ServletException, IOException
  {
    StringBuffer responseBuffer = new StringBuffer(5000);
    responseBuffer.append("<env:Envelope
xmlns:env=\"http://www.w3c.org/2002/06/soap-envelope\""
                  + " xmlns:tcapp=\"http://com.wiley.compBooks/EJwithUML2e\">");
    buildHeaderTag(responseBuffer);
    try
    {
      HashMap requestData = filter.filter(request);
      // Obtain remote reference to ExtractTimeEntriesWorkflow session bean.
      Context initial = new InitialContext();
      Object rtwobjref = initial.lookup(EjbReferenceNames.EXTRACT_
TIME_ENTRY_WORKFLOW_HOME);
      ExtractTimeEntriesWorkflowHome home = (ExtractTimeEntriesWorkflowHome)
          PortableRemoteObject.narrow(rtwobjref,
ExtractTimeEntriesWorkflowHome.class);
      ExtractTimeEntriesWorkflow rtw = home.create();
      Date startDate = DateUtil.createDate(
      (String)requestData.get(XmlTimeEntryReportRequestTags.START_DATE));
      Date endDate = DateUtil.createDate(
      (String)requestData.get(XmlTimeEntryReportRequestTags.END_DATE));
      ExtractCriteriaDTO criteria = new ExtractCriteriaDTO((
String)requestData.get(
                            XmlTimeEntryReportRequestTags.CLIENT_NAME),
                            startDate,
                            endDate);

      ArrayList users = (ArrayList)requestData.get(
                            XmlTimeEntryReportRequestTags.USERS);
      if (users != null)
      {
        criteria.setUsers(users);
```

```
      }
      HashMap reports = rtw.extractForCriteria(criteria);
      buildBodyTag(responseBuffer, reports, users);
    }
    catch (Exception e)
    {
      System.out.println("e= " +e);
      buildFaultTag(responseBuffer, e);
    }
    responseBuffer.append("</env:Envelope>");
    response.getWriter().print(responseBuffer.toString());
    response.getWriter().flush();
    response.getWriter().close();
  }

  private void buildFaultTag(StringBuffer response, Exception exp)
  {
    response.append("<env:Fault><env:Code><env:Value>");
    if (exp instanceof IOException ||
        exp instanceof SAXException)
    {
      response.append("env:Sender");
    }
    else
    {
      response.append("env:Receiver");
    }
    response.append("</env:Value><env:Subcode><env:Value>" +
            ((ApplicationException)exp).getOrigin() +
            "</env:Value></env:Subcode></env:Code><env:Reason>" +
             exp.getClass().getName() +
            "</env:Reason><env:Detail>" +
            exp.toString() +
            "</env:Detail></env:Fault>");
  }

  private void buildHeaderTag(StringBuffer response)
  {
    response.append(
    "<env:Header xmlns:tcapp=\"http://com.wiley.compBooks/EJwithUML2e\">" +
    "<tcapp:Responder env:mustUnderstand=\"1\">");
    response.append("TimecardApplication</tcapp:Responder></env:Header>");
  }

  private void buildBodyTag(StringBuffer response, HashMap responseData,
                            ArrayList users)
  {
    response.append("<env:Body><tcapp:TimeEntries>");
    buildUserTags(response, responseData);
    if (users.size() > responseData.size())
    {
      //Some of the users do not exist.
      ArrayList userNotInDatabase = new ArrayList();
      for(int i=0; i < users.size(); i++)
      {
```

```
          if (!responseData.containsKey((String)users.get(i)))
          {
            userNotInDatabase.add(users.get(i));
          }
        }
        buildUserNotInDatabaseTag(response, userNotInDatabase);
      }
      response.append("</tcapp:TimeEntries></env:Body>");
    }

    private void buildUserTags(StringBuffer response, HashMap responseData)
    {
      Iterator userIterator = responseData.entrySet().iterator();
      while(userIterator.hasNext())
      {
        TimeEntryReportDTO userData = (TimeEntryReportDTO)((Map.Entry)
                                         userIterator.next()).getValue();
        response.append("<tcapp:User><tcapp:Name>"+userData.getName()+
                        "</tcapp:Name>");
        buildTimeEntryTags(response, userData.getTimeEntries());
        response.append("</tcapp:User>");
      }
    }

    private void buildTimeEntryTags(StringBuffer response, Iterator timeentries)
    {
      while(timeentries.hasNext())
      {
        TimeEntryDTO timeentryData = (TimeEntryDTO)timeentries.next();
        response.append("<tcapp:TimeEntry><tcapp:Project>"+
                        timeentryData.getProjectName()+"</tcapp:Project>");
        response.append("<tcapp:ChargeCode>"+
                        timeentryData.getChargeCodeName()+"</tcapp:ChargeCode>");
        response.append("<tcapp:Date>"+
                        DateUtil.toDateString(timeentryData.
getDate())+"</tcapp:Date>");
        response.append("<tcapp:Hours>"+
                        timeentryData.getHours()+"</tcapp:Hours></tcapp:TimeEntry>");
      }
    }

    private void buildUserNotInDatabaseTag(StringBuffer response, ArrayList users)
    {
      response.append("<tcapp:UserNotInDatabase>");
      for(int i=0; i < users.size(); i++)
      {
        response.append("<tcapp:UserName>"+users.get(i)+
                        "</tcapp:UserName>");
      }
      response.append("</tcapp:UserNotInDatabase>");
    }


  }
}
```

ExtractTimeEntriesWorkflow Stateless Session Bean

Recall the implementation decision that we made in Chapter 15, "Design for the Time-cardDomain and TimecardWorkflow," regarding the EJBs. We define a business interface that ties the EJB remote interface and the corresponding bean together and allows the compiler to apply compile-time type checking. The ExtractTimeEntriesWorkflow stateless session bean consists of four files:

- **ExtractTimeEntriesWorkflowInt.** The Business interface
- **ExtractTimeEntriesWorkflowLocal.** The remote EJB interface
- **ExtractTimeEntriesWorkflowLocalHome.** The EJB Home interface
- **ExtractTimeEntriesWorkflowBean.** The Bean implementation class

ExtractTimeEntriesWorkflowInt.java

ExtractTimeEntriesWorkflowInt.java is the local Business interface for the Extract-TimeEntriesWorkflow stateless session bean. It defines the business methods for the ExtractTimeEntriesWorkflow bean.

```
package com.wiley.compBooks.EJwithUML.TimeCardWorkflow;

import java.rmi.*;
import javax.ejb.*;
import com.wiley.compBooks.EJwithUML.Base.ApplicationExceptions.*;
import com.wiley.compBooks.EJwithUML.Dtos.*;
import java.util.HashMap;
import java.util.Collection;


/**
 * The ExtractTimeEntriesWorkflowInt is the interface that ties the Bean with
 * the Remote interface to provide compile time type checking.
 */
public interface ExtractTimeEntriesWorkflowInt
{
  /**
   * Answers a HashMap of TimeEntryReportDTO objects for the given search
   * criteria for a single client.
   */
  public HashMap extractForCriteria(ExtractCriteriaDTO criteria) throws
  FatalApplicationException, DataNotFoundException, InvalidDataException,
  RemoteException;

  /**
   * Answers a Collection of TimeCardDTO objects for a user.
   */
  public Collection getAllTimecardsForUser(String userName) throws
  FatalApplicationException, DataNotFoundException, InvalidDataException,
                      RemoteException;
}
```

ExtractTimeEntriesWorkflow.java

ExtractTimeEntriesWorkflow.java is the remote EJB interface that inherits from Extract-TimeEntriesWorkflowInt and hence it has an empty body. This is in line with what we have set as our implementation strategy for all of our EJBs. This is shown in Figure 17.5.

```
package com.wiley.compBooks.EJwithUML.TimeCardWorkflow;

import javax.ejb.*;
import com.wiley.compBooks.EJwithUML.Base.ApplicationExceptions.*;
import com.wiley.compBooks.EJwithUML.Dtos.*;
import java.util.HashMap;
import java.util.Collection;

/**
 * The ExtractTimeEntriesWorkflow allows clients to retrieve time entries based
 * on extract criteria.
 * ExtractTimeEntriesWorkflow is the remote interface through which clients
 * access the underlying session bean.
 */
public interface ExtractTimeEntriesWorkflow extends EJBObject,
ExtractTimeEntriesWorkflowInt
{
}
```

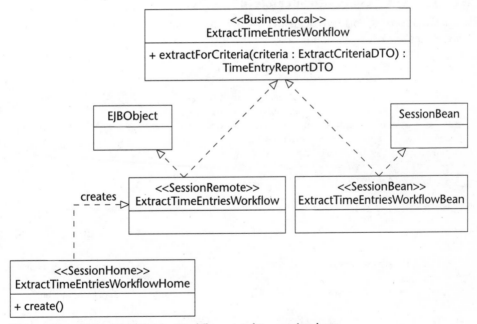

Figure 17.5 ExtractTimeEntriesWorkflow stateless session bean.

ExtractTimeEntriesWorkflowHome.java

ExtractTimeEntriesWorkflowHome.java is the Home interface for the ExtractTimeEntriesWorkflow session bean. It contains the method by which ExtractTimeEntriesWorkflow session beans are created.

```java
package com.wiley.compBooks.EJwithUML.TimeCardWorkflow;

import java.util.*;
import java.rmi.*;
import javax.ejb.*;

/**
 * The ExtractTimeEntriesWorkflow allows clients to retrieve time entries based
 * on extract criteria.
 * ExtractTimeEntriesHome is the remote interface through which clients find and
 * create the underlying session beans.
 */
public interface ExtractTimeEntriesWorkflowHome extends EJBHome
{
  /** Answers a reference to the newly created ExtractTimeEntriesWorkflow bean. */
  public ExtractTimeEntriesWorkflow create() throws CreateException,
RemoteException;
}
```

ExtractTimeEntriesWorkflowBean.java

ExtractTimeEntriesWorkflowBean.java is the implementation class for the ExtractTimeEntriesWorkflow session bean.

```java
package com.wiley.compBooks.EJwithUML.TimeCardWorkflow;

import com.wiley.compBooks.EJwithUML.Base.EjbUtil.*;
import com.wiley.compBooks.EJwithUML.TimeCardDomain.*;
import com.wiley.compBooks.EJwithUML.Base.ApplicationExceptions.*;
import com.wiley.compBooks.EJwithUML.Base.*;
import com.wiley.compBooks.EJwithUML.Dtos.*;
import java.util.*;
import java.rmi.*;
import javax.ejb.*;
import javax.naming.*;


/**
 * The ExtractTimeEntriesWorkflow allows clients to retrieve time entries based
 * on extract criteria.
 * ExtractTimeEntriesWorkflowBean is the actual session bean implementation.
 */
public class ExtractTimeEntriesWorkflowBean extends BasicSessionBean
{
  public void ejbCreate() throws CreateException
  {
    System.out.println("created ExtractTimeEntriesWorkflowBean!");
```

```
        }

    public void ejbPostCreate()
    {
    }

    /**
     * Answers a HashMap of TimeEntryReportDTO objects for the given search
     * criteria for a single client.
     */
    public HashMap extractForCriteria(ExtractCriteriaDTO criteria) throws
    FatalApplicationException, DataNotFoundException,
InvalidDataException,RemoteException
    {
      try
      {
        System.out.println("In extractForCriteria()");
        Context initialContext = getInitialContext();
        UserLocalHome uhome = (UserLocalHome)initialContext.lookup(
                                            EjbReferenceNames.USER_HOME);
        ClientLocalHome chome = (ClientLocalHome)initialContext.lookup(
                                            EjbReferenceNames.CLIENT_HOME);
        Collection users = null;
        Collection clients = chome.findByName(criteria.getClient());
        //makes sure that only one client found.
        if (clients.size() > 1)
        {
          // the client name has more than one hit in the database.
          // requires one client.
          System.out.println("More than one client found by the name " +
                          criteria.getClient());
          throw new InvalidDataException(Origin.EXTRACT_TIME_ENTRY_WORKFLOW,
                                    "More than one client found.");
        }
        else if ( clients.size() == 0)
        {
          System.out.println("no client found by the name " +
                          criteria.getClient());
          throw new InvalidDataException(Origin.EXTRACT_TIME_ENTRY_WORKFLOW,
                                    "no client found.");
        }
        // uses a HashMap to collect all the time entries by user. User name is
        // key to the corresponding time entry report
        HashMap reports = new HashMap();
        ArrayList userNames = criteria.getUsers();
        if (userNames == null)
        {
          //all users
          System.out.println("extracting time entries for all users.");
          users = uhome.findAll();
          generateTimeReportsForUsers((ClientLocal)clients.iterator().next(), users,
          criteria.getStartDate().getTime(), criteria.getEndDate().getTime(),
reports);
        }
```

```
    else
    {
      System.out.println("extracting time entries for " + userNames.size()
                          + " user(s).");
      //a list of specific users
      for(int i = 0; i < userNames.size(); i++)
      {
        users = uhome.findByUserName((String)userNames.get(i));
        if (users.isEmpty())
        {
          System.out.println("warning:user(" + userNames.get(i) +
                              ") does not exist.");
        }
        generateTimeReportsForUsers((ClientLocal)clients.iterator().next(), ⊃
users,
        criteria.getStartDate().getTime(), criteria.getEndDate().getTime(), ⊃
reports);
      }
    }
    System.out.println("Done extractForCriteria()");
    return reports;
  }
  catch (NamingException e)
  {
    throw new FatalApplicationException(Origin.EXTRACT_TIME_ENTRY_WORKFLOW, e,
                                        "User/Client Bean Not Found");
  }
  catch (FinderException e)
  {
    throw new DataNotFoundException(Origin.EXTRACT_TIME_ENTRY_WORKFLOW, e,
                                    "User/Client Not Found");
  }
}


/**
 * Answers a Collection of TimeCardDTO objects for a user.
 */
public Collection getAllTimecardsForUser(String userName) throws
FatalApplicationException, DataNotFoundException, InvalidDataException, ⊃
RemoteException
{
  try
  {
    System.out.println("In getAllTimecardsForUser()");
    Context initialContext = getInitialContext();
    UserLocalHome uhome = (UserLocalHome)initialContext.lookup(
                                         EjbReferenceNames.USER_HOME);
    Collection users = uhome.findByUserName(userName);
    //makes sure that only one user found.
    if (users.size() > 1)
    {
      // the user name has more than one hit in the database.
      // requires one user.
      System.out.println("More than one user found by the name " +
```

```
                                        userName);
          throw new InvalidDataException(Origin.EXTRACT_TIME_ENTRY_WORKFLOW,
                                     "More than one user found.");
      }
      else if (users.size() == 0)
      {
        System.out.println("no user found by the name " +
                             userName);
        throw new InvalidDataException(Origin.EXTRACT_TIME_ENTRY_WORKFLOW,
                                     "no user found by the name " + userName);
      }
      TimecardLocalHome tchome = (TimecardLocalHome)initialContext.lookup(
                                             EjbReferenceNames.
TIMECARD_HOME);
      Collection cards = tchome.findAllForUser(((UserPK)((UserLocal)
          users.iterator().next()).getPrimaryKey()).id);
      ArrayList cardDtos = new ArrayList();
      Iterator cardIterator = cards.iterator();
      System.out.println("total cards#" + cards.size());
      while(cardIterator.hasNext())
      {
        TimecardLocal card = (TimecardLocal) cardIterator.next();
        cardDtos.add(retrieveTimeEntriesForCard(card));
      }
      System.out.println("Done getAllTimecardsForUser()");
      return cardDtos;
    }
    catch (NamingException e)
    {
      throw new FatalApplicationException(Origin.EXTRACT_TIME_ENTRY_WORKFLOW, e,
                                     "User Bean Not Found");
    }
    catch (FinderException e)
    {
      throw new DataNotFoundException(Origin.EXTRACT_TIME_ENTRY_WORKFLOW, e,
                                "User Not Found");
    }
  }

  private TimecardDTO retrieveTimeEntriesForCard(TimecardLocal timecard)
      throws InvalidDataException
  {
    System.out.println("In retrieveTimeEntriesForCard()");
    TimecardDTO tcDTO = new TimecardDTO(new Date(timecard.getStartDate()),
                                    new Date(timecard.getEndDate())));
    Collection timeEntries = timecard.getTimeEntries();
    Iterator timeEntryIterator = timeEntries.iterator();
    System.out.println("total entries#" + timeEntries.size());
    while(timeEntryIterator.hasNext())
    {
      TimeEntryLocal timeEntry = (TimeEntryLocal) timeEntryIterator.next();
      ChargeCodeLocal chargeCode = (ChargeCodeLocal) timeEntry.getChargeCode();
      TimeEntryDTO timeEntryDTO = new TimeEntryDTO(
          ((TimeEntryPK)timeEntry.getPrimaryKey()).id,
```

```
        chargeCode.getProject().getClient().getName(),
        chargeCode.getName(), chargeCode.getProject().getName(),
        timeEntry.getHours(), timeEntry.getDate());
    tcDTO.addEntry(timeEntryDTO);
  }
  System.out.println(tcDTO);
  System.out.println("Done retrieveTimeEntriesForCard()");
  return tcDTO;
}


private void generateTimeReportsForUsers(ClientLocal client, Collection users,
long start, long end, HashMap reportsByUsers) throws FatalApplicationException,
                                        RemoteException
{
  try
  {
    System.out.println("In generateTimeReportsForUsers()");
    Context initialContext = getInitialContext();
    TimecardLocalHome tchome = (TimecardLocalHome)initialContext.lookup(
                                        EjbReferenceNames.TIMECARD_HOME);
    Collection projects = client.getProjects();
    Iterator userIterator = users.iterator();
    while(userIterator.hasNext())
    {
      UserLocal user = (UserLocal) userIterator.next();
      System.out.println("for user- " + user.getName() + " ..." );
      TimeEntryReportDTO report = new TimeEntryReportDTO(user.getName());
      try
      {
        Collection timecards = tchome.findTimecard(((UserPK)user.
getPrimaryKey()).id,
                                        start, end);
        if (timecards.isEmpty())
        {
          System.out.println("no timecard found for " + user.getName());
        }
        else
        {
          System.out.println( user.getName() + "'s timecard count#" +
timecards.size());
          filterTimeEntries(report, projects, timecards);
        }
      }
      catch (FinderException e)
      {
        // there may not be any time entered by the user for timecards between
        // start and end. Igonre the exception.
        System.out.println("no timecard found for " + user.getName() +
        " between " + DateUtil.toDateString(new Date(start)) + "and " +
        DateUtil.toDateString(new Date(end)));
      }
      reportsByUsers.put(user.getName(), report);
    } // end of while
```

```
          System.out.println("Done generateTimeReportsForUsers()");
      }
      catch (NamingException e)
      {
         throw new FatalApplicationException(Origin.EXTRACT_TIME_ENTRY_WORKFLOW, e,
                                          "Timecard Bean Not Found");
      }
   }


   /**
    * Populates TimeEntryReportDTO object with all the entries that have a has
    * charge code belonging to one of the projects provided
    */
   private void filterTimeEntries(TimeEntryReportDTO report, Collection projects,
                                  Collection timecards)
   {
      System.out.println("In filterTimeEntries()");
      Iterator cardIterator = timecards.iterator();
      int cardCount = 0;
      //Loops through each timecard
      while(cardIterator.hasNext())
      {
         cardCount++;
         System.out.println("timecard#" + cardCount);
         TimecardLocal card = (TimecardLocal) cardIterator.next();
         Collection entries = card.getTimeEntries();
         Iterator entryIterator = entries.iterator();
         int entryCount = 0;
         System.out.println("entry count#" + entries.size());
         //Loops through each entry in the timecard
         while(entryIterator.hasNext())
         {
            entryCount++;
            System.out.println("time entry#" + entryCount);
            TimeEntryLocal entry = (TimeEntryLocal) entryIterator.next();
            Iterator projectIterator =  projects.iterator();
            // Adds the entry to the report if the entry was charged to any of
the project
            // in the list. Breaks out of the loop as soon as we have a hit.
            while(projectIterator.hasNext())
            {
               ProjectLocal project = (ProjectLocal) projectIterator.next();
               if (project.getChargeCodes().contains(entry.getChargeCode()))
               {
                  System.out.println("adding entry...");
                  TimeEntryDTO entryDto = new TimeEntryDTO(((TimeEntryPK)entry.
getPrimaryKey()).id,
                  project.getClient().getName(), entry.getChargeCode().getName(),
                  project.getName(), entry.getHours(), entry.getDate());
                  report.addTimeEntry(entryDto);
                  break;
               }
```

```
        } // End of project loop
      } // End of time entry loop
    } // End of timecard loop

    System.out.println("Done filterTimeEntries()");
  }
}
```

Supporting Classes

The classes in this section are some of the helper classes that collaborate with the core classes mentioned in the previous section. As mentioned in Chapter 14, "Introduction to Design," these classes usually are discovered in the process of design refinement and do not affect the architectural constraints.

ExtractCriteriaDTO.java

ExtractCriteriaDTO's entire purpose is to completely encapsulate the criteria data. It is fairly lightweight and is implemented as a DTO, as described in Chapter 14. This is in line with the design decisions made in Chapter 14, that is, the servlets and the Work-flow beans should exchange strongly typed data implemented as DTOs

```
package com.wiley.compBooks.EJwithUML.Dtos;

import java.util.*;
import java.io.*;
import java.text.*;

/**
 * The ExtractCriteria class that holds criteria for extracting time entries
from
 * the database. The ExtractTimeEntriesWorkflow bean uses the criteria object to
 * actually perform the search.
 */
public class ExtractCriteriaDTO implements Serializable
{
  private String client;
  private ArrayList users;
  private Date startDate;
  private Date endDate;
  private boolean loaded = false;

  /**
   * Create an ExtractCriteriaDto using the raw criteria found in the request
   * from the external system.
   */
  public ExtractCriteriaDTO(String client, Date startDate, Date endDate)
  {
    this.startDate = startDate;
    this.endDate = endDate;
```

```java
  this.client = client;
}

/** Answers with the start date of the search */
public Date getStartDate()
{
  return this.startDate;
}

/** Answers with the end date of the search */
public Date getEndDate()
{
  return this.endDate;
}

/** Answers with the list of users whose time entries need to be retrieved */
public ArrayList getUsers()
{
  return this.users;
}

/** Answers with the client for whom time entries need to be retrieved */
public String getClient()
{
  return this.client;
}

/** Sets the client for whom the time entries need to be retrieved */
public void setUsers(ArrayList users)
{
  this.users = users;
}

/** Sets the list of users for whom the time entries need to be retrieved */
public void setClient(String client)
{
  this.client = client;
}

public String toString()
{
  StringBuffer buffer = new StringBuffer();
  buffer.append("ExtractCriteria[start date="+ startDate +
                ",end date=" + endDate);
  if (client != null)
  {
    buffer.append(",client{" + client + "}");
  }
  if (users != null)
  {
    buffer.append(",users{");
    for(int i = 0; i < users.size();i++)
    {
```

```
            buffer.append(" " +users.get(i));
          }
        buffer.append(" }");
      }
    buffer.append("]");
    return buffer.toString();
  }

  public  int hashCode()
  {
    int hashCode = this.startDate.hashCode() ^ this.endDate.hashCode();
    if (this.client != null)
    {
      hashCode = hashCode ^ this.client.hashCode();
    }

    if (this.users != null)
    {
      hashCode = hashCode ^ this.users.hashCode();
    }
    return hashCode;
  }

  public boolean equals(Object obj)
  {
    if (obj == null)
    {
      return false;
    }
    else
    {
      if (!obj.getClass().equals(this.getClass()))
      {
        return false;
      }
      else
      {
        ExtractCriteriaDTO criteria = (ExtractCriteriaDTO)obj;
        return ((criteria.startDate.equals(this.startDate)) &&
                (criteria.endDate.equals(this.endDate)));
      }
    }
  }
}
```

TimeEntryReportDTO.java

The TimeEntryReportDTO class holds the time entry data for a client for a list of users. As with ExtractCriteriaDTO, TimeEntryReportDTO is a lightweight data container used to ship just the required data from the TimeEntry entity bean and other related beans to ExtractTimeEntriesServlet.

```
  package com.wiley.compBooks.EJwithUML.Dtos;
```

```java
import java.util.*;
import java.io.*;
import com.wiley.compBooks.EJwithUML.Base.DateUtil;

/**
 * This class captures time entries by user. The time entries captured will
 * be based on some search criteria in the context of a use case.
 */
public class TimeEntryReportDTO implements Serializable
{
  private String name;
  private ArrayList entries = new ArrayList();

  public TimeEntryReportDTO(String name)
  {
    setName(name);
  }

  public String getName()
  {
    return this.name;
  }

  public void setName(String name)
  {
    this.name = name;
  }

  public Iterator getTimeEntries()
  {
    return this.entries.iterator();
  }

  public void setTimeEntries(ArrayList entries)
  {
    this.entries = entries;
  }

  public void addTimeEntry(TimeEntryDTO entry)
  {
    this.entries.add(entry);
  }

  public String toString()
  {
    StringBuffer buffer = new StringBuffer();
    Iterator entryIterator = entries.iterator();
    buffer.append("TimeEntryReport[name="+name);
    int count = 0;
    while(entryIterator.hasNext())
    {
     count++;
     TimeEntryDTO entry = (TimeEntryDTO) entryIterator.next();
```

```
          buffer.append(",#"+count +"{" + entry.toString()+ "}");
        }
      buffer.append("]");
      return buffer.toString();
    }


  public  int hashCode()
  {
    return (name.hashCode() ^ entries.hashCode());
  }


  public boolean equals(Object obj)
  {
    if (obj == null)
    {
      return false;
    }
    else
    {
      if (!obj.getClass().equals(this.getClass()))
      {
        return false;
      }
      else
      {
        TimeEntryReportDTO report = (TimeEntryReportDTO)obj;
        return ((report.name.equals(this.name)) &&
                (report.entries.equals(this.entries)));
      }
    }
  }
}
```

XmlContentHandler.java

The XmlContentHandler contains the core logic for parsing the XML extract time entry request messages. It implements all the appropriate callbacks that are invoked by the SAX parser during the parsing of an XML request. Notice how it remembers the elements as they are reported by the parser. Based on the name of the tag, the XmlContentHandler takes different actions. For example, it builds an ArrayList of names when it sees the occurrence of the Users tag. At the end, it returns a HashMap of the request data.

```
    package com.wiley.compBooks.EJwithUML.BillingSystemInterface;

    import org.xml.sax.Attributes;
    import org.xml.sax.ContentHandler;
    import org.xml.sax.Locator;
    import org.xml.sax.SAXException;
    import java.util.HashMap;
    import java.util.ArrayList;

    /**
     * This is a ContentHandler class for SOAP/XML request messages. It ignores
```

```
 * namespace information as well as attributes associated with elements.
 */
class XMLContentHandler implements ContentHandler
{
    private String currentElement = "";
    private HashMap xmlRequest;
    private ArrayList users = new ArrayList();

    /**
     * Holds onto the locator for location information
     */
    private Locator locator;

    /**
     * Creates a ContentHandler that populates HashMap with request data
     * from SOAP message. It uses the tag name as the key.
     */
    public XMLContentHandler(HashMap request)
    {
        this.xmlRequest = request;
    }

    public void setDocumentLocator(Locator locator)
    {
        this.locator = locator;
    }

    /**
     * This indicates the start of a SOAP message - <...Envelope...>
     */
    public void startDocument() throws SAXException
    {
        System.out.println("XMLContentHandler.startDocument()- parsing begins.");
    }

    /**
     * This indicates the end of a SOAP request message - </Envelope>
     */
    public void endDocument() throws SAXException
    {
        System.out.println("XMLContentHandler.endDocument()- parsing ends.");
    }

    /**
     * This indicates that a processing instruction (other than
     * the XML declaration) has been encountered. This is not used.
     */
    public void processingInstruction(String target, String data) throws
SAXException
    {
        //Ignore
    }
```

```
/**
 * This is not used - No OP!
 */
public void startPrefixMapping(String prefix, String xmlSource)
{
   // Ignore
}


/**
 * This is not used - No OP!
 */
public void endPrefixMapping(String prefix)
{
   // Ignore
}


/**
 * This captures the name of the request data as well as the request name.
 * The namespace is ignored. Attributes are also ignored.
 */
public void startElement(String namespaceURI, String localName, String        ⊃
rawName,
                    Attributes atts) throws SAXException
{
   if (currentElement.equals(XmlTimeEntryReportRequestTags.BODY))
   {
      xmlRequest.put(XmlTimeEntryReportRequestTags.REQUEST_NAME,
                     localName);
      System.out.println("XMLContentHandler.startElement()- Request name:"
                         + localName);
   }
   else
   {
      System.out.println("XMLContentHandler.startElement()-request data name: "
                         + localName);
   }
   currentElement = localName;
   if (currentElement.equals(XmlTimeEntryReportRequestTags.USERS))
   {
      xmlRequest.put(XmlTimeEntryReportRequestTags.USERS, users);
   }
   if (currentElement.equals(XmlTimeEntryReportRequestTags.ALL_USERS))
   {
      xmlRequest.put(XmlTimeEntryReportRequestTags.ALL_USERS,
                  new Boolean(true));
   }
}


/**
 * This indicates the end of an element of a SOAP request. It is ignored.
 */
public void endElement(String namespaceURI, String localName, String rawName)
    throws SAXException
{
```

```
        // Ignore
    }


    /**
     * This reports the value of the current request data as character data
     */
    public void characters(char[] ch, int start, int end) throws SAXException
    {
        String value = new String(ch, start, end).trim();
        if (!value.equals(""))
        {
            if (currentElement.equals(XmlTimeEntryReportRequestTags.USER_NAME))
            {
              users.add(value);
            }
            else
            {
              xmlRequest.put(currentElement, value);
            }
        }
        System.out.println("XMLContentHandler.characters()-data(" +
                        currentElement + ", " + value + ").");
    }


    /**
     * This reports whitespace that can be ignored in the originating document.
     * This is typically invoked only when validation is ocurring in the parsing
     * process. This is ignored.
     */
    public void ignorableWhitespace(char[] ch, int start, int end) throws
SAXException
    {
        // Ignored
    }


    /**
     * This reports an entity that is skipped by the parser. This should only
     * occur for nonvalidating parsers, and then is still
     * implementation-dependent behavior. This is ignored.
     */
    public void skippedEntity(String name) throws SAXException
    {
        // Ignored
    }
}
```

Unit Testing using JUnit

As mentioned in Chapter 15, "Design for the TimecardDomain and TimecardWorkflow," the container classes (Servlet, EJBs) pose a challenge to performing unit testing.

We need to deploy them in a container to be able to perform any meaningful testing. The following sections show unit test classes to test the ExtractTimeEntriesWorkflow bean and ExtractTimeEntriesServlet.

TestExtractTimeEntriesWorkflow.java

The TestExtractTimeEntriesWorkflow implements different test cases for the Extract-TimeEntriesWorkflow bean class. These test cases can be run together or can be run separately.

```java
package com.wiley.compBooks.EJwithUML.Clients;

import javax.naming.*;
import javax.ejb.*;
import java.rmi.*;
import javax.rmi.PortableRemoteObject;
import java.util.*;
import java.text.ParseException;
import com.wiley.compBooks.EJwithUML.TimeCardDomain.*;
import com.wiley.compBooks.EJwithUML.Dtos.*;
import com.wiley.compBooks.EJwithUML.TimeCardWorkflow.*;
import com.wiley.compBooks.EJwithUML.Base.ApplicationExceptions.*;
import com.wiley.compBooks.EJwithUML.Base.*;
import com.wiley.compBooks.EJwithUML.Base.EjbUtil.*;
import junit.framework.*;

/**
 * This is JUnit test class for testing ExtractTimeEntriesWorkflow EJB. This
 * test assumes that the EJB is running and accessible.
 */
public class TestExtractTimeEntriesWorkflow extends TestCase
{
  private static ExtractTimeEntriesWorkflow xtewf;
  private static String testCaseToRun;
  private ExtractCriteriaDTO criteria;

  public TestExtractTimeEntriesWorkflow(String name)
  {
    super(name);
  }

  /** Executes all the test cases */
  public static void main(String[] args)throws CreateException,
NamingException, RemoteException
  {
    Context initial = new InitialContext();
    Object objref =
initial.lookup(EjbReferenceNames.EXTRACT_TIME_ENTRY_WORKFLOW_HOME);
    ExtractTimeEntriesWorkflowHome xtewhome = (ExtractTimeEntriesWorkflowHome)
        PortableRemoteObject.narrow(objref,
ExtractTimeEntriesWorkflowHome.class);
    xtewf = xtewhome.create();
```

```
   if (args.length > 0)
   {
     TestExtractTimeEntriesWorkflow.testCaseToRun= args[0];
   }
   junit.textui.TestRunner.run(suite());
}

/** Groups all test cases into a test suite */
public static Test suite()
{
   TestSuite suite = null;
   if (TestExtractTimeEntriesWorkflow.testCaseToRun == null)
   {
      // Runs all test cases
      suite = new TestSuite(TestExtractTimeEntriesWorkflow.class);
   }
   else
   {
      suite = new TestSuite();
      suite.addTest(new TestExtractTimeEntriesWorkflow(
                           TestExtractTimeEntriesWorkflow.testCaseToRun));
   }
   return suite;
}


/**
 * Sets common test fixture (input test data) for all the test cases<br>
 * Prepares the testing environment before a testXXX() method is executed
 */
protected void setUp()throws ParseException
{
   criteria = new ExtractCriteriaDTO("Ford",
     DateUtil.createDate("10/10/2002"), DateUtil.createDate("11/27/2002"));
}


/**
 * tearDown method for test case<br>
 * Resets the testing environment after a testXXX() method is executed
 */
protected void tearDown()
{
   criteria.setClient("Ford");
}

public void testGetAllTimecardsForUser()throws Exception
{
   try
   {
     Collection timecards = xtewf.getAllTimecardsForUser("fred");
     Iterator cardIterator = timecards.iterator();
     while(cardIterator.hasNext())
     {
       System.out.println((TimecardDTO)cardIterator.next());
```

```
        }

      }
    catch(ApplicationException e)
    {
      fail("expected exception, but received none.");
    }
  }


public void testExtractForCriteriaWithInvalidClient()throws Exception
{
  try
  {
    criteria.setClient("nissan");
    HashMap reports = xtewf.extractForCriteria(criteria);
    fail("expected exception, but received none.");
  }
  catch(InvalidDataException e)
  {
    System.out.println("received expected exception-" + e);
  }
}


public void testExtractForCriteriaWithInvalidUser()throws Exception
{
  try
  {
    ArrayList users = new ArrayList();
    users.add("syed");
    criteria.setUsers(users);
    HashMap reports = xtewf.extractForCriteria(criteria);
    fail("expected exception, but received none.");
  }
  catch(InvalidDataException e)
  {
    System.out.println("received expected exception-" + e);
  }
}

public void testExtractForCriteriaWithAllUser()
{
  try
  {
    HashMap reports = xtewf.extractForCriteria(criteria);
    Iterator reportIterator = reports.entrySet().iterator();
    while(reportIterator.hasNext())
    {
      Map.Entry entry = (Map.Entry) reportIterator.next();
      System.out.println(entry.getValue());
    }
  }
  catch(Exception e)
  {
```

```
        fail("received unexpected exception-" + e);
    }
}

public void testExtractForCriteriaWithAUserList()
{
  try
  {
    ArrayList users = new ArrayList();
    users.add("fred");
    criteria.setUsers(users);
    HashMap reports = xtewf.extractForCriteria(criteria);
    Iterator reportIterator = reports.entrySet().iterator();
    while(reportIterator.hasNext())
    {
      Map.Entry entry = (Map.Entry) reportIterator.next();
      System.out.println(entry.getValue());
    }
  }
  catch(Exception e)
  {
    fail("received unexpected exception-" + e);
  }
}
}
```

Conclusion

This chapter completed the implementation of the Timecard application. Throughout the development process, UML helped us describe the problem and the solution in a clear and comprehensible form. In a real project, this allows a community of developers and stakeholders to evolve a consensus on what the system should do and how it should do it. Less time is lost in communicating ideas. This time is more profitably spent debating the merits of the ideas.

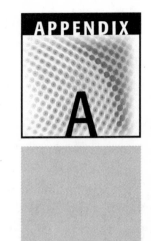

APPENDIX

A

The Web Site

The Web site for this book, www.wiley.com/compbooks/arrington, features the UML design model for the Timecard application, as well as the Java source code and deployment instructions that can be used to deploy the application.

The model is intended to provide a coherent picture of the design that was developed over many chapters in the book. Some figures that are in the book are not in the model, and vice versa.

The Java source code and deployment instructions allow the reader to see one possible implementation of the design and to experiment with various alternatives. These instructions guide you as you install the required software and deploy the Timecard application. The instructions are broken into several sections, with each section shown in its own table. The leftmost column of the table shows the major steps required for the section. The middle column describes the details for each step. Finally, the rightmost column describes any expected results.

If your interest and patience are high, you may wish to deploy the Enterprise Java-Beans from scratch. An additional page of custom installation instructions guides you through this tedious process. You can also view the deployment instructions or the custom installation instructions as Word documents.

In addition, the Web site also features a Visual Glossary, which shows how several object-oriented concepts are shown in UML.

Hardware Requirements

To deploy the sample application, your system must meet the following requirements:

Platform/processor/operating system: Windows NT, 2000, or XP.

RAM: 128 MB

Hard drive space: 120 MB

Processor: 400 MHz Pentium or equivalent

User Assistance and Information

The software on the accompanying Web site is being provided as is without warranty or support of any kind. Should you require basic installation assistance, please call our product support number at (201) 748-6194 weekdays between 9 A.M. and 4 P.M. eastern standard time. Or, we can be reached via email at: techhelp@wiley.com.

To place additional orders or to request information about other Wiley products, please call (800) 879-4539.

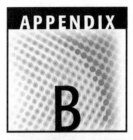

APPENDIX B

Additional Resources

Here are additional resources for several categories.

Object-Oriented Analysis and Design

Booch, Grady. *Object-Oriented Analysis and Design with Applications*. Reading, MA: Addison-Wesley-Longman, Inc., 1994.

> This is still the classic text for OO analysis and design. It has a unique combination of academic precision and clear explanations.

Booch, Grady, James Rumbaugh, and Ivar Jacobson. *The Unified Modeling Language User Guide*. Reading, MA: Addison-Wesley-Longman, Inc., 1999.

> Excellent reference for the UML and its application.

Coad, Peter, and Mark Mayfield. *Java Design*. Upper Saddle River, NJ: Prentice-Hall PTR, 1997.

> A very concise and readable book that stresses design by composition.

Fowler, Martin, with Kendall Scott. *UML Distilled: Applying the Standard Object Modeling Language*. Reading, MA: Addison-Wesley-Longman, Inc., 1997.

> A very concise guide to the UML.

Patterns

Buschmann, Frank, Regine Meunier, Hans Rohnert, Peter Sommerlad, and Michael Stal. *Pattern-Oriented Software Architecture: A System of Patterns*. West Sussex, England: John Wiley & Sons, Ltd., 1996.

> Introduces several important architectural patterns, including MVC and layers.

Fowler, Martin. *Analysis Patterns: Reusable Object Models*. Reading, MA: Addison-Wesley-Longman, Inc., 1997.

> Very interesting book on analysis and domain modeling. Contains a lot of examples and clear explanations of the author's thought process as he creates his designs.

Gamma, Erich, Richard Helm, Ralph Johnson, and John Vlissides. *Design Patterns Elements of Reusable Object-Oriented Software*. Reading, MA: Addison-Wesley-Longman, Inc., 1995.

> The book for design patterns. Invaluable resource.

Software Development Process

Jacobson, Ivar, Grady Booch, and James Rumbaugh. *The Unified Software Development Process*. Reading, MA: Addison-Wesley-Longman, Inc., 1999.

> Excellent reference for the proprietary process and for OO software engineering in general.

Kruchten, Philippe. *The Rational Unified Process: An Introduction*. Reading, MA: Addison-Wesley-Longman, Inc., 1999.

> Concise guide to the RUP.

McConnell, Steve. *Rapid Development*. Redmond, WA: Microsoft Press, 1996.

> Incredibly easy-to-read coverage of some difficult and important topics. This is not an OO book, rather the definitive software engineering book for the practitioner.

McConnell, Steve. *Software Project Survival Guide*. Redmond, WA: Microsoft Press, 1998.

> Contains a lot of the same material as *Rapid Development*, above, but in a convenient easy-to-gift-wrap size. Makes a great gift for your favorite unenlightened manager or customer.

Webster, Bruce F. *Pitfalls of Object-Oriented Development*. New York: M&T Books, 1995.

> A clearly organized and easy-to-read guide to the dangers inherent in OO software development. It contains excellent advice for both managers and developers as they adopt OO technology.

XML

Megginson, David. *Structuring XML Documents.* Upper Saddle River, NJ: Prentice-Hall, Inc., 1998.

> Goes way beyond the basics for a complete discussion of XML DTDs and how to construct them.

St. Laurent, Simon. *XML: A Primer.* Foster City, CA: MIS Press, 1998.

> Concise guide to creating XML DTDs and documents.

Java

Asbury, Stephen, and Scott R. Weiner. *Developing Java Enterprise Applications.* New York: John Wiley & Sons, Inc., 1999.

> An excellent introduction to Sun's Enterprise Java class libraries.

Bloch, Joshua. *Effective Java Programming Language Guide.* Palo Alto, CA: Sun Microsystems, Inc., 2001.

> A concise and readable list of dos and don'ts for Java programming and OO design.

Chan, Patrick, Rosanna Lee, and Douglas Kramer. *The Java Class Libraries Second Edition, Volumes 1, 2, and Supplemental edition for the Java 2 Platform.* Reading, MA: Addison-Wesley-Longman, Inc., 1998.

> An amazing series of books, with the best low-level explanations of the packages and classes that make up the core class libraries for Java.

Eckstein, Robert, Marc Loy, and Dave Wood. *Java Swing.* Sebastopol, CA: O'Reilly & Associates, Inc., 1998.

> Very readable explanations of a complex topic. Exhaustive and evenly written coverage of a huge amount of material.

Flanagan, David. *Java in a Nutshell.* Sebastopol, CA: O'Reilly & Associates, Inc., 1996.

> Excellent guide and reference for the language, tools, and basic classes.

Hamilton, Graham, Rick Cattell, and Maydene Fisher. *JDBC Database Access with Java: A Tutorial and Annotated Reference.* Reading, MA: Addison-Wesley-Longman, Inc., 1997.

> Thorough coverage of JDBC, but a little heavy on the reprinted JavaDocs for our taste.

Hunter, Jason, with William Crawford. *Java Servlet Programming.* Sebastopol, CA: O'Reilly & Associates, Inc., 1998.

> Solid coverage of servlets, from fundamentals to advanced topics.

Oaks, Scott, and Henry Wong. *Java Threads*. Sebastopol, CA: O'Reilly & Associates, Inc., 1997.

> Excellent coverage of multi-threaded programming in Java, with a good balance of theory and details.

Reese, George. *Database Programming with JDBC and JAVA*. Sebastopol, CA: O'Reilly & Associates, Inc., 1997.

> Excellent coverage of JDBC, and a thought-provoking introduction to the design of object-to-relational frameworks.

Roman, Ed, Scott Ambler, and Tyler Jewell. *Mastering Enterprise JavaBeans, 2nd Edition*. New York: John Wiley & Sons, Inc., 2001.

> Excellent coverage of a wide range of enterprise technologies, especially Enterprise JavaBeans.

Index